Praise for the *Sun Certified Programmer & Developer for Java 2 Study Guide*

"Kathy Sierra is one of the few people in the world who can make complicated things seem damn simple. And as if that isn't enough, she can make boring things seem interesting. I always look forward to reading whatever Kathy writes—she's one of my favorite authors."

—Paul Wheaton, Trail Boss JavaRanch.com

"Who better to write a Java study guide than Kathy Sierra, the reigning queen of Java instruction? Kathy Sierra has done it again—here is a study guide that almost guarantees you a certification!"

—James Cubeta, Systems Engineer, SGI

"The thing I appreciate most about Kathy is her quest to make us all remember that we are teaching people and not just lecturing about Java. Her passion and desire for the highest quality education that meets the needs of the individual student is positively unparalleled at SunEd. Undoubtedly there are hundreds of students who have benefited from taking Kathy's classes."

—Victor Peters, founder Next Step Education & Software Sun Certified Java Instructor

"I want to thank Kathy for the EXCELLENT Study Guide. The book is well written, every concept is clearly explained using a real life example, and the book states what you specifically need to know for the exam. The way it's written, you feel that you're in a classroom and someone is actually teaching you the difficult concepts, but not in a dry, formal manner. The questions at the end of the chapters are also REALLY good, and I am sure they will help candidates pass the test. Watch out for this Wickedly Smart book."

—Alfred Raouf, Web Solution Developer

"The Sun Certification exam was certainly no walk in the park, but Kathy's material allowed me to not only pass the exam, but Ace it!"

—Mary Whetsel, Sr. Technology Specialist,
Application Strategy and Integration, The St. Paul Companies

"Bert has an uncanny and proven ability to synthesize complexity into simplicity offering a guided tour into learning what's needed for the certification exam."

—Thomas Bender, President, Gold Hill Software Design, Inc.

"With his skill for clearly expressing complex concepts to his training audience, every student can master what Bert has to teach."

—David Ridge, CEO, Ridge Associates

Sun® Certified Programmer & Developer for Java™ 2 Study Guide

(Exams 310-035 & 310-027)

Sun® Certified Programmer & Developer for Java™ 2 Study Guide

(Exams 310-035 & 310-027)

McGraw-Hill/Osborne is an independent entity from Sun Microsystems and is not affiliated with Sun Microsystems in any manner. This publication and CD may be used in assisting students to prepare for a Sun Certified Java 2 Exam. Neither Sun Microsystems nor McGraw-Hill/Osborne warrants that use of this publication and CD will ensure passing the relevant Exam. Sun, Sun Microsystems, and the Sun Logo are trademarks or registered trademarks of Sun Microsystems, Inc. in the United States and other countries. Java and all Java-based marks are trademarks or registered trademarks of Sun Microsystems, Inc. in the United States and other countries. McGraw-Hill/Osborne is independent of Sun Microsystems, Inc.

Kathy Sierra
Bert Bates

McGraw-Hill/Osborne

New York Chicago San Francisco Lisbon London Madrid
Mexico City Milan New Delhi San Juan Seoul Singapore Sydney Toronto

The **McGraw-Hill** *Companies*

McGraw-Hill/Osborne
2600 Tenth Street
Berkeley, California 94710
U.S.A.

To arrange bulk purchase discounts for sales promotions, premiums, or fund-raisers, please contact McGraw-Hill/Osborne at the above address. For information on translations or book distributors outside the U.S.A., please see the International Contact Information page immediately following the index of this book.

Sun® Certified Programmer & Developer for Java™ 2 Study Guide (Exam 310-035 & 310-027)

234567890 DOC DOC 019876543

Book p/n 0-07-222685-4 and CD p/n 0-07-222686-2
parts of
ISBN 0-07-222684-6

Publisher
Brandon A. Nordin

Vice President & Associate Publisher
Scott Rogers

Acquisitions Editor
Timothy Green

Project Editor
Mark Karmendy

Acquisitions Coordinator
Jessica Wilson

Technical Editor
John Nyquist

Copy Editor
Dennis Weaver

Proofreader
Pat Mannion

Indexer
Rebecca Plunkett

Composition
Lucie Ericksen
Apollo Publishing Services

Illustrators
Jackie Sieben
Michael Mueller

Series Design
Roberta Steele

This book was published with Corel VENTURA™ Publisher.

ABOUT THE CONTRIBUTORS

About the Author

Kathy Sierra is a co-developer of the SCJP 1.4 exam (310-035) and Sun's ePractice exam. She is also a Sun Certified Java Instructor and master trainer for Sun Educational Services, where she teaches other Java instructors. Her full-time job since 1998 has been to help others learn Java and prepare for the SCJP exam, and she also is also the sole founder of what is arguably the world's largest Java certification web site, Javaranch.com. Kathy has worked for Sun Educational Services worldwide headquarters in the course development, customer training, and certification departments. Prior to that, she worked as an instructor for UCLA Extension's IBM New Media Lab, and developed games for Virgin, MGM, and Amblin' Entertainment. She can be reached at Kathy.Sierra@wickedlysmart.com.

About the Co-Author

Bert Bates is a Sun Certified Programmer for Java 1.4, and has been developing software for the last 20 years. He participated both in the beta development of the 1.4 exam and Sun's ePractice exam. Bert has also been teaching software development, including Java programming, for many years, with a particular interest and background in artificial intelligence. His clients have included Rockwell, Timken, The Weather Channel, and Arts & Entertainment Network (A&E). Recently he has been developing a "smart" adaptive eLearning system for delivering technical training in the most learner-friendly way. He can be reached at Bert.Bates@wickedlysmart.com.

About the Technical Editor

John R. Nyquist is currently Programming Manager for Klein Buendel (kleinbuendel.com), leading development of both server- and client-side applications. He spent two years at Sun Microsystems teaching programmers Java as well as preparing them for certification. John is one of the technical reviewers for "Advanced Java How to Program." He has co-authored two books on Lingo and technical edited two more. He has programmed in a wide variety of languages from the well-known C/C++ to the almost unknown (but great) Prograph CPX. Kathy Sierra evangelized the virtues of Java to him many years ago, and for that he is grateful. John enjoys living in Colorado with his beautiful wife, Laura, and his two cool kids, Alice and Richard (he is still negotiating a dog). He can be reached at http://nyquist.net/.

To Java, for being a language worth pulling all-nighters studying for the exam.

CONTENTS AT A GLANCE

CONTENTS

ACKNOWLEDGMENTS

Kathy and Bert would like to thank the following people:

- All the incredibly hard-working folks at Osborne: Brandon Nordin, Scott Rogers, Gareth Hancock, Tim Green, Mark Karmendy, Dennis Weaver, and Jessica Wilson for all their help, and for being so responsive and patient—well, OK, not all that patient—but so professional and the nicest group of people you could hope to work with.
- The terrific java experts/testers from Javaranch.com: Mikalai Zaikin, Katherine Rogers, Dan Chisholm, Alfred Raouf—Egypt, Valentin Crettaz, Junilu Lacar, Hoai "Peter" Tran, Angelo Celeste, Aniruddha Mukherjee, Oussama Azizi, Mohamed Mazahim, Shweta Mathur, James Chegwidden, Manish Hatwalne, Mike Gallihugh, Michael Taupitz, Emiko Hori, John Paverd, Joseph Bih, Skulrat Patanavanich, Sunil Palicha, Suddhasatwa Ghosh, R. Srinivasan, and, of course, to the Javaranch Trail Boss Paul Wheaton, for running the best Java community site on the Web.
- Some of the software professionals who helped us in the early days: Tom Bender, Peter Loerincs, Craig Matthews, Morgan Porter, and Mike Kavenaugh.
- Our JavaJam III Geek Cruise students Kevin, Dave, Mary, and Bill for letting us experiment on them, and for being the most amazing, smartest, and fun group. They studied and drilled each other, even when we were all seasick.
- Above all, the wonderful and talented Certification team at Sun Educational Services, especially Certification Program Manager Steve ("Goose") Moore, and the most persistent get-it-done person we know, Evelyn Cartagena.
- Our best friends and Java gurus, Simon Roberts and Solveign Haugland.
- The kids, Eden and Skyler, for being horrified that adults—out of school—would study this hard for an exam; we wondered the same thing when *we*

were preparing for the exam. The 'rents', Ann and Jim for supporting this hare-brained scheme.

- Finally, all the other past and present Sun Ed Java instructors for helping to make learning Java a fun experience including (to name only a few): Alan Petersen, Jean Tordella, Georgianna Meagher, Anthony Orapallo, Jacqueline Jones, James Cubeta, Teri Cubeta, David Marsland, Mark Smith, Kathy Collina, Bryan Basham, Joel Budgor, David Hamilton, Rob Weingruber, John Nyquist, Asok Perumainar, Steve Stelting, Dave Zaffery, Flip Medley, Kimberly Bobrow, Keith Ratliff, and the most caring and inspiring Java guy on the planet, Jari Paukku, from Sun Microsystems, Finland.
- Our thanks to the following sharp-eyed readers: Jessica Sant, Johannes de Jong, Dan Culache, Mark Jackson, Leshec Claassens, Phillip Houston, Kenneth Thomas, John Adair, Craig Baker, Ellen Zhao, Christopher Thompson, Srinivasu Mandava, Clay Graham, Barry Gaunt, Bruce Graham, Selcuk Sonmezer, and Clover the dog.

INTRODUCTION

In This Book

This book is organized in such a way as to serve as an in-depth review for the Sun Certified Programmer for the Java 2 Platform 1.4 exam for both experienced Java professionals and those in the earlier stages of experience with Java technologies. Each chapter covers a major aspect of the exam, with an emphasis on the "why" as well as the "how to" of programming in the Java language. The book also includes an in-depth review of the essential ingredients for a successful assessment of a project submitted for the Sun Certified Java Developer exam.

What This Book Is Not

You will not find a beginners guide to learning Java in this book. All 700+ pages of this book are dedicated solely to helping you pass the exams. If you are brand new to Java, we suggest you spend a little time learning the basics, and should not start with this book until you know how to write, compile, and run simple Java programs. We do not, however, assume any level of prior knowledge of the individual topics covered. In other words, for any given topic (driven exclusively by the actual exam objectives), we start with the assumption that you are new to that *topic*. So we assume you're new to the individual topics, but we assume that you are *not* new to Java.

We also do not pretend to be both preparing you for the exam *and simultaneously making you a complete Java being*. This is a certification exam study guide, and it's very clear about its mission. That's not to say that preparing for the exam won't help you become a better Java programmer! On the contrary, even the most experienced Java developer often claims that having to prepare for the certification exam made him a far more knowledgeable and well-rounded programmer than he would have been without the exam-driven studying.

On the CD

For more information on the CD-ROM, please see Appendix A.

In Every Chapter

In the Programmer's Exam section of the book (Part I), we've created a set of chapter components that call your attention to important items, reinforce important points, and provide helpful exam-taking hints. Take a look at what you'll find in every chapter:

- Every chapter begins with the **Certification Objectives**—what you need to know in order to pass the section on the exam dealing with the chapter topic. The Objective headings identify the objectives within the chapter, so you'll always know an objective when you see it!

- **Exam Watch** notes call attention to information about, and potential pitfalls in, the exam. These helpful hints are written by authors who have taken the exams and received their certification—who better to tell you what to worry about? They know what you're about to go through!
- **Practice Exercises** are interspersed throughout the chapters. These are step-by-step exercises that allow you to get the hands-on experience you need in order to pass the exams. They help you master skills that are likely to be an area of focus on the exam. Don't just read through the exercises! They provide hands-on practice that you should be comfortable completing. Learning by doing is an effective way to increase your competency.

- **On The Job** notes describe the issues that come up most often in real-world settings. They provide a valuable perspective on certification-related topics. They point out common mistakes and address questions that have arisen from on the job discussions and experience.
- **From The Classrooms** describe the issues that come up most often in the training classroom setting. These sidebars highlight some of the most common and confusing problems that students encounter when taking a live Java training course. You can get a leg up on those difficult-to-understand subjects by focusing extra attention on these sidebars.
- **Scenario and Solutions** sections lay out potential problems and solutions in a quick-to-read format:

SCENARIO & SOLUTION	
What benefits do you gain from encapsulation?	Ease of code maintenance, extensibility, and code clarity.
What is the object-oriented relationship between a tree and an oak?	An IS-A relationship: Oak IS-A Tree.
What is the object-oriented relationship between a city and a road?	A HAS-A relationship. City HAS-A Road.

- The **Certification Summary** is a succinct review of the chapter and a restatement of salient points regarding the exam.

- The **Two-Minute Drill** at the end of every chapter is a checklist of the main points of the chapter. It can be used for last-minute review.

Q&A

- The **Self Test** offers questions that closely simulate the topics, structure, and nature of those found on the certification exam. The answers to these questions, as well as explanations of the answers, can be found at the end of each chapter. By taking the Self Test after completing each chapter, you'll reinforce what you've learned from that chapter while becoming familiar with the tricky structure of the exam questions. You can also use the Self Test questions as a way to assess your readiness to take the actual exam. The author helped to develop the *real* exam, so she has a pretty good idea of how the real questions are structured!

Some Pointers

Once you've finished reading this book, set aside some time to do a thorough review. You might want to return to the book several times and make use of all the methods it offers for reviewing the material:

1. *Re-read all the Two-Minute Drills*, or have someone quiz you. You also can use the drills as a way to do a quick cram before the exam. You might want

to make some flash cards out of 3 × 5 index cards that have the Two-Minute Drill material on them.

2. *Re-read all the Exam Watch notes.* Remember that these notes are written by authors who have taken the exam and passed. They know what you should expect—and what you should be on the lookout for.
3. *Review all the S&S sections* for quick problem solving.
4. *Re-take the Self Tests.* Taking the tests right after you've read the chapter is a good idea, because the questions help reinforce what you've just learned. However, it's an even better idea to go back later and do all the questions in the book in one sitting. Pretend that you're taking the live exam. (When you go through the questions the first time, you should mark your answers on a separate piece of paper. That way, you can run through the questions as many times as you need to until you feel comfortable with the material.)
5. *Complete the Exercises.* Did you do the exercises when you read through each chapter? If not, do them! These exercises are designed to cover exam topics, and there's no better way to get to know this material than by practicing. Be sure you understand why you are performing each step in each exercise. If there is something you are not clear on, re-read that section in the chapter.

Introduction to the Material in the Book

This section will help prepare you to take the Programmer exam. Tips and preparation notes for the Developer exam are presented in the Developer Exam chapters in Part II (Chapters 10–17). The Sun Certified Java Programmer (SCJP) exam is considered one of the hardest (if not *the* hardest) in the IT industry, and we can tell you from experience that a large chunk of exam candidates go in to the test unprepared. And we're talking about the ones who already know Java quite well and have been programming in it for years! As programmers, we tend to learn only what we need to complete our current project, given the insane deadlines we're usually under. But this exam attempts to prove your complete understanding of the Java language, not just the parts of it you've become familiar with in your work.

Experience alone will rarely get you through this exam with a passing mark, because even the things you *think* you know might work just a little different than you imagined. It isn't enough to be able to get your code to work correctly; you *must* understand the core fundamentals in a deep way, and with enough breadth to cover virtually anything that could crop up in the course of using the language.

The Sun Certified Developer Exam is unique to the IT certification realm, because it actually evaluates your skill as a developer rather than simply your knowledge of the language or tools. Becoming a Certified Java Developer is, by definition, development experience.

Who Cares About Certification?

Employers do. Headhunters do. Programmers do. Sun's programmer exam has been considered the fastest-growing certification in the IT world, and the number of candidates taking the exam continues to grow each year. Passing this exam proves three important things to a current or prospective employer: you're smart; you know how to study and prepare for a challenging test; and, most of all, you know the Java language. If an employer has a choice between a candidate that's passed the exam and one who hasn't, the employer knows that the certified programmer does not have to take time to learn the Java language.

But does it mean that you can actually develop software in Java? Not necessarily, but it's a good head start. To really demonstrate your ability to develop (as opposed to just your knowledge of the language), you should consider the Developer Exam, where you're given an assignment to build a program, start to finish, and submit it for an assessor to evaluate and score.

Sun's Certification Program

Currently there are four Java certification exams. They are the *Programmer*, the *Developer*, the *Web Component Developer*, and the *Architect* exams. The Programmer and Web Component Developer exams are exclusively multiple-choice exams taken at a testing center, while the Developer and Architect exams involve submitting a project.

The Programmer Exam (CX-310-035)

Sun Certified Programmer for Java 2 Platform 1.4

The Programmer exam is designed to test your knowledge of the Java programming language itself. It requires detailed knowledge of language syntax, core concepts, and a small number of application programming interfaces (APIs). It does not test any issues related to program design or architecture, and it does not ask why one approach is better than another, but rather it asks whether the given approach works in a particular situation.

The Developer Exam (CX-310-252A, CX-310-027)

Sun Certified Developer for Java 2 Platform 1.4
The Developer exam picks up where the Programmer exam leaves off. Passing the Programmer exam is required before you can start the Developer exam. The Developer exam requires you to develop an actual program and then defend your design decisions. It is designed to test your understanding of why certain approaches are better than others in certain circumstances, and to prove your ability to follow a specification and implement a correct, functioning, and user-friendly program.

The Developer exam consists of two pieces: a project assignment, and a follow-up essay exam. Candidates have an unlimited amount of time to complete the project, but once the project is submitted, the candidate then must go to a testing center and complete a short follow-up essay exam, designed primarily to validate and verify that it was *you* who designed and built the project.

The Web Component Developer Exam (CX-310-080)

Sun Certified Web Component Developer for J2EE Platform
The web developer exam is for those who are using Java technology servlet and JSP (Java Server Pages) to build Web applications. It's based on the Servlet and JSP specifications defined in the Java 2 Enterprise Edition (J2EE). Like the Developer exam, it also requires that the candidate is a Sun Certified Java Programmer.

The Architect Exam (CX-310-051)

Sun Certified Enterprise Architect for J2EE Technology
This certification is for enterprise architects, and thus does not require that the candidate pass the Programmer exam. The Architect exam is in three pieces: a knowledge-based multiple-choice exam, an architectural design assignment, and a follow-up essay exam. You must successfully pass the multiple-choices exam before registering and receiving the design assignment.

Taking the Programmer's Exam

In a perfect world, you would be assessed for your true knowledge of a subject, not simply how you respond to a series of test questions. But life isn't perfect, and it just isn't practical to evaluate everyone's knowledge on a one-to-one basis.

For the majority of its certifications, Sun evaluates candidates using a computer-based testing service operated by Sylvan Prometric. This service is quite popular in the industry, and it is used for a number of vendor certification programs, including Novell's CNE and Microsoft's MCSE. Thanks to Sylvan Prometric's large number of facilities, exams can be administered worldwide, generally in the same town as a prospective candidate.

For the most part, Sylvan Prometric exams work similarly from vendor to vendor. However, there is an important fact to know about Sun's exams: they use the traditional Sylvan Prometric test format, not the newer adaptive format. This gives the candidate an advantage, since the traditional format allows answers to be reviewed and revised during the test.

exam Watch ***Many experienced test takers do not go back and change answers unless they have a good reason to do so. Only change an answer when you feel you may have misread or misinterpreted the question the first time. Nervousness may make you second-guess every answer and talk yourself out of a correct one.***

To discourage simple memorization, Sun exams present a potentially different set of questions to different candidates. In the development of the exam, hundreds of questions are compiled and refined using beta testers. From this large collection, questions are pulled together from each objective, and assembled into several different versions of the exam.

Each Sun exam has a specific number of questions (the Programmer's exam contains 61 questions) and test duration (120 minutes for the Programmer's exam). Testing time is typically generous; the 310-035 exam has (for the first time in the Programmer's exam history) generated comments that time *could* be a factor for those not well prepared. The time remaining is always displayed in the corner of the testing screen, along with the number of remaining questions. If time expires during an exam, the test terminates, and incomplete answers are counted as incorrect.

At the end of the exam, your test is immediately graded, and the results are displayed on the screen. Scores for each subject area are also provided, but the system will not indicate which specific questions were missed. A report is automatically printed at the proctor's desk for your files. The test score is electronically transmitted back to Sun.

exam Watch

When you find yourself stumped answering multiple-choice questions, use your scratch paper to write down the two or three answers you consider the strongest, then underline the answer you feel is most likely correct. Here is an example of what your scratch paper might look like when you've gone through the test once:

21. B or C

33. A or C

This is extremely helpful when you mark the question and continue on. You can then return to the question and immediately pick up your thought process where you left off. Use this technique to avoid having to re-read and re-think questions. You will also need to use your scratch paper during complex, text-based scenario questions to create visual images to better understand the question. This technique is especially helpful if you are a visual learner.

Question Format

Sun's Java exams pose questions in multiple-choice format. In earlier versions of the exam, you were not told how many answers were correct, but with each version of the exam, the questions have become more difficult, so today each question tells you how many answers to choose. The Self Test questions at the end of each chapter are closely matched to the format, wording, and difficulty of the real exam questions.

Tips on Taking the Exam

There are 61 questions on the 310-035 (1.4) exam. You will need to get at least 32 of them correct to pass—just over 52 percent. You are given two hours to complete the exam. This information is subject to change. Always check with Sun before taking the exam, at www.suned.sun.com.

You are allowed to answer questions in any order, and you can go back and check your answers after you've gone through the test. There are no penalties for wrong answers, so it's better to at least attempt an answer than to not give one at all.

A good strategy for taking the exam is to go through once and answer all the questions that come to you quickly. You can then go back and do the others. Answering one question might jog your memory for how to answer a previous one.

Be very careful on the code examples. Check for syntax errors first, count curly braces, semicolons, and parenthesis and make sure there are as many left ones as right ones. Look for capitalization errors and other such syntax problems before trying to figure out what the code does.

Many of the questions on the exam will hinge on subtleties of syntax. You will need to have a thorough knowledge of the Java language in order to succeed.

Tips on Studying for the Exam

First and foremost, give yourself plenty of time to study. Java is a complex programming language, and you can't expect to cram what you need to know into a single study session. It is a field best learned over time, by studying a subject and then applying your knowledge. Build yourself a study schedule and stick to it, but be reasonable about the pressure you put on yourself, especially if you're studying in addition to your regular duties at work.

One easy technique to use in studying for certification exams is the 15-minutes-per-day effort. Simply study for a minimum of 15 minutes every day. It is a small but significant commitment. If you have a day where you just can't focus, then give up at 15 minutes. If you have a day where it flows completely for you, study longer. As long as you have more of the "flow days," your chances of succeeding are extremely high.

We strongly recommend you use flash cards when preparing for the Programmer's exam. A flash card is simply a 3 × 5 or 4 × 6 index card with a question on the front, and the answer on the back. You construct these cards yourself as you go through a chapter, capturing anything you think you might need more memorization or practice time. You can drill yourself with them by reading the question, thinking through the answer, then turning the card over to see if you're correct. Or you can get another person to help you by holding up the card with the question facing you, and then verifying your answer. Most of our students have found these to be tremendously helpful, especially because they're so portable that while you're in study mode, you can take them everywhere. Best not to use them while driving, though, except at red lights. We've taken ours everywhere—the doctor's office, restaurants, theaters, you name it.

Certification study groups are another excellent resource, and you won't find a larger or more willing community than on the javaranch.com Big Moose Saloon certification forums. If you have a question from this book, or any other mock exam question you may have stumbled upon, posting a question in a certification forum will get you an answer, in nearly all cases, within a day, usually, within a few hours. You'll find us (the authors) there several times a week, helping those just starting out on their exam preparation journey. (You won't actually think of it as anything as pleasant-sounding as a "journey" by the time you're ready to take the exam.)

Scheduling Your Exam

The Sun exams are purchased directly from Sun, but are scheduled by calling Sylvan Prometric directly. For locations outside the United States, your local number can be found on Sylvan's Web site at http://www.2test.com. Sylvan representatives can schedule your exam, but they don't have information about the certification programs. Questions about certifications should be directed to Sun's Worldwide Training department.

These representatives are familiar enough with the exams to find them by name, but it's best if you have the specific exam number handy when you call. After all, you wouldn't want to be scheduled and charged for the wrong exam.

Exams can be scheduled up to a year in advance, although it's really not necessary. Generally, scheduling a week or two ahead is sufficient to reserve the day and time you prefer. When scheduling, operators will search for testing centers in your area. For convenience, they can also tell which testing centers you've used before.

When registering for the exam, you will be asked for your ID number. This number is used to track your exam results back to Sun. It's important that you use the same ID number each time you register, so that Sun can follow your progress. Address information provided when you first register is also used by Sun to ship certificates and other related material. In the United States, your Social Security Number is commonly used as your ID number. However, Sylvan can assign you a unique ID number if you prefer not to use your Social Security Number.

Arriving at the Exam

As with any test, you'll be tempted to cram the night before. Resist that temptation. You should know the material by this point, and if you're too groggy in the morning, you won't remember what you studied anyway. Get a good night's sleep.

Arrive early for your exam; it gives you time to relax and review key facts. Take the opportunity to review your notes. If you get burned out on studying, you can usually start your exam a few minutes early. On the other hand, I don't recommend arriving late. Your test could be cancelled, or you may not be left with enough time to complete the exam.

When you arrive at the testing center, you'll need to sign in with the exam administrator. In order to sign in, you need to provide two forms of identification. Acceptable forms include government-issued IDs (for example, passport or driver's license), credit cards, and company ID badge. One form of ID must include a photograph. They just want to be sure that you don't send your brilliant Java guru next-door-neighbor-who-you've-paid in to take the exam for you.

Aside from a brain full of facts, you don't need to bring anything else to the exam. In fact, your brain is about all you're allowed to take into the exam! All the tests are closed-book, meaning you don't get to bring any reference materials with you. You're also not allowed to take any notes out of the exam room. The test administrator will provide you with paper and a pencil. Some testing centers may provide a small marker board instead. We do recommend that you bring a water bottle. Two hours is a long time to keep your brain active, and it functions much better when well hydrated.

Leave your pager and telephone in the car, or turn them off. They only add stress to the situation, since they are not allowed in the exam room, and can sometimes still be heard if they ring outside of the room. Purses, books, and other materials must be left with the administrator before entering the exam. While in the exam room, it's important that you don't disturb other candidates; talking is not allowed during the exam.

Once in the testing room, the exam administrator logs onto your exam, and you have to verify that your ID number and the exam number are correct. If this is the first time you've taken a Sun test, you can select a brief tutorial of the exam software. Before the test begins, you will be provided with facts about the exam, including the duration, the number of questions, and the score required for passing. Then the clock starts ticking and the fun begins.

The testing software is Windows-based, but you won't have access to the main desktop or any of the accessories. The exam is presented in full screen, with a single question per screen. Navigation buttons allow you to move forward and backward between questions. In the upper-right corner of the screen, counters show the number of questions and time remaining. Most important, there is a Mark check box in the upper-left corner of the screen—this will prove to be a critical tool in your testing technique.

Test-Taking Techniques

Without a plan of attack, candidates are overwhelmed by the exam or become side-tracked and run out of time. For the most part, if you are comfortable with the material, the allotted time is more than enough to complete the exam. The trick is to keep the time from slipping away during any one particular problem.

The obvious goal of an exam is to answer the questions effectively, although other aspects of the exam can distract from this goal. Here are some tips for taking the exam more efficiently.

Size Up the Challenge

First, take a quick pass through all the questions in the exam. "Cherry-pick" the easy questions, answering them on the spot. Briefly read each question, noticing the type of question and the subject. As a guideline, try to spend less than 25 percent of your testing time in this pass.

This step lets you assess the scope and complexity of the exam, and it helps you determine how to pace your time. It also gives you an idea of where to find potential answers to some of the questions. Often, the answer to one question is shown in the exhibit of another. Sometimes the wording of one question might lend clues or jog your thoughts for another question.

If you're not entirely confident with your answer to a question, answer it anyway, but check the Mark box to flag it for later review. In the event that you run out of time, at least you've provided a "first guess" answer, rather than leaving it blank.

Second, go back through the entire test, using the insight you gained from the first go-through. For example, if the entire test looks difficult, you'll know better than to spend more than a minute or so each question. Break down the pacing into small milestones—for example, "I need to answer 10 questions every 15 minutes."

At this stage, it's probably a good idea to skip past the time-consuming questions, marking them for the next pass. Try to finish this phase before you're 50–60 percent through the testing time.

Third, go back through all the questions you marked for review, using the Review Marked button in the question review screen. This step includes taking a second look at all the questions you were unsure of in previous passes, as well as tackling the time-consuming ones you deferred until now. Chisel away at this group of questions until you've answered them all.

If you're more comfortable with a previously marked question, unmark it now. Otherwise, leave it marked. Work your way through the time-consuming questions now, especially those requiring manual calculations. Unmark them when you're satisfied with the answer.

By the end of this step, you've answered every question in the test, despite having reservations about some of your answers. If you run out of time in the next step, at least you won't lose points for lack of an answer. You're in great shape if you still have 10–20 percent of your time remaining.

Review Your Answers

Now you're cruising! You've answered all the questions, and you're ready to do a quality check. Take yet another pass (yes, one more) through the entire test, briefly re-reading each question and your answer.

Carefully look over the questions again to check for "trick" questions. Be particularly wary of those that include a choice of "Does not compile." Be alert for last-minute clues. You're pretty familiar with nearly every question at this point, and you may find a few clues that you missed before.

The Grand Finale

When you're confident with all your answers, finish the exam by submitting it for grading. After what will seem like the longest 10 seconds of your life, the testing software will respond with your score. This is usually displayed as a bar graph, showing the minimum passing score, your score, and a PASS/FAIL indicator.

If you're curious, you can review the statistics of your score at this time. Answers to specific questions are not presented; rather, questions are lumped into categories, and results are tallied for each category. This detail is also on a report that has been automatically printed at the exam administrator's desk.

As you leave the exam, you'll need to leave your scratch paper behind or return it to the administrator. (Some testing centers track the number of sheets you've been given, so be sure to return them all.) In exchange, you'll receive a copy of the test report.

This report will be embossed with the testing center's seal, and you should keep it in a safe place. Normally, the results are automatically transmitted to Sun, but occasionally you might need the paper report to prove that you passed the exam.

In a few weeks, Sun will send you a package in the mail containing a nice paper certificate, a lapel pin, and a letter. You may also be sent instructions for how to obtain artwork for a logo that you can use on personal business cards.

Re-Testing

If you don't pass the exam, don't be discouraged. Try to have a good attitude about the experience, and get ready to try again. Consider yourself a little more educated. You know the format of the test a little better, and the report shows which areas you need to strengthen.

If you bounce back quickly, you'll probably remember several of the questions you might have missed. This will help you focus your study efforts in the right area. Serious go-getters will re-schedule the exam for a couple of days after the previous attempt, while the study material is still fresh in their mind.

Ultimately, remember that Sun certifications are valuable because they're hard to get. After all, if anyone could get one, what value would it have? In the end, it takes a good attitude and a lot of studying, but you can do it!

Part I

The Programmer's Exam

CHAPTERS

1

Language Fundamentals

CERTIFICATION OBJECTIVES

- Java Programming Language Keywords
- Literals and Ranges of All Primitive Data Types
- Array Declaration, Construction, and Initialization
- Using a Variable or Array Element That Is Uninitialized and Unassigned
- Command-Line Arguments to Main

✓ Two-Minute Drill

Q&A Self Test

This chapter looks at the Java fundamentals that you need to pass the Java 1.4 Programmer exam. Because you're planning on becoming Sun certified, we assume you already know the basics of Java, so this chapter concentrates just on the details you'll need for the exam. If you're completely new to Java, this chapter (and the rest of the book) will be confusing, despite our spectacularly cogent writing. That's our story and we're sticking to it!

CERTIFICATION OBJECTIVE

Java Programming Language Keywords (Exam Objective 4.4)

Identify all Java programming language keywords and correctly constructed identifiers.

Keywords are special reserved words in Java that you cannot use as identifiers (names) for classes, methods, or variables. They have meaning to the compiler; it uses them to figure out what your source code is trying to do. Table 1-1 contains all 49 of the reserved keywords.

You *must* memorize these for the test; you can count on being asked to select the keywords (and nonkeywords) from a list. Notice none of the reserved words have

TABLE 1-1 Complete List of Java Keywords

abstract	boolean	break	byte	case	catch
char	class	const	continue	default	do
double	else	extends	final	finally	float
for	goto	if	implements	import	instanceof
int	interface	long	native	new	package
private	protected	public	return	short	static
strictfp	super	switch	synchronized	this	throw
throws	transient	try	void	volatile	while
assert					

capital letters; this is a good first step when weeding out nonkeywords on the exam. You're probably familiar with most of them, but we'll review them anyway. Don't worry right now about what each keyword means or does; we'll cover most of them in more detail in later chapters.

exam Watch

Look for questions that include reserved words from languages other than Java. You might see `include`, `overload`, `unsigned`, `virtual`, `friend`, and the like. Besides appearing in questions specifically asking for keyword identification, the "imposter" words may show up in code examples used anywhere in the exam. Repeat after me, "Java is not C++."

Access Modifiers

The following are access modifiers:

- **`private`** Makes a method or a variable accessible only from within its own class.
- **`protected`** Makes a method or a variable accessible only to classes in the same package or subclasses of the class.
- **`public`** Makes a class, method, or variable accessible from any other class.

Class, Method, and Variable Modifiers

The following are class, method, and/or variable modifiers:

- **`abstract`** Used to declare a class that cannot be instantiated, or a method that must be implemented by a nonabstract subclass.
- **`class`** Keyword used to specify a class.
- **`extends`** Used to indicate the superclass that a subclass is extending.
- **`final`** Makes it impossible to extend a class, override a method, or reinitialize a variable.
- **`implements`** Used to indicate the interfaces that a class will implement.
- **`interface`** Keyword used to specify an interface.
- **`native`** Indicates a method is written in a platform-dependent language, such as C.
- **`new`** Used to instantiate an object by invoking the constructor.

- **`static`** Makes a method or a variable belong to a class as opposed to an instance.
- **`strictfp`** Used in front of a method or class to indicate that floating-point numbers will follow FP-strict rules in all expressions.
- **`synchronized`** Indicates that a method can be accessed by only one thread at a time.
- **`transient`** Prevents fields from ever being serialized. *Transient* fields are always skipped when objects are serialized.
- **`volatile`** Indicates a variable may change out of sync because it is used in threads.

Flow Control

The following are keywords used to control the flow through a block of code:

- **`break`** Exits from the block of code in which it resides.
- **`case`** Executes a block of code, dependent on what the *switch* tests for.
- **`continue`** Stops the rest of the code following this statement from executing in a loop and then begins the next iteration of the loop.
- **`default`** Executes this block of code if none of the switch-case statements match.
- **`do`** Executes a block of code one time, then, in conjunction with the *while* statement, it performs a test to determine whether the block should be executed again.
- **`else`** Executes an alternate block of code if an *if* test is false.
- **`for`** Used to perform a conditional loop for a block of code.
- **`if`** Used to perform a logical test for *true* or *false.*
- **`instanceof`** Determines whether an object is an instance of a class, superclass, or interface.
- **`return`** Returns from a method without executing any code that follows the statement (can optionally return a variable).

- **`switch`** Indicates the variable to be compared with the *case* statements.
- **`while`** Executes a block of code repeatedly while a certain condition is *true.*

Error Handling

The following are keywords used in error handling:

- **`catch`** Declares the block of code used to handle an exception.
- **`finally`** Block of code, usually following a *try-catch* statement, which is executed no matter what program flow occurs when dealing with an exception.
- **`throw`** Used to pass an exception up to the method that called this method.
- **`throws`** Indicates the method will pass an exception to the method that called it.
- **`try`** Block of code that will be tried, but which may cause an exception.
- **`assert`** Evaluates a conditional expression to verify the programmer's assumption.

Package Control

The following are keywords used for package control:

- **`import`** Statement to import packages or classes into code.
- **`package`** Specifies to which package all classes in a source file belong.

Primitives

The following keywords are primitives:

- **`boolean`** A value indicating *true* or *false.*
- **`byte`** An 8-bit integer (signed).
- **`char`** A single Unicode character (16-bit unsigned)
- **`double`** A 64-bit floating-point number (signed).

- **`float`** A 32-bit floating-point number (signed).
- **`int`** A 32-bit integer (signed).
- **`long`** A 64-bit integer (signed).
- **`short`** A 16-bit integer (signed).

Variable Keywords

The following keywords are a special type of reference variable:

- **`super`** Reference variable referring to the immediate superclass.
- **`this`** Reference variable referring to the current instance of an object.

Void Return Type Keyword

The `void` keyword is used only in the return value placeholder of a method declaration.

- **`void`** Indicates no return type for a method.

Unused Reserved Words

There are two keywords that are reserved in Java but which are not used. If you try to use one of these, the Java compiler will scold you with the following:

```
KeywordTest.java:4: 'goto' not supported.
               goto MyLabel;
1 error
```

The engineers' first-draft of the preceding compiler warning resembled the following:

```
KeywordTest.java:4: 'goto' not supported. Duh.
You have no business programming in Java. Begin erasing Java
Software Development Kit? (Yes/OK)
1 life-altering error
```

- **`const`** Do not use to declare a constant; use `public static final`.
- **`goto`** Not implemented in the Java language. It's considered harmful.

exam Watch

Look for questions that use a keyword as the name of a method or variable. The question might appear to be asking about, say, a runtime logic problem, but the real problem will be that the code won't even compile because of the illegal use of a keyword. For example, the following code will not compile:

```
class Foo {
public void go() {
     // complex code here
    }
    public int break(int b) {
      // code that appears to break something
  }
}
```

You might be fooled by the use of the keyword `break` as a method name, because the method might genuinely appear to be code that "breaks" something, and therefore the method name makes sense. Meanwhile, you're trying to figure out the complex code within the methods, when you needn't look beyond the illegal method name and choose the "Code does not compile" answer.

According to the Java Language Specification, `null`, `true`, and `false` are technically literal values (sometimes referred to as manifest constants) and not keywords. Just as with the other keywords, if you try to create an identifier with one of these literal values, you'll get a compiler error. For the purposes of the exam, treat them just as you would the other reserved words. You will *not* be asked to differentiate between reserved words and these reserved literals.

exam Watch

Be careful of practice exams with questions that, for example, ask if `false` is a keyword. Many exam candidates worry about how to answer such a question, but the real exam does not expect you to make a distinction between the reserved keywords and the literals of `null`, `true`, and `false`. Because the certainty of this being on the exam has reached urban legend status, Sun modified the objectives for exam 310-035 to clear up any confusion. Objective 4.4 now includes the statement, "Note: There will not be any questions regarding esoteric distinctions between keywords and manifest constants." Contrary to popular belief, the exam creators are not evil or malicious. (I will admit, however, that while creating the exam, we experienced a giddy joy when one of us came up with a particularly tricky, er, clever question. High-fives all around!)

```
class LiteralTest {
     public static void main (String [] args) {
          int true = 100; // this will cause error
     }
}
```

Compiling this code gives us the following error (or something similar depending on which compiler you are using):

```
%javac LiteralTest.java
LiteralTest.java:3: not a statement.
                    int true = 100; // this will cause error
                    ^
```

In other words, trying to assign a value to *true* is much like saying:

```
int 200 = 100;
```

exam Watch

***Look for words that differ from the Java reserved words in subtle ways. For example, you might see* protect *rather than* `protected`, *extend* *rather than* `extends`.**

CERTIFICATION OBJECTIVE

Literals and Ranges of All Primitive Data Types (Exam Objective 4.6)

State the range of all primitive data types and declare literal values for String and all primitive types using all permitted formats, bases, and representations.

For the exam, you'll need to know the ranges of all primitive data types. Primitives include `byte`, `short`, `int`, `long`, `float`, `double`, `boolean`, and `char`. The primitive `long`, for instance, has a range of -9,223,372,036,854,775,808 to 9,223,372,036,854,775,807. But you knew that. Go memorize them all and come back when you've burned it in. *Just kidding.* The good news is you don't have to memorize such ridiculous numbers. There's an easier method to calculate the ranges, and for the larger integer values it will be enough to know that 16 bits gives you more than 60,000 possibilities, 32 bits gives you approximately 4 billion, and so on. But you *will* need to know that the number types (both integer and floating-point types) are all signed, and how that affects the range. First, let's review the concepts.

Range of Primitive Types

All six number types in Java are signed, meaning they can be negative or positive. The leftmost bit (the most significant digit) is used to represent the sign, where a `1` means negative (glass half empty) and `0` means positive (glass half full), as shown in Figure 1-1. The rest of the bits represent the value, using two's complement notation.

Table 1-2 shows the primitive types with their sizes and ranges. Figure 1-2 shows that with a byte, for example, there are 256 possible numbers (or 2^8). Half of these are negative, and half -1 are positive. The positive range is one less than the negative range because the number zero is stored as a positive binary number. We use the formula $-2^{(bits - 1)}$ to calculate the negative range, and we use $2^{(bits - 1)}-1$ for the positive range.

The range for floating-point numbers is complicated to determine, but luckily you don't need to know these for the exam (although you *are* expected to know that a `double` holds 64 bits and a `float` 32).

For `boolean` types there is not a range; a `boolean` can be only `true` or `false`. If someone asks you for the bit depth of a boolean, look them straight in the eye and say, "That's virtual-machine dependent." They'll be impressed.

The `char` type (a character) contains a single, 16-bit Unicode character. Although the extended ASCII set known as ISO Latin-1 needs only 8 bits (256 different characters), a larger range is needed to represent characters found in languages other than English. Unicode characters are actually represented by unsigned 16-bit integers, which means 2^{16} possible values, ranging from 0 to 65535 (2^{16})-1. You'll learn in

FIGURE 1-1

The sign bit for a byte

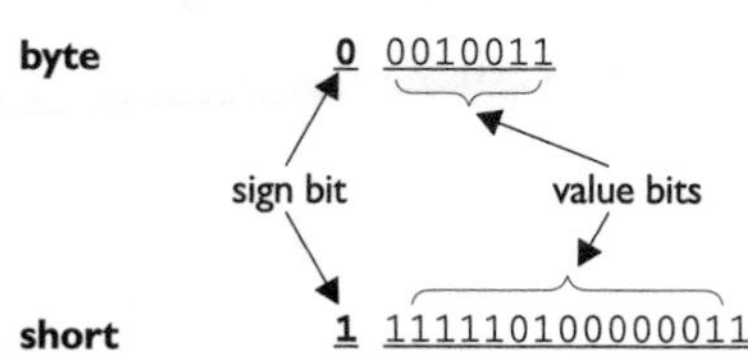

sign bit: 0 = positive
1 = negative

value bits:

byte: 7 bits can represent 2^7 or 128 different values:
0 thru 127 -or- –128 thru –1

short: 15 bits can represent 2^{15} or 32768 values:
0 thru 32767 -or- –32768 thru –1

TABLE 1-2 Ranges of Primitive Numbers

Type	Bits	Bytes	Minimum Range	Maximum Range
`byte`	8	1	-2^7	2^7-1
`short`	16	2	-2^{15}	$2^{15}-1$
`int`	32	4	-2^{31}	$2^{31}-1$
`long`	64	8	-2^{63}	$2^{63}-1$
`float`	32	4	Not needed	Not needed
`double`	64	8	Not needed	Not needed

Chapter 3 that because a `char` is really an integer type, it can be assigned to any number type large enough to hold 65535.

Literal Values for All Primitive Types

A primitive literal is merely a source code representation of the primitive data types—in other words, an integer, floating-point number, boolean, or character that you type in while writing code. The following are examples of primitive literals:

```
'b'  //  char literal
42  // int literal
false  // boolean literal
2546789.343  // double literal
```

Integer Literals

There are three ways to represent integer numbers in the Java language: decimal (base 10), octal (base 8), and hexadecimal (base 16). Most exam questions with integer literals use decimal representations, but the few that use octal or hexadecimal are worth studying for. Even though the odds that you'll ever actually *use* octal in the real world are astronomically tiny, they were included in the exam just for fun.

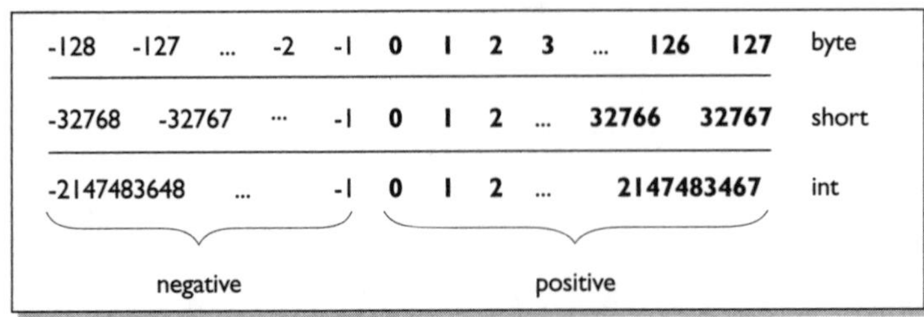

FIGURE 1-2 The range of a byte

Decimal Literals Decimal integers need no explanation; you've been using them since grade one or earlier. Chances are, you don't keep your checkbook in hex. (If you *do*, there's a Geeks Anonymous (GA) group ready to help.) In the Java language, they are represented as is, with no prefix of any kind, as follows:

```
int length = 343;
```

Octal Literals Octal integers use only the digits 0 to 7. In Java, you represent an integer in octal form by placing a zero in front of the number, as follows:

```
class Octal {
     public static void main(String [] args) {
          int six = 06; // Equal to decimal 6
          int seven = 07; // Equal to decimal 7
          int eight = 010; // Equal to decimal 8
          int nine = 011; // Equal to decimal 9
          System.out.println("Octal 010 = " + eight);
     }
}
```

Notice that when we get past seven and are out of digits to use (we are only allowed the digits 0 through 7 for octal numbers), we revert back to zero, and one is added to the beginning of the number. You can have up to 21 digits in an octal number, not including the leading zero. If we run the preceding program, it displays the following:

```
Octal 010 = 8
```

Hexadecimal Literals Hexadecimal (*hex* for short) numbers are constructed using 16 distinct symbols. Because we never invented single digit symbols for the numbers 10 through 15, we use alphabetic characters to represent these digits. Counting from 0 through 15 in hex looks like this:

```
0 1 2 3 4 5 6 7 8 9 a b c d e f
```

Java will accept capital or lowercase letters for the extra digits (one of the few places Java is not case-sensitive!). You are allowed up to 16 digits in a hexadecimal number, not including the prefix *0x* or the optional suffix extension *L*, which will be explained later.

All of the following hexadecimal assignments are legal:

```
class HexTest {
     public static void main (String [] args) {
          int x = 0X0001;
```

```
            int y = 0x7fffffff;
            int z = 0xDeadCafe;
            System.out.println("x = " + x + " y = " + y + " z = " + z);
        }
    }
```

Running HexTest produces the following output:

```
x = 1 y = 2147483647 z = -559035650
```

Don't be misled by changes in case for a hexadecimal digit or the 'x' preceding it. 0XCAFE and 0xcafe are both legal.

All three integer literals (octal, decimal, and hexadecimal) are defined as int by default, but they may also be specified as long by placing a suffix of *L* or *l* after the number:

```
long jo = 110599L;
long  so = 0xFFFFl;  // Note the lowercase 'l'
```

Floating-Point Literals

Floating-point numbers are defined as a number, a decimal symbol, and more numbers representing the fraction.

```
double d = 11301874.9881024;
```

In the preceding example, the number 11301874.9881024 is the literal value. Floating-point literals are defined as double (64 bits) by default, so if you want to assign a floating-point literal to a variable of type float (32 bits), you *must* attach the suffix *F* or *f* to the number. If you don't, the compiler will complain about a possible loss of precision, because you're trying to fit a number into a (potentially) less precise "container." The *F* suffix gives you a way to tell the compiler, "Hey, I know what I'm doing and I'll take the risk, thank you very much."

```
float f = 23.467890;  // Compiler error, possible loss of precision
float g = 49837849.029847F; // OK; has the suffix "F"
```

You may also optionally attach a *D* or *d* to double literals, but it is not necessary because this is the default behavior. But for those who enjoy typing, knock yourself out.

```
double d = 110599.995011D; // Optional, not required
double  g = 987.897; // No 'D' suffix, but OK because the
                     // literal is a double
```

Look for numeric literals that include a comma, for example,

```
int x = 25,343;   // Won't compile because of the comma
```

Boolean Literals

Boolean literals are the source code representation for `boolean` values. A `boolean` value can only be defined as `true` or `false`. Although in C (and some other languages) it is common to use numbers to represent `true` or `false`, *this will not work in Java.* Again, repeat after me, "Java is not C++."

```
boolean t = true; // Legal
boolean  f = 0; // Compiler error!
```

Be on the lookout for questions that use numbers where booleans are required. You might see an *if* ***test that uses a number, as in the following:***

```
int x = 1;   if (x) {   } // Compiler error!
```

Character Literals

A `char` literal is represented by a single character in single quotes.

```
char a = 'a';
char b = '@';
```

You can also type in the Unicode value of the character, using the Unicode notation of prefixing the value with `\u` as follows:

```
char letterN = '\u004E'; // The letter 'N'
```

Remember, characters are just 16-bit unsigned integers under the hood. That means you can assign a number literal, assuming it will fit into the unsigned 16-bit range (65535 or less). For example, the following are all legal:

```
char a = 0x892; // hexadecimal literal
char b = 982; // int literal
char c = (char) 70000; // The cast is required; 70000 is out of char range
char d = (char) -98; // Ridiculous, but legal
```

And the following are *not* ***legal and produce compiler errors:***

```
char e = -29; // Possible loss of precision; needs a cast
char f = 70000 // Possible loss of precision; needs a cast
```

You can also use an escape code if you want to represent a character that can't be typed in as a literal, including the characters for linefeed, newline, horizontal tab, backspace, and double and single quotes.

```
char c = '\"'; // A double quote
char  d = '\n'; // A newline
```

Now that you're familiar with the primitive data types and their ranges, you should be able to identify the proper data type to use in a given situation. Next are some examples of real-life quantities. Try to pick the primitive type that best represents the quantity.

Literal Values for Strings

A string literal is a source code representation of a value of a String object. For example, the following is an example of two ways to represent a string literal:

```
String s = "Bill Joy";
System.out.println("Bill" + " Joy");
```

SCENARIO & SOLUTION	
Which primitive type would be best to represent the number of stars in the universe?	`long`
Which primitive type would be best to represent a single multiple choice question on a test, with only one answer allowed?	`char`
Which primitive type would be best to represent a single multiple choice question on a test, with more than one answer allowed?	`char []`
Which primitive type would be best to represent the population of the U.S. in 2003?	`int` (or `long` for the world population)
Which primitive type would be best to represent the amount of money (in dollars and cents) you plan on having at retirement?	`float` (or `double` if you are a CEO of a software company)

Although strings are not primitives, they're included in this section because they can be represented as literals—in other words, *typed directly into code*. The only other nonprimitive type that has a literal representation is an array, which we'll look at in the next section.

```
Thread t = ???  // what literal value could possibly go here?
```

CERTIFICATION OBJECTIVE

Array Declaration, Construction, and Initialization (Exam Objective 1.1)

Write code that declares, constructs, and initializes arrays of any base type using any of the permitted forms both for declaration and for initialization.

Arrays are objects in Java that store multiple variables of the same type. Arrays can hold either primitives or object references, but the array itself will always be an object on the heap, even if the array is declared to hold primitive elements. In other words, there is no such thing as a primitive array, but you *can* make an array of primitives.

For this objective, you need to know three things:

- How to make an array *reference* variable (declare)
- How to make an array *object* (construct)
- How to *populate* the array with elements (initialize)

There are several different ways to do each of those, and you need to know about all of them for the exam.

on the job

Arrays are efficient, but most of the time you'll want to use one of the Collection types from java.util (including HashMap, ArrayList, TreeSet). Collection classes offer more flexible ways to access an object (for insertion, deletion, reading, etc.) and unlike arrays, can expand or contract dynamically as you add or remove elements (they're really managed arrays, since they use arrays behind the scenes). There's a Collection type for a wide range of needs. Do you need a fast sort? A group of objects with no duplicates? A way to access a name/value pair? A linked list? Chapter 6 covers them in more detail.

Declaring an Array

Arrays are declared by stating the type of element the array will hold, which can be an object or a primitive, followed by square brackets to the left or right of the identifier.

Declaring an Array of Primitives

```
int[] key; // Square brackets before name (recommended)
int key []; // Square brackets after name (legal but less readable)
```

Declaring an Array of Object References

```
Thread[] threads; // Recommended
Thread threads []; // Legal but less readable
```

on the Job

When declaring an array reference, you should always put the array brackets immediately after the declared type, rather than after the identifier (variable name). That way, anyone reading the code can easily tell that, for example, *key* ***is a reference to an*** `int` *array object,* ***and not an*** `int` *primitive.*

We can also declare multidimensional arrays, which are in fact arrays of arrays. This can be done in the following manner:

```
String[][][] occupantName;
String[] ManagerName [];
```

The first example is a three-dimensional array (an array of arrays of arrays) and the second is a two-dimensional array. Notice in the second example we have one square bracket before the variable name and one after. This is perfectly legal to the compiler, proving once again that *just because it's legal doesn't mean it's right.*

exam Watch

It is *never* ***legal to include the size of the array in your declaration. Yes, we know you can do that in some other languages, which is why you might see a question or two that include code similar to the following:***

```
int[5] scores;
```

The preceding code won't make it past the compiler. Remember, the JVM doesn't allocate space until you actually instantiate the array object. *That's* ***when size matters.***

Constructing an Array

Constructing an array means creating the array object on the heap—in other words, doing a `new` on the array type. To create an array object, Java needs to know how much space to allocate on the heap, so you must specify the size of the array at construction time. The size of the array is the number of elements the array will hold.

Constructing One-Dimensional Arrays

The most straightforward way to construct an array is to use the keyword `new` followed by the array type, with a bracket specifying how many elements of that type the array will hold. The following is an example of constructing an array of type `int`:

```
int[] testScores; // Declares the array of ints
testScores = new int[4]; //constructs an array and assigns it
//the testScores variable
```

The preceding code puts one new object on the heap—an array object holding four elements—with each element containing an `int` with a default value of 0. Think of this code as saying to the compiler, "Create an array object on the heap that will hold four primitives of type `int`, and assign it to the previously declared reference variable named testScores. And while you're at it, go ahead and set each `int` element to zero. Thanks." (The compiler appreciates good manners.) Figure 1-3 shows how the *testScores* array appears on the heap, after construction.

The next objective (4.5) covers more detail on the default values for array *elements*, but for now we're more concerned with how the *array object* itself is initialized.

FIGURE 1-3

A one-dimensional array on the heap

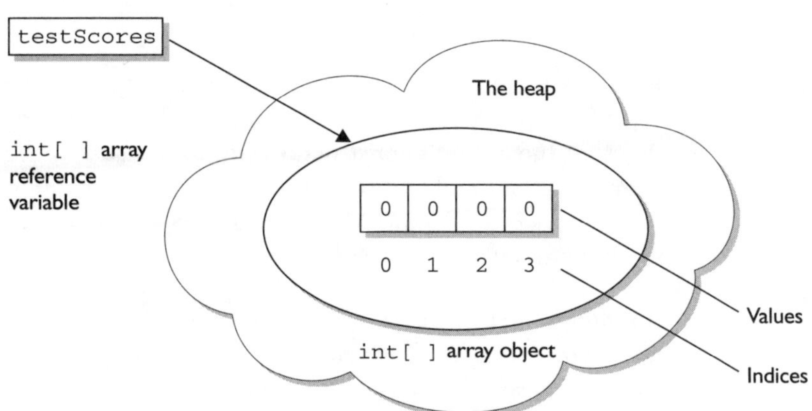

You can also declare and construct an array in one statement as follows:

```
int[] testScores = new int[14];
```

This single statement produces the same result as the two previous statements. Arrays of object types can be constructed in the same way:

```
Thread[] threads = new Thread[5];
```

The key point to remember here is that—despite how the code appears—*the Thread constructor is not being invoked.* We're not creating a *Thread instance,* but rather a single *Thread array* object. After the preceding statements, there are still no actual Thread objects!

exam Watch

Think carefully about how many objects are on the heap after a code statement or block executes. The exam will expect you to know, for example, that the preceding code produces just one object (the array assigned to the reference variable named *threads*___***). The single object referenced by*** *threads* ***holds five Thread*** *reference variables,* ***but no Thread*** *objects* ***have been created or assigned to those references.***

Remember, arrays must *always* be given a size at the time they are constructed. The JVM needs the size to allocate the appropriate space on the heap for the new array object. It is never legal, for example, to do the following:

```
int[] carList = new int[]; // Will not compile; needs a size
```

So don't do it, and if you see it on the test, run screaming toward the nearest answer marked "Compilation fails."

exam Watch

You may see the words *construct,* *create,* ***and*** *instantiate* ***used interchangeably. They all mean, "An object is built and placed on the heap." These words also imply that the object's constructor runs, as a result of the contruct/create/instantiate code. You can say with certainty, for example, that any code that uses the keyword*** `new` ***will (if it runs successfully) cause the class constructor and all superclass constructors to run.***

In addition to being constructed with `new`, arrays can also be created using a kind of syntax shorthand that creates the array while simultaneously initializing the array elements to values supplied in code (as opposed to default values). We'll look at that in detail in the section on initialization. For now, understand that because of these syntax shortcuts, objects can still be created even without you ever using or seeing the keyword `new`.

Constructing Multidimensional Arrays

Multidimensional arrays, remember, are simply arrays of arrays. So a two-dimensional array of type `int` is really an object of type `int` array (`int []`), with each element in that array holding a reference to another `int` array. The second dimension holds the actual `int` primitives.

The following code declares and constructs a two-dimensional array of type `int`:

```
int[][] ratings = new int[3][];
```

Notice that only the first brackets are given a size. That's acceptable in Java, since the JVM needs to know only the size of the object assigned to the variable `ratings`.

Figure 1-4 shows how a two-dimensional `int` array works on the heap.

Initializing an Array

Initializing an array means putting things into it. *Things* (why, yes that *is* a technical term) in the array are the array's elements, and they're either primitive values (`2`, `'a'`, `false`, etc.), or objects referred to by the reference variables in the array. If you have an array of objects (as opposed to primitives) the array doesn't actually *hold* the objects, just as any other nonprimitive variable never actually holds the *object*, but instead holds a *reference* to the object. But we talk about arrays as, for example, "an array of five strings", even though what we really mean is, "an array of five *references* to String objects." Then the big question becomes whether or not those references are actually pointing (oops, this is Java, we mean *referring)* to real String objects, or are simply *null*. Remember, a reference that has not had an object assigned to it is a *null* reference. And if you try to actually use that *null* reference by, say, applying the dot operator to invoke a method on it, you'll get the infamous *NullPointerException*.

The individual elements in the array can be accessed with an index number. The index number always begins with zero, so for an array of ten objects the index numbers will run from 0 through 9. Suppose we create an array of three Animals as follows:

```
Animal [] pets = new Animal[3];
```

FIGURE 1-4

A two-dimensional array on the heap

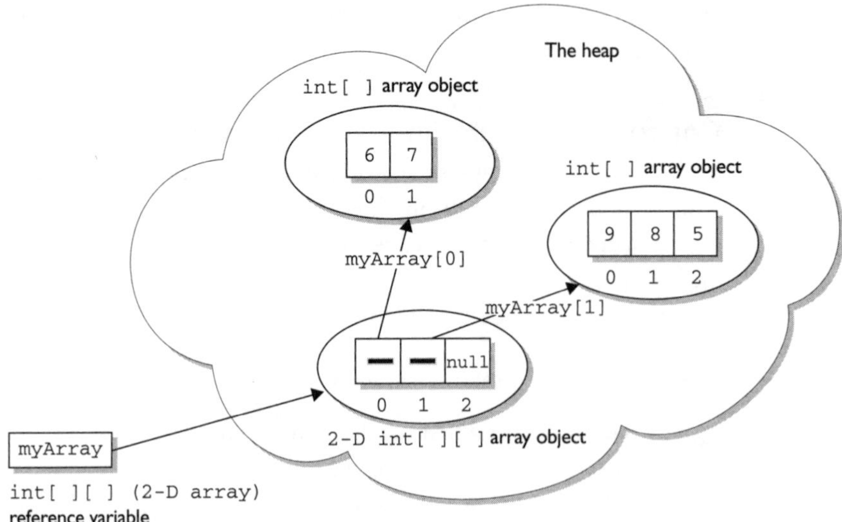

Picture demonstrates the result of the following code:

```
int[ ][ ] myArray = new int[3][ ];
myArray[0] = new int[2];
myArray[0][0] = 6;
myArray[0][1] = 7;
myArray[1] = new int[3];
myArray[1][0] = 9;
myArray[1][1] = 8;
myArray[1][2] = 5;
```

We have one array object on the heap, with three *null* references of type Animal, but we still do not have any Animal objects. The next step is to create some Animal objects and assign them to index positions in the array referenced by *pets*:

```
pets[0] = new Animal();
pets[1] = new Animal();
pets[2] = new Animal();
```

This code puts three new Animal objects on the heap and assigns them to the three index positions (elements) in the *pets* array.

Look for code that tries to access an out of range array index. For example, if an array has three elements, trying to access the [3] element will raise an `ArrayIndexOutOfBoundsException`***, because in an array of three elements, the legal index values are 0, 1, and 2. You also might see an attempt to use a negative number as an array index. The following are examples of legal and illegal array access attempts. Be sure to recognize that these cause runtime exceptions and not compiler errors! Nearly all of the exam questions list both runtime exception and compiler error as possible answers.***

```
int[] x = new int[5];
x[4] = 2; // OK, the last element is at index 4
x[5] = 3; // Runtime exception. There is no element at index 5!

int [] z = new int[2];
int y = -3;
z[y] = 4; // Runtime exception.; y is a negative number
```

These can be hard to spot in a complex loop, but that's where you're most likely to see array index problems in exam questions.

A two-dimensional array (an array of arrays) can be initialized as follows:

```
int[][] scores = new int[3][];
// Declare and create an array holding three references to int arrays

scores[0] = new int[4];
// the first element in the scores array is an int array of four int element

scores[1] = new int[6];
// the second element in the scores array is an int array of six int elements

scores[2] = new int[1];
// the third element in the scores array is an int array of one int element
```

Initializing Elements in a Loop

Array objects have a single public variable *length* that gives you the number of elements in the array. The last index value, then, is always one less than the length. For example, if the length of an array is 4, the index values are from 0 through 3. Often, you'll see array elements initialized in a loop as follows:

```
Dog[] myDogs = new Dog[6]; // creates an array of 6 Dog references
for (int x = 0; x < myDogs.length; x++) {
```

```
    myDogs[x] = new Dog(); // assign a new Dog to the index position x
}
```

The *length* variable tells us how many elements the array holds, but it does *not* tell us whether those elements have been initialized.

Declaring, Constructing, and Initializing on One Line

You can use two different array-specific syntax shortcuts to both initialize (put explicit values into an array's elements) and construct (instantiate the array object itself) in a single statement. The first is used to declare, create, and initialize in one statement as follows:

```
1.  int x = 9;
2.  int[] dots = {3,6,x,8};
```

Line 2 in the preceding code does four things:

- Declares an `int` array reference variable named `dots`.
- Creates an `int` array with a length of four (four elements).
- Populates the elements with the values 3, 6, 9, and 8.
- Assigns the new array object to the reference variable `dots`.

The size (length of the array) is determined by the number of items between the comma-separated curly braces. The code is functionally equivalent to the following longer code:

```
int[] dots;
dots = new int[4];
int x = 9;
dots[0] = 3;
dots[1] = 6;
dots[2] = x;
dots[3] = 8;
```

This begs the question, "Why would anyone use the longer way?" Two reasons come to mind. First, you might not know—at the time you create the array—the values that will be assigned to the array's elements. Second, you might just *prefer* doing it the long, slower-to-type way. Or third (OK, that's *three* reasons), maybe you just didn't know it was possible. This array shortcut alone is worth the price of this book (well, that combined with the delightful prose).

With object references rather than primitives, it works exactly the same way:

```
Dog puppy = new Dog("Frodo");
Dog[] myDogs = {puppy, new Dog("Clover"), new Dog("Aiko")};
```

The preceding code creates one Dog array, referenced by the variable *myDogs*, with a length of three elements. It assigns a previously created Dog object (assigned to the reference variable puppy) to the first element in the array, and also creates two new Dog objects ("Clover" and "Aiko"), and assigns the two newly created instances to the last two Dog reference variable elements in the *myDogs* array. Figure 1-5 shows the result of the preceding code.

FIGURE 1-5

Declaring, constructing, and initializing an array of objects

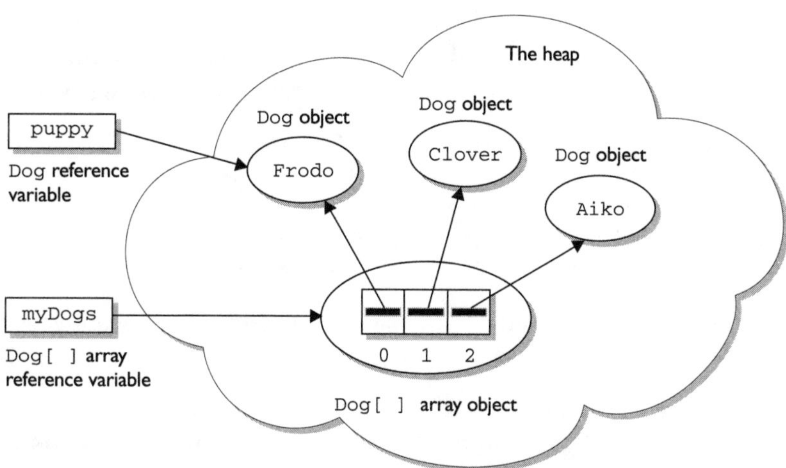

Picture demonstrates the result of the following code:

```
Dog puppy = new Dog("Frodo");
Dog[ ] myDogs = {puppy, new Dog("Clover"), new Dog("Aiko")};
```

Four objects are created:
1 Dog object referenced by puppy and by myDogs(0)
1 Dog[ ] array referenced by myDogs
2 Dog objects referenced by myDogs[1] and myDogs[2]

You can also use the shortcut syntax with multidimensional arrays, as follows:

```
int[][] scores = {{5,2,4,7}, {9,2}, {3,4}};
```

The preceding code creates a total of four objects on the heap. First, an array of `int` arrays is constructed (the object that will be assigned to the `scores` reference variable). The *scores* array has a length of three, derived from the number of items (comma-separated) between the outer curly braces. Each of the three elements in the `scores` array is a reference variable to an `int` array, so the three `int` arrays are constructed and assigned to the three elements in the *scores* array.

The size of each of the three `int` arrays is derived from the number of items within the corresponding inner curly braces. For example, the first array has a length of four, the second array has a length of two, and the third array has a length of two. So far we have four objects: one array of `int` arrays (each element is a reference to an `int` array), and three `int` arrays (each element in the three `int` arrays is an `int` value). Finally, the three `int` arrays are initialized with the actual `int` values within the inner curly braces. Thus, the first `int` array contains the values 5, 2, 4, and 7. The following code shows the values of some of the elements in this two-dimensional array:

```
scores[0] // an array of four ints
scores[1] // an array of 2 ints
scores[2] // an array of 2 ints
scores[0][1] // the int value 2
scores[2][1] // the int value 4
```

Figure 1-6 shows the result of declaring, constructing, and initializing a two-dimensional array in one statement.

Constructing and Initializing an Anonymous Array

The second shortcut is called *anonymous array creation* and can be used to construct and initialize an array, and then assign the array to a previously declared array reference variable:

```
int[] testScores;
testScores = new int[] {4,7,2};
```

The preceding code creates a new `int` array with three elements, initializes the three elements with the values 4, 7, and 2, and then assigns the new array to the previously declared `int` array reference variable *testScores.* We call this anonymous array creation because with this syntax you don't even need to assign the new array to anything.

FIGURE 1-6 Declaring, constructing, and initializing a two-dimensional array

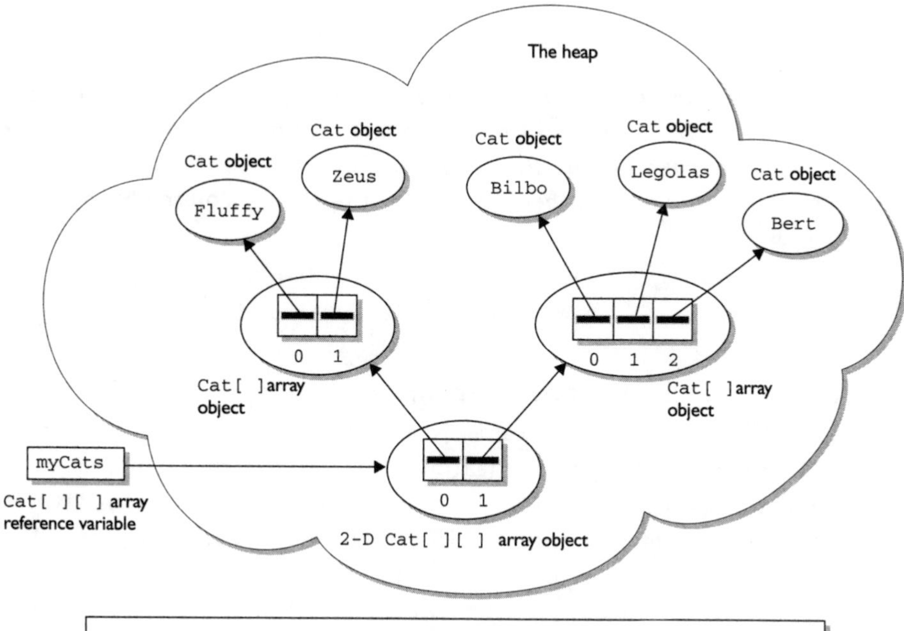

Picture demonstrates the result of the following code:

```
Cat[ ][ ] myCats = {{new Cat("Fluffy"), new Cat("Zeus")},
{new Cat("Bilbo"), new Cat("Legolas"), new Cat("Bert")}}
```

Eight objects are created:
1 2-D `Cat[ ][ ]` array object
2 `Cat[ ]` array objects
5 `Cat` objects

Maybe you're wondering, "What good is an array if you don't assign it to a reference variable?" You can use it to create a *just-in-time* array to use, for example, as an argument to a method that takes an array parameter. The following code demonstrates a just-in-time array argument:

```
public class Foof {
     void takesAnArray(int []  someArray) {
     // use the array parameter
     ...
      }
```

```
      public static void main (String [] args) {
         Foof f = new Foof();
         f.takesAnArray(new int[] {7,7,8,2,5}); //we need an array argument
      }
   }
```

exam Watch

Remember that you** do not specify a size **when using anonymous array creation syntax. The size is derived from the number of items (comma-separated) between the curly braces. Pay very close attention to the array syntax used in exam questions (and there will be a lot of them). You might see syntax such as

```
new Object[3] {null, new Object(), new Object()};
  // not legal;size must not be specified
```

Legal Array Element Assignments

What can you put in a particular array? For the exam, you need to know that arrays can have only one declared type (`int [ ]`, `Dog[ ]`, `String [ ]`, and so on) but that doesn't necessarily mean that only objects or primitives of the declared type can be assigned to the array elements. And what about the array reference itself? What kind of array object can be assigned to a particular array reference? For the exam, you'll need to know the answer to all of these questions. And, as if by magic, we're actually covering those very same topics in the following sections. Pay attention.

Arrays of Primitives

Primitive arrays can accept any value that can be promoted implicitly to the declared type of the array. Chapter 3 covers the rules for promotion in more detail, but for an example, an `int` array can hold any value that can fit into a 32-bit `int` variable. Thus, the following code is legal:

```
int[] weightList = new int[5];
byte b = 4;
char c = 'c';
short s = 7;
weightList[0] = b; // OK, byte is smaller than int
weightlist[1] = c;  // OK, char is smaller than int
weightList[2] = s;  // OK, short is smaller than int
```

Arrays of Object References

If the declared array type is a class, you can put objects of any subclass of the declared type into the array. For example, if Dog is a subclass of Animal, you can put both Dog objects and Animal objects into the array as follows:

```
class Car {}
class Subaru extends Car {}
class Honda extends Car {}
class Ferrari extends Car {}
Car [] myCars = {new Subaru(), new Honda(), new Ferrari()};
```

It helps to remember that the elements in a Car array are nothing more than Car reference variables. So anything that can be assigned to a Car reference variable can be legally assigned to a Car array element. Chapter 5 covers *polymorphic assignments* in more detail.

If the array is declared as an interface type, the array elements can refer to any instance of any class that implements the declared interface. The following code demonstrates the use of an interface as an array type:

```
interface Sporty {
     void beSporty();
}

class Ferrari extends Car implements Sporty {
     public void beSporty() {
      …
     // implement cool sporty method in a Ferrari-specific way
     }
}
class RacingFlats extends AthleticShoe implements Sporty {
     public void beSporty() {
      …
     // implement cool sporty method in a RacingShoe-specific way
     }
}
class GolfClub { }
class TestSportyThings {
     public static void main (String [] args) {
        Sporty[] sportyThings = new Sporty [3];
        sportyThings[0] = new Ferrari(); // OK, Ferrari implements Sporty
        sportyThings[1] = new RacingFlats();
        // OK, RacingFlats implements Sporty
        sportyThings[2] = new GolfClub();
```

```
            // Not OK; GolfClub does not implement Sporty
            // I don't care what anyone says
        }
    }
```

The bottom line is this: any object that passes the "IS-A" test for the declared array type can be assigned to an element of that array.

Array Reference Assignments for One-Dimensional Arrays

For the exam, you need to recognize legal and illegal assignments for array reference variables. We're not talking about references *in* the array (in other words, array *elements*), but rather references *to* the array object. For example, if you declare an `int` array, the reference variable you declared *can* be reassigned to any `int` array (of any size), but *cannot* be reassigned to anything that is *not* an `int` array, including an `int` value. Remember, all arrays are objects, so an `int` *array reference* cannot refer to an `int` *primitive*. The following code demonstrates legal and illegal assignments for primitive arrays:

```
int[] splats;
int[] dats = new int[4];
char[] letters = new char[5];
splats = dats; // OK, dats refers to an int array
splats = letters; // NOT OK, letters refers to a char array
```

It's tempting to assume that because a variable of type `byte`, `short`, or `char` can be explicitly promoted and assigned to an `int`, an array of any of those types could be assigned to an `int` array. You can't do that in Java, but it would be just like those cruel, heartless (but otherwise attractive) exam developers to put tricky array assignment questions in the exam.

Arrays that hold object references, as opposed to primitives, aren't as restrictive. Just as you can put a Honda object in a Car array (because Honda `extends` Car), you can assign an array of type Honda to a Car array reference variable as follows:

```
Car[] cars;
Honda[] cuteCars = new Honda[5];
cars = cuteCars; // OK because Honda is a type of Car
Beer[] beers = new Beer [99];
cars = beers; // NOT OK, Beer is not a type of Car
```

Apply the IS-A test to help sort the legal from the illegal. Honda IS-A Car, so a Honda array can be assigned to a Car array. Beer IS-A Car is not true; Beer does *not* extend Car (not to mention the fact that it doesn't make logical sense, unless you've already had too much of it).

exam Watch

You cannot reverse the legal assignments. ***A Car array cannot be assigned to a Honda array. A Car is not necessarily a*** `Honda`***, so if you've declared a Honda array, it might blow up if you were allowed to assign a Car array to the Honda reference variable. Think about it: a Car array could hold a reference to a Ferrari, so someone who thinks they have an array of Hondas could suddenly find themselves with a Ferrari. Remember that the IS-A test can be checked in code using the*** `instanceof` ***operator. The*** `instanceof` ***operator is covered in more detail in Chapter 3. Figure 1-7 shows an example of legal and illegal assignments for references to an array.***

FIGURE 1-7 Legal and illegal array assignments

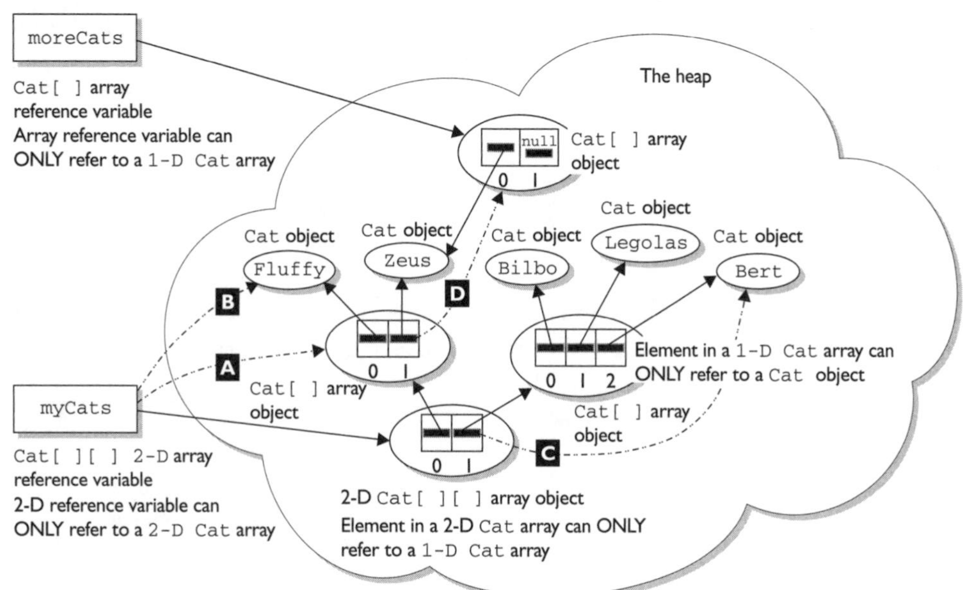

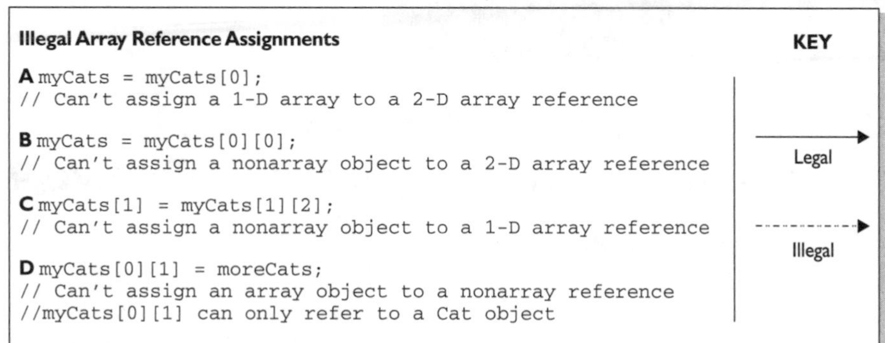

Illegal Array Reference Assignments

A `myCats = myCats[0];`
`// Can't assign a 1-D array to a 2-D array reference`

B `myCats = myCats[0][0];`
`// Can't assign a nonarray object to a 2-D array reference`

C `myCats[1] = myCats[1][2];`
`// Can't assign a nonarray object to a 1-D array reference`

D `myCats[0][1] = moreCats;`
`// Can't assign an array object to a nonarray reference`
`//myCats[0][1] can only refer to a Cat object`

KEY

Legal (solid arrow)

Illegal (dashed arrow)

The rules for array assignment apply to interfaces as well as classes. An array declared as an interface type can reference an array of any type that implements the interface. Remember, any object from a class implementing a particular interface will pass the IS-A (`instanceof`) test for that interface. For example, if Box implements Foldable, the following is legal:

```
Foldable[]  foldingThings;
Box[] boxThings = new Box[3];
foldingThings = boxThings;
// OK, Box implements Foldable, so Box IS-A Foldable
```

Array Reference Assignments for Multidimensional Arrays

When you assign an array to a previously declared array reference, *the array you're assigning must be the same dimension as the reference you're assigning it to.* For example, a two-dimensional array of `int` arrays *cannot* be assigned to a regular `int` array reference, as follows:

```
int[]  blots;
int[][] squeegees = new int[3][];
blots = squeegees;  // NOT OK, squeegees is a two-d array of int arrays
int[] blocks = new int[6];
blots = blocks; // OK, blocks is an int array
```

Pay particular attention to array assignments using different dimensions. You might, for example, be asked if it's legal to assign an `int` array to the first element in an array of `int` arrays, as follows:

```
int[][]  books = new int[3][];
int[] numbers = new int[6];
int aNumber = 7;
books[0] = aNumber; //NOT OK, expecting an int array instead of an int
books[0] = numbers; //OK, numbers is an int array
```

CERTIFICATION OBJECTIVE

Using a Variable or Array Element That Is Uninitialized and Unassigned (Exam Objective 4.5)

Identify all Java programming language keywords and correctly constructed identifiers.

Java gives us the option of initializing a declared variable or leaving it uninitialized. When we attempt to *use* the uninitialized variable, we can get different behavior depending on what type of variable or array we are dealing with (primitives or objects). The behavior also depends on the level (scope) at which we are declaring our variable. An *instance variable* is declared within the class but outside any method or constructor, whereas a *local variable* is declared within a method (or in the argument list of the method).

exam Watch

Local variables are sometimes called *stack, temporary, automatic,* ***or*** *method* ***variables, but the rules for these variables are the same regardless of what you call them. Although you can leave a local variable uninitialized, the compiler complains if you try to*** *use* ***a local variable before initializing it with a value, as we shall see.***

Primitive and Object Type Instance Variables

Instance variables (also called *member variables*) are variables defined at the class level. That means the variable declaration is not made within a method, constructor, or any other initializer block. Instance variables are initialized to a default value each time a new instance is created. Table 1-3 lists the default values for primitive and object types.

Primitive Instance Variables

In the following example, the integer *year* is defined as a class member because it is within the initial curly braces of the class and not within a method's curly braces:

```
public class BirthDate {
    int year; // Instance variable
    public static void main(String [] args) {
       BirthDate bd = new BirthDate();
       bd.showYear();
    }
    public void showYear() {
       System.out.println("The year is " + year);
     }
}
```

When the program is started, it gives the variable *year* a value of zero, the default value for primitive number instance variables.

TABLE 1-3 Default Values for Primitive and Reference Types

Variable Type	Default Value
Object reference	`null` (not referencing any object)
`byte, short, int, long`	`0`
`float, double`	`0.0`
`boolean`	`false`
`char`	`'\u0000'`

It's a good idea to initialize all your variables, even if you're assigning them with the default value. Your code will be easier to read; programmers who have to maintain your code (after you win the lottery and move to Tahiti) will be grateful.

Object Reference Instance Variables

When compared with uninitialized primitive variables, Object references that aren't initialized are a completely different story. Let's look at the following code:

```
public class Book {
     private String title;
     public String getTitle() {
        return title;
     }
     public static void main(String [] args) {
        Book b = new Book();
        System.out.println("The title is " + b.getTitle());
     }
}
```

This code will compile fine. When we run it, the output is

```
The title is null
```

The *title* variable has not been explicitly initialized with a String assignment, so the instance variable value is *null*. Remember that *null* is not the same as an empty String (""). A *null* value means the reference variable is not referring to any object on the heap. Thus, the following modification to the Book code runs into trouble:

```
public class Book {
    private String title;
```

```
    public String getTitle() {
       return title;
    }
    public static void main(String [] args) {
       Book b = new Book();
       String s = b.getTitle(); // Compiles and runs
       String t = s.toLowerCase(); // Runtime Exception!
    }
}
```

When we try to run the Book class, the JVM will produce the following error:

```
%java Book
Exception in thread "main" java.lang.NullPointerException
     at Book.main(Book.java:12
```

We get this error because the reference variable `title` does not point (refer) to an object. We can check to see whether an object has been instantiated by using the keyword `null`, as the following revised code shows:

```
public class Book {
    private String title;
    public String getTitle() {
       return title;
    }
    public static void main(String [] args) {
       Book b = new Book();
       String s = b.getTitle(); // Compiles and runs
       if (s != null) {
          String t = s.toLowerCase();
       }
     }
}
```

The preceding code checks to make sure the object referenced by the variable `s` is not `null` before trying to use it. Watch out for scenarios on the exam where you might have to trace back through the code to find out whether an object reference will have a value of `null`. In the preceding code, for example, you look at the instance variable declaration for *title*, see that there's no explicit initialization, recognize that the *title* variable will be given the default value of `null`, and then realize that the variable *s* will also have a value of `null`. Remember, the value of *s* is a copy of the value of *title* (as returned by the `getTitle()` method), so if *title* is a *null* reference, *s* will be too.

Array Instance Variables

An array is an object; thus, an array instance variable that's declared but not explicitly initialized will have a value of `null`, just as any other object reference instance variable. But…if the array *is* initialized, what happens to the elements contained in the array? All array elements are given their default values—the same default values that elements of that type get when they're instance variables. The bottom line: *Array elements are always always always given default values, regardless of where the array itself is declared or instantiated.* By the way, if you see the word *always* three times in a row, reread the sentence three times. Now, once more, with feeling!

If we initialize an array, object reference elements will equal `null` if they are not initialized individually with values. If primitives are contained in an array, they will be given their respective default values. For example, in the following code, the array *year* will contain 100 integers that all equal zero by default:

```
public class BirthDays {
     static int [] year = new int[100];
     public static void main(String [] args) {
          for(int i=0;i<100;i++)
               System.out.println("year[" + i + "] = " + year[i]);
     }
}
```

When the preceding code runs, the output indicates that all 100 integers in the array equal zero.

Local (Stack, Automatic) Primitives and Objects

Local variables are defined within a method, including method parameters.

"Automatic" is just another term for "local variable." It does not mean the automatic variable is automatically assigned a value! The opposite is true; an automatic variable must be assigned a value in the code; otherwise, the compiler will complain.

Local Primitives

In the following time travel simulator, the integer *year* is defined as an automatic variable because it is within the curly braces of a method.

```
public class TimeTravel {
     public static void main(String [] args) {
          int year = 2050;
          System.out.println("The year is " + year);
     }
}
```

Okay, so we've still got work to do on the physics. *Local variables, including primitives, always always always must be initialized before you attempt to use them* (though not necessarily on the same line of code). Java does not *give* local variables a default value; *you must explicitly initialize them* with a value, as in the preceding example. If you try to use an uninitialized primitive in your code, you'll get a compiler error:

```
public class TimeTravel {
     public static void main(String [] args) {
          int year; // Local variable (declared but not initialized)
          System.out.println("The year is " + year); // Compiler error
     }
}
```

Compiling produces the following output:

```
%javac TimeTravel.java
TimeTravel.java:4: Variable year may not have been initialized.
          System.out.println("The year is " + year);
1 error
```

To correct our code, we must give the integer `year` a value. In this updated example, we declare it on a separate line, which is perfectly valid:

```
public class TimeTravel {
     public static void main(String [] args) {
          int year; // Declared but not initialized
          int day; // Declared but not initialized
          System.out.println("You step into the portal.");
          year = 2050; // Initialize (assign an explicit value)
          System.out.println("Welcome to the year " + year);
     }
}
```

Notice in the preceding example we declared an integer called *day* that never gets initialized, yet the code compiles and runs fine. Legally, you can declare a local variable without initializing it as long as you don't *use* the variable, but let's face it, if you declared it, you probably had a reason. (Although we have heard of programmers declaring random local variables just for sport, to see if they can figure out how and why they're being used.)

The compiler can't always tell whether a local variable has been initialized before use. For example, if you initialize within a logically conditional block (in other words, a code block that may not run, such as an if block or for loop without a literal value of `true` or `false` in the test), the compiler knows that the initialization might not happen, and can produce an error. The following code upsets the compiler:

```
public class TestLocal {
    public static void main(String [] args) {
        int x;
        if (args[0] != null) { //assume you know this will always be true
            x = 7; // compiler can't tell that this statement will run
        }
        int y = x;
    }
}
```

The preceding code produces the following error when you attempt to compile it:

```
TestLocal.java:8: variable x might not have been initialized
  int y = x;
1 error
```

Because of the compiler-can't-tell-for-certain problem, you will sometimes need to initialize your variable outside the conditional block, just to make the compiler happy. You know why that's important if you've seen the bumper sticker: "When the compiler's not happy, ain't *nobody* happy."

Local Objects

Objects, too, behave differently when declared within a method rather than as instance variables. With instance variable object references, you can get away with leaving an object reference uninitialized, as long as the code checks to make sure the reference isn't *null* before using it. Remember, to the compiler, `null` *is* a value. You can't use the dot operator on a `null` reference, because there *is* no object at the other end of it, but *a null reference is not the same as an uninitialized reference.* Locally declared references can't get away with checking for *null* before use, unless you explicitly initialize the local variable to `null`. The compiler will complain about the following code:

```
import java.util.Date;
public class TimeTravel {
     public static void main(String [] args) {
          Date date;
          if (date == null)
               System.out.println("date is null");
     }
}
```

Compiling the code results in the following error:

```
%javac TimeTravel.java
TimeTravel.java:5: Variable date may not have been initialized.
          If (date == null)
1 error
```

Instance variable references are always given a default value of `null`, until explicitly initialized to something else. But local references are *not* given a default value; in other words, *they aren't null.* If you don't initialize a local reference variable, then by default, its value is…well that's the whole point—it doesn't have *any* value at all! So we'll make this simple: Just set the darn thing to `null` explicitly, until you're ready to initialize it to something else. The following local variable will compile properly:

```
Date date = null; // Explicitly set the local reference variable to null
```

Local Arrays

Just like any other object reference, array references declared within a method must be assigned a value before use. That just means you must declare and construct the array. You do not, however, need to explicitly initialize the elements of an array. We've said it before, but it's important enough to repeat: *array elements are given their default values (*`0`*,* `false`*,* `null`*,* `'\u0000'`*, etc.) regardless of whether the array is declared as an instance or local variable.* The array object itself, however, will not be initialized if it's declared locally. In other words, you must explicitly initialize an array reference if it's declared and used within a method, but at the moment you construct an array object, all of its elements are assigned their default values.

CERTIFICATION OBJECTIVE

Command-Line Arguments to Main (Exam Objective 4.3)

State the correspondence between index values in the argument array passed to a main method and command line arguments.

Now that you know all about arrays, command-line arguments will be a piece of cake. Remember that the main method—the one the JVM invokes—must take a String array parameter. That String array holds the arguments you send along with the command to run your Java program, as follows:

```
class TestMain {
  public static void main (String [] args) {
     System.out.println("First arg is " + args[0]);
  }
}
```

When invoked at the command line as follows,

```
%java TestMain  Hello
```

the output is

```
First arg is Hello
```

The length of the *args* array will always be equal to the number of command-line arguments. In the following code, `args.length` is one, meaning there is one element in the array, and it is at index zero. If you try to access beyond `length-1`, you'll get an `ArrayIndexOutOfBoundsException`! This causes your entire program to explode in a spectacular JVM shutdown, so be sure the right number of arguments are being passed, perhaps with a nice user suggestion. The following code is an example of a main method expecting three arguments:

```
    public static void main (String [] args) {
      if (args.length < 3) {
        System.out.println("Usage: [name] [social security #]
  [IQ] Try again when you have a clue");
      }
    }
```

exam Watch

The String array parameter does not have to be named** args **or** arg. **It can be named, for example,** freddie. **Also, remember that the** main **argument is just an array! There's nothing special about it, other than how it gets passed into** main **(from the JVM).

EXERCISE 1-1

Creating a Program That Outputs Command-Line Arguments

In the following exercise...

1. Create a program that outputs every command-line argument, then displays the number of arguments.
2. You should use the array variable *length* to retrieve the length of the array.

An example of how you might write your code is at the end of this chapter.

CERTIFICATION SUMMARY

After absorbing the material in this chapter, you should be familiar with some of the nuances of the Java language. You may also be experiencing confusion around why you ever wanted to take this exam in the first place. That's normal at this point. If you hear yourself saying, "What was I thinking?" just lie down until it passes. We would *like* to tell you that it gets easier... that this was the toughest chapter and it's all downhill from here.

Let's briefly review what you'll need to know for the exam.

There will be more than one question dealing with keywords, so be sure you can identify which are keywords and which aren't. Make sure you're familiar with the ranges of integer primitives, and the bit depth of all primitives. And, although this isn't Java language specific, you must be able to convert between octal, decimal, and hexadecimal literals. You have also learned about arrays, and how they behave when declared in a class or a method.

Be certain that you know the effects of leaving a variable uninitialized, and how the variable's scope changes the behavior. You'll also be expected to know what happens to the elements of an array when they're not explicitly initialized.

For the exam, knowing what you can't do with the Java language is just as important as knowing what you can do. Give the sample questions a try! They're very similar to the difficulty and structure of the real exam questions, and should be an eye opener for how difficult the exam can be. Don't worry if you get a lot of them wrong. If you find a topic that you are weak in, spend more time reviewing and studying. Many programmers need two or three serious passes through a chapter (or an individual objective) before they can answer the questions confidently.

TWO-MINUTE DRILL

Java Programming Language Keywords

- ❑ Keywords cannot be used as identifiers (names) for classes, methods, variables, or anything else in your code.
- ❑ All keywords start with a lowercase letter.

Literals and Ranges of All Primitive Data Types

- ❑ All six number types in Java are signed, so they can be positive or negative.
- ❑ Use the formula $-2^{(bits-1)}$ to $2^{(bits-1)}-1$ to determine the range of an integer type.
- ❑ A `char` is really a 16-bit unsigned integer.
- ❑ Literals are source code representations of primitive data types, or String.
- ❑ Integers can be represented in octal (0127), decimal (1245), and hexadecimal (0XCAFE).
- ❑ Numeric literals cannot contain a comma.
- ❑ A `char` literal can be represented as a single character in single quotes ('A').
- ❑ A `char` literal can also be represented as a Unicode value ('\u0041').
- ❑ A `char` literal can also be represented as an integer, as long as the integer is less than 65536.
- ❑ A `boolean` literal can be either `true` or `false`.
- ❑ Floating-point literals are always double by default; if you want a `float`, you must append an *F* or *f* to the literal.

Array Declaration, Construction, and Initialization

- ❑ Arrays can hold primitives or objects, but the array itself is *always* an object.
- ❑ When you declare an array, the brackets can be to the left or right of the variable name.
- ❑ It is never legal to include the size of an array in the declaration.

- You must include the size of an array when you construct it (using `new`) unless you are creating an anonymous array.
- Elements in an array of objects are not automatically created, although primitive array elements are given default values.
- You'll get a `NullPointerException` if you try to use an array element in an object array, if that element does not refer to a real object.
- Arrays are indexed beginning with zero. In an array with three elements, you can access element 0, element 1, and element 2.
- You'll get an `ArrayIndexOutOfBoundsException` if you try to access outside the range of an array.
- Arrays have a *length* variable that contains the number of elements in the array.
- The last index you can access is always one less than the length of the array.
- Multidimensional arrays are just arrays of arrays.
- The dimensions in a multidimensional array can have different lengths.
- An array of primitives can accept any value that can be promoted implicitly to the declared type of the array. For example, a `byte` variable can be placed in an `int` array.
- An array of objects can hold any object that passes the IS-A (or `instanceof`) test for the declared type of the array. For example, if Horse extends Animal, then a Horse object can go into an Animal array.
- If you assign an array to a previously declared array reference, the array you're assigning must be the same dimension as the reference you're assigning it to.
- You can assign an array of one type to a previously declared array reference of one of its supertypes. For example, a Honda array can be assigned to an array declared as type Car (assuming Honda `extends` Car).

Using a Variable or Array Element That Is Uninitialized and Unassigned

- When an array of objects is instantiated, objects within the array are not instantiated automatically, but all the references get the default value of `null`.
- When an array of primitives is instantiated, all elements get their default values.

- Just as with array elements, instance variables are always initialized with a default value.
- Local/automatic/method variables are never given a default value. If you attempt to use one before initializing it, you'll get a compiler error.

Command-Line Arguments to Main

- Command-line arguments are passed to the String array parameter in the *main* method.
- The first command-line argument is the first element in the main String array parameter.
- If no arguments are passed to *main*, the length of the *main* String array parameter will be zero.

SELF TEST

The following questions will help you measure your understanding of the material presented in this chapter. Read all the choices carefully! These questions are *very* similar to the kinds of questions you'll see on the latest exam. Again, don't worry if you have trouble with them at first; the style of the exam questions can take some getting used to. For example, you might find yourself looking at the answers and wanting to kick yourself for missing little things that you actually knew, but just didn't see in the question. The best advice we have for both the practice questions and the real exam is to *always look again.* As soon as you get an idea in your head about the answer to a question, imagine someone standing next to you and whispering in your ear, "Are you sure? Look again." Much of the time, you'll look again and say, "I'm sure," especially since your first reaction is often the best one to go with. But you'll be surprised by how often that second look brings up something new.

Java Programming Language Keywords (Objective 4.4)

1. Given the following,

```
public class Test {
   public static void main(String [] args) {
      signed int x = 10;
         for (int y=0; y<5; y++, x--)
            System.out.print(" " + x);
   }
}
```

what is the result? (Choose one.)

A. `10 9 8 7 6`

B. `9 8 7 6 5`

C. Compilation fails

D. An exception is thrown at runtime

2. Which is a reserved word in the Java programming language? (Choose one.)

A. `method`

B. `native`

C. `subclasses`

D. `reference`

E. `array`

3. Which one of these lists contains only Java programming language keywords? (Choose one.)

A. `class, if, void, long, Int, continue`

B. `goto, instanceof, native, finally, default, throws`

C. `try, virtual, throw, final, volatile, transient`

D. `strictfp, constant, super, implements, do`

E. `byte, break, assert, switch, include`

4. Which two are keywords? (Choose two.)

A. `interface`

B. `unsigned`

C. `Float`

D. `this`

E. `string`

Literals and Ranges of All Primitive Data Types (Objective 4.6)

5. Which three are valid declarations of a `char`? (Choose three.)

A. `char c1 = 064770;`

B. `char c2 = 'face';`

C. `char c3 = 0xbeef;`

D. `char c4 = \u0022;`

E. `char c5 = '\iface';`

F. `char c6 = '\uface';`

6. Which two are valid declarations of a String? (Choose two.)

A. `String s1 = null;`

B. `String s2 = 'null';`

C. `String s3 = (String) 'abc';`

D. `String s4 = (String) '\ufeed';`

E. `String s5 = "strings rule";`

7. Which one is a valid declaration of a `boolean`? (Choose one.)

   A. `boolean b1 = 0;`

   B. `boolean b2 = 'false';`

   C. `boolean b3 = false;`

   D. `boolean b4 = Boolean.false();`

   E. `boolean b5 = no;`

8. What is the numerical range of a `char`? (Choose one.)

   A. –128 to 127

   B. –(2 ^ 15) to (2 ^ 15) - 1

   C. 0 to 32767

   D. Platform dependent

   E. 0 to 65535

9. Which three are valid declarations of a `float`? (Choose three.)

   A. `float f1 = -343;`

   B. `float f2 = 3.14;`

   C. `float f3 = 0x12345;`

   D. `float f4 = 42e7;`

   E. `float f5 = 2001.0D;`

   F. `float f6 = 2.81F;`

Array Declaration, Construction, and Initialization (Objective 1.1)

10. Which three are legal array declarations? (Choose three.)

    A. `int [] myScores [];`

    B. `char [] myChars;`

    C. `int [6] myScores;`

    D. `Dog myDogs [];`

    E. `Dog myDogs [7];`

11. Given the following,

```
public class Test {
    public static void main(String [] args) {
```

```
    int [] [] [] x = new int [3] [] [];
    int i,j;
    x[0] = new int[4][];
    x[1] = new int[2][];
    x[2] = new int[5][];
    for (i=0; i<x.length; i++)
       for (j=0; j<x[i].length; j++) {
          x[i][j] = new int [i + j + 1];
          System.out.println("size = " + x[i][j].length);
       }
    }
}
```

how many lines of output will be produced? (Choose one.)

A. 7

B. 9

C. 11

D. 13

E. Compilation fails

F. An exception is thrown at runtime

12. Given the following,

```
1.  public class Test {
2.     public static void main(String [] args) {
3.        byte [][] big = new byte [7][7];
4.        byte [][] b = new byte [2][1];
5.        byte b3 = 5;
6.        byte b2 [][][][] = new byte [2][3][1][2];
7.
8.     }
9.  }
```

which of the following lines of code could be inserted at line 7, and still allow the code to compile? (Choose four that would work.)

A. `b2[0][1] = b;`

B. `b[0][0] = b3;`

C. `b2[1][1][0] = b[0][0];`

D. `b2[1][2][0] = b;`

E. `b2[0][1][0][0] = b[0][0];`

F. `b2[0][1] = big;`

13. Which two will declare an array and initialize it with five numbers? (Choose two.)

A. `Array a = new Array(5);`

B. `int [] a = {23,22,21,20,19};`

C. `int [] array;`

D. `int array [] = new int [5];`

E. `int a [] = new int(5);`

F. `int [5] array;`

14. Which will legally declare, construct, and initialize an array? (Choose one.)

A. `int [] myList = {"1", "2", "3"};`

B. `int [] myList = (5, 8, 2);`

C. `int myList [] [] = {4,9,7,0};`

D. `int myList [] = {4, 3, 7};`

E. `int [] myList = [3, 5, 6];`

F. `int myList [] = {4; 6; 5};`

Using a Variable or Array Element That Is Uninitialized and Unassigned (Objective 4.5)

15. Which four describe the correct default values for array elements of the types indicated? (Choose four.)

A. `int     -> 0`

B. `String  -> "null"`

C. `Dog     -> null`

D. `char    -> '\u0000'`

E. `float   -> 0.0f`

F. `boolean -> true`

16. Given the following,

```
public class TestDogs {
   public static void main(String [] args) {
      Dog [][] theDogs = new Dog[3][];
      System.out.println(theDogs[2][0].toString());
   }
}
```

```

class Dog {}
```

what is the result? (Choose one.)

A. `null`

B. `theDogs`

C. Compilation fails

D. An exception is thrown at runtime

17. Given the following,

```
public class X {
   public static void main(String [] args) {
      String names [] = new String[5];
         for (int x=0; x < args.length; x++)
            names[x] = args[x];
         System.out.println(names[2]);
   }
}
```

and the command line invocation is

```
java X a b
```

what is the result? (Choose one.)

A. `names`

B. `null`

C. Compilation fails

D. An exception is thrown at runtime

Command-Line Arguments to Main (Objective 4.3)

18. Given the following,

```
public class CommandArgs {
   public static void main(String [] args) {
      String s1 = args[1];
      String s2 = args[2];
      String s3 = args[3];
      String s4 = args[4];
      System.out.print(" args[2] = " + s2);
   }
}
```

and the command-line invocation,

```
java CommandArgs 1 2 3 4
```

what is the result?

A. `args[2] = 2`

B. `args[2] = 3`

C. `args[2] = null`

D. `args[2] = 1`

E. Compilation fails

F. An exception is thrown at runtime

19. Given the following,

```
public class CommandArgsTwo {
   public static void main(String [] argh) {
      String [] args;
      int x;
      x = argh.length;
      for (int y = 1; y <= x; y++) {
         System.out.print(" " + argh[y]);
      }
   }
}
```

and the command-line invocation,

```
java CommandArgsTwo 1 2 3
```

what is the result?

A. 0 1 2

B. 1 2 3

C. 0 0 0

D. `null null null`

E. Compilation fails

F. An exception is thrown at runtime

20. Given the following,

```
public class CommandArgsThree {
   public static void main(String [] args) {
      String [][] argCopy = new String[2][2];
      int x;
      argCopy[0] = args;
      x = argCopy[0].length;
      for (int y = 0; y < x; y++) {
         System.out.print(" " + argCopy[0][y]);
      }
   }
}
```

and the command-line invocation,

```
java CommandArgsThree 1 2 3
```

what is the result?

A. 0 0

B. 1 2

C. 0 0 0

D. 1 2 3

E. Compilation fails

F. An exception is thrown at runtime

SELF TEST ANSWERS

Java Programming Language Keywords (Objective 4.4)

1. ☑ C. The word "signed" is not a valid modifier keyword in the Java language. All number primitives in Java are signed. Always.

2. ☑ B. The word `native` is a valid keyword, used to modify a method declaration.
☒ A, D, and E are not keywords. C is wrong because the keyword for subclassing in Java is `extends`, not 'subclasses'.

3. ☑ B. All the words in answer **B** are among the 49 Java keywords.
☒ A is wrong because the keyword for the primitive `int` starts with a lowercase *i*. C is wrong because "virtual" is a keyword in C++, but not Java. **D** is wrong because "constant" is not a keyword. Constants in Java are marked `static` and `final`. **E** is wrong because "include" is a keyword in C, but not Java.

4. ☑ A and D. Both `interface` and `this` are both valid keywords.
☒ B is wrong because "unsigned" is a keyword in C/C++ but not in Java. C is wrong because "Float" is a class type. The keyword for the Java primitive is `float`. E is wrong because although "String" is a class type in Java, "string" is not a keyword.

Literals and Ranges of All Primitive Data Types (Objective 4.6)

5. ☑ A, C, and F. **A** is an octal representation of the integer value 27128, which is legal because it fits into an unsigned 16-bit integer. **C** is a hexadecimal representation of the integer value 48879, which fits into an unsigned 16-bit integer. **F** is a Unicode representation of a character.
☒ B is wrong because you can't put more than one character in a `char` literal. You know that **B** is a literal character because it comes between single quotes. The only other acceptable `char` literal that can go between single quotes is a Unicode value, and Unicode literals must always start with a '`\u`'. **D** is wrong because the single quotes are missing. **E** is wrong because it appears to be a Unicode representation (notice the backslash), but starts with '`\i`' rather than '`\u`'.

6. ☑ A and E. **A** sets the String reference to null; **E** initializes the String reference with a literal.
☒ B is wrong because null cannot be in single quotes. **C** is wrong because there are multiple characters between the single quotes ('abc'). **D** is wrong because you can't cast a `char` (primitive) to a String (object).

7. ☑ C. A boolean can only be assigned the literal `true` or `false`.
☒ A, B, D, and E are all invalid assignments for a boolean.

8. ☑ E. A `char` is really an unsigned 16-bit integer behind the scenes, so it supports 2^{16} (from 0 to 65535) values.

9. ☑ A, C, and F. A and C are integer literals (32 bits), and integers can be legally assigned to floats (also 32 bits). F is correct because *F* is appended to the literal, declaring it as a `float` rather than a `double` (the default for floating point literals).
☒ B, D, and E are all doubles.

Array Declaration, Construction, and Initialization (Objective 1.1)

10. ☑ A, B, and D. With an array declaration, you can place the brackets to the right or left of the identifier. A looks strange, but it's perfectly legal to split the brackets in a multidimensional array, and place them on both sides of the identifier. Although coding this way would only annoy your fellow programmers, for the exam, you need to know it's legal.
☒ C and E are wrong because you can't declare an array with a size. The size is only needed when the array is actually instantiated (and the JVM needs to know how much space to allocate for the array, based on the type of array and the size).

11. ☑ C. The loops use the array sizes (length).
If you think this question is unfairly complicated, get used to it. Question 11 is a good example of the kinds of questions you'll see on the exam. You should approach complex loop questions by using a pencil and paper and stepping through the loop (or loops, in this case), keeping track of the variable values at each iteration. Tedious, we know, but you can expect a lot of questions like this on the exam. Take your time and recheck your work.

12. ☑ A, B, E, and F. This question covers the issue of, "What can I assign to an array reference variable?" The key is to get the dimensions right. For example, if an array is declared as a two-dimensional array, you can't assign a one-dimensional array to a one-dimensional array reference.
☒ C is wrong because it tries to assign a primitive byte where a byte *array* (one dimension) is expected. D is wrong because it tries to assign a two-dimensional array where a one-dimensional array is expected.

13. ☑ B and D. Both are legal ways to declare and initialize an array with five elements.
☒ A is wrong because it shows an example of instantiating a *class* named Array, passing the integer value 5 to the object's constructor. If you don't see the brackets, you can be

certain there is no actual array object! In other words, an Array object (instance of class Array) is not the same as an array object. C is wrong because it shows a legal array declaration, but with no initialization. E is wrong (and will not compile) because the initialization uses parens () rather than brackets. F is wrong (and will not compile) because it declares an array with a size. Arrays must never be given a size when declared.

14. ☑ D. The only legal array declaration and assignment statement is D.
☒ A is wrong because it initializes an `int` array with String literals. B and E are wrong because they use something other than curly braces for the initialization. C is wrong because it provides initial values for only one dimension, although the declared array is a two-dimensional array. F is wrong because it uses semicolons where it should use commas, to separate the items in the initialization.

Using a Variable or Array Element That Is Uninitialized and Unassigned (Objective 4.5)

15. ☑ A, C, D, and E.
☒ B is wrong because the default value for a String (and any other object reference) is `null`, with no quotes. F is wrong because the default value for `boolean` elements is `false`.

16. ☑ D. The second dimension of the array referenced by `theDogs` has not been initialized. Attempting to access an uninitialized object element (line 4) raises a `NullPointerException`.

17. ☑ B. The *names* array is initialized with five *null* elements. Then elements 0 and 1 are assigned the String values "a" and "b" respectively (the command-line arguments passed to main). Elements 2, 3, and 4 remain unassigned, so they have a value of `null`.

Command-line Arguments to Main (Objective 4.3)

18. ☑ F. An exception is thrown because at line 6, the array index (the fifth element) is out of bounds. The exception thrown is the cleverly named `ArrayIndexOutOfBoundsException`.

19. ☑ F. An exception is thrown because at some point in line 7, the value of x will be equal to y, resulting in an attempt to access an index out of bounds for the array. Remember that you can access only as far as *length*-1, so loop logical tests should use `x<someArray.length` as opposed to `x <= someArray.length`.

20. ☑ D. In line 5, the reference variable `argCopy[0]`, which was referring to an array with two elements, is reassigned to an array (args) with three elements.

EXERCISE ANSWERS

Exercise 1.1: Command-Line Arguments to Main

Your completed code should look something like the following:

```
public class MainTest {
     public static void main (String [] args) {
          for (int i = 0;i < args.length;i++) {
               System.out.println(args[i]);
          }
          System.out.println("Total words:  " + args.length);
     }
}
```

2

Declarations and Access Control

CERTIFICATION OBJECTIVES

- Declarations and Modifiers
- Declaration Rules
- Interface Implementation
- ✓ Two-Minute Drill

Q&A Self Test

We're on a roll. We've covered the fundamentals of keywords, primitives, arrays, and variables. Now it's time to drill deeper into rules for declaring classes, methods, and variables. We'll tackle access modifiers, abstract method implementation, interface implementation, and what you can and can't return from a method. Chapter 2 includes the topics asked most often on the exam, so you really need a solid grasp of this chapter's content. Grab your caffeine and let's get started.

CERTIFICATION OBJECTIVE

Declarations and Modifiers (Exam Objective 1.2)

Declare classes, nested classes, methods, instance variables, static variables, and automatic (method local) variables making appropriate use of all permitted modifiers (such as `public`, `final`, `static`, `abstract`, *and so forth). State the significance of each of these modifiers both singly and in combination, and state the effect of package relationships on declared items qualified by these modifiers.*

When you write code in Java, you're writing classes. Within those classes, as you know, are variables and methods (plus a few other things). *How* you declare your classes, methods, and variables dramatically affects your code's behavior. For example, a `public` method can be accessed from code running anywhere in your application. Mark that method `private`, though, and it vanishes from everyone's radar (except the class in which it was declared). For this objective, we'll study the ways in which you can modify (or not) a class, method, or variable declaration. You'll find that we cover modifiers in an extreme level of detail, and though we know you're already familiar with them, we're starting from the very beginning. Most Java programmers *think* they know how all the modifiers work, but on closer study often find out that they don't (at least not to the degree needed for the exam). Subtle distinctions are everywhere, so you need to be absolutely certain you're *completely* solid on everything in this objective before taking the exam.

Class Declarations and Modifiers

We'll start this objective by looking at how to declare and modify a class. Although nested (often called *inner*) classes are on the exam, we'll save nested class declarations for Chapter 8. You're going to love that chapter. No, *really*. Seriously. No kidding around.

Before we dig into class declarations, let's do a quick review of the rules:

- There can be only one `public` class per source code file.
- The name of the file must match the name of the `public` class.
- If the class is part of a package, the package statement must be the first line in the source code file.
- If there are import statements, they must go between the package statement and the class declaration. If there isn't a package statement, then the import statement(s) must be the first line(s) in the source code file. If there are no package or import statements, the class declaration must be the first line in the source code file. (Comments don't count; they can appear anywhere in the source code file.)
- Import and package statements apply to all classes within a source code file.

The following code is a bare-bones class declaration:

```
class MyClass { }
```

This code compiles just fine, but you can also add modifiers before the class declaration. Modifiers fall into two categories:

- Access modifiers: `public`, `protected`, `private`
- Nonaccess modifiers (including `strictfp`, `final`, and `abstract`)

We'll look at access modifiers first, so you'll learn how to restrict or allow access to a class you create. Access control in Java is a little tricky because there are *four* access *controls* (levels of access) but only *three* access *modifiers*. The fourth access control level (called *default* or *package* access) is what you get when you don't use any of the three access modifiers. In other words, every class, method, and instance variable you declare has an access control, whether you explicitly type one or not. Although all four access controls (which means all three modifiers) work for most method and variable declarations, a class can be declared with only public or default access; the other two access control levels don't make sense for a class, as you'll see.

on the job

Java is a package-centric language; the developers assumed that for good organization and name scoping, you would put all your classes into packages. They were right, and you should. Imagine this nightmare: three different programmers, in the same company but working on different parts of a project, write a class named Utilities. If those three Utilities classes have not been declared in any explicit package, and are in the classpath, you won't have any way to tell the compiler or JVM which of the three you're trying to reference. Sun recommends that developers use reverse domain names, appended with division and/or project names. For example, if your domain name is geeksanonymous.com, and you're working on the client code for the TwelvePointOSteps program, you would name your package something like com.geeksanonymous.steps.client. That would essentially change the name of your class to `com.geeksanonymous.steps.client.Utilities`***. You might still have name collisions within your company, if you don't come up with your own naming schemes, but you're guaranteed not to collide with classes developed outside your company (assuming they follow Sun's naming convention, and if they don't, well, Really Bad Things could happen).***

Class Access

What does it mean to access a class? When we say code from one class (class A) has access to another class (class B), it means class A can do one of three things:

- Create an instance of class B
- Extend class B (in other words, become a subclass of class B)
- Access certain methods and variables within class B, depending on the access control of those methods and variables.

In effect, access means *visibility*. If class A can't see class B, the access level of the methods and variables *within* class B won't matter; class A won't have any way to access those methods and variables.

Default Access A class with *default* access has no modifier preceding it in the declaration. In other words, it's the access control you get when you don't type a modifier in the class declaration. Think of default access as package-level access, because *a class with default access can be seen only by classes within the same package.* For example, if class A and class B are in different packages, and class A has default access, class B won't be able to create an instance of class A, or even declare a variable or return type of class A. In fact, class B has to pretend that class A doesn't even exist, or the compiler will complain. Look at the following source file:

```
package cert;
class Beverage {
 }
```

Now look at the second source file:

```
package exam.stuff;
import cert.Beverage;
class Tea extends Beverage {
 }
```

As you can see, the superclass (Beverage) is in a different package from the subclass (Tea). The import statement at the top of the Tea file is trying (fingers crossed) to import the Beverage class. The Beverage file compiles fine, but watch what happens when we try to compile the Tea file:

```
 >javac Tea.java
Tea.java:1: Can't access class cert.Beverage. Class or
interface must be public, in same package, or an accessible member
class.
import cert.Beverage;
..
```

Tea won't compile because its superclass, Beverage, has default access and is in a different package. You can do one of two things to make this work. You could put both classes in the same package, or declare Beverage as `public`, as the next section describes.

When you see a question with complex logic, be sure to look at the access modifiers first. That way, if you spot an access violation (for example, a class in package A trying to access a default class in package B), you'll know the code won't compile so you don't have to bother working through the logic. It's not as if, you know, you don't have anything* better *to do with your time while taking the exam. Just choose the "Compilation fails" answer and zoom on to the next question.

Public Access A class declaration with the `public` keyword gives all classes from all packages access to the public class. In other words, *all* classes in the Java Universe (JU) (you'll be tested on this acronym) have access to a public class. Don't forget, though, that if a public class you're trying to use is in a different package from the class you're writing, you'll still need to import the public class. (Just kidding about the JU acronym. We just made that up to keep you on your toes.)

In the example from the preceding section, we may not want to place the subclass in the same package as the superclass. To make the code work, we need to add the keyword `public` in front of the superclass (Beverage) declaration, as follows:

```
package cert;
public class Beverage {
 }
```

This changes the Beverage class so it will be visible to all classes in all packages. The class can now be instantiated from all other classes, and any class is now free to subclass (extend from) it—*unless*, that is, the class is also marked with the nonaccess modifier `final`. Read on.

Other (Nonaccess) Class Modifiers

You can modify a class declaration using the keyword `final`, `abstract`, or `strictfp`. These modifiers are in addition to whatever access control is on the class, so you could, for example, declare a class as both `public` *and* `final`. But you can't *always* mix nonabstract modifiers. You're free to use `strictfp` in combination with `abstract` or `final`, but you must never, ever, *ever* mark a class as both `final` *and* `abstract`. You'll see why in the next two sections.

You won't need to know how `strictfp` works, so we're focusing only on modifying a class as `final` or `abstract`. For the exam, you need to know only that `strictfp` is a keyword and can be used to modify a class or a method, but never a variable. Marking a class as `strictfp` means that any method code in the class will conform to the IEEE754 standard rules for floating points. Without that modifier, floating points used in the methods might behave in a platform-dependent way. If you don't declare a class as `strictfp`, you can still get `strictfp` behavior on a method-by-method basis, by declaring a *method* as `strictfp`. If you don't know the IEEE754 standard, now's not the time to learn it. You have, as we say, *bigger fish to fry*.

Final Classes When used in a class declaration, the `final` keyword means the class can't be subclassed. In other words, no other class can ever *extend* (inherit from) a `final` class, and any attempts to do so will give you a compiler error.

So why would you ever mark a class `final`? After all, doesn't that violate the whole OO notion of inheritance? You should make a final class *only* if you need an absolute guarantee that *none* of the methods in that class will ever be overridden. If you're deeply dependent on the implementations of certain methods, then using `final` gives you the security that nobody can change the implementation out from under you.

You'll notice many classes in the Java core libraries are final. For example, the String class cannot be subclassed. Imagine the havoc if you couldn't guarantee how a String object would work on any given system your application is running on! If programmers were free to extend the String class (and thus substitute their new String subclass instances where `java.lang.String` instances are expected), civilization—as we know it—could collapse. So use `final` for safety, but *only* when you're certain that your final class has indeed said all that ever needs to be said in its methods. Marking a class final means, in essence, your class can't ever be improved upon, or even specialized, by another programmer.

Another benefit of having nonfinal classes is this scenario: imagine you find a problem with a method in a class you're using, but you don't have the source code. So you can't modify the source to improve the method, but you *can* extend the class and override the method in your new subclass, and substitute the subclass everywhere the original superclass is expected. If the class is final, though, then you're stuck.

Let's modify our Beverage example by placing the keyword `final` in the declaration:

```
package cert;
public final class Beverage{
   public void importantMethod() {
   }
}
```

Now, if we try to compile the Tea subclass:

```
package exam.stuff;
import cert.Beverage;
class Tea extends Beverage {
 }
```

We get the following error:

```
>javac Tea.java
Tea.java:3: Can't subclass final classes: class
cert.Beverage class Tea extends Beverage{
1 error
```

In practice, you'll almost never make a final class. A final class obliterates a key benefit of OO—extensibility. So unless you have a serious safety or security issue, assume that some day another programmer will need to extend your class. If you don't, the next programmer forced to maintain your code will hunt you down and <insert really scary thing>.

Abstract Classes An *abstract class* can never be instantiated. Its sole purpose, mission in life, *raison d'être,* is to be extended (subclassed). Why make a class if you can't make objects out of it? Because the class might be just too, well, *abstract.* For example, imagine you have a class Car that has generic methods common to all vehicles. But you don't want anyone actually *creating* a generic, abstract Car object. How would they initialize its state? What color would it be? How many seats? Horsepower? All-wheel drive? Or more importantly, *how would it behave*? In other words, how would the methods be implemented?

No, you need programmers to instantiate *actual* car types such as SubaruOutback, BMWBoxster, and the like, and we'll bet the Boxster owner will tell you his car does things the Subaru can do "only in its dreams!" Take a look at the following abstract class:

```
abstract class Car {
   private double price;
   private Color carColor;
   private String model;
   private String year;
   public abstract void goFast();
   public abstract void goUpHill();
```

```
    public abstract void impressNeighbors();
    // Additional, important, and serious code goes here
}
```

The preceding code will compile fine. However, if you try to instantiate a Car in another body of code, you'll get a compiler error:

```
AnotherClass.java:7: class Car is an abstract
class. It can't be instantiated.
      Car x = new Car();
1 error
```

Notice that the methods marked `abstract` end in a semicolon rather than curly braces.

exam watch

Look for questions with a method declaration that ends with a semicolon, rather than curly braces. If the method is in a class—as opposed to an interface—then both the method and the class** must **be marked** `abstract`**. You might get a question that asks how you could fix a code sample that includes a method ending in a semicolon, but without an** `abstract` **modifier on the class or method. In that case, you could either mark the method and class** `abstract`**, or remove the** `abstract` **modifier from the method. Oh, and if you change a method from abstract to nonabstract, *don't forget to change the semicolon at the end of the method declaration into a curly brace pair!*

We'll look at abstract *methods* in more detail later in this objective, but always remember that *if even a single method is abstract, the whole class must be declared* `abstract`. One abstract method spoils the whole bunch. You can, however, put nonabstract methods in an abstract class. For example, you might have methods with implementations that shouldn't change from car type to car type, such as `getColor()` or `setPrice()`. By putting nonabstract methods in an abstract class, you give all concrete subclasses (concrete just means *not abstract*) inherited method implementations. The good news there is that concrete subclasses get to inherit functionality, and need to implement only the methods that define subclass-specific behavior.

(By the way, if you think we misused *raison d'être*, for gosh sakes don't send an email. We're rather pleased with ourselves, and let's see *you* work it into a programmer certification book.)

on the Job

Coding with abstract class types (including interfaces, discussed later in this chapter) let's you take advantage of polymorphism, and gives you the greatest degree of flexibility and extensibility. You'll learn more about polymorphism in Chapter 5.

exam Watch

You can't mark a class as both abstract and final. They have nearly opposite meanings. An abstract class *must* ***be subclassed, whereas a final class*** *must not* ***be subclassed. If you see this combination of*** `abstract` ***and*** `final` ***modifiers, used for a class or method declaration,*** *the code will not compile.*

EXERCISE 2-1

Creating an Abstract Superclass and Concrete Subclass

The following exercise will test your knowledge of public, default, final, and abstract classes. Create an abstract superclass named Fruit and a concrete subclass named Apple. The superclass should belong to a package called *food* and the subclass can belong to the default package (meaning it isn't put into a package explicitly). Make the superclass `public` and give the subclass default access.

1. Create the superclass as follows:

```
package food;
public abstract class Fruit{ /* any code you want */}
```

2. Create the subclass in a separate file as follows:

```
import food.Fruit;
class Apple extends Fruit{ /* any code you want */}
```

3. Create a directory called *food* off the directory in your class path setting.
4. Attempt to compile the two files. If you want to use the Apple class, make sure you place the Fruit.class file in the food subdirectory.

Method and Variable Declarations and Modifiers

We've looked at what it means to use a modifier in a *class* declaration, and now we'll look at what it means to modify a *method* or *variable* declaration.

Methods and instance (nonlocal) variables are collectively known as *members*. You can modify a member with both access and nonaccess modifiers, and you have more modifiers to choose from (and combine) than when you're declaring a class.

Member Access

Because method and variable members are usually given access control in exactly the same way, we'll cover both in this section.

Whereas a class can use just two of the four access control levels (`default` or `public`), members can use all four:

- public
- protected
- *default*
- private

Default protection is what you get when you don't type an access modifier in the member declaration. The default and protected access control types have almost identical behavior, except for one difference that will be mentioned later.

exam Watch

It's crucial that you know access control inside and out for the exam. There will be quite a few questions with access control playing a role. Some questions test several concepts of access control at the same time, so not knowing one small part of access control could blow an entire question.

What does it mean for code in one class to have access to a *member* of another class? For now, ignore any differences between methods and variables. If class A has access to a member of class B, it means that class B's member is *visible* to class A. When a class does *not* have access to another member, the compiler will slap you for trying to access something that you're not even supposed to know exists!

You need to understand two different access issues:

- Whether method code in one class can access a member of another class
- Whether a subclass can inherit a member of its superclass

The first type of access is when a method in one class tries to access a method or a variable of another class, using the dot operator (.) to invoke a method or retrieve a variable. For example,

```
class Zoo {
   public String coolMethod() {
      return "Wow  baby";
   }
}

class Moo {
   public void useAZoo() {
      Zoo z = new Zoo();
      // If the preceding line compiles Moo has access
      // to the Zoo class
      // But… does it have access to the coolMethod()?

      System.out.println("A Zoo says, " + z.coolMethod());
     // The preceding line works because Moo can access the
     // public method
   }
}
```

The second type of access revolves around which, if any, members of a superclass a subclass can access *through inheritance.* We're not looking at whether the subclass can, say, invoke a method on an instance of the superclass (which would just be an example of the first type of access). Instead, we're looking at whether the subclass *inherits* a member of its superclass. Remember, if a subclass inherits a member, it's exactly as if the subclass actually declared the member itself. In other words, if a subclass *inherits* a member, the subclass *has* the member.

```
class Zoo {
   public String coolMethod() {
      return "Wow  baby";
   }
}

class Moo extends Zoo {
   public void useMyCoolMethod() {
      // Does an instance of Moo inherit the coolMethod()?
     System.out.println("Moo says, " + this.coolMethod());
     // The preceding line works because Moo can inherit the public method

     // Can an instance of Moo invoke coolMethod() on an instance of Zoo?
     Zoo z = new Zoo();
     System.out.println("Zoo says, " + z.coolMethod());
     // coolMethod() is public, so Moo can invoke it on a Zoo reference

   }
}
```

Figure 2-1 compares the effect of access modifiers on whether a class can inherit a member of another class, or access a member of another class using a reference of an instance of that class.

Much of access control (both types) centers on whether the two classes involved are in the same or different packages. Don't forget, though, if class A *itself* can't be accessed by class B, then no *members* within class A can be accessed by class B.

FIGURE 2-1

Comparison of inheritance vs. dot operator for member access

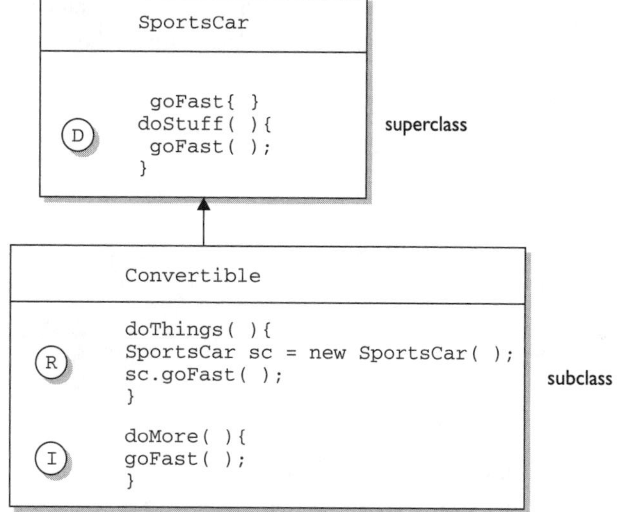

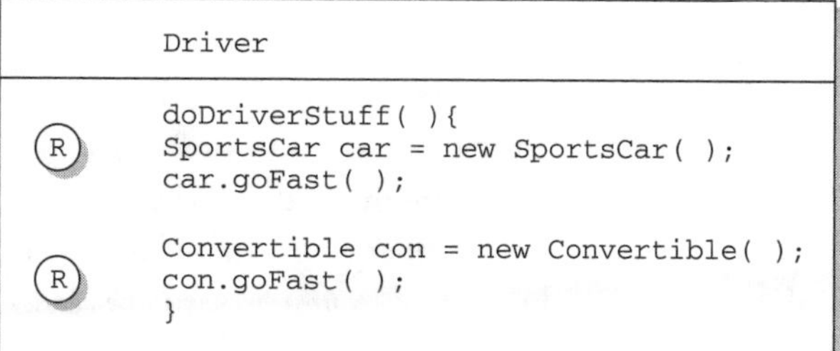

Three ways to access a method:

(D) Invoking a method declared in the same class

(R) Invoking a method using a reference of the class

(I) Invoking an inherited method

exam Watch

You need to know the effect of different combinations of class and member access (such as a default class with a public variable). To figure this out, first look at the access level of the class. If the class itself will not be visible to another class, then none of the members will be either, even if the member is declared `public`. Once you've confirmed that the class is visible, then it makes sense to look at access levels on individual members.

Public Members When a method or variable member is declared `public`, it means all other classes, regardless of the package they belong to, can access the member (assuming the class itself is visible). Look at the following source file:

```
package book;
import cert.*;  // Import all classes in the cert package
class Goo {
   public static void main(String [] args) {
      Sludge o = new Sludge();
      o.testIt();
   }
}
```

Now look at the second file:

```
package cert;
public class Sludge {
   public void testIt() {
      System.out.println("sludge");
   }
}
```

As you can see, Goo and Sludge are in different packages. However, Goo can invoke the method in Sludge without problems because both the Sludge class and its `testIt()` method are marked `public`.

For a subclass, if a member of its superclass is declared `public`, the subclass inherits that member *regardless of whether both classes are in the same package.* Read the following code:

```
package cert;
public class Roo {
   public String doRooThings() {
    // imagine the fun code that goes here
   }
}
```

The Roo class declares the `doRooThings()` member as `public`. So if we make a subclass of Roo, any code in that Roo subclass can call its own inherited `doRooThings()` method.

```
package notcert; //Not the package Roo is in
import cert.Roo;
class  Cloo extends Roo {
   public void testCloo() {
      System.out.println(doRooThings());
   }
}
```

Notice in the preceding code that the `doRooThings()` method is invoked without having to preface it with a reference. Remember, if you see a method invoked (or a variable accessed) without the dot operator (.), it means the method or variable belongs to the class where you see that code. It also means that the method or variable is implicitly being accessed using the `this` reference. So in the preceding code, the call to `doRooThings()` in the Cloo class could also have been written as *`this`*`.doRooThings()`. The reference `this` always refers to the currently executing object—in other words, the object running the code where you see the `this` reference. Because the `this` reference is implicit, you don't need to preface your member access code with it, but it won't hurt. Some programmers include it to make the code easier to read for new (or non) java programmers.

Besides being able to invoke the `doRooThings()` method on itself, code from some *other* class can call `doRooThings()` on a Cloo instance, as in the following:

```
class Toon {
   public static void main (String [] args) {
      Cloo c = new Cloo();
      System.out.println(c.doRooThings()); //No problem; method is public
   }
}
```

Private Members Members marked `private` can't be accessed by code in any class other than the class in which the private member was declared. Let's make a small change to the Roo class from an earlier example.

```
package cert;
public class Roo {
   private String doRooThings() {
    // imagine the fun code that goes here, but only the Roo class knows
   }
}
```

The `doRooThings()` method is now private, so no other class can use it. If we try to invoke the method from any other class, we'll run into trouble.

```
package notcert;
import cert.Roo;
class  UseARoo {
   public void testIt() {
      Roo r = new Roo(); //So far so good; class Roo is still public
      System.out.println(r.doRooThings()); //Compiler error!
   }
}
```

If we try to compile the `UseARoo` class, we get the following compiler error:

```
%javac Balloon.java
Balloon.java:6: No method matching doRooThings() found in class
cert.Roo.
      r.doRooThings();
1 error
```

It's as if the method `doRooThings()` doesn't exist, and as far as any code outside of the Roo class is concerned, it's true. *A private member is invisible to any code outside the member's own class.*

What about a subclass that tries to *inherit* a private member of its superclass? When a member is declared private, a subclass can't inherit it. For the exam, you need to recognize that a subclass can't see, use, or even *think about* the private members of its superclass. You can, however, declare a matching method in the subclass. But regardless of how it looks, it is *not* an overriding method! It is simply a method that happens to have the same name as a private method (which you're not supposed to know about) in the superclass. The rules of overriding do not apply, so you can make this newly-declared-but-just-happens-to-match method declare new exceptions, or change the return type, or anything else you want to do with it.

```
package cert;
public class Roo {
   private String doRooThings() {
    // imagine the fun code that goes here, but no other class will know
   }
}
```

The `doRooThings()` method is now off limits to all subclasses, even those in the same package as the superclass.

```
package cert;  //Cloo and Roo are in the same package
class  Cloo extends Roo {  //Still OK, superclass Roo is public
   public void testCloo() {
      System.out.println(doRooThings()); //Compiler error!
   }
}
```

If we try to compile the subclass Cloo, the compiler is delighted to spit out the following error:

```
%javac Cloo.java
Cloo.java:4: Undefined method: doRooThings()
      System.out.println(doRooThings());
1 error
```

on the Job

Although you're allowed to mark instance variables as `public`, in practice it's nearly always best to keep all variables `private` or `protected`. If variables need to be changed, set, or read, programmers should use public accessor methods, so that code in any other class has to ask to get or set a variable (by going through a method), rather than access it directly. Accessor methods should usually take the form `get<propertyName>` and `set<propertyName>`, and provide a place to check and/or validate before returning or modifying a value. Without this protection, the weight variable of a Cat object, for example, could be set to a negative number if the offending code goes straight to the public variable as in `someCat.weight = -20`. But an accessor method, `setWeight(int wt)`, could check for an inappropriate number. (OK, wild speculation, but we're guessing a negative weight might be inappropriate for a cat. And no wisecracks from you cat haters.) Chapter 5 will discuss this data protection (encapsulation) in more detail.

Can a private method be overridden by a subclass? That's an interesting question, but the answer is *technically* no. Since the subclass, as we've seen, cannot *inherit* a private method, it therefore cannot *override* the method—overriding *depends* on inheritance. We'll cover the implications of this in more detail a little later in this section as well as in Chapter 5, but for now just remember that a method marked `private` cannot be overridden. Figure 2-2 illustrates the effects of the public and private access modifiers on classes from the same or different packages.

Protected and Default Members The protected and default access control levels are almost identical, but with one critical difference. A default member may

FIGURE 2-2

The effects of public and private access

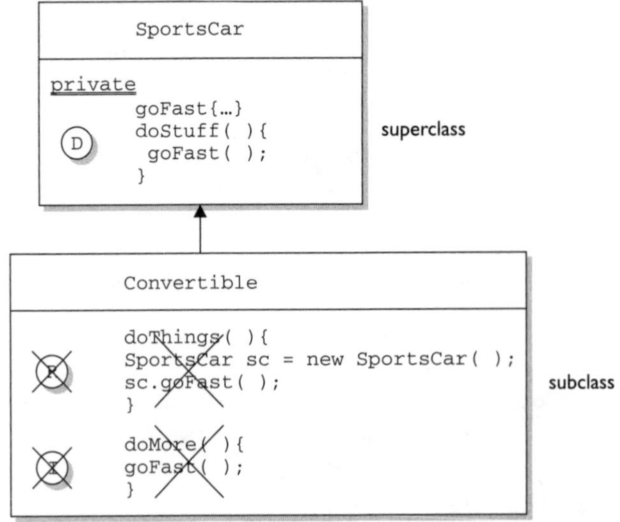

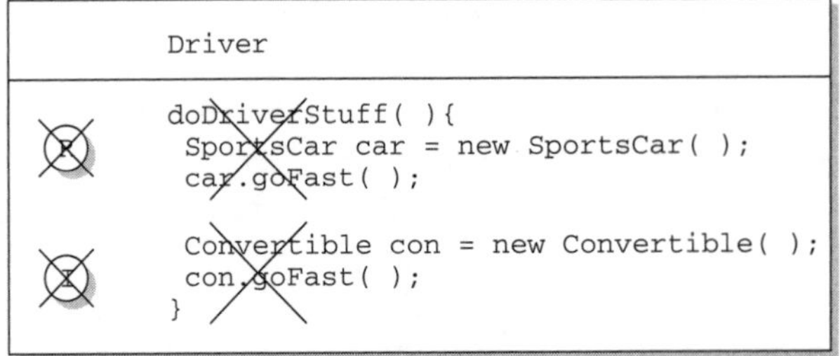

Three ways to access a method:

(D) Invoking a method declared in the same class

(R) Invoking a method using a reference of the class

(I) Invoking an inherited method

be accessed only if the class accessing the member belongs to the same package, whereas a protected member can be accessed (through inheritance) by a subclass even if the subclass is in a different package. Take a look at the following two classes:

```
package certification;
public class OtherClass {
```

```
   void testIt() {   // No modifier means method has default access
      System.out.println("OtherClass");
   }
}
```

In another source code file you have the following:

```
package somethingElse;
import certification.OtherClass;
class AccessClass {
   static public void main(String [] args) {
      OtherClass o = new OtherClass();
      o.testIt();
   }
}
```

As you can see, the `testIt()` method in the second file has default (think: *package-level*) access. Notice also that class OtherClass is in a different package from the AccessClass. Will AccessClass be able to use the method `testIt()`? Will it cause a compiler error? Will Daniel ever marry Francesca? Stay tuned.

```
%javac AccessClass.java
AccessClass.java:5: No method matching testIt() found in class
certification.OtherClass.
      o.testIt();
1 error
```

From the preceding results, you can see that AccessClass can't use the OtherClass method `testIt()` because `testIt()` has default access, and AccessClass is not in the same package as OtherClass. So AccessClass can't see it, the compiler complains, and we have no idea who Daniel and Francesca are.

Default and protected behavior differ *only* when we talk about subclasses. This difference is not often used in actual practice, but that doesn't mean it won't be on the exam! Let's look at the distinctions between protected and default access.

If the `protected` keyword is used to define a member, any subclass of the class declaring the member can access it. It doesn't matter if the superclass and subclass are in different packages, the protected superclass member is still visible to the subclass (although visible only in a very specific way as we'll see a little later). This is in contrast to the default behavior, which doesn't allow a subclass to access a superclass member unless the subclass is in the same package as the superclass.

Whereas default access doesn't extend any *special* consideration to subclasses (you're either in the package or you're not), the `protected` modifier respects the parent-child relationship, even when the child class moves away (and joins a new package). So, when you think of default access, think package restriction. *No exceptions.* But when you think `protected`, think *package + kids.* A class with a protected member is marking that member as having package-level access for all classes, but with a special exception for subclasses outside the package.

But what does it mean for a subclass-outside-the-package to have access (visibility) to a superclass (parent) member? It means the subclass *inherits* the member. It does not, however, mean the subclass-outside-the-package can access the member using a reference to an instance of the superclass. In other words, protected = inheritance. Protected does *not* mean that the subclass can treat the protected superclass member as though it were public. So if the subclass-outside-the-package gets a reference to the superclass (by, for example, creating an instance of the superclass somewhere in the subclass' code), the subclass *cannot* use the dot operator on the superclass reference to access the protected member. To a subclass-outside-the-package, a protected member might as well be default (or even private), when the subclass is using a reference to the superclass. *The subclass can* only *see the protected member through inheritance.*

Are you confused? So are we. Hang in there and it will all become clear with the next batch of code examples. (And don't worry; we're not *actually* confused. We're just trying to make you feel better if *you* are. You know, like it's *OK* for you to feel as though nothing makes sense, and that it isn't your fault. *Or is it?* <insert evil laugh>)

Let's take a look at a protected instance variable (remember, an instance variable is a member) of a superclass.

```
package certification;
public class Parent {
   protected int x = 9; // protected access
}
```

The preceding code declares the variable *x* as `protected`. This makes the variable accessible to all other classes in the certification package, as well as inheritable by any subclasses outside the package. Now let's create a subclass in a different package, and attempt to use the variable *x* (that the subclass inherits).

```
package other; // Different package
import certification.Parent;
class Child extends Parent {
```

```
    public void testIt() {
       System.out.println("x is " + x); // No problem; Child inherits x
    }
}
```

The preceding code compiles fine. Notice, though, that the Child class is accessing the protected variable *through inheritance.* Remember, anytime we talk about a subclass having *access* to a superclass member, we could be talking about the subclass *inheriting* the member, not simply accessing the member through a reference to an instance of the superclass (the way any other nonsubclass would access it). Watch what happens if the subclass Child (outside the superclass' package) tries to access a protected variable using a Parent class reference.

```
package other;
import certification.Parent;
class Child extends Parent {
   public void testIt() {
      System.out.println("x is " + x); // No problem; Child inherits x
      Parent p = new Parent(); // Can we access x using the p reference?
      System.out.println("X in parent is " + p.x); // Compiler error!
   }
}
```

The compiler is more than happy to show us the problem:

```
%javac -d . other/Child.java
other/Child.java:9: x has protected access in certification.Parent
System.out.println("X in parent is " + p.x);
                                        ^
1 error
```

So far we've established that a protected member has essentially package-level or *default* access to all classes except for subclasses. We've seen that subclasses outside the package can inherit a protected member. Finally, we've seen that subclasses outside the package can't use a superclass reference to access a protected member. For a subclass outside the package, *the protected member can be accessed only through inheritance.*

But there's still one more issue we haven't looked at…what does a protected member look like to *other* classes trying to use the subclass-outside-the-package to get to the subclass' inherited protected superclass member? For example, using our previous Parent/Child classes, what happens if some other class—Neighbor, say—in the same package as the Child (subclass), has a reference to a Child instance and wants to access the member variable *x*? In other words, how does that protected member behave once the subclass has inherited it? Does it maintain its protected status, such that classes in the Child's package can see it?

No! Once the subclass-outside-the-package inherits the protected member, that member (as inherited by the subclass) becomes private to any code outside the subclass. So if class Neighbor instantiates a Child object, then even if class Neighbor is in the same package as class Child, class Neighbor won't have access to the Child's inherited (but protected) variable *x*. The bottom line: when a subclass-outside-the-package inherits a protected member, the member is essentially private inside the subclass, such that only the subclass' own code can access it. Figure 2-3 illustrates the effect of protected access on classes and subclasses in the same or different packages.

Whew! That wraps up `protected`, the most misunderstood modifier in Java. Again, it's used only in very special cases, but you can count on it showing up on the exam. Now that we've covered the `protected` modifier, we'll switch to default member access, a piece of cake compared to `protected`.

Let's start with the default behavior of a member in a superclass. We'll modify the Parent's member *x* to make it default.

```
package certification;
public class Parent {
   int x = 9; // No access modifier, means default (package) access
}
```

Notice we didn't place an access modifier in front of the variable *x*. Remember that if you don't type an access modifier before a class or member declaration, the access control is default, which means *package level*. We'll now attempt to access the default member from the Child class that we saw earlier. When we compile the Child file, we get the following error:

```
%javac Child.java
Child.java:4: Undefined variable: x
      System.out.println("Variable x is " + x);
1 error
```

The compiler gives the same error as when a member is declared as `private`. The subclass Child (in a different package from the superclass Parent) can't see or

FIGURE 2-3 The effects of protected access

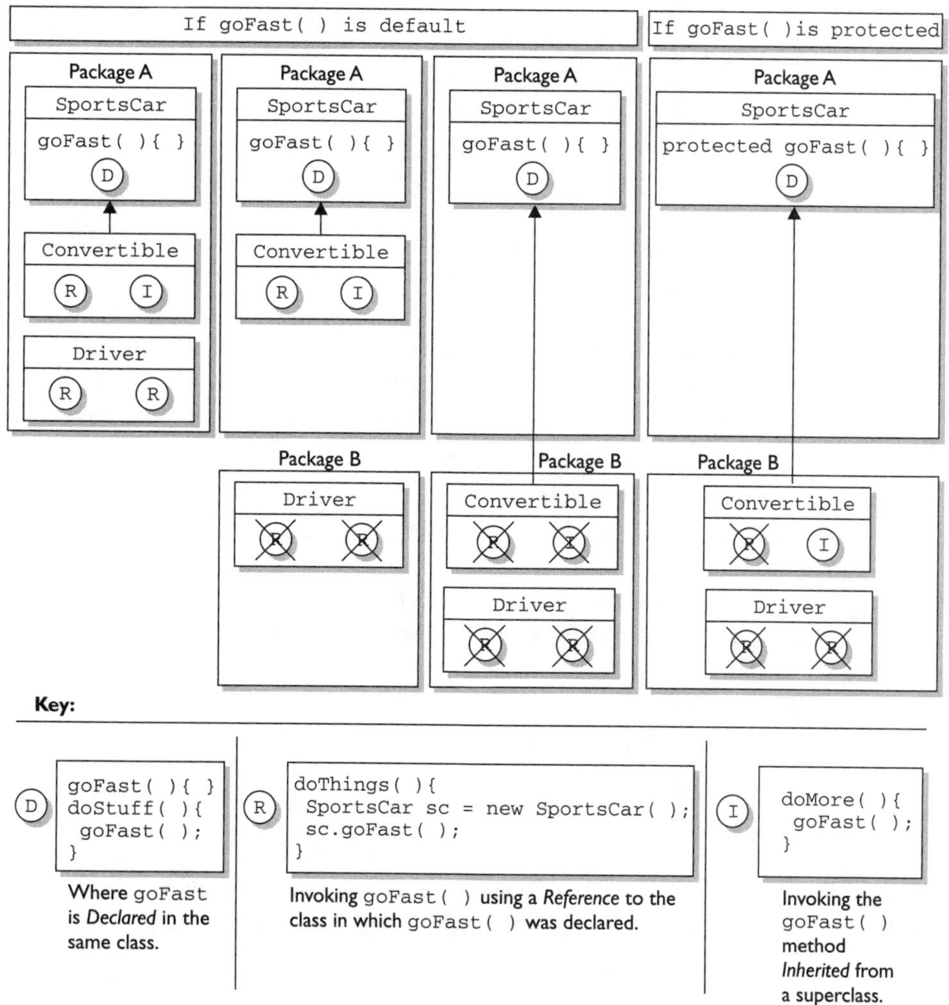

use the default superclass member *x*! Now, what about default access for two classes in the same package?

```
package certification;
public class Parent{
   int x = 9; // default access
}
```

And in the second class you have the following:

```
package certification;
class Child extends Parent{
   static public void main(String [] args) {
      Child sc = new Child();
      sc.testIt();
   }
   public void testIt() {
      System.out.println("Variable x is " + x); // No problem;
   }
}
```

The preceding source file compiles fine, and the class Child runs and displays the value of *x*. Just remember that default members are visible only to the subclasses that are in the same package as the superclass.

Local Variables and Access Modifiers Can access modifiers be applied to local variables? This one should be simple to remember: *NO!*

exam Watch

There is** never **a case where an access modifier can be applied to a local variable, so watch out for code like the following:

```
class Foo {
  void doStuff() {
    private int x = 7;
    this.doMore(x);
  }
}
```

You can be certain that any local variable declared with an access modifier will not compile. In fact, there is only one modifier that can ever be applied to local variables—`final`.

That about does it for our discussion on member *access* modifiers. Table 2-1 shows all the combinations of access and visibility; you really should spend some time with it. Next, we're going to dig into the other (nonaccess) modifiers that you can apply to member declarations.

TABLE 2-1 Determining Access to Class Members

Visibility	Public	Protected	*Default*	Private
From the same class	Yes	Yes	Yes	Yes
From any class in the same package	Yes	Yes	Yes	No
From any non-subclass class outside the package	Yes	No	No	No
From a subclass in the same package	Yes	Yes	Yes	No
From a subclass outside the same package	Yes	Yes	No	No

Nonaccess Member Modifiers

We've discussed member *access*, which refers to whether or not code from one class can invoke a method (or access an instance variable) from another class. That still leaves a boatload of *other* modifiers you can use on member declarations. Two you're already familiar with—`final` and `abstract`—because we applied them to class declarations earlier in this chapter. But we still have to take a quick look at `transient`, `synchronized`, `native`, `strictfp`, and then a long look at the Big One—`static`. We'll look first at modifiers applied to *methods*, followed by a look at modifiers applied to *instance variables*. We'll wrap up this objective with a look at how `static` works when applied to variables and methods.

Final Methods The `final` keyword prevents a method from being overridden in a subclass, and is often used to enforce the API functionality of a method. For example, the Thread class has a method called `isAlive()` that checks whether a thread is still active. If you extend the Thread class, though, there is really no way that you can correctly implement this method yourself (it uses native code, for one thing), so the designers have made it final. Just as you can't subclass the String class (because we need to be able to trust in the behavior of a String object), you can't override many of the methods in the core class libraries. This can't-be-overridden restriction provides for safety and security, but you should use it with great caution. Preventing a subclass from overriding a method stifles many of the benefits of OO including extensibility through polymorphism.

A typical final method declaration looks like this:

```
class SuperClass{
   public final void showSample() {
      System.out.println("One thing.");
   }
}
```

It's legal to extend SuperClass, since the class itself isn't marked `final`, but we can't override the final method `showSample()`, as the following code attempts to do:

```
class SubClass extends SuperClass{
   public void showSample() { // Try to override the final superclass method
      System.out.println("Another thing.");
   }
}
```

Attempting to compile the preceding code gives us the following:

```
%javac FinalTest.java
FinalTest.java:5: The method void showSample() declared in class
SubClass cannot override the final method of the same signature
declared in class SuperClass. Final methods cannot be overridden.
     public void showSample() { }
1 error
```

Final Arguments Method arguments are the variable declarations that appear in between the parentheses in a method declaration. A typical method declaration with multiple arguments looks like this:

```
public Record getRecord(int fileNumber, int recordNumber) {}
```

Method arguments are essentially the same as local variables. In the preceding example, the variables *fileNumber* and *recordNumber* will both follow all the rules applied to local variables. This means they can also have the modifier `final`:

```
public Record getRecord(int fileNumber, final int recordNumber) {}
```

In this example, the variable *recordNumber* is declared as `final`, which of course means it can't be modified within the method. In this case, "modified" means reassigning a new value to the variable. In other words, a final argument must keep the same value that the parameter had when it was passed into the method.

Abstract Methods An *abstract method* is a method that's been declared (as `abstract`) but not implemented. In other words, the method contains no functional code. And if you recall from the previous section on abstract classes, an abstract method declaration doesn't even have curly braces for where the implementation code goes, but instead closes with a semicolon. You mark a method `abstract` when you want to force subclasses to provide the implementation. For example, if you write an abstract class Car with a method `goUpHill()`, you might want to force each subtype of car to define its own `goUpHill()` behavior, specific to that particular type of car. (If you've ever lived in the Rockies, you know that the differences in how cars go uphill (or *fail* to) is not, um, subtle.)

A typical abstract method declaration is as follows:

```
public abstract void showSample();
```

Notice that the abstract method ends with a semicolon instead of curly braces. It is illegal to have an abstract method in a class that is not declared abstract. Look at the following illegal class:

```
public class IllegalClass{
   public abstract void doIt();
}
```

The preceding class will produce the following error if you try to compile it:

```
%javac IllegalClass.java
IllegalClass.java:1: class IllegalClass must be declared abstract.
It does not define void doIt() from class IllegalClass.
public class IllegalClass{
1 error
```

You can, however, have an abstract class with no abstract methods. The following example will compile fine:

```
public abstract class LegalClass{
   void goodMethod() {
      // lots of real implementation code here
   }
 }
```

In the preceding example, `goodMethod()` is not abstract. Three different clues tell you it's not an abstract method:

- The method is not marked abstract.
- The method declaration includes curly braces, as opposed to ending in a semicolon.
- The method provides actual implementation code.

Any class that extends an abstract class *must* implement all abstract methods of the superclass. *Unless the subclass is also abstract.* The rule is

> *The first concrete subclass of an abstract class must implement all abstract methods of the superclass.*

Concrete just means nonabstract, so if you have an abstract class extending another abstract class, the abstract subclass doesn't need to provide implementations for the inherited abstract methods. Sooner or later, though, somebody's going to make a nonabstract subclass (in other words, a class that can be instantiated), and that subclass will have to implement all the abstract methods from up the inheritance tree. The following example demonstrates an inheritance tree with two abstract classes and one concrete class:

```
public abstract class Vehicle {
   private String type;
   public abstract void goUpHill();   // Abstract method
   public String getType() {
      return type;
   }    // Non-abstract method
}

public abstract class Car extends Vehicle {
   public abstract void goUpHill(); // Still abstract
   public void doCarThings() {
      // special car code goes here
   }
}

public class Mini extends Car {
   public void goUpHill() {
```

```
            // Mini-specific going uphill code
        }
    }
```

So how many methods does class Mini have? Three. It inherits both the `getType()` and `doCarThings()` methods, because they're public and concrete (nonabstract). But because `goUpHill()` is abstract in the superclass Vehicle, and is never implemented in the Car class (so it remains abstract), it means class Mini—as the first concrete class below Vehicle—*must* implement the `goUpHill()` method. In other words, *class Mini can't pass the buck* (of abstract method implementation) to the next class down the inheritance tree, but class Car *can* since Car, like Vehicle, is abstract. Figure 2-4 illustrates the effects of the abstract modifier on concrete and abstract subclasses.

FIGURE 2-4

The effects of abstract on subclasses

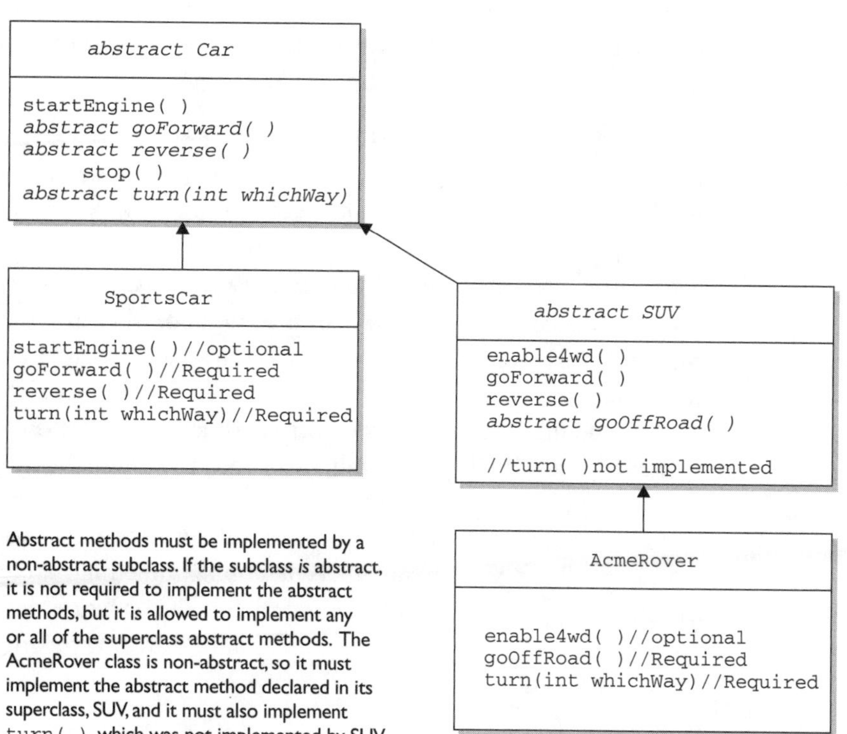

exam Watch

Look for concrete classes that don't provide method implementations for abstract methods of the superclass. For example, the following code won't compile:

```
public abstract class A {
    abstract void foo();
}
class B extends A {
    void foo(int I) {
    }
}
```

Class B won't compile because it doesn't implement the inherited abstract method* `foo()`*. Although the* `foo(int I)` *method in class B might appear to be an implementation of the superclass' abstract method, it is simply an overloaded method (a method using the same identifier, but different arguments), so it doesn't fulfill the requirements for implementing the superclass' abstract method. We'll look at the differences between overloading and overriding in detail in Chapter 5.

A method can never, ever, ever be marked as both `abstract` *and* `final`, or both `abstract` *and* `private`. Think about it—abstract methods *must* be implemented (which essentially means overridden by a subclass) whereas final and private methods cannot *ever* be overridden by a subclass. Or to phrase it another way, an `abstract` designation means *the superclass doesn't know anything* about how the subclasses should behave in that method, whereas a `final` designation means *the superclass knows everything* about how all subclasses (however far down the inheritance tree they may be) should behave in that method. The `abstract` and `final` modifiers are virtually opposites. Because `private` methods cannot even be *seen* by a subclass (let alone inherited) they too cannot be overridden, so they too cannot be marked `abstract`.

Abstract methods also cannot be marked as `synchronized`, `strictfp`, or `native`, all of which are modifiers describing something about the *implementation* of a method. Because abstract methods define the signature, access, and return type, but can say nothing about implementation, be watching for any of the following illegal method declarations:

```
abstract synchronized void foo();
abstract strictfp void foof();
abstract native void poof();
```

The preceding declarations will deliver you a nice compiler error message similar to

```
MyClass.java:18: illegal combination of modifiers: abstract and synchronized
   abstract synchronized void foo();
                              ^
MyClass.java:19: illegal combination of modifiers: abstract and strictfp
   abstract strictfp void foof();
                          ^
MyClass.java:20: illegal combination of modifiers: abstract and native
   abstract native void poof();
                        ^
```

Finally, you need to know that the `abstract` modifier can never be combined with the `static` modifier. We'll cover static methods later in this objective, but for now just remember that the following would be illegal:

```
abstract static void doStuff();
```

And it would give you an error that should be familiar by now:

```
MyClass.java:2: illegal combination of modifiers: abstract and static
  abstract static void doStuff();
                       ^
```

Synchronized Methods The `synchronized` keyword indicates that a method can be accessed by only one thread at a time. We'll discuss this nearly to death in Chapter 9, but for now all we're concerned with is knowing that *the* `synchronized` *modifier can be applied only to methods*—not variables, not classes, just methods. A typical synchronized declaration looks like this:

```
public synchronized Record retrieveUserInfo(int id) { }
```

You should also know that the `synchronized` modifier can be matched with any of the four access control levels (which means it can be paired with any of the three access modifier keywords). And you can also combine `synchronized` with `final`, but *never with* `abstract`. Synchronization is an implementation issue; only the programmer can decide whether a method needs to be marked as synchronized. If you declare a method like the following,

```
abstract synchronized void doStuff();
```

you'll get a compiler error similar to this:

```
MyClass.java:2: illegal combination of modifiers: abstract and synchronized
abstract synchronized void doStuff();
                      ^
```

Native Methods The `native` modifier indicates that a method is implemented in a platform-dependent language, such as C. You don't need to know how to use native methods for the exam, other than knowing that `native` is a modifier (thus a reserved keyword), `native` can *never* be combined with `abstract`, and `native` can be applied only to methods—not classes, not variables, just methods.

Strictfp Methods We looked earlier at using `strictfp` as a class modifier, but even if you don't declare a *class* as `strictfp`, you can still declare an individual *method* as `strictfp`. Remember, `strictfp` forces floating points (and any floating-point operations) to adhere to the IEE754 standard. With `strictfp`, you can predict how your floating points will behave regardless of the underlying platform the JVM is running on. The downside is that if the underlying platform is capable of supporting greater precision, a `strictfp` method won't be able to take advantage of it.

You'll need to have the IEEE754 standard pretty much memorized—that is, if you need something to help you fall asleep. For the exam, however, you don't need to know anything about `strictfp` other than what it's used for, that it can modify a class or *nonabstract* method declaration, and that *a variable can never be declared* `strictfp`.

Variable Declarations

We've already discussed variable *access*, which refers to the ability of code in one class to access a variable in another class. In this section we'll look at the other keywords that apply to variable declarations, but first we'll do a quick review of the difference between *instance* and *local* variables.

Instance Variables *Instance variables* are defined inside the class, but outside of any method, and are only initialized when the class is instantiated. Instance variables are the *fields* that belong to each unique object. For example, the following code defines fields (instance variables) for the name, title, and manager for employee objects:

```
class Employee {
   //  define fields (instance variables) for employee instances
   private String name;
   private String title,
   private String manager;
   // other code goes here including access methods for private fields
}
```

The preceding Employee class says that each employee instance will know its own name, title, and manager. In other words, each instance can have its own unique values for those three fields. If you see the term "field," "instance variable," "property," or "attribute," they mean virtually the same thing. (There actually *are* subtle but occasionally important distinctions between the terms, but those distinctions aren't used on the exam.)

For the exam, you need to know that instance variables

- Can use any of the four access levels (which means they can be marked with any of the three access modifiers)
- Can be marked `final`
- Can be marked `transient`
- Cannot be marked `abstract`
- Cannot be marked `synchronized`
- Cannot be marked `strictfp`
- Cannot be marked `native`

We've already covered the effects of applying access control to instance variables (it works the same way as it does for member methods). A little later in this chapter we'll look at what it means to apply the `final` or `transient` modifier to an instance variable. First, though, we'll take a quick look at the difference between instance and local variables. Figure 2-5 compares the way in which modifiers can be applied to methods vs. variables.

Local (Automatic/Stack/Method) Variables *Local variables* are variables *declared* within a method. That means the variable is not just *initialized* within the method, but also *declared within the method.* Just as the local variable starts its life inside the method, it's also destroyed when the method has completed. *Local*

FIGURE 2-5

Comparison of modifiers on variables vs. methods

Local Variables	Variables (non-local)	Methods
final	final public protected private static transient volatile	final public protected private static abstract synchronized strictfp native

variables are always on the stack, not the heap. Although the *value* of the variable might be passed into, say, another method that then stores the *value* in an instance variable, the variable itself lives only within the scope of the method.

Just don't forget that while the local variable is on the stack, if the variable is an object reference *the object itself will still be created on the heap.* There is no such thing as a stack *object*, only a stack *variable.* You'll often hear programmers use the phrase, "local object," but what they really mean is, "locally declared reference variable." So if you hear a programmer use that expression, you'll know that he's just too lazy to phrase it in a technically precise way. You can tell him we said that—unless he's really really big and knows where we live.

Local variable declarations can't use most of the modifiers that can be applied to instance variables, such as `public` (or the other access modifiers), `transient`, `volatile`, `abstract`, or `static`, but as we saw earlier, local variables *can* be marked `final`. And if you remember Chapter 1 (which we know you do, since it is, in fact, *unforgettable*), before a local variable can be used, it must be initialized with a value.

```
class TestServer {
   public void logIn() {
      int count = 10;
   }
}
```

Typically, you'll initialize a local variable in the same line in which you declare it, although you might still need to reinitialize it later in the method. The key is to remember that a local variable *must* be initialized before you try to *use* it. The compiler will reject any code that tries to use a local variable that hasn't been assigned a value, because—unlike instance variables—*local variables don't get default values.*

A local variable can't be referenced in any code outside the method in which it's declared. In the preceding code example, it would be impossible to refer to the variable *count* anywhere else in the class except within the scope of the method `logIn()`. Again, that's not to say that the *value* of *count* can't be passed out of the method to take on a new life. But the *variable* holding that value, *count*, can't be accessed once the method is complete, as the following illegal code demonstrates:

```
class TestServer {
   public void logIn() {
      int count = 10;
   }
   public void doSomething(int i) {
      count = i;  // Won't compile! Can't access count outside method login()
   }
}
```

It *is* possible to declare a local variable with the same name as an instance variable. That's known as shadowing, and the following code demonstrates this in action:

```
class TestServer {
   int count = 9;  // Declare an instance variable named count
   public void logIn() {
      int count = 10;  // Declare a local variable named count
      System.out.println("local variable count is " + count);
   }
   public void count() {
      System.out.println("instance variable count is " + count);
   }
   public static void main(String[] args) {
      new TestServer().logIn();
      new TestServer().count();
   }
}
```

The preceding code produces the following output:

```
local variable count is 10
instance variable count is 9
```

Why on earth (or the planet of your choice) would you want to do that? Normally, you won't. But one of the more common reasons is to name an argument with the same name as the instance variable to which the parameter will be assigned. The following (but wrong) code is trying to set an instance variable's value using a parameter:

```
class Foo {
   int size = 27;
   public void setSize(int size) {
      size = size;   // ??? which size equals which size???
   }
}
```

So you've decided that—for overall readability—you want to give the argument the same name as the instance variable its value is destined for, but how do you resolve the naming collision? Use the keyword `this`. The keyword `this` always always always refers to the object currently running. The following code shows this in action:

```
class Foo {
   int size = 27;
   public void setSize(int size) {
      this.size = size;   // this.size means the current object's
      // instance variable for size
   }
}
```

Final Variables Declaring a variable with the `final` keyword makes it impossible to reinitialize that variable once it has been initialized with an *explicit* value (notice we said *explicit* rather than *default*). For primitives, this means that once the variable is assigned a value, the value can't be altered. For example, if you assign 10 to the `int` variable *x*, then *x* is going to *stay* 10, forever. So that's straightforward for primitives, but what does it mean to have a final *object reference* variable? A reference variable marked `final` can't ever be reassigned to refer to a different object. The data *within* the object, however, *can* be modified, but the reference variable cannot be changed. In other words, you can use a final reference to *modify the object* it refers to, but you *can't modify the reference* variable to make it refer to a *different* object. Burn this in: *there are no final objects*, only final *references.*

You might need to remind yourself what the *value* of a reference variable actually *is*. A reference variable's value—in other words, the bit pattern the variable holds—*is not an object*. Just as the value of a primitive variable is the bit pattern representing the primitive (for example, the bits representing the integer value 2), the value of a reference variable is a bit pattern representing, well, a *reference*. We're not using "traditional" pointers in Java, but you can still *think* of it as a pointer (not necessarily a pointer to an object, but a pointer to a pointer to…). A reference variable holds bits that represent, in a platform-dependent format, *a way to get to an object*. That's really all we care about, and all we're even allowed to *know* about reference variables in Java, unless you happen to be one of the developers of a JVM.

Final instance variables don't have to be explicitly initialized in the same line in which they're declared, but the compiler will make sure that the final variable has a value by the time the constructor has completed. Don't count on the default value for final variables, though, because a final variable—even if it's an instance variable—won't be given one. The rule is: if you declare a final instance variable, you're obligated to give it an explicit value, and you must do so by the time the constructor completes. Look at the following code:

```
class FinalTest{
   final int x; // Will not work unless x is assigned in the constructor
   public void showFinal() {
      System.out.println("Final x = " + x);
   }
}
```

Attempting to compile the preceding code gives us the following:

```
%javac FinalTest.java
FinalTest.java:2: Blank final variable 'x' may not have been
initialized. It must be assigned a value in an initializer, or in
every constructor.
   final int x;
1 error
```

If you declare an instance variable as `final`, but don't give it an explicit value at the time you declare it, the variable is considered a *blank* `final`. The final instance variable can stay *blank* only until the constructor completes.

```
class FinalTest{
   final int x; // Will work because it's initialized in the constructor
```

```
    public FinalTest() {
       x = 28;  // Whew! The compiler is relieved that we took care of it
       System.out.println("Final x = " + x);
    }
 }
```

So now we've seen that you need to assign a value to a final variable, but *then* what? As we mentioned earlier, *you can't change a final variable once it's been initialized!* Let's look at declaring an object reference variable as `final`:

```
import java.util.Date;
class TestClass {
   final Date d = new Date();
   public void showSample() {
      d.setYear(2001); //Altering Date object, not d variable, so it's OK
   }
}
```

In the `showSample()` method in the preceding class, the *year* of the Date instance is modified by invoking `setYear()` on the final reference variable *d*. That's perfectly legal, and the class compiles fine, because an instance can have its data modified even though the reference to it is declared `final`. But now let's see what happens when we try to assign a new object to the final reference variable *d*, after *d* has been initialized.

```
import java.util.Date;
class FinalTest {
   final Date d = new Date(); // Initialize d
   public void showSample() {
      d.setYear(2001);
      d = new Date(); // Won't work! Can't change the value of d
   }
}
```

Code within the `showSample()` method tries to reassign a new object to *d*. If we try to compile the preceding class, we're treated to this error:

```
%javac FinalTest.java
FinalTest.java:6: Can't assign a value to a final variable: d
         d = new Date();
1 error
```

Look for code that tries to reassign a final variable, but don't expect it to be obvious. For example, *a variable declared in an interface is always implicitly final, whether you declare it that way or not!* ***So you might see code similar to the following:***

```
interface Foo {
    Integer x = new Integer(5); // x is implicitly final
}
class FooImpl implements Foo {
    void doStuff() {
       x = new Integer(5); // Big Trouble! Can't assign new object to x
    }
}
```

The reference variable *x* ***is*** `final`***. No matter what. You're allowed to explicitly declare it as*** **`final`** ***if you like, but it doesn't matter to the compiler whether you do or not. It simply*** *is* ***final****, just* ***because it's an interface variable, and they are always implicitly*** `public static final`***. We'll look at interface variables again later in this chapter, but for now just remember that a final variable can't be reassigned, and that in the case of interface variables, they're final even if they don't say it out loud. The exam expects you to spot any attempt to violate this rule.***

We've now covered how the `final` modifier can be applied to classes, methods, and variables. Figure 2-6 highlights the key points and differences of the various applications of `final`.

Transient Variables If you mark an instance variable as `transient`, you're telling the JVM to skip (ignore) this variable when you attempt to serialize the object declaring it. Serialization is one of the coolest features of Java; it lets you save (sometimes called "flatten") an object by writing its state (in other words, the *value of its instance variables*) to a special type of IO stream. With serialization you can save an object to a file, or even ship it over a wire for reinflating (deserializing) at the other end, in another JVM. For the exam, you aren't required to know how serialization works, but you need to know that `transient` *can be applied only to instance variables.*

Don't be surprised, though, if serialization shows up in some future version of the exam. Regardless of its relevance for the exam, serialization is one of the most

FIGURE 2-6 The effect of `final` on variables, methods, and classes

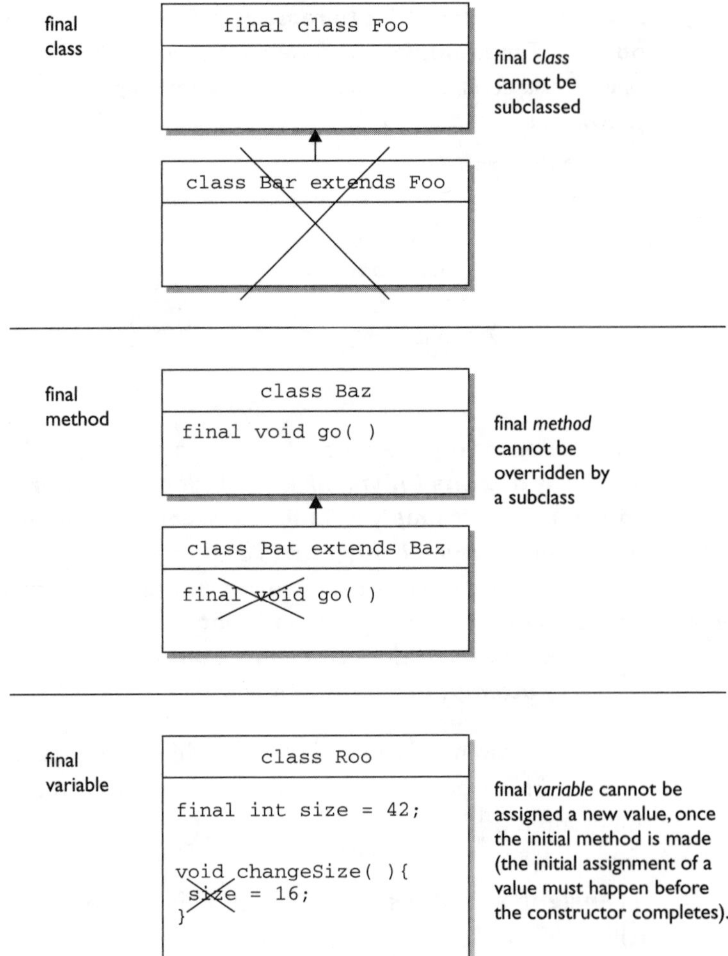

powerful aspects of Java and is worth your learning all about it. Most advanced uses of Java—RMI, EJB, and Jini, for example—depend on it. OK, we'll step off the serialization soapbox now, and resume our exam prep already in progress.

Volatile Variables The `volatile` modifier tells the JVM that a thread accessing the variable must always reconcile its own private copy of the variable with the master copy in memory. *Say what?* Don't worry about it. For the exam, all you need to know about `volatile` is that, as with `transient`, it can be applied only to instance variables. Make no mistake, the idea of multiple threads accessing an instance variable is scary stuff, and very important for any Java programmer to understand. But as you'll see in Chapter 9, you'll probably use synchronization, rather than the `volatile` modifier, to make your data thread-safe.

The* `volatile` *modifier may also be applied to project managers.

Static Variables and Methods

The `static` modifier has such a profound impact on the behavior of a method or variable that we're treating it as a concept entirely separate from the other modifiers. To understand the way a static member works, we'll look first at a reason for using one. Imagine you've got a utility class with a method that always runs the same way; its sole function is to return, say, a random number. It wouldn't matter which instance of the class performed the method—it would always behave exactly the same way. In other words, the method's behavior has no dependency on the state (instance variable values) of an object. So why, then, do you need an object when the method will never be instance-specific? Why not just ask *the class itself* to run the method?

Let's imagine another scenario: suppose you want to keep a running count of all instances instantiated from a particular class. Where do you actually keep that variable? It won't work to keep it as an instance variable within the class whose instances you're tracking, because the count will just be initialized back to a default value with each new instance. The answer to both the utility-method-always-runs-the-same scenario and the keep-a-running-total-of-instances scenario is to use the `static` modifier. Variables and methods marked `static` belong to the *class*, rather than to any particular instance. In fact, you can use a static method or variable *without having any instances of that class at all.* You need only have the class available to be able to invoke a static method or access a static variable. Static variables, too, can be accessed without having an instance of a class. But if there are instances, a static variable of a class will be shared by *all* instances of that class; there is only one copy.

The following code declares and uses a static counter variable:

```
class Frog {
   static int frogCount = 0;  // Declare and initialize static variable
   public Frog() {
      frogCount += 1;  // Modify the value in the constructor
   }
   public static void main (String [] args) {
      new Frog();
      new Frog();
```

```
        new Frog();
        System.out.println("Frog count is now " + frogCount);
    }
}
```

In the preceding code, the static *frogCount* variable is set to zero when the Frog class is first loaded by the JVM, *before any Frog instances are created!* (By the way, you don't actually *need* to initialize a static variable to zero; static variables get the same default values instance variables get.) Whenever a Frog instance is created, the Frog constructor runs and increments the static *frogCount* variable. When this code executes, three Frog instances are created in `main()`, and the result is

```
Frog count is now 3
```

Now imagine what would happen if *frogCount* were an instance variable (in other words, *nonstatic*):

```
class Frog {
   int frogCount = 0;  // Declare and initialize instance variable
   public Frog() {
      frogCount += 1;  // Modify the value in the constructor
   }
   public static void main (String [] args) {
      new Frog();
      new Frog();
      new Frog();
      System.out.println("Frog count is now " + frogCount);
   }
}
```

When this code executes, it should still create three Frog instances in `main()`, but the result is...a compiler error! We can never get this code to run because it won't even compile.

```
Frog.java:11: non-static variable frogCount cannot be referenced
from a static context
     System.out.println("Frog count is " + frogCount);
                                           ^
     1 error
```

The JVM doesn't know *which* Frog object's *frogCount* you're trying to access. The problem is that `main()` is itself a static method, and thus isn't running against any particular *instance* of the class, rather just on the class itself. A static method can't access a nonstatic (instance) variable, because *there is no instance!* That's not to say there aren't instances of the class alive on the heap, but rather that even if there are, the static method doesn't know anything about them. The same applies to instance methods; a static method can't directly invoke a nonstatic method. Think static = class, nonstatic = instance. Making the method called by the JVM (`main()`) a static method means the JVM doesn't have to create an instance of your class just to start running code.

exam Watch

One of the mistakes most often made by new Java programmers is attempting to access an instance variable (which means nonstatic variable) from the static `main()` method (which doesn't know anything about any instances, so it can't access the variable). The following code is an example of illegal access of a nonstatic variable from a static method:

```
class Foo {
   int x = 3;
   public static void main (String [] args) {
     System.out.println("x is " + x);
   }
}
```

Understand that this code will never compile, because you can't access a nonstatic (instance) variable from a static method. Just think of the compiler saying, "Hey, I have no idea which ***Foo object's*** x ***variable you're trying to print!" Remember, it's the*** class ***running the `main()` method, not an*** instance ***of the class. Of course, the tricky part for the exam is that the question won't look as obvious as the preceding code. The problem you're being tested for—accessing a nonstatic variable from a static method—will be buried in code that might appear to be testing something else. For example, the code above would be more likely to appear as***

```
class Foo {
   int x = 3;
   float y = 4.3f;
   public static void main (String [] args) {
     for (int z = x; z < ++x; z--, y = y + z) {
       // complicated looping and branching code
     }
}
```

So while you're off trying to follow the logic, the real ***issue is that*** x ***and*** y ***can't be used within `main()`, because*** x ***and*** y ***are instance, not static, variables! The same applies for accessing nonstatic methods from a static method. The rule is, a static method of a class can't access a nonstatic (instance) member—method or variable—of its own class.***

Accessing Static Methods and Variables

Since you don't need to have an instance in order to invoke a static method or access a static variable, then how *do* you invoke or use a static member? What's the syntax? We know that with a regular old instance method, you use the dot operator on a reference to an instance:

```
class Frog {
   int frogSize = 0;
   public int getFrogSize() {
      return frogSize;
   }
   public Frog(int s) {
      frogSize = s;
   }
   public static void main (String [] args) {
      Frog f = new Frog(25);
      System.out.println(f.getFrogSize()); // Access instance method using f
   }
}
```

In the preceding code, we instantiate a Frog, assign it to the reference variable *f*, and then use that *f* reference to invoke a method *on the Frog instance we just created.* In other words, the `getFrogSize()` method is being invoked on a specific Frog object on the heap.

But this approach (using a reference to an object) isn't appropriate for accessing a static method, because there might not be any instances of the class at all! So, the way we access a static method (or static variable) is to use the dot operator *on the class name*, as opposed to on a reference to an instance, as follows:

```
class Frog {
   static int frogCount = 0;  // Declare and initialize static variable
   public Frog() {
      frogCount += 1;  // Modify the value in the constructor
   }
}

class TestFrog {
   public static void main (String [] args) {
     new Frog();
     new Frog();
     new Frog();
     System.out.print("frogCount:"+Frog.frogCount); //Access static variable
   }
}
```

But just to make it really confusing, the Java language also allows you to use an object reference *variable* to access a static member:

```
Frog f = new Frog();
int frogs = f.getFrogCount(); // Access static method getFrogCount using f
```

In the preceding code, we instantiate a Frog, assign the new Frog object to the reference variable *f*, and then use the *f* reference to invoke a static method! But even though we are using a specific Frog instance to access the static method, the rules haven't changed. This is merely a syntax trick to let you *use* an object reference *variable* (but not the object it refers to) to get to a static method or variable, but the static member is still unaware of the particular instance used to invoke the static member. In the Frog example, the compiler knows that the reference variable *f* is of type Frog, and so the Frog class static method is run with no awareness or concern for the Frog instance at the other end of the *f* reference. In other words, the compiler cares only that reference variable *f* is declared as type Frog. Figure 2-7 illustrates the effects of the static modifier on methods and variables.

Another point to remember is that *static methods can't be overridden*! This doesn't mean they can't be redefined in a subclass, as we'll see a little later when we look at overriding in more detail, but redefining and overriding aren't the same thing.

Things you can mark as `static`:

- Methods
- Variables
- Top-level nested classes (we'll look at nested classes in Chapter 8)

Things you *can't* mark as `static`:

- Constructors (makes no sense; a constructor is used only to create instances)
- Classes
- Interfaces
- Inner classes (unless you want them to be top-level nested classes; we'll explore this in Chapter 8)
- Inner class methods and instance variables
- Local variables

FIGURE 2-7

The effects of static on methods and variables

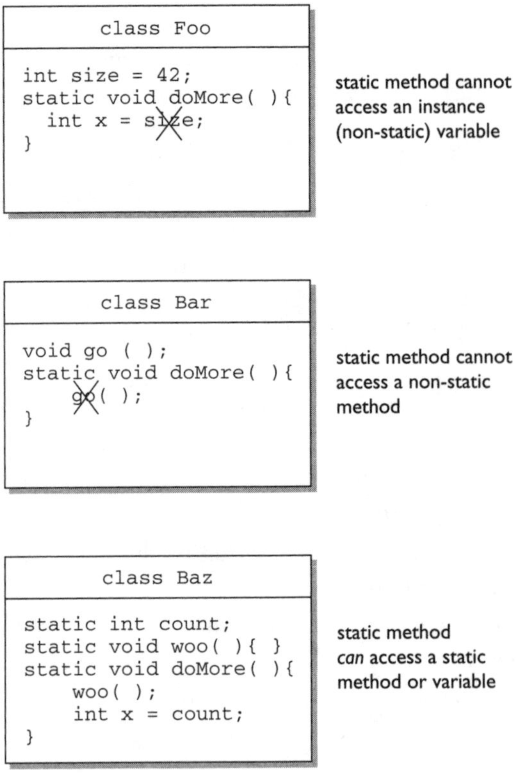

```
class Foo

int size = 42;
static void doMore( ){
  int x = size;
}
```

static method cannot access an instance (non-static) variable

```
class Bar

void go ( );
static void doMore( ){
    go( );
}
```

static method cannot access a non-static method

```
class Baz

static int count;
static void woo( ){ }
static void doMore( ){
    woo( );
    int x = count;
}
```

static method *can* access a static method or variable

CERTIFICATION OBJECTIVE

Declaration Rules (Exam Objective 4.1)

Identify correctly constructed source files, package declarations, import statements, class declarations (of all forms, including nested classes), interface declarations, method declarations (including the `main()` *method that is used to start execution of a class), variable declarations, and identifiers.*

The previous objective, 1.2, covered the fundamentals of declarations including modifiers applied to classes, methods, and variables. In this objective, we'll look at how those fundamentals must be applied in a few specific situations. We're not covering all of Objective 4.1 in this section, however. Inner classes won't be discussed here because they're already in Chapter 8, the chapter on inner classes (what are the odds?), and we'll hold off on interfaces until we get to Objective 4.2, the section immediately following this one.

We promise that this section will be much shorter than the previous one. We promise that we'll introduce very little new information. We promise you'll win friends and influence people with your declaration prowess. We promise to stop making promises.

Source Files, Package Declarations, and Import Statements

It's been awhile since we looked at source declaration rules (about 30+ pages ago), so let's do a quick review of the rules *again*:

- There can be only one public class per source code file.
- The name of the file must match the name of the public class.
- If the class is part of a package, the package statement must be the first line in the source code file.
- Import and package statements apply to *all* classes within a source code file.
- If there are import statements, they must go between the package statement and the class declaration. If there isn't a package statement, the import statement(s) must be the first line(s) in the source code file. If there are no package or import statements, the class declaration must be the first line in the source code file. (Comments don't count; they can appear anywhere in the source code file.)

Source File Structure

We know that you know all this, so we'll just focus on the kinds of import and package issues you might see on the exam. The following legal (albeit pretty useless) code declares a class `Foo`, in package `com.geeksanonymous`:

```
package com.geeksanonymous;   // Notice the semicolon
class Foo { }
```

There can be only one package statement per source code file, so the following would not be legal:

```
package com.geeksanonymous;
package com.wickedlysmart;  // Illegal! Only one package declaration allowed
class Foo { }
```

If class Foo adds any import statements, they must be below the package declaration and above the class declaration, as follows:

```
package  com.geeksanonymous;
import java.util.*; // Wildcard package import
import com.wickedlysmart.Foo;  // Explicit class import
class Bob { }
```

If class Foo has no package declaration, the import statements must be above the class declaration, as follows:

```
import java.util.*; // Wildcard package import
import com.wickedlysmart.Foo;  // Explicit class import
class Bob { }
```

You can have only one public class per source code file. You can put as many classes in a source code file as you like, but only one (or none) can be public. The file name should match the name of the public class, but if no public class is in the file, you can name it whatever you like. The following source code file, with two public classes, would be illegal:

```
package com.geeksanonymous;
public class Foo { }
public class Bat { }
```

But the following is fine:

```
package com.geeksanonymous;
class Foo { }
public class Bat { }
```

The order in which the classes appear makes no difference; as long as the package and import statements appear before the first class (and in the correct order), the class order doesn't matter.

You should group classes into a single source code file only when those classes should only be used together as one component. Typically, you'll keep each class in a separate file, with the file name matching the class name (a requirement if the class is public; optional, but good practice, if the class has default access). Putting multiple classes into a single source code file makes it much harder to locate the source for a particular class, and makes the source code less reusable.

Keep in mind that *package and import declarations apply to* all *classes in a source file!* For the exam, you'll need to recognize that the package declaration at the top of a code example means that all classes in that file are in the same package.

exam Watch

The exam uses a line numbering scheme that indicates whether the code in the question is a snippet (a partial code sample taken from a larger file), or a complete file. If the line numbers start at 1, you're looking at a complete file. If the numbers start at some arbitrary (but always greater than 1) number, you're looking at only a fragment of code rather than the complete source code file. For example, the following indicates a complete file:

```
1. package fluffy;
2. class Bunny {
3.     public void hop() { }
4.       }
```

whereas the following indicates a snippet:

```
 9. public void hop() {
10.   System.out.println("hopping");
11. }
```

Using Import Statements

Import statements come in two flavors—*wildcard* import and *explicit class* import. Before we look at both in more detail, say it with me again, "Java is not C." An *import* statement is not an *include*! Import statements are little more than a way for you to save keystrokes when you're typing your code. When you put a class in a package (through the package declaration), you essentially give the class a longer name, which we call the *fully qualified name.* The fully qualified name of a class, as opposed to *just* the class name, is like talking about the difference between your full name (say, Albert James Bates IV) and your first name (Albert).

For example, if class Foo is in a package `com.geeksanonymous`, the Foo class is still named Foo, but it also has a fully qualified name of `com.geeksanonymous.Foo`. As we looked at earlier, package organization helps prevent name collisions—in case other programmers build a class named Foo, for example. But if a programmer from WickedlySmart builds a Foo class, its fully qualified name will be `com.wickedlysmart.Foo` (or possibly even `com.wickedlysmart.projectx.Foo`), while a programmer from GeeksAnonymous gives her Foo class the fully qualified name of `com.geeksanonymous.Foo`. Once you put Foo in a package, if you refer to the Foo class in some other code, the compiler needs to know *which* Foo you're talking about.

OK, so given that there might be more than one Foo floating around, and that even within a single application you might want to use, say, two different Foo classes, you need a way to distinguish between them. Otherwise, the compiler would never know what you meant if you typed the following:

```
class Bar {
   void doStuff() {
      Foo f = new Foo(); // Here you want the WickedlySmart version
   }                     // But how will the compiler know?
}
```

To eliminate the confusion, you're required to do one of two things to help the compiler:

1. Use an `import` statement,

```
import com.wickedlysmart.Foo;
class Bar {
   void doStuff() {
      Foo f = new Foo(); // Now the compiler knows which one to use
   }
}
```

or

2. Use the fully qualified name throughout your code:

```
class Bar {
   void doStuff() {
      com.wickedlysmart.Foo f = new com.wickedlysmart.Foo() // No doubts
   }
}
```

OK, we don't know about *you*, but we'd prefer the one with less typing. The `import` statement is almost always the way to go. You need to recognize that either option is legal, however. And using *both together* is legal as well. It's not a problem, for example, to do the following:

```
import com.wickedlysmart.Foo;  // Import class Foo
class Bar {
  void doStuff() {
     com.wickedlysmart.Foo f = new com.wickedlysmart.Foo() //OK; not needed
   }
}
```

exam Watch

You might see questions that appear to be asking about classes and packages in the core Java API that you haven't studied, because you didn't think they were part of the exam objectives. For example, if you see a question like

```
class Foo extends java.rmi.UnicastRemoteObject {
   /// more code
}
```

don't panic! You're not actually being tested on your RMI knowledge, but rather a language and/or syntax issue. If you see code that references a class you're not familiar with, you can assume you're being tested on the way in which the code is *structured,* ***as opposed to what the class actually*** *does.* ***In the preceding code example, the question might really be about whether you need an import statement if you use the fully qualified name in your code (the answer is no, by the way).***

When do you use wildcard package imports vs. explicit class imports? Most of the time the compiler is just as happy with either, so the choice is more a matter of style and/or convenience. The tradeoffs usually come down to readability vs. typing.

If you use the wildcard import, other programmers reading your code will know that you're referencing classes from a particular package, but they won't be able to know how many classes—and what those classes are—from the package you've used unless they wade through the rest of the code! So the explicit class import helps folks reading your code (including you, if you're like most programmers and forget what you wrote a week after writing it) know exactly which classes you're using. On the other hand, if you're using, say, seven classes from a single package, it gets tedious to type each class in specifically. If we were forced at gunpoint to pick sides, we'd prefer the explicit class import, because of its, well, *explicitness.*

The one difference that might matter to you (but which you won't need to know for the exam) is that the order in which the compiler resolves imports is not simply top to bottom. Explicit imports are resolved first, then the classes from the current package, and last—the implicit imports.

exam watch

Look for syntax errors on import statements. Can you spot what's wrong with the following code?

```
import java.util.Arraylist.*; // Wildcard import
import java.util; // Explicit class import
```

The first import looks like it should be a valid wildcard import, but ArrayList is a class, not a package, so it makes no sense (not to mention making the compiler cranky) to use the wildcard import on a single class. Pay attention to the syntax detail of the import statement, by looking at how the statement ends. If it ends with `.*;` (dot, asterisk, semicolon), then it must be a wildcard statement; therefore, the* thing *immediately preceding the `.*;` must be a package name, not a class name. Conversely, the second import looks like an explicit class import, but* util *is a package, not a class, so you can't end that statement with a semicolon.

Think about another dilemma for a moment: what happens if you have two classes with the same name, from two different packages, and you want to use *both* in the same source code? In that case, you have to use the fully qualified names in code. Even in the core class libraries you'll find more than one class using the same name. You'll find a List class, for example, in both `java.awt` and `java.util`. If you want to use both, you'll have to make it clear to the compiler.

Wildcard imports alone won't work properly since importing both *packages* still doesn't help the compiler figure out *which* version of the List class you want. The following code shows the problem of trying to use two classes of the same name (although different packages):

```
import java.awt.*;
import java.util.*;

class TestImport {
   void doStuff() {
      List fromAWT = new List(); // How will the compiler know which to use?
      List fromUtil = new List(); // How will the compiler know which to use?
   }
}
```

The preceding code confuses the compiler (*never* a pretty thing), and you'll get a message similar to this:

```
TestImport.java:6: reference to List is ambiguous, both class
java.util.List in java.util and class java.awt.List in java.awt
match
```

```
List w = new List();
^
```

Formatting the Main() Method

When you want your code to actually run, you have to get the ball rolling with a `main()` method. The following rules apply to the `main()` method:

- It must be marked `static`.
- It must have a `void` return type.
- It must have a single String array argument.
- You can name the argument anything you want.
- It should be declared `public` (for the purposes of the exam, assume it *must* be public).

There's nothing special about the `main()` method; it's just another static method in your class. The only thing that makes it different from other methods is that it has the signature the JVM is looking for when you invoke Java as follows:

```
java MyClass
```

Typing that at the command line starts the JVM looking for the class file named `MyClass`, and when it finds it, it looks for the `main()` method—the one with a signature matching what the JVM is searching for. If it finds the matching method, you're good to go. If it doesn't, you get a runtime error like this:

```
Exception in thread "main" java.lang.NoSuchMethodError: main
```

The tricky thing about this error is that you can get it even when there *is* a `main()` method. The following code compiles fine, but still produces the previous `NoSuchMethodError` when you try to invoke this class from the command line:

```
class MyClass {
   public void main (String [] args) { }
}
```

Did you spot the problem? There *is* a `main()` method, but it isn't static. So when we say "the `main()` method," you need to know whether we mean "*a* method that happens to be named `main()`" (which you're allowed to have) or "*the* Main() Method"—the one the JVM looks for.

exam
Watch

Look for lots of subtle variations surrounding the `main()` method. You might see classes with a `main()` method similar to the preceding example, where the signature doesn't match what the JVM wants. You must know that* not having a proper `main()` method is a runtime error, not a compiler error! *So while you're completely free to have as many methods named `main()` as you like (or none at all), if no methods match the `main()` method the JVM looks for, then you won't be able to* run *the class by invoking Java using that class' name. You can still instantiate the class from other code (or invoke its static methods once the JVM is already running), it just can't be used to crank up a virtual machine and bootstrap your program. If the `main()` method doesn't look like this:

```
public static void main (String [] args) { }
```

you won't be able to* run *the class. You actually do have a few* slight *variations you can make to the `main()` method. For example, the following is a perfectly legal, executable `main()` method:

```
static public void main (String whatever []) { }
```

In other words, you're allowed to name the String array argument whatever you like, and the `static` and `public` modifiers can be used in a different order. The most important point for the exam is to know that not having the "able-to-run" `main()` method is a runtime, rather than compiler, error. A class with a legal, nonstatic `main()` method, for example, will compile just fine, and other code is free to call that method. But when it comes time to use that class to invoke the JVM, that nonstatic `main()` method just won't cut it, and you'll get the runtime error.

We've covered everything we need for this objective except for interface declarations, which we'll look at next, and inner class declarations, which we'll look at in Chapter 8. The key points for this objective are the structure of a source code file (where to place the package, import, and class declarations) and the signature of the `main()` method (`public static void main (String [] args)`). Next, we're going to dive into the rules for declaring and implementing interfaces.

CERTIFICATION OBJECTIVE

Interface Implementation (Exam Objective 4.2)

Identify classes that correctly implement an interface where that interface is either java.lang.Runnable or a fully specified interface in the question.

So far in this chapter, we began with Objective 1.2—a look at how to use modifiers in class, method, and variable declarations. Next, for Objective 4.1, we covered the rules for structuring a source code file and declaring the `main()` method. In this objective, we'll focus on interface declarations and implementations.

exam Watch

You must know how to implement the `java.lang.Runnable` interface, without being shown the code in the question. In other words, you might be asked to choose from a list of six classes which one provides a correct implementation of `Runnable`. Be sure you memorize the signature of the one and only one `Runnable` interface method:

```
public void run() { }
```

For any other interface-related question not dealing with `Runnable`, if the specification of the interface matters, the interface code will appear in the question. A question, for example, might show you a complete interface and a complete class, and ask you to choose whether or not the class correctly implements the interface. But if the question is about `Runnable`, you won't be shown the interface. You're expected to have `Runnable` memorized!

Declaring an Interface

When you create an interface, you're defining a contract for *what* a class can do, without saying anything about *how* the class will do it. An interface is a contract. You could write an interface `Bounceable`, for example, that says in effect, "This is the Bounceable interface. Any class type that implements this interface must agree to write the code for the `bounce()` and `setBounceFactor()` methods."

By defining an interface for Bounceable, any class that wants to be treated as a *Bounceable thing* can simply implement the Bounceable interface and provide code for the interface's two methods.

Interfaces can be implemented by *any* class, *from any inheritance tree.* This lets you take radically different classes and give them a common characteristic. For example, you might want both a Ball and a Tire to have bounce behavior, but Ball and Tire don't share any inheritance relationship; Ball extends Toy while Tire extends only `java.lang.Object`. But by making both Ball and Tire implement Bounceable, you're saying that Ball and Tire can be treated as, "Things that can bounce," which in Java translates to "Things on which you can invoke the `bounce()` and `setBounceFactor()` methods." Figure 2-8 illustrates the relationship between interfaces and classes.

Think of an interface as a 100-percent abstract class. Like an abstract class, an interface defines abstract methods that take the form,

```
abstract void bounce();  // Ends with a semicolon rather than curly braces
```

But while an abstract class can define both abstract and nonabstract methods, an interface can have *only* abstract methods. Another place interfaces differ from

FIGURE 2-8

The relationship between interfaces and classes

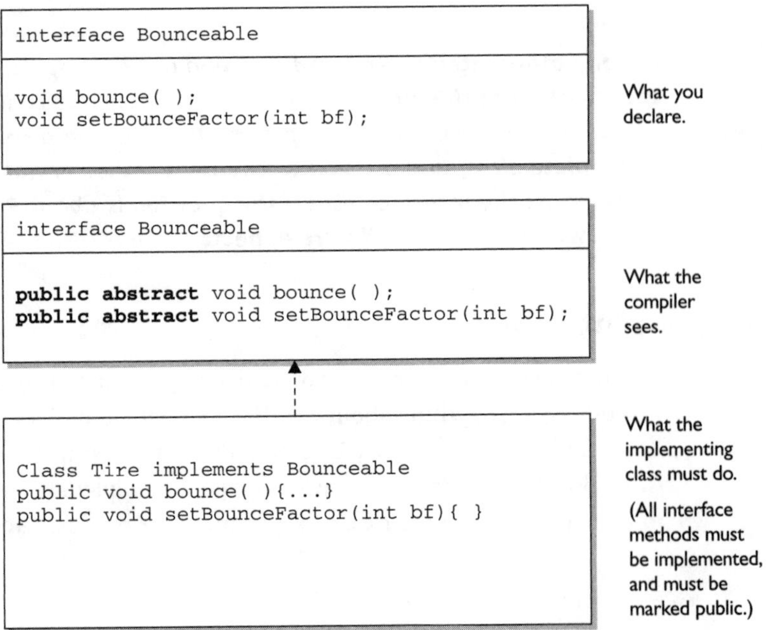

abstract classes is that interfaces have very little flexibility in how the methods and variables defined in the interface are declared. The rules are strict, but simple:

- All interface methods are implicitly public and abstract.
- Interface methods must not be static.
- You do not need to actually *type* the `public` or `abstract` modifiers in the method declaration, but the method is still always public and abstract.
- All *variables* defined in an interface must be public, static, and final—in other words, interfaces can declare only constants, not instance variables.
- Because interface methods are abstract, they cannot be marked `final`, `native`, `strictfp`, or `synchronized`.
- An interface can *extend* one or more other interfaces.
- An interface cannot extend anything *but* another interface.
- An interface cannot *implement* another interface or class.
- An interface must be declared with the keyword `interface`.
- Interface types can be used polymorphically (see Chapter 5 for more details).

The following is a legal interface declaration:

```
public abstract interface Rollable { }
```

Typing in the `abstract` modifier is considered redundant; interfaces are implicitly abstract whether you type `abstract` or not. You just need to know that both of these declarations are legal, and functionally identical:

```
public abstract interface Rollable { }
public interface Rollable { }
```

The `public` modifier *is* required if you want the interface to have public rather than default access.

We've looked at the interface declaration but now we'll look closely at the *methods* within an interface:

```
public interface Bounceable {
    public abstract void bounce();
    public abstract void setBounceFactor(int bf);
}
```

Typing in the `public` and `abstract` modifiers on the methods is redundant, though, since all interface methods are implicitly public and abstract. Given that rule, you can see that the following code is exactly equivalent to the preceding interface:

```
public interface Bounceable {
      void bounce();  // No modifiers
      void setBounceFactor(int bf);  // No modifiers
}
```

You must remember that all interface methods are public and abstract *regardless of what you see in the interface definition.*

exam Watch

Look for interface methods declared with any combination of public, abstract, or no modifiers. For example, the following five method declarations, if declared within an interface, are legal *and identical!*

```
void bounce();
public void bounce();
abstract void bounce();
public abstract void bounce();
abstract public void bounce();
```

The following interface method declarations won't compile:

```
final void bounce(); // final and abstract can never be used
static void bounce(); // interfaces define instance methods
private void bounce(); // interface methods are always public
protected void bounce(); // (same as above)
synchronized void bounce(); // can't mix abstract and synchronized
native void bounce(); // can't mix abstract and native
strictfp void bounce(); // can't mix abstract and strictfp
```

Declaring Interface Constants

You're allowed to put constants in an interface. By doing so, you guarantee that any class implementing the interface will have access to the same constant. Imagine that a Bounceable thing works by using `int` values to represent gravity where the Bounceable thing is, its degree of bounciness (bounce-osity?), and so on. Now imagine that for a Bounceable thing, gravity is set such that a 1 is low, 2 is medium, 3 is high, and for bounciness, 4 is a little bouncy, 8 is very bouncy, and 12 is extremely bouncy. Those numbers are tough to remember when you're trying to decide how to set the values ("let's see, was it 8 for high gravity and 3 for medium bounce? Or was it the other way around…"). Now let's say that you (the developer of Bounceable) decide that it would be much easier for programmers to remember names like *HIGH_GRAVITY*, *LOW_BOUNCE*, and *HIGH_BOUNCE* as opposed to knowing the exact *int* values corresponding to each of those. So, you know you want to define some constants so the programmer can just use the constant name rather than the *int* value. You need something like the following:

```
public final static int LOW_BOUNCE = 4;
public final static int HIGH_GRAVITY = 3;
... // and so on
```

That way, if a method takes the `int` values,

```
public void animateIt(int gravity, int bounceFactor) {  }
```

then the code that calls `animateIt()` can substitute the constants wherever the `int` values are expected, as follows:

```
animator.animateIt(LOW_GRAVITY, HIGH_BOUNCE);
```

So we've made a case for using constants with easy-to-remember names (as opposed to using nearly arbitrary numbers), but where do you *put* these constants so that all Bounceable things (things as in "things that implement the Bounceable interface") can substitute the `int` constant name everywhere one of the `int` values is needed? You could define them in some companion class called, for example, BounceableConstants. But why not just put them in the Bounceable interface? That way you can guarantee that all Bounceable things will always have access to the constants, without having to create another class. Look at the changes we've made to the `Bounceable` interface:

```
public interface Bounceable {
   int LOW_GRAVITY = 1;
   int MEDIUM_GRAVITY = 2;
   int HIGH_GRAVITY = 3;
   int LOW_BOUNCE = 4;
   int MEDIUM_BOUNCE = 8;
   int HIGH_BOUNCE = 12;

   void bounce();
```

```
    void setBounceFactor(int bounceFactor);
    void setGravity(int gravity);
}
```

By placing the constants right in the interface, *any class that implements the interface has direct access to the constants, just as if the class had inherited them.* For example, the following would be legal for a Bounceable implementation class:

```
class Ball implements Bounceable {
   // Lots of exciting code goes here
   public void bounce() {
      animator.animateIt(LOW_GRAVITY, HIGH_BOUNCE);  // MUCH easier this way
   }
   // Still more action-packed code goes here
}
```

You need to remember a few rules for interface constants. They must always be

- public
- static
- final

So that sounds simple, right? After all, interface constants are no different from any other publicly accessible constants, so they obviously must be declared `public`, `static`, and `final`. But before you breeze past the rest of this discussion, think about the implications. First, because interface constants are defined in an interface, they don't have to be *declared* as `public`, `static`, or `final`. They must *be* public, static, and final, but you don't have to actually *declare* them that way. Just as interface methods are always public and abstract whether you say so in the code or not, *any variable defined in an interface must be—and implicitly is—a public constant.* See if you can spot the problem with the following implementation of Bounceable:

```
class Check implements Bounceable {
   // Implementation code goes here
   public void adjustGravityFactors(int x) {
      if (x > LOW_GRAVITY) {
      LOW_GRAVITY = x;
      MEDIUM_GRAVITY = x + 1;
      HIGH-GRAVITY = x + 2;
      }
   }
}
```

You can't change the value of a constant! Once the value has been assigned, the value can never be modified. The assignment happens in the interface itself (where the constant is declared), so the implementing class can access it and use it, but as a read-only value.

exam Watch

Look for interface definitions that define constants, but without explicitly using the required modifiers. For example, the following are all identical:

```
public int x = 1; // Looks non-static and non-final, but isn't!
int x = 1; // Looks default, non-final, and non-static, but isn't!
static int x = 1; // Doesn't show final or public
final int x = 1; // Doesn't show static or public
public static int x = 1; // Doesn't show final
public final int x = 1; // Doesn't show static
static final int x = 1 // Doesn't show public
public static final int x = 1; // Exactly what you get implicitly
```

Any combination of the required (but implicit) modifiers is legal, as is using no modifiers at all! On the exam, you can expect to see questions you won't be able to answer correctly unless you know, for example, that an interface variable is final and can never be given a value by the implementing (or any other) class.

Implementing an Interface

When you implement an interface, you're agreeing to adhere to the contract defined in the interface. That means you're agreeing to provide legal implementations for every method defined in the interface, and that anyone who knows what the interface methods look like (not how they're *implemented*, but how they can be *called* and what they *return*) can rest assured that they can invoke those methods on an instance of your implementing class.

For example, if you create a class that implements the `Runnable` interface (so that your code can be executed by a specific thread), you *must* provide the `public void run()` method. Otherwise, the poor thread could be told to go execute your `Runnable` object's code and—surprise surprise—the thread then discovers the object has no `run()` method! (At which point, the thread would blow up and the JVM would crash in a spectacular yet horrible explosion.) Thankfully, Java prevents this meltdown from occurring by running a compiler check on any class that claims to implement an interface. If the class *says* it's implementing an interface, it darn well better have an implementation for each method in the interface (with a few exceptions we'll look at in a moment).

We looked earlier at several examples of implementation classes, including the `Ball` class that implements `Bounceable`, but the following class would also compile legally:

```
public class Ball implements Bounceable {  // Keyword 'implements'
   public void bounce() { }
   public void setBounceFactor(int bf) { }
}
```

OK, we know what you're thinking: "This has got to be the worst implementation class in the history of implementation classes." It compiles, though. And runs. The interface contract guarantees that a class will have the method (in other words, others can call the method subject to access control), but it never guaranteed a good implementation—or even any actual implementation code in the body of the method. The compiler will never say to you, "Um, excuse me, but did you *really* mean to put *nothing* between those curly braces? *HELLO.* This *is* a method after all, so shouldn't it do something?"

Implementation classes must adhere to the same rules for method implementation as a class extending an abstract class. In order to be a legal implementation class, a nonabstract implementation class *must* do the following:

- Provide concrete (nonabstract) implementations for all methods from the declared interface.
- Follow all the rules for legal overrides (see Chapter 5 for details).
- Declare no checked exceptions on implementation methods other than those declared by the interface method, or subclasses of those declared by the interface method.
- Maintain the signature of the interface method, and maintain the same return type (but does not have to declare the exceptions declared in the interface method declaration).

But wait, there's more! An implementation class can itself be abstract! For example, the following is legal for a class Ball implementing the Bounceable interface:

```
abstract class Ball implements Bounceable { }
```

Notice anything missing? We never provided the implementation methods. And that's OK. If the implementation class is abstract, it can simply pass the buck to its first concrete subclass. For example, if class BeachBall extends Ball, and BeachBall is not abstract, then BeachBall will have to provide all the methods from Bounceable:

```
class BeachBall extends Ball {
  // Even though we don't say it in the class declaration above,
  //BeachBall implements Bounceable, since BeachBall's abstract
  //superclass (Ball) implements Bounceable

   public void bounce() {
      // interesting BeachBall-specific bounce code
   }
   public void setBounceFactor(int bf) {
      // clever BeachBall-specific code for setting a bounce factor
   }
   // if class Ball defined any abstract methods, they'll have to be
   // implemented here as well.
}
```

exam Watch

Look for methods that* claim *to implement an interface but don't provide the correct method implementations. Unless the implementing class is abstract, the implementing class must provide implementations for all methods defined in the interface.

Two more rules you need to know and then we can put this topic to sleep (or put *you* to sleep; we always get those two confused):

1. **A class can implement more than one interface.**

   It's perfectly legal to say, for example, the following:

   ```
   public class Ball implements Bounceable, Serializable,
   Runnable { ... }
   ```

   You can extend only one class, but implement many. But remember that *subclassing* defines who and what you are, whereas *implementing* defines a role you can play or a hat you can wear, despite how different you might be from some other class implementing the same interface (but from a different inheritance tree). For example, a person *extends* `HumanBeing` (although for some, that's debatable). But a person may also *implement* `programmer`, `snowboarder`, `employee`, `parent`, or `personcrazyenoughtotakethisexam`.

2. **An interface can itself *extend* another interface, but never *implement* anything.**

   The following code is perfectly legal:

   ```
   public interface Bounceable extends Moveable { }
   ```

   What does that mean? The first concrete (nonabstract) implementation class of `Bounceable` must implement all the methods of Bounceable, plus all the methods of Moveable! The subinterface, as we call it, simply adds more requirements to the contract of the superinterface. You'll see this concept applied in many areas of Java, especially J2EE where you'll often have to build your own interface that extends one of the J2EE interfaces.

Hold on though, because here's where it gets strange. *An interface can extend more than one interface!* Think about that for a moment. You know that when we're talking about classes, the following is illegal:

```
public class Programmer extends Employee, Geek { } // Illegal!
```

A class is not allowed to extend multiple classes in Java. It that were allowed, it would be multiple inheritance, a potential nightmare in some scenarios (more on that in Chapter 5). An interface, however, is free to extend multiple interfaces.

```
interface Bounceable extends Moveable, Spherical {
   void bounce();
   void setBounceFactor(int bf);
}

interface Moveable {
   void moveIt();
}

interface Spherical {
   void doSphericalThing();
}
```

Ball is required to implement Bounceable, plus all methods from the interfaces that Bounceable extends (including any interfaces *those* interfaces extend and so on until you reach the top of the stack—or is it *bottom* of the stack?—well, you know what we mean). So Ball would need to look like the following:

```
class Ball implements Bounceable {
   // Implement the methods from Bounceable
   public void bounce() { }
   public void setBounceFactor(int bf) { }

   // Implement the methods from Moveable
   public void moveIt() { }

   // Implement the methods from Spherical
   public void doSphericalThing() { }
}
```

If class Ball fails to implement any of the methods from Bounceable, Moveable, or Spherical, the compiler will jump up and down wildly, red in the face, until it does. *Unless*, that is, *class Ball is marked abstract*. In that case, Ball could choose to implement any, all, or none of the methods from any of the interfaces, thus leaving the rest of the implementations to a concrete subclass of Ball, as follows:

```
abstract class Ball implements Bounceable {
   public void bounce() { … }  // Define bounce behavior
   public void setBounceFactor(int bf) { … }
   // Don't implement the rest; leave it for a subclass
}

class SoccerBall extends Ball {
   // class SoccerBall must implement the interface methods that Ball didn't
   public void moveIt() { … }
   public void doSphericalThing() { … }
   // SoccerBall can choose to override the Bounceable methods
   // implemented by Ball
   public void bounce() { … }
}
```

Figure 2-9 compares the legal and illegal use of extends and implements, for both classes and interfaces.

FIGURE 2-9 Legal and illegal uses of extends and implements

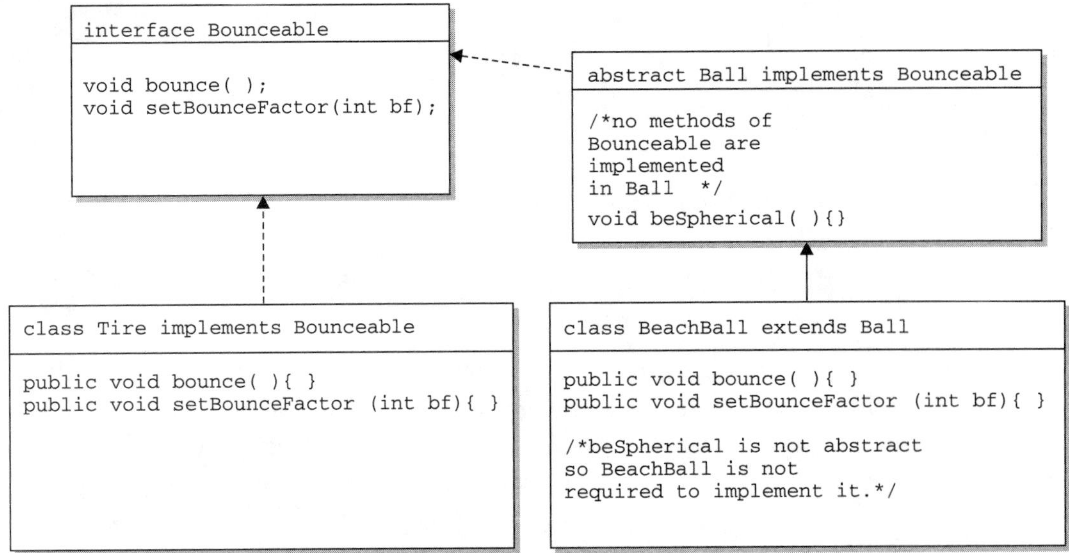

Because BeachBall is the first concrete class to implement Bounceable, it must provide implementations for all methods of Bounceable, except those defined in the abstract class Ball. Because Ball did not provide implementations of Bounceable methods, BeachBall was required to implement all of them.

exam Watch

Look for illegal uses of extends and implements. The following shows examples of legal and illegal class and interface declarations:

```
class Foo { } // OK
class Bar implements Foo  { } // No! Can't implement a class
interface Baz { } // OK
interface Fi { } // OK
interface Fee implements Baz { } // No! Interface can't implement an interface
interface Zee implements Foo { } // No! Interface can't implement a class
interface Zoo extends Foo { }  // No! Interface can't extend a class
interface Boo extends Fi  { } // OK. Interface can extend an interface
class Toon extends Foo, Button { } // No! Class can't extend multiple classes
class Zoom implements Fi, Fee { }  // OK. class can implement multiple interfaces
interface Vroom extends Fi, Fee { }  // OK. interface can extend multiple interfaces
```

Burn these in, and watch for abuses in the questions you get on the exam. Regardless of what the question *appears* ***to be testing, the*** *real* ***problem might be the class or interface declaration. Before you get caught up in, say, tracing a complex threading flow, check to see if the code will even compile. (Just that tip alone may be worth your putting us in your will!) (You'll be impressed by the effort the exam developers put into distracting you from the*** *real* ***problem.) (How did people manage to write anything before parentheses were (was?) invented?)***

CERTIFICATION SUMMARY

You now have a good understanding of access control as it relates to classes, methods, and variables. You've looked at how access modifiers (`public`, `protected`, `private`) define the access control of a class or member. You've also looked at the other modifiers including `static`, `final`, `abstract`, `synchronized`, etc. You've learned how some modifiers can never be combined in a declaration, such as mixing `final` with `abstract` or `abstract` with `private`.

Keep in mind that there are no final objects in Java. A reference *variable* marked `final` can never be changed, but the *object* it refers to can be modified. You've seen that `final` applied to methods means a subclass can't override them, and when applied to a class, the final class can't be subclassed.

You learned that abstract classes can contain both abstract and nonabstract methods, but that if even a single method is marked `abstract`, the class must be marked abstract. Don't forget that a concrete (nonabstract) subclass of an abstract class must provide implementations for all the abstract methods of the superclass, but that an abstract class does not have to implement the abstract methods from its superclass. An abstract subclass can "pass the buck" to the first concrete subclass.

Remember what you've learned about static variables and methods, especially that static members are *per-class* as opposed to *per-instance*. Don't forget that a static method can't directly access an instance variable from the class it's in, because it doesn't have an explicit reference to any particular instance of the class.

You've also looked at source code declarations, including the use of package and import statements. Don't forget that you can have a `main()` method with any legal signature you like, but if it isn't `public static void main (String [] args)`, the JVM won't be able to invoke it to start your program running.

Finally, you covered interface implementation, including the requirement to implement `public void run()` for a class that implements Runnable. You also saw that interfaces can extend another interface (even multiple interfaces), and that any class that implements an interface must implement all methods from *all* the interfaces in the inheritance tree of the interface the class is implementing.

Before you hurl yourself at the practice test, spend some time with the following optimistically named "Two-Minute Drill." Come back to this particular drill often, as you work through this book and especially when you're doing that last-minute cramming. Because—and here's the advice you wished your mother had given you before you left for college—*it's not what you know, it's when you know it.*

TWO-MINUTE DRILL

Class Access Modifiers

- There are three access *modifiers*: `public`, `protected`, and `private`.
- There are four access *levels*: `public`, `protected`, default, and `private`.
- Classes can have only public or default access.
- Class visibility revolves around whether code in one class can:
  - Create an instance of another class
  - Extend (or subclass), another class
  - Access methods and variables of another class
- A class with default access can be seen only by classes within the same package.
- A class with public access can be seen by all classes from all packages.

Class Modifiers (nonaccess)

- Classes can also be modified with `final`, `abstract`, or `strictfp`.
- A class cannot be both final *and* abstract.
- A final class cannot be subclassed.
- An abstract class cannot be instantiated.
- A single abstract method in a class means the whole class must be abstract.
- An abstract class can have both abstract and nonabstract methods.
- The first concrete class to extend an abstract class must implement all abstract methods.

Member Access Modifiers

- ❑ Methods and instance (nonlocal) variables are known as "members."
- ❑ Members can use all four access levels: `public`, `protected`, default, `private`.
- ❑ Member access comes in two forms:
  - ❑ Code in one class can access a member of another class.
  - ❑ A subclass can inherit a member of its superclass.
- ❑ If a class cannot be accessed, its members cannot be accessed.
- ❑ Determine class visibility before determining member visibility.
- ❑ Public members can be accessed by all other classes, even in different packages.
- ❑ If a superclass member is public, the subclass inherits it—regardless of package.
- ❑ Members accessed without the dot operator (.) must belong to the same class.
- ❑ `this.` always refers to the currently executing object.
- ❑ `this.aMethod()` is the same as just invoking `aMethod()`.
- ❑ Private members can be accessed only by code in the same class.
- ❑ Private members are not visible to subclasses, so private members cannot be inherited.
- ❑ Default and protected members differ only in when subclasses are involved:
  - ❑ Default members can be accessed only by other classes in the same package.
  - ❑ Protected members can be accessed by other classes in the same package, plus subclasses regardless of package.
- ❑ Protected = package plus kids (kids meaning subclasses).
- ❑ For subclasses outside the package, the protected member can be accessed only through inheritance; a subclass outside the package cannot access a protected member by using a reference to an instance of the superclass (in other words, inheritance is the only mechanism for a subclass outside the package to access a protected member of its superclass).
- ❑ A protected member inherited by a subclass from another package is, in practice, private to all other classes (in other words, no other classes from

the subclass' package or any other package will have access to the protected member from the subclass).

Local Variables

- Local (method, automatic, stack) variable declarations cannot have access modifiers.
- `final` is the only modifier available to local variables.
- Local variables don't get default values, so they must be initialized before use.

Other Modifiers—Members

- Final methods cannot be overridden in a subclass.
- Abstract methods have been declared, with a signature and return type, but have not been implemented.
- Abstract methods end in a semicolon—no curly braces.
- Three ways to spot a nonabstract method:
  - The method is not marked abstract.
  - The method has curly braces.
  - The method has code between the curly braces.
- The first nonabstract (concrete) class to extend an abstract class must implement all of the abstract class' abstract methods.
- Abstract methods must be implemented by a subclass, so they must be inheritable. For that reason:
  - Abstract methods cannot be private.
  - Abstract methods cannot be final.
- The `synchronized` modifier applies only to methods.
- Synchronized methods can have any access control and can also be marked `final`.
- Synchronized methods cannot be abstract.
- The `native` modifier applies only to methods.
- The `strictfp` modifier applies only to classes and methods.

- Instance variables can
  - Have any access control
  - Be marked `final` or `transient`
- Instance variables cannot be declared `abstract`, `synchronized`, `native`, or `strictfp`.
- It is legal to declare a local variable with the same name as an instance variable; this is called "shadowing."
- Final variables have the following properties:
  - Final variables cannot be reinitialized once assigned a value.
  - Final reference variables cannot refer to a different object once the object has been assigned to the final variable.
  - Final reference variables must be initialized before the constructor completes.
- There is no such thing as a final object. An object reference marked `final` does not mean the object itself is immutable.
- The `transient` modifier applies only to instance variables.
- The `volatile` modifier applies only to instance variables.

Static variables and methods

- They are not tied to any particular instance of a class.
- An instance of a class does not need to exist in order to use static members of the class.
- There is only one copy of a static variable per class and all instances share it.
- Static variables get the same default values as instance variables.
- A static method (such as `main()`) cannot access a nonstatic (instance) variable.
- Static members are accessed using the class name:
  `ClassName.theStaticMethodName()`
- Static members can also be accessed using an instance reference variable,
  `someObj.theStaticMethodName()`
  but that's just a syntax trick; the static method won't know anything about the instance referred to by the variable used to invoke the method. The

compiler uses the *class type* of the reference variable to determine which static method to invoke.

- ❑ Static methods cannot be *overridden*, although they can be redeclared/redefined by a subclass. So although static methods can sometimes *appear* to be overridden, polymorphism will not apply (more on this in Chapter 5).

Declaration Rules

- ❑ A source code file can have only one public class.
- ❑ If the source file contains a public class, the file name should match the public class name.
- ❑ A file can have only one package statement, but can have multiple import statements.
- ❑ The package statement (if any) must be the first line in a source file.
- ❑ The import statements (if any) must come after the package and before the class declaration.
- ❑ If there is no package statement, import statements must be the first statements in the source file.
- ❑ Package and import statements apply to all classes in the file.
- ❑ A file can have more than one nonpublic class.
- ❑ Files with no public classes have no naming restrictions.
- ❑ In a file, classes can be listed in any order (there is no forward referencing problem).
- ❑ Import statements only provide a typing shortcut to a class' fully qualified name.
- ❑ Import statements cause no performance hits and do not increase the size of your code.
- ❑ If you use a class from a different package, but do not import the class, you must use the fully qualified name of the class everywhere the class is used in code.
- ❑ Import statements can coexist with fully qualified class names in a source file.
- ❑ Imports ending in `'.*;'` are importing all classes within a package.

- Imports ending in `';'` are importing a single class.
- You must use fully qualified names when you have different classes from different packages, with the same class name; an import statement will not be explicit enough.

Properties of main()

- It must be marked `static`.
- It must have a `void` return type.
- It must have a single String array argument; the name of the argument is flexible, but the convention is *args*.
- For the purposes of the exam, assume that *the* `main()` method must be public.
- Improper `main()` method declarations (or the lack of a `main()` method) cause a runtime error, not a compiler error.
- In the declaration of `main()`, the order of `public` and `static` can be switched, and *args* can be renamed.
- Other overloaded methods named `main()` can exist legally in the class, but if none of them match the expected signature for *the* `main()` method, then the JVM won't be able to use that class to start your application running.

java.lang.Runnable

- You must memorize the `java.lang.Runnable` interface; it has a single method you must implement: `public void run {}`.

Interface Implementation

- Interfaces are contracts for what a class can do, but they say nothing about the way in which the class must do it.
- Interfaces can be implemented by any class, from any inheritance tree.
- An interface is like a 100-percent abstract class, and is implicitly abstract whether you type the `abstract` modifier in the declaration or not.
- An interface can have only abstract methods, no concrete methods allowed.

- Interfaces are by default public and abstract—explicit declaration of these modifiers is optional.
- Interfaces can have constants, which are always implicitly `public`, `static`, and `final`.
- Interface constant declarations of `public`, `static`, and `final` are optional in any combination.
- A legal nonabstract implementing class has the following properties:
  - It provides concrete implementations for all methods from the interface.
  - It must follow all legal override rules for the methods it implements.
  - It must not declare any new *checked* exceptions for an implementation method.
  - It must not declare any checked exceptions that are broader than the exceptions declared in the interface method.
  - It may declare runtime exceptions on any interface method implementation regardless of the interface declaration.
  - It must maintain the exact signature and return type of the methods it implements (but does not have to declare the exceptions of the interface).
- A class implementing an interface can itself be abstract.
- An abstract implementing class does not have to implement the interface methods (but the first concrete subclass must).
- A class can extend only one class (no multiple inheritance), but it can implement many.
- Interfaces *can* extend one or more other interfaces.
- Interfaces *cannot* extend a class, or implement a class or interface.
- When taking the exam, verify that interface and class declarations are legal before verifying other code logic.

SELF TEST

The following questions will help you measure your understanding of the material presented in this chapter. Read all of the choices carefully, as there may be more than one correct answer. Choose all correct answers for each question.

Declarations and Modifiers (Sun Objective 1.2)

1. What is the most restrictive access modifier that will allow members of one class to have access to members of another class in the same package?

   A. `public`

   B. `abstract`

   C. `protected`

   D. `synchronized`

   E. default access

2. Given a method in a `public` class, what access modifier do you use to restrict access to that method to only the other members of the same class?

   A. `final`

   B. `static`

   C. `private`

   D. `protected`

   E. `volatile`

   F. default access

3. Given the following,

```
abstract class A {
  abstract short m1() ;
  short m2() { return (short) 420; }
}

abstract class B extends A {
  // missing code ?
  short m1() { return (short) 42; }
}
```

   which three of the following statements are true? (Choose three.)

A. The code will compile with no changes.

B. Class B must either make an `abstract` declaration of method `m2()` or implement method `m2()` to allow the code to compile.

C. It is legal, but not required, for class B to either make an abstract declaration of method `m2()` or implement method `m2()` for the code to compile.

D. As long as line 8 exists, class A must declare method `m1()` in some way.

E. If line 6 were replaced with `'class B extends A {'` the code would compile.

F. If class A was not abstract and method `m1()` on line 2 was implemented, the code would not compile.

4. Which two of the following are legal declarations for nonnested classes and interfaces? (Choose two.)

A. `final abstract class Test {}`

B. `public static interface Test {}`

C. `final public class Test {}`

D. `protected abstract class Test {}`

E. `protected interface Test {}`

F. `abstract public class Test {}`

5. How many of the following are legal method declarations?

```
1 - protected abstract void m1();
2 - static final void m1(){}
3 - transient private native void m1() {}
4 - synchronized public final void m1() {}
5 - private native void m1();
6 - static final synchronized protected void m1() {}
```

A. 1

B. 2

C. 3

D. 4

E. 5

F. All of them

6. Given the following,

```
package testpkg.p1;
public class ParentUtil {
  public int x = 420;
  protected int doStuff() { return x; }
}
```

```
1.  package testpkg.p2;
2.  import testpkg.p1.ParentUtil;
3.  public class ChildUtil extends ParentUtil {
4.    public static void main(String [] args) {
5.      new ChildUtil().callStuff();
6.    }
7.    void callStuff() {
8.      System.out.print("this " + this.doStuff() );
9.      ParentUtil p = new ParentUtil();
10.     System.out.print(" parent " + p.doStuff() );
11.   }
12. }
```

which statement is true?

A. The code compiles and runs, with output `this 420 parent 420`.

B. If line 8 is removed, the code will compile and run.

C. If line 10 is removed, the code will compile and run.

D. Both lines 8 and 10 must be removed for the code to compile.

E. An exception is thrown at runtime.

Declaration Rules (Sun Objective 4.1)

7. Given the following,

```
interface Count {
  short counter = 0;
  void countUp();
}
public class TestCount implements Count {

  public static void main(String [] args) {
    TestCount t = new TestCount();
    t.countUp();
  }
```

```
    public void countUp() {
      for (int x = 6; x>counter; x--, ++counter) {
         System.out.print(" " + counter);
      }
    }
  }
```

what is the result?

A. 0 1 2

B. 1 2 3

C. 0 1 2 3

D. 1 2 3 4

E. Compilation fails

F. An exception is thrown at runtime

8. Given the following,

```
1.  import java.util.*;
2.  public class NewTreeSet2 extends NewTreeSet {
3.    public static void main(String [] args) {
4.      NewTreeSet2 t = new NewTreeSet2();
5.      t.count();
6.    }
7.  }
8.  protected class NewTreeSet {
9.    void count() {
10.     for (int x = 0; x < 7; x++,x++ ) {
11.       System.out.print(" " + x);
12.     }
13.   }
14. }
```

what is the result?

A. 0 2 4

B. 0 2 4 6

C. Compilation fails at line 4

D. Compilation fails at line 5

E. Compilation fails at line 8

F. Compilation fails at line 10

9. Given the following,

```
1.
2.    public class NewTreeSet extends java.util.TreeSet{
3.      public static void main(String [] args) {
4.        java.util.TreeSet t = new java.util.TreeSet();
5.        t.clear();
6.      }
7.      public void clear() {
8.         TreeMap m = new TreeMap();
9.         m.clear();
10.     }
11.   }
```

which two statements, added independently at line 1, allow the code to compile? (Choose two.)

A. No statement is required

B. `import java.util.*;`

C. `import.java.util.Tree*;`

D. `import java.util.TreeSet;`

E. `import java.util.TreeMap;`

10. Which two are valid declarations within an interface? (Choose two.)

A. `public static short stop = 23;`

B. `protected short stop = 23;`

C. `transient short stop = 23;`

D. `final void madness(short stop);`

E. `public Boolean madness(long bow);`

F. `static char madness(double duty);`

11. Which of the following class level (*nonlocal*) variable declarations will not compile?

A. `protected int a;`

B. `transient int b = 3;`

C. `public static final int c;`

D. `volatile int d;`

E. `private synchronized int e;`

Interface Implementation (Sun Objective 4.2)

12. Given the following,

```
1.  interface DoMath {
2.     double getArea(int rad); }
3.
4.   interface MathPlus {
5.     double getVol(int b, int h); }
6.
7.
8.
```

which two code fragments inserted at lines 7 and 8 will compile? (Choose two.)

A. `class AllMath extends DoMath {`
`public double getArea(int r); }`

B. `interface AllMath implements MathPlus {`
`public double getVol(int x, int y); }`

C. `interface AllMath extends DoMath {`
`public float getAvg(int h, int l); }`

D. `class AllMath implements MathPlus {`
`public double getArea(int rad); }`

E. `abstract class AllMath implements DoMath, MathPlus {`
`public double getArea(int rad) { return rad * rad * 3.14; } }`

13. Which three are valid method signatures in an interface? (Choose three.)

A. `private int getArea();`

B. `public float getVol(float x);`

C. `public void main(String [] args);`

D. `public static void main(String [] args);`

E. `boolean setFlag(Boolean [] test []);`

14. Which two statements are true for any concrete class implementing the `java.lang.Runnable` interface? (Choose two.)

A. You can extend the `Runnable` interface as long as you override the `public run()` method.

B. The class must contain a method called `run()` from which all code for that thread will be initiated.

C. The class must contain an empty `public void` method named `run()`.

D. The class must contain a `public void` method named `runnable()`.

E. The class definition must include the words `implements Threads` and contain a method called `run()`.

F. The mandatory method must be `public`, with a return type of `void`, must be called `run()`, and cannot take any arguments.

15. Given the following,

```
interface Base {
  boolean m1 ();
  byte m2(short s);
}
```

which two code fragments will compile? (Choose two.)

A. `interface Base2 implements Base {}`

B.
```
abstract class Class2 extends Base {
  public boolean m1() { return true; } }
```

C. `abstract class Class2 implements Base { }`

D.
```
abstract class Class2 implements Base {
  public boolean m1() { return (7 > 4); } }
```

E.
```
class Class2 implements Base {
  boolean m1() { return false; }
  byte m2(short s) { return 42; } }
```

SELF TEST ANSWERS

Declarations and Modifiers

1. ☑ **E.** `default access` is the "package oriented" access modifier.
☒ **A** and **C** are wrong because `public` and `protected` are less restrictive. **B** and **D** are wrong because `abstract` and `synchronized` are not access modifiers.

2. ☑ **C.** The `private` access modifier limits access to members of the same class.
☒ **A, B, D, E,** and **F** are wrong because `protected` and `default` are the wrong access modifiers, and `final`, `static`, and `volatile` are modifiers but not access modifiers.

3. ☑ **A, C,** and **E. A** and **C** are correct, because an `abstract` class does not need to implement any of its superclass' methods. **E** is correct because as it stands, it is a valid concrete extension of class A.
☒ **B** is wrong because an `abstract` class does not need to implement any of its superclass' methods. **D** is wrong because a class that extends another class is free to add new methods. **F** is wrong because it is legal to extend an `abstract` class from a concrete class.

4. ☑ **C, F.** Both are legal class declarations.
☒ **A** is wrong because a class cannot be `abstract` and `final`—there would be no way to use such a class. **B** is wrong because interfaces and classes cannot be marked as `static`. **D** and **E** are wrong because classes and interfaces cannot be marked as `protected`.

5. ☑ **E.** Statements 1, 2, 4, 5, and 6 are legal declarations.
☒ **A, B, C, D,** and **F** are incorrect because the only illegal declaration is 3; `transient` applies only to variable declarations, not to method declarations. As you can see from these other examples, method declarations can be very extensive.

6. ☑ **C.** The ParentUtil instance `p` cannot be used to access the `doStuff()` method. Because `doStuff()` has `protected` access, and the ChildUtil class is not in the same package as the ParentUtil class, `doStuff()` can be accessed only by instances of the ChildUtil class (a subclass of `ParentUtil`).
☒ **A, B, D,** and **E** are incorrect because of the access rules described previously.

Declaration Rules

7. ☑ **E.** The code will not compile because the variable `counter` is an interface variable that is by default `final static`. The compiler will complain at line 12 when the code attempts to

increment `counter`.
☒ A, B, C, and D are incorrect because of the explanation given above.

8. ☑ E. Nonnested classes cannot be marked `protected` (or `final` for that matter), so the compiler will fail at line 8.
☒ A, B, C, and D are incorrect because of the explanation given above.

9. ☑ B and E. TreeMap is the only class that must be imported. TreeSet does not need an import statement because it is described with a fully qualified name.
☒ A is incorrect because TreeMap must be imported. C is incorrect syntax for an import statement. D is incorrect because it will not import TreeMap, which is required.

10. ☑ A and E are valid interface declarations.
☒ B and C are incorrect because interface variables cannot be either `protected` or `transient`. D and F are incorrect because interface methods cannot be `final` or `static`.

11. ☑ E will not compile; the `synchronized` modifier applies only to methods.
☒ A and B will compile because `protected` and `transient` are legal variable modifiers. C will compile because when a variable is declared `final` it does not have to be initialized with a value at the same time. D will compile because `volatile` is a proper variable modifier.

Interface Implementation

12. ☑ C and E. C are E are correct because interfaces and abstract classes do not need to fully implement the interfaces they extend or implement (respectively).
☒ A is incorrect because a class cannot extend an interface. B is incorrect because an interface cannot implement anything. D is incorrect because the method being implemented is from the wrong interface.

13. ☑ B, C, and E. These are all valid interface method signatures.
☒ A, is incorrect because an interface method must be `public`; if it is not explicitly declared `public` it will be made `public` implicitly. D is incorrect because interface methods cannot be `static`.

14. ☑ B and F. When a thread's `run()` method completes, the thread will die. The `run()` method must be declared `public void` and not take any arguments.
☒ A is incorrect because classes can never extend interfaces. C is incorrect because the

`run()` method is typically not empty; if it were, the thread would do nothing. **D** is incorrect because the mandatory method is `run()`. **E** is incorrect because the class implements `Runnable`.

15. ☑ **C** and **D**. **C** is correct because an `abstract` class doesn't have to implement any or all of its interface's methods. **D** is correct because the method is correctly implemented ((7 > 4) is a `boolean`).
☒ **A** is incorrect because interfaces don't implement anything. **B** is incorrect because classes don't extend interfaces. **E** is incorrect because interface methods are implicitly `public`, so the methods being implemented must be `public`.

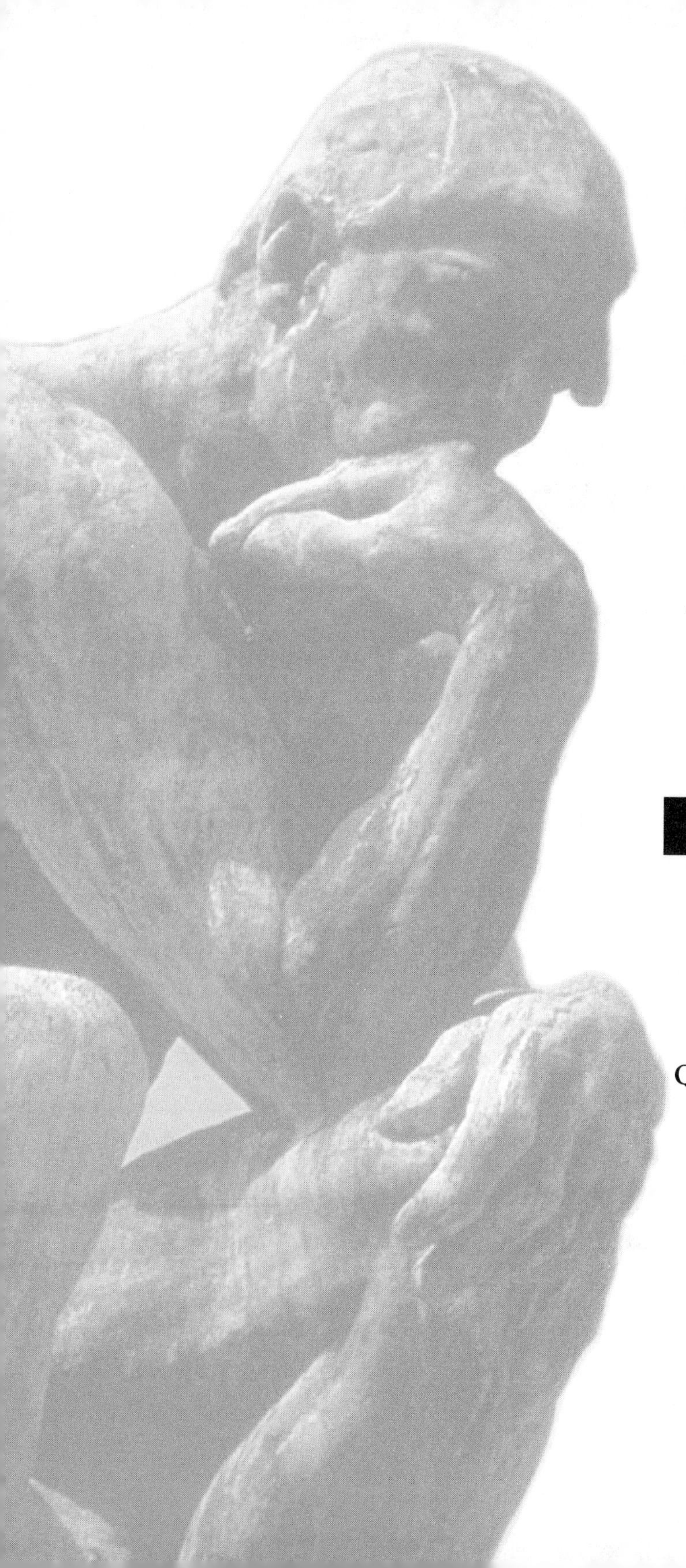

JAVA™ 2

SUN™ CERTIFIED PROGRAMMER & DEVELOPER

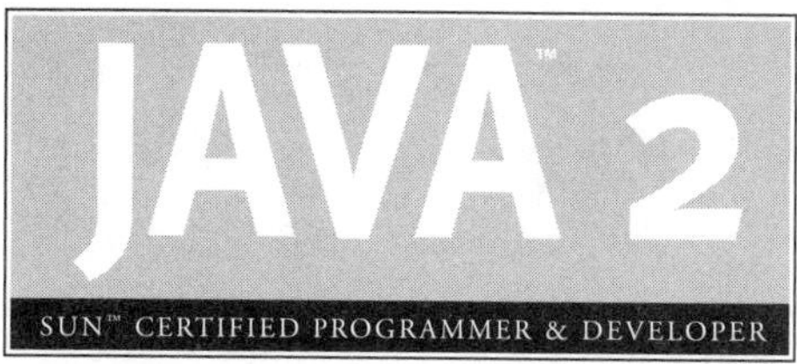

3

Operators and Assignments

CERTIFICATION OBJECTIVES

- Java Operators
- Logical Operators
- Passing Variables into Methods
- ✓ Two-Minute Drill
- Q&A Self Test

If you've got variables, you're going to modify them. You'll increment them, add them together, shift their bits, flip their bits, and compare one to another. In this chapter you'll learn how to do all that in Java. We'll end the chapter exploring the effect of passing variables of all types into methods. For an added bonus, you'll learn how to do things that you'll probably never use in the real world, but that will almost certainly be on the exam. After all, what fun would it be if you were tested only on things you already use?

CERTIFICATION OBJECTIVE

Java Operators (Exam Objective 5.1)

Determine the result of applying any operator (including assignment operators and instanceof) to operands of any type, class, scope, or accessibility, or any combination of these.

Java *operators* produce new values from one or more *operands* (just so we're all clear, the *operands* are things on the right or left side of the operator). The result of most operations is either a boolean or numeric value. And because you know by now that *Java is not C++*, you won't be surprised that Java operators can't be overloaded. There is, however, one operator that comes overloaded out of the box: If applied to a String, the + operator concatenates the right-hand operand to the operand on the left.

Stay awake. The operators and assignments portion of the exam is typically the one where exam takers see their lowest scores. We aren't naming names or anything, but even some of the exam *creators* (including one whose last name is a mountain range in California) have been known to get a few of these wrong.

Assignment Operators

Assigning a value to a variable seems straightforward enough; you simply assign the stuff on the right side of the = to the variable on the left. Well, sure, but don't expect to be tested on something like this:

```
x = 6;
```

No, you won't be tested on the *no-brainer* (technical term) assignments. You will, however, be tested on the trickier assignments involving complex expressions and casting. We'll look at both primitive and reference variable assignments. But before we begin, let's back up and peek inside of a variable. What *is* a variable? How are the *variable* and its *value* related?

Variables are just bit holders, with a designated type. You can have an *int* holder, a *double* holder, a Button holder, and even a `String[]` holder. Within that holder is a bunch of bits representing the value. For primitives, the bits represent a numeric value (although we don't know what that bit pattern looks like for `boolean`, but we don't care). A `byte` with a value of 6, for example, means that the bit pattern in the variable (the *byte* holder) is 00000110, representing the 8 bits.

So the value of a *primitive* variable is clear, but what's inside an *object* holder? If you say

```
Button b = new Button();
```

what's inside the Button holder *b*? Is it the Button object? *No!* A variable referring to an object is just that—a *reference variable.* A reference variable bit holder contains bits representing *a way to get to the object.* We don't know what the format is; the way in which object references are stored is virtual-machine specific (it's a pointer to *something*, we just don't know what that something really is). All we can say for sure is that the variable's value is not the object, but rather a value representing *a specific object on the heap.* Or `null`. If the reference variable has not been assigned a value, or has been explicitly assigned a value of `null`, the variable holds bits representing—you guessed it—`null`. You can read

```
Button b = null;
```

as "The `Button` variable *b* is not referring to any object."

So now that we know a variable is just a little box o' bits, we can get on with the work of changing those bits. We'll look first at assigning values to primitives, and finish with assignments to reference variables.

Primitive Assignments

The equal (=) sign is used for *assigning* a value to a variable, and it's cleverly named the *assignment operator.* There are actually 12 assignment operators, but the other 11 are all combinations of the equal sign and other arithmetic operators, as shown in Table 3-1. These *compound assignment operators* have a couple of special properties we'll look at in this section.

TABLE 3-1 Compound Assignment Operators

=	*=	/=	%=
+=	-=	<<=	>>=
>>>=	&=	^=	|=

You can assign a primitive variable using a literal or the result of an expression. Take a look at the following:

```
int x = 7; // literal assignment
int y = x + 2; // assignment with an expression (including a literal)
int z = x * y; // assignment with an expression
```

The most important point to remember is that a literal integer (such as 7) is always implicitly an `int`. Thinking back to Chapter 1, you'll recall that an int is a 32-bit value. No big deal if you're assigning a value to an `int` or a `long` variable, but what if you're assigning to a *byte* variable? After all, a *byte*-sized holder can't hold as many bits as an *int*-sized holder. Here's where it gets weird. The following is legal,

```
byte b = 27;
```

but only because the compiler *automatically* narrows the literal value to a *byte*. In other words, *the compiler puts in the cast.* The preceding code is identical to the following:

```
byte b = (byte) 27; // Explicitly cast the int literal to a byte
```

It looks as though the compiler gives you a break, and let's you take a shortcut with assignments to integer variables smaller than an *int.* (Everything we're saying about *byte* applies equally to *char* and *short,* both of which are smaller than an *int.*) We're not actually at the weird part yet, by the way.

We know that a literal integer is always an *int,* but more importantly—the result of an expression involving anything *int*-sized or smaller is always an *int.* In other words, add two *bytes* together and you'll get an *int*—even if those two *bytes* are tiny. Multiply an *int* and a *short* and you'll get an *int.* Divide a *short* by a *byte* and you'll get…an *int.* OK, now we're at the weird part. Check this out:

```
byte b = 3; // No problem, 3 fits in a byte
byte c = 8; // No problem, 8 fits in a byte
byte d = b + c; // Should be no problem, sum of the two bytes
                // fits in a byte
```

The last line won't compile! You'll get the following error:

```
TestBytes.java:5: possible loss of precision
found    : int
required: byte
    byte c = a + b;
               ^
```

We tried to assign the sum of two *bytes* to a *byte* variable, the result of which (11) was definitely small enough to fit into a *byte*, but the compiler didn't care. It knew the rule about *int*-or-smaller expressions always resulting in an *int*. It would have compiled if we'd done the explicit cast:

```
byte c = (byte) (a + b);
```

Assigning Floating-Point Numbers Floating-point numbers have slightly different assignment behavior than integer types. We've already discussed this in Chapter 1, but we'll do another quick review here while we're on the subject. First, you must know that *every floating-point literal is implicitly a double (64 bits), not a float.* So the literal 2.3, for example, is considered a *double.* If you try to assign a *double* to a *float,* the compiler knows you don't have enough room in a 32-bit float container to hold the precision of a 64-bit *double,* and it lets you know. The following code looks good, but won't compile:

```
float f = 32.3;
```

You can see that 32.3 should fit just fine into a *float*-sized variable, but the compiler won't allow it. In order to assign a floating-point literal to a *float* variable, you must either cast the value or append an *f* to the end of the literal. The following assignments will compile:

```
float f = (float) 32.3;
float g = 32.3f;
float h = 32.3F;
```

Assigning a Literal That Is Too Large for the Variable We'll also get a compiler error if we try to assign a literal value that the compiler knows is too big to fit into the variable.

```
byte a = 128; // byte can only hold up to 127
```

The preceding code gives us this error:

```
TestBytes.java:5: possible loss of precision
found   : int
required: byte
byte a = 128;
```

We can fix it with a cast:

```
byte a = (byte) 128;
```

But then what's the result? When you narrow a primitive, Java simply truncates the higher-order bits that won't fit. In other words, it loses all the bits to the left of the bits you're narrowing to.

Let's take a look at what happens in the preceding code. There, 128 is the bit pattern `10000000`. It takes a full 8 bits to represent 128. But because the literal 128 is an *int*, we actually get 32 bits, with the 128 living in the right-most (lower-order) 8 bits. So a literal 128 is actually

```
00000000000000000000000010000000
```

Take our word for it; there are 32 bits there.

To narrow the 32 bits representing 128, Java simply lops off the leftmost (higher-order) 24 bits. We're left with just the `10000000`. But remember that a *byte* is signed, with the leftmost bit representing the sign (and not part of the value of the variable). So we end up with a negative number (the 1 that used to represent 128 now represents the negative sign bit). Remember, to find out the value of a negative number using two's complement notation, you flip all of the bits and then add 1. Flipping the 8 zeroes give us: `01111111`, and adding 1 to that gives us `10000000`, or back to 128! And when we apply the sign bit, we end up with -128.

You must use an explicit cast to assign 128 to a *byte*, and the assignment leaves you with the value -128. A cast is nothing more than your way of saying to the compiler, "Trust me. I'm a professional. I take full responsibility for anything weird that happens when those top bits are chopped off."

That brings us to the compound assignment operators. The following will compile,

```
byte b = 3;
b += 7;  // No problem - adds 7 to b (result is 10)
```

and is equivalent to

```
byte b = 3;
b = (byte) (b + 7);   // Won't compile without the
                      // cast, since b + 7 results in an int
```

The compound assignment operator += let's you add to the value of *b*, without putting in an explicit cast.

Assigning One Primitive Variable to Another Primitive Variable

When you assign one primitive variable to another, *the contents of the right-hand variable are copied*, for example,

```
int a = 6;
int b = a;
```

The preceding code can be read as, "Assign the bit pattern for the number 6 to the *int* variable *a*. Then copy the bit pattern in *a*, and place the copy into variable *b*. So, both variables now hold a bit pattern for 6, but the two variables have no other relationship. We used the variable *a* only to copy its contents. At this point, *a* and *b* have identical contents (in other words, identical *values*), but if we change the contents of *a* or *b*, the other variable won't be affected."

Take a look at the following example:

```
class ValueTest {
   public static void main (String [] args) {
      int a = 10;  // Assign a value to a
      System.out.println("a = " + a);
      int b = a;
      b = 30;
      System.out.println("a = " + a + "after change to b");
   }
}
```

The output from this program is

```
%java ValueTest
a = 10
a = 10 after change to b
```

Notice the value of *a* stayed at 10. The key point to remember is that even after you assign *a* to *b*, *a* and *b* are not referring to the same place in memory. The *a* and *b* variables do not share a single value; they have identical *copies.*

Reference Variable Assignments

You can assign a newly created object to an object reference variable as follows:

```
Button b = new Button();
```

The preceding line does three key things:

- Makes a reference variable named *b*, of type Button
- Creates a new Button object on the heap
- Assigns the newly created Button object to the reference variable *b*

You can also assign `null` to an object reference variable, which simply means the variable is not referring to any object:

```
Button c = null;
```

The preceding line creates space for the Button *reference* variable (the bit holder for a reference value), but doesn't create an actual Button *object.*

You can also use a reference variable to refer to any object that is a subclass of the declared reference variable type, as follows:

```
public class Foo {
   public void doFooStuff() {
   }
}
public class Bar extends Foo {
   public void doBarStuff() { }
   }
}
class Test {
   public static void main (String [] args) {
      Foo reallyABar = new Bar();  // Legal because Bar is a subclass of Foo
      Bar reallyAFoo = new Foo(); // Illegal! Foo is not a subclass of Bar
   }
}
```

We'll look at the concept of reference variable assignments in much more detail in Chapter 5, so for now you just need to remember the rule that you can assign a subclass of the declared type, but not a superclass of the declared type. But think about it…a Bar object is guaranteed to be able to do anything a Foo can do, so anyone with a Foo reference can invoke Foo methods even though the object is actually a Bar.

In the preceding code, we see that Foo has a method `doFooStuff()` that someone with a Foo reference might try to invoke. If the object referenced by the Foo variable is really a Foo, no problem. But it's also no problem if the object is a Bar, since Bar inherited the `doFooStuff()` method. You can't make it work in reverse, however. If a somebody has a Bar reference, they're going to invoke `doBarStuff()`, but if the object being referenced is actually a Foo, it won't know how to respond.

Assigning One Reference Variable to Another

With primitive variables, an assignment of one variable to another means the contents (bit pattern) of one variable are copied into another. Object reference variables work exactly the same way. The contents of a reference variable are a bit pattern, so if you assign reference variable *a* to reference variable *b*, the bit pattern in *a* is copied and the new copy is placed into *b*. If we assign an existing instance of an object to a new reference variable, then two reference variables will hold the same bit pattern—a bit pattern referring to a specific object on the heap. Look at the following code:

```
import java.awt.Dimension;
class ReferenceTest {
   public static void main (String [] args) {
      Dimension a = new Dimension(5,10);
      System.out.println("a.height = " + a.height);
      Dimension b = a;
      b.height = 30;
      System.out.println("a.height = " + a.height +
         "after change to b");
   }
}
```

In the preceding example, a Dimension object *a* is declared and initialized with a width of 5 and a height of 10. Next, Dimension *b* is declared, and assigned the value of *a*. At this point, both variables (*a* and *b)* hold identical values, because the contents of *a* were copied into *b*. There is still only one Dimension object—the one that both *a* and *b* refer to. Finally, the height property is changed using the *b* reference. Now think for a minute: Is this going to change the height property of *a* as well? Let's see what the output will be:

```
%java ReferenceTest
a.height = 10
a.height = 30 after change to b
```

From this output, we can conclude that both variables refer to the *same* instance of the Dimension object. When we made a change to *b*, the height property was also changed for *a*.

One exception to the way object references are assigned is String. In Java, String objects are given special treatment. For one thing, *String objects are immutable*; you can't change the value of a String object. But it sure *looks* as though you can. Examine the following code:

```
class Strings {
    public static void main(String [] args) {
        String x = "Java";  // Assign a value to x
        String y = x;       // Now y and x refer to the same String object
        System.out.println("y string = " + y);
        x = x + " Bean";    // Now modify the object using the x reference
        System.out.println("y string = " + y);
    }
}
```

You might think String *y* will contain the characters *Java Bean* after the variable *x* is changed, because strings are objects. Let's see what the output is:

```
%java String
y string = Java
y string = Java
```

As you can see, even though *y* is a reference variable to the same object that *x* refers to, when we change *x* it doesn't change *y*! For any other object type, where two references refer to the same object, if either reference is used to modify the object, both references will see the change because there is still only a single object. But with a string, the VM creates a brand new String object every time we use the + operator to concatenate two strings, or any time we make any changes at all to a string. You need to understand what happens when you use a String reference variable to modify a string:

- A new string is created, leaving the original String object untouched.
- The reference used to modify the String (or rather, make a new String by modifying a copy of the original) is then assigned the brand new String object.

So when you say,

```
1. String s = "Fred";
2. String t = s;   // Now t and s refer to the same String object
3. t.toUpperCase(); // Invoke a String method that changes the String
```

you actually haven't changed the original String object created on line 1. When line 2 completes, both *t* and *s* reference the same String object. But when line 3 runs, rather than modifying the object referred to by t (which is the one and only String object up to this point), a brand new String object is created. And then abandoned. Because the new String isn't assigned to a String variable, the newly created String (which holds the string "FRED") is toast. So while two String objects were created in the preceding code, only one is actually referenced, and both *t* and *s* refer to it. The behavior of strings is extremely important in the exam, so we'll cover it in much more detail in Chapter 6.

Comparison Operators

Comparison operators always result in a boolean (`true` or `false`) value. This boolean value is most often used in an *if* test, as follows,

```
int x = 8;
if (x < 9) {
    // do something
}
```

but the resulting value can also be assigned directly to a boolean primitive:

```
class CompareTest {
   public static void main(String [] args) {
      boolean b = 100 > 99;
      System.out.println("The value of b is " + b);
   }
}
```

You have four comparison operators that can be used to compare any combination of integers, floating-point numbers, or characters:

- > greater than
- >= greater than or equal to
- < less than
- <= less than or equal to

Let's look at some legal comparisons:

```
class GuessAnimal {
   public static void main(String [] args) {
      String animal = "unknown";
      int weight = 700;
      char sex = 'm';
      double colorWaveLength = 1.630;
      if (weight >= 500) animal = "elephant";
      if (colorWaveLength > 1.621) animal = "gray " + animal;
      if (sex <= 'f') animal = "female " + animal;
      System.out.println("The animal is a " + animal);
   }
}
```

In the preceding code, we are using a comparison between characters. It's also legal to compare a character primitive with any number (though it isn't great programming style). Running the preceding class will output the following:

```
%java GuessAnimal
The animal is a gray elephant
```

We mentioned that characters can be used in comparison operators. When comparing a character with a character, or a character with a number, Java will take the ASCII or Unicode value of the character as the numerical value, and compare the numbers.

instanceof Comparison

The `instanceof` operator is used for object reference variables only, and you can use it to check whether an object is of a particular type. By type, we mean class or interface type—in other words, if the object referred to by the variable on the left side of the operator passes the IS-A test for the class or interface type on the right side (Chapter 5 covers IS-A relationships in detail). Look at the following example:

```
public static void main (String [] args) {
   String s = new String("foo");
   if (s instanceof String) {
      System.out.print("s is a String");
   }
}
```

Even if the object being tested is not an actual instantiation of the class type on the right side of the operator, `instanceof` will still return true if the object being compared is assignment compatible with the type on the right. The following example demonstrates testing an object using `instanceof`, to see if it's an instance of one of its superclasses:

```
class A { }
class B extends A { }
 public static void main (String [] args) {
   B b = new B();
   if (b instanceof A) {
      System.out.print("b is an A");
   }
}
```

The preceding code shows that *b* is an *a*. So you can test an object reference against its own class type, or any of its superclasses. This means that *any* object reference will evaluate to true if you use the `instanceof` operator against type Object, as follows,

```
B b = new B();
if (b instanceof Object) {
   System.out.print("b is definitely an Object");
}
```

which prints

```
b is definitely an Object
```

You can use the `instanceof` operator on interface types as well:

```
interface Foo { }
class Bar implements Foo { }
class TestBar {
   public static void main (String [] args) {
      Bar b = new Bar()
      if ( b instanceof Bar) {
         System.out.println("b is a Bar");
      }
      if (b instanceof Foo) {
         System.out.println("b is a Foo");
      }
    }
}
```

Running the TestBar class proves that the Bar object referenced by *b* is both a Bar and a Foo:

```
b is a Bar
b is a Foo
```

Look for instanceof questions that test whether an object is an instance of an interface, when the object's class implements indirectly. An indirect implementation occurs when one of an object's superclasses implements an interface, but the actual class of the instance does not—for example,

```
interface Foo { }
class A implements Foo { }
class B extends A { }
```

Using the definitions above, if we instantiate an A and a B as follows,

```
A a = new A();
B b = new B();
```

the following are true:

```
a instanceof A
a instanceof Foo
b instanceof A
b instanceof B
b instanceof Foo  // Even though class B doesn't implement Foo
directly!
```

An object is said to be of a particular interface type (meaning it will pass the instanceof test) if any of the object's superclasses implement the interface.

In addition, it is legal to test whether a null object (or `null` itself) is an instance of a class. This will always result in false, of course. The following code demonstrates this:

```
class InstanceTest {
   public static void main(String [] args) {
      String a = null;
      boolean b = null instanceof String;
      boolean c = a instanceof String;
      System.out.println(b + " " + c);
   }
}
```

When this code is run, we get the following output:

```
false false
```

So even though variable *a* was defined as a String, the underlying object is null; therefore, `instanceof` returns a value of false when compared to the String class.

exam Watch

Remember that arrays are objects, even if the array is an array of primitives. Look for questions that might look like this:

```
int [] nums = new int[3];
if (nums instanceof Object) { } // result is true
```

An array is always an instance of Object. Any array.

Table 3-2 shows results from several instanceof comparisons. For this table, assume the following:

```
interface Face { }
class Bar implements Face{ }
class Foo extends Bar { }
```

Equality Operators

Equality can be tested with the operators equals and not equals:

- == equals (also known as "equal to")
- != not equals (also known as "not equal to")

Equality operators compare two *things* and return a *boolean* value. Each individual comparison can involve two numbers (including *char*), two *boolean* values, or two

TABLE 3-2 Operands and Results Using `instanceof` Operator

First Operand (Reference Being Tested)	`instanceof` Operand (Type We're Comparing the Reference Against)	Result
null	Any Class or Interface type	false
Foo instance	Foo, Bar, Face, Object	true
Bar instance	Bar, Face, Object	true
Bar instance	Foo	false
Foo []	Foo, Bar, Face	false
Foo []	Object	true
Foo[1]	Foo, Bar, Face, Object	true

object reference variables. You can't compare incompatible types, however. What would it mean to ask if a *boolean* is equal to a *char*? Or if a Button is equal to a String array? (Exactly, nonsense, which is why you can't do it.) There are four different types of *things* that can be tested:

- Numbers
- Characters
- Boolean primitives
- Object reference variables

So what does == actually look at? The value in the variable—in other words, the bit pattern.

Equality for Primitives

Most programmers are familiar with comparing primitive values. The following code shows some equality tests on primitive variables:

```
class ComparePrimitives {
   public static void main(String [] args) {
      System.out.println("character 'a' == 'a'? " + ('a' == 'a'));
      System.out.println("character 'a' == 'b'? " + ('a' == 'b'));
      System.out.println("5 != 6? " + (5 != 6));
      System.out.println("5.0 == 5L? " + (5.0 == 5L));
      System.out.println("true == false? " + (true == false));
   }
}
```

This program produces the following output:

```
%java ComparePrimitives
character 'a' == 'a'? true
character 'a' == 'b'? false
5 != 6? true
5.0 == 5L? true   // Compare a floating point to an int
true == false? false
```

As we can see, if a floating-point number is compared with an integer and the values are the same, the == operator returns *true* as expected.

Don't mistake = for == in a boolean expression. The following is legal:

```
1. boolean b = false;
2. if (b = true) {
3.    System.out.println("b is true");
4.} else {
5.   System.out.println("b is false");
6.}
```

Look carefully! You might be tempted to think the output is "b is false," but look at the** boolean **test in line 2. The** boolean **variable** b **is not being** compared **to** `true`**, it's being** set to `true`**, so line 3 executes and we get "b is true." Keeping in mind that the result of any assignment expression is the value of the variable following the assignment, you can see that in line 3, the result of the expression will be** true–**the value of** (b = `true`)**. This substitution of = for == works only with** boolean **variables, since the if test can be done only on** boolean **expressions. Thus, the following does not compile:

```
7. int x = 1;
8. if (x = 0) { }
```

Because** x **is an integer (and not a boolean), the result of (**x **= 0) is 0 (the result of the assignment). Integers cannot be used where a** boolean **value is expected, so the code in line 8 won't work unless changed from an assignment (=) to an equality test (==) as follows:

```
if (x == 0) { }
```

Equality for Reference Variables

As we saw earlier, two reference variables can refer to the same object, as the following code snippet demonstrates:

```
Button a = new Button("Exit");
Button b = a;
```

After running this code, both variable *a* and variable *b* will refer to the same object (a Button with the label *Exit*). Reference variables can be tested to see if they refer to the same object by using the == operator. Remember, the == operator is looking at the bits in the variable, so for reference variables if the bits in both variables are identical, then both refer to the same object. Look at the following code:

```
import java.awt.Button;
class CompareReference {
   public static void main(String [] args) {
```

```
            Button a = new Button("Exit");
            Button b = new Button("Exit");
            Button c = a;
            System.out.println("Is reference a == b? " + (a == b));
            System.out.println("Is reference a == c? " + (a == c));
        }
    }
```

This code creates three reference variables. The first two, *a* and *b*, are separate Button objects that happen to have the same label. The third reference variable, *c*, is initialized to refer to the same object that *a* refers to. When this program runs, the following output is produced:

```
Is reference a == b? false
Is reference a == c? true
```

This shows us that *a* and *c* reference the same instance of a Button. We'll take another look at the implications of testing object references for equality in Chapters 6 and 7, where we cover String comparison and the `equals()` *method* (as opposed to the equals *operator* we're looking at here).

Arithmetic Operators

We're sure you're familiar with the basic arithmetic operators.

- + addition
- – subtraction
- × multiplication
- / division

These can be used in the standard way:

```
class MathTest {
    public static void main (String [] args) {
        int x = 5 * 3;
        int y = x - 4;
        System.out.println("x - 4 is " +  y);  // Prints 11
    }
}
```

(Warning: if you don't know how to use the basic arithmetic operators, your fourth-grade teacher, Mrs. Beasley, should be hunted down and forced to take the programmer's exam. That's assuming you actually ever *went* to your fourth-grade class.)

One operator you might not be as familiar with (and we won't hold Mrs. Beasley responsible) is the remainder operator, %. The remainder operator divides the left operand by the right operand, and the result is the remainder, as the following code demonstrates:

```
class MathTest {
   public static void main (String [] args) {
      int x = 15;
      int y = x % 4;
      System.out.println("The result of 15 % 4 is the remainder of
15 divided by 4. The remainder is " + y);
   }
}
```

Running class MathTest prints the following:

```
The result of 15 % 4 is the remainder of 15 divided by 4. The remainder is 3
```

You can also use a compound assignment operator (shown in Table 3-1) if the operation is being done to a single variable. The following demonstrates using the %= compound assignment operator:

```
class MathTest {
   public static void main (String [] args) {
      int x = 15;
      x %= 4; // same as x = x % 4;
      System.out.println("The remainder of 15 % 4 is " + x);
   }
}
```

You're expected to know what happens when you divide by zero. With integers, you'll get a runtime exception (ArithmeticException), but with floating-point numbers you won't. Floating-point numbers divided by zero return either positive infinity or negative infinity, depending on whether or not the zero is positive or negative! That's right, some floating-point operators can distinguish between positive and negative zero. Rules to remember are these:

- Dividing an integer by zero will violate an important law of thermodynamics, and cause an ArithmeticException (can't divide by zero).
- Using the remainder operator (%) will result in an ArithmeticException if the right operand is zero (can't divide by zero).

- Dividing a floating-point number by zero will *not* result in an ArithmeticException, and the universe will remain intact.
- Using the remainder operator on floating-point numbers, where the right operand is zero, will *not* result in an ArithmeticException.

String Concatenation Operator

The plus sign can also be used to concatenate two strings together, as we saw earlier (and we'll definitely see again):

```
String animal = "Grey " + "elephant";
```

String concatenation gets interesting when you combine numbers with Strings. Check out the following:

```
String a = "String";
int b = 3;
int c = 7;
System.out.println(a + b + c);
```

Will the + operator act as a plus sign when adding the *int* variables *b* + *c*? Or will the + operator treat 3 and 7 as characters, and concatenate them individually? Will the result be `String10` or `String37`? OK, you've had long enough to think about it. The result is

```
String37
```

The int values were simply treated as characters and glued on to the right side of the string. So we could read the previous code as:

> "Start with String *a*, "String", and add the character 3 (the value of *b*) to it, to produce a new string "String3", and then add the character 7 (the value of *c*) to that, to produce a new string "String37", then print it out."

However, if you put parentheses around the two *int* variables, as follows,

```
System.out.println(a + (b + c));
```

you'll get

```
String10
```

Using parentheses causes the (*b* + *c*) to evaluate first, so the + operator functions as the addition operator, given that both operands are *int* values. The key point here is that the left-hand operand is not a String. If it were, then the + operator would perform String concatenation. The previous code can be read as:

"Add the values of *b* + *c* together, then take the sum and convert it to a String and concatenate it with the String from variable *a*."

The rule to remember is

If either operand is a String, the + operator becomes a String concatenation operator. If both operands are numbers, the + operator is the addition operator.

You'll find that sometimes you might have trouble deciding whether, say, the left hand operator is a String or not. On the exam, don't expect it to always be obvious. (Actually, now that we think about it, don't expect it *ever* to be obvious.) Look at the following code:

```
System.out.println(x.foo() + 7);
```

You can't know how the + operator is being used until you find out what the `foo()` method returns! If `foo()` returns a `String`, then 7 is concatenated to the returned String. But if `foo()` returns a number, then the + operator is used to add 7 to the return value of `foo()`.

exam watch

If you don't understand how String concatenation works, especially within a print statement, you could actually fail the exam even if you know the rest of the answer to the question! Because so many questions ask, "What is the result?", you need to know not only the result of the code running, but also how that result is printed. Although there will be at least a half-dozen questions directly testing your String knowledge, String concatenation shows up in other questions on virtually every objective, and if you get the concatenation wrong, you'll miss that question regardless of your ability to work out the rest of the code. Experiment! For example, you might see a line such as

```
int b = 2;
int c = 3;
System.out.println("" + b + c);
```

which prints

```
23
```

but if the print statement changes to

```
System.out.println(b + c);
```

then the result becomes

```
5.
```

Increment and Decrement

Java has two operators that will increment or decrement a variable by exactly one. These operators are composed of either two plus signs (++) or two minus signs (--):

- ++ increment (prefix and postfix)
- -- decrement (prefix and postfix)

The operator is placed either before (prefix) or after (postfix) a variable to change the value. Whether the operator comes before or after the operand can change the outcome of an expression. Examine the following:

```
1.  class MathTest {
2.     static int players = 0;
3.     public static void main (String [] args) {
4.        System.out.println("players online: " + players++);
5.        System.out.println("The value of players is " + players);
6.        System.out.println("The value of players is now " + ++players);
7.     }
8.  }
```

Notice that in the fourth line of the program the increment operator is *after* the variable *players.* That means we're using the postfix increment operator, which causes the variable *players* to be incremented by one *but only after the value of players is used in the expression.* When we run this program, it outputs the following:

```
%java MathTest
players online: 0
The value of players is 1
The value of players is now 2
```

Notice that when the variable is written to the screen, at first it says the value is `0`. Because we used the *postfix* increment operator, the increment doesn't happen until *after* the *players* variable is used in the print statement. Get it? The *post* in postfix means *after.* The next line, line 5, doesn't increment *players;* it just outputs it to the screen, so the newly incremented value displayed is 1. Line 6 applies the *prefix* operator to players, which means the increment happens *before* the value of the variable is used (*pre* means *before*). So the output is 2.

Expect to see questions mixing the increment and decrement operators with other operators, as in the following example:

```
int x = 2;
int y = 3;
```

```
if ((y == x++) | (x < ++y)) {
   System.out.println("x = " + x + " y = " + y);
 }
```

The preceding code prints

```
x = 3 y = 4
```

You can read the code as

"If 3 is equal to 2 OR 3 < 4…"

The first expression compares *x* and *y*, and the result is *false*, because the increment on *x* doesn't happen until after the == test is made. Next, we increment *x*, so now *x* is 3. Then we check to see if *x* is less than *y*, but *we increment y before comparing it with x*! So the second logical test is (3 < 4). The result is *true*, so the print statement runs.

exam watch

Look out for questions that use the increment or decrement operators on a final variable. Because final variables can't be changed, the increment and decrement operators can't be used with them, and any attempt to do so will result in a compiler error. The following code won't compile,

```
final int x = 5;
int y = x++;
```

and produces the error

```
Test.java:4: cannot assign a value to final variable x
int y = x++;
         ^
```

You can expect a violation like this to be buried deep in a complex piece of code. If you spot it, you know the code won't compile and you can move on without working through the rest of the code (unless, of course, you're into the sport of Extreme Test-Taking, and you want the running-out-of-time challenge).

As with String concatenation, the increment and decrement operators are used throughout the exam, even on questions that aren't trying to test your knowledge of how those operators work. You might see them in questions on *for* loops, exceptions, even threads. Be ready.

Shift Operators

The following are shift operators:

- >> right shift
- << left shift
- >>> unsigned right shift (also called *zero-filled right shift*)

The more obscure the topic, the more likely it will appear on the exam. Operators such as +, -, *, and / aren't likely to be tested for on the exam because they're so commonly used. Shift operators are rarely used by most programmers; therefore, they will most definitely be on the exam.

The shift operators shift the bits of a number to the right or left, producing a new number. Shift operators are used on integral numbers only (not floating-point numbers). To determine the result of a shift, you have to convert the number into binary. Let's look at an example of a bit shift:

```
8 >> 1;
```

First, we must convert this number to a binary representation:

```
0000 0000 0000 0000 0000 0000 0000 1000
```

An *int* is a 32-bit integer, so all 32 bits must be displayed. If we apply a bit shift of one to the right, using the >> operator, the new bit number is

```
0000 0000 0000 0000 0000 0000 0000 0100
```

Notice how the 1 bit moved over to the right, one place.

We can now convert this back to a decimal number (base 10) to get 4. The following code shows the complete example:

```
class BitShift {
   public static void main(String [] args) {
      int x = 8;
      System.out.println("Before shift x equals " + x);
      x = x >> 1;
      System.out.println("After shift x equals " + x);
   }
}
```

When we compile and run this program we get the following output:

```
%java BitShift
Before shift x equals 8
After shift x equals 4
```

As you can see, the results are exactly what we expected them to be. Shift operations can work on all integer numbers, regardless of the base they're displayed in (octal, decimal, or hexadecimal). The left shift works in exactly the same way, except all bits are shifted in the opposite direction. The following code uses a hexadecimal number to shift:

```
class BitShift {
   public static void main(String [] args) {
      int x = 0x80000000;
      System.out.println("Before shift x equals " + x);
      x = x << 1;
      System.out.println("After shift x equals " + x);
   }
}
```

To understand the preceding example, we'll convert the hexadecimal number to a bit number. Fortunately, it's pretty simple to convert from hexadecimal to bits. Each hex digit converts to a four-bit representation, as we can see here:

```
8    0    0    0    0    0    0    0
1000 0000 0000 0000 0000 0000 0000 0000
```

In the preceding example, the very leftmost bit represents the sign (positive or negative). When the leftmost bit is 1, the number is negative; and when it is 0, the number is positive. Running our program gives us the following:

```
%java BitShift
Before shift x equals -2147483648
After shift x equals 0
```

Shifting the bits one to the left moves the sign bit out where it simply drops off the left edge (it doesn't wrap around or anything like that) leaving us with 0 in the leftmost bit. What about the right side? What gets filled in on the right side as the previous rightmost bits move to the left? With the left shift operator, the right side is always filled with zeroes.

Then what about the left side of a right shift operation? When we shift to the right, what gets filled in on the left as the previous leftmost bit moves to the right? What takes its place? The answer depends on which of the two right shift operators we're using.

When using the right shift operator (>>) to shift the bits of a negative number, the sign bit gets shifted to the right, but the leftmost bits are filled in on the left with whatever the sign bit was. So the bottom line is that *with the right shift operator (>>), a negative number stays negative.* For example, let's use the hex number 0x80000000 again:

```
1000 0000 0000 0000 0000 0000 0000 0000
```

Now we'll shift the bits, using >>, one to the right:

```
1100 0000 0000 0000 0000 0000 0000 0000
```

As we can see, the sign bit is shifted to the right but (and this is important) the leftmost bit is filled with the original sign bit. Let's try some code that shifts it *four* to the right rather than just one:

```
class BitShift {
   public static void main(String [] args) {
      int x = 0x80000000;
      System.out.println("Before shift x equals " + x);
      x = x >> 4;
      System.out.println("After shift x equals " + x);
   }
}
```

In line 5 of this program, the number will be bit shifted four to the right. Running this program gives us the following output:

```
%java BitShift
Before shift x equals -2147483648
After shift x equals -134217728
```

The number now equals the following in bit representation:

```
1111 1000 0000 0000 0000 0000 0000 0000
```

Notice how the four new bits on the left have all been filled in with the original sign bit.

We can use a special shift operator if we don't want to keep the sign bit. This is the unsigned right shift operator >>>. Let's change the code slightly to use this operator:

```
class BitShift {
   public static void main(String [] args) {
      int x = 0x80000000;
      System.out.println("Before shift x equals " + x);
      x >>>= 4; //Assignment operator
      System.out.println("After shift x equals " + x);
   }
}
```

The output for this program is now the following:

```
%java BitShift
Before shift x equals -2147483648
After shift x equals 134217728
```

As we can see, the new number is positive because the negative bit wasn't kept. In bit representation, the old number is

```
1000 0000 0000 0000 0000 0000 0000 0000
```

and the new number is

```
0000 1000 0000 0000 0000 0000 0000 0000
```

Notice how the leftmost bits are filled in with zeroes, even though the original sign bit was a 1. That's why the unsigned right shift operator is often referred to as the "zero filled right shift operator." One important implication of using >>> vs. >> is that, except for a few special cases that we'll discuss next, *the result of an unsigned right shift is always positive, regardless of the original sign bit.*

You also need to know that all operands in a bit shift are promoted to at least an *int*. And what happens if you try to shift by more places than the number of bits in the number being shifted? For example, what happens if you try to shift an *int* by 33? The rule to remember is: the number of bits shifted is always going to be the right operand modulus the total number of bits for that primitive type. So for an *int*, that means you'll shift by the right operand modulus 32, and for a *long*, the right operand modulus 64. For example, if you try to shift an *int* by, say, 34, it looks like this,

```
int x = 2;
int y = x >> 34;
```

but because it's meaningless to shift by 34, since you don't even have that many bits, you actually end up shifting by 34 % 32 (we can use the remainder operator to figure this out), which leaves us with a remainder of 2. So the result is actually

```
int y = x >> 2;
```

Note that when using any of the shift operators, if you shift an *int* by any multiple of 32, or a *long* by any multiple of 64, the original value will not change.

exam Watch

You need to know what the bit shifts are actually doing in practical terms. A right shift operator is actually causing the number being shifted to be* divided *by 2 to the power of the number of bits to shift. For example, shifting* x >> 4 *is exactly the same as saying* $x / 2^4$*. And* x >> 8 *is exactly the same as* $x / 2^8$*. With the left shift operator, the result is exactly the same as* multiplying *the number being shifted by 2 to the power of the number of bits to shift. So shifting* x << 3 *is the same as saying* $x * 2^3$*. One day, you* will *thank us for pointing this out. (We accept checks and chocolate!)

EXERCISE 3-1

Using Shift Operators

1. Try writing a class that takes an integer of 1, shifts the bit 31 to the left, then 31 to the right.
2. What number does this now represent?
3. What is the bit representation of the new number?

Bitwise Operators

The bitwise operators take two individual bit numbers, then use AND/OR to determine the result on a bit-by-bit basis. There are three bitwise operators:

- & AND
- | inclusive OR
- ^ exclusive OR

The & operator compares corresponding bits between two numbers. If both bits are 1, the final bit is also 1. If only one of the bits is 1, the resulting bit is 0.

Once again, for bitwise operations we must convert numbers to bit representations. Table 3-3 displays the truth table for each of these operators. The left side of the table displays the *x* and *y* values, and the right side shows the result of the operator on these two values.

Let's compare two numbers, 10 and 9, with the & operator:

```
1010 & 1001 = 1000
```

Try putting the second operand directly beneath the first, to make it easier to see the result. For the preceding comparison (10 and 9), you can look at it as

```
  1 0 1 0
&
  1 0 0 1
__________
  1 0 0 0
```

As we can see, only the first bit (8) is a 1 in both locations, hence the final number is 1000 in bit representation (or 8 in decimal). Let's see this in some code:

```
class Bitwise {
   public static void main(String [] args) {
      int x = 10 & 9; // 1010 and 1001
      System.out.println("1010 & 1001 = " + x);
   }
}
```

When we run this code, the following output is produced:

```
%java Bitwise
1010 & 1001 = 8
```

The | (OR) operator is different from the & (AND) operator when it compares corresponding bits. Whereas the & operator will set a resulting bit to 1 only if *both*

TABLE 3-3 Calculating Values from a Truth Table

X	Y	& (AND)	| (OR)	^ (XOR)
0	0	0	0	0
0	1	0	1	1
1	0	0	1	1
1	1	1	1	0

operand bits in the same position are 1, the | operator will set the resulting bit to 1 if *either* (of both) of the bits is a 1. So, for the numbers 10 and 9, we get the following,

```
1010 | 1001 = 1011
```

which is easier to see as

```
    1 0 1 0
|
    1 0 0 1
-----------
    1 0 1 1
```

In this case because we have 1s in the 1, 2, and 8 bit slots, those bits are carried in to the result. This expression produces the number 11 (in decimal). Let's look at this in code:

```
class Bitwise {
   public static void main(String [] args) {
      int x = 10 | 9; // 1010 and 1001
      System.out.println("1010 | 1001 = " + x);
   }
}
```

When we run the preceding code, we receive the following:

```
%java Bitwise
1010 | 1001 = 11
```

The ^ (Exclusive OR, also known as XOR) operator compares two bits to see if they are different. If they *are* different, the result is a 1. Look at the numbers 10 and 5 in bit representation:

```
1010 ^ 0101 = 1111
```

As we can see, the result is 15 in decimal form. To see it a little more clearly:

```
    1 0 1 0
^
    0 1 0 1
-----------
    1 1 1 1
```

Now let's look at doing an XOR on 8 and13:

```
1000 ^ 1101 = 0101
```

The result is 5 in decimal form.

```
    1 0 0 0
^
    1 1 0 1
___________
    0 1 0 1
```

Bitwise Complement Operator

The ~ operator is a flip-the-bits operator. It will change all 1s to 0s and vice versa. Look at the following code:

```
class Bitwise {
   public static void main(String [] args) {
      int x = 5;
      System.out.println("x is initially " + x);
      x = ~x;
      System.out.println("~x is equal to " + x);
   }
}
```

This program is changing every bit into its complement; thus, the output from this program is the following:

```
%java Bitwise
x is initially 5
~x is equal to -6
```

In bit representation, the conversion looks like this,

```
~0000 0000 0000 0000 0000 0000 0000 0101
```

and converts to

```
 1111 1111 1111 1111 1111 1111 1111 1010
```

Conditional Operator

The *conditional operator* is a ternary operator (it has three operands) and is used to evaluate boolean expressions, much like an *if* statement except instead of executing a block of code if the test is *true*, a conditional operator will assign a value to a variable. In other words, the goal of the conditional operator is to decide which of two values to assign to a variable. A conditional operator is constructed using a ? (question mark) and a : (colon). The parentheses are optional. Its structure is as follows:

someVariable = (boolean expression) ? value to assign if true : value to assign if false

Let's take a look at a conditional operator in code:

```
class Salary {
   public static void main(String [] args) {
      int numOfPets = 3;
      String status = (numOfPets<4)?"Pet limit not exceeded":"too many pets";
      System.out.println("This pet status is " + status);
   }
}
```

You can read the preceding code as:

"Set `numOfPets` equal to 3. Next we're going to assign a `String` to the *status* variable. If *numOfPets* is less than 4, assign "Pet limit not exceeded" to the *status* variable; otherwise, assign "too many pets" to the *status* variable."

A conditional operator starts with a boolean operation, followed by two possible values for the variable to the left of the conditional operator. The first value (the one to the left of the colon) is assigned if the conditional (boolean) test is *true*, and the second value is assigned if the conditional test is *false*. You can even nest conditional operators into one statement.

```
class AssignmentOps {
   public static void main(String [] args) {
      int sizeOfYard = 10;
      int numOfPets = 3;
      String status = (numOfPets<4)?"Pet count OK"
           :(sizeOfYard > 8)? "Pet limit on the edge"
           :"too many pets";
      System.out.println("Pet status is " + status);
   }
}
```

Don't expect many questions using conditional operators, but you need to be able to spot them and respond correctly. Conditional operators are sometimes confused with assertion statements, so be certain you can tell the difference. Chapter 4 covers assertions in detail.

Primitive Casting

Casting lets you convert primitive values from one type to another. We looked at primitive casting earlier in this chapter, in the assignments section, but now we're going to take a deeper look. Object casting is covered in Chapter 5.

Casts can be *implicit* or *explicit*. An *implicit cast* means you don't have to write code for the cast; the conversion happens automatically. Typically, an implicit cast happens when you're doing a *widening* conversion. In other words, putting a smaller thing (say, a *byte*) into a bigger container (like an *int*). Remember those "possible loss of precision" compiler errors we saw in the assignments section? Those happened when you tried to put a larger thing (say, a *long*) into a smaller container (like a *short*). The large-value-into-small-container conversion is referred to as narrowing and requires an *explicit* cast, where you tell the compiler that you're aware of the danger and accept full responsibility. First we'll look at an implicit cast:

```
int a = 100;
long b = a; // Implicit cast, an int value always fits in a long
```

An explicit casts looks like this:

```
float a = 100.001;
int b = (int)a; // Explicit cast, a float can lose info as an int
```

Integer values may be assigned to a *double* variable without explicit casting, because any integer value can fit in a 64-bit `double`. The following line demonstrates this:

```
double d = 100L; // Implicit cast
```

In the preceding statement, a *double* is initialized with a *long* value (as denoted by the *L* after the numeric value). No cast is needed in this case because a *double* can hold every piece of information that a *long* can store. If, however, we want to assign a *double* value to an integer type, we're attempting a narrowing conversion and the compiler knows it:

```
class Casting {
   public static void main(String [] args) {
      int x = 3957.229; // illegal
   }
}
```

If we try to compile the preceding code, the following error is produced:

```
%javac Casting.java
Casting.java:3: Incompatible type for declaration. Explicit cast
needed to convert double to int.
      int x = 3957.229; // illegal
1 error
```

In the preceding code, a floating-point value is being assigned to an integer variable. Because an integer is not capable of storing decimal places, an error occurs. To make this work, we'll cast the floating-point number into an integer:

```
class Casting {
   public static void main(String [] args) {
      int x = (int)3957.229; // legal cast
      System.out.println("int x = " + x);
   }
}
```

When you a cast a floating-point number to an integer type, the value loses all the digits after the decimal. Running the preceding code will produce the following output:

```
%java Casting
int x = 3957
```

We can also cast a larger number type, such as a *long*, into a smaller number type, such as a *byte*. Look at the following:

```
class Casting {
   public static void main(String [] args) {
      long l = 56L;
      byte b = (byte)l;
      System.out.println("The byte is " + b);
   }
}
```

The preceding code will compile and run fine. But what happens if the *long* value is larger than 127 (the largest number a byte can store)? Let's modify the code and find out:

```
class Casting {
   public static void main(String [] args) {
      long l = 130L;
      byte b = (byte)l;
```

```
        System.out.println("The byte is " + b);
    }
}
```

The code compiles fine, and when we run it we get the following:

```
%java Casting
The byte is -126
```

You don't get a runtime error, even when the value being narrowed is too large for the type. The bits to the left of the lower 8 just…go away. As we saw in the assignments section, if the leftmost bit in the byte now happens to be a 1, the 1 is no longer part of the value and instead becomes the sign bit for the new byte.

EXERCISE 3-2

Casting Primitives

Create a `float` number type of any value, and assign it to a short using casting.

1. Declare a float variable: `float f = 234.56F;`
2. Assign the float to a short: `short s = (short)f;`

CERTIFICATION OBJECTIVE

Logical Operators (Exam Objective 5.3)

In an expression involving the operators &, |, &&, and ||, and variables of known values, state which operands are evaluated and the value of the expression.

There are four logical operators. Two you've seen before; the & and | bitwise operators can be used in boolean expressions. The other two we haven't yet covered, and are known as the *short-circuit* logical operators:

- && short-circuit AND
- || short-circuit OR

Short-Circuit Logical Operators

The && operator is similar to the & operator, except it evaluates only boolean values and can't be used as a bitwise operator. Remember, for an AND expression to be true, both operands must be true—for example,

```
if ((2 < 3) && (3 < 4)) { }
```

The preceding expression evaluates to *true* only because *both* operand one (2 < 3) and operand two (3 < 4) evaluate to *true.*

The short-circuit feature of the && operator is that *it doesn't waste its time on pointless evaluations.* A short-circuit && evaluates the left side of the operation first (operand one), and if operand one resolves to *false,* the && operator doesn't bother looking at the right side of the equation (operand two). The operator already knows that the complete expression can't possibly be true, since one operand has already proven to be *false.*

```
class Logical {
   public static void main(String [] args) {
      boolean b = true && false;
      System.out.println("boolean b = " + b);
   }
}
```

When we run the preceding code, we get

```
C:\Java Projects\BookTest>java Logical
boolean b = false
```

The || operator is similar to the && operator, except that it evaluates the left side first, this time looking for *true.* If the first operand in an OR operation is *true,* the result will be *true,* so the short-circuit || doesn't waste time looking at the right side of the equation. If the first operand is *false,* however, the short-circuit || has to evaluate the second operand to see if the result of the OR operation will be *true* or *false.* Pay close attention to the following example; you'll see quite a few questions like this on the exam:

```
class TestOR {
   public static void main (String [] args) {
    if ((isItSmall(3)) || (isItSmall(7))) {
       System.out.println("Result is true");
```

```
 5.       }
 6.       if ((isItSmall(6)) || (isItSmall(9))) {
 7.          System.out.println("Result is true");
 8.       }
 9.    }
10.
11.    public static boolean isItSmall(int i) {
12.       if (i < 5) {
13.          System.out.println("i less than 5");
14.          return true;
15.       } else {
16.       System.out.println("i greater than 5");
17.          return false;
18.       }
19.    }
20. }
```

What is the result?

```
[localhost:~/javatests] kathy% java TestOR
i less than 5
Result is true
i greater than 5
i greater than 5
```

Here's what happened when the `main()` method ran:

1. When we hit line 3, the first operand in the || expression (in other words, the left side of the || operation) is evaluated.
2. The `isItSmall(3)` method is invoked and prints "`i less than 5`".
3. The `isItSmall(3)` method returns *true*.
4. Because the first operand in the || expression on line 3 is `true`, the || operator doesn't bother evaluating the second operand. So we never see the "`i greater than 5`" that would have printed had the second operand been evaluated (which would have invoked `isItSmall(7)`).
5. Line 6 is now evaluated, beginning with the first operand in the || expression on line 6.
6. The `isItSmall(6)` method is invoked and prints "`i greater than 5`".
7. The `isItSmall(6)` method returns *false*.

8. Because the first operand in the || expression on line 6 is *false*, the || operator can't skip the second operand; there's still a chance the expression can be *true*, if the second operand evaluates to *true*.
9. The `isItSmall(9)` method is invoked and prints `"i greater than 5"`.
10. The `isItSmall(9)` method returns *false*, so the expression on line 6 is *false*, and thus line 7 never executes.

exam Watch

The || and && operators only work with boolean operands. The exam may try to fool you by using integers with these operators, so be on guard for questions such as,

```
if (5 && 6) { }
```

where it looks as though we're trying to do a bitwise AND on the bits representing the integers 5 and 6, but the code won't even compile.

Logical Operators (not Short-Circuit)

The bitwise operators, & and |, can also be used in logical expressions. But because they aren't the short-circuit operators, *they evaluate both sides of the expression, always!* They're inefficient. For example, even if the first operand (left side) in an & expression is *false*, the second operand will still be evaluated—*even though it's now impossible for the result to be true!* And the | is just as inefficient; if the first operand is *true*, it still plows ahead and evaluates the second operand *even when it* knows *the expression will be true.*

The rule to remember is

The short-circuit operators (&& and ||) can be used only in logical (not bitwise) expressions. The bitwise operators (& and |) can be used in both logical and bitwise expressions, but are rarely used in logical expressions because they're not efficient.

You'll find a lot of questions on the exam that use both the short-circuit and non-short-circuit logical operators. You'll have to know exactly which operands are evaluated and which are not, since the result will vary depending on whether the second operand in the expression is evaluated. The "Self Test" at the end of this chapter includes several logical operator questions similar to those on the exam.

Now that you have a better idea how operators work in Java, the following chart shows some operators in action:

<table>
<tr><th colspan="2">SCENARIO & SOLUTION</th></tr>
<tr><td>What is the result of (1 & 3)?</td><td>1</td></tr>
<tr><td>What is the result of (1 | 3)?</td><td>3</td></tr>
<tr><td>What is the result of (1 << 2)?</td><td>4</td></tr>
<tr><td>What is the resulting value of (new String(“fred”) instanceof Object)?</td><td><code>true</code></td></tr>
</table>

CERTIFICATION OBJECTIVE

Passing Variables into Methods (Exam Objective 5.4)

Determine the effect upon objects and primitive values of passing variables into methods and performing assignments or other modifying operations in that method.

Methods can be declared to take primitives and/or object references. You need to know how (or if) the *caller's* variable can be affected by the *called* method. The difference between object reference and primitive variables, when passed into methods, is huge and important. To understand this section, you'll need to be comfortable with the assignments section covered in the first part of this chapter.

Passing Object Reference Variables

When you pass an object variable into a method, you must keep in mind that you're passing the object *reference*, and not the actual *object* itself. Remember that a reference variable holds bits that represent (to the underlying VM) a way to get to a specific object in memory (on the heap). More importantly, you must remember that you aren't even passing the actual reference variable, but rather a *copy* of the reference variable. A copy of a variable means you get a copy of the bits in that variable, so when you pass a reference variable, you're passing a copy of the bits representing how to get to a specific object. In other words, both the caller and the called method will now have identical copies of the reference, and thus both will refer to the same exact (not a copy) object on the heap.

For this example, we'll use the Dimension class from the java.awt package:

```
 1. import java.awt.Dimension;
 2. class ReferenceTest {
 3.  public static void main (String [] args) {
 4.     Dimension d = new Dimension(5,10);
 5.     ReferenceTest rt = new ReferenceTest();
 6.     System.out.println("Before modify() d.height = " + d.height);
 7.     rt.modify(d);
 8.     System.out.println("After modify() d.height = " + d.height);
 9.  }
10.   void modify(Dimension dim) {
11.     dim.height = dim.height + 1;
12.     System.out.println("dim = " + dim.height);
13.  }
14. }
```

When we run this class, we can see that the `modify()` method was indeed able to modify the original (and only) Dimension object created on line 4.

```
C:\Java Projects\Reference>java ReferenceTest
Before modify() d.height = 10
dim = 11
After modify() d.height = 11
```

Notice when the Dimension object on line 4 is passed to the `modify()` method, any changes to the object that occur inside the method are being made to the object whose reference was passed. In the preceding example, reference variables *d* and *dim* both point to the same object.

Does Java Use Pass-By-Value Semantics?

If Java passes objects by passing the reference variable instead, does that mean Java uses *pass-by-reference* for objects? Not exactly, although you'll often hear and read that it does. Java is actually *pass-by-value* for *all* variables running within a single VM. Pass-by-value means pass-by-*variable*-value. And that means, *pass-by-copy-of-the-variable*!

It makes no difference if you're passing primitive or reference variables, you are always passing a copy of the bits in the variable. So for a primitive variable, you're passing a copy of the bits representing the value. For example, if you pass an `int` variable with the value of 3, you're passing a *copy* of the bits representing 3. The called method then gets its own copy of the value, to do with it what it likes.

And if you're passing an object reference variable, you're passing a *copy* of the bits representing the reference to an object. The called method then gets its own copy of the reference variable, to do with it what it likes. But because two identical reference variables refer to the exact same object, if the called method modifies the object (by invoking setter methods, for example), the caller will see that the *object* the caller's original variable refers to has also been changed. In the next section, we'll look at how the picture changes when we're talking about primitives.

The bottom line on pass-by-value: the called method can't change the caller's *variable*, although for object reference variables, the called method *can* change the object the variable referred to. What's the difference between changing the variable and changing the object? For object references, it means the called method can't reassign the caller's original reference variable and make it refer to a different object, or null. For example, in the following code,

```
void bar() {
   Foo f = new Foo();
   doStuff(f);
}

void doStuff(Foo g) {
   g = new Foo();
}
```

reassigning *g* does not reassign *f*! At the end of the `bar()` method, two Foo objects have been created, one referenced by the local variable *f* and one referenced by the local (argument variable) *g*. Because the `doStuff()` method has a *copy* of the reference variable, it has a way to get to the original Foo object, but *the* `doStuff()` *method does* not *have a way to get to the* f *reference variable*. So `doStuff()` can change what *f* refers to, but can't change the actual contents (bit pattern) of *f*.

Passing Primitive Variables

Let's look at what happens when a primitive variable is passed to a method:

```
class ReferenceTest {
   public static void main (String [] args) {
      int a = 1;
      ReferenceTest rt = new ReferenceTest();
      System.out.println("Before modify() a = " + a);
      rt.modify(a);
```

```
      System.out.println("After modify() a = " + a);
   }
   void modify(int number) {
      number = number + 1;
      System.out.println("number = " + number);
   }
}
```

In this simple program, the variable *a* is passed to a method called `modify()`, which increments the variable by 1. The resulting output looks like this:

```
C:\Java Projects\Reference>java ReferenceTest
Before modify() a = 1
number = 2
After modify() a = 1
```

Notice that *a* did not change after it was passed to the method. Remember, it was only a *copy* of *a* that was passed to the method. When a primitive variable is passed to a method, it is *passed by value*, which means pass-by-copy-of-the-bits-in-the-variable.

FROM THE CLASSROOM

The Shadowy World of Variables

Just when you think you've got it all figured out, you see a piece of code with variables not behaving the way you think they should. You might have stumbled into code with a shadowed variable. You can shadow a variable in several ways; we'll look just at the one most likely to trip you up—*hiding an instance variable by shadowing it with a local variable.*

Shadowing involves redeclaring a variable that's already been declared somewhere else. The effect of shadowing is to hide the previously declared variable in such a way that it may *look* as though you're using the hidden variable, but you're actually using the shadowing variable. You might find reasons to shadow a variable intentionally, but typically it happens by accident and causes hard-to-find bugs. On the exam, you can expect to see questions where shadowing plays a role.

FROM THE CLASSROOM

You can shadow an instance variable by declaring a local variable of the same name, either directly or as part of an argument as follows:

```
class Foo {
   static int size = 7;
   static void changeIt(int size) {
      size = size + 200;
      System.out.println("size in changeIt is " + size);
   }
   public static void main (String [] args) {
      Foo f = new Foo();
      System.out.println("size = " + size);
      changeIt(size);
      System.out.println("size after changeIt is " + size);
    }
}
```

The preceding code appears to change the *size* instance variable in the `changeIt()` method, but because `changeIt()` has a parameter named *size*, the local *size* variable is modified while the instance variable *size* is untouched. Running class Foo prints

```
%java Foo
size = 7
size in changeIt is 207
size after changeIt is 7
```

Things become more interesting when the shadowed variable is an object reference, rather than a primitive:

```
class Bar {
   int barNum = 28;
}
class Foo {
   Bar myBar = new Bar();
   void changeIt(Bar myBar) {
      myBar.barNum = 99;
```

FROM THE CLASSROOM

```
      System.out.println("myBar.barNum in changeIt is " + barNum);
      myBar = new Bar();
      myBar.barNum = 420;
      System.out.println("myBar.barNum in changeIt is now " + barNum);
   }
   public static void main (String [] args) {
      Foo f = new Foo();
      System.out.println("f.myBar.barNum is " + f.myBar.barNum);
      changeIt(f.myBar);
      System.out.println("myBar.barNum after changeIt is " + f.myBar.barNum);
    }
}
```

The preceding code prints out this:

```
f.myBar.barNum is 28
myBar.barNum in changeIt is 99
myBar.barNum in changeIt is now 420
f.myBar.barNum after changeIt is 99
```

You can see that the shadowing variable (the local parameter *myBar* in `changeIt()`) can still affect the *myBar* instance variable, because the *myBar* parameter receives a reference to the same Bar object. But when the local *myBar* is reassigned a new Bar object, which we then modify by changing its *barNum* value, Foo's original *myBar* instance variable is untouched.

CERTIFICATION SUMMARY

If you've studied this chapter diligently, and thought of nothing else except this chapter for the last 72 hours, you should have a firm grasp on Java operators. You should understand what equality means when tested with the == operator, and you know how primitives and objects behave when passed to a method. Let's review the highlights of what you've learned in this chapter.

To understand what a bit-shift operation is doing, you need to look at the number being shifted in its binary form. The left shift (<<) shifts all bits to the left, filling the right side with zeroes, and the right shift (>>) shifts all bits right, *filling in the left side with whatever the sign bit was.* The unsigned right shift (>>>) moves all bits to the right, but fills the left side with zeroes, regardless of the original sign bit. Thus, the result of an unsigned right shift is always a positive number, except that when using any of the shift operators, if you shift an *int* by any multiple of 32, or a *long* by any multiple of 64, the original value will not change.

The logical operators (&& and ||) can be used only to evaluate two boolean expressions. The bitwise operators (& and |) can be used on integral numbers to produce a resulting numeric value, or on boolean values to produce a resulting *boolean* value. The difference between && and & is that the && operator won't bother testing the right operand if the left evaluates to *false*, because the result of the && expression can never be *true*. The difference between || and | is that the || operator won't bother testing the right operand if the left evaluates to *true*, because the result is already known to be *true* at that point.

The == operator can be used to compare values of primitives, but it can also be used to determine whether two reference variables refer to the same object.

Although both objects and primitives are passed by value into a method, key differences exist between how they behave once passed. Objects are passed *by a copy of the reference value*, while primitives are passed *by a copy of the variable value.* This means that if an object is modified within a method, other code referring to that object will notice the change. Both the caller and called methods have identical copies of reference variables; therefore, they both refer to the exact same object in memory.

Be prepared for a lot of exam questions involving the topics from this chapter. Even within questions testing your knowledge of another objective, the code will frequently use operators, assignments, object and primitive passing, etc., so be on your toes for this topic, and take the "Self Test" seriously.

TWO-MINUTE DRILL

Here are some of the key points from each certification objective in Chapter 3.

Java Operators (Sun Objective 5.1)

- ❑ The result of performing most operations is either a boolean or a numeric value.
- ❑ Variables are just bit holders with a designated type.
- ❑ A reference variable's bits represent a way to get to an object.
- ❑ An unassigned reference variable's bits represent *null.*
- ❑ There are 12 assignment operators: =, *=, /=, %=, +=, -=, <<=, >>=, >>>=, &=, ^=, |=.
- ❑ Numeric expressions always result in at least an *int*-sized result—never smaller.
- ❑ Floating-point numbers are implicitly doubles (64 bits).
- ❑ Narrowing a primitive truncates the high-order bits.
- ❑ Two's complement means: flip all the bits, then add 1.
- ❑ Compound assignments (e.g. +=) perform an automatic cast.

Reference Variables

- ❑ When creating a new object, e.g., Button b = new Button();, three things happen:
  - ❑ Make a reference variable named *b*, of type Button
  - ❑ Create a new Button object
  - ❑ Refer the reference variable b to the Button object
- ❑ Reference variables can refer to subclasses of the declared type but not superclasses.

String Objects and References

- ❑ String *objects* are immutable, cannot be changed.

- ❑ When you use a String reference variable to modify a String:
  - ❑ A new string is created (the old string *is immutable*).
  - ❑ The reference variable refers to the new string.

Comparison Operators

- ❑ Comparison operators always result in a boolean value (`true` or `false`).
- ❑ There are four comparison operators: >, >=, <, <=.
- ❑ When comparing characters, Java uses the ASCII or Unicode value of the number as the numerical value.

instanceof Operator

- ❑ `instanceof` is for reference variables only, and checks for whether this object is of a particular type.
- ❑ The `instanceof` operator can be used only to test objects (or *null*) against class types that are in the same class hierarchy.
- ❑ For interfaces, an object is "of a type" if any of its superclasses implement the interface in question.

Equality Operators

- ❑ Four types of things can be tested: numbers, characters, booleans, reference variables.
- ❑ There are two equality operators: == and !=.

Arithmetic Operators

- ❑ There are four primary operators: add, subtract, multiply, and divide.
- ❑ The remainder operator returns the remainder of a division.
- ❑ When floating-point numbers are divided by zero, they return positive or negative infinity, except when the dividend is also zero, in which case you get NaN.
- ❑ When the remainder operator performs a floating-point divide by zero, it will not cause a runtime exception.

- When integers are divided by zero, a runtime ArithmeticException is thrown.
- When the remainder operator performs an integer divide by zero, a runtime ArithmeticException is thrown.

String Concatenation Operator

- If either operand is a String, the + operator concatenates the operands.
- If both operands are numeric, the + operator adds the operands.

Increment/Decrement Operators

- Prefix operator runs before the value is used in the expression.
- Postfix operator runs after the value is used in the expression.
- In any expression, both operands are fully evaluated before the operator is applied.
- Final variables cannot be incremented or decremented.

Shift Operators

- There are three shift operators: >>, <<, >>>; the first two are signed, the last is unsigned.
- Shift operators can only be used on integer types.
- Shift operators can work on all bases of integers (octal, decimal, or hexadecimal).
- Except for the unusual cases of shifting an *int* by a multiple of 32 or a *long* by a multiple of 64 (these shifts result in no change to the original values), bits are filled as follows:
    - << fills the right bits with zeros.
    - >> fills the left bits with whatever value the original sign bit (leftmost bit) held.
    - >>> fills the left bits with zeros (negative numbers will become positive).
- All bit shift operands are promoted to at least an int.
- For int shifts > 32 or long shifts > 64, the actual shift value is the remainder of the right operand / divided by 32 or 64, respectively.

Bitwise Operators

- ❑ There are three bitwise operators—&, ^, |—and a bitwise complement, operator ~.
- ❑ The & operator sets a bit to 1 if both operand's bits are set to 1.
- ❑ The ^ operator sets a bit to 1 if exactly one operand's bit is set to 1.
- ❑ The | operator sets a bit to 1 if at least one operand's bit is set to 1.
- ❑ The ~ operator reverses the value of every bit in the single operand.

Ternary (Conditional Operator)

- ❑ Returns one of two values based on whether a boolean expression is *true* or *false*.
- ❑ The value after the ? is the 'if *true* return'.
- ❑ The value after the : is the 'if *false* return'.

Casting

- ❑ Implicit casting (you write no code) happens when a widening conversion occurs.
- ❑ Explicit casting (you write the cast) is required when a narrowing conversion is desired.
- ❑ Casting a floating point to an integer type causes all digits to the right of the decimal point to be lost (truncated).
- ❑ Narrowing conversions can cause loss of data—the most significant bits (leftmost) can be lost.

Logical Operators (Sun Objective 5.3)

- ❑ There are four logical operators: &, |, &&, ||.
- ❑ Logical operators work with two expressions that must resolve to boolean values.
- ❑ The && and & operators return `true` only if both operands are *true*.
- ❑ The || and | operators return `true` if either or both operands are *true*.

- The && and || operators are known as short-circuit operators.
- The && operator does not evaluate the right operand if the left operand is *false*.
- The || does not evaluate the right operand if the left operand is *true*.
- The & and | operators always evaluate both operands.

Passing Variables into Methods (Sun Objective 5.4)

- Methods can take primitives and/or object references as arguments.
- Method arguments are always copies—of either primitive variables or reference variables.
- Method arguments are never actual objects (they can be references to objects).
- In practice, a primitive argument is a completely detached copy of the original primitive.
- In practice, a reference argument is another copy of a reference to the original object.

SELF TEST

The following questions will help you measure your understanding of the material presented in this chapter. Read all of the choices carefully, as there may be more than one correct answer. Choose all correct answers for each question.

Java Operators (Sun Objective 5.1)

1. Which two are equal? (Choose two.)

A. `32 / 4;`

B. `(8 >> 2) << 4;`

C. `2 ^ 5;`

D. `128 >>> 2;`

E. `(2 << 1) * (32 >> 3);`

F. `2 >> 5;`

2. Given the following,

```
1.  import java.awt.*;
2.  class Ticker extends Component {
3.     public static void main (String [] args) {
4.        Ticker t = new Ticker();
5.
6.     }
7.  }
```

which two of the following statements, inserted independently, could legally be inserted into line 5 of this code? (Choose two.)

A. `boolean test = (Component instanceof t);`

B. `boolean test = (t instanceof Ticker);`

C. `boolean test = t.instanceof(Ticker);`

D. `boolean test = (t instanceof Component);`

E. `boolean test = t.instanceof(Object);`

F. `boolean test = (t instanceof String);`

3. Given the following,

```
class Equals {
    public static void main(String [] args) {
        int x = 100;
        double y = 100.1;
        boolean b = (x = y);
        System.out.println(b);
    }
}
```

what is the result?

A. `true`

B. `false`

C. Compilation fails

D. An exception is thrown at runtime

4. Given the following,

```
import java.awt.Button;
class CompareReference {
    public static void main(String [] args) {
        float f = 42.0f;
        float [] f1 = new float[2];
        float [] f2 = new float[2];
        float [] f3 = f1;
        long x = 42;
        f1[0] = 42.0f;
    }
}
```

which three statements are true? (Choose three.)

A. `f1 == f2`

B. `f1 == f3`

C. `f2 == f1[1]`

D. `x == f1[0]`

E. `f == f1[0]`

5. Given the following,

```
class BitShift {
    public static void main(String [] args) {
```

```
        int x = 0x80000000;
        System.out.print(x + " and  ");
        x = x >>> 31;
        System.out.println(x);
    }
}
```

what is the output from this program?

A. `-2147483648 and 1`

B. `0x80000000 and 0x00000001`

C. `-2147483648 and -1`

D. `1 and -2147483648`

E. None of the above

6. Given the following,

```
class Bitwise {
    public static void main(String [] args) {
        int x = 11 & 9;
        int y = x ^ 3;
        System.out.println( y | 12 );
    }
}
```

what is the result?

A. `0`

B. `7`

C. `8`

D. `14`

E. `15`

7. Which of the following are legal lines of code? (Choose all that apply.)

A. `int w = (int)888.8;`

B. `byte x = (byte)1000L;`

C. `long y = (byte)100;`

D. `byte z = (byte)100L;`

Logical Operators (Sun Objective 5.3)

8. Given the following,

```
class Test {
  public static void main(String [] args) {
    int x= 0;
    int y= 0;
    for (int z = 0; z < 5; z++) {
       if (( ++x > 2 ) || (++y > 2)) {
          x++;
       }
    }
    System.out.println(x + " " + y);
  }
}
```

what is the result?

A. 5 3

B. 8 2

C. 8 3

D. 8 5

E. 10 3

F. 10 5

9. Given the following,

```
class Test {
  public static void main(String [] args) {
    int x= 0;
    int y= 0;
    for (int z = 0; z < 5; z++) {
       if (( ++x > 2 ) && (++y > 2)) {
          x++;
       }
    }
    System.out.println(x + " " + y);
  }
}
```

What is the result?

A. 5 2

B. 5 3

C. 6 3

D. `6 4`

E. `7 5`

F. `8 5`

10. Given the following,

```
class SSBool {
  public static void main(String [] args) {
    boolean b1 = true;
    boolean b2 = false;
    boolean b3 = true;
    if ( b1 & b2 | b2 & b3 | b2 )
      System.out.print("ok ");
    if ( b1 & b2 | b2 & b3 | b2 | b1 )
      System.out.println("dokey");
  }
}
```

what is the result?

A. `ok`

B. `dokey`

C. `ok dokey`

D. No output is produced

E. Compilation error

F. An exception is thrown at runtime

11. Given the following,

```
class Test {
    public static void main(String [] args) {
       int x=20;
       String sup = (x<15)?"small":(x<22)?"tiny":"huge";
       System.out.println(sup);
    }
}
```

what is the result of compiling and running this code?

A. `small`

B. `tiny`

C. `huge`

D. Compilation fails

12. Given the following,

```
class BoolArray {
  boolean [] b = new boolean[3];
  int count = 0;

  void set(boolean [] x, int i) {
    x[i] = true;
    ++count;
  }

  public static void main(String [] args) {
    BoolArray ba = new BoolArray();
    ba.set(ba.b, 0);
    ba.set(ba.b, 2);
    ba.test();
  }

  void test() {
    if ( b[0] && b[1] | b[2] )
      count++;
    if ( b[1] && b[(++count - 2)] )
      count += 7;
    System.out.println("count = " + count);
  }
}
```

what is the result?

A. `count = 0`

B. `count = 2`

C. `count = 3`

D. `count = 4`

E. `count = 10`

F. `count = 11`

Passing Variables into Methods (Sun Objective 5.4)

13. Given the following,

```
class Test {
   static int s;

```

```
    public static void main(String [] args) {
      Test p = new Test();
      p.start();
      System.out.println(s);
    }

    void start() {
      int x = 7;
      twice(x);
      System.out.print(x + " ");
    }

    void twice(int x) {
      x = x*2;
      s = x;
    }
  }
```

what is the result?

A. 7 7

B. 7 14

C. 14 0

D. 14 14

E. Compilation fails

F. An exception is thrown at runtime

14. Given the following,

```
class Test {
    public static void main(String [] args) {
      Test p = new Test();
      p.start();
    }

    void start() {
      boolean b1 = false;
      boolean b2 = fix(b1);
      System.out.println(b1 + " " + b2);
    }

    boolean fix(boolean b1) {
      b1 = true;
```

```
            return b1;
        }
    }
```

what is the result?

A. `true true`

B. `false true`

C. `true false`

D. `false false`

E. Compilation fails

F. An exception is thrown at runtime

15. Given the following,

```
class PassS {
    public static void main(String [] args) {
      PassS p = new PassS();
      p.start();
    }

    void start() {
      String s1 = "slip";
      String s2 = fix(s1);
      System.out.println(s1 + " " + s2);
    }

    String fix(String s1) {
      s1 = s1 + "stream";
      System.out.print(s1 + " ");
      return "stream";
    }
}
```

what is the result?

A. `slip stream`

B. `slipstream stream`

C. `stream slip stream`

D. `slipstream slip stream`

E. Compilation fails

F. An exception is thrown at runtime

16. Given the following,

```
class SC2 {
  public static void main(String [] args) {
    SC2 s = new SC2();
    s.start();
  }

  void start() {
    int a = 3;
    int b = 4;
    System.out.print(" " + 7 + 2 + " ");
    System.out.print(a + b);
    System.out.print(" " + a + b + " ");
    System.out.print(foo() + a + b + " ");
    System.out.println(a + b + foo());
  }

  String foo() {
    return "foo";
  }
}
```

what is the result?

A. 9 7 7 foo 7 7foo

B. 72 34 34 foo34 34foo

C. 9 7 7 foo34 34foo

D. 72 7 34 foo34 7foo

E. 9 34 34 foo34 34foo

17. Given the following,

```
class PassA {
   public static void main(String [] args) {
     PassA p = new PassA();
     p.start();
   }

   void start() {
     long [] a1 = {3,4,5};
     long [] a2 = fix(a1);
     System.out.print(a1[0] + a1[1] + a1[2] + " ");
     System.out.println(a2[0] + a2[1] + a2[2]);
```

```
    }

    long [] fix(long [] a3) {
      a3[1] = 7;
      return a3;
    }
}
```

what is the result?

A. 12 15

B. 15 15

C. 3 4 5 3 7 5

D. 3 7 5 3 7 5

E. Compilation fails

F. An exception is thrown at runtime

18. Given the following,

```
class Two {
  byte x;
}

class PassO {
   public static void main(String [] args) {
     PassO p = new PassO();
     p.start();
   }

   void start() {
     Two t = new Two();
     System.out.print(t.x + " ");
     Two t2 = fix(t);
     System.out.println(t.x + " " + t2.x);
   }

   Two fix(Two tt) {
     tt.x = 42;
     return tt;
   }
 }
```

what is the result?

A. `null null 42`

B. `0 0 42`

C. `0 42 42`

D. `0 0 0`

E. Compilation fails

F. An exception is thrown at runtime

SELF TEST ANSWERS

Java Operators (Sun Objective 5.1)

1. ☑ B and D. B and D both evaluate to 32. B is shifting bits right then left using the signed bit shifters >> and <<. D is shifting bits using the unsigned operator >>>, but since the beginning number is positive the sign is maintained.
   ☒ A evaluates to 8, C looks like 2 to the 5th power, but ^ is the Exclusive OR operator so C evaluates to 7. E evaluates to 16, and F evaluates to 0 (2 >> 5 is not 2 to the 5th).

2. ☑ B and D. B is correct because class type Ticker is part of the class hierarchy of *t*; therefore it is a legal use of the *instanceof* operator. D is also correct because Component is part of the hierarchy of *t*, because Ticker extends Component in line 2.
   ☒ A is incorrect because the syntax is wrong. A variable (or `null`) always appears before the *instanceof* operator, and a type appears after it. C and E are incorrect because the statement is used as a method, which is illegal. F is incorrect because the String class is not in the hierarchy of the *t* object.

3. ☑ C. The code will not compile because in line 5, the line will work only if we use (`x == y`) in the line. The == operator compares values to produce a `boolean`, whereas the = operator assigns a value to variables.
   ☒ A, B, and D are incorrect because the code does not get as far as compiling. If we corrected this code, the output would be *false*.

4. ☑ B, D, and E. B is correct because the reference variables *f1* and *f3* refer to the same array object. D is correct because it is legal to compare integer and floating-point types. E is correct because it is legal to compare a variable with an array element.
   ☒ C is incorrect because *f2* is an array object and *f1[1]* is an array element.

5. ☑ A. The >>> operator moves all bits to the right, zero filling the left bits. The bit transformation looks like this:

   Before: `1000 0000 0000 0000 0000 0000 0000 0000`
   After: `0000 0000 0000 0000 0000 0000 0000 0001`

   ☒ C is incorrect because the >>> operator zero fills the left bits, which in this case changes the sign of *x*, as shown. B is incorrect because the output method `print()` always displays integers in base 10. D is incorrect because this is the reverse order of the two output numbers. E is incorrect because there was a correct answer.

6. ☑ **D**. The & operator produces a 1 bit when both bits are 1. The result of the & operation is 9. The ^ operator produces a 1 bit when exactly one bit is 1; the result of this operation is 10. The | operator produces a 1 bit when at least one bit is 1; the result of this operation is 14.
☒ **A, B, C,** and **E,** are incorrect based on the program logic described above.

7. ☑ **A, B, C,** and **D**. **A** is correct because when a floating-point number (a *double* in this case) is cast to an *int,* it simply loses the digits after the decimal. **B** and **D** are correct because a *long* can be cast into a *byte.* If the *long* is over 127, it loses its most significant (leftmost) bits. **C** actually works, even though a cast is not necessary, because a *long* can store a *byte.*
☒ There are no incorrect answer choices.

Logical Operators (Sun Objective 5.3)

8. ☑ **B.** The first two iterations of the *for* loop both *x* and *y* are incremented. On the third iteration *x* is incremented, and for the first time becomes greater than 2. The short circuit `or` operator || keeps *y* from ever being incremented again and *x* is incremented twice on each of the last three iterations.
☒ **A, C, D, E,** and **F** are incorrect based on the program logic described above.

9. ☑ **C.** In the first two iterations *x* is incremented once and *y* is not because of the short circuit && operator. In the third and fourth iterations *x* and *y* are each incremented, and in the fifth iteration *x* is doubly incremented and *y* is incremented.
☒ **A, B, D, E,** and **F** are incorrect based on the program logic described above.

10. ☑ **B.** The & operator has a higher precedence than the | operator so that on line 6 *b1* and *b2* are evaluated together as are *b2* & *b3.* The final *b1* in line 8 is what causes that *if* test to be *true.*
☒ **A, C,** and **D** are incorrect based on the program logic described above.

11. ☑ **B.** This is an example of a nested ternary operator. The second evaluation `(x < 22)` is true, so the "tiny" value is assigned to `sup`.
☒ **A, C,** and **D** are incorrect based on the program logic described above.

12. ☑ **C.** The reference variables *b* and *x* both refer to the same `boolean` array. `Count` is incremented for each call to the `set()` method, and once again when the first *if* test is true. Because of the && short circuit operator, *count* is not incremented during the second *if* test.
☒ **A, B, D, E,** and **F** are incorrect based on the program logic described above.

Passing Variables into Methods (Sun Objective 5.4)

13. ☑ B. The `int` *x* in the `twice()` method is not the same `int` *x* as in the `start()` method. `Start()'s` *x* is not affected by the `twice()` method. The instance variable *s* is updated by `twice()`'s *x*, which is 14.
☒ A, C, and D are incorrect based on the program logic described above.

14. ☑ B. The `boolean` *b1* in the `fix()` method is a different `boolean` than the *b1* in the `start()` method. The *b1* in the `start()` method is not updated by the `fix()` method.
☒ A, C, D, E, and F are incorrect based on the program logic described above.

15. ☑ D. When the `fix()` method is first entered, `start()`'s *s1* and `fix()`'s *s1* reference variables both refer to the same String object (with a value of "slip"). `Fix()`'s *s1* is reassigned to a new object that is created when the concatenation occurs (this second String object has a value of "slipstream"). When the program returns to `start()`, another String object is created, referred to by *s2* and with a value of "stream".
☒ A, B, C, and E are incorrect based on the program logic described above.

16. ☑ D. Because all of these expressions use the + operator, there is no precedence to worry about and all of the expressions will be evaluated from left to right. If either operand being evaluated is a String, the + operator will concatenate the two operands; if both operands are numeric, the + operator will add the two operands.
☒ A, B, C, and E are incorrect based on the program logic described above.

17. ☑ B. The reference variables *a1* and *a3* refer to the same `long` array object. When the `[1]` element is updated in the `fix()` method, it is updating the array referred to by *a1*. The reference variable *a2* refers to the same array object.
☒ A, C, D, E, and F are incorrect based on the program logic described above.

18. ☑ C. In the `fix()` method, the reference variable *tt* refers to the same object (class Two) as the *t* reference variable. Updating *tt.x* in the `fix()` method updates *t.x* (they are one in the same object). Remember also that the instance variable *x* in the Two class is initialized to 0.
☒ A, B, D, E, and F are incorrect based on the program logic described above.

EXERCISE ANSWERS

Exercise 3-1: Using Shift Operators

The program should look something like the following:

```
class BitShift {
   public static void main(String [] args) {
      int x = 0x00000001; // or simply 1
      x <<= 31;
      x >>= 31;
      System.out.println("After shift x equals " + x);
   }
}
```

The number should now equal -1. In bits, this number is

```
1111 1111 1111 1111 1111 1111 1111 1111
```

Exercise 3-2: Casting Primitives

The program should look something like the following:

```
class Cast {
   public static void main(String [] args) {
      float f = 234.56F;
      short s = (short)f;
   }
}
```

4

Flow Control, Exceptions, and Assertions

CERTIFICATION OBJECTIVES

- Writing Code Using *if* and *switch* Statements
- Writing Code Using Loops
- Handling Exceptions
- Working with the Assertion Mechanism
- ✓ Two-Minute Drill
- Q&A Self Test

Can you imagine trying to write code using a language that didn't give you a way to execute statements conditionally? In other words, a language that didn't let you say, "If this thing over here is *true*, then I want this thing to happen; otherwise, do this other thing instead." Flow control is a key part of most any useful programming language, and Java offers several ways to do it. Some, like *if* statements and *for* loops, are common to most languages. But Java also throws in a couple flow control features you might not have used before—exceptions and assertions.

The *if* statement and the *switch* statement are types of conditional/decision controls that allow your program to perform differently at a "fork in the road," depending on the result of a logical test. Java also provides three different looping constructs—`for`, `while`, and `do-while`—so you can execute the same code over and over again depending on some condition being *true*. Exceptions give you a clean, simple way to organize code that deals with problems that might crop up at runtime. Finally, the assertion mechanism, added to the language with version 1.4, gives you a way to do debugging checks on conditions you expect to smoke out while developing, when you don't necessarily need or want the runtime overhead associated with exception handling.

With these tools, you can build a robust program that can handle any logical situation with grace. Expect to see a wide range of questions on the exam that include flow control as part of the question code, even on questions that aren't testing your knowledge of flow control.

CERTIFICATION OBJECTIVE

Writing Code Using if and switch Statements (Exam Objective 2.1)

Write code using if *and* switch *statements and identify legal argument types for these statements.*

The *if* and *switch* statements are commonly referred to as *decision statements.* When you use decision statements in your program, you're asking the program to evaluate a given expression to determine which course of action to take. We'll look at the *if* statement first.

if-else Branching

The basic format of an `if` statement is as follows:

```
if (booleanExpression) {
    System.out.println("Inside if statement");
}
```

The expression in parentheses *must* evaluate to a boolean `true` or `false` result. Typically you're testing something to see if it's *true*, and then running a code block (one or more statements) if it *is true*, and (optionally) another block of code if it isn't. We consider it good practice to enclose the blocks within curly braces, even if there's only one statement in the block. The following code demonstrates a legal `if` statement:

```
if (x > 3) {
   System.out.println("x is greater than 3");
} else {
   System.out.println("x is not greater than 3");
}
```

The `else` block is optional, so you can also use the following:

```
if (x > 3) {
   y = 2;
}
z += 8;
a = y + x;
```

The preceding code will assign 2 to *y* if the test succeeds (meaning *x* really is greater than 3), but the other two lines will execute regardless.

Even the curly braces are optional if you have only one statement to execute within the body of the conditional block. The following code example is legal (although not recommended for readability):

```
if (x > 3)
   y = 2;
z += 8;
a = y + x;
```

Be careful with code like this, because you might think it should read as, "*If x* is greater than 3, *then* set *y* to 2, *z* to *z* + 8, and *a* to *y* + *x*." But the last two lines are going to execute no matter what! They aren't part of the conditional flow. You might find it even more misleading if the code were indented as follows:

```
if (x > 3)
   y = 2;
   z += 8;
   a = y + x;
```

You might have a need to nest *if-else* statements (although, again, not recommended for readability, so nested *if* tests should be kept to a minimum). You can set up an *if-else* statement to test for multiple conditions. The following example uses two conditions so that *if* the first test fails, we want to perform a second test before deciding what to do:

```
if (price < 300) {
   buyProduct();
} else {
   if (price < 400) {
      getApproval();
   }
   else {
      dontBuyProduct();
   }
}
```

Sometimes you can have a problem figuring out which *if* your *else* goes to, as follows:

```
if (exam.done())
if (exam.getScore() < 0.61)
System.out.println("Try again.");
// Which if does this belong to?
else System.out.println("Java master!");
```

We intentionally left out the indenting in this piece of code so it doesn't give clues as to which *if* statement the *else* belongs to. Did you figure it out? Java law decrees that an *else* clause belongs to the innermost *if* statement to which it might possibly belong (in other words, the closest preceding `if` that doesn't have an `else`). In the case of the preceding example, the `else` belongs to the *second* `if` statement in the listing. With proper indenting, it would look like this:

```
if (exam.done())
   if (exam.getScore() < 0.61)
      System.out.println("Try again.");
```

```
  // Which if does this belong to?
else
      System.out.println("Java master!");
```

Following our coding conventions by using curly braces, it would be even easier to read:

```
if (exam.done()) {
   if (exam.getScore() < 0.61) {
      System.out.println("Try again.");
   // Which if does this belong to?
   } else {
      System.out.println("Java master!");
   }
}
```

Don't get your hopes up about the exam questions being all nice and indented properly. Some exam takers even have a slogan for the way questions are presented on the exam: *anything that* can *be made more confusing,* will *be.*

exam Watch

Be prepared for questions that not only fail to indent nicely, but intentionally indent in a misleading way: Pay close attention for misdirection like the following example:

```
if (exam.done())
  if (exam.getScore() < 0.61)
     System.out.println("Try again.");
else
  System.out.println("Java master!"); // Hmmmmm… now where does it belong?
```

Of course, the preceding code is exactly the same as the previous two examples, except for the way it *looks.*

Legal Arguments for if Statements

if statements can test against only a boolean. Any expression that resolves down to a boolean is fine, but some of the expressions can be complex. Assume doStuff() returns true,

```
int y = 5;
int x = 2;
if ((((x > 3) && (y < 2)) | doStuff()) {
System.out.println("true");
}
```

which prints

```
true
```

You can read the preceding code as, "If both ($x > 3$) and ($y < 2$) are *true*, or if the result of `doStuff()` is *true*, then print "true." So basically, if just `doStuff()` alone is *true*, we'll still get "true." If `doStuff()` is false, though, then both ($x > 3$) and ($y < 2$) will have to be *true* in order to print "true."

The preceding code is even more complex if you leave off one set of parentheses as follows,

```
int y = 5;
int x = 2;
if ((x > 3) && (y < 2) | doStuff()) {
System.out.println("true");
}
```

which now prints…nothing! Because the preceding code (with one less set of parentheses) evaluates as though you were saying, "If ($x > 3$) is *true, and* either ($y < 2$) or the result of `doStuff()` is *true*, then print "true." So if ($x > 3$) is not *true*, no point in looking at the rest of the expression." Because of the short-circuit && and the fact that at runtime the expression is evaluated as though there were parentheses around `((y< 2) | doStuff())`, it reads as though both the test before the && ($x > 3$) *and* then the rest of the expression *after* the && `(y<2 | doStuff())` must be *true.*

Remember that the only legal argument to an *if* test is a boolean. Table 4-1 lists illegal arguments that might look tempting, compared with a modification to make each argument legal.

exam Watch

One common mistake programmers make (and that can be difficult to spot), is assigning a `boolean` variable when you meant to test a `boolean` variable. Look out for code like the following:

```
boolean boo = false;
if (boo = true) { }
```

You might think one of three things:

1. ***The code compiles and runs fine, and the if test fails because boo is false.***
2. ***The code won't compile because you're using an assignment (=) rather than an equality test (==).***
3. ***The code compiles and runs fine and the if test succeeds because boo is set to `true` (rather than tested for `true`) in the if argument!***

Well, number 3 is correct. Pointless, but correct. Given that the result of any assignment is the value of the variable after the assignment, the expression (`boo = true`) has a result of `true`. Hence, the if test succeeds. But the only variable that can be assigned (rather than tested against something else) is a boolean; all other assignments will result in something nonboolean, so they're not legal, as in the following:

```
int x = 3;
if (x = 5) { }  // Won't compile because x is not a boolean!
```

Because *if* tests require boolean expressions, you need to be really solid on *both* logical operators and *if* test syntax and semantics.

switch Statements

Another way to simulate the use of multiple *if* statements is with the *switch* statement. Take a look at the following *if-else* code, and notice how confusing it can be to have nested *if* tests, even just a few levels deep:

```
int x = 3;
if(x == 1) {
   System.out.println("x equals 1");
}
else if(x == 2) {
      System.out.println("x equals 2");
   }
   else if(x == 3) {
         System.out.println("x equals 3");
      }
      else {
         System.out.println("No idea what x is");
      }
```

TABLE 4-1 Illegal and Legal Arguments to *if*

Illegal Arguments to *if*	Legal Arguments to *if*
`int x = 1;` `if (x) { }`	`int x = 1;` `if (x == 1) { }`
`if (0) { }`	`if (false)`
`if (x = 6)`	`if (x == 6)`

Now let's see the same functionality represented in a *switch* construct:

```
int x = 3;
switch (x) {
   case 1:
      System.out.println("x is equal to 1");
      break;
   case 2:
      System.out.println("x is equal to 2");
      break;
   case 3:
      System.out.println("x is equal to 3");
      break;
   default:
      System.out.println("Still no idea what x is");
}
```

Legal Arguments to switch and case

The only type that a *switch* can evaluate is the primitive `int`! That means only variables and values that can be automatically promoted (in other words, implicitly cast) to an `int` are acceptable. So you can switch on any of the following, but nothing else: `byte`, `short`, `char`, `int`.

You won't be able to compile if you use anything else, including the remaining numeric types of `long`, `float`, and `double`.

The only argument a *case* can evaluate is one of the same type as *switch* can use, with one additional—*and big*—constraint: *the* case *argument must be final!* The *case* argument has to be resolved at compile time, so that means you can use *only a constant final* variable that is assigned a literal value. It is not enough to be final, it must be a compile time constant. For example:

```
final int a = 1;
final int b;
int x = 0;
switch (x) {
  case a:      // ok
  case b:      // compiler error
               // thx to John Paverd !
```

Also, the switch *can only check for equality.* This means that the other relational operators such as *greater than* are rendered unusable in a *case.* The following is an example of a valid expression using a method invocation in a *switch* statement. Note that for this code to be legal, the method being invoked on the object reference must return a value compatible with an `int`.

```
String s = "xyz";
switch (s.length()) {
```

```
    case 1:
       System.out.println("length is one");
       break;
    case 2:
       System.out.println("length is two");
       break;
    case 3:
       System.out.println("length is three");
       break;
    default:
       System.out.println("no match");
}
```

The following example uses final variables in a *case* statement. Note that if the `final` keyword is omitted, this code will not compile.

```
final int one = 1;
final int two = 2;
int x = 1;
switch (x) {
   case one:  System.out.println("one");
              break;
   case two:  System.out.println("two");
              break;
}
```

One other rule you might not expect involves the question, "What happens if I switch on a variable smaller than an `int`?" Look at the following `switch` example:

```
byte g = 2;
switch(g) {
case 23:
case 128:
}
```

This code won't compile. Although the *switch* argument is legal—a `byte` is implicitly cast to an `int`—the second case argument (128) is too large for a `byte`, and the compiler knows it! Attempting to compile the preceding example gives you an error:

```
Test.java:6: possible loss of precision
found   : int
required: byte
    case 128:
         ^
```

It's also illegal to have more than one *case* label using the same value. For example, the following block of code won't compile because it uses two *cases* with the same value of 80:

```
int temp = 90;
switch(temp) {
   case 80 :
      System.out.println("80");
      break;
   case 80 :
      System.out.println("80");
      break;
   case 90:
      System.out.println("90");
      break;
   default:
      System.out.println("default");
}
```

exam Watch

Look for any violation of the rules for* switch *and* case *arguments. For example, you might find illegal examples like the following three snippets:

```
Integer in = new Integer(4);
switch (in) { }

==================
switch(x) {
   case 0 {
      y = 7;
    }
 }
==================
switch(x) {
   0: { }
   1: { }
}
```

In the first example, you can't switch on an Integer object, only an* `int` *primitive. In the second example, the case uses a curly brace and omits the colon. The third example omits the keyword* `case`*.

Default, Break, and Fall-Through in switch Blocks

When the program encounters the keyword `break` during the execution of a *switch* statement, execution will immediately move out of the `switch` block to the next statement *after* the `switch`. If break is omitted, the program just keeps executing the different *case* blocks until either a `break` is found or the *switch* statement ends. Examine the following code:

```
int x = 1;
switch(x) {
   case 1:  System.out.println("x is one");
   case 2:  System.out.println("x is two");
   case 3:  System.out.println("x is three");
}
System.out.println("out of the switch");
```

The code will print the following:

```
x is one
x is two
x is three
out of the switch
```

This combination occurs because the code didn't hit a *break* statement; thus, execution just kept dropping down through each `case` until the end. This dropping down is actually called "fall through," because of the way execution falls from one `case` to the next. *Think of the matching* `case` *as simply your entry point into the* `switch` *block!* In other words, you must *not* think of it as, "Find the matching case, execute just that code, and get out." That's not how it works. If you do want that "just the matching code" behavior, you'll insert a *break* into each `case` as follows:

```
int x = 1;
switch(x) {
   case 1:  {
      System.out.println("x is one");
      break;
   }
   case 2:  {
      System.out.println("x is two");
      break;
   }
   case 3:  {
      System.out.println("x is two");
```

```
        break;
    }
}
System.out.println("out of the switch");
```

Running the preceding code, now that we've added the *break* statements, will print

```
x is one
out of the switch
```

and that's it. We entered into the *switch* block at `case` 1. Because it matched the `switch()` argument, we got the `println` statement, then hit the `break` and jumped to the end of the *switch*.

Another way to think of this fall-through logic is shown in the following code:

```
int x = someNumberBetweenOneAndTen;

switch (x) {
   case 2:
   case 4:
   case 6:
   case 8:
   case 10: {
      System.out.println("x is an even number");
      break;
   }
}
```

This *switch* statement will print "x is an even number" or nothing, depending on whether the number is between one and ten and is odd or even. For example, if *x* is 4, execution will begin at `case` 4, but then fall down through 6, 8, and 10, where it prints and then breaks. The `break` at `case` 10, by the way, is not needed; we're already at the end of the *switch* anyway.

The Default Case

What if, using the preceding code, you wanted to print "x is an odd number" if none of the cases (the even numbers) matched? You couldn't put it after the *switch* statement, or even as the last *case* in the *switch*, because in both of those situations it would always print "x is an odd number." To get this behavior, you'll use the `default` keyword. (By the way, if you've wondered why there is a `default` keyword even though we don't use a modifier for default access control, now you'll see that the `default` keyword is used for a completely different purpose.) The only change we need to make is to add the *default case* to the preceding code:

```
int x = someNumberBetweenOneAndTen;

switch (x) {
   case 2:
   case 4:
   case 6:
   case 8:
   case 10: {
      System.out.println("x is an even number");
      break;
   }
   default: System.out.println("x is an odd number");
}
```

exam Watch

The `default` case doesn't have to come at the end of the switch. Look for it in strange places such as the following:

```
int x = 2;
switch (x) {
   case 2:  System.out.println("2");
   default: System.out.println("default");
   case 3: System.out.println("3");
   case 4: System.out.println("4");
}
```

Running the preceding code prints

```
2
default
3
4
```

and if we modify it so that the only match is the `default` case:

```
int x = 7;
switch (x) {
   case 2:  System.out.println("2");
   default: System.out.println("default");
   case 3: System.out.println("3");
   case 4: System.out.println("4");
}
```

Running the preceding code prints

```
default
3
4
```

The rule to remember is `default` ***works just like any other*** case ***for fall-through!***

EXERCISE 4-1

Creating a switch-case Statement

Try creating a *switch-case* statement using a `char` value as the *case*. Include a default behavior if none of the `char` values match.

1. Make sure a `char` variable is declared before the *switch* statement.
2. Each *case* statement should be followed by a `break`.
3. The `default` value can be located at the end, middle, or top.

CERTIFICATION OBJECTIVE

Writing Code Using Loops (Exam Objective 2.2)

Write code using all forms of loops including labeled and unlabeled, use of break and continue, and state the values taken by loop counter variables during and after loop execution.

Java loops come in three flavors: *while*, *do-while*, and *for*. All three let you repeat a block of code as long as some condition is *true*, or for a specific number of iterations. You're probably familiar with loops from other languages, so even if you're somewhat new to Java, these won't be a problem to learn.

Using while Loops

The *while* loop is good for scenarios where you don't know how many times block or statement should repeat, but you want it to continue as long as some condition is *true*. A *while* statement looks like this:

```
int x = 2;
while(x == 2) {
   System.out.println(x);
   ++x;
}
```

In this case, as in all loops, the expression (test) must evaluate to a boolean result. Any variables used in the expression of a *while* loop must be declared before the expression is evaluated. In other words, you can't say

```
while (int x = 2) { }
```

Then again, why would you? Instead of testing the variable, you'd be declaring and initializing it, so it would always have the exact same value. Not much of a test condition!

The body of the *while* loop will *only* execute if the condition results in a *true* value. Once inside the loop, the loop body will repeat until the condition is no longer met and evaluates to *false*. In the previous example, program control will enter the loop body because *x* is equal to 2. However, *x* is incremented in the loop, so when the condition is checked again it will evaluate to *false* and exit the loop.

The key point to remember about a *while* loop is that it might not *ever* run. If the test expression is *false* the first time the *while* expression is checked, the loop body will be skipped and the program will begin executing at the first statement *after* the *while* loop. Look at the following example:

```
int x = 8;
while (x > 8) {
   System.out.println("in the loop");
   x = 10;
}
System.out.println("past the loop");
```

Running this code produces

```
past the loop
```

Although the test variable *x* is incremented within the *while* loop body, the program will never see it. This is in contrast to the *do-while* loop that executes the loop body once, and *then* does the first test.

Using do-while Loops

The following shows a `do-while` statement in action:

```
do {
   System.out.println("Inside loop");
} while(false);
```

The `System.out.println()` statement will print once, *even though the expression evaluates to false.* The *do-while* loop will *always* run the code in the loop *body at least once.* Be sure to note the use of the semicolon at the end of the *while* expression.

exam watch

As with* if *tests, look for* while *loops (and the* while *test in a* do-while *loop) with an expression that does not resolve to a* boolean. *Take a look at the following examples of legal and illegal* `while` *expressions:

```
int x = 1;
while (x) { }  // Won't compile; x is not a boolean
while (x = 5) { } // Won't compile; resolves to 5 (result of assignment)
while (x == 5) { }  // Legal, equality test
while (true) { } // Legal
```

Using for Loops

The *for* loop is especially useful for flow control when you already know how many times you need to execute the statements in the loop's block. The *for* loop declaration has three main parts, besides the body of the loop:

- Declaration and initialization of variables
- The boolean expression (conditional test)
- The iteration expression

Each of the three *for* declaration parts is separated by a semicolon. The following two examples demonstrate the *for* loop. The first example shows the parts of a *for* loop in a pseudocode form, and the second shows typical syntax of the loop.

```
for (/*Initialization*/ ; /*Condition*/ ;  /* Iteration */) {
   /* loop body */
}

for (int i = 0; i<10; i++) {
   System.out.println("i is " + i);
}
```

Declaration and Initialization

The first part of the *for* statement lets you declare and initialize zero, one, or multiple variables of the same type inside the parentheses after the `for` keyword. If you declare more than one variable of the same type, then you'll need to separate them with commas as follows:

```
for (int x = 10, y = 3; y > 3; y++) { }
```

The declaration and initialization happens before anything else in a for *loop.* And whereas the other two parts—the boolean test and the iteration expression—will run with each iteration of the loop, the declaration and initialization happens just once, at the very beginning. You also must know that *the scope of variables declared in the* for *loop ends with the* for *loop*! The following demonstrates this:

```
for (int x = 1; x < 2; x++) {
   System.out.println(x);  // Legal
}
System.out.println(x);  // Not Legal! x is now out of scope and
can't be accessed.
```

If you try to compile this, you'll get

```
Test.java:19: cannot resolve symbol
symbol  : variable x
location: class Test
  System.out.println(x);
                     ^
```

Conditional (boolean) Expression

The next section that executes is the conditional expression, which (like all other conditional tests) *must* evaluate to a boolean value. You can have only one logical expression, but it can be very complex. Look out for code that uses logical expressions like this:

```
for (int x = 0; ((((x < 10) && (y-- > 2)) | x == 3)); x++) { }
```

The preceding code is legal, but the following is *not*:

```
for (int x = 0; (x > 5), (y < 2); x++) { } // too many
                                            //expressions
```

The compiler will let you know the problem:

```
TestLong.java:20: ';' expected
for (int x = 0; (x > 5), (y < 2); x++) { }
                        ^
```

The rule to remember is this: *You can have only one test expression.* In other words, you can't use multiple tests separated by commas, even though the *other* two parts of a *for* statement can have multiple parts.

Iteration Expression

After each execution of the body of the *for* loop, the iteration expression is executed. This part is where you get to say what you want to happen with each iteration of the loop. Remember that it always happens *after* the loop body runs! Look at the following:

```
for (int x = 0; x < 1; x++) {
    // body code here
}
```

The preceding loop executes just once. The first time into the loop *x* is set to 0, then *x* is tested to see if it's less than 1 (which it is), and then the body of the loop executes. After the body of the loop runs, the iteration expression runs, incrementing *x* by 1. Next, the conditional test is checked, and since the result is now *false*, execution jumps to *below* the `for` loop and continues on. Keep in mind that this *iteration expression is always the last thing that happens*! So although the body may never execute again, the iteration expression *always* runs at the end of the loop block, as long as no other code within the loop causes execution to leave the loop. For example, a `break`, `return`, exception, or `System.exit()` will all cause a loop to terminate abruptly, without running the iteration expression. Look at the following code:

```
static boolean doStuff() {
   for (int x = 0; x < 3; x++) {
      System.out.println("in for loop");
      return true;
   }
   return true;
}
```

Running this code produces

```
in for loop
```

The statement only prints once, because a `return` causes execution to leave not just the current iteration of a loop, but the entire method. So the iteration expression never runs in that case. Table 4-2 lists the causes and results of abrupt loop termination.

for Loop Issues

None of the three sections of the `for` declaration are required! The following example is perfectly legal (although not necessarily good practice):

```
for( ; ; ) {
   System.out.println("Inside an endless loop");
}
```

In the preceding example, all the declaration parts are left out so it will act like an endless loop. For the exam, it's important to know that with the absence of the

TABLE 4-2 Causes of Early Loop Termination

Code in Loop	What Happens
`break`	Execution jumps immediately to the first statement after the *for* loop.
`return`	Execution immediately jumps back to the calling method.
`System.exit()`	All program execution stops; the VM shuts down.

initialization and increment sections, the loop will act like a *while* loop. The following example demonstrates how this is accomplished:

```
int i = 0;

for (;i<10;) {
   i++;
   //do some other work
}
```

The next example demonstrates a *for* loop with multiple variables in play. A comma separates the variables, and they must be of the same type. Remember that the variables declared in the *for* statement are all local to the *for* loop, and can't be used outside the scope of the loop.

```
for (int i = 0,j = 0; (i<10) && (j<10); i++, j++) {
   System.out.println("i is " + i + "j is " +j);
}
```

exam Watch

Variable scope plays a large role in the exam. You need to know that a variable* declared *in the* for *loop can't be used beyond the* for *loop. But a variable only* initialized *in the* for *statement (but declared earlier) can be used beyond the loop. For example, the following is legal,

```
int x = 3;
for (x = 12; x < 20, x++) { }
System.out.println(x);
```

while this is not,

```
for (int x = 3; x < 20; x++) { }System.out.println(x);
```

The last thing to note is that *all three sections of the* for *loop are independent of each other.* The three expressions in the *for* statement don't need to operate on the same variables, although they typically do. But even the iterator expression, which many mistakenly call the "increment expression," doesn't need to increment or set anything; you can put in virtually any arbitrary code statements that you want to happen with each iteration of the loop. Look at the following:

```
int b = 3;
for (int a = 1;  b != 1; System.out.println("iterate")) {
   b = b - a;
}
```

The preceding code prints

```
iterate
iterate
```

exam Watch

Most questions in the new (1.4) exam list "Compilation fails" and "An exception occurs at runtime" as possible answers. This makes it more difficult because you can't simply work through the behavior of the code. You must first make sure the code isn't violating any fundamental rules that will lead to compiler error, and then look for possible exceptions, and only after you've satisfied those two should you dig into the logic and flow of the code in the question.

Using break and continue in for Loops

The `break` and `continue` keywords are used to stop either the entire loop (*break*) or just the current iteration (*continue*). Typically if you're using `break` or `continue`, you'll do an *if* test within the loop, and if some condition becomes *true* (or *false* depending on the program), you want to get out immediately. The difference between them is whether or not you continue with a new iteration or jump to the first statement below the loop and continue from there.

exam Watch

`continue` ***statements must be inside a loop; otherwise, you'll get a compiler error.*** *`break`* ***statements must be used inside either a loop or switch statement. (Note: This does not apply to labeled*** *`break`* ***statements.)***

The `break` statement causes the program to stop execution of the innermost looping and start processing the next line of code after the block.

The `continue` statement causes only the current *iteration* of the innermost loop to cease and the next iteration of the same loop to start if the condition of the loop is met. When using a `continue` statement with a *for* loop, you need to consider the effects that *continue* has on the loop iteration. Examine the following code, which will be explained afterward.

```
for (int i = 0; i < 10; i++) {
   System.out.println("Inside loop");
   continue;
}
```

The question is, is this an endless loop? The answer is no. When the `continue` statement is hit, the iteration expression still runs! It runs just as though the current iteration ended "in the natural way." So in the preceding example, *i* will still increment before the condition (*i* < 10) is checked again. Most of the time, a `continue` is used within an `if` test as follows:

```
for (int i = 0; i < 10; i++) {
   System.out.println("Inside loop");
   if (foo.doStuff() == 5) {
     continue;
   }
   // more loop code, that won't be reached when the above if
   //test is true
}
```

Unlabeled Statements

Both the `break` statement and the `continue` statement can be unlabeled or labeled. Although it's far more common to use `break` and `continue` unlabeled, the exam expects you to know how labeled `break` and `continue` work. As stated before, a `break` statement (unlabeled) will exit out of the innermost looping construct and proceed with the next line of code beyond the loop block. The following example demonstrates a `break` statement:

```
boolean problem = true;
while (true) {
   if (problem) {
      System.out.println("There was a problem");
      break;
   }
}
//next line of code
```

In the previous example, the `break` statement is unlabeled. The following is another example of an unlabeled `continue` statement:

```
while (!EOF) {
   //read a field from a file
   if (there was a problem) {
      //move to the next field in the file
      continue;
   }
}
```

In this example, there is a file being read from one field at a time. When an error is encountered, the program moves to the next field in the file and uses the `continue` statement to go back into the loop (if it is not at the end of the file) and keeps reading the various fields. If the `break` command were used instead, the code would stop reading the file once the error occurred and move on to the next line of code. The `continue` statement gives you a way to say, "This particular iteration of the loop needs to stop, but not the whole loop itself. I just don't want the rest of the code in this iteration to finish, so do the iteration expression and then start over with the test, and don't worry about what was below the `continue` statement."

Labeled Statements

You need to understand the difference between labeled and unlabeled `break` and `continue`. The labeled varieties are needed only in situations where you have a nested loop, and need to indicate *which* of the nested loops you want to *break* from, or from which of the nested loops you want to `continue` with the next iteration. A `break` statement will exit out of the *labeled* loop, as opposed to the *innermost* loop, if the `break` keyword is combined with a label. An example of what a label looks like is in the following code:

```
foo:
   for (int x = 3; x < 20; x++) {
      while(y > 7) {
         y--;
      }
  }
```

The label must adhere to the rules for a valid variable name and should adhere to the Java naming convention. The syntax for the use of a label name in conjunction with a `break` statement is the `break` keyword, then the label name, followed by a semicolon. A more complete example of the use of a labeled `break` statement is as follows:

```
outer:
   for(int i=0; i<10; i++) {
      while (y > 7) {
         System.out.println("Hello");
         break outer;
      } // end of inner for loop
      System.out.println("Outer loop."); // Won't print
```

```
   } // end of outer for loop
System.out.println("Good-Bye");
```

Running this code produces

```
Hello
Good-Bye
```

In this example the word *Hello* will be printed one time. Then, the labeled `break` statement will be executed, and the flow will exit out of the loop labeled *outer.* The next line of code will then print out *Good-Bye.* Let's see what will happen if the `continue` statement is used instead of the `break` statement. The following code example is the same as the preceding one, with the exception of substituting `continue` for `break`:

```
outer:
   for (int i=0; i<10; i++) {
      for (int j=0; j<5; j++) {
         System.out.println("Hello");
         continue outer;
      } // end of inner loop
     System.out.println("outer"); // Never prints
   }
System.out.println("Good-Bye");
```

Running this code produces

```
Hello
Hello
Hello
Hello
Hello
Hello
Hello
Hello
Hello
Hello
Good-Bye
```

In this example, *Hello* will be printed ten times. After the `continue` statement is executed, the flow continues with the next iteration of the loop identified with the label. Finally, when the condition in the outer loop evaluates to `false`, the *i* loop will finish and *Good-Bye* will be printed.

EXERCISE 4-2

Creating a Labeled while Loop

Try creating a labeled *while* loop. Make the label *outer* and provide a condition to check whether a variable age is less than or equal to 21. Within the loop, it should increment the age by one. Every time it goes through the loop, it checks whether the age is 16. If it is, it will print a message to get your driver's license and continue to the outer loop. If not, it just prints "Another year."

1. The outer label should appear just before the *while* loop begins. It does not matter if it is on the same line or not.
2. Make sure *age* is declared outside of the *while* loop.

exam Watch

Labeled `continue` and `break` statements must be inside the loop that has the same label name; otherwise, the code will not compile.

CERTIFICATION OBJECTIVE

Handling Exceptions (Exam Objectives 2.3 and 2.4)

Write code that makes proper use of exceptions and exception handling clauses (try, catch, finally) and declares methods and overriding methods that throw exceptions.

Recognize the effect of an exception arising at a specified point in a code fragment. Note that the exception may be a runtime exception, a checked exception, or an error (the code may include try, catch, or finally clauses in any legitimate combination).

An old maxim in software development says that 80 percent of the work is used 20 percent of the time. The 80 percent refers to the effort required to check and handle errors. In many languages, writing program code that checks for and deals with errors is tedious and bloats the application source into confusing spaghetti. Still, error detection and handling may be the most important ingredient of any robust application. Java arms developers with an elegant mechanism for handling errors that produces efficient and organized error-handling code: *exception handling*.

Exception handling allows developers to detect errors easily without writing special code to test return values. Even better, it lets us keep exception-handling code cleanly separated from the exception-generating code. It also lets us use the same exception-handling code to deal with a range of possible exceptions.

The exam has two objectives covering exception handling, but because they're covering the same topic we're covering both objectives with the content in this section.

Catching an Exception Using try and catch

Before we begin, let's introduce some terminology. The term *exception* means "exceptional condition" and is an occurrence that alters the normal program flow. A bunch of things can lead to exceptions, including hardware failures, resource exhaustion, and good old bugs. When an exceptional event occurs in Java, an exception is said to be *thrown.* The code that's responsible for doing something about the exception is called an *exception handler,* and it *catches* the thrown exception.

Exception handling works by transferring the execution of a program to an appropriate exception handler when an exception occurs. For example, if you call a method that opens a file but the file cannot be opened, execution of that method will stop, and code that you wrote to deal with this situation will be run. Therefore, we need a way to tell the JVM what code to execute when a certain exception happens. To do this, we use the `try` and `catch` keywords. The `try` is used to define a block of code in which exceptions may occur. This block of code is called a *guarded region* (which really means "risky code goes here"). One or more `catch` clauses match a specific exception (or class of exceptions—more on that later) to a block of code that handles it. Here's how it looks in pseudocode:

```
try {
   // This is the first line of the "guarded region"
   // that is governed by the try keyword.
   // Put code here that might cause some kind of exception.
   // We may have many code lines here or just one.
}
catch(MyFirstException) {
   // Put code here that handles this Exception.
   // This is the next line of the exception handler.
   // This is the last line of the exception handler.
}
catch(MySecondException) {
   // Put code here that handles this exception
}
```

```
15.
16. // Some other unguarded (normal, non-risky) code begins here
```

In this pseudocode example, lines 2 through 5 constitute the guarded region that is governed by the `try` clause. Line seven is an exception handler for an exception of type MyFirstException. Line 12 is an exception handler for an exception of type MySecondException. Notice that the `catch` blocks immediately follow the `try` block. This is a requirement; *if you have one or more* `catch` *blocks, they must immediately follow the* `try` *block.* Additionally, the `catch` blocks must all follow each other, *without any other statements or blocks in between.* Also, the order in which the catch blocks appear matters, as we'll see a little later.

Execution starts at line 2. If the program executes all the way to line 5 with no exceptions being thrown, execution will transfer to line 15 and continue downward. However, if at any time in lines 2 through 5 (the `try` block) an exception is thrown of type MyFirstException, execution will immediately transfer to line 8. Lines 8 through 10 will then be executed so that the entire `catch` block runs, and then execution will transfer to line 15 and continue.

Note that if an exception occurred on, say, line 3 of the `try` block, the rest of the lines in the `try` block (3 through 5) would never be executed. Once control jumps to the `catch` block, it never returns to complete the balance of the `try` block. This is exactly what you want, though. Imagine your code looks something like this pseudocode:

```
try {
   getTheFileFromOverNetwork
   readFromTheFileAndPopulateTable
}
catch(CantGetFileFromNetwork) {
   useLocalFileInstead
}
```

The preceding pseudocode demonstrates how you typically work with exceptions. Code that's dependent on a risky operation (as populating a table with file data is dependent on getting the file from the network) is grouped into a `try` block in such a way that if, say, the first operation fails, you won't continue trying to run other code that's guaranteed to also fail. In the pseudocode example, you won't be able to read from the file if you can't get the file off the network in the first place.

One of the benefits of using exception handling is that code to handle any particular exception that may occur in the governed region needs to be written only once. Returning to our earlier code example, there may be three different places in our `try` block that can generate a MyFirstException, but wherever it occurs it will be handled by the same `catch` block (on line 7). We'll discuss more benefits of exception handling near the end of this chapter.

Using finally

Try and *catch* provide a terrific mechanism for trapping and handling exceptions, but we are left with the problem of how to clean up after ourselves. Because execution transfers out of the `try` block as soon as an exception is thrown, we can't put our cleanup code at the bottom of the `try` block and expect it to be executed if an exception occurs. Almost as bad an idea would be placing our cleanup code in the `catch` blocks.

Exception handlers are a poor place to clean up after the code in the `try` block because each handler then requires its own copy of the cleanup code. If, for example, you allocated a network socket or opened a file somewhere in the guarded region, each exception handler would have to close the file or release the socket. That would make it too easy to forget to do cleanup, and also lead to a lot of redundant code. To address this problem, Java offers the `finally` block.

A `finally` block encloses code that is *always* executed at some point after the `try` block, *whether an exception was thrown or not.* Even if there is a *return* statement in the `try` block, the finally block executes right after the *return* statement! This is the right place to close your files, release your network sockets, and perform any other cleanup your code requires. If the `try` block executes with no exceptions, the `finally` block is executed immediately after the `try` block completes. If there was an exception thrown, the `finally` block executes immediately after the proper `catch` block completes.

Let's look at another pseudocode example:

```
try {
   // This is the first line of the "guarded region".
}
catch(MyFirstException) {
   // Put code here that handles this error.
}
catch(MySecondException) {
   // Put code here that handles this error.
}
finally {
   // Put code here to release any resource we
   // allocated in the try clause.
```

```
13: }
14:
15: // More code here
```

As before, execution starts at the first line of the `try` block, line 2. If there are no exceptions thrown in the `try` block, execution transfers to line 11, the first line of the `finally` block. On the other hand, if a MySecondException is thrown while the code in the `try` block is executing, execution transfers to the first line of that exception handler, line 8 in the `catch` clause. After all the code in the `catch` clause is executed, the program moves to line 11, the first line of the `finally` clause. Repeat after me: finally *always runs*! OK, we'll have to refine that a little, but for now, start burning in the idea that *finally always* runs. If an exception is *thrown*, *finally* runs. If an exception is *not* thrown, *finally* runs. If the exception is *caught*, *finally* runs. If the exception is *not* caught, *finally* runs. Later we'll look at the few scenarios in which *finally* might not run or complete.

`finally` clauses are not required. If you don't write one, your code will compile and run just fine. In fact, if you have no resources to clean up after your `try` block completes, you probably don't need a `finally` clause. Also, because the compiler doesn't even require `catch` clauses, sometimes you'll run across code that has a `try` block immediately followed by a `finally` block. Such code is useful when the exception is going to be passed back to the calling method, as explained in the next section. Using a `finally` block allows the cleanup code to execute even when there isn't a `catch` clause.

The following legal code demonstrates a *try* with a *finally* but no *catch*:

```
try {
  // do stuff
} finally {
    //clean up
}
```

The following legal code demonstrates a *try*, *catch*, and *finally*:

```
try {
   // do stuff
} catch (SomeException ex) {
  // do exception handling
} finally {
   // clean up
}
```

The following *illegal* code demonstrates a *try* without *catch* or *finally*:

```
try {
  // do stuff
}
// need a catch or finally here
System.out.println("out of try block");
```

The following *illegal* code demonstrates a misplaced `catch` block:

```
try {
   // do stuff
}
// can't have code between try/catch
System.out.println("out of try block");
catch(Exception ex) { }
```

exam Watch

It is illegal to use a `try` clause without either a `catch` clause or a `finally` clause. A `try` clause by itself will result in a compiler error. Any `catch` clauses must immediately follow the `try` block. Any `finally` clauses must immediately follow the last `catch` clause. It is legal to omit either the `catch` clause or the `finally` clause, but not both.

exam Watch

You can't sneak any code in between the `try` and `catch` (or `try` and `finally`) blocks. The following won't compile:

```
try {
   // do stuff
}
System.out.print("below the try");  //Illegal!
catch(Exception ex) { }
```

Propagating Uncaught Exceptions

Why aren't `catch` clauses required? What happens to an exception that's thrown in a `try` block when there is no `catch` clause waiting for it? Actually, there's no requirement that you code a `catch` clause for every possible exception that could be thrown from the corresponding `try` block. In fact, it's doubtful that you could accomplish such a feat! If a method doesn't provide a `catch` clause for a particular exception, that method is said to be "ducking" the exception (or "passing the buck").

So what happens to a ducked exception? Before we discuss that, we need to briefly review the concept of the *call stack.* Most languages have the concept of a method stack or a call stack. Simply put, the call stack is the chain of methods that your program executes to get to the current method. If your program starts in method `main()` and `main()` calls method `a()`, which calls method `b()` that in turn calls method `c()`, the call stack consists of the following:

```
c
b
a
main
```

A stack can be represented as growing upward (although it can also be visualized as growing downward). As you can see, the last method called is at the top of the stack, while the first calling method is at the bottom. If you could print out the state of the stack at any given time, you would produce a *stack trace.* The method at the very top of the stack trace would be the method you were currently executing. If we move back down the call stack, we're moving from the current method to the previously called method. Figure 4-1 illustrates a way to think about how the call stack in Java works.

Now let's examine what happens to ducked exceptions. Imagine a building, say, five stories high, and at each floor there is a deck or balcony. Now imagine that on each deck, one person is standing holding a baseball mitt. Exceptions are like balls dropped from person to person, starting from the roof. An exception is first thrown

FIGURE 4-1

The Java method call stack

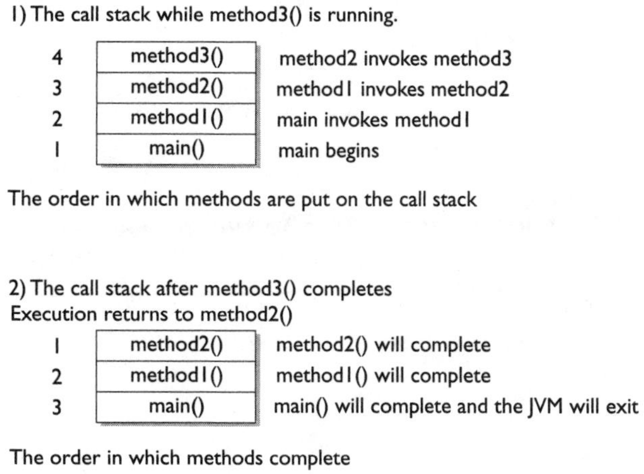

1) The call stack while method3() is running.

4	method3()	method2 invokes method3
3	method2()	method1 invokes method2
2	method1()	main invokes method1
1	main()	main begins

The order in which methods are put on the call stack

2) The call stack after method3() completes
Execution returns to method2()

1	method2()	method2() will complete
2	method1()	method1() will complete
3	main()	main() will complete and the JVM will exit

The order in which methods complete

from the top of the stack (in other words, the person on the roof), and if it isn't caught by the same person who threw it (the person on the roof), it drops down the call stack to the previous method, which is the person standing on the deck one floor down. If not caught there, by the person one floor down, the exception/ball again drops down to the previous method (person on the next floor down), and so on until they are caught or until they reach the very bottom of the call stack. This is called *exception propagation.*

If they reach the bottom of the call stack, it's like reaching the bottom of a very long drop; the ball explodes, and so does your program. An exception that's never caught will cause your application to stop running. A description (if one is available) of the exception will be displayed, and the call stack will be "dumped." This helps you debug your application by telling you what exception was thrown, from what method it was thrown, and what the stack looked like at the time.

exam Watch

You can keep throwing an exception down through the methods on the stack. But what about when you get to the `main()` method at the bottom? You can throw the exception out of `main()` as well. This results in the Java virtual machine (JVM) halting, and the stack trace will be printed to the output. The following code throws an exception,

```
class TestEx {
   public static void main (String [] args) {
       doStuff();
   }
   static void doStuff() {
      doMoreStuff();
   }
   static void doMoreStuff() {
    int x = 5/0;  // Can't divide by zero! ArithmeticException is thrown here
   }
}
```

which prints out the stack trace,

```
 %java TestEx
Exception in thread "main" java.lang.ArithmeticException: / by zero
at TestEx.doMoreStuff(TestEx.java:10)
at TestEx.doStuff(TestEx.java:7)
at TestEx.main(TestEx.java:3)
```

EXERCISE 4-3

Propagating and Catching an Exception

So far you have only seen exceptions displayed in this chapter with pseudocode. In this exercise we attempt to create two methods that deal with exceptions. One of the methods is the `main()` method, which will call another method. If an exception is thrown in the other method, it must deal with it. A `finally` statement will be included to indicate it is all done. The method it will call will be named `reverse()`, and it will reverse the order of the characters in the string. If the string contains no characters, it will propagate an exception up to the `main()` method.

1. Create an enclosing class called Propagate and a `main()` method, which will remain empty for now.
2. Create a method called `reverse()`. It takes an argument of a string and returns a String.
3. Check if the String has a length of 0 by using the `length()` method. If the length is 0, it will throw a new exception.
4. Now let's include the code to reverse the order of the String. Because this isn't the main topic of this chapter, the reversal code has been provided, but feel free to try it on your own.

```
String reverseStr = "";
for(int i=s.length()-1;i>=0;--i) {
   reverseStr += s.charAt(i);
}
return reverseStr;
```

5. Now in the `main()` method we will attempt to call this method and deal with any potential exceptions. Additionally, we will include a `finally` statement that tells us it has finished.

Defining Exceptions

We have been discussing exceptions as a concept. We know that they are thrown when a problem of some type happens, and we know what effect they have on the flow of our program. In this section we will develop the concepts further and use exceptions in functional Java code. Earlier we said that an exception is an occurrence that alters the normal program flow. But because this is Java, anything that's not a primitive must be…an object. Exceptions are no, well, *exception* to this rule. Every exception is as an instance of a class that has class Exception in its inheritance hierarchy. In other words, exceptions are always some subclass of `java.lang.Exception`.

When an exception is thrown, an object of a particular Exception subtype is instantiated and handed to the exception handler as an argument to the `catch` clause. An actual `catch` clause looks like this:

```
try {
   // some code here
}
catch (ArrayIndexOutOfBoundsException e) {
   e.printStackTrace();
}
```

In this example, *e* is an instance of a class with the tersely named ArrayIndexOutOfBoundsException. As with any other object, you can call its methods.

Exception Hierarchy

All exception classes are subtypes of class Exception. This class derives from the class Throwable (which derives from the class Object). Figure 4-2 shows the hierarchy for the exception classes.

As you can see, there are two subclasses that derive from Throwable: Exception and Error. Classes that derive from Error represent unusual situations that are not caused by program errors or by anything that would normally happen during program execution, such as the JVM running out of memory. Generally, your application won't be able to recover from an Error, so you're not required to handle them. If your code does *not* handle them (and it usually won't), it will still compile with no trouble. Although often thought of as exceptional conditions, Errors are technically not exceptions because they do not derive from class Exception.

In general, an exception represents something that happens not as a result of a programming error, but rather because some resource is not available or some other condition required for correct execution is not present. For example, if your application is supposed to communicate with another application or computer that is not

FIGURE 4-2

Exception class hierarchy

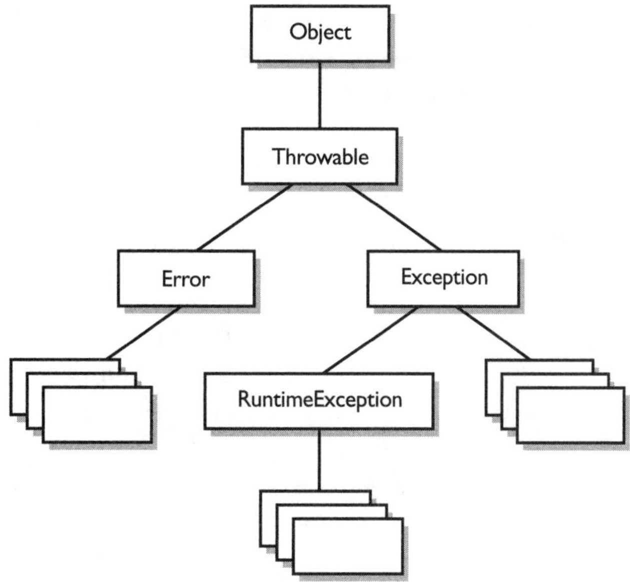

answering, this is an exception that is not caused by a bug. Figure 4-2 also shows a subtype of Exception called RuntimeException. These exceptions are a special case because they actually do indicate program errors. They can also represent rare, difficult to handle exceptional conditions. Runtime exceptions are discussed in greater detail later in this chapter.

Java provides many exception classes, most of which have quite descriptive names. There are two ways to get information about an exception. The first is from the type of the exception itself. The next is from information that you can get from the exception object. Class Throwable (at the top of the inheritance tree for exceptions) provides its descendants with some methods that are useful in exception handlers. One of these is `printStackTrace()`. As expected, if you call an exception object's `printStackTrace()` method, as in the earlier example, a stack trace from where the exception occurred will be printed.

We discussed that a call stack builds upward with the most recently called method at the top. You will notice that the `printStackTrace()` method prints the most recently entered method first and continues down, printing the name of each method as it works its way down the call stack (this is called *unwinding the stack*) from the top.

For the exam, it is not necessary to know any of the* methods *contained in the Throwable classes, including Exception and Error. You are expected to know that Exception, Error, RuntimeException, and Throwable types can all be thrown using the* `throws` *keyword, and can all be caught (although you rarely will catch anything other than Exception subtypes).

Handling an Entire Class Hierarchy of Exceptions

We've discussed that the `catch` keyword allows you to specify a particular type of exception to catch. You can actually catch *more* than one type of exception in a single `catch` clause. If the exception class that you specify in the `catch` clause has no subclasses, then only the specified class of exception will be caught. However, if the class specified in the `catch` clause does have subclasses, *any exception object that subclasses the specified class will be caught* as well.

For example, class IndexOutOfBoundsException has two subclasses, ArrayIndexOutOfBoundsException and StringIndexOutOfBoundsException. You may want to write one exception handler that deals with exceptions produced by either type of boundary error, but you might not be concerned with which exception you actually have. In this case, you could write a `catch` clause like the following:

```
try {
   // Some code here that can throw a boundary exception
}
catch (IndexOutOfBoundsException e) {
   e.printStackTrace();
}
```

If any code in the `try` block throws ArrayIndexOutOfBoundsException or StringIndexOutOfBoundsException, the exception will be caught and handled. This can be convenient, but it should be used sparingly. By specifying an exception class' superclass in your `catch` clause, you're discarding valuable information about the exception. You can, of course, find out exactly what exception class you have, but if you're going to do that, you're better off writing a separate `catch` clause for each exception type of interest.

on the job

Resist the temptation to write a single catchall exception handler such as the following:

```
try {
   // some code
```

```
}
catch (Exception e) {
   e.printStackTrace();
}
```

This code will catch every exception generated. Of course, no single exception handler can properly handle every exception, and programming in this way defeats the design objective. Exception handlers that trap many errors at once will probably reduce the reliability of your program because it's likely that an exception will be caught that the handler does not know how to handle.

Exception Matching

If you have an exception hierarchy composed of a superclass exception and a number of subtypes, and you're interested in handling one of the subtypes in a special way but want to handle all the rest together, you need write only two `catch` clauses.

When an exception is thrown, Java will try to find a `catch` clause for the exception type. If it doesn't find one, it will search for a handler for a supertype of the exception. If it does *not* find a `catch` clause that matches a supertype for the exception, then the exception is propagated down the call stack. This process is called *exception matching*.

Let's look at an example:

```
import java.io.*;
public class ReadData {
   public static void main(String args[]) {
      try {
         RandomAccessFile raf =
            new RandomAccessFile("myfile.txt", "r");
         byte b[] = new byte[1000];
         raf.readFully(b, 0, 1000);
      }
      catch(FileNotFoundException e) {
         System.err.println("File not found");
         System.err.println(e.getMessage());
         e.printStackTrace();
      }
      catch(IOException e) {
         System.err.println("IO Error");
         System.err.println(e.toString());
         e.printStackTrace();
      }
```

```
20:     }
21: }
```

This short program attempts to open a file and to read some data from it. Opening and reading files can generate many exceptions, most of which are some type of IOException. Imagine that in this program we're interested in knowing only whether the exact exception is a FileNotFoundException. Otherwise, we don't care exactly what the problem is.

FileNotFoundException is a subclass of IOException. Therefore, we could handle it in the `catch` clause that catches all subtypes of IOException, but then we would have to test the exception to determine whether it was a FileNotFoundException. Instead, we coded a special exception handler for the FileNotFoundException and a separate exception handler for all other IOException subtypes.

If this code generates a FileNotFoundException, it will be handled by the `catch` clause that begins at line 10. If it generates another IOException—perhaps EOFException, which is a subclass of IOException—it will be handled by the `catch` clause that begins at line 15. If some other exception is generated, such as a runtime exception of some type, neither `catch` clause will be executed and the exception will be propagated down the call stack.

Notice that the `catch` clause for the FileNotFoundException was placed above the handler for the IOException. *This is really important!* If we do it the opposite way, the program will not compile. *The handlers for the most specific exceptions must always be placed above those for more general exceptions.* The following will not compile:

```
try {
   // do risky IO things
} catch (IOException e) {
  // handle general IOExceptions
} catch (FileNotFoundException ex) {
  // handle just FileNotFoundException
}
```

You'll get the following compiler error:

```
TestEx.java:15: exception java.io.FileNotFoundException has
 already been caught
} catch (FileNotFoundException ex) {
         ^
```

If you think of the people with baseball mitts, imagine that the most general mitts are the largest, and can thus catch many different kinds of balls. An IOException mitt is large enough and flexible enough to catch any type of IOException. So if the person on the fifth floor (say, Fred) has a big 'ol IOException mitt, he can't help but catch a FileNotFoundException ball with it. And if the guy (say, Jimmy) on the second floor is holding a FileNotFoundException mitt, that FileNotFoundException ball will never get to him, since it will always be stopped by Fred on the fifth floor, standing there with his big-enough-for-any-IOException mitt.

So what do you do with exceptions that are siblings in the class hierarchy? If one Exception class is not a subtype or supertype of the other, then the order in which the `catch` clauses are placed doesn't matter.

Exception Declaration and the Public Interface

So, how do we know that some method throws an exception that we have to catch? Just as a method must specify what type and how many arguments it accepts and what is returned, the exceptions that a method can throw *must* be declared (unless the exceptions are subclasses of `RuntimeException`). The list of thrown exceptions is part of a method's public interface. The `throws` keyword is used as follows to list the exceptions that a method can throw:

```
void myFunction() throws MyException1, MyException2 {
   // code for the method here
}
```

This method has a `void` return type, accepts no arguments, and declares that it `throws` two exceptions of type MyException1 and MyException2. (Just because the method *declares* that it `throws` an exception doesn't mean it always *will.* It just tells the world that it *might.*)

Suppose your method doesn't directly throw an exception, but calls a method that *does.* You can choose not to handle the exception yourself and instead just declare it, as though it were *your* method that actually `throws` the exception. If you do declare the exception that your method might get from another method, and you don't provide a `try/catch` for it, then the method will propagate back to the method that called *your* method, and either be caught there or continue on to be handled by a method further down the stack.

Any method that might *throw* an exception (unless it's a subclass of RuntimeException) must *declare* the exception. That includes methods that aren't actually throwing it directly, but are "ducking" and letting the exception pass down to the next method in the stack. If you "duck" an exception, it is just as if you were the one actually throwing the exception. RuntimeException subclasses are exempt, so the compiler won't check to see if you've declared them. But all non-RuntimeExceptions are considered "checked" exceptions, because the compiler checks to be certain you've acknowledged that "bad things could happen here."

Remember this: Each method must either handle *all* checked exceptions by supplying a `catch` clause *or* list each unhandled checked exception as a thrown exception. This rule is referred to as Java's *handle or declare requirement.* (Sometimes called *catch* or *declare.*)

exam Watch

Look for code that invokes a method declaring an exception, where the calling method doesn't handle or declare the checked exception. The following code has two big problems that the compiler will prevent:

```
void doStuff() {
   doMore();
}
void doMore() {
    throw new IOException();
}
```

First, the `doMore()` ***method throws a checked exception, but does not declare it! But suppose we fix the*** `doMore()` ***method as follows:***

```
void doMore() throws IOException { … }
```

The `doStuff()` ***method is still in trouble because it, too, must declare the IOException,*** unless ***it handles it by providing a*** `try`/`catch`***, with a*** `catch` ***clause that can take an IOException.***

Again, some exceptions are exempt from this rule. An object of type RuntimeException may be thrown from any method without being specified as part of the method's public interface (and a handler need not be present). And even if a method does declare a RuntimeException, the calling method is under no obligation to handle or declare it. RuntimeException, Error, and all of their subtypes are *unchecked* exceptions and *unchecked exceptions do not have to be specified or handled.*

Here is an example:

```
import java.io.*;
class Test {
   public int myMethod1() throws EOFException {
      return myMethod2();
   }
   public int myMethod2() throws EOFException {
```

```
        // Some code that actually throws the exception goes here
        return 1;
    }
}
```

Let's look at myMethod1(). Because EOFException subclasses IOException and IOException subclasses Exception, it is a checked exception and must be declared as an exception that may be thrown by this method. But where will the exception actually come from? The public interface for method myMethod2() called here declares that an exception of this type can be thrown. Whether that method actually throws the exception itself or calls another method that throws it is unimportant to us; we simply know that we have to either catch the exception or declare that we throw it. The method myMethod1() does not catch the exception, so it declares that it throws it.

Now let's look at another legal example, myMethod3().

```
public void myMethod3() {
   // Some code that throws a NullPointerException goes here
}
```

According to the comment, this method can throw a NullPointerException. Because RuntimeException is the immediate superclass of NullPointerException, it is an *unchecked* exception and need not be declared. We can see that myMethod3() does not declare any exceptions.

Runtime exceptions are referred to as *unchecked exceptions.* All other exceptions, meaning all those that do not derive from java.lang.RuntimeException, are *checked exceptions.* A checked exception must be caught somewhere in your code. If you invoke a method that throws a checked exception but you don't catch the checked exception somewhere, your code will not compile. That's why they're called checked exceptions; the compiler checks to make sure that they're handled or declared. A number of the methods in the Java 2 Standard Edition libraries throw checked exceptions, so you will often write exception handlers to cope with exceptions generated by methods you didn't write.

You can also throw an exception yourself, and that exception can be either an existing exception from the Java API or one of your own. To create your own exception, you simply subclass Exception (or one of its subclasses) as follows:

```
class MyException extends Exception { }
```

And if you throw the exception, the compiler will guarantee that you declare it as follows:

```
class TestEx {
   void doStuff() {
     throw new MyException();  // Throw a checked exception
   }
}
```

The preceding code upsets the compiler:

```
TestEx.java:6: unreported exception MyException; must be caught or
declared to be thrown
  throw new MyException();
  ^
```

exam Watch

When an object of a subtype of Exception is thrown, it* must *be handled or declared. These objects are called* checked *exceptions, and include all exceptions except those that are subtypes of RuntimeException, which are* unchecked *exceptions. Be ready to spot methods that don't follow the handle or declare rule, such as

```
class MyException extends Exception {
void someMethod () {
    doStuff();
}
void doStuff() throws MyException {
   try {
      throw new MyException();
    }
   catch(MyException me) {
      throw me;
    }
}
```

You need to recognize that this code won't compile. If you try, you'll get

```
TestEx.java:8: unreported exception MyException; must be caught or
declared to be thrown
doStuff();
^
```

exam
Watch

The exam objectives specifically state that you need to know how an Error compares with checked and unchecked exceptions. Objects of type Error are *not* ***Exception objects, although they do represent exceptional conditions. Both Exception and Error share a common superclass, Throwable, thus both can be thrown using the*** `throws` ***keyword. When an Error or a subclass of Error is thrown, it's unchecked.*** *You are not required to catch Error objects or Error subtypes.* ***You can also throw an Error yourself (although you probably won't ever want to) and you*** *can* ***catch one, but again, you probably*** *won't.* ***What, for example, would you actually do if you got an OutOfMemoryError? It's not like you can tell the garbage collector to run; you can bet the JVM fought desperately to save itself (and reclaimed all the memory it could) by the time you got the error. In other words, don't expect the JVM at that point to say, "Run the garbage collector? Oh, thanks*** *so* ***much for telling me. That just never occurred to me. Sure, I'll get right on it…" Even better, what would you do if a VirtualMachineError arose? Your program is toast by the time you'd catch the Error, so there's really no point in trying to catch one of these babies. Just remember, though, that you*** *can!* ***The following compiles just fine:***

```
class TestEx {
   public static void main (String [] args) {
      badMethod();
   }
   static void badMethod() {  // No need to declare an Error
      doStuff()
   }
   static void doStuff() {  //No need to declare an Error
      try {
        throw new Error();
      }
      catch(Error me) {
         throw me; // We catch it, but then rethrow it
      }
    }
}
```

If we were throwing a checked exception rather than Error, then the `doStuff()` ***method would need to declare the exception. But remember, since Error is not a subtype of Exception, it doesn't need to be declared. You're free to declare it if you like, but the compiler just doesn't care one way or another when or how the Error is thrown, or by whom.***

Because Java has checked exceptions, it's commonly said that Java forces developers to handle errors. Yes, Java forces us to write exception handlers for each exception that can occur during normal operation, but it's up to us to make the exception handlers actually* do *something useful. We know software managers who melt down when they see a programmer write

```
try {
    callBadMethod();
} catch (Exception ex) { }
```

Notice anything missing? Don't "eat" the exception by catching it without actually handling it. You won't even be able to tell that the exception occurred, because you'll never see the stack trace.

Rethrowing the Same Exception

Just as you can throw a new exception from a `catch` clause, you can also throw the same exception you just caught. Here's a `catch` clause that does this:

```
catch(IOException e) {
   // Do things, then if you decide you can't handle it…
        throw e;
}
```

All other `catch` clauses associated with the same `try` are ignored, and the exception is thrown back to the calling method (the next method down the call stack). If you *throw* a checked exception from a `catch` clause, you must also *declare* that exception! In other words, you must handle *and* declare, as opposed to handle *or* declare. The following example is illegal:

```
public void doStuff() {
   try {
      // risky IO things
   } catch(IOException ex) {
      // can't handle it
       throw ex;  // Can't throw it unless you declare it
   }
}
```

In the preceding code, the `doStuff()` method is clearly able to throw a checked exception—in this case an IOException—so the compiler says, *"Well, that's just peachy that you have a* `try/catch` *in there, but it's not good enough. If you* might *rethrow the IOException you catch, then you* must *declare it!"*

EXERCISE 4-4

Creating an Exception

In this exercise we attempt to create a custom exception. We won't put in any new methods (it will have only those inherited from Exception), and because it extends Exception, the compiler considers it a checked exception. The goal of the program is to check to see if a command-line argument, representing a particular food (as a string), is considered bad or OK.

1. Let's first create our exception. We will call it BadFoodException. This exception will be thrown when a bad food is encountered.
2. Create an enclosing class called MyException and a `main()` method, which will remain empty for now.
3. Create a method called `checkFood()`. It takes a String argument and throws our exception if it doesn't like the food it was given. Otherwise, it tells us it likes the food. You can add any foods you aren't particularly fond of to the list.
4. Now in the `main()` method, you'll get the command-line argument out of the String array, and then pass that String on to the `checkFood()` method. Because it's a checked exception, the `checkFood()` method must declare it, and `the main()` method must handle it (using a *try/catch*). Do *not* have `main()` declare the method, because if `main()` ducks the exception, who else is back there to catch it?

As useful as exception handling is, it's still up to the developer to make proper use of it. Exception handling makes organizing our code and signaling problems easy, but the exception handlers still have to be written. You'll find that even the most complex situations can be handled, and keep your code reusable, readable, and maintainable.

CERTIFICATION OBJECTIVE

Working with the Assertion Mechanism (Exam Objectives 2.4 and 2.5)

Write code that makes proper use of assertions, and distinguish appropriate from inappropriate uses of assertions.

Identify correct statements about the assertion mechanism.

You know you're not supposed to make assumptions, but you can't help it when you're writing code. You put them in comments:

```
if (x > 2 && y) {
   // do something
} else if (x < 2 || y) {
   // do something
} else {
   // x must be 2
   // do something else
}
```

You write *print* statements with them:

```
while (true) {
   if (x > 2) {
       break;
   }
   System.out.print("If we got here something went horribly
wrong");
}
```

Added to the Java language beginning with version 1.4, assertions let you test your assumptions during development, without the expense (in both your time and program overhead) of writing exception handlers for exceptions that *you assume will never happen* once the program is out of development and fully deployed.

Starting with exam 310-035 (version 1.4 of the Sun Certified Java Programmer exam), you're expected to know the basics of how assertions (in Java) work, including how to enable them, how to use them, and how *not* to use them. Because both objectives test the same concepts, the things you need to know for both are covered together in this section.

Assertions Overview

Suppose you assume that a number passed into a method (say, `methodA()`) will never be negative. While testing and debugging, you want to validate your assumption, but you don't want to have to strip out *print* statements, runtime exception handlers, or *if/else* tests when you're done with development. But leaving any of those in is, at the least, a performance hit. Assertions to the rescue! Check out the following preassertions code:

```
private void methodA(int num) {
   if (num >= 0) {
      // do stuff
   } else {  // num must be < 0
     // This code will never be reached!
     System.out.println("Yikes! num is a negative number! " + num);
   }
   useNum(num + x);
}
```

Because you're so certain of your assumption, you don't want to take the time (or program performance hit) to write exception-handling code. And at runtime, you don't want the *if/else* in there either because if you *do* reach the `else` condition, it means your earlier logic (whatever was running prior to this method being called) is flawed. Assertions let you test your assumptions during development, but the assertion code—in effect—*evaporates* when the program is deployed, leaving behind no overhead or debugging code to track down and remove. Let's rewrite `methodA()` to validate that the argument was not negative:

```
private void methodA(int num) {
   assert (num>=0);  // throws an AssertionError
                     // if this test isn't true
   useNum(num + x);
}
```

Not only do assertions let your code stay cleaner and smaller, but because assertions are inactive unless specifically "turned on" (enabled), the code will run as though it were written like this:

```
private void methodA(int num) {
   useNum(num + x); // we've tested this;
                    // we now know we're good here
}
```

Assertions work quite simply. *You always assert that something is* true. If it *is*, no problem. Code keeps running. But if your assertion turns out to be wrong (*false*), then a stop-the-world AssertionError is thrown (that you should never, ever handle!) right then and there, so you can fix whatever logic flaw led to the problem.

Assertions come in two flavors: simple and *really* simple, as follows:

Really Simple

```
private void doStuff() {
   assert (y > x);
   // more code assuming y is greater than x
}
```

Simple

```
private void doStuff() {
   assert (y > x): "y is " + y " " x is " + x;
   // more code assuming y is greater than x
}
```

The difference between them is that the simple version adds a second expression, separated from the first (boolean expression) by a colon, that adds a little more information to the stack trace. Both versions throw an immediate AssertionError, but the simple version gives you a little more debugging help while the really simple version simply tells you that your assumption was *false*.

Assertions are typically enabled when an application is being tested and debugged, but* disabled *when the application is deployed. The assertions are still in the code, although ignored by the JVM, so if you do have a deployed application that starts misbehaving, you can always choose to enable assertions in the field for additional testing.

Assertion Expression Rules

Assertions can have either one or two expressions, depending on whether you're using the *simple* or *really simple* flavor. The first expression must always result in a `boolean` value! Follow the same rules you use for *if* and *while* tests. The whole point is to assert *aTest*, which means you're asserting that *aTest* is *true*. If it *is true*, no problem. If it's *not true*, however, then your assumption was wrong and you get an AssertionError.

The second expression, used only with the simple version of an `assert` statement, can be *anything that results in a value.* Remember, the second expression is used to generate a String message that displays in the stack trace to give you a little more debugging information. It works much like `System.out.println()` in that you can pass it a primitive or an object, and it will convert it into a String representation. It *must* resolve to a value!

Table 4-3 lists legal and illegal expressions for both parts of an `assert` statement. Remember, expression2 is used only with the simple `assert` statement, where the second expression exists solely to give you a little more debugging detail.

exam Watch

If you see the word "expression" in a question about assertions, and the question doesn't specify whether it means *expression1* ***(the boolean test) or*** *expression2* ***(the value to print in the stack trace), then always assume the word*** *expression* ***refers to*** *expression1****, the boolean test. For example, if we asked you the following question,***

"An assert expression must result in a boolean value, true or false?",

assume that the word *expression* ***refers to*** *expression1* ***of an*** `assert`***, so the question statement is correct. If the statement were referring to expression2, however, the statement would not be correct, since expression2 can have a result of*** *any* ***value, not just a boolean.***

Enabling Assertions

If you want to use assertions, you have to think first about how to *compile* with assertions in your code, and then about how to *run* with assertions turned on. Both require version 1.4 or greater, and that brings us to the first issue: how to compile with assertions in your code.

TABLE 4-3 Legal and Illegal `assert` Expressions

Expression1		Expression2	
Legal	**Illegal**	**Legal**	**Illegal**
`assert (x ==2)`	`assert (x = 2)`	`: "x is " + x`	`: void`
`boolean z = true;` `assert (z)`	`int z = 0;` `assert (z)`	`public int go() { return 1; }` `: go();`	`public void go() { }` `: go();`
`assert false`	`assert 1`	`: new Foo();`	`: Foo f;`

Compiling with Assertions

Prior to version 1.4, you might very well have written code like this:

```
int assert = getInitialValue();
if (assert == getActualResult()) {
   // do something
}
```

Notice that in the preceding code, `assert` is used as an identifier. No problem prior to 1.4. But remember that you cannot use a keyword/reserved word as an identifier, and beginning with version 1.4, *`assert` is now a keyword!* The bottom line is

You can use "assert" as a keyword or as an identifier, but not both.

You get a choice whenever you compile with version 1.4, as to whether you're compiling *"assertion aware"* code or code written in the old way, where assert is not a reserved word. Let's look at both. You must know this: in version 1.4, *assertions are disabled by default!* If you don't specifically "turn them on" at compile time, then assert will not be recognized as a keyword, because the compiler will act as a version 1.3 compiler, with respect to the word "assert" (in which case your code can happily use `assert` as an identifier).

Compiling Assertion-Aware Code If you're using `assert` as a keyword (in other words, you're actually trying to *assert* something in your code), then you must explicitly enable assertion-awareness at compile time, as follows:

```
javac -source 1.4 com/geeksanonymous/TestClass
```

You can read that as "compile the class TestClass, in the directory com/geeksanonymous, and do it in the 1.4 way, where `assert` is a recognized keyword."

Compiling with Code That Uses Assert as an Identifier If you don't use the `-source 1.4` flag, then the default behavior is as though you said to the compiler, "Compile this code as if you didn't known anything about `assert` as a keyword, so that I may use the word `assert` as an identifier for a method or variable." The following is what you get by default:

```
javac -source 1.3 com/geeksanonymous/TestClass
```

But since that's the default behavior, it's redundant to actually type `-source 1.3`.

Running with Assertions

Here's where it gets cool. Once you've written your assertion-aware code (in other words, code that uses `assert` as a keyword, to actually perform assertions at runtime), you can choose to enable or disable them! Remember, *assertions are disabled by default.*

Enabling Assertions at Runtime You enable assertions at runtime with

```
java -ea com.geeksanonymous.TestClass
```

or

```
java -enableassertions com.geeksanonymous.TestClass
```

The preceding command-line switches tell the JVM to run with assertions enabled.

Disabling Assertions at Runtime You must also know the command-line switches for disabling assertions,

```
java -da com.geeksanonymous.TestClass
```

or

```
java -disableassertions com.geeksanonymous.TestClass
```

Because assertions are disabled by default, using the disable switches might seem unnecessary. Indeed, using the switches the way we do in the preceding example just gives you the default behavior (in other words, you get the same result regardless of whether you use the disabling switches). But…you can also selectively enable and disable assertions in such a way that they're enabled for some classes and/or packages, and disabled for others, while a particular program is running.

Selective Enabling and Disabling The command-line switches to enable and disable assertions can be used in various ways:

- **With no arguments** (as in the preceding examples) Enables or disables assertions in all classes, except for the system classes.
- **With a package name** Enables or disables assertions in the package specified, and any packages below this package in the same directory hierarchy (more on that in a moment).
- **With a class name** Enables or disables assertions in the class specified.

You can combine switches to, say, disable assertions in a single class, but keep them enabled for all others, as follows:

```
java -ea  -da:com.geeksanonymous.Foo
```

The preceding command line tells the JVM to enable assertions in general, but disable them in the class `com.geeksanonymous.Foo`. You can do the same selectivity for a package as follows:

```
java -ea -da:com.geeksanonymous...
```

The preceding command line tells the JVM to enable assertions in general, but disable them in the package *com.geeksanonymous, and all of its subpackages!* You may not be familiar with the term *subpackages,* since there wasn't much use of that term prior to assertions. A *subpackage* is any package in a subdirectory of the named package. For example, look at the following directory tree:

```
com
   |_geeksanonymous
                  |_Foo
                  |_Bar
                  |_twelvesteps
                              |_StepOne
                              |_StepTwo
```

This tree lists three directories,

```
com
geeksanonymous
twelvesteps
```

and four classes:

```
com.geeksanonymous.Foo
com.geeksanonymous.Bar
com.geeksanonymous.twelvesteps.StepOne
com.geeksanonymous.twelvesteps.StepTwo
```

The subpackage of *com.geeksanonymous* is the *twelvesteps* package. Remember that in Java, the *com.geeksanonymous.twelvesteps* package is treated as a completely *distinct* package that has no relationship with the packages above it (in this example, the *com.geeksanonymous* package), except they just *happen* to share a couple of directories. Table 4-4 lists examples of command-line switches for enabling and disabling assertions.

TABLE 4-4 Assertion Command-Line Switches

Command-Line Example	What It Means
`java -ea` `java -enableassertions`	Enable assertions
`java -da` `java -disableassertions`	Disable assertions (the default behavior of version 1.4)
`java -ea:com.foo.Bar`	Enable assertions in class com.foo.Bar
`java -ea:com.foo...`	Enable assertions in package *com.foo*, and *any of its subpackages*
`java -ea -dsa`	Enable assertions in general, but disable assertions in system classes
`java -ea -da:com.foo...`	Enable assertions in general, but disable assertions in package *com.foo and any of its subpackages*

Using Assertions Appropriately

Not all *legal* uses of assertions are considered *appropriate.* As with so much of Java, you can abuse the intended use for assertions, despite the best efforts of Sun's Java engineers to discourage you. For example, you're *never* supposed to handle an assertion failure. That means don't catch it with a `catch` clause and attempt to recover. Legally, however, AssertionError is a subclass of Throwable, so it *can* be caught. But just don't do it! If you're going to try to recover from something, it should be an exception. To discourage you from trying to substitute an assertion for an exception, the AssertionError doesn't provide access to the object that generated it. All you get is the String message.

So who gets to decide what is and is not *appropriate*? Sun. Both the exam and this section use Sun's "official" assertion documentation to determine appropriate and inappropriate uses.

exam Watch

If you see the word "appropriate" on the exam, do not mistake that for "legal." *Appropriate* ***always refers to the way in which something is*** *supposed* ***to be used, according to either the developers of the mechanism or best practices officially embraced by Sun. If you see the word "correct" in the context of assertions, as in, "Line 3 is a correct use of assertions," you should also assume that*** *correct* ***is referring to how assertions*** *should* ***be used rather than how they legally*** *could* ***be used.***

Do not use assertions to validate arguments to a *public* method.

The following is an inappropriate use of assertions:

```
public void doStuff(int x) {
   assert (x > 0);
   // do things with x
}
```

A *public* method might be called from code that you don't control (or have ever seen). Because *public* methods are part of your exposed interface to the outside world, you're supposed to guarantee that any constraints on the arguments will be enforced by the method itself. But since assertions aren't guaranteed to actually run (they're typically disabled in a deployed application), the enforcement won't happen if assertions aren't enabled. You don't want publicly accessible code that works only *conditionally*, depending on whether assertions are enabled or disabled.

If you need to validate *public* method arguments, you'll probably use exceptions to throw, say, an IllegalArgumentException if the values passed to the *public* method are invalid.

Do use assertions to validate arguments to a private method.

If you write a *private* method, you almost certainly wrote (or control) any code that calls it. When you assume that the logic in code calling your *private* method is correct, you can test that assumption with an `assert` as follows:

```
private void doMore(int x) {
   assert (x > 0);
   // do things with x
}
```

The only difference that matters between the preceding example and the one before it is the access modifier. So, *do* enforce constraints on *private* arguments, but do *not* enforce constraints on *public* methods. You're certainly free to compile assertion code with an inappropriate validation of *public* arguments, but for the exam (and real life) you need to know that you *shouldn't* do it.

Do not use assertions to validate command-line arguments.

This is really just a special case of the "Do not use assertions to validate arguments to a *public* method" rule. If your program requires command-line arguments, you'll probably use the exception mechanism to enforce them.

Do use assertions, *even in public methods*, to check for cases that you know are never, ever supposed to happen.

This can include code blocks that should never be reached, including the default of a *switch* statement as follows:

```
switch(x) {
   case 2: y = 3;
   case 3: y = 17;
   case 4: y = 27;
   default: assert false; // We're never supposed to get here!
}
```

If you assume that a particular code block won't be reached, as in the preceding example where you assert that *x* must be either 2, 3, or 4, then you can use `assert false` to cause an AssertionError to be thrown immediately if you ever *do* reach that code. So in the *switch* example, we're not performing a boolean test—we've already asserted that we should never be there, so just *getting* to that point is an automatic failure of our assertion/assumption.

Do not use assert expressions that can cause side effects!

The following would be a very bad idea:

```
public void doStuff() {
   assert (modifyThings());
   // continues on
}
public boolean modifyThings() {
   x++ = y;
   return true;
}
```

The rule is: *An assert expression should leave the program in the same state it was in before the expression!* Think about it. Assert expressions aren't guaranteed to always run, so you don't want your code to behave differently depending on whether assertions are enabled. Assertions must not cause any side effects. If assertions are enabled, the only change to the way your program runs is that an AssertionError can be thrown if one of your assertions (think: *assumptions*) turns out to be false.

CERTIFICATION SUMMARY

This chapter covered a lot of ground, all of which involves ways of controlling your program flow, based on a conditional test. First you learned about *if* and *switch* statements. The `if` statement evaluates one or more expressions to a boolean result. If the result is *true*, the program will execute the code in the block that is encompassed by the *if*. If an `else` statement is used and the expression evaluates to *false*, then the code following the *else* will be performed. If the *else* is not used, then none of the code associated with the *if* statement will execute.

You also learned that the `switch` statement is used to replace multiple *if-else* statements. The *switch* statement can evaluate only integer primitive types that can be implicitly cast to an `int`. Those types are `byte`, `short`, `int`, and `char`. At runtime, the JVM will try to find a match between the argument to the *switch* statement and an argument in a corresponding *case* statement. If a match is found, execution will begin at the matching *case*, and continue on from there until a `break` statement is found or the end of the `switch` statement occurs. If there is no match, then the `default` case will execute, if there is one.

You've learned about the three looping constructs available in the Java language. These constructs are the *for* loop, the *while* loop, and the *do-while* loop. In general, the *for* loop is used when you know how many times you need to go through the loop. The *while* loop is used when you do not know how many times you want to go through, whereas the *do-while* is used when you need to go through at least once. In the *for* loop and the *while* loop, the expression will have to evaluate to `true` to get inside the block and will check after every iteration of the loop. The *do-while* loop does not check the condition until after it has gone through the loop once. The major benefit of the *for* loop is the ability to initialize one or more variables and increment or decrement those variables in the *for* loop definition.

The `break` and `continue` statements can be used in either a labeled or unlabeled fashion. When unlabeled, the `break` statement will force the program to stop processing the innermost looping construct and start with the line of code following the loop. Using an unlabeled `continue` command will cause the program to stop execution of the current iteration of the innermost loop and proceed with the next iteration. When a `break` or a `continue` statement is used in a labeled manner, it will perform in the same way, with one exception. The statement will not apply to the innermost loop; instead, it will apply to the loop with the label. The `break` statement is used most often in conjunction with the `switch` statement.

When there is a match between the *switch* expression and the *case* value, the code following the *case* value will be performed. To stop the execution of the code, the `break` statement is needed.

You've seen how Java provides an elegant mechanism in exception handling. Exception handling allows you to isolate your error-correction code into separate blocks so that the main code doesn't become cluttered by error-checking code. Another elegant feature allows you to handle similar errors with a single error-handling block, without code duplication. Also, the error handling can be deferred to methods further back on the call stack.

You learned that Java's `try` keyword is used to specify a guarded region—a block of code in which problems might be detected. An exception handler is the code that is executed when an exception occurs. The handler is defined by using Java's `catch` keyword. All `catch` clauses must immediately follow the related `try` block. Java also provides the `finally` keyword. This is used to define a block of code that is *always* executed, either immediately after a `catch` clause completes or immediately after the associated `try` block in the case that no exception was thrown (or there was a *try* but no *catch*). Use `finally` blocks to release system resources and to perform any cleanup required by the code in the `try` block. A `finally` block is not required, but if there is one it must follow the *catch*. It is guaranteed to be called *except* in the special cases where the *try* or *catch* code issues a `System.exit()`.

An exception object is an instance of class Exception or one of its subclasses. The `catch` clause takes, as a parameter, an instance of an object of a type derived from the Exception class. Java requires that each method either *catch* any checked exception it can throw or else *declare* that it *throws* the exception. The exception declaration is part of the method's *public* interface. To declare an exception may be thrown, the `throws` keyword is used in a method definition, along with a list of all checked exceptions that might be thrown.

Runtime exceptions are of type RuntimeException (or one of its subclasses). These exceptions are a special case because they do *not* need to be handled or declared, and thus are known as "unchecked" exceptions. Errors are of type java.lang.Error or its subclasses, and like runtime exceptions, they do *not* need to be handled or declared. Checked exceptions include any exception types that are not of type RuntimeException or Error. If your code fails to either handle a checked exception or declare that it is thrown, your code won't compile. But with *un*checked exceptions or objects of type Error, it doesn't matter to the compiler whether you declare them, or handle them, do nothing about them, or do some combination of declaring and handling. In other words, you're free to declare them and handle them, but the compiler won't care one way or the other. It is not good practice to handle an Error, though, because rarely can you do anything to recover from one.

Assertions, added to the language in version 1.4, are a useful new debugging tool. You learned how you can use them for testing, by enabling them, but keep them disabled when the application is deployed. If you have older Java code that uses the word *assert* an identifier, then you won't be able to use assertions, and you must recompile your older code using the default `-source 1.3` flag. If you do want to enable assertions in your code, then you must use the `-source 1.4` flag, causing the compiler to see *assert* as a keyword rather than an identifier.

You learned how *assert* statements always include a boolean expression, and if the expression is `true` the code continues on, but if the expression is *false*, an AssertionError is thrown. If you use the two-expression `assert` statement, then the second expression is evaluated, converted to a String representation and inserted into the stack trace to give you a little more debugging info. Finally, you saw why assertions should not be used to enforce arguments to `public` methods, and why *assert* expressions must not contain side effects!

TWO-MINUTE DRILL

Here are some of the key points from each certification objective in Chapter 4. You might want to *loop* through them several times, but only *if* you're interested in passing the exam.

Writing Code Using if and switch Statements

- ❑ The *if* statement must have all expressions enclosed by at least one pair of parentheses.
- ❑ The only legal argument to an *if* statement is a boolean, so the *if* test can be only on an expression that resolves to a boolean or a boolean variable.
- ❑ Watch out for boolean assignments (=) that can be mistaken for boolean equality (==) tests:

```
boolean x = false;
if (x = true) { } // an assignment, so x will always be true!
```

- ❑ Curly braces are optional for *if* blocks that have only one conditional statement. But watch out for misleading indentations.
- ❑ Switch statements can evaluate only the `byte`, `short`, `int`, and `char` data types. You can't say

```
long s = 30;
switch(s) { }
```

- ❑ The `case` argument must be a literal or final variable! You cannot have a *case* that includes a non-final variable, or a range of values.
- ❑ If the condition in a *switch* statement matches a *case* value, execution will run through all code in the *switch* following the matching `case` statement until a *break* or the end of the *switch* statement is encountered. In other words, *the matching case is just the entry point into the case block*, but unless there's a `break` statement, the matching *case* is not the only *case* code that runs.
- ❑ The `default` keyword should be used in a `switch` statement if you want to execute some code when none of the *case* values match the conditional value.
- ❑ The default block can be located anywhere in the *switch* block, so if no *case* matches, the `default` block will be entered, and if the *default* does not contain a *break*, then code will continue to execute (fall-through) to the end of the *switch* or until the `break` statement is encountered.

Writing Code Using Loops

- A *for* statement does not require any arguments in the declaration, but has three parts: declaration and/or initialization, boolean evaluation, and the iteration expression.
- If a variable is incremented or evaluated within a *for* loop, it must be declared before the loop, or within *for* loop declaration.
- A variable declared (not just initialized) within the *for* loop declaration cannot be accessed outside the *for* loop (in other words, code below the *for* loop won't be able to use the variable).
- You can initialize more than one variable in the first part of the *for* loop declaration; each variable initialization must be separated by a comma.
- You cannot use a number (old C-style language construct) or anything that does not evaluate to a boolean value as a condition for an *if* statement or looping construct. You can't, for example, say:
  ```
  if (x)
  ```
  unless `x` is a boolean variable.
- The *do-while* loop will enter the body of the loop at least once, even if the test condition is not met.

Using break and continue

- An unlabeled `break` statement will cause the current iteration of the innermost looping construct to stop and the next line of code following the loop to be executed.
- An unlabeled `continue` statement will cause the current iteration of the innermost loop to stop, and the condition of that loop to be checked, and if the condition is met, perform the loop again.
- If the `break` statement or the `continue` statement is labeled, it will cause similar action to occur on the labeled loop, not the innermost loop.
- If a `continue` statement is used in a *for* loop, the iteration statement is executed, and the condition is checked again.

Catching an Exception Using try and catch

- Exceptions come in two flavors: checked and unchecked.

- ❑ Checked exceptions include all subtypes of Exception, *excluding* classes that extend RuntimeException.
- ❑ Checked exceptions are subject to the *handle or declare* rule; any method that *might* throw a checked exception (including methods that invoke methods that can throw a checked exception) must either declare the exception using the `throws` keyword, or handle the exception with an appropriate *try/catch*.
- ❑ Subtypes of Error or RuntimeException are unchecked, so the compiler doesn't enforce the handle or declare rule. You're free to handle them, and you're free to declare them, but the compiler doesn't care one way or the other.
- ❑ If you use an optional `finally` block, it will always be invoked, regardless of whether an exception in the corresponding *try* is thrown or not, and regardless of whether a thrown exception is caught or not.
- ❑ The only exception to the *finally*-will-always-be-called rule is that a *finally* will *not* be invoked if the JVM shuts down. That could happen if code from the `try` or `catch` blocks calls `System.exit()`, in which case the JVM will not start your `finally` block.
- ❑ Just because `finally` is invoked does not mean it will complete. Code in the `finally` block could itself raise an exception or issue a `System.exit()`.
- ❑ Uncaught exceptions propagate back through the call stack, starting from the method where the exception is thrown and ending with either the first method that has a corresponding `catch` for that exception type or a JVM shutdown (which happens if the exception gets to `main()`, and `main()` is "ducking" the exception by declaring it).
- ❑ You can create your own exceptions, normally by extending Exception or one of its subtypes. Your exception will then be considered a checked exception, and the compiler will enforce the handle or declare rule for that exception.
- ❑ All `catch` blocks must be ordered from most specific to most general. For example, if you have a `catch` clause for both IOException and Exception, you must put the `catch` for IOException first (in order, top to bottom in your code). Otherwise, the IOException would be caught by `catch(Exception e)`, because a `catch` argument can catch the specified exception or any of its subtypes! The compiler will stop you from defining `catch` clauses that can never be reached (because it sees that the more specific exception will be caught first by the more general *catch*).

Working with the Assertion Mechanism

- ❑ Assertions give you a way to test your assumptions during development and debugging.
- ❑ Assertions are typically enabled during testing but disabled during deployment.
- ❑ You can use `assert` as a keyword (as of version 1.4) or an identifier, but not both together. To compile older code that uses *assert* as an identifier (for example, a method name), use the `-source 1.3` command-line flag to `javac`.
- ❑ Assertions are disabled at runtime by default. To enable them, use a command-line flag `-ea` or `-enableassertions`.
- ❑ You can selectively disable assertions using the `-da` or `-disableassertions` flag.
- ❑ If you enable or disable assertions using the flag without any arguments, you're enabling or disabling assertions in general. You can combine enabling and disabling switches to have assertions enabled for some classes and/or packages, but not others.
- ❑ You can enable or disable assertions in the system classes with the `-esa` or `-dsa` flags.
- ❑ You can enable and disable assertions on a class-by-class basis, using the following syntax:
  ```
  java -ea  -da:MyClass  TestClass
  ```
- ❑ You can enable and disable assertions on a package basis, and any package you specify also includes any subpackages (packages further down the directory hierarchy).
- ❑ Do *not* use assertions to validate arguments to *public* methods.
- ❑ Do *not* use assert expressions that cause side effects. Assertions aren't guaranteed to always run, so you don't want behavior that changes depending on whether assertions are enabled.
- ❑ *Do* use assertions—even in *public* methods—to validate that a particular code block will never be reached. You can use
  ```
  assert false;
  ```
  for code that should never be reached, so that an assertion error is thrown immediately if the *assert* statement is executed.
- ❑ Do not use *assert* expressions that can cause side effects.

SELF TEST

The following questions will help you measure your understanding of the material presented in this chapter. You've heard this before, and this time we really mean it: this chapter's material is crucial for the exam! Regardless of what the exam question is really testing, there's a good chance that flow control code will be part of the question. Expect to see loops and *if* tests used in questions throughout the entire range of exam objectives.

Flow Control (if and switch) (Sun Objective 2.1)

1. Given the following,

```
1.   public class Switch2 {
2.     final static short x = 2;
3.     public static int y = 0;
4.     public static void main(String [] args) {
5.       for (int z=0; z < 3; z++) {
6.         switch (z) {
7.           case y: System.out.print("0 ");
8.           case x-1: System.out.print("1 ");
9.           case x: System.out.print("2 ");
10.        }
11.      }
12.    }
13.  }
```

what is the result?

A. 0 1 2

B. 0 1 2 1 2 2

C. Compilation fails at line 7.

D. Compilation fails at line 8.

E. Compilation fails at line 9.

F. An exception is thrown at runtime.

2. Given the following,

```
1.   public class Switch2 {
2.     final static short x = 2;
3.     public static int y = 0;
4.     public static void main(String [] args) {
5.       for (int z=0; z < 3; z++) {
6.         switch (z) {
```

```
7.              case x: System.out.print("0 ");
8.              case x-1: System.out.print("1 ");
9.              case x-2: System.out.print("2 ");
10.          }
11.        }
12.      }
13.   }
```

what is the result?

A. 0 1 2

B. 0 1 2 1 2 2

C. 2 1 0 1 0 0

D. 2 1 2 0 1 2

E. Compilation fails at line 8.

F. Compilation fails at line 9.

3. Given the following,

```
1.    public class If1 {
2.      static boolean b;
3.      public static void main(String [] args) {
4.        short hand = 42;
5.        if ( hand < 50 & !b ) hand++;
6.        if ( hand > 50 ) ;
7.        else if ( hand > 40 ) {
8.           hand += 7;
9.           hand++;     }
10.         else
11.          --hand;
12.        System.out.println(hand);
13.      }
14.   }
```

what is the result?

A. 41

B. 42

C. 50

D. 51

E. Compiler fails at line 5.

F. Compiler fails at line 6.

4. Given the following,

```
public class Switch2 {
    final static short x = 2;
    public static int y = 0;
  public static void main(String [] args) {
    for (int z=0; z < 4; z++) {
      switch (z) {
        case x: System.out.print("0 ");
        default: System.out.print("def ");
        case x-1: System.out.print("1 ");  break;
        case x-2: System.out.print("2 ");
      }
    }
  }
}
```

what is the result?

A. `0 def 1`

B. `2 1 0 def 1`

C. `2 1 0 def def`

D. `2 1 def 0 def 1`

E. `2 1 2 0 def 1 2`

F. `2 1 0 def 1 def 1`

5. Given the following,

```
public class If2 {
  static boolean b1, b2;
  public static void main(String [] args) {
    int x = 0;
    if ( !b1 ) {
      if ( !b2 ) {
        b1 = true;
        x++;
        if ( 5 > 6 ) {
          x++;
        }
        if ( !b1 ) x = x + 10;
        else if ( b2 = true ) x = x + 100;
        else if ( b1 | b2 ) x = x + 1000;
      }
    }
```

```
            System.out.println(x);
        }
    }
```

what is the result?

A. 0

B. 1

C. 101

D. 111

E. 1001

F. 1101

Flow Control (loops) (Sun Objective 2.2)

6. Given the following,

```
1. public class While {
2.    public void loop() {
3.       int x= 0;
4.       while ( 1 ) {
5.          System.out.print("x plus one is " + (x + 1));
6.       }
7.    }
8. }
```

Which statement is true?

A. There is a syntax error on line 1.

B. There are syntax errors on lines 1 and 4.

C. There are syntax errors on lines 1, 4, and 5.

D. There is a syntax error on line 4.

E. There are syntax errors on lines 4 and 5.

F. There is a syntax error on line 5.

7. Given the following,

```
class For {
  public void test() {

      System.out.println("x = "+ x);
```

```
        }
      }
  }
```

and the following output,

```
x = 0
x = 1
```

which two lines of code (inserted independently) will cause this output? (Choose two.)

A. `for (int x = -1; x < 2; ++x) {`

B. `for (int x = 1; x < 3; ++x ) {`

C. `for (int x = 0; x > 2; ++x ) {`

D. `for (int x = 0; x < 2; x++ ) {`

E. `for (int x = 0; x < 2; ++x ) {`

8. Given the following,

```
public class Test {
  public static void main(String [] args) {
    int I = 1;
    do while ( I < 1 )
      System.out.print("I is " + I);
    while ( I > 1 ) ;
  }
}
```

what is the result?

A. `I is 1`

B. `I is 1 I is 1`

C. No output is produced.

D. Compilation error

E. `I is 1 I is 1 I is 1` in an infinite loop.

9. Given the following,

```
int I = 0;
outer:
  while (true) {
    I++;
    inner:
      for (int j = 0; j < 10; j++) {
```

```
            I += j;
            if (j == 3)
              continue inner;
            break outer;
          }
          continue outer;
      }
    System.out.println(I);


```

what is the result?

A. 1

B. 2

C. 3

D. 4

10. Given the following,

```
int I = 0;
label:
   if (I < 2) {
      System.out.print("I is " + I);
      I++;
      continue label;
   }
```

what is the result?

A. `I is 0`

B. `I is 0 I is 1`

C. Compilation fails.

D. None of the above

Exceptions (Sun Objectives 2.3 and 2.4)

11. Given the following,

```
System.out.print("Start ");
try {
   System.out.print("Hello world");
   throw new FileNotFoundException();
```

```
}
System.out.print(" Catch Here ");
catch(EOFException e) {
   System.out.print("End of file exception");
}
catch(FileNotFoundException e) {
   System.out.print("File not found");
}
```

and given that EOFException and FileNotFoundException are both subclasses of IOException, and further assuming this block of code is placed into a class, which statement is most true concerning this code?

A. The code will not compile.

B. Code output: `Start Hello world File Not Found.`

C. Code output: `Start Hello world End of file exception.`

D. Code output: `Start Hello world Catch Here File not found.`

12. Given the following,

```
public class MyProgram {
   public static void main(String args[]){
      try {
         System.out.print("Hello world ");
      }
      finally {
         System.out.println("Finally executing ");
      }
   }
}
```

what is the result?

A. Nothing. The program will not compile because no exceptions are specified.

B. Nothing. The program will not compile because no `catch` clauses are specified.

C. `Hello world.`

D. `Hello world Finally executing`

13. Given the following,

```
import java.io.*;
public class MyProgram {
   public static void main(String args[]){
      FileOutputStream out = null;
```

```
 5.        try {
 6.           out = new FileOutputStream("test.txt");
 7.           out.write(122);
 8.        }
 9.        catch(IOException io) {
10.            System.out.println("IO Error.");
11.        }
12.        finally {
13.           out.close();
14.        }
15.     }
16.  }
```

and given that all methods of class FileOutputStream, including `close()`, throw an IOException, which of these is true? (Choose one.)

A. This program will compile successfully.

B. This program fails to compile due to an error at line 4.

C. This program fails to compile due to an error at line 6.

D. This program fails to compile due to an error at line 9.

E. This program fails to compile due to an error at line 13.

14. Given the following,

```
public class MyProgram {
   public static void throwit() {
     throw new RuntimeException();
   }
   public static void main(String args[]){
      try {
         System.out.println("Hello world ");
         throwit();
         System.out.println("Done with try block ");
      }
      finally {
         System.out.println("Finally executing ");
      }
   }
}
```

which answer most closely indicates the behavior of the program?

A. The program will not compile.

B. The program will print `Hello world`, then will print that a RuntimeException has occurred, then will print `Done with try block`, and then will print `Finally executing`.

C. The program will print `Hello world`, then will print that a RuntimeException has occurred, and then will print `Finally executing`.

D. The program will print `Hello world`, then will print `Finally executing`, then will print that a `RuntimeException` has occurred.

15. Given the following,

```
public class RTExcept {
  public static void throwit () {
    System.out.print("throwit ");
    throw new RuntimeException();
  }
  public static void main(String [] args) {
    try {
      System.out.print("hello ");
      throwit();
    }
    catch (Exception re ) {
      System.out.print("caught ");
    }
    finally {
      System.out.print("finally ");
    }
    System.out.println("after ");
  }
}
```

what is the result?

A. `hello throwit caught`

B. Compilation fails

C. `hello throwit RuntimeException caught after`

D. `hello throwit RuntimeException`

E. `hello throwit caught finally after`

F. `hello throwit caught finally after RuntimeException`

Assertions (Sun Objectives 2.5 and 2.6)

16. Which of the following statements is true?

A. In an *assert* statement, the expression after the colon (:) can be *any* Java expression.

B. If a *switch* block has no default, adding an *assert* default is considered appropriate.

C. In an *assert* statement, if the expression after the colon (:) does not have a value, the assert's error message will be empty.

D. It is appropriate to handle assertion failures using a `catch` clause.

17. Which two of the following statements are true? (Choose two.)

A. It is sometimes good practice to throw an AssertionError explicitly.

B. It is good practice to place assertions where you think execution should never reach.

C. Private `getter()` and `setter()` methods should not use assertions to verify arguments.

D. If an AssertionError is thrown in a `try-catch` block, the `finally` block will be bypassed.

E. It is proper to handle assertion statement failures using a *catch* (`AssertionException ae`) block.

18. Given the following,

```
public class Test {
  public static int y;
  public static void foo(int x) {
    System.out.print("foo ");
    y = x;
  }
  public static int bar(int z) {
    System.out.print("bar ");
    return y = z;
  }
  public static void main(String [] args ) {
    int t = 0;
    assert t > 0 : bar(7);
    assert t > 1 : foo(8);
    System.out.println("done ");
  }
}
```

what is the result?

A. `bar`

B. `bar done`

C. `foo done`

D. `bar foo done`

E. Compilation fails

F. An error is thrown at runtime.

19. Which two of the following statements are true? (Choose two.)

A. If assertions are compiled into a source file, and if no flags are included at runtime, assertions will execute by default.

B. As of Java version 1.4, assertion statements are compiled by default.

C. With the proper use of runtime arguments, it is possible to instruct the VM to disable assertions for a certain class, and to enable assertions for a certain package, at the same time.

D. The following are all valid runtime assertion flags:
`-ea`, `-esa`, `-dsa`, `-enableassertions`,
`-disablesystemassertions`

E. When evaluating command-line arguments, the VM gives `-ea` flags precedence over `-da` flags.

20. Given the following,

```
public class Test2 {
  public static int x;
  public static int foo(int y) {
    return y * 2;
  }
  public static void main(String [] args) {
    int z = 5;
    assert z > 0;
    assert z > 2: foo(z);
    if ( z < 7 )
    assert z > 4;
    switch (z) {
      case 4: System.out.println("4 ");
      case 5: System.out.println("5 ");
      default: assert z < 10;
    }
    if ( z < 10 )
      assert z > 4: z++;
    System.out.println(z);
  }
}
```

which line is an example of an inappropriate use of assertions?

A. Line 8

B. Line 9

C. Line 11

D. Line 15

E. Line 18

SELF TEST ANSWERS

Flow Control (if and switch) (Sun Objective 2.1)

1. ☑ C. Case expressions must be constant expressions. Since *x* is marked `final`, lines 8 and 9 are legal; however *y* is not a `final` so the compiler will fail at line 7.
   ☒ A, B, D, E, and F, are incorrect based on the program logic described above.

2. ☑ D. The *case* expressions are all legal because `x` is marked `final`, which means the expressions can be evaluated at compile time. In the first iteration of the *for* loop `case x-2` matches, so 2 is printed. In the second iteration, `x-1` is matched so 1 and 2 are printed (remember, once a match is found all remaining statements are executed until a break statement is encountered). In the third iteration, `x` is matched so 0 1 and 2 are printed.
   ☒ A, B, C, E, **and** F are incorrect based on the program logic described above.

3. ☑ D. In Java, `boolean` instance variables are initialized to *false*, so the *if* test on line 5 is `true` and `hand` is incremented. Line 6 is legal syntax, a do nothing statement. The *else-if* is *true* so `hand` has 7 added to it and is then incremented.
   ☒ A, B, C, E, and F are incorrect based on the program logic described above.

4. ☑ F. When `z == 0 , case x-2` is matched. When `z == 1, case x-1` is matched and then the `break` occurs. When `z == 2, case x`, then `default`, then `x-1` are all matched. When `z == 3, default`, then `x-1` are matched. The rules for `default` are that it will fall through from above like any other `case` (for instance when `z == 2`), and that it will match when no other `cases` match (for instance when `z == 3`).
   ☒ A, B, C, D, and E are incorrect based on the program logic described above.

5. ☑ C. As instance variables, `b1` and `b2` are initialized to `false`. The *if* tests on lines 5 and 6 are successful so `b1` is set to `true` and `x` is incremented. The next *if* test to succeed is on line 13 (note that the code is not testing to see if `b2` is `true`, it is setting `b2` to be `true`). Since line 13 was successful, subsequent *else-if's* (line 14) will be skipped.
   ☒ A, B, D, E, and F are incorrect based on the program logic described above.

Flow Control (loops) (Sun Objective 2.2)

6. ☑ D. Using the integer 1 in the *while* statement, or any other looping or conditional construct for that matter, will result in a compiler error. This is old C syntax, not valid Java.
   ☒ A, B, C, E, and F are incorrect because line 1 is valid (Java is case sensitive so While is a valid class name). Line 5 is also valid because an equation may be placed in a String operation as shown.

7. ☑ D and E. It doesn't matter whether you preincrement or postincrement the variable in a *for* loop; it is always incremented after the loop executes and before the iteration expression is evaluated.
☒ A and B are incorrect because the first iteration of the loop must be zero. C is incorrect because the test will fail immediately and the *for* loop will not be entered.

8. ☑ C. There are two different looping constructs in this problem. The first is a *do-while* loop and the second is a *while* loop, nested inside the *do-while.* The body of the *do-while* is only a single statement—brackets are not needed. You are assured that the *while* expression will be evaluated at least once, followed by an evaluation of the *do-while* expression. Both expressions are *false* and no output is produced.
☒ A, B, D, and E are incorrect based on the program logic described above.

9. ☑ A. The program flows as follows: `I` will be incremented after the *while* loop is entered, then `I` will be incremented (by zero) when the *for* loop is entered. The *if* statement evaluates to *false,* and the `continue` statement is never reached. The `break` statement tells the JVM to break out of the *outer* loop, at which point `I` is printed and the fragment is done.
☒ B, C, and D are incorrect based on the program logic described above.

10. ☑ C. The code will not compile because a `continue` statement can only occur in a looping construct. If this syntax were legal, the combination of the `continue` and the *if* statements would create a kludgey kind of loop, but the compiler will force you to write cleaner code than this.
☒ A, B, and D are incorrect based on the program logic described above.

Exceptions (Sun Objectives 2.3 and 2.4)

11. ☑ A. Line 6 will cause a compiler error. The only legal statements after `try` blocks are either `catch` or `finally` statements.
☒ B, C, and D are incorrect based on the program logic described above. If line 6 was removed, the code would compile and the correct answer would be **B**.

12. ☑ D. `Finally` clauses are always executed. The program will first execute the `try` block, printing `Hello world`, and will then execute the `finally` block, printing `Finally executing`.
☒ A, B, and C are incorrect based on the program logic described above. Remember that either a `catch` or a `finally` statement must follow a `try`. Since the *finally* is present, the *catch* is not required.

13. ☑ E. Any method (in this case, the `main()` method) that throws a checked exception (in this case, `out.close()`) must be called within a `try` clause, or the method must declare that it throws the exception. Either `main()` must declare that it throws an exception, or the call to `out.close()` in the `finally` block must fall inside a (in this case nested) `try-catch` block.
☒ A, B, C, and D are incorrect based on the program logic described above.

14. ☑ D. Once the program throws a RuntimeException (in the `throwit()` method) that is not caught, the `finally` block will be executed and the program will be terminated. If a method does not handle an exception, the `finally` block is executed before the exception is propagated.
☒ A, B, and C are incorrect based on the program logic described above.

15. ☑ E. The `main()` method properly catches and handles the RuntimeException in the `catch` block, *finally* runs (as it always does), and then the code returns to normal.
☒ A, B, C, D, and F are incorrect based on the program logic described above. Remember that properly handled exceptions do not cause the program to stop executing.

Assertions (Sun Objectives 2.5 and 2.6)

16. ☑ B. Adding an assertion statement to a `switch` statement that previously had no default case is considered an excellent use of the assert mechanism.
☒ A is incorrect because only Java expressions that return a value can be used. For instance, a method that returns `void` is illegal. C is incorrect because the expression after the colon must have a value. D is incorrect because assertions throw errors and not exceptions, and assertion errors do cause program termination and should not be handled.

17. ☑ A and B. A is correct because it is sometimes advisable to thrown an assertion error even if assertions have been disabled. B is correct. One of the most common uses of `assert` statements in debugging is to verify that locations in code that have been designed to be unreachable are in fact never reached.
☒ C is incorrect because it is considered appropriate to check argument values in *private* methods using assertions. D is incorrect; *finally* is never bypassed. E is incorrect because AssertionErrors should never be handled.

18. ☑ E. The `foo()` method returns `void`. It is a perfectly acceptable method, but because it returns `void` it cannot be used in an *assert* statement, so line 14 will not compile.
☒ A, B, C, D, and F are incorrect based on the program logic described above.

19. ☑ C and **D. C** is true because multiple VM flags can be used on a single invocation of a Java program. **D** is true, these are all valid flags for the VM.
☒ A is incorrect because at runtime assertions are ignored by default. **B** is incorrect because as of Java 1.4 you must add the argument `-source 1.4` to the command line if you want the compiler to compile assertion statements. **E** is incorrect because the VM evaluates all assertion flags left to right.

20. ☑ E. *Assert* statements should not cause side effects. Line 18 changes the value of `z` if the assert statement is *false*.
☒ A is fine; a second expression in an *assert* statement is not required. **B** is fine because it is perfectly acceptable to call a method with the second expression of an *assert* statement. **C** is fine because it is proper to call an *assert* statement conditionally. **D** is fine because it is considered good form to add a default *assert* statement to *switch* blocks that have no default case.

EXERCISE ANSWERS

Exercise 4.1: Creating a switch-case Statement

The code should look something like this:

```
char temp = 'c';
switch(temp) {
   case 'a': {
      System.out.println("A");
      break;
   }
   case 'b': {
      System.out.println("B");
      break;
   }
   case 'c':
      System.out.println("C");
      break;
   default:
      System.out.println("default");
}
```

Exercise 4-2: Creating a Labeled while Loop

The code should look something like this:

```
class LoopTest {
   public static void main(String [] args) {
      int age = 12;
      outer:
      while(age < 21) {
         age += 1;
         if(age == 16) {
            System.out.println("Obtain driver's license");
            continue outer;
         }
         System.out.println("Another year.");
      }
   }
}
```

Exercise 4-3: Propagating and Catching an Exception

The code should look something like this:

```
class Propagate {
   public static void main(String [] args) {
      try {
         System.out.println(reverse("Hello"));
      }
      catch (Exception e) {
         System.out.println("The string was blank");
      }
      finally {
         System.out.println("All done!");
      }
   }
   public static String reverse(String s) throws Exception {
      if (s.length() == 0 ) {
         throw new Exception();
      }
      String reverseStr = "";
      for(int i=s.length()-1;i>=0;--i) {
         reverseStr += s.charAt(i);
      }
      return reverseStr;
   }
}
```

Exercise 4-4: Creating an Exception

The code should look something like this:

```
class BadFoodException extends Exception {}
class MyException {
   public static void main(String [] args) {
     try {
       checkFood(args[0]);
     } catch(BadFoodException e) {
        e. printStackTrace();
     }
   }
   public static void checkWord(String s) {
      String [] badFoods = {"broccoli","brussel sprouts","sardines"};
      for(int i=0;i<badFoods.length;++i) {
         if (s.equals(badFoods[i]))
            throw new BadWFoodException();
      }
      System.out.println(s + " is ok with me.");
   }
}
```

5

Object Orientation, Overloading and Overriding, Constructors, and Return Types

CERTIFICATION OBJECTIVES

- Benefits of Encapsulation
- Overridden and Overloaded Methods
- Constructors and Instantiation
- Legal Return Types
- ✓ Two-Minute Drill
- Q&A Self Test

The objectives in this section revolve (mostly) around object-oriented (OO) programming including encapsulation, inheritance, and polymorphism. For the exam, you need to know whether a code fragment is correctly or incorrectly implementing some of the key OO features supported in Java. You also need to recognize the difference between overloaded and overridden methods, and be able to spot correct and incorrect implementations of both.

Because this book focuses on your passing the programmer's exam, only the critical exam-specific aspects of OO software will be covered here. If you're not already well versed in OO concepts, you could (and should) study a dozen books on the subject of OO development to get a broader and deeper understanding of both the benefits and the techniques for analysis, design, and implementation. But for passing the exam, the relevant concepts and rules you need to know are covered here. (That's a disclaimer, because we can't say you'll be a "complete OO being" by reading this chapter.) (We can say, however, that your golf swing will improve.)

We think you'll find this chapter a nice treat after slogging your way through the technical (and picky) details of the previous chapters. Object-oriented programming is a festive topic, so may we suggest you don the appropriate clothing—say, a Hawaiian shirt and a party hat. Grab a margarita (if you're new to OO, maybe nonalcoholic is best) and let's have some fun!

(OK so maybe we exaggerated a *little* about the whole party aspect. Still, you'll find this section both smaller and less detailed than the previous four.) (And this time we really mean it.)

CERTIFICATION OBJECTIVE

Benefits of Encapsulation (Exam Objective 6.1)

State the benefits of encapsulation in object-oriented design and write code that implements tightly encapsulated classes and the relationships IS-A and HAS-A.

Imagine you wrote the code for a class, and another dozen programmers from your company all wrote programs that used your class. Now imagine that you didn't like the way the class behaved, because some of its instance variables were being set (by the other programmers from within their code) to values you hadn't anticipated. *Their* code brought out errors in *your* code. (Relax, this is just hypothetical...) Well, it *is* a Java program, so you should be able just to ship out a newer version of the class, which they could replace in their programs without changing any of their own code.

This scenario highlights two of the promises/benefits of OO: flexibility and maintainability. But those benefits don't come automatically. You have to *do* something. You have to write your classes and code in a way that *supports* flexibility and maintainability. So *what* if Java supports OO? It can't design your code for you. For example, imagine if you (not the *real* you, but the *hypothetical-not-as-good-a-programmer you*) made your class with `public` instance variables, and those other programmers were setting the instance variables directly, as the following code demonstrates:

```
public class BadOO {
   public int size;
   public int weight;
   ...
}
public class ExploitBadOO {
   public static void main (String [] args) {
      BadOO b = new BadOO();
      b.size = -5; // Legal but bad!!
   }
}
```

And now you're in trouble. How are you going to change the class in a way that lets you handle the issues that come up when somebody changes the *size* variable to a value that causes problems? Your only choice is to go back in and write method code for adjusting *size* (a `setSize(int a)` method, for example), and then protect the *size* variable with, say, a `private` access modifier. But as soon as you make that change to *your* code, *you break everyone else's!*

The ability to make changes in your implementation code *without* breaking the code of others who use your code is a key benefit of encapsulation. *You want to hide implementation details behind a* `public` *programming interface.* By interface, we mean the set of accessible methods your code makes available for other code to call—in other words, *your code's API.* By hiding implementation details, you can rework your method code (perhaps also altering the way variables are used by your class) without forcing a change in the code that calls your changed method.

If you want maintainability, flexibility, and extensibility (and of course, you do), your design must include encapsulation. How do you do that?

- Keep your instance variables protected (with an access modifier, often `private`).
- Make *public* accessor methods, and force calling code to use those methods.
- For the methods, use the JavaBeans naming convention of set<someProperty> and get<someProperty>.

Figure 5-1 illustrates the idea that encapsulation forces callers of our code to go through methods rather than accessing variables directly.

We call the access methods *getters and setters* although some prefer the fancier terms (more impressive at dinner parties) *accessors and mutators.* Personally, we don't

FIGURE 5-1 The nature of encapsulation

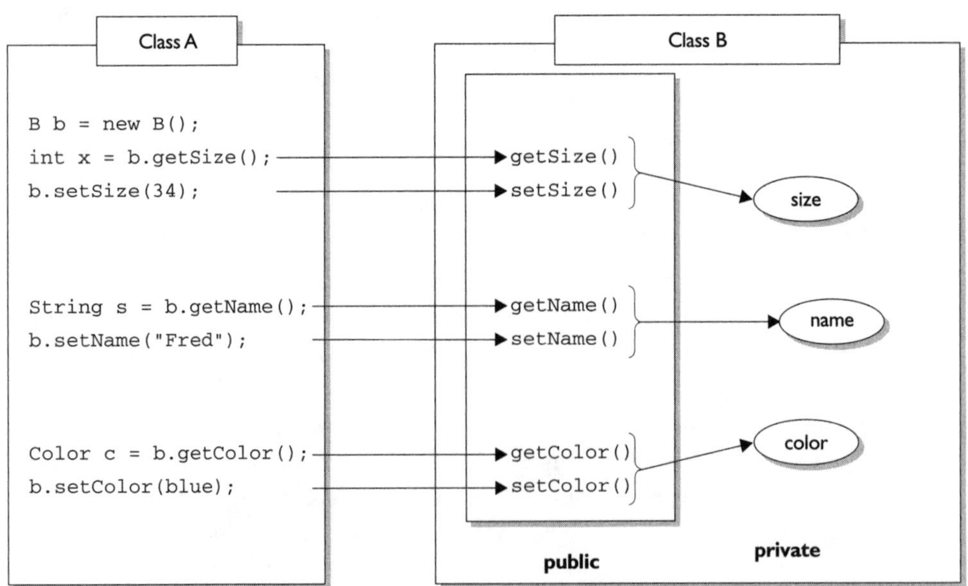

Class A cannot access Class B instance variable data without going through getter and setter methods. Data is marked private; only the accessor methods are public.

like the word *mutate.* Regardless of what you call them, they're methods that others must go through in order to access your instance variables. They look simple, and you've probably been using them forever:

```
public class Box {
   // protect the instance variable; only an instance
   // of Box can access it
   private int size;
   // Provide public getters and setters
   public int getSize() {
      return size;
   }
   public void setSize(int newSize) {
      size = newSize;
   }
}
```

Wait a minute…how useful is the previous code? It doesn't even do any validation or processing. What benefit can there be from having getters and setters that add no additional functionality? The point is, *you can change your mind later*, and add more code to your methods without breaking your API. Even if you don't think you really need validation or processing of the data, good OO design dictates that you plan for the future. To be safe, *force calling code to go through your methods rather than going directly to instance variables.* Always. Then you're free to rework your method implementations later, without risking the wrath of those dozen programmers who know where you live. And have been doing Tae-bo. And drink way too much Mountain Dew.

exam Watch

Look out for code that appears to be asking about the behavior of a method, when the problem is actually a lack of encapsulation. Look at the following example, and see if you can figure out what's going on:

```
class Foo {
   public int left = 9;
   public int right = 3;
   public void setLeft(int leftNum) {
      left = leftNum;
      right = leftNum/3;
   }
 // lots of complex test code here
}
```

Now consider this question: *Is the value of right always going to be one-third the value of left?* ***It looks like it will, until you realize that users of the Foo class don't*** *need* ***to use the*** `setLeft()` ***method! They can simply go straight to the instance variables and change them to any arbitrary*** *int* ***value.***

IS-A and HAS-A Relationships

For the exam you need to be able to look at code and determine whether the code demonstrates an IS-A or HAS-A relationship. The rules are simple, so this should be one of the few areas where answering the questions correctly is almost a no-brainer. (Well, at least it *would* have been a no-brainer if we (exam creators) hadn't tried our best to obfuscate the real problem.) (If you don't know the word "obfuscate", stop and look it up, then write and tell us what it means.)

IS-A

In OO, the concept of IS-A is based on inheritance. IS-A is a way of saying, "this thing *is a* type of that thing." For example, a Mustang is a type of horse, so in OO terms we can say, "Mustang IS-A Horse." Subaru IS-A Car. Broccoli IS-A Vegetable (not a very fun one, but it still counts). You express the IS-A relationship in Java through the keyword `extends`:

```
public class Car {
  // Cool Car code goes here
}

public class Subaru extends Car {
   // Important Subaru-specific stuff goes here
   // Don't forget Subaru inherits accessible Car members
}
```

A Car is a type of Vehicle, so the inheritance tree might start from the Vehicle class as follows:

```
public class Vehicle { … }
public class Car extends Vehicle { … }
public class Subaru extends Car { … }
```

In OO terms, you can say the following:

- Vehicle is the superclass of Car.
- Car is the subclass of Vehicle.

- Car is the superclass of Subaru.
- Subaru is the subclass of Vehicle.
- Car inherits from Vehicle.
- Subaru inherits from Car.
- Subaru inherits from Vehicle.
- Subaru is derived from Car.
- Car is derived from Vehicle.
- Subaru is derived from Vehicle.
- Subaru is a subtype of Car.
- Subaru is a subtype of Vehicle.

Returning to our IS-A relationship, the following statements are true:

> "Car extends Vehicle" means *"Car IS-A Vehicle."*
> "Subaru extends Car" means *"Subaru IS-A Car."*

And we can also say:

> "Subaru IS-A Vehicle" because a class is said to be "a type of" anything further up in its inheritance tree. If Foo `instanceof` Bar, then class Foo IS-A Bar, even if Foo doesn't directly extend Bar, but instead extends some other class that is a subclass of Bar. Figure 5-2 illustrates the inheritance tree for Vehicle, Car, and Subaru. The arrows move from the subclass to the superclass. In other words, a class' arrow points toward the class it extends from.

FIGURE 5-2

Inheritance tree for Vehicle, Car, and Subaru

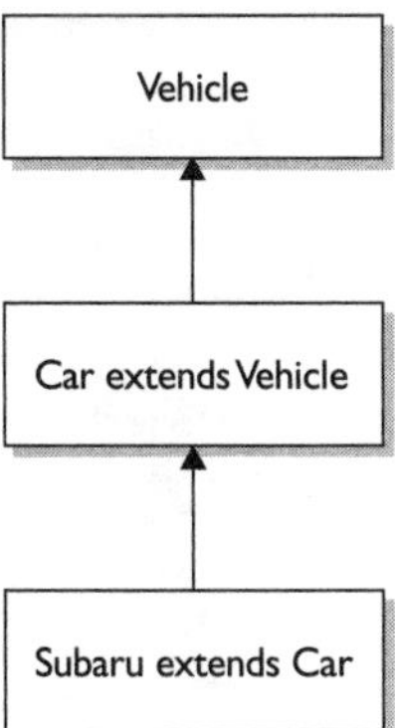

HAS-A

HAS-A relationships are based on usage, rather than inheritance. In other words, class A HAS-A B if *code in class A* has a *reference to an instance of class B.* For example, you can say the following,

A Horse IS-A Animal. A Horse HAS-A Halter.

and the code looks like this:

```
public class Animal { }
public class Horse extends Animal {
   private Halter myHalter;
}
```

In the preceding code, the Horse class has an instance variable of type Halter, so you can say that "Horse HAS-A Halter." In other words, *Horse has a reference to a Halter.* Horse code can use that Halter reference to invoke methods on the Halter, and get Halter behavior without having Halter-related code (methods) in the Horse class itself. Figure 5-3 illustrates the HAS-A relationship between Horse and Halter.

HAS-A relationships allow you to design classes that follow good OO practices by not having monolithic classes that do a gazillion different things. Classes (and thus the *objects* instantiated from those classes) should be specialists. The more specialized the class, the more likely it is that you can reuse the class in other applications. If you put all the Halter-related code directly into the Horse class, you'll end up duplicating code in the Cow class, Sheep class, UnpaidIntern class, and any other class that might need Halter behavior. By keeping the Halter code in a separate, specialized Halter class, you have the chance to reuse the Halter class in multiple applications.

FIGURE 5-3

HAS-A relationship between Horse and Halter

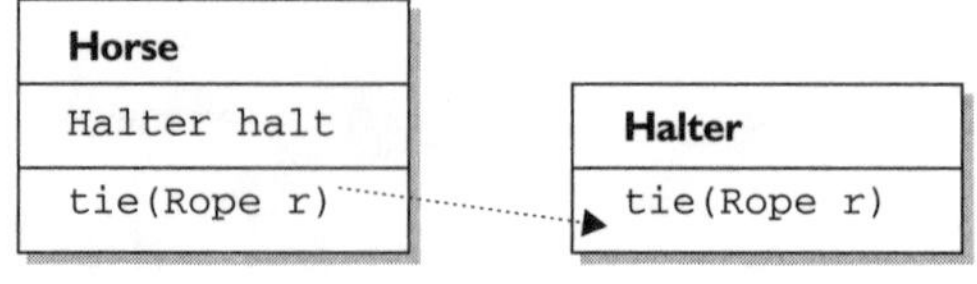

Horse class has a Halter, because Horse declares an instance variable of type Halter. When code invokes `tie()` on a Horse instance, the Horse invokes `tie()` on the Horse object's Halter instance variable.

Users of the Horse class (that is, code that calls methods on a Horse instance), *think* that the Horse class has Halter behavior. The Horse class might have a `tie(LeadRope rope)` method, for example. Users of the Horse class should never have to know that when they invoke the `tie()` method, the Horse object turns around and delegates the call to its Halter class by invoking `myHalter.tie(rope)`. The scenario just described might look like this:

```
public class Horse extends Animal {
   private Halter myHalter;
   public void tie(LeadRope rope) {
      myHalter.tie(rope);  // Delegate tie behavior to the
                           // Halter object
   }
}
public class Halter {
   public void tie(LeadRope aRope) {
      // Do the actual tie work here
   }
}
```

In OO, we don't want callers to worry about which class or which object is actually doing the real work. To make that happen, the Horse class hides implementation details from Horse users. Horse users ask the Horse object to do things (in this case, tie itself up), and the Horse will either do it or, as in this example, ask something else to do it. To the caller, though, it always appears that *the Horse object takes care of itself.* Users of a Horse should not even need to know that there *is* such a thing as a Halter class.

Now that we've looked at some of the OO characteristics, here are some possible scenario questions and their solutions.

SCENARIO & SOLUTION	
What benefits do you gain from encapsulation?	Ease of code maintenance, extensibility, and code clarity.
What is the object-oriented relationship between a tree and an oak?	An IS-A relationship: Oak IS-A Tree.
What is the object-oriented relationship between a city and a road?	A HAS-A relationship: City HAS-A Road.

FROM THE CLASSROOM

Object-Oriented Design

IS-A and HAS-A relationships and encapsulation are just the tip of the iceberg when it comes to object-oriented design. Many books and graduate theses have been dedicated to this topic. The reason for the emphasis on proper design is simple: money. The cost to deliver a software application has been estimated to be as much as 10 times more expensive for poorly designed programs. Having seen the ramifications of poor designs, I can assure you that this estimate is not far-fetched.

Even the best object-oriented designers make mistakes. It is difficult to visualize the relationships between hundreds, or even thousands, of classes. When mistakes are discovered during the implementation (code writing) phase of a project, the amount of code that has to be rewritten can sometimes cause programming teams to start over from scratch.

The software industry has evolved to aid the designer. Visual object modeling languages, such as the Unified Modeling Language (UML), allow designers to design and easily modify classes without having to write code first, because object-oriented components are represented graphically. This allows the designer to create a map of the class relationships and helps them recognize errors before coding begins. Another recent innovation in object-oriented design is design patterns. Designers noticed that many object-oriented designs apply consistently from project to project, and that it was useful to apply the same designs because it reduced the potential to introduce new design errors. Object-oriented designers then started to share these designs with each other. Now, there are many catalogs of these design patterns both on the Internet and in book form.

Although passing the Java certification exam does not require you to understand object-oriented design this thoroughly, hopefully this background information will help you better appreciate why the test writers chose to include encapsulation and *is a* and *has a* relationships on the exam.

—Jonathan Meeks, Sun Certified Java Programmer

CERTIFICATION OBJECTIVE

Overridden and Overloaded Methods (Exam Objective 6.2)

Write code to invoke overridden or overloaded methods and parental or overloaded constructors, and describe the effect of invoking these methods.

Methods can be overloaded or overridden, but constructors can be only overloaded. *Overloaded* methods and constructors let you use the same method name (or constructor) but with different argument lists. *Overriding* lets you redefine a method in a subclass, when you need new subclass-specific behavior.

Overridden Methods

Anytime you have a class that inherits a method from a superclass, you have the opportunity to override the method (unless, as you learned earlier, the method is marked `final`). The key benefit of overriding is the ability to define behavior that's specific to a particular subclass type. The following example demonstrates a Horse subclass of Animal overriding the Animal version of the `eat()` method:

```
public class Animal {
   public void eat() {
      System.out.println("Generic Animal Eating Generically");
   }
}
class Horse extends Animal {
   public void eat() {
       System.out.println("Horse eating hay, oats, and horse treats");
   }
}
```

For abstract methods you inherit from a superclass, you have no choice. You must implement the method in the subclass unless the subclass is *also* abstract. Abstract methods are said to be *implemented* by the concrete subclass, but this is virtually the same as saying that the concrete subclass *overrides* the abstract methods of the superclass. So you should *think of abstract methods as methods you're forced to override.*

The Animal class creator might have decided that for the purposes of polymorphism, all Animal subtypes should have an `eat()` method defined in a unique, specific way. Polymorphically, when someone has an Animal reference that refers not to an

Animal instance, but to an Animal *subclass* instance, the caller should be able to invoke `eat()` on the Animal reference, but the actual runtime object (say, a Horse instance) will run its own specific `eat()` method. Marking the `eat()` method abstract is the Animal programmer's way of saying to all subclass developers, "It doesn't make any sense for your new subtype to use a generic `eat()` method, so you have to come up with your own `eat()` method implementation!" An example of using polymorphism looks like this:

```
public class TestAnimals {
   public static void main (String [] args) {
      Animal a = new Animal();
      Animal b = new Horse();  //Animal ref, but a Horse object
      a.eat(); // Runs the Animal version of eat()
      b.eat(); // Runs the Horse version of eat()
   }
}
class Animal {
   public void eat() {
      System.out.println("Generic Animal Eating Generically");
   }
}
class Horse extends Animal {
   public void eat() {
       System.out.println("Horse eating hay, oats, and horse treats");
   }
   public void buck() { }
}
```

In the preceding code, the test class uses an Animal reference to invoke a method on a Horse object. Remember, the compiler will allow only methods in class Animal to be invoked when using a reference to an Animal. The following would not be legal given the preceding code:

```
Animal c = new Horse();
c.buck();   // Can't invoke buck();
            // Animal class doesn't have that method
```

The compiler looks only at the *reference* type, not the *instance* type. Polymorphism lets you use a more abstract supertype (including an interface) reference to refer to one of its subtypes (including interface implementers).

The overriding method *cannot have a more restrictive access modifier* than the method being overridden (for example, you can't override a method marked `public` and make it `protected`). Think about it: if the Animal class advertises a public `eat()`

method and someone has an Animal reference (in other words, a reference declared as type Animal), that someone will assume it's safe to call `eat()` on the Animal reference regardless of the actual instance that the Animal reference is referring to. If a subclass were allowed to sneak in and change the access modifier on the overriding method, then suddenly at runtime—when the JVM invokes the true *object's* (Horse) version of the method rather than the *reference type's* (Animal) version—the program would die a horrible death. (Not to mention the emotional distress for the one who was betrayed by the rogue subclass.) Let's modify the polymorphic example we saw earlier:

```
public class TestAnimals {
   public static void main (String [] args) {
      Animal a = new Animal();
      Animal b = new Horse();  //Animal ref, but a Horse object
      a.eat(); // Runs the Animal version of eat()
      b.eat(); // Runs the Horse version of eat()
   }
}
class Animal {
   public void eat() {
      System.out.println("Generic Animal Eating Generically");
   }
}
class Horse extends Animal {
   private void eat() {
       System.out.println("Horse eating hay, oats,
                          and horse treats");
   }
}
```

If this code were allowed to compile (which it's not, by the way—the compiler wants you to know that it didn't just fall off the turnip truck), the following would fail at runtime:

```
Animal b = new Horse();  // Animal ref, but a Horse
                         // object , so far so good
b.eat();                 // Meltdown!
```

The variable *b* is of type Animal, which has a `public eat()` method. But remember that at runtime, Java uses *virtual method invocation* to dynamically select the *actual* version of the method that will run, based on the *actual* instance. An Animal reference can always refer to a Horse instance, because Horse IS-A(n) Animal. What makes that superclass reference to a subclass instance possible is that *the subclass is guaranteed to be able to do everything the superclass can do.* Whether the Horse instance overrides the inherited methods of Animal or simply inherits them, anyone with an Animal reference to a Horse instance is free to call all accessible Animal methods. For that reason, an overriding method must fulfill the contract of the superclass.

The rules for overriding a method are as follows:

- The *argument list must exactly match* that of the overridden method.
- The *return type must exactly match* that of the overridden method.
- The *access level must not be more restrictive* than that of the overridden method.
- The *access level can be less restrictive* than that of the overridden method.
- The overriding method *must not throw new or broader checked exceptions* than those declared by the overridden method. For example, a method that declares a FileNotFoundException cannot be overridden by a method that declares a SQLException, Exception, or any other non-runtime exception unless it's a subclass of FileNotFoundException.
- The overriding method *can throw narrower or fewer exceptions.* Just because an overridden method "takes risks" doesn't mean that the overriding subclass' exception takes the same risks. Bottom line: An overriding method doesn't have to declare any exceptions that it will never throw, regardless of what the overridden method declares.
- You *cannot override a method marked* `final`.
- *If a method can't be inherited, you cannot override it.* For example, the following code is not legal:

```
public class TestAnimals {
   public static void main (String [] args) {
      Horse h =  new Horse();
      h.eat(); // Not  legal because Horse didn't inherit eat()
   }
}
class Animal {
   private void eat() {
      System.out.println("Generic Animal Eating Generically");
   }
}
class Horse extends Animal { }
```

Invoking a Superclass Version of an Overridden Method

Often, you'll want to take advantage of some of the code in the superclass version of a method, yet still override it to provide some additional specific behavior. It's like saying, "Run the superclass version of the method, then come back down here and finish with my subclass additional method code." (Note that there's no requirement that the superclass version run before the subclass code.) It's easy to do in code using the keyword `super` as follows:

```
public class Animal {

   public void eat() { }
   public void printYourself() {
      // Useful printing code goes here
   }
}
class Horse extends Animal {
   public void printYourself() {
      // Take advantage of Animal code, then add some more
      super.printYourself();  // Invoke the superclass
                              // (Animal) code
                              // Then come back and do
                              // additional Horse-specific
                              // print work here
   }
}
```

Examples of Legal and Illegal Method Overrides

Let's take a look at overriding the `eat()` method of Animal:

```
public class Animal {
   public void eat() { }
}
```

Table 5-1 lists examples of illegal overrides of the Animal `eat()` method, given the preceding version of the Animal class.

Overloaded Methods

Overloaded methods let you reuse the same method name in a class, but with different arguments (and optionally, a different return type). Overloading a method often means you're being a little nicer to those who call your methods, because *your* code

TABLE 5-1 Examples of Illegal Overrides

Illegal Override Code	Problem with the Code
`private void eat() { }`	Access modifier is more restrictive
`public void eat() throws IOException { }`	Declares a checked exception not declared by superclass version
`public void eat(String food) { }`	A legal overload, not an override, because the argument list changed
`public String eat() { }`	Not an override because of the return type, but not an overload either because there's no change in the argument list

takes on the burden of coping with different argument types rather than forcing the *caller* to do conversions prior to invoking your method. The rules are simple:

- Overloaded methods *must* change the argument list.
- Overloaded methods *can* change the return type.
- Overloaded methods *can* change the access modifier.
- Overloaded methods *can* declare new or broader checked exceptions.
- A method *can* be overloaded in the same class or in a subclass.

Legal Overloads

Let's look at a method we want to overload:

```
public void changeSize(int size, String name, float pattern) { }
```

The following methods are *legal overloads* of the `changeSize()` method:

```
public void changeSize(int size, String name) { }
public int changeSize(int size, float pattern) { }
public void changeSize(float pattern, String name)
                          throws IOException { }
```

exam watch

Be careful to recognize when a method is overloaded rather than overridden. You might see a method that appears to be violating a rule for overriding, but which is actually a legal overload, as follows:

```
public class Foo {
   public void doStuff(int y, String s) { }
   public void moreThings(int x) { }
}
class Bar extends Foo {
   public void doStuff(int y, float s) throws IOException { }
}
```

You might be tempted to see the IOException as the problem, seeing that the overridden `doStuff()` method doesn't declare an exception, and knowing that IOException is checked by the compiler. But the `doStuff()` method is* not *overridden at all! Subclass Bar* overloads *the `doStuff()` method, by varying the argument list, so the IOException is fine.

Invoking Overloaded Methods

When a method is invoked, more than one method of the same name might exist for the object type you're invoking a method on. For example, the Horse class might have three methods with the same name but with different argument lists, which means the method is overloaded.

Deciding which of the matching methods to invoke is based on the arguments. If you invoke the method with a String argument, the overloaded version that takes a String is called. If you invoke a method of the same name but pass it a *float*, the overloaded version that takes a *float* will run. If you invoke the method of the same name but pass it a Foo object, and there isn't an overloaded version that takes a Foo, then the compiler will complain that it can't find a match. The following are examples of invoking overloaded methods:

```
class Adder {
   public int addThem(int x, int y) {
      return x + y;
   }

   // Overload the addThem method to add doubles instead of ints
   public double addThem(double x, double y) {
      return x + y;
   }
}
// From another class, invoke the addThem() method
public class TestAdder {
   public static void main (String [] args) {
```

```
        Adder a = new Adder();
        int b = 27;
        int c = 3;
        int result = a.addThem(b,c); // Which addThem is invoked?
        double doubleResult = a.addThem(22.5,89.36);
        // Which addThem?
    }
}
```

In the preceding TestAdder code, the first call to `a.addThem(b,c)` passes two *ints* to the method, so the first version of `addThem()`—the overloaded version that takes two *int* arguments—is called. The second call to `a.addThem(22.5, 89.36)` passes two *doubles* to the method, so the second version of `addThem()`—the overloaded version that takes two *double* arguments—is called.

Invoking overloaded methods that take object references rather than primitives is a little more interesting. Say you have an overloaded method such that one version takes an Animal and one takes a Horse (subclass of Animal). If you pass a Horse object in the method invocation, you'll invoke the overloaded version that takes a Horse. Or so it looks at first glance:

```
class Animal { }
class Horse extends Animal { }
class UseAnimals {
    public void doStuff(Animal a) {
        System.out.println("In the Animal version");
    }
    public void doStuff(Horse h) {
        System.out.println("In the Horse version");
    }
    public static void main (String [] args) {
        UseAnimals ua = new UseAnimals();
        Animal animalObj = new Animal();
        Horse horseObj = new Horse();
        ua.doStuff(animalObj);
        ua.doStuff(horseObj);
    }
}
```

The output is what you expect:

```
in the Animal version
in the Horse version
```

But what if you use an Animal reference to a Horse object?

```
Animal animalRefToHorse = new Horse();
 ua.doStuff(animalRefToHorse);
```

Which of the overloaded versions is invoked? You might want to say, "The one that takes a Horse, since it's a Horse object at runtime that's being passed to the method." But that's not how it works. The preceding code would actually print

```
in the Animal version
```

Even though the actual object at runtime is a Horse and not an Animal, the choice of which *overloaded* method to call is not dynamically decided at runtime. Just remember, *the reference type (not the object type) determines which overloaded method is invoked!* To summarize, which *overridden* method to call (in other words, from which class in the inheritance tree) is decided at *runtime* based on *object* type, but which *overloaded* version of the method to call is based on the *reference* type passed at *compile* time.

Polymorphism in Overloaded and Overridden Methods How does polymorphism work with overloaded methods? From what we just looked at, it doesn't appear that polymorphism matters when a method is *overloaded*. If you pass an Animal reference, the overloaded method that takes an Animal will be invoked, *even if the actual object passed is a Horse.* Once the Horse masquerading as Animal gets *in* to the method, however, the Horse object is still a Horse despite being passed into a method expecting an Animal. So it's true that polymorphism doesn't determine which *overloaded* version is called; polymorphism does come into play when the decision is about which *overridden* version of a method is called. But sometimes, a method is both overloaded *and* overridden. Imagine the Animal and Horse classes look like this:

```
public class Animal {
   public void eat() {
      System.out.println("Generic Animal Eating Generically");
```

```
    }
}
public class Horse extends Animal {
   public void eat() {
       System.out.println("Horse eating hay ");
   }
   public void eat(String s) {
      System.out.println("Horse eating " + s);
   }
}
```

Notice that the Horse class has both overloaded *and* overridden the `eat()` method. Table 5-2 shows which version of the three `eat()` methods will run depending on how they are invoked.

TABLE 5-2 Overloaded and Overridden Method Invocations

Method Invocation Code	Result
`Animal a = new Animal();` `a.eat();`	`Generic Animal Eating Generically`
`Horse h = new Horse();` `h.eat();`	`Horse eating hay`
`Animal ah = new` **`Horse`**`();` `ah.eat();`	`Horse eating hay` Polymorphism works—the actual object type (Horse), not the reference type (Animal), is used to determine which `eat()` is called.
`Horse he = new Horse();` `he.eat("Apples");`	`Horse eating Apples` The overloaded `eat(String s)` method is invoked.
`Animal a2 = new Animal();` `a2.eat("treats");`	Compiler error! Compiler sees that Animal class doesn't have an `eat()` method that takes a String.
`Animal ah2 = new` **`Horse`**`();` `ah2.eat("Carrots");`	Compiler error! Compiler *still* looks only at the reference type, and sees that Animal doesn't have an `eat()` method that takes a string. Compiler doesn't care that the actual object might be a Horse at runtime.

exam Watch

Don't be fooled by a method that's overloaded but not overridden by a subclass. It's perfectly legal to do the following:

```
public class Foo {
   void doStuff() { }
}
class Bar extends Foo {
   void doStuff(String s) { }
}
```

The Bar class has two `doStuff()` methods: the no-arg version it inherits from Foo (and does not override), and the overloaded `doStuff(String s)` defined in the Bar class. Code with a reference to a Foo can invoke only the no-arg version, but code with a reference to a Bar can invoke *either* ***of the overloaded versions.***

Table 5-3 summarizes the difference between overloaded and overridden methods.

TABLE 5-3 Difference Between Overloaded and Overridden Methods

	Overloaded Method	Overridden Method
argument list	Must change	Must not change
return type	Can change	Must not change
exceptions	Can change	Can reduce or eliminate. Must not throw new or broader checked exceptions
access	Can change	Must not make more restrictive (can be less restrictive)
invocation	*Reference* type determines which overloaded version (based on declared argument types) is selected. Happens at *compile* time. The actual *method* that's invoked is still a virtual method invocation that happens at runtime, but the compiler will already know the *signature* of the method to be invoked. So at runtime, the argument match will already have been nailed down, just not the actual *class* in which the method lives.	*Object* type (in other words, *the type of the actual instance on the heap*) determines which method is selected. Happens at *runtime.*

FIGURE 5-4

Overloaded and overridden methods in class relationships

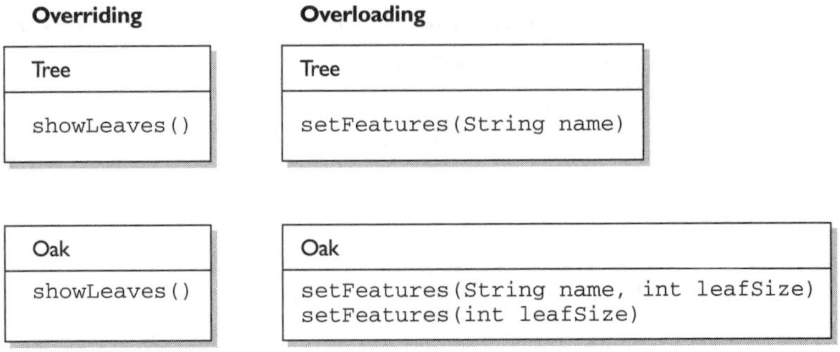

The current objective (5.2) covers both method and constructor overloading, but we'll cover constructor overloading in the next section, where we'll also cover the other constructor-related topics that are on the exam. Figure 5-4 illustrates the way overloaded and overridden methods appear in class relationships.

CERTIFICATION OBJECTIVE

Constructors and Instantiation (Exam Objectives 1.3, 6.3, 6.2)

For a given class, determine if a default constructor will be created, and if so, state the prototype of that constructor.

Write code to construct instances of any concrete class, including normal top-level classes and nested classes.

Write code to invoke parental or overloaded constructor, and describe the effect of those invocations.

Objects are constructed. *You can't make a new object without invoking a constructor.* In fact, you can't make a new object without invoking not just the constructor of the object's actual class type, but also *the constructor of each of its superclasses!* Constructors are the code that runs whenever you use the keyword `new`. We've got plenty to talk about here—we'll look at how constructors are coded, *who* codes them, and how they work at runtime. So grab your hardhat and a hammer, and let's do some object building. (Don't forget your lunch box and thermos.)

Constructor Basics

Every class, *including abstract classes*, must have a constructor. Burn that into your brain. But just because a class must have one, doesn't mean the *programmer* has to type it. A constructor looks like this:

```
class Foo {
   Foo() { } // The constructor for the Foo class
}
```

Notice what's missing? *There's no return type!* Remember from Chapter 2 that a constructor has no return type and its name must exactly match the class name. Typically, constructors are used to initialize instance variable state, as follows:

```
class Foo {
   int size;
   String name;
   Foo(String name, int size) {
      this.name = name;
      this.size = size;
   }
}
```

In the preceding code example, the Foo class does not have a no-arg constructor. That means the following will *fail* to compile,

```
Foo f = new Foo();  // Won't compile, no matching constructor
```

but the following *will* compile,

```
Foo f = new Foo("Fred", 43);  // No problem. Arguments match Foo constructor.
```

So it's very common (and desirable) for a class to have a no-arg constructor, regardless of how many other overloaded constructors are in the class (yes, constructors can be overloaded). You can't always make that work for your classes; occasionally you have a class where it makes no sense to create an instance without supplying information to the constructor. A java.awt.Color object, for example, can't be created by calling a no-arg constructor, because that would be like saying to the JVM, "Make me a new Color object, and I really don't care what color it is…*you* pick." (Imagine if the JVM were allowed to make aesthetic decisions. What if it's favorite color is mauve?)

Constructor Chaining

We know that constructors are invoked at runtime when you say `new` on some class type as follows:

```
Horse h = new Horse();
```

But what really happens when you say `new Horse()` ?

1. Horse constructor is invoked.
2. Animal constructor is invoked (Animal is the superclass of Horse).
3. Object constructor is invoked (Object is the ultimate superclass of *all* classes, so class Animal extends Object even though you don't actually type "`extends Object" in to the Animal class declaration. It's implicit.) At this point we're` on the top of the stack.
4. Object instance variables are given their explicit values (if any).
5. Object constructor completes.
6. Animal instance variables are given their explicit values (if any).
7. Animal constructor completes.
8. Horse instance variables are given their explicit values (if any).
9. Horse constructor completes.

Figure 5-5 shows how constructors work on the call stack.

FIGURE 5-5

Constructors on the call stack

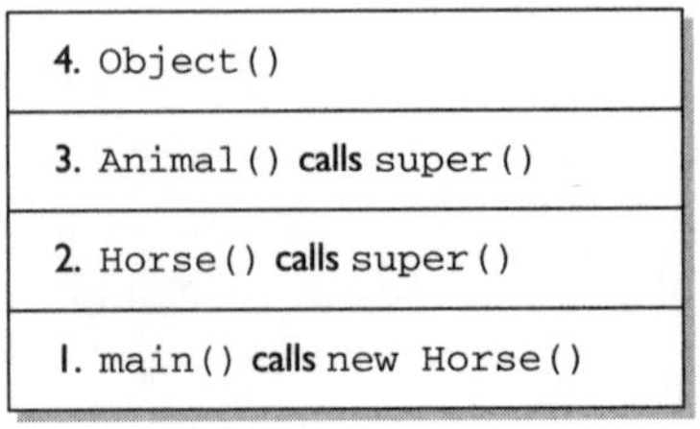

4. `Object()`
3. `Animal()` calls `super()`
2. `Horse()` calls `super()`
1. `main()` calls `new Horse()`

Rules for Constructors

The following list summarizes the rules you'll need to know for the exam (and to understand the rest of this section):

- Constructors can use any access modifier, including `private`. (A *private* constructor means only code within the class itself can instantiate an object of that type, so if the *private*-constructor class wants to allow an instance of the class to be used, the class must provide a static method or variable that allows access to an instance created from within the class.)
- The constructor name must match the name of the class.
- Constructors must not have a return type.
- It's legal (but stupid) to have a method with the same name as the class, but that doesn't make it a constructor. If you see a return type, it's a method rather than a constructor.
- If you don't type a constructor into your class code, a default constructor will be automatically generated by the compiler.
- The default constructor is *always* a no-arg constructor.
- If you want a no-arg constructor and you've typed any other constructor(s) into your class code, the compiler won't provide the no-arg constructor (or any other constructor) for you. In other words, *if you've typed in a constructor with arguments, you won't have a no-arg constructor unless you type it in yourself!*
- Every constructor must have as its first statement either a call to an overloaded constructor (`this()`) or a call to the superclass constructor (`super()`).
- If you *do* type in a constructor (as opposed to relying on the compiler-generated default constructor), and you do *not* type in the call to `super()`, *the compiler will insert a no-arg call to* `super()` *for you.*
- A call to `super()` can be either a no-arg call or can include arguments passed to the super constructor.
- A no-arg constructor is not necessarily the *default* constructor, although the default constructor is always a no-arg constructor. *The default constructor is the one the compiler provides!* While the default constructor is *always* a no-arg constructor, you're free to put in your *own* no-arg constructor.

- You *cannot* make a call to an instance method, or access an instance variable, until *after* the super constructor runs.
- You *can* access static variables and methods, although you can use them only as part of the call to `super()` or `this()`. (Example: `super(Animal.DoThings())`)
- Abstract classes have constructors, and those constructors are *always* called when a concrete subclass is instantiated.
- Interfaces do *not* have constructors. Interfaces are not part of an object's inheritance tree.
- The only way a constructor can be invoked is from within another constructor. In other words, you can't write code that actually calls a constructor as follows:

```
class Horse {
   Horse() { } // constructor
   void doStuff() {
     Horse();   // calling the constructor - illegal!
   }
}
```

Determine Whether a Default Constructor Will Be Created

The following example shows a Horse class with two constructors:

```
class Horse {
   Horse() { }
   Horse(String name) { }
 }
```

Will the compiler put in a default constructor for the class above? No!

How about for the following variation of the class?

```
class Horse {
   Horse(String name) { }
}
```

Now will the compiler insert a default constructor? No!

What about this class?

```
class Horse { }
```

Now we're talking. The compiler will generate a default constructor for the preceding class, because the class doesn't have any constructors defined.

OK, what about *this* class?

```
class Horse {
   void Horse() { }
}
```

It might *look* like the compiler won't create one, since there already is a constructor in the Horse class. Or is there? Take another look at the preceding Horse class.

What's wrong with the `Horse()` constructor? It isn't a constructor at all! It's simply a method that happens to have the same name as the class. Remember, the return type is a dead giveaway that we're looking at a method, and not a constructor.

How do you know for sure whether a default constructor will be created? Because *you* didn't write *any* constructors in your class.

How do you know what the default constructor will look like?
Because…

- The default constructor has the *same access modifier as the class.*
- The default constructor has *no arguments.*
- The default constructor includes a *no-arg call to the super constructor* (`super()`).

The Table 5-4 shows what the compiler will (or won't) generate for your class.

TABLE 5-4 Compiler-Generated Constructor Code

Class Code (What *You* Type)	Compiler-Generated Constructor Code (In Bold Type)

`class Foo {}`	`class Foo {`
	  `Foo() {`
	    `super();`
	  `}`
	`}`

TABLE 5-4 Compiler-Generated Constructor Code *(continued)*

Class Code (What *You* Type)	Compiler-Generated Constructor Code (In Bold Type)

`class Foo {`
`   Foo() { }`
`}`
	class Foo {
	Foo() {
	super();
	}
	}

`public class Foo {}`	*class Foo {* **public Foo() {** **super();** **}** *}*

`class Foo {`
`   Foo(String s) { }`
`}`
	class Foo {
	Foo(String s) {
	super();
	}
	}

`class Foo {`
`   Foo(String s) {`
`      super();`
`   }`
`}`
	Nothing—compiler doesn't need to insert anything.

`class Foo {`
`   void Foo() {}`
`}`
	class Foo {
	void Foo() {}
	Foo() {
	super();
	}
	}
	(`void Foo()` is a method, not a constructor)

What happens if the super constructor has arguments? Constructors can have arguments just as methods can, and if you try to invoke a method that takes, say, an *int*, but you don't pass anything to the method, the compiler will complain as follows:

```
class Bar {
    void takeInt(int x) { }
}

class UseBar {
```

```
    public static void main (String [] args) {
      Bar b = new Bar();
      b.takeInt();   // Try to invoke a no-arg takeInt() method
    }
}
```

The compiler will complain that you can't invoke `takeInt()` without passing an *int*. Of course, the compiler enjoys the occasional riddle, so the message it spits out on some versions of the JVM (your mileage may vary) is less than obvious:

```
UseBar.java:7: takeInt(int) in Bar cannot be applied to ()
     b.takeInt();
      ^
```

But you get the idea. The bottom line is that there must be a match for the method. And by match, we mean that the argument types must be able to accept the values or variables you're passing, and in the order you're passing them. Which brings us back to constructors (and here you were thinking we'd never get there), which work exactly the same way.

So if your super constructor (that is, the constructor of your immediate superclass/parent) has arguments, you must type in the call to `super()`, supplying the appropriate arguments. Crucial point: if your superclass does *not* have a no-arg constructor, you *must* type a constructor in your class (the subclass) because *you need a place to put in the call to super with the appropriate arguments.*

The following is an example of the problem:

```
class Animal {
   Animal(String name) { }
}

class Horse extends Animal {
   Horse() {
      super();   // Problem!
   }
}
```

And once again the compiler treats us with the stunningly lucid:

```
Horse.java:7: cannot resolve symbol
symbol   : constructor Animal  ()
location: class Animal
      super();   // Problem!
      ^
```

If you're lucky (and eat all your vegetables, including broccoli), your compiler might be a little more explicit. But again, the problem is that there just isn't a match for what we're trying to invoke with `super()`—an Animal constructor with no arguments.

Another way to put this—and you can bet your favorite Grateful Dead t-shirt it'll be on the exam—is *if your superclass does not have a no-arg constructor, then in your subclass you will not be able to use the default constructor supplied by the compiler.* It's that simple. Because the compiler can only put in a call to a no-arg `super()`, you won't even be able to compile something like the following:

```
class Clothing {
   Clothing(String s) { }
}
class TShirt extends Clothing { }
```

Trying to compile this code gives us exactly the same error we got when we put a constructor in the subclass with a call to the no-arg version of `super()`:

```
Clothing.java:4: cannot resolve symbol
symbol  : constructor Clothing  ()
location: class Clothing
class TShirt extends Clothing { }
^
```

In fact, the preceding Clothing and TShirt code is implicitly the same as the following code, where we've supplied a constructor for TShirt that's identical to the default constructor supplied by the compiler:

```
class Clothing {
   Clothing(String s) { }
}
class TShirt extends Clothing {
   // Constructor identical to compiler-supplied default constructor
   TShirt() {
      super();
   }
}
```

One last point on the whole default constructor thing (and it's probably very obvious, but we have to say it or we'll feel guilty for years), *constructors are never inherited.* They aren't methods. They can't be *overridden* (because they aren't methods and only methods can be overridden). So the type of constructor(s) your superclass has in no way determines the type of default constructor you'll get. Some folks mistakenly believe that the default constructor somehow matches the super constructor, either by the arguments the default constructor will have (remember, *the default constructor is always a no-arg*), or by the arguments used in the compiler-supplied call to `super()`.

But although constructors can't be overridden, you've already seen that they can be overloaded, and typically are.

Overloaded Constructors

Overloading a constructor means typing in multiple versions of the constructor, each having a different argument lists, like the following examples:

```
class Foo {
   Foo() { }
   Foo(String s) { }
}
```

The preceding Foo class has two overloaded constructors, one that takes a string, and one with no arguments. Because there's no code in the no-arg version, it's actually identical to the default constructor the compiler supplies, but remember—since there's already a constructor in this class (the one that takes a string), the compiler won't supply a default constructor. If you want a no-arg constructor to overload the with-args version you already have, you're going to have to type it yourself, just as in the Foo example.

Overloading a constructor is used typically to provide alternate ways for clients to instantiate objects of your class. For example, if a client knows the animal name, they can pass that to an Animal constructor that takes a string. But if they don't know the name, the client can call the no-arg constructor and that constructor can supply a default name. Here's what it looks like:

```
public class Animal {
  String name;
  Animal(String name) {
    this.name = name;
 }

 Animal() {
  this(makeRandomName());
 }

 static String makeRandomName() {
```

```
12.      int x = (int) (Math.random() * 5);
13.      String name = new String[] {"Fluffy", "Fido",
                                     "Rover", "Spike",
                                     "Gigi"}[x];
14.      return name;
15.   }
16.
17.   public static void main (String [] args) {
18.     Animal a = new Animal();
19.     System.out.println(a.name);
20.     Animal b = new Animal("Zeus");
21.     System.out.println(b.name);
22.   }
23. }
```

Running this code four times produces the output:

```
% java Animal
Gigi
Zeus

% java Animal
Fluffy
Zeus

% java Animal
Rover
Zeus

% java Animal
Fluffy
Zeus
```

There's a lot going on in the preceding code. Figure 5-6 shows the call stack for constructor invocations when a constructor is overloaded. Take a look at the call stack, and then let's walk through the code straight from the top.

- **Line 2** Declare a String instance variable *name*.
- **Lines 3–5** Constructor that takes a String, and assigns it to instance variable *name*.
- **Line 7** Here's where it gets fun. Assume every animal needs a name, but the client (calling code) might not always know what the name should be, so you'll assign a random name. The no-arg constructor generates a name by invoking the `makeRandomName()` method.

FIGURE 5-6

Overloaded constructors on the call stack

4. `Object()`
3. `Animal(String s)` calls `super()`
2. `Animal()` calls `this(randomlyChosenNameString)`
1. `main()` calls `new Animal()`

- **Line 8** The no-arg constructor invokes its own overloaded constructor that takes a string, in effect calling it the same way it would be called if client code were doing a `new` to instantiate an object, passing it a string for the name. The overloaded invocation uses the keyword `this`, but uses it as though it were a method name, `this()`. So line 8 is simply calling the constructor on line 3, passing it a randomly selected string rather than a client-code chosen name.
- **Line 11** Notice that the `makeRandomName()` method is marked `static`! That's because you *cannot* invoke an instance (in other words, *nonstatic*) method (or access an instance variable) until *after* the super constructor has run. And since the super constructor will be invoked from the constructor on line 3, rather than from the one on line 7, line 8 can use only a *static* method to generate the name. If we wanted all animals not specifically named by the caller to have the same default name, say, "Fred," then line 8 could have read

  ```
  this("Fred");
  ```

  rather than calling a method that returns a string with the randomly chosen name.
- **Line 12** Line 12 doesn't have anything to do with constructors, but since we're all here to learn...it generates a random number between 0 and 5.
- **Line 13** Weird syntax, we know. We're creating a new String object (just a single String instance), but we want the string to be selected randomly from a list. Except we don't have the list, so we need to make it. So in that one line of code we

  1. Declare a String variable, *name.*
  2. Create a String array (anonymously—we don't assign the array itself to anything).
  3. Retrieve the string at index [*x*] (*x* being the random number generated on line 12) of the newly created String array.

4. Assign the string retrieved from the array to the declared instance variable *name.* We could have made it *much* easier to read if we'd just written
```
String[] nameList = {"Fluffy", "Fido", "Rover",
"Spike", "Gigi"};
String name = nameList[x];
```
But where's the fun in that? Throwing in unusual syntax (especially for code wholly unrelated to the real question) is in the spirit of the exam. Don't be startled! (OK, be startled, but then just say to yourself, "Whoa" and get on with it.)

- **Line 18** We're invoking the no-arg version of the constructor (causing a random name from the list to be selected and passed to the *other* constructor).
- **Line 20** We're invoking the overloaded constructor that takes a string representing the *name.*

The key point to get from this code example is in line 8. Rather than calling `super()`, we're calling `this()`, and `this()` *always means a call to another constructor in the same class.* OK, fine, but what happens *after* the call to `this()`? Sooner or later the `super()` constructor gets called, right? Yes indeed. A call to `this()` just means you're delaying the inevitable. Some constructor, somewhere, must make the call to `super()`.

Key Rule: The first line in a constructor must be a call to `super()` or a call to `this()`.

No exceptions. If you have *neither* of those calls in your constructor, the compiler will insert the no-arg call to `super()`. In other words, if constructor `A()` has a call to `this()`, the compiler knows that constructor `A()` will *not* be the one to invoke `super()`.

exam Watch

The preceding rule means a constructor can never have both a call to `super()` and a call to `this()`. Because each of those calls must be the very first statement in a constructor, you can't legally use both in the same constructor. That also means the compiler will not put a call to `super()` in any constructor that has a call to `this()`.

Thought Question: What do you think will happen if you try to compile the following code?

```
class A {
   A() {
```

```
      this("foo");
    }
    A(String s) {
       this();
    }
}
```

Your compiler may not actually catch the problem (it varies depending on your compiler, but most won't catch the problem). It assumes you know what you're doing. Can you spot the flaw? Given that a super constructor must always be called, where would the call to `super()` go? Remember, the compiler won't put in a default constructor if you've already got one or more constructors in your class. And when the compiler doesn't put in a default constructor, it *still* inserts a call to `super()` in any constructor that doesn't explicitly have a call to the super constructor—unless, that is, the constructor already has a call to `this()`. So in the preceding code, where can `super()` go? The only two constructors in the class both have calls to `this()`, and in fact you'll get exactly what you'd get if you typed the following method code:

```
public void go() {
   doStuff();
}

public void doStuff() {
   go();
}
```

Now can you see the problem? Of course you can. *The stack explodes!* It gets higher and higher and higher until it just bursts open and method code goes spilling out, oozing out of the JVM right onto the floor. Two overloaded constructors both calling `this()` are two constructors calling each other. Over and over and over, resulting in

```
% java A
Exception in thread "main" java.lang.StackOverflowError
```

The benefit of having overloaded constructors is that you offer flexible ways to instantiate objects from your class. The benefit of having one constructor invoke another overloaded constructor is to avoid code duplication. In the Animal example, there wasn't any code other than setting the name, but imagine if after line 4 there was still more work to be done in the constructor. By putting all the other constructor work in just one constructor, and then having the other constructors invoke it, you don't have to write and maintain multiple versions of that other important constructor code. Basically, each of the other not-the-real-one overloaded constructors will call another overloaded constructor, passing it whatever data it needs (data the client code didn't supply).

Constructors and instantiation become even *more* exciting (just when you thought it was safe) when you get to inner classes, but we know you can only stand to have so much fun in one chapter, so we're holding the rest of the discussion on instantiating inner classes until Chapter 8.

CERTIFICATION OBJECTIVE

Legal Return Types (Exam Objective 1.4)

Identify legal return types for any method given the declarations of all related methods in this or parent classes.

This objective covers two aspects of return types: What you can *declare* as a return type, and what you can actually *return* as a value. What you can and cannot declare is pretty straightforward, but it all depends on whether you're overriding an inherited method or simply declaring a new method (which includes overloaded methods). We'll take just a quick look at the difference between return type rules for overloaded and overriding methods, because we've already covered that in this chapter. We'll cover a small bit of new ground, though, when we look at polymorphic return types and the rules for what is and is not legal to actually *return.*

Return Type Declarations

This section looks at what you're allowed to declare as a return type, which depends primarily on whether you are overriding, overloading, or declaring a new method.

Return Types on Overloaded Methods

Remember that method overloading is not much more than name reuse. The overloaded method is a completely different method from any other method of the same name. So if you inherit a method but *overload* it in a subclass, you're not subject to the restrictions of overriding, which means you can declare any return type you like. What you *can't* do is change *just* the return type. To overload a method, remember, *you must change the argument list.* The following code shows an overloaded method:

```
public class Foo{
   void go() { }
}
public class Bar extends Foo {
   String go(int x) {
     return null;
   }
}
```

Notice that the Bar version of the method uses a different return type. That's perfectly fine. As long as you've changed the argument list, you're overloading the method, so the return type doesn't have to match that of the superclass version. What you're not allowed to do is this:

```
public class Foo{
   void go() { }
}
public class Bar extends Foo {
   String go() { // Not legal! Can't change only the return type
      return null;
   }
}
```

Overriding and Return Types

When a subclass wants to change the method implementation of an inherited method, the subclass must define a method that matches the inherited version *exactly*. As we saw earlier in this chapter, an exact match means the arguments and return types must be identical. Other rules apply to overriding, including those for access modifiers and declared exceptions, but those rules aren't relevant to the return type discussion.

For the exam, be sure you know that *overloaded* methods *can* change the return type, but *overriding* methods *cannot*. Just that knowledge alone will help you through a wide range of exam questions.

Returning a Value

You have to remember only six rules for returning a value:

1. You can return `null` in a method that has an object reference return type.

```
public Button doStuff() {
   return null;
}
```

2. An array is a perfectly legal return type.

```
public String [] go() {
    return new String[] {"Fred", "Barney", "Wilma"};
}
```

3. In a method with a primitive return type, you can return any value or variable that can be implicitly converted to the declared return type.

```
public int foo() {
   char c = 'c';
   return c;  // char is compatible with int
}
```

4. In a method with a primitive return type, you can return any value or variable that can be explicitly cast to the declared return type.

```
public int foo () {
     float f = 32.5f;
     return (int) f;
}
```

5. You must *not* return anything from a method with a `void` return type.

```
public void bar() {
   return "this is it";   // Not legal!!
}
```

6. In a method with an object reference return type, you can return any object type that can be implicitly cast to the declared return type.

```
public Animal getAnimal() {
   return new Horse();   // Assume Horse extends Animal
}

public Object getObject() {
    int[] nums = {1,2,3};
    return nums;  // Return an int array, which is still an object
}

public interface Chewable { }
public class Gum implements Chewable { }

public class TestChewable {

    // Method with an interface return type
    public Chewable getChewable {
```

```
        return new Gum();  // Return interface implementer
    }
}
```

exam Watch

Watch for methods that declare an abstract class or interface return type, and know that any object that passes the IS-A test (in other words, would test `true` ***using the*** `instanceof` ***operator) can be returned from that method—for example:***

```
public abstract class Animal { }
public class Bear extends Animal { }
public class Test {
   public Animal go() {
      return new Bear();  // OK, Bear "is-a" Animal
   }
}
```

exam Watch

Be sure you understand the rules for casting primitives. Take a look at the following:

```
public short s = (short) (90 + 900000);
```

The preceding code compiles fine. But look at this variation:

```
public short s = (short) 90 + 900000;  // Illegal!
```

By leaving off the parentheses around the arithmetic expression, the cast (short) applies only to the first number! So the compiler gives us

```
Test.java:4: possible loss of precision
found   : int
required: short
   short s = (short) 90 + 900000;
                        ^
```

Casting rules matter when returning values, so the following code would not compile,

```
public short foo() {
   return (short) 90 + 900000;
}
```

but with parentheses around `(90 + 900000)`***, it compiles fine.***

CERTIFICATION SUMMARY

Let's take a stroll through Chapter 5 and see where we've been. You looked at how encapsulation can save you from being ripped to shreds by programmers whose code you could break if you change the way client code accesses your data. Protecting the instance variables (often by marking them private) and providing more accessible getter and setter methods represent the good OO practice of encapsulation, and support flexibility and maintainability by hiding your implementation details from other code.

You learned that inheritance relationships are described using IS-A, as in "Car IS-A Vehicle," and that the keyword `extends` is used to define IS-A relationships in Java:

```
class Car extends Vehicle
```

You also learned that reference relationships are described using HAS-A, as in "Car HAS-A Engine." HAS-A relationships in Java often are defined by giving one class a reference to another, usually through instance variable declarations:

```
class Car extends Vehicle {
    private Engine eng;  // Now Car has-a Engine,
                         // and can thus invoke
methods on it.
}
```

We looked at the difference between overridden and overloaded methods, learning that an overridden method occurs when a subclass inherits a method from a superclass, but the subclass redefines it to add more specialized behavior. We learned that at runtime, the JVM will invoke the subclass version on an instance of a subclass, and the superclass version on an instance of the superclass. Remember that abstract methods *must* be overridden (*technically* abstract methods must be *implemented*, as opposed to overridden, since there really isn't anything *to* override in an abstract method, but who's counting?).

We saw that overriding methods must keep the same argument list and return type as the overridden method, and that the access modifier can't be more restrictive. The overriding method also can't throw any new or broader checked exceptions that weren't declared in the overridden method. You also learned that the overridden method can be invoked using the syntax `super.doSomething();`.

Overloaded methods let you reuse the same method name in a class, but with different arguments (and optionally, a different return type). Whereas *overriding* methods must *not* change the argument list, *overloaded* methods *must.* But unlike overriding methods, overloaded methods are free to vary the return type, access modifier, and declared exceptions any way they like.

We covered constructors in detail, learning that even if you don't provide a constructor for your class, the compiler will always insert one. The compiler-generated constructor is called the *default* constructor, and it is *always* a no-arg constructor with a no-arg call to `super()`. The default constructor will never be generated if there is even a single constructor in your class (and regardless of the arguments of that constructor), so if you need more than one constructor in your class and you want a no-arg constructor, you'll have to write it yourself. We also saw that constructors are not inherited, and that you can be confused by a method that has the same name as the class (which is legal). The return type is the giveaway that a method is not a constructor, since constructors do not have return types.

We saw how all of the constructors in an object's inheritance tree will always be invoked when the object is instantiated using `new`. We also saw that constructors can be overloaded, which means defining constructors with different argument lists. A constructor can invoke another constructor of the same class using the keyword `this()`, as though the constructor were a method named `this()`. We saw that every constructor *must* have either `this()` or `super()` as the first statement.

We also looked at method return types, and saw that you can declare any return type you like (assuming you have access to a class for an object reference return type), unless you're overriding a method. An overriding method must have the same return type as the overridden method of the superclass. We saw that while overriding methods must *not* change the return type, overloaded methods *can* (as long as they *also* change the argument list).

Finally, you learned that it is legal to return any value or variable that can be implicitly converted to the declared return type. So, for example, a *short* can be returned when the return type is declared as an *int.* And a Horse reference can be returned when the return type is declared an Animal (assuming Horse extends Animal).

And once again, you learned that the exam includes tricky questions designed largely to test your ability to recognize just how tricky the questions can be. If you took our advice about the margarita, you might want to review the following Two-Minute Drill again after you're sober.

TWO-MINUTE DRILL

Here are some of the key points from each certification objective in Chapter 5.

Encapsulation, IS-A, HAS-A (Sun Objective 6.1)

- ❑ The goal of encapsulation is to hide implementation behind an interface (or API).
- ❑ Encapsulated code has two features:
  - ❑ Instance variables are kept protected (usually with the `private` modifier).
  - ❑ Getter and setter methods provide access to instance variables.
- ❑ IS-A refers to inheritance.
- ❑ IS-A is expressed with the keyword `extends`.
- ❑ "IS-A," "inherits from," "is derived from," and "is a subtype of" are all equivalent expressions.
- ❑ HAS-A means an instance of one class "has a" reference to an instance of another class.

Overriding and Overloading (Sun Objective 6.2)

- ❑ Methods can be overridden or overloaded; constructors can be overloaded but not overridden.
- ❑ Abstract methods *must* be overridden by the first concrete (nonabstract) subclass.
- ❑ With respect to the method it overrides, the overriding method
  - ❑ Must have the same argument list
  - ❑ Must have the same return type
  - ❑ Must not have a more restrictive access modifier
  - ❑ May have a less restrictive access modifier
  - ❑ Must not throw new or broader checked exceptions
  - ❑ May throw fewer or narrower checked exceptions, or any unchecked exception

- ❑ Final methods cannot be overridden.
- ❑ Only inherited methods may be overridden.
- ❑ A subclass uses `super.overriddenMethodName` to call the superclass version of an overridden method.
- ❑ Overloading means reusing the same method name, but with different arguments.
- ❑ Overloaded methods
  - ❑ Must have different argument lists
  - ❑ May have different return types, as long as the argument lists are also different
  - ❑ May have different access modifiers
  - ❑ May throw different exceptions
- ❑ Methods from a superclass can be overloaded in a subclass.
- ❑ Polymorphism applies to overriding, not to overloading
- ❑ Object type determines which overridden method is used at runtime.
- ❑ Reference type determines which overloaded method will be used at compile time.

Instantiation and Constructors (Sun Objectives 6.3 and 1.3)

- ❑ Objects are constructed:
  - ❑ You cannot create a new object without invoking a constructor.
  - ❑ Each superclass in an object's inheritance tree will have a constructor called.
- ❑ Every class, even abstract classes, has at least one constructor.
- ❑ Constructors must have the same name as the class.
- ❑ Constructors do not have a return type. If there *is* a return type, then it is simply a method with the same name as the class, and not a constructor.
- ❑ Constructor execution occurs as follows:
  - ❑ The constructor calls its superclass constructor, which calls its superclass constructor, and so on all the way up to the Object constructor.

- The Object constructor executes and then returns to the calling constructor, which runs to completion and then returns to *its* calling constructor, and so on back down to the completion of the constructor of the actual instance being created.
- Constructors can use any access modifier (even `private`!).
- The compiler will create a *default* constructor if you don't create any constructors in your class.
- The *default* constructor is a no-arg constructor with a no-arg call to `super()`.
- The first statement of every constructor must be a call to either `this()` (an overloaded constructor) or `super()`.
- The compiler will add a call to `super()` if you do not, unless you have already put in a call to `this()`.
- Instance methods and variables are only accessible *after* the super constructor runs.
- Abstract classes have constructors that are called when a concrete subclass is instantiated.
- Interfaces do not have constructors.
- If your superclass does not have a no-arg constructor, you must create a constructor and insert a call to `super()` with arguments matching those of the superclass constructor.
- Constructors are never inherited, thus they cannot be overridden.
- A constructor can be directly invoked only by another constructor (using a call to `super()` or `this()`).
- Issues with calls to `this()`:
  - May appear only as the first statement in a constructor.
  - The argument list determines which overloaded constructor is called.
  - Constructors can call constructors can call constructors, and so on, but sooner or later *one* of them better call `super()` or the stack will explode.
  - `this()` and `super()` *cannot* be in the same constructor. You can have one or the other, but never both.

Return Types (Sun Objectives 1.4)

- ❑ Overloaded methods can change return types; overridden methods cannot.
- ❑ Object reference return types can accept `null` as a return value.
- ❑ An array is a legal return type, both to declare and return as a value.
- ❑ For methods with primitive return types, any value that can be implicitly converted to the return type can be returned.
- ❑ Nothing can be returned from a `void`, *but you can return nothing.* You're allowed to simply say `return`, in any method with a void return type, to bust out of a method early. But you can't return *nothing* from a method with a non-`void` return type.
- ❑ For methods with an object reference return type, a subclass of that type can be returned.
- ❑ For methods with an interface return type, any implementer of that interface can be returned.

SELF TEST

The following questions will help you measure your understanding of the material presented in this chapter. Don't even *think* about skipping this test. You really need to see what the questions on the exam can be like, and check your grasp and memorization of this chapter's topics.

Encapsulation, IS-A, HAS-A (Sun Objective 6.1)

1. Given the following,

```
1.   public class Barbell {
2.     public int getWeight() {
3.       return weight;
4.     }
5.     public void setWeight(int w) {
6.       weight = w;
7.     }
8.     public int weight;
9.   }
```

which is true about the class described above?

A. Class Barbell is tightly encapsulated.

B. Line 2 is in conflict with encapsulation.

C. Line 5 is in conflict with encapsulation.

D. Line 8 is in conflict with encapsulation.

E. Lines 5 and 8 are in conflict with encapsulation.

F. Lines 2, 5, and 8 are in conflict with encapsulation.

2. Given the following,

```
public class B extends A {
  private int bar;
  public void setBar(int b) {
    bar = b;
  }
}
class A {
  public int foo;
}
```

which is true about the classes described above?

A. Class A is tightly encapsulated.

B. Class B is tightly encapsulated.

C. Classes A and B are both tightly encapsulated.

D. Neither class A nor class B is tightly encapsulated.

3. Which is true?

A. Tightly encapsulated classes are typically easier to reuse.

B. Tightly encapsulated classes typically use inheritance more than unencapsulated classes.

C. Methods in tightly encapsulated classes cannot be overridden.

D. Methods in tightly encapsulated classes cannot be overloaded.

E. Tightly encapsulated classes typically do not use HAS-A relationships.

4. Which two are *not* benefits of encapsulation? (Choose two.)

A. Clarity of code

B. Code efficiency

C. The ability to add functionality later on

D. Modifications require fewer coding changes

E. Access modifiers become optional

5. Given the following,

```
class B extends A {
  int getID() {
    return id;
  }
}
class C {
  public int name;
}
class A {
  C c = new C();
  public int id;
}
```

which two are true about instances of the classes listed above? (Choose two.)

A. `A is-a B`

B. `C is-a A`

C. `A has-a C`

D. `B has-a A`

E. `B has-a C`

Overriding and Overloading (Sun Objective 6.2)

6. Given the following,

```
class A {
 public void baz() {
   System.out.println("A");
 }
}
public class B extends A {
  public static void main(String [] args) {
    A a = new B();
    a.baz();
  }
  public void baz() {
    System.out.println("B");
  }
}
```

what is the result?

A. `A`

B. `B`

C. Compilation fails.

D. An exception is thrown at runtime.

7. Given the following,

```
class Foo {
  String doStuff(int x) { return "hello"; }
}
```

which method would not be legal in a subclass of Foo?

A. `String doStuff(int x) { return "hello"; }`

B. `int doStuff(int x) { return 42; }`

C. `public String doStuff(int x) { return "Hello"; }`

D. `protected String doStuff(int x) { return "Hello"; }`

E. `String doStuff(String s) { return "Hello"; }`

F. `int doStuff(String s) { return 42; }`

8. Given the following,

```
class ParentClass {
  public int doStuff(int x) {
    return x * 2;
```

```
4.     }
5.   }
6.
7.   public class ChildClass extends ParentClass {
8.     public static void main(String [] args ) {
9.       ChildClass cc = new ChildClass();
10.      long x = cc.doStuff(7);
11.      System.out.println("x = " + x);
12.    }
13.
14.    public long doStuff(int x) {
15.      return x * 3;
16.    }
17.  }
```

What is the result?

A. `x = 14`

B. `x = 21`

C. Compilation fails at line 2.

D. Compilation fails at line 11.

E. Compilation fails at line 14.

F. An exception is thrown at runtime.

9. Given the following,

```
1.  class Over {
2.    int doStuff(int a, float b) {
3.      return 7;
4.    }
5.  }
6.
7.  class Over2 extends Over {
8.      // insert code here
9.  }
```

which two methods, if inserted independently at line 8, will not compile? (Choose two.)

A. `public int doStuff(int x, float y) { return 4; }`

B. `protected int doStuff(int x, float y) {return 4; }`

C. `private int doStuff(int x, float y) {return 4; }`

D. `private int doStuff(int x, double y) { return 4; }`

E. `long doStuff(int x, float y) { return 4; }`

F. `int doStuff(float x, int y) { return 4; }`

Instantiation and Constructors (Sun Objectives 6.3 and 1.3)

10. Given the following,

```
public class TestPoly {
  public static void main(String [] args ){
    Parent p = new Child();
  }
}

class Parent {
  public Parent() {
    super();
    System.out.println("instantiate a parent");
  }
}

class Child extends Parent {
  public Child() {
    System.out.println("instantiate a child");
  }
}
```

what is the result?

A. `instantiate a child`

B. `instantiate a parent`

C. `instantiate a child`
`instantiate a parent`

D. `instantiate a parent`
`instantiate a child`

E. Compilation fails.

F. An exception is thrown at runtime.

11. Given the following,

```
public class TestPoly {
  public static void main(String [] args ){
    Parent p = new Child();
  }
}

class Parent {
  public Parent() {
    super();
```

```
        System.out.println("instantiate a parent");
    }
}

class Child extends Parent {
    public Child() {
        System.out.println("instantiate a child");
        super();
    }
}
```

what is the result?

A. `instantiate a child`

B. `instantiate a parent`

C. `instantiate a child`
   `instantiate a parent`

D. `instantiate a parent`
   `instantiate a child`

E. Compilation fails.

F. An exception is thrown at runtime.

12. Given the following,

```
class MySuper {
    public MySuper(int i) {
        System.out.println("super " + i);
    }
}

public class MySub extends MySuper {
    public MySub() {
        super(2);
        System.out.println("sub");
    }

    public static void main(String [] args) {
        MySuper sup = new MySub();
    }
}
```

what is the result?

A. `sub`
   `super 2`

B. `super 2`
`sub`

C. Compilation fails at line 2.

D. Compilation fails at line 8.

E. Compilation fails at line 9.

F. Compilation fails at line 14.

13. Given the following,

```
public class ThreeConst {
  public static void main(String [] args) {
    new ThreeConst(4L);
  }
  public ThreeConst(int x) {
    this();
    System.out.print(" " + (x * 2));
  }
  public ThreeConst(long x) {
    this((int) x);
    System.out.print(" " + x);
  }

  public ThreeConst() {
    System.out.print("no-arg ");
  }
}
```

what is the result?

A. `4`

B. `4 8`

C. `8 4`

D. `8 4 no-arg`

E. `no-arg 8 4`

F. Compilation fails.

14. Given the following,

```
public class ThreeConst {
  public static void main(String [] args) {
    new ThreeConst();
  }
```

```
    public void ThreeConst(int x) {
      System.out.print(" " + (x * 2));
    }
    public void ThreeConst(long x) {
     System.out.print(" " + x);
    }

    public void ThreeConst() {
      System.out.print("no-arg ");
    }
  }
```

what is the result?

A. `no-arg`

B. `8 4 no-arg`

C. `no-arg 8 4`

D. Compilation fails.

E. No output is produced.

F. An exception is thrown at runtime.

15. Given the following,

```
  class Dog {
    Dog(String name) { }
  }
```

if class Beagle extends Dog, and class Beagle has only one constructor, which of the following could be the legal constructor for class Beagle?

A. `Beagle() { }`

B. `Beagle() { super(); }`

C. `Beagle() { super("fido"); }`

D. `No constructor, allow the default constructor`

16. Which two of these statements are true about constructors? (Choose two.)

A. Constructors must not have arguments if the superclass constructor does not have arguments.

B. Constructors are not inherited.

C. Constructors cannot be overloaded.

D. The first statement of every constructor is a legal call to the `super()` or `this()` method.

Return Types (Sun Objective 1.4)

17. Given the following,

```
13.   int x;
14.   x = n.test();
18.   int test() {
19.
20.     return y;
21.   }
```

which line of code, inserted at line 19, will not compile?

A. `short y = 7;`

B. `int y = (int) 7.2d;`

C. `Byte y = 7;`

D. `char y = 's';`

E. `int y = 0xface;`

18. Given the following,

```
14.   long test( int x, float y) {
15.
16.   }
```

which two of the following lines, inserted independently, at line 15 would not compile? (Choose two.)

A. `return x;`

B. `return (long) x / y;`

C. `return (long) y;`

D. `return (int) 3.14d;`

E. `return ( y / x );`

F. `return  x / 7;`

19. Given the following,

```
1.   import java.util.*;
2.   class Ro {
3.      public static void main(String [] args) {
4.         Ro r = new Ro();
5.         Object o = r.test();
6.      }
```

```
7.
8.       Object test() {
9.
10.
11.      }
12.  }
```

which two of the following code fragments inserted at lines 9/10 will not compile? (Choose two.)

A. `return null;`

B. `Object t = new Object();`
`return t;`

C. `int [] a = new int [2];`
`return a;`

D. `char [] [] c = new char [2][2];`
`return c[0] [1];`

E. `char [] [] c = new char [2][2];`
`return c[1];`

F. `return 7;`

20. Given the following,

```
1.   import java.util.*;
2.   class Ro {
3.      public static void main(String [] args) {
4.         Ro r = new Ro();
5.         Object o = r.test();
6.      }
7.
8.      Object test() {
9.
10.
11.     }
12.  }
```

which two of the following code fragments inserted at lines 9/10 will not compile? (Choose two.)

A. `char [] [] c = new char [2][2];`
`return c;`

B. `return (Object) 7;`

C. `return (Object) (new int [] {1,2,3} );`

D. `ArrayList a = new ArrayList();`
`return a;`

E. `return (Object) "test";`

F. `return (Float) 4.3;`

21. Given the following,

```
class Test {
   public static Foo f = new Foo();
   public static Foo f2;
   public static Bar b = new Bar();

   public static void main(String [] args) {
      for (int x=0; x<6; x++) {
         f2 = getFoo(x);
         f2.react();
      }
   }
   static Foo getFoo(int y) {
         if ( 0 == y % 2 ) {
           return f;
         } else {
           return b;
         }
   }
}

class Bar extends Foo {
   void react() { System.out.print("Bar "); }
}

class Foo {
   void react() { System.out.print("Foo "); }
}
```

what is the result?

A. `Bar Bar Bar Bar Bar Bar`

B. `Foo Bar Foo Bar Foo Bar`

C. `Foo Foo Foo Foo Foo Foo`

D. Compilation fails.

E. An exception is thrown at runtime.

SELF TEST ANSWERS

Encapsulation, IS-A, HAS-A (Sun Objective 6.1)

1. ☑ **D.** If a class has an instance variable that is marked `public`, the class cannot be said to be encapsulated.
   ☒ **A, B, C, E,** and **F** are incorrect based on the program logic described above. `Public` getter and setter methods are compatible with the concept of encapsulation.

2. ☑ **D.** Class A is clearly not encapsulated because it has a `public` instance variable. At first glance class B appears to be encapsulated, however because it extends from class A it inherits the `public` instance variable *foo*, which is not encapsulated.
   ☒ **A, B,** and **C** are incorrect based on the program logic described above.

3. ☑ **A.** One of the main benefits of encapsulation is that encapsulated code is much easier to reuse than unencapsulated code.
   ☒ **B, C, D,** and **E** are incorrect. **B** is incorrect because inheritance is a concept that is independent of encapsulation. **C** and **D** are incorrect because encapsulation does not restrict the use of overloading or overriding. **E** is incorrect because HAS-A relationships are independent of encapsulation.

4. ☑ **B** and **E.** Encapsulation tends to make code more maintainable, extensible, and debuggable, but not necessarily any more efficient at runtime. Encapsulation is a design approach and in no way affects any Java language rules such as the use of access modifiers.
   ☒ **A, C,** and **D** are well-known benefits of encapsulation.

5. ☑ **C** and **E. C** is correct because class A has an instance variable, *c*, that is a reference to an object of class C. **E** is correct because class B extends from class A, which HAS-A class C reference, so class B, through inheritance, HAS-A class C.
   ☒ **A, B,** and **D** are incorrect based on the program logic described. **A** is incorrect because class B extends from class A, not the other way around. **B** is incorrect because class C is not in class A's inheritance tree. **D** is incorrect because class B IS-A class A; HAS-A is not used to describe inheritance relationships.

Overriding and Overloading (Sun Objective 6.2)

6. ☑ **B.** Reference variable '*d*' is of type `A`, but it refers to an object of type `B`. Line 9 is a polymorphic call, and the VM will use the version of the `baz()` method that is in the class that the reference variable refers to at that point.
   ☒ **A, C,** and **D** are incorrect because of the logic described above.

7. ☑ **B**. **B** is neither a legal override (the return type has been changed) nor a legal overload (the arguments have not changed).
☒ **A**, **C**, and **D** are legal overrides of the `doStuff()` method, and **E** and **F** are legal overloads of the `doStuff()` method.

8. ☑ **E**. Line 14 is an illegal override of the `doStuff()` method in ParentClass. When you override a method, you must leave both the arguments and the return types the same.
☒ **A**, **B**, **C**, **D**, and **F** are incorrect based on the program logic described above. If line 14 had returned an *int*, then **B** would be correct.

9. ☑ **C** and **E**. **C** is an illegal override because the `private` modifier is more restrictive than `doStuff()`'s default modifier in class Over. **E** is an illegal override because you can't change an overridden method's return type, or **E** is an illegal overload because you must change an overloaded method's arguments.
☒ **A** and **B** are simple overrides (`protected` is less restrictive than default). **D** and **F** are simple overloads (swapping arguments of different types creates an overload).

Instantiation and Constructors (Sun Objectives 6.3 and 1.3)

10. ☑ **D**. The class Child constructor calls the class Parent constructor implicitly before any code in the Child constructor runs. When the class Parent constructor's code runs, it prints the first line of output, finishes, and returns control to the Child constructor, which prints out its line of output and finishes. The call to `super()` is redundant.
☒ **A**, **B**, **C**, **E**, and **F** are incorrect based on the program logic described above.

11. ☑ **E**. Line 17 will cause the compiler to fail. The call to `super()` must be the first statement in a constructor.
☒ **A**, **B**, **C**, **D**, and **F** are incorrect based on the program logic described above. If line 17 were removed, **D** would be correct.

12. ☑ **B**. Class MySuper does not need a no-args constructor because MySub explicitly calls the MySuper constructor with an argument.
☒ **A** is incorrect because other than the implicit calls to `super()`, constructors run in order from base class to extended class, so MySuper's output will print first. **C**, **D**, **E**, and **F** are incorrect based on the program logic described above.

13. ☑ **E**. The `main()` method calls the *long* constructor which calls the *int* constructor, which calls the no-arg constructor, which runs, then returns to the *int* constructor, which runs, then returns to the *long* constructor, which runs last.
☒ **A**, **B**, **C**, **D**, and **F** are incorrect based on the program logic described above.

14. ☑ E. The class elements declared in lines 5, 8, and 12 are badly named methods, not constructors. The default constructor runs with no output, and these methods are never called.
☒ A, B, C, D, and F are incorrect because of the logic described above.

15. ☑ C. Only C is correct because the Dog class does not have a no-arg constructor; therefore, you must explicitly make the call to `super()`, passing in a string.
☒ A, B, and D are incorrect based on the program logic described above.

16. ☑ B and D are simply stating two rules about constructors.
☒ A is wrong because subclass constructors do not have to match the arguments of the superclass constructor. Only the call to `super()` must match. C is incorrect because constructors can be and are frequently overloaded.

Return Types (Sun Objective 1.4)

17. ☑ C. Byte is a wrapper object, not a primitive.
☒ A and D are primitives that are shorter than *int* so they are cast implicitly. B is a *double* explicitly cast to an *int*. E is a valid integer initialized with a hexadecimal value.

18. ☑ B and E. B won't compile because the *long* cast only applies to *x*, not to the expression *x / y*. (We know it's tricky, but so is the test.) E won't compile because the result of (*y / x*) is a *float*.
☒ A, C, D, and F all return either *longs* or *ints* (which are automatically cast to *longs*).

19. ☑ D and F. D is a reference to a *char* primitive that happens to be in an array. F returns a primitive, not an object.
☒ A, B, C, and E all return objects. For A, `null` is always a valid object return. For C, an array is an object that holds other things (either objects or primitives). For E, we are returning an array held in an array, and it's still an object!

20. ☑ B and F are both attempting to cast a primitive to an object—can't do it.
☒ A, C, D, and E all return objects. A is an array object that holds other arrays. C is an array object. D is an ArrayList object. E is a string cast to an object.

21. ☑ B. Line 8 is an example of a polymorphic return type. The VM will determine on a case-by-case basis what class of object `f2` refers to, Bar or Foo. This is only possible because the classes Foo and Bar are in the same inheritance tree.
☒ A, C, D, and E, are incorrect based on the logic described above.

6

Java.lang—The Math Class, Strings, and Wrappers

CERTIFICATION OBJECTIVES

- Using the java.lang.String Class
- Using the java.lang.Math Class
- Using Wrapper Classes
- Using the `equals()` Method with Strings and Wrappers and Objects

✓ Two-Minute Drill

Q&A Self Test

This chapter focuses on the aspects of the java.lang package that you'll need to understand for the exam. The java.lang package contains many of the most fundamental and often-used classes in the Java API. The exam will test your knowledge of String and StringBuffer basics, including the infamous immutability of String objects, and how the more common String and StringBuffer methods work. You will be tested on many of the basic methods included in the Math class (extremely interesting), and you will need to know all about wrappers—those methods that allow you to encapsulate your favorite primitives into objects, so that you can do object-like stuff with them (like put them in collections). Finally, we'll reveal more than you've ever wanted to know about how the `equals()` method and == operator work when dealing with String objects and wrappers.

As always, our focus will be on the knowledge you'll really need to pass the exam. Undoubtedly some very wonderful methods will be overlooked in our tour of java.lang, but we're dedicated to helping you pass this test.

CERTIFICATION OBJECTIVE

Using the String Class (Exam Objective 8.2)

Describe the significance of the immutability of String objects.

This section covers the String and StringBuffer classes. The key concepts we'll cover will help you understand that once a String object is created, it can never be changed—so what *is* happening when a String object *seems* to be changing? We'll find out. We'll also cover the differences between the String and StringBuffer classes and when to use which.

Strings Are Immutable Objects

Let's start with a little background information about strings. Strictly speaking you may not need this information for the test, but a little context will help you learn what you *do* have to know. Handling "strings" of characters is a fundamental aspect of most programming languages. In Java, each character in a string is a 16-bit

Unicode character. Because Unicode characters are 16 bits (not the skimpy 7 or 8 bits that ASCII provides), a rich, international set of characters is easily represented in Unicode.

In Java, strings are objects. Just like other objects, you can create an instance of a String with the `new` keyword, as follows:

```
String s = new String();
```

This line of code creates a new object of class String, and assigns the reference variable *s* to it. So far String objects seem just like other objects. Now, let's give the String a value:

```
s = "abcdef";
```

As you might expect the String class has about a zillion constructors, so you can use a more efficient shortcut:

```
String s = new String("abcdef");
```

And just because you'll use strings all the time, you can even say this:

```
String s = "abcdef";
```

There are some subtle differences between these options that we'll discuss later, but what they have in common is that they all create a new String object, with a value of "abcdef", and assign it to a reference variable *s*. Now let's say that you want a second reference to the String object referred to by *s*:

```
String s2 = s;   //  refer s2 to the same String as s
```

So far so good. String objects seem to be behaving just like other objects, so what's all the fuss about? The certification objective states: "describe the significance of the immutability of String objects." Ah-ha! Immutability! (What the heck is immutability?) Once you have assigned a String a value, that value can never change— it's immutable, frozen solid, won't budge, fini, done. (We'll also talk about why later, don't let us forget.) The good news is that while the String *object* is immutable, its *reference variable* is not, so to continue with our previous example:

```
s = s.concat(" more stuff");  // the concat() method 'appends
                              // a literal to the end
```

Now wait just a minute, didn't we just say that Strings were immutable? So what's all this "appending to the end of the string" talk? Excellent question; let's look at what really happened…

The VM took the value of String *s* (which was `"abcdef"`), and tacked `" more stuff"` onto the end, giving us the value `"abcdef more stuff"`. Since Strings are immutable, the VM couldn't stuff this new String into the old String referenced by *s*, so it created a new String object, gave it the value `"abcdef more stuff"`, and made *s* refer to *it.* At this point in our example, we have two String objects: the first one we created, with the value `"abcdef"`, and the second one with the value `"abcdef more stuff"`. Technically there are now *three* String objects, because the literal argument to concat `" more stuff"` is *itself* a new String object. But we have references only to `"abcdef"` (referenced by *s2*) and `"abcdef more stuff"` (referenced by *s*).

What if we didn't have the foresight or luck to create a second reference variable for the `"abcdef"` String *before* we called: `s = s.concat(" more stuff");`? In that case the original, unchanged String containing `"abcdef"` would still exist in memory, but it would be considered "lost." No code in our program has any way to reference it—it is lost to us. Note, however, that the original "abcdef" String didn't change (it can't, remember, it's *immutable*); only the reference variable *s* was changed, so that it would refer to a different String. Figure 6-1 shows what happens on the heap when you reassign a reference variable. Note that the dashed line indicates a deleted reference.

To review our first example:

```
String s = "abcdef";     // create a new String object, with value "abcdef",
                         // refer s to it
String s2 = s;           // create a 2nd reference variable referring to
                         // the same String

s = s.concat(" more stuff");    // create a new String object, with value
                                // "abcdef more stuff", refer s to it.
                                // (change s's reference from the old
                                // String to the new String.  ( Remember
                                // s2 is still referring to the original
                                // "abcdef" String.
```

FIGURE 6-1

String objects and their reference variables

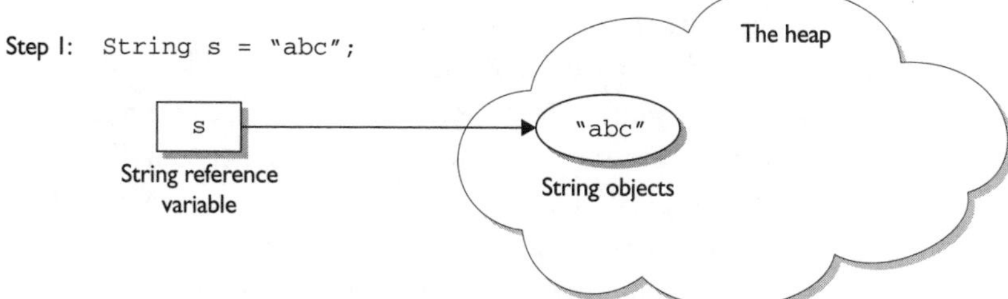

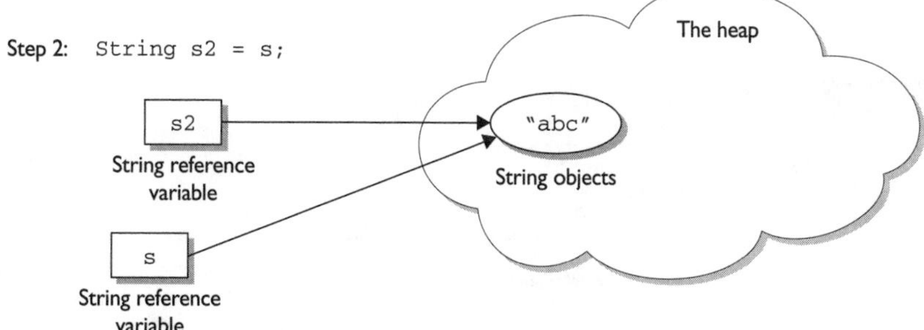

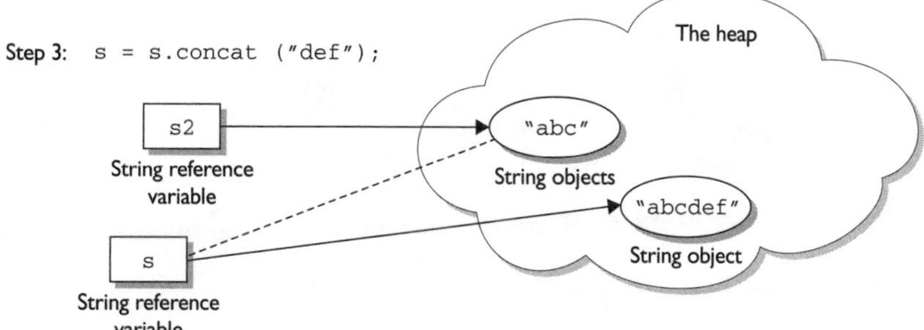

Let's look at another example:

```
String x = "Java";
x.concat(" Rules!");
System.out.println("x = " + x);
```

The output will be `x = Java`.

The first line is straightforward: create a new String object, give it the value `"Java"`, and refer *x* to it. What happens next? The VM creates a second String object with the value `"Java Rules!"` but nothing refers to it!!! The second String object is instantly lost; no one can ever get to it. The reference variable *x* still refers to the original String with the value `"Java"`. Figure 6-2 shows creating a String object without assigning to a reference.

Let's expand this current example. We started with

```
String x = "Java";
x.concat(" Rules!");
System.out.println("x = " + x);     // the output is:   x = Java
```

FIGURE 6-2

A String object is abandoned upon creation

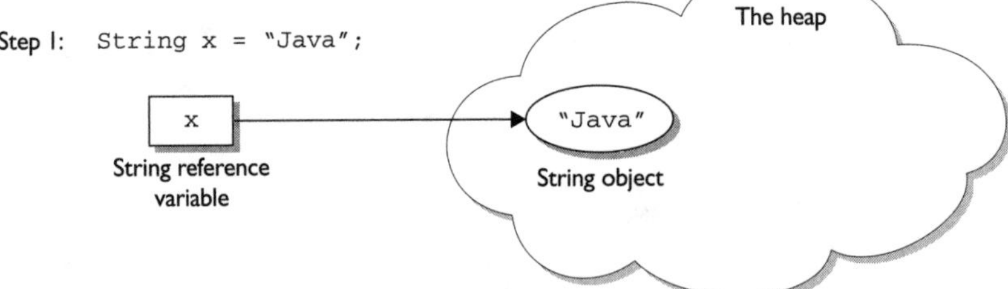

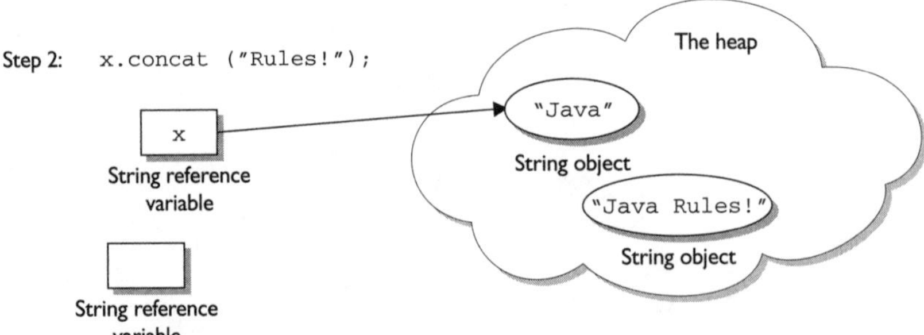

Now let's add

```
x.toUpperCase();
System.out.println("x = " + x);      // the output is still:   x = Java
```

(We actually *did* just create a new String object with the value "JAVA", but it was lost, and *x still* refers to the original, unchanged String "Java".)

How about adding

```
x.replace('a', 'X');
System.out.println("x = " + x);     // the output is still:  x = Java
```

Can you determine what happened? The VM created yet another new String object, with the value "JXvX", (replacing the *a*'s with *X*'s), but once again this new String was lost, leaving *x* to refer to the original unchanged and *unchangeable* String object, with the value "Java". In all of these cases we called various String methods to create a new String by altering an existing String, but we never *assigned* the newly created String to a reference variable.

But we can put a small spin on the previous example:

```
String x = "Java";
x = x.concat(" Rules!");      //  Now we're assigning x to the new String
System.out.println("x = " + x);     // the output will be:
                                    // x = Java Rules!
```

This time, when the VM runs the second line, a new String object is created with the value of "Java Rules!", and *x* is set to reference it. But wait, there's more—now the original String object, "Java", has been lost, and no one is referring to it. So in both examples we created *two* String objects and only *one* reference variable, so one of the two String objects was left out in the cold. See Figure 6-3 for a graphic depiction of this sad story. The dashed line indicates a deleted reference.

Let's take this example a little further:

```
String x = "Java";
x = x.concat(" Rules!");
System.out.println("x = " + x);     //     the output is:   x = Java Rules!

x.toLowerCase();         //  no assignment, create a new, abandoned String

System.out.println("x = " + x);       //     no assignment, the output is
                                      //     still:    x = Java Rules
```

```
x = x.toLowerCase();                //   create a new String, assigned to x
System.out.println("x = " + x);     //   the assignment causes the output:
                                    //   x = java rules!
```

The previous discussion contains the keys to understanding Java String immutability. If you really, really *get* the examples and diagrams, backwards and forwards, you should get 80 percent of the String questions on the exam correct. We will cover more details about Strings next, but make no mistake—in terms of bang for your buck, what we've already covered is by far the most important part of understanding how String objects work in Java.

We'll finish this section by presenting an example of the kind of devilish String question you might expect to see on the exam. Take the time to work it out on paper (as a hint, try to keep track of how many objects and reference variables there are, and which ones refer to which).

FIGURE 6-3

An old String object being abandoned

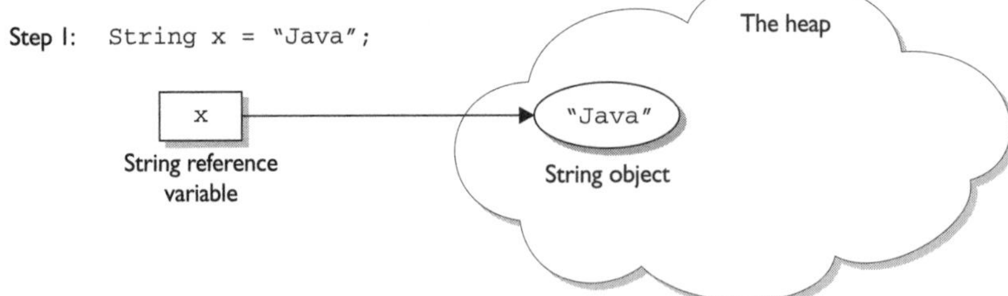

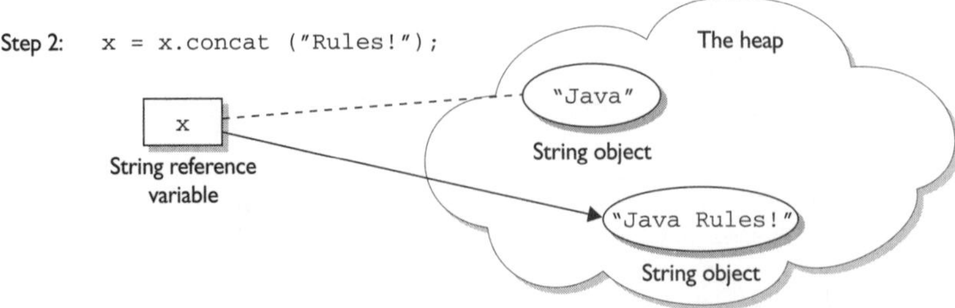

Notice in step 2 that there is no valid reference to the "Java" String; that object has been "abandoned," and a new object created.

```
String s1 = "spring ";
String s2 = s1 + "summer ";
s1.concat("fall ");
s2.concat(s1);
s1 += "winter ";
System.out.println(s1 + " " + s2);
```

What is the output?

For extra credit, how many String objects and how many reference variables were created prior to the `println` statement? Answer:

The result of this code fragment is "`spring winter spring summer`". There are two reference variables, *s1* and *s2*. There were a total of eight String objects created as follows: “spring”, “summer ” (lost), “spring summer”, “fall” (lost), “spring fall” (lost), “spring summer spring” (lost), “winter” (lost), “spring winter” (at this point “spring” is lost). Only two of the eight String objects are not lost in this process.

Important Facts About Strings and Memory

In this section we’ll discuss how Java handles string objects in memory, and some of the reasons behind these behaviors.

One of the key goals of any good programming language is to make efficient use of memory. As applications grow, it’s very common that String literals occupy large amounts of a program’s memory, and that there is often a lot of redundancy within the universe of String literals for a program. To make Java more memory efficient, the JVM sets aside a special area of memory called the “String constant pool.” When the compiler encounters a String literal, it checks the pool to see if an identical String already exists. If a match is found, the reference to the new literal is directed to the existing String, and no new String literal object is created. (The existing String simply has an additional reference.) Now we can start to see why making String objects immutable is such a good idea. If several reference variables refer to the same String without even knowing it, it would be *very* bad if any of them could change the String’s value.

You might say, “Well that’s all well and good, but what if someone overrides the String class functionality; couldn’t that cause problems in the pool?” That’s one of the main reasons that the String class is marked `final`. Nobody can override the behaviors of any of the String methods, so you can rest assured that the String objects you are counting on to be immutable will, in fact, *be* immutable.

Creating New Strings

Earlier we promised to talk more about the subtle differences between the various methods of creating a String. Let's look at a couple of examples of how a String might be created, and let's further assume that no other String objects exist in the pool:

```
1 - String s = "abc";     //  creates one String object and one reference
                         //  variable
```

In this simple case, "abc" will go in the pool and *s* will refer to it.

```
2 - String s = new String("abc");     // creates two objects, and one
                                     // reference variable
```

In this case, because we used the new keyword, Java will create a new String object in normal (nonpool) memory, and *s* will refer to it. In addition, the literal "abc" will be placed in the pool.

Important Methods in the String Class

The following methods are some of the more commonly used methods in the String class, and also the ones that you're most likely to encounter on the exam.

public char charAt(int index)

This method returns the character located at the String's specified index. Remember that String indexes are zero-based—for example,

```
String x = "airplane";
System.out.println( x.charAt(2) );              //  output is 'r'
```

public String concat(String s)

This method returns a String with the value of the String *passed* in to the method appended to the end of the String used to *invoke* the method—for example,

```
String x = "taxi";
System.out.println( x.concat(" cab") );      // output is "taxi cab"
```

The overloaded + and += operators perform functions similar to the concat() method—for example,

```
String x = "library";
System.out.println( x + " card");         // output is "library card"
```

```
1. String x = "Atlantic";
2. x += " ocean"
3. System.out.println( x );        // output is "Atlantic ocean"
```

In the preceding "Atlantic Ocean" example, notice that the value of *x really did change!* Remember that the += operator is an *assignment* operator, so line 2 is really creating a new String, "Atlantic Ocean", and assigning it to the *x* variable. After line 2 executes, the original String *x* was referring to, "Atlantic", is abandoned.

`public boolean equalsIgnoreCase(String s)`

This method returns a *boolean* value (`true` or `false`) depending on whether the value of the String in the *argument* is the same as the value of the String *used to invoke the method.* This method will return `true` even when characters in the String objects being compared have differing cases—for example,

```
String x = "Exit";
System.out.println( x.equalsIgnoreCase("EXIT"));    // returns "true"

System.out.println( x.equalsIgnoreCase("tixe"));    // returns "false"
```

`public int length()`

This method returns the length of the String used to invoke the method—for example,

```
String x = "01234567";
System.out.println( x.length() );      // returns "8"
```

exam Watch

Arrays have an attribute (not a method), called `length`. You may encounter questions in the exam that attempt to use the `length()` method on an array, or that attempt to use the `length` attribute on a String. Both cause compiler errors—for example,

```
String x = "test";
System.out.println( x.length );    // compiler error
```

or

```
String [] x = new String[3];
System.out.println( x.length() );
```

`public String replace(char old, char new)`

This method returns a String whose value is that of the String used to invoke the method, updated so that any occurrence of the *char* in the first argument is replaced by the *char* in the second argument—for example,

```
String x = "oxoxoxox";
System.out.println( x.replace('x', 'X') );    // output is  "oXoXoXoX"
```

`public String substring(int begin)`
`public String substring(int begin, int end)`

The `substring()` method is used to return a part (or *sub*string) of the String used to invoke the method. The first argument represents the starting location (zero-based) of the substring. If the call has only *one* argument, the substring returned will include the characters to the end of the original String. If the call has *two* arguments, the substring returned will end with the character located in the *n*th position of the original String where *n* is the second argument. Unfortunately, the ending argument is not zero-based, so if the second argument is 7, the last character in the returned String will be in the original String's 7 position, which is index 6 (ouch). Let's look at some examples:

```
String x = "0123456789";          // as if by magic, the value of each char
                                  // is the same as its index!
System.out.println( x.substring(5) );      //   output is  "56789"
System.out.println( x.substring(5, 8));   // output is "567"
```

The first example should be easy: start at index 5 and return the rest of the String. The second example should be read as follows: start at index 5 and return the characters up to and including the 8th position (index 7).

`public String toLowerCase()`

This method returns a String whose value is the String used to invoke the method, but with any uppercase characters converted to lowercase—for example,

```
String x = "A New Moon";
System.out.println( x.toLowerCase() );    // output is  "a new moon"
```

`public String toString()`

This method returns the value of the String used to invoke the method. What? Why would you need such a seemingly "do nothing" method? All objects in Java must have a `toString()` method, which typically returns a String that in some meaningful way describes the object in question. In the case of a String object, what more meaningful way than the String's value? For the sake of consistency, here's an example:

```
String x = "big surprise";
System.out.println( x.toString() );     // output - reader's exercise
```

`public String toUpperCase()`

This method returns a String whose value is the String used to invoke the method, but with any lowercase characters converted to uppercase—for example,

```
String x = "A New Moon";
System.out.println( x.toUpperCase() );    // output is  "A NEW MOON"
```

`public String trim()`

This method returns a String whose value is the String used to invoke the method, but with any leading or trailing blank spaces removed—for example,

```
String x = "       hi        ";

System.out.println( x + "x" );              // result is "     hi    x"
System.out.println( x.trim() + "x");        // result is "hix"
```

The StringBuffer Class

The StringBuffer class should be used when you have to make a lot of modifications to strings of characters. As we discussed in the previous section, String objects are immutable, so if you choose to do a lot of manipulations with String objects, you will end up with a lot of abandoned String objects in the String pool. On the other hand, objects of type StringBuffer can be modified over and over again without leaving behind a great effluence of discarded String objects.

A common use for StringBuffers is file I/O when large, ever-changing streams of input are being handled by the program. In these cases, large blocks of characters are handled as units, and StringBuffer objects are the ideal way to handle a block of data, pass it on, and then reuse the same memory to handle the next block of data.

In the previous section, we saw how the exam might test your understanding of String immutability with code fragments like this:

```
String x = "abc";
x.concat("def");
System.out.println("x = " + x);      //  output is "x = abc"
```

Because no new assignment was made, the new String object created with the `concat()` method was abandoned instantly. We also saw examples like this:

```
String x = "abc";
x = x.concat("def");
System.out.println("x = " + x);     // output is "x = abcdef"
```

We got a nice new String out of the deal, but the downside is that the old String "`abc`" has been lost in the String pool, thus wasting memory. If we were using a StringBuffer instead of a String, the code would look like this:

```
StringBuffer sb = new StringBuffer("abc");
sb.append("def");
System.out.println("sb = " + sb);       // output is "sb = abcdef"
```

All of the StringBuffer methods we will discuss operate on the value of the StringBuffer object invoking the method. So a call to `sb.append("def");` *is actually appending* "`def`" *to itself* (`StringBuffer sb`). In fact, these method calls can be *chained* to each other—for example,

```
StringBuffer sb = new StringBuffer("abc");
sb.append("def").reverse().insert(3, "---");
System.out.println( sb );                        // output is  "fed---cba"
```

exam Watch

The exam will probably test your knowledge of the difference between String and StringBuffer objects. Because StringBuffer objects are changeable, the following code fragment will behave differently than a similar code fragment that uses String objects:

```
StringBuffer sb = new StringBuffer("abc");
sb.append("def");
System.out.println( sb );
```

In this case, the output will be

"abcdef"

Important Methods in the StringBuffer Class

The following method returns a StringBuffer object with the argument's value appended to the value of the object that invoked the method:

```
public synchronized StringBuffer append(String s)
```

As we've seen earlier, this method will update the value of the object that invoked the method, whether or not the return is assigned to a variable. This method will take many different arguments, *boolean, char, double, float, int, long,* and others, but the most likely use on the exam will be a String argument—for example,

```
StringBuffer sb = new StringBuffer("set ");
sb.append("point");
System.out.println( sb );       // output is "set point"
```

or

```
StringBuffer sb = new StringBuffer("pi = ");
sb.append(3.14159f);
System.out.println( sb );           // output is  "pi = 3.14159"
```

```
public synchronized StringBuffer insert(int offset, String s)
```

This method returns a StringBuffer object and updates the value of the StringBuffer object that invoked the method call. In both cases, the String passed in to the second argument is inserted into the original StringBuffer starting at the offset location represented by the first argument (the offset is zero-based). Again, other types of data can be passed in through the second argument (*boolean, char, double, float, int, long,* etc.), but the String argument is the one you're most likely o see:

```
StringBuffer sb = new StringBuffer("01234567");
sb.insert(4, "---");
System.out.println( sb );          //   output is  "0123---4567"
```

```
public synchronized StringBuffer reverse()
```

This method returns a StringBuffer object and updates the value of the StringBuffer object that invoked the method call. In both cases, the characters in the StringBuffer are reversed, the first character becoming the last, the second becoming the second to the last, and so on:

```
StringBuffer sb = new StringBuffer("A man a plan a canal Panama");
sb.reverse();
System.out.println(sb);        // output is "amanaP lanac a nalp a nam A"
```

public String toString()

This method returns the value of the StringBuffer object that invoked the method call as a String:

```
StringBuffer sb = new StringBuffer("test string");
System.out.println( sb.toString() );        //  output is "test string"
```

That's it for StringBuffers. If you take only one thing away from this section, it's that *unlike Strings, StringBuffer objects can be changed.*

exam Watch

Many of the exam questions covering this chapter's topics use a tricky bit of Java syntax known as *chained methods.* ***A statement with chained methods has the general form:***

`result = method1().method2().method3();`

In theory, any number of methods can be *chained* ***in this fashion, although typically you won't see more than three. Here's how to decipher these "handy Java shortcuts" when you encounter them:***

1. ***Determine what the leftmost method call will return (let's call it*** *x****).***
2. ***Use*** *x* ***as the object invoking the second (from the left) method. If there are only two chained methods, the result of the second method call*** *is* ***the expression's result.***
3. ***If there is a third method, the result of the second method call is used to invoke the third method, whose result*** *is* ***the expression's result— for example,***

```
String x = "abc";
String y = x.concat("def").toUpperCase().replace('C','x'); //chained methods
System.out.println("y = " + y); // result is "ABxDEF"
```

Let's look at what happened. The literal `"def"` ***was concatenated to*** `"abc"`***, creating a temporary, intermediate String (soon to be lost), with the value*** `"abcdef"`***. The*** `toUpperCase()` ***method created a new (soon to be lost) temporary String with the value*** `"ABCDEF"`***. The*** `replace()` ***method created a final String with the value*** `"ABxDEF"`***, and referred*** *y* ***to it.***

CERTIFICATION OBJECTIVE

Using the Math Class (Exam Objective 8.1)

Write code using the following methods of the java.lang.Math class: abs, ceil, floor, max, min, random, round, sin, cos, tan, sqrt.

The java.lang package defines classes that are fundamental to the Java language. For this reason, all classes in the java.lang package are imported automatically, so there is no reason to write an `import` statement for them. The package defines object wrappers for all primitive types. The class names are Boolean, Byte, Character, Double, Float, Integer, Long, Short, and Void as well as Object, the class from which all other Java classes inherit.

The java.lang package also contains the Math class, which is used to perform basic mathematical operations. The Math class defines approximations for the mathematical constants *pi* and *e.* Their signatures are as follows:

```
public final static double Math.PI
public final static double Math.E
```

Because all methods of the Math class are defined as `static`, you don't need to create an instance to use them. In fact, it's not *possible* to create an instance of the Math class because the constructor is `private`. You can't extend the Math class either, because it's marked `final`.

Methods of the java.lang.Math Class

The methods of the Math class are static and are accessed like any static method—through the class name. For these method calls the general form is

```
result = Math.aStaticMathMethod();
```

The following sections describe the Math methods and include examples of how to use them.

abs()

The `abs()` method returns the absolute value of the argument—for example,

```
x = Math.abs(99);        // output is 99
x = Math.abs(-99)        // output is 99
```

The method is overloaded to take an *int*, a *long*, a *float*, or a *double* argument. In all but two cases, the returned value is non-negative. The signatures of the `abs()` method are as follows:

```
public static int abs(int a)
public static long abs(long a)
public static float abs(float a)
public static double abs(double a)
```

ceil()

The `ceil()` method returns the smallest integer, as a *double*, that is *greater than or equal to the argument* and *equal to the nearest integer value*. In other words, the argument is rounded up to the nearest integer equivalent.

Let's look at some examples of this in action, just to make sure you are familiar with the concept. All the following calls to `Math.ceil()` return the *double* value 9.0:

```
Math.ceil(9.0)     // result is 9.0
Math.ceil(8.8)     // rises to 9.0
Math.ceil(8.02)    // still rises to 9.0
```

Negative numbers are similar, but just remember that –9 is greater than –10. All the following calls to `Math.ceil()` return the *double* value -9.0:

```
Math.ceil(-9.0)    // result is -9.0
Math.ceil(-9.4)    // rises to -9.0
Math.ceil(-9.8)    // still rises to -9.0
```

There is only one `ceil()` method and it has the following signature:

```
public static double ceil(double a)
```

floor()

The `floor()` method returns the largest *double* that is less than or equal to the argument and equal to the nearest integer value. This method is the antithesis of the `ceil()` method.

All the following calls to `Math.floor()` return the *double* value 9.0:

```
Math.floor(9.0)      // result is 9.0
Math.floor(9.4)      // drops to 9.0
Math.floor(9.8)      // still drops to 9.0
```

As before, keep in mind that with negative numbers, –9 is less than –8! All the following calls to `Math.floor()` return the *double* value –9.0:

```
Math.floor(-9.0)     // result is -9.0
Math.floor(-8.8)     // drops to -9.0
Math.floor(-8.1)     // still drops to -9.0
```

The signature of the `floor()` method is as follows:

```
public static double floor(double a)
```

exam watch

The `floor()` and `ceil()` methods take only* doubles. *There are no overloaded methods for integral numbers, because the methods would just end up returning the integral numbers they were passed. The whole point of `floor()` and `ceil()` is to convert floating-point numbers `(doubles)`, to integers, based on the rules of the methods. It may seem strange (it does to us) that the integer values are returned in a* double *sized container, but don't let that throw you.

max()

The `max()` method takes two numeric arguments and returns the greater of the two—for example,

```
x = Math.max(1024, -5000);      //  output is 1024.
```

This method is overloaded to handle *int*, *long*, *float*, or *double* arguments. If the input parameters are the same, `max()` returns a value equal to the two arguments. The signatures of the `max()` method are as follows:

```
public static int max(int a, int b)
public static long max(long a, long b)
public static float max(float a, float b)
public static double max(double a, double b)
```

min()

The `min()` method is the antithesis of the `max()` method; it takes two numeric arguments and returns the lesser of the two—for example,

```
x = Math.min(0.5, 0.0);    //   output is  0.0
```

This method is overloaded to handle *int*, *long*, *float*, or *double* arguments. If the input parameters are the same, `min()` returns a value equal to the two arguments. The signatures of the `min()` method are as follows:

```
public static int min(int a, int b)
public static long min(long a, long b)
public static float min(float a, float b)
public static double min(double a, double b)
```

And for the record, we're pretty impressed with our use of the word "antithesis".

EXERCISE 6-1

Using the Math Class

In this exercise we will examine some numbers using the `abs()`, `ceil()`, and `floor()` methods of the Math class. Find the absolute, ceiling, and floor values of the following numbers: 10.5, –10.5, Math.PI, and 0.

- Create a class and a `main()` method to perform the calculations.
- Store these numbers in an array of *double* values.
- Use a *for* loop to go through the array and perform the tests on each of these numbers.
- Try to determine what the results of your program will be before running it.
- An example solution is provided at the end of the chapter.

random()

The `random()` method returns a random *double* that is greater than or equal to 0.0 and less than 1.0. The `random()` method does not take any parameters—for example,

```
public class RandomTest {
  public static void main(String [] args) {
    for (int x=0; x < 15; x++)
      System.out.print( (int)(Math.random()*10) + " " );
  }
}
```

The `println()` method multiplies the result of the call to `Math.random()` by 10, and then casts the resulting *double* (whose value will be between 0.0 and 9.99999999...), to an integer. Here are some sample results:

```
6 3 3 1 2 0 5 9 3 5 6 6 0 3 5
4 9 3 6 6 8 1 1 3 0 3 2 5 3 4
```

The signature of the `random()` method is as follows:

```
public static double random( )
```

round()

The `round()` method returns the integer closest to the argument. The algorithm is to add 0.5 to the argument and truncate to the nearest integer equivalent. This method is overloaded to handle a *float* or a *double* argument.

The methods `ceil()`, `floor()`, and `round()` all take floating-point arguments and return integer equivalents (although again, delivered in a *double* variable). If the number after the decimal point is *less than* 0.5, `Math.round()` is equal to `Math.floor()`. If the number after the decimal point is *greater than or equal to* 0.5, `Math.round()` is equal to `Math.ceil()`. Keep in mind that with negative numbers, a number at the .5 mark will round up to the *larger* number—for example,

```
Math.round(-10.5);      // result is -10
```

The signatures of the `round()` method are as follows:

```
public static int round(float a)
public static long round(double a)
```

sin()

The `sin()` method returns the sine of an angle. The argument is a *double* representing an angle *in radians*. Degrees can be converted to radians by using `Math.toRadians()`—for example,

```
Math.sin(Math.toRadians(90.0)) //  returns 1.0
```

The signature of the `sin()` method is as follows:

```
public static double sin(double a)
```

cos()

The `cos()` method returns the cosine of an angle. The argument is a *double* representing an angle *in radians*—for example,

```
Math.cos(Math.toRadians(0.0)) // returns 1.0
```

The signature of the `cos()` method is as follows:

```
public static double cos(double a)
```

tan()

The `tan()` method returns the tangent of an angle. The argument is a *double* representing an angle *in radians*—for example,

```
Math.tan(Math.toRadians(45.0))    // returns 1.0
```

The signature of the `tan()` method is as follows:

```
public static double tan(double a)
```

exam Watch

Sun does not expect you to be a human calculator. The certification exam will not contain questions that require you to verify the result of calling methods such as `Math.cos(0.623)`. (Although we thought it would be fun to include questions like that...)

sqrt()

The `sqrt()` method returns the square root of a *double*—for example,

```
Math.sqrt(9.0) // returns 3.0
```

What if you try to determine the square root of a negative number? After all, the actual mathematical square root function returns a complex number (comprised of real and imaginary parts) when the operand is negative. The Java `Math.sqrt()` method returns `NaN` instead of an object representing a complex number. `NaN` is a bit pattern that denotes "not a number." The signature of the `sqrt()` method is as follows:

```
public static double sqrt(double a)
```

EXERCISE 6-2

Rounding Random Numbers

In this exercise we will round a series of random numbers. The program will generate ten random numbers from 0 through 100. Round each one of them, then print the results to the screen. Try to do this with as little code as possible.

1. Create a class and a `main()` method to perform the calculations.
2. Use a *for* loop to go through ten iterations.
3. Each iteration should generate a random number using `Math.random()`. To get a number from 0 through 100 simply multiply the random number by 100. Print this number to the screen. Without rounding it, though, you can't ever get to 100 (the `random()` method always returns something *less* than 1.0).
4. Round the number using the `Math.round()` method. Print the rounded number to the screen.
5. A sample solution is listed at the end of the chapter.

As a bonus, note whether the numbers look random. Is there an equal number of even and odd numbers? Are they grouped more towards the top half of 100 or the bottom half? What happens to the distribution as you generate more random numbers?

toDegrees()

The `toDegrees()` method takes an argument representing an angle in radians and returns the equivalent angle in degrees—for example,

```
Math.toDegrees(Math.PI * 2.0)   //  returns 360.0
```

The signature of the `toDegrees()` method is as follows:

```
public static double toDegrees(double a)
```

toRadians()

The `toRadians()` method takes an argument representing an angle in degrees and returns the equivalent angle in radians—for example,

```
Math.toRadians(360.0)   //  returns 6.283185, which is 2 * Math.PI
```

This method is useful for converting an angle in degrees to an argument suitable for use with the trigonometric methods (`cos()`, `sin()`, `tan()`, `acos()`, `asin()`, and `atan()`). For example, to determine the sin of 60 degrees:

```
double d = Math.toRadians(60);
System.out.println("sin 60 = " + Math.sin(d) ); // "sin 60 = 0.866..."
```

The signature of the `toRadians()` method is as follows:

```
public static double toRadians(double a)
```

Table 6-1 summarizes the key static methods of the Math class.

TABLE 6-1 Important Static Math Class Method Signatures

Static Math Methods
double ceil (double a)
double floor (double a)
double random ( )
double abs (double a)
float abs (float a)
int abs (int a)
long abs (long a)
double max (double a, double b)
float max (float a, float b)
int max (int a, int b)
long max (long a, long b)
double min (double a, double b)
float min (float a, float b)double sqrt (double a)
int min (int a, int b)
long min (long a, long b)
double toDegrees (double angleInRadians)
double toRadians (double angleInDegrees)
double tan (double a)

TABLE 6-1

Important Static Math Class Method Signatures *(continued)*

Static Math Methods
double sin (double a)
double cos (double a)
double sqrt (double a)
int round (float a)
long round (double a)

Miscellaneous Math Class Facts

The following program demonstrates some of the unusual results that can occur when pushing some of the limits of the Math class or performing mathematical functions that are "on the edge" (such as dividing floating-point numbers by 0). These are some of the basic special cases. There are many more, but if you know these you will be in good shape for the exam.

exam Watch

If you want to live dangerously, or you're running out of study time before the big day, just focus on the examples below with the **.

```
double d;
float p_i = Float.POSITIVE_INFINITY;     // The floating point classes have
double n_i = Double.NEGATIVE_INFINITY;   // these three special fields.
double notanum = Double.NaN;             // They can be Float or Double

if ( notanum != notanum )                // ** NaN isn't == to anything, not
                                         // even itself!
  System.out.println("NaNs not equal"); // result is  "NaNs not equal"

if ( Double.isNaN(notanum))              // Float and Double have isNan()
                                         // methods to test for NaNs
  System.out.println("got a NaN");       // result is  "got a NaN"

d = Math.sqrt(n_i);                      // square root of negative infinity?
if ( Double.isNaN(d) )
  System.out.println("got sqrt NaN");    // result is "got sqrt NaN"

System.out.println( Math.sqrt(-16d));    // result is "NaN"

System.out.println( 16d / 0.0 );        // ** result is (positive) "Infinity"
System.out.println( 16d / -0.0 );       // ** result is (negative) "-Infinity"

     // divide by 0 only works for floating point numbers
     // divide by 0 with integer numbers results in ArithmeticException

System.out.println("abs(-0) = "+ Math.abs(-0));  // result is "abs(-0) = 0"
```

The exam will test your knowledge of implicit casting. For the numeric primitives, remember that from narrowest to widest the numeric primitives types are** byte, short, int, long, float, double. **Any numeric primitive can be implicitly cast to any numeric primitive type that is wider than itself. For instance, a** byte **can be implicitly cast to any other numeric primitive, but a** float **can only be implicitly cast to a** double. **Remembering implicit casting, and the method signatures in Table 6-1, will help you answer many of the exam questions.

CERTIFICATION OBJECTIVE

Using Wrapper Classes (Exam Objective 8.3)

Describe the significance of wrapper classes, including making appropriate selections in the wrapper classes to suit specified behavior requirements, stating the result of executing a fragment of code that includes an instance of one of the wrapper classes, and writing code using the following methods of the wrapper classes (e.g., Integer, Double, etc.): doubleValue, floatValue, intValue, longValue, parseXxx, getXxx, toString, toHexString.

The wrapper classes in the Java API serve two primary purposes:

- To provide a mechanism to "wrap" primitive values in an object so that the primitives can be included in activities reserved for objects, like as being added to Collections, or returned from a method with an object return value.
- To provide an assortment of utility functions for primitives. Most of these functions are related to various conversions: converting primitives to and from String objects, and converting primitives and String objects to and from different bases (or radix), such as binary, octal, and hexadecimal.

An Overview of the Wrapper Classes

There is a wrapper class for every primitive in Java. For instance the wrapper class for *int* is Integer, for *float* is Float, and so on. *Remember that the primitive name is simply the lowercase name of the wrapper except for char, which maps to Character, and int, which maps to Integer.* Table 6-2 lists the wrapper classes in the Java API.

Creating Wrapper Objects

For the exam you need to understand the three most common approaches for creating wrapper objects. Some approaches take a String representation of a primitive as an argument. Those that take a String throw NumberFormatException if the String provided cannot be parsed into the appropriate primitive. For example "two" can't be parsed into "2". Like another class previously discussed in this chapter, wrapper objects are immutable. Once they have been given a value, that value cannot be changed. (Can you guess which other class we're talking about?)

The Wrapper Constructors

All of the wrapper classes except Character provide two constructors: one that takes a primitive of the type being constructed, and one that takes a String representation of the type being constructed—for example,

```
Integer i1 = new Integer(42);
Integer i2 = new Integer("42");
```

or

```
Float f1 = new Float(3.14f);
Float f2 = new Float("3.14f");
```

TABLE 6-2 Wrapper Classes and Their Constructor Arguments

Primitive	Wrapper Class	Constructor Arguments
boolean	Boolean	boolean or String
byte	Byte	byte or String
char	Character	char
double	Double	double or String
float	Float	float, double, or String
int	Integer	int or String
long	Long	long or String
short	Short	short or String

The Character class provides only one constructor, which takes a *char* as an argument—for example,

```
Character c1 = new Character('c');
```

The constructors for the Boolean wrapper take either a boolean value `true` or `false`, or a case-insensitive String with the value "true" or "false". But a Boolean object can't be used as an expression in a boolean test—for instance,

```
Boolean b = new Boolean("false");
if (b)    // won't compile, expecting a boolean not a Boolean
```

The valueOf() Methods

The static `valueOf()` methods provided in most of the wrapper classes give you another approach to creating wrapper objects. Both methods take a String representation of the appropriate type of primitive as their first argument, the second method (when provided) takes an additional argument, `int radix`, which indicates in what base (for example binary, octal, or hexadecimal) the first argument is represented—for example,

```
Integer i2 = Integer.valueOf("101011", 2);  // converts 101011 to 43 and
                                             // assigns the value 43 to the
                                             // Integer object i2
```

or

```
Float f2 = Float.valueOf("3.14f");   // assigns 3.14 to the Float object f2
```

Using Wrapper Conversion Utilities

As we said earlier, a wrapper's second big function is converting stuff. The following methods are the most commonly used, and are the ones you're most likely to see on the test.

xxxValue()

When you need to convert the value of a wrapped numeric to a primitive, use one of the many `xxxValue()` methods. All of the methods in this family are no-arg methods. As you can see by referring to Table 6-3, there are 36 `xxxValue()` methods. Each of the six numeric wrapper classes has six methods, so that any numeric wrapper can be converted to any primitive numeric type—for example,

```
Integer i2 = new Integer(42);  //  make a new wrapper object
byte b = i2.byteValue();       //  convert i2's value to a byte
                               //  primitive
short s = i2.shortValue();     //  another of Integer's xxxValue
                               //  methods
double d = i2.doubleValue();   //  yet another of Integer's
                               //  xxxValue methods
```

or

```
Float f2 = new Float(3.14f);   // make a new wrapper object
short s = f2.shortValue();     // convert f2's value to a short
                               // primitive
System.out.println(s);         // result is 3  (truncated, not
                               // rounded)
```

TABLE 6-3 Common Wrapper Conversion Methods

Method s = static n = NFE exception	**Boolean**	**Byte**	**Character**	**Double**	**Float**	**Integer**	**Long**	**Short**
byteValue		x		x	x	x	x	x
doubleValue		x		x	x	x	x	x
floatValue		x		x	x	x	x	x
intValue		x		x	x	x	x	x
longValue		x		x	x	x	x	x
shortValue		x		x	x	x	x	x
parseXxx *s,n*		x		x	x	x	x	x
parseXxx *s,n* (with radix)		x				x	x	x
valueOf *s,n*	x	x		x	x	x	x	x
valueOf *s,n* (with radix)		x				x	x	x

TABLE 6-3 Common Wrapper Conversion Methods *(continued)*

Method s = static n = NFE exception	Boolean	Byte	Character	Double	Float	Integer	Long	Short
toString	x	x	x	x	x	x	x	x
toString *s* (primitive)		x		x	x	x	x	x
toString *s* (primitive, radix)						x	x	
toBinaryString *s*						x	x	
toHexString *s*						x	x	
toOctalString *s*						x	x	

In summary, the essential method signatures for Wrapper conversion methods are

- primitive xxxValue() - to convert a Wrapper to a String
- primitive parseXxx(String) - to convert a String to a primitive
- Wrapper valueOf(String) - to convert a String to a Wrapper

parseXxx() and valueOf()

The six `parseXxx()` methods (one for each numeric wrapper type) are closely related to the `valueOf()` method that exists in all of the numeric wrapper classes (plus Boolean). Both `parseXxx()` and `valueOf()` take a String as an argument, throw a NumberFormatException if the String argument is not properly formed, and can convert String objects from different bases (radix), when the underlying primitive type is any of the four integer types. (See Table 6-3.)

The difference between the two methods is

- `parseXxx()` returns the named primitive.
- `valueOf()` returns a newly created wrapped object of the type that invoked the method.

Some examples of these methods in action:

```
double d4 = Double.parseDouble("3.14");     // convert a String to a primitive
System.out.println("d4 = " + d4);           // result is  "d4 = 3.14"

Double d5 = Double.valueOf("3.14");         // create a Double object
System.out.println(d5 instanceof Double ); // result is "true"
```

The next examples involve using the radix argument, (in this case binary):

```
long L2 = Long.parseLong("101010", 2);      // binary String to a primitive
System.out.println("L2 = " + L2);           // result is "L2 = 42"

Long L3 = Long.valueOf("101010", 2);        // binary String to Long object
System.out.println("L3 value = " + L3);     // result is "L2 value = 42"
```

toString()

The class Object, the alpha class, the top dog, has a `toString()` method. Since we know that all other Java classes inherit from class Object, we also know (stay with me here) that all other Java classes have a `toString()` method. The idea of the `toString()` method is to allow you to get some *meaningful representation* of a given object. For instance, if you have a Collection of various types of objects, you can loop through the Collection and print out some sort of meaningful representation of each object using the `toString()` method, which is guaranteed to be in every class. We'll talk more about the `toString()` method in the Collections chapter, but for now let's focus on how the `toString()` method relates to the wrapper classes which, as we know, are marked `final`. All of the wrapper classes have a *no-arg, nonstatic, instance* version of `toString()`. This method returns a String with the value of the primitive wrapped in the object—for instance,

```
Double d = new Double("3.14");
System.out.println("d = " + d.toString() );    //  result is "d = 3.14"
```

All of the numeric wrapper classes provide an overloaded, `static toString()` method that takes a primitive numeric of the appropriate type (`Double.toString()` takes a *double*, `Long.toString()` takes a *long*, etc.), and, of course, returns a String with that primitive's value—for example,

```
System.out.println("d = " + Double.toString(3.14);    // result is "d = 3.14"
```

Finally, Integer and Long provide a third `toString()` method. It is `static`, its first argument is the appropriate primitive, and its second argument is a *radix*. The radix argument tells the method to take the first argument (which is radix 10 or base 10 by default), and convert it to the radix provided, then return the result as a String—for instance,

```
System.out.println("hex = " + Long.toString(254,16); // result is "hex = fe"
```

toXxxString() (Binary, Hexadecimal, Octal)

The Integer and Long wrapper classes let you convert numbers in base 10 to other bases. These conversion methods, `toXxxString()`, take an *int* or *long*, and return a String representation of the converted number, for example,

```
String s3 = Integer.toHexString(254);        // convert 254 to hex
System.out.println("254 in hex = " + s3);    // result is "254 in hex = fe"

String s4 = Long.toOctalString(254);         // convert 254 to octal
System.out.println("254 in octal = "+ s4);   // result is "254 in octal = 376"
```

Studying Table 6-3 is the single best way to prepare for this section of the test. If you can keep the differences between `xxxValue()`, `parseXxx()`, and `valueOf()` straight, you should do well on this part of the exam.

CERTIFICATION OBJECTIVE

Using equals()(Exam Objective 5.2)

Determine the result of applying the boolean `equals(Object)` *method to objects of any combination of the classes java.lang.String, java.lang.Boolean, and java.lang.Object.*

In this chapter we begin our discussion of == and the `equals()` method, and in the Collections chapter we'll dive deeper into these two mysterious comrades. For now, we'll limit our discussion to how == and the `equals()` method relate to String, and the wrapper classes, and an overview of other object classes.

An Overview of == and the equals() Method

There are three kinds of entities in Java that we might want to compare to determine if they're equivalent: primitive variables, reference variables, and objects. Part of this discussion looks at a critical question: *What exactly does "equivalent" mean?*

Comparing Variables

Let's start with primitive and reference variables. You always compare primitive variables using ==; the `equals()` method obviously can't be used on primitives.

The == operator returns a *boolean* value: `true` if the variables are equivalent, `false` if they're not. Primitive variables are stored in memory as some absolute number of bits, depending on the type of primitive being handled (*short* is 16 bits, *int* is 32 bits, *long* is 64 bits, etc.). On the other hand, we can't know from one Java implementation to the next how big a reference variable is—it might be 64 bits, it might be 97 bits (probably not!)—but the key thing to remember is that wherever a Java program might run, all of the reference variables running on a single VM will be the same size (in bits) and format. When we use the == operator to compare two reference variables, we're *really* testing to see if the two reference variables *refer to the same object!* So remember that when you compare variables (of either type, primitive or reference), you are really comparing two sets of bit patterns.

Either bit patterns are the same, or they're not. If primitive *a* holds a 5, and primitive *b* holds a 5, then the bits in *a* and *b* are the same and *a* == *b* will be true. If a reference variable *c* refers to object `X017432` and reference variable *d* also refers to object `X017432`, then the bits in *c* and *d* are the same, and *c* == *d* will be true.

When comparing reference variables with the == operator, you can only compare reference variables that refer to objects that are in the same class or class hierarchy. Attempting to use == to compare reference variables for objects in different class hierarchies will result in a compiler error.

exam Watch

Key facts to remember about comparing variables:

1. ***The rule is the same for reference variables and primitive variables: == returns true if the two bit patterns are identical.***
2. ***Primitive variables must use ==; they cannot use the*** `equals()` ***method.***
3. ***For reference variables, == means that both reference variables are referring to the same object.***

Comparing Objects

We saw what it means to compare reference variables (to see if they refer to the same object), but what does it mean to compare the objects themselves? For an object as simple as a String, it's fairly intuitive to say that if two String objects have the same value (in other words the same characters), we consider them equal. When you want to determine if two objects are *meaningfully equivalent,* use the `equals()` method. Like ==, the `equals()` method returns a *boolean* `true` if the objects are considered equivalent; otherwise, it returns *false.* (Remember, if we want to know whether two String reference variables refer to the same String, we must use ==.) Given the following code sample,

```
String x1 = "abc";
String x2 = "ab";
x2 = x2 + "c";
```

we might want to know, much later on in our code, whether the *contents* of the two different String objects *x1* and *x2* are in fact the same. This is where the `equals()` method comes in:

```
if ( x1 != x2 ) {                          // comparing reference vars
   System.out.println("different objects");
}
if ( x1.equals(x2) ) {                     // comparing values
   System.out.println("same values");
}
```

In the example above we could also have written this:

```
if ( x2.equals(x1) ) {                     // same result
```

In a similar vein, it's a pretty safe bet that when we want to compare two wrapper objects, we're really interested in the primitive *values* that they're wrapping. However, it's important to know that all of the wrapper class' `equals()` methods only return `true` if *both* the primitive values *and* the wrapper's classes are the same.

```
Double d1 = new Double("3.0");
Integer i1 = new Integer(3);             // create a couple of wrappers

if ( d1.equals(i1) )  {                  // are the values equal ?
   System.out.println("wraps are equal"); // no output, different classes
}

Double d2 = d1.valueOf("3.0d");             // create a third wrapper
if (d1.equals(d2) )  {                      // are the Doubles equal ?
   System.out.println("Doubles are equal"); // result is "Doubles are equal"
}
```

The equals() Method Revealed (or at Least a Little Bit Revealed)

We'll be diving in to the `equals()` method much more deeply in the Collections chapter, but for now let's just cover a few key points. The class Object, the granddaddy of all classes (and from which all classes extend), has an `equals()` method. That means every other Java class (including those in the API or those that you create) inherits an `equals()` method. In `java.lang`, the String and wrapper classes have overridden the `equals()` method to behave as we just discussed. And remember, the String and wrapper classes are all marked `final`, so you can't override any of their methods, *including* the `equals()` method.

When you create your own classes, you'll have to decide what it means for two distinct objects to be meaningfully equivalent. Your class may have reference variables that collectively represent the value of an instance. If you want to compare instances of a class to one another, it will be up to you to override the `equals()` method to define what it means for two different instances to be *meaningfully* equal.

Remember the following key points about the `equals()` ***method:***

1. `equals()` ***is used only to compare objects.***
2. `equals()` ***returns a boolean,*** `true` ***or*** `false`.
3. ***The StringBuffer class has not overridden*** `equals()`.
4. ***The String and wrapper classes are*** `final` ***and have overridden*** `equals()`.

CERTIFICATION SUMMARY

Strings

At the risk of being pedantic, remember that String *objects* are immutable, *references* to Strings are not! You learned that you can make a new String by using an existing String as a starting point, but if you don't *assign* a reference variable to a new String it will be lost to your program—you will have no way to access your new String. Review the important methods in the String class. They're all fairly intuitive except for `substring()`, which needs a little extra brainpower. (And did we mention how annoying—*possibly evil*—it is that the developers of the `substring()` method didn't follow the Java naming convention? It should have been `subString()`!)

StringBuffers are not immutable—you can change them over and over again. The StringBuffer methods are fairly intuitive, but remember that unlike String methods, they *do* modify the StringBuffer object, even if you don't assign the result to anything.

Math

As the Math class relates to the certification exam, you won't be expected to reproduce complicated mathematical algorithms in your head or know the cosine of an angle. But remember that you *will* need to know how to calculate the result of calling `abs()`, `ceil()`, `floor()`, `max()`, `min()`, and `round()` with any given values. Know the method signatures in Table 6-1. The exam will test your ability to remember method signatures and follow simple algorithms. Most questions on the Math class are quite simple as long as you've spent the time to commit to memory the Math class methods and their calling signatures. Table 6-1 will really help.

While you're at it, spend some time studying Table 6-1. It's important to know which methods are overridden and which are not. And just in case we're not making ourselves clear, *we really want you to study Table 6-1.*

Wrappers

Remember that wrappers have two main functions: to wrap primitives so they can be treated like objects, and to provide utility methods for primitives (typically conversions). All the wrapper classes have the same name, capitalized, as their primitive counterparts except for Character and Integer. Remember that Boolean objects can't be used like *boolean* primitives. In terms of return on investment for your studying time, make sure that you know the details of the `xxxValue()` methods, the `parseXxx()` methods, the `valueOf()` methods, and the `toString()` methods. Pay attention to which methods are `static` and which throw NumberFormatException. Study Table 6-3. Copy it by hand, and then place it under your pillow. Frame it and hang it on your wall.

Equals()

Compare primitives with ==. To determine if two reference variables refer to the *same object, use* ==. To determine if two objects are *meaningfully equivalent, use* `equals()`. When using == to compare reference variables, the compiler will verify that the classes are the same or in the same inheritance hierarchy. Remember that the *StringBuffer class does not override the* `equals()` *method,* which means that there is no built-in method to determine if the contents of one StringBuffer object are the same as the contents of another StringBuffer object.

TWO-MINUTE DRILL

Here are some of the key points from the certification objectives in this chapter.

Using the java.lang.String Class (Exam Objective 8.2)

- ❑ String objects are immutable, and String reference variables are not.
- ❑ If you create a new String without assigning it, it will be lost to your program.
- ❑ If you redirect a String reference to a new String, the old String can be lost.
- ❑ String methods use zero-based indexes, except for the second argument of `substring()`.
- ❑ The String class is `final`—its methods can't be overridden.
- ❑ When a String literal is encountered by the VM, it is added to the pool.
- ❑ Strings have a method named `length()`, arrays have an attribute named *length*.
- ❑ StringBuffers are mutable—they can change without creating a new object.
- ❑ StringBuffer methods act on the invoking object, but objects can change without an explicit assignment in the statement.
- ❑ StringBuffer `equals()` is not overridden; it doesn't compare values.
- ❑ In all sections, remember that *chained* methods are evaluated from left to right.

Using the java.lang.Math Class (Exam Objective 8.1)

- ❑ The `abs()` method is overloaded to take an *int*, a *long*, a *float*, or a *double*.
- ❑ The `abs()` method can return a negative if the argument is the minimum *int* or *long* value equal to the value of Integer.MIN_VALUE or Long.MIN_VALUE, respectively.
- ❑ The `max()` method is overloaded to take *int*, *long*, *float*, or *double* arguments.
- ❑ The `min()` method is overloaded to take *int*, *long*, *float*, or *double* arguments.
- ❑ The `random()` method returns a *double* greater than or equal to 0.0 and less than 1.0.

- The `random()` does not take any arguments.
- The methods `ceil()`, `floor()`, and `round()` all return integer equivalent floating-point numbers, `ceil()` and `floor()` return *doubles*, `round()` returns an *int* if it was passed a *float*, or it returns a *long* if it was passed a *double*.
- The `round()` method is overloaded to take a *float* or a *double*.
- The methods `sin()`, `cos()`, and `tan()` take a *double* angle in radians.
- The method `sqrt()` can return `NaN` if the argument is `NaN` or less than zero.
- Floating-point numbers can be divided by 0.0 without error; the result is either positive or negative infinity.
- `NaN` is not equal to anything, not even itself.

Using Wrappers (Exam Objective 8.3)

- The wrapper classes correlate to the primitive types.
- Wrappers have two main functions:
  - To wrap primitives so that they can be handled like objects
  - To provide utility methods for primitives (usually conversions)
- Other than Character and Integer, wrapper class names are the primitive's name, capitalized.
- Wrapper constructors can take a String or a primitive, except for Character, which can only take a *char*.
- A Boolean object can't be used like a *boolean* primitive.
- The three most important method families are
  - `xxxValue()` Takes no arguments, returns a primitive
  - `parseXxx()` Takes a String, returns a primitive, is static, throws NFE
  - `valueOf()` Takes a String, returns a wrapped object, is static, throws NFE
- Radix refers to bases (typically) other than 10; binary is radix 2, octal = 8, hex = 16.

Using equals() (Exam Objective 5.2)

- ❑ Use == to compare primitive variables.
- ❑ Use == to determine if two reference variables refer to the *same object.*
- ❑ == compares bit patterns, either primitive bits or reference bits.
- ❑ Use `equals()` to determine if two objects are *meaningfully equivalent.*
- ❑ The String and Wrapper classes override `equals()` to check for values.
- ❑ The StringBuffer class `equals()` is *not* overridden; it uses == under the covers.
- ❑ The compiler will not allow == if the classes are not in the same hierarchy.
- ❑ Wrappers won't pass `equals()` if they are in different classes.

SELF TEST

The following questions will help you measure your understanding of the material presented in this chapter. Read all of the choices carefully, as there may be more than one correct answer. Choose all correct answers for each question.

Using the java.lang.String Class (Exam Objective 8.2)

1. Given the following,

```
public class StringRef {
  public static void main(String [] args) {
    String s1 = "abc";
    String s2 = "def";
    String s3 = s2;
    s2 = "ghi";
    System.out.println(s1 + s2 + s3);
  }
}
```

what is the result?

A. `abcdefghi`

B. `abcdefdef`

C. `abcghidef`

D. `abcghighi`

E. Compilation fails.

F. An exception is thrown at runtime.

2. Given the following,

```
String x = "xyz";
x.toUpperCase();
String y = x.replace('Y', 'y');
y = y + "abc";
System.out.println(y);
```

what is the result?

A. `abcXyZ`

B. `abcxyz`

C. `xyzabc`

D. `XyZabc`

E. Compilation fails.

F. An exception is thrown at runtime.

3. Given the following,

```
String x = new String("xyz");
y = "abc";
x = x + y;
```

how many String objects have been created?

A. 2

B. 3

C. 4

D. 5

4. Given the following,

```
String a = "newspaper";
a = a.substring(5,7);
char b = a.charAt(1);
a = a + b;
System.out.println(a);
```

what is the result?

A. `apa`

B. `app`

C. `apea`

D. `apep`

E. `papp`

F. `papa`

5. Given the following,

```
String d = "bookkeeper";
d.substring(1,7);
d = "w" + d;
d.append("woo");
System.out.println(d);
```

what is the result?

A. `wookkeewoo`

B. `wbookkeeper`

C. `wbookkeewoo`

D. `wbookkeeperwoo`

E. Compilation fails.

F. An exception is thrown at runtime.

Using the java.lang.Math Class (Exam Objective 8.1)

6. Given the following,

```
public class Example {
  public static void main(String [] args) {
    double values[] = {-2.3, -1.0, 0.25, 4};
    int cnt = 0;
    for (int x=0; x < values.length; x++) {
      if (Math.round(values[x] + .5) == Math.ceil(values[x])) {
        ++cnt;
      }
    }
   System.out.println("same results " + cnt + " time(s)");
  }
}
```

what is the result?

A. same results 0 time(s)

B. same results 2 time(s)

C. same results 4 time(s)

D. Compilation fails.

E. An exception is thrown at runtime.

7. Which of the following are valid calls to Math.max? (Choose all that apply.) (Yeah, yeah, we know that on the *real* exam you'd know how many were correct, but we just want you to work a little harder here.)

A. `Math.max(1,4)`

B. `Math.max(2.3, 5)`

C. `Math.max(1, 3, 5, 7)`

D. `Math.max(-1.5, -2.8f)`

8. What two statements are true about the result obtained from calling `Math.random()`? (Choose two.)

A. The result is less than 0.0.

B. The result is greater than or equal to 0.0..

C. The result is less than 1.0.

D. The result is greater than 1.0.

E. The result is greater than or equal to 1.0.

F. The result is less than or equal to 1.0.

9. Given the following,

```
public class SqrtExample {
  public static void main(String [] args) {
    double value = -9.0;
    System.out.println( Math.sqrt(value));
  }
}
```

what is the result?

A. 3.0

B. –3.0

C. NaN

D. Compilation fails.

E. An exception is thrown at runtime.

10. Given the following,

```
1. public class Degrees {
2.   public static void main(String [] args) {
3.     System.out.println( Math.sin(75) );
4.     System.out.println( Math.toDegrees(Math.sin(75) ));
5.     System.out.println( Math.sin(Math.toRadians(75) ));
6.     System.out.println( Math.toRadians(Math.sin(75) ));
7.   }
8. }
```

at what line will the sine of 75 degrees be output?

A. Line 3

B. Line 4

C. Line 5

D. Line 6

E. Line 3 and either line 4, 5, or 6

F. None of the above

Using Wrapper Classes (Exam Objective 8.3)

11. Given the following,

```
1.  public class WrapTest2 {
2.     public static void main(String [] args) {
3.       Long b = new Long(42);
4.       int x = Integer.valueOf("345");
5.       int x2 = (int) Integer.parseInt("345", 8);
6.       int x3 = Integer.parseInt(42);
7.       int x4 = Integer.parseInt("42");
8.       int x5 = b.intValue();
9.     }
10. }
```

which two lines will cause compiler errors? (Choose two.)

A. Line 3

B. Line 4

C. Line 5

D. Line 6

E. Line 7

F. Line 8

12. Given the following,

```
public class NFE {
  public static void main(String [] args) {
    String s = "42";
    try {
      s = s.concat(".5");
      double d = Double.parseDouble(s);
      s = Double.toString(d);
      int x = (int) Math.ceil(Double.valueOf(s).doubleValue());
      System.out.println(x);
```

```
    }
    catch (NumberFormatException e) {
      System.out.println("bad number");
    }
  }
}
```

what is the result?

A. `42`

B. `42.5`

C. `43`

D. `bad number`

E. Compilation fails.

F. An uncaught exception is thrown at runtime.

13. Given the following,

```
public class BoolTest {
  public static void main(String [] args) {
    Boolean b1 = new Boolean("false");
    boolean b2;
    b2 = b1.booleanValue();
    if (!b2) {
      b2 = true;
      System.out.print("x ");
    }
    if (b1 & b2) {
      System.out.print("y ");
    }
    System.out.println("z");
  }
}
```

what is the result?

A. `z`

B. `x z`

C. `y z`

D. `x y z`

E. Compilation fails.

F. An exception is thrown at runtime.

14. Given the following,

```
1.   public class WrapTest3 {
2.     public static void main(String [] args) {
3.       String s = "98.6";
4.       // insert code here
5.     }
6.   }
```

which three lines inserted independently at line 4 will cause compiler errors? (Choose three.)

A. `float f1 = Float.floatValue(s);`

B. `float f2 = Float.valueOf(s);`

C. `float f3 = new Float(3.14f).floatValue();`

D. `float f4 = Float.parseFloat(1.23f);`

E. `float f5 = Float.valueOf(s).floatValue();`

F. `float f6 = (float) Double.parseDouble("3.14");`

15. Given the following,

```
11.    try {
12.      Float f1 = new Float("3.0");
13.      int x = f1.intValue();
14.      byte b = f1.byteValue();
15.      double d = f1.doubleValue();
16.      System.out.println(x + b + d);
17.    }
18.    catch (NumberFormatException e) {
19.      System.out.println("bad number");
20.    }
```

what is the result?

A. `9.0`

B. `bad number`

C. Compilation fails on line 13.

D. Compilation fails on line 14.

E. Compilation fails on lines 13 and 14.

F. An uncaught exception is thrown at runtime.

Using equals() (Exam Objective 5.2)

16. Given the following,

```
public class WrapTest {
  public static void main(String [] args) {
    int result = 0;
    short s = 42;
    Long x = new Long("42");
    Long y = new Long(42);
    Short z = new Short("42");
    Short x2 = new Short(s);
    Integer y2 = new Integer("42");
    Integer z2 = new Integer(42);

    if (x == y) result = 1;
    if (x.equals(y) ) result = result + 10;
    if (x.equals(z) ) result = result + 100;
    if (x.equals(x2) ) result = result + 1000;
    if (x.equals(z2) ) result = result + 10000;

    System.out.println("result = " + result);
  }
}
```

what is the result?

A. `result = 1`

B. `result = 10`

C. `result = 11`

D. `result = 11010`

E. `result = 11011`

F. `result = 11111`

17. Given the following,

```
public class BoolTest {
  public static void main(String [] args) {
    int result = 0;

    Boolean b1 = new Boolean("TRUE");
    Boolean b2 = new Boolean("true");
```

```
        Boolean b3 = new Boolean("tRuE");
        Boolean b4 = new Boolean("false");

        if (b1 == b2)  result = 1;
        if (b1.equals(b2) ) result = result + 10;
        if (b2 == b4)  result = result + 100;
        if (b2.equals(b4) ) result = result + 1000;
        if (b2.equals(b3) ) result = result + 10000;

        System.out.println("result = " + result);
    }
}
```

what is the result?

A. 0

B. 1

C. 10

D. 1100

E. 10001

F. 10010

18. Given the following,

```
public class ObjComp {
  public static void main(String [] args ) {
    int result = 0;
    ObjComp oc = new ObjComp();
    Object o = oc;

    if (o == oc)  result = 1;
    if (o != oc)  result = result + 10;
    if (o.equals(oc) )  result = result + 100;
    if (oc.equals(o) )  result = result + 1000;

    System.out.println("result = " + result);
  }
}
```

what is the result?

A. 1

B. 10

C. `101`

D. `1001`

E. `1101`

19. Which two statements are true about wrapper or String classes? (Choose two.)

A. If *x* and *y* refer to instances of different wrapper classes, then the fragment `x.equals(y)` will cause a compiler failure.

B. If *x* and *y* refer to instances of different wrapper classes, then *x* == *y* can sometimes be `true`.

C. If *x* and *y* are String references and if `x.equals(y)` is `true`, then *x* == *y* is `true`.

D. If *x*, *y*, and *z* refer to instances of wrapper classes and `x.equals(y)` is `true`, and `y.equals(z)` is `true`, then `z.equals(x)` will always be `true`.

E. If *x* and *y* are String references and *x* == *y* is `true`, then `y.equals(x)` will be `true`.

SELF TEST ANSWERS

Strings (Exam Objective 8.2)

1. ☑ C. After line 5 executes, both *s2* and *s3* refer to a String object that contains the value "def". When line 6 executes, a new String object is created with the value "ghi", to which *s2* refers. The reference variable *s3* still refers to the (immutable) String object with the value "def".
   ☒ A, B, D, E, and F are incorrect based on the logic described above.

2. ☑ C. Line 12 creates a new String object with the value "XYZ", but this new object is immediately lost because there is no reference to it. Line 13 creates a new String object referenced by *y*. This new String object has the value "xyz" because there was no "Y" in the String object referred to by *x*. Line 14 creates a new String object, appends "abc" to the value "xyz", and refers *y* to the result.
   ☒ A, B, D, E, and F are incorrect based on the logic described above.

3. ☑ C. Line 13 creates two, one referred to by *x* and the lost String "xyz". Line 14 creates one (for a total of three). Line 15 creates one more (for a total of four), the concatenated String referred to by *x* with a value of "xyzabc".
   ☒ A, B, and D are incorrect based on the logic described above.

4. ☑ B. Both `substring()` and `charAt()` methods are indexed with a zero-base, and `substring()` returns a String of length arg2 – arg1.
   ☒ A, C, D, E, and F are incorrect based on the logic described above.

5. ☑ E. In line 7 the code calls a StringBuffer method, `append()` on a String object.
   ☒ A, B, C, D, and F are incorrect based on the logic described above.

Math (Exam Objective 8.1)

6. ☑ B. `Math.round()` adds .5 to the argument then performs a `floor()`. Since the code adds an additional .5 before `round()` is called, it's as if we are adding 1 then doing a `floor()`. The values that start out as integer values will in effect be incremented by 1 on the `round()` side but not on the `ceil()` side, and the noninteger values will end up equal.
   ☒ A, C, D, and E are incorrect based on the logic described above.

7. ☑ A, B, and D. The `max()` method is overloaded to take two arguments of type *int, long, float*, or *double*.
   ☒ C is incorrect because the `max()` method only takes two arguments.

8. ☑ B and C. The result range for `random()` is 0.0 to < 1.0; 1.0 is not in range.
   ☒ A, D, E, and F are incorrect based on the logic above.

9. ☑ C. The `sqrt()` method returns `NaN` (not a number) when it's argument is less than zero.
   ☒ A, B, D, and E are incorrect based on the logic described above.

10. ☑ C. The Math class' trigonometry methods expect their arguments to be in radians, not degrees. Line 5 can be decoded: "Convert 75 (degrees) into radians, then find the sine of that result."
    ☒ A, B, D, E, and F are incorrect based on the logic described above.

Wrappers (Exam Objective 8.3)

11. ☑ B and D. B is incorrect because the `valueOf()` method returns an Integer object. D is incorrect because the `parseInt()` method takes a String.
    ☒ A, C, E, and F all represent valid syntax. Line 5 takes the String "345" to be octal number, and converts it to an integer value 229.

12. ☑ C. All of this code is legal, and line 5 creates a new String with a value of "42.5". Lines 6 and 7 convert the String to a *double* and then back again. Line 8 is fun—`Math.ceil()`'s argument expression is evaluated first. We invoke the `valueOf()` method that returns an anonymous Double object (with a value of 42.5). Then the `doubleValue()` method is called (invoked on the newly created Double object), and returns a *double* primitive (there and back again), with a value of (you guessed it) 42.5. The `ceil()` method converts this to 43.0, which is cast to an *int* and assigned to *x*. We know, we know, but stuff like this is on the exam.
    ☒ A, B, D, E, and F are incorrect based on the logic described above.

13. ☑ E. The compiler fails at line 10 because *b1* is a reference variable to a Boolean wrapper object, not a *boolean* primitive. Logical *boolean* tests can't be made on Boolean objects.
    ☒ A, B, C, D, and F are incorrect based on the logic described above.

14. ☑ A, B, and D. A won't compile because the `floatValue()` method is an instance method that takes no arguments. B won't compile because the `valueOf()` method returns a wrapper object. D won't compile because the `parseFloat()` method takes a String.
    ☒ C, E, and F are all legal (if not terribly useful) ways to return a primitive *float*.

15. ☑ A is correct. The `xxxValue()` methods convert any numeric wrapper object's value to any primitive type. When narrowing is necessary, significant bits are dropped and the results are difficult to calculate.
☒ B, C, D, E, and F are incorrect based on the logic described above.

Equals() (Exam Objective 5.2)

16. ☑ B. Line 12 fails because == compares reference values, not object values. Line 13 succeeds because both String and primitive wrapper constructors resolve to the same value (except for the Character wrapper). Lines 14, 15, and 16 fail because the `equals()` method fails if the object classes being compared are different and not in the same tree hierarchy.
☒ A, C, D, E, and F are incorrect based on the logic described above.

17. ☑ F. Line 10 fails because *b1* and *b2* are two different objects. Lines 11 and 14 succeed because the Boolean String constructors are case insensitive. Lines 12 and 13 fail because `true` is not equal to `false`.
☒ A, B, C, D, and E are incorrect based on the logic described above.

18. ☑ E. Even though *o* and *oc* are reference variables of different types, they are both referring to the same object. This means that == will resolve to `true` and that the default `equals()` method will also resolve to `true`.
☒ A, B, C, and D are incorrect based on the logic described above.

19. ☑ D and E. D describes an example of the `equals()` method behaving transitively. By the way, *x*, *y*, and *z* will all be the same type of wrapper. E is true because *x* and *y* are referring to the same String object.
☒ A is incorrect—the fragment will compile. B is incorrect because *x* == *y* means that the two reference variables are referring to the same object. C will only be true if *x* and *y* refer to the same String. It is possible for *x* and *y* to refer to two different String objects with the same value.

EXERCISE ANSWERS

Exercise 6-1: Using the Math Class

The following code listing is an example of how you might have written code to complete the exercise:

```
class NumberInterrogation {
   public static void main(String [] argh) {
      double [] num = {10.5, -10.5, Math.PI, 0};
      for(int i=0;i<num.length;++i) {
         System.out.println("abs("+num[i]+")="+Math.abs(num[i]));
         System.out.println("ceil("+num[i]+")="+Math.ceil(num[i]));
         System.out.println("floor("+num[i]+")="+Math.floor(num[i]));
         System.out.println();
      }
   }
}
```

Exercise 6-2: Rounding Random Numbers

The following code listing is an example of how you might have written code to complete the exercise:

```
class RandomRound {
   public static void main(String [] argh) {
      for(int i=0;i<10;++i) {
         double num = Math.random() * 100;
         System.out.print("The number " + num);
         System.out.println(" rounds to " + Math.round(num));
      }
   }
}
```

7

Objects and Collections

CERTIFICATION OBJECTIVES

- Overriding hashCode() and equals()
- Collections
- Garbage Collection
- ✓ Two-Minute Drill
- Q&A Self Test

CERTIFICATION OBJECTIVE

Overriding hashCode() and equals() (Exam Objective 9.2)

Distinguish between correct and incorrect implementations of hashcode methods.

You're an object. Get used to it. You have state, you have behavior, you have a job. (Or at least your chances of getting one will go up after passing the exam.) If you exclude primitives, everything in Java is an object. Not just object, but Object with a capital 'O'. Every exception, every event, *every array* extends from java.lang.Object. We've already talked about it in Chapter 6 when we looked at overriding `equals()`, but there's more to the story, and that *more* is what we'll look at now.

For the exam, you don't need to know every method in Object, but you *will* need to know about the methods listed in Table 7-1.

Chapter 9 covers `wait()`, `notify()`, and `notifyAll()`. The `finalize()` method is covered later in this chapter. So in this section we'll look at just the `hashCode()` and `equals()` methods. Oh, that leaves out `toString()`, doesn't it. OK, we'll cover that right now because it takes two seconds.

TABLE 7-1 Methods of Class Object Covered on the Exam

Method	Description
`boolean equals(Object obj)`	Decides whether two objects are meaningfully equivalent.
`void finalize()`	Called by the garbage collector when the garbage collector sees that the object cannot be referenced.
`int hashCode()`	Returns a hashcode *int* value for an object, so that the object can be used in Collection classes that use hashing, including Hashtable, HashMap, and HashSet.
`final void notify()`	Wakes up a thread that is waiting for this object's lock.
`final void notifyAll()`	Wakes up *all* threads that are waiting for this object's lock.
`final void wait()`	Causes the current thread to wait until another thread calls `notify` or `notifyAll` on this object.
`String toString()`	Returns a "text representation" of the object.

The toString() Method Override `toString()` when you want a mere mortal to be able to read something meaningful about the objects of your class. Code can call `toString()` on your object when it wants to read useful details about your object. For example, when you pass an object reference to the `System.out.println()` method, the object's `toString()` method is called, and the return of `toString()` is what you see displayed as follows:

```
public class HardToRead {
   public static void main (String [] args) {
     HardToRead h = new HardToRead();
     System.out.println(h);
   }
}
```

Running the HardToRead class gives us the lovely and meaningful,

```
% java HardToRead
HardToRead@a47e0
```

The preceding output is what you get when you *don't* override the `toString()` method of class Object. It gives you the class name (at least *that's* meaningful) followed by the @ symbol, followed by the unsigned hexadecimal representation of the object's hashcode.

Seeing this perhaps motivates you to override the `toString()` method in your classes, for example,

```
public class BobTest {
   public static void main (String[] args) {
     Bob f = new Bob("GoBobGo", 19);
     System.out.println(f);
   }
}

class Bob {
   int shoeSize;
   String nickName;
   Bob(String nickName, int shoeSize) {
     this.shoeSize = shoeSize;
     this.nickName = nickName;
   }
   public String toString() {
      return ("I am a Bob, but you can call me " + nickName +
              ". My shoe size is " + shoeSize);
   }
}
```

This ought to be a bit more readable:

```
% java BobTest
I am a Bob, but you can call me GoBobGo. My shoe size is 19
```

Some people affectionately refer to `toString()` as "the spill-your-guts method," because the most common implementations of `toString()` simply spit out the object's state (in other words, the current values of the important instance variables).

So that's it for `toString()`. Now we'll tackle `equals()` and `hashCode()`.

Overriding equals()

You learned about the `equals()` method in Chapter 6, where we looked at the wrapper classes. We discussed how comparing two object references using the == operator evaluates true only when both references refer to the same object (because == simply looks at the bits in the variable, and they're either identical or they're not). You saw that the String class and the wrapper classes have overridden the `equals()` method (inherited from class Object), so that you could compare two different objects (of the same type) to see if their *contents* are meaningfully equivalent. If two different Integer instances both hold the *int* value 5, as far as you're concerned they *are* equal. The fact that the value 5 lives in two separate objects doesn't matter.

When you really need to know if two *references* are identical, use ==. But when you need to know if the *objects themselves* (not the references) are equal, use the `equals()` method. For each class you write, you must decide if it makes sense to consider two different instances equal. For some classes, you might decide that two objects can *never* be equal. For example, imagine a class Car that has instance variables for things like make, model, year, configuration—you certainly don't want your car suddenly to be treated as the very *same* car as someone with a car that has *identical attributes.* Your car is your car and you don't want your neighbor Billy driving off in it just because, "hey, it's really the same car; the `equals()` method said so." So *no two cars should ever be considered exactly equal.* If two references refer to *one* car, then you know that both are talking about *one* car, not two cars that have the same attributes. So in the case of a Car you might not ever need, or want, to override the `equals()` method. Of course, you know that can't be the end of the story.

What It Means if You *Don't* Override equals()

There's a potential limitation lurking here: if you don't override the `equals()` method, *you won't be able to use the object as a key in a hashtable.* The `equals()` method in Object uses only the == operator for comparisons, so unless you override `equals()`, two objects are considered equal *only if the two references refer to the same object.*

Let's look at what it means to not be able to use an object as a hashtable key. Imagine you have a car, a very *specific* car (say, John's red Subaru Outback as opposed to Moe and Mary's purple Mini) that you want to put in a HashMap (a type of hashtable we'll look at later in this chapter), so that you can search on a particular car and retrieve the corresponding Person object that represents the owner. So you add the car instance as the *key* to the HashMap (along with a corresponding Person object as the *value*). But now what happens when you want to do a search? You want to say to the HashMap collection, "Here's the car, now give me the Person object that goes with this car." But now you're in trouble *unless you still have a reference to the exact object you used as the key when you added it to the Collection.* In other words, you can't make an identical Car object and use *it* for the search.

The bottom line is this: if you want objects of your class to be used as keys for a hashtable (or as elements in any data structure that uses equivalency for searching for—and/or retrieving—an object), then *you must override* `equals()` *so that two different instances can be considered the same.* So how would we fix the car? You might override the `equals()` method so that it compares the unique VIN (Vehicle Identification Number) as the basis of comparison. That way, you can use one instance when you add it to a Collection, and essentially *re-create* an identical instance when you want to do a search based on that object as the key. Of course, overriding the `equals()` method for Car also allows the potential that more than one object representing a single unique car can exist, which might not be safe in your design. Fortunately, the String and wrapper classes work well as keys in hashtables—they override the `equals()` method. So rather than using the actual *car instance* as the key into the car/owner pair, you could simply use a String that represents the unique identifier for the car. That way, you'll never have more than one instance representing a specific car, but you can still use the car—or rather, *one of the car's attributes*—as the search key.

Implementing an equals() Method

So let's say you decide to override `equals()` in your class. It might look something like this:

```
public class EqualsTest {
   public static void main (String [] args) {
      Moof one = new Moof(8);
      Moof two = new Moof(8);
      if (one.equals(two)) {
        System.out.println("one and two are equal");
      }
   }
}
class Moof {
   private int moofValue;
   Moof(int val) {
     moofValue = val;
   }
  public int getMoofValue() {
     return moofValue;
   }
  public boolean equals(Object o) {
    if ((o instanceof Moof) && (((Moof)o).getMoofValue()
         == this.moofValue)) {
      return true;
     } else {
       return false;
     }
   }
}
```

Let's look at this code in detail. In the main method of EqualsTest, we create two Moof instances, passing the same value (8) to the Moof constructor. Now look at the Moof class and let's see what it does with that constructor argument—it assigns the value to the *moofValue* instance variable. Now imagine that you've decided two Moof objects are the same if their *moofValue* is identical. So you override the `equals()` method and compare the two *moofValues*. It *is* that simple. But let's break down what's happening in the `equals()` method:

```
public boolean equals(Object o) {
  if ((o instanceof Moof) && (((Moof)o).getMoofValue()
         == this.moofValue)) {
     return true;
```

```
4.      } else {
5.        return false;
6.      }
7.  }
```

First of all, you *must* observe all the rules of overriding, and in line 1 we are indeed declaring a valid override of the `equals()` method we inherited from Object.

Line 2 is where all the action is. Logically, we have to do *two* things in order to make a valid equality comparison:

1. *Be sure that the object being tested is of the correct type!* It comes in polymorphically as type Object, so you need to do an `instanceof` test on it. Having two objects of different class types be considered equal is usually *not* a good idea, but that's a design issue we won't go into here. Besides, you'd *still* have to do the `instanceof` test just to be sure that you could cast the object argument to the correct type *so that you can access its methods* or variables in order to actually *do* the comparison. Remember, if the object doesn't pass the `instanceof` test, then you'll get a runtime `ClassCastException` if you try to do, for example, this:

   ```
   public boolean equals(Object o) {
      if (((Moof)o).getMoofValue() == this.moofValue){
         // the preceding line compiles, but it's BAD!
         return true;
       } else {
         return false;
       }
     }
   ```

   The `(Moof)o` cast will fail if *o* doesn't refer to something that IS-A Moof.

2. *Compare the attributes we care about* (in this case, just *moofValue*). Only the developers can decide what makes two instances equal. (For performance you're going to want to check the fewest number of attributes.)

By the way, in case you were a little surprised by the whole `((Moof)o).getMoofValue()` syntax, we're simply casting the object reference, *o*, just-in-time as we try to call a method that's in the Moof class but not in Object. Remember *without* the cast, you can't compile because the compiler would see the object referenced by *o* as simply, well, an Object. And since the Object class doesn't have a `moofvalue()` method, the compiler would squawk (technical term). But then as we said earlier, even *with* the cast the code fails at runtime if the object referenced by *o* isn't something that's castable to a Moof. So don't ever forget to use the `instanceof` test first. Here's another reason to appreciate the short circuit && operator—if the `instanceof` test fails, we'll never *get* to the code that does the cast, so we're always safe at runtime with the following:

```
if ((o instanceof Moof) && (((Moof)o).getMoofValue()
      == this.moofValue)) {
    return true;
} else {
    return false;
}
```

exam Watch

Remember that the `equals()`, `hashCode()`, and `toString()` methods are all public. **The following would not be a valid override of the `equals()` method, although it might appear to be if you don't look closely enough during the exam:**

```
class Foo {
   boolean equals(Object o) { }
  }
}
```

And watch out for the argument types as well. The following method is an overload, **but** not an override **of the equals() method:**

```
class Boo {
   public boolean equals(Boo b) { }
}
```

Be sure you're very comfortable with the rules of overriding so that you can identify whether a method from Object is being overridden, overloaded, or illegally redeclared in a class. The `equals()` method in class Boo changes the argument from Object to Boo, so it becomes an overloaded method and won't be called unless it's from your own code that knows about this new, different method that happens to also be named equals.

So that takes care of `equals()`.

Whoa… not so fast. If you look at the Object class in the Java API documentation, you'll find what we call a *contract* specified in the `equals()` method. A Java *contract* is a set of rules that *should* be followed, or rather *must be followed if you want to provide a "correct" implementation as others will expect it to be.* Or to put it another way, if you don't follow the contract, you may still compile and run, but your code (or someone else's) may break at runtime in some unexpected way.

The equals() Contract

Pulled straight from the Java docs, the `equals()` contract says:

- *It is reflexive:* For any reference value `x`, `x.equals(x)` should return `true`.
- *It is symmetric:* For any reference values `x` and `y`, `x.equals(y)` should return `true` if and only if `y.equals(x)` returns `true`.
- *It is transitive:* For any reference values `x`, `y`, and `z`, if `x.equals(y)` returns `true` and `y.equals(z)` returns `true`, then `x.equals(z)` should return `true`.
- *It is consistent:* For any reference values `x` and `y`, multiple invocations of `x.equals(y)` consistently return `true` or consistently return `false`, provided no information used in `equals` comparisons on the object is modified.
- For any nonnull reference value `x`, `x.equals(null)` should return `false`.

And you're so not off the hook yet. We haven't looked at the `hashCode()` method, but `equals()` and `hashCode()` are bound together by a joint contract that specifies *if two objects are considered equal using the* `equals()` *method, then they must have identical hashcode values.* So to be truly safe, your rule of thumb should be *if you override* `equals()`, *override* `hashCode()` *as well.* So let's switch over to `hashCode()` and see how that method ties in to `equals()`.

Overriding hashCode()

The hashcode value of an object is used by some collection classes (we'll look at the collections later in this chapter). Although you can think of it as kind of an object ID number, it isn't necessarily unique. Collections such as HashMap and HashSet use the hashcode value of an object to determine where the object should be *stored* in the collection, and the hashcode is used again to help *locate* the object in the collection. For the exam you do *not* need to understand the deep details of how the collection classes that use hashing are implemented, but you *do* need to know which collections use them (but, um, they all have *hash* in the name so you should be good there). You must also be able to recognize an *appropriate* or *correct* implementation of `hashCode()`. This does not mean *legal* and does not even mean *efficient*. It's perfectly legal to have a terribly inefficient hashcode method in your class, as long as it doesn't violate the contract specified in the Object class documentation (we'll look at that contract in a moment). So for the exam, if you're asked to pick out an appropriate or correct use of hashcode, don't mistake appropriate for *legal* or *efficient*.

Understanding Hashcodes

In order to understand what's appropriate and correct, we have to look at how some of the collections use hashcodes.

Imagine a set of buckets lined up on the floor. Someone hands you a piece of paper with a name on it. You take the name and calculate an integer code from it by using A is 1, B is 2, etc., and adding the numeric values of all the letters in the name together. *A specific name will always result in the same code;* for example, see Figure 7-1.

We don't introduce anything random, we simply have an algorithm that will always run the same way given a specific input, so the output will always be identical for any two identical inputs. So far so good? Now the way you *use* that code (and we'll call it a *hashcode* now) is to determine which bucket to place the piece of paper into (imagine that each bucket represents a different code number you might get). Now imagine that someone comes up and shows you a name and says, "Please retrieve the piece of paper that matches this name." So you look at the name they show you, and run the same hashcode-generating algorithm. The hashcode tells you in which bucket you should look to find the name.

You might have noticed a little flaw in our system, though. *Two different names might result in the same value.* For example, the names *Amy* and *May* have the same

FIGURE 7-1

A simplified hashcode example

Key	Hashcode Algorithm	Hashcode
Alex	A(1) + L(12) + E(5) + X(24)	= 42
Bob	B(2) + O(15) + B(2)	= 19
Dirk	D(4) +I(9) + R(18) + K(11)	= 42
Fred	F(6) + R(18) + E(5) + (D)	= 33

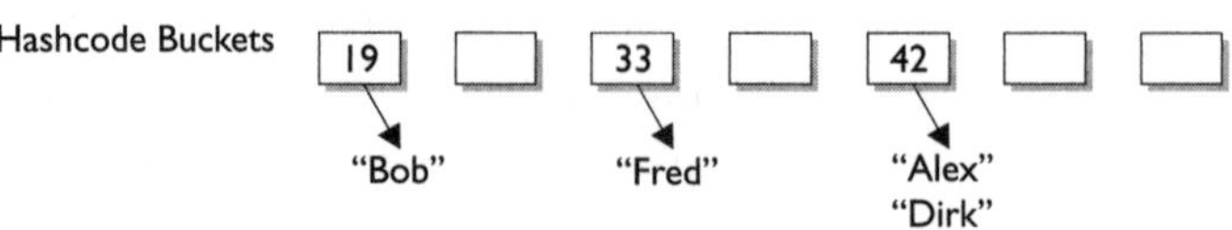

letters, so the hashcode will be identical for both names. That's acceptable, but it does mean that when someone asks you (the bucket-clerk) for the *Amy* piece of paper, you'll still have to search through the target bucket reading each *name* until we find *Amy* rather than *May*. The code tells you only which *bucket* to go into, but not how to locate the name once we're *in* that bucket.

on the job

In real-life hashing, it's not uncommon to have more than one entry in a bucket. Good hashing retrieval is typically a two-step process:

1. Find the right bucket.
2. Search the bucket for the right element.

So for efficiency, your goal is to have the papers distributed as evenly as possible across all buckets. Ideally, you might have just one name per bucket so that when someone asked for a paper you could simply calculate the hashcode and just grab the *one* paper from the correct bucket (without having to go flipping through different papers in that bucket until you locate the exact one you're looking for). The least efficient (but still functional) hashcode generator would return the *same* hashcode (say, 42) *regardless* of the name, so that *all* the papers landed in the same bucket while the others stood empty. The bucket-clerk would have to keep going to that one bucket and flipping painfully through each one of the names in the bucket until the right one was found. And if *that's* how it works, they might as well not use the hashcodes at all but just go to the one big bucket and start from one end and look through each paper until they find the one they want.

This distributed-across-the-buckets example is similar to the way hashcodes are used in collections. When you put an object in a collection that uses hashcodes, the collection uses the hashcode of the object to decide in which bucket/slot the object should land. Then when you want to *fetch* that object (or, for a hashtable, retrieve the associated value for that object), you have to give the collection a reference to an object which *the collection compares to the objects it holds in the collection.* As long as the object (stored in the collection, like a paper in the bucket) you're trying to search for has the *same hashcode* as the object you're using for the search (the name you *show* to the person working the buckets), then the object will be found. But…and this is a Big One, imagine what would happen if, going back to our name example, you showed the bucket-worker a name and they calculated the code based on only *half* the letters in the name instead of *all* of them. They'd never find the name in the bucket because they wouldn't be looking in the correct bucket!

Now can you see why if two objects are considered equal, their hashcodes must also be equal? Otherwise, you'd never be able to find the object since the default hashcode method in class Object virtually always comes up with a unique number for each object, *even if the equals method is overridden in such a way that two or more objects are considered equal.* It doesn't matter how equal the objects are if their hashcodes don't reflect that. So one more time: *If two objects are equal, their* ***hashcodes*** *must be equal as well.*

Implementing hashCode()

What the heck does a *real* hashcode algorithm look like? People get their PhDs on hashing algorithms, so from a computer science viewpoint, it's beyond the scope of the exam. The part we care about here is the issue of *whether you follow the contract.* And to follow the contract, think about what you do in the `equals()` method. *You compare attributes.* Because that comparison almost always involves instance variable values (remember when we looked at two Moof objects and considered them equal if their *int moofValues* were the same?). Your `hashCode()` implementation should use the same instance variables. Here's an example:

```
class HasHash {
   public int x;
   HasHash(int xVal) {
     x = xVal;
   }
  public boolean equals(Object o) {
    HasHash h = (HasHash) o; // Don't try at home without
                             // instanceof test
    if (h.x == this.x) {
      return true;
    } else {
      return false;
    }
  }
  public int hashCode() {
    return (x * 17);
  }
}
```

Because the `equals()` method considers two objects equal if they have the same *x* value, we have to be sure that objects with the same *x* value will return identical hashcodes.

exam
Watch

A `hashCode()` that returns the same value for* all *instances whether they're equal or not is still a legal—even* appropriate*—`hashCode()` method! For example,

```
public int hashCode() {
    return 1492;
  }
```

***would not violate the contract. Two objects with an* x *value of 8 will have the same hashcode. But then again, so will two* unequal *objects, one with an* x *value of 12 and the other a value of -920. This `hashCode()` method is horribly inefficient, remember, because it makes* all *objects land in the same bucket, but even so, the object can still be found as the collection cranks through the one and only bucket—using `equals()`—trying desperately to finally, painstakingly, locate the correct object. In other words, the hashcode was really no help at all in speeding up the search, even though search speed is hashcode's intended purpose! Nonetheless, this one-hash-fits-all method would be considered appropriate and even correct because it doesn't violate the contract. Once more,* correct *does not necessarily mean* good.**

Typically, you'll see `hashCode()` methods that do some combination of ^-ing (XOR-ing) the instance variables, along with perhaps multiplying them by a prime number. In any case, while the goal is to get a wide and random distribution of objects across buckets, the contract (and whether or not an object can be found) requires only that two equal objects have equal hashcodes. The exam does *not* expect you to rate the efficiency of a `hashCode()` method, but you must be able to recognize which ones will and will not work (work meaning "will cause the object to be found in the collection").

Now that we know that two equal objects must have identical hashcodes, is the reverse true? Do two objects with identical hashcodes have to be considered equal? Think about it—you might have lots of objects land in the same bucket because their hashcodes are identical, but unless they *also pass the* `equals()` *test,* they won't come up as a match in a search through the collection. This is exactly what you'd get with our very inefficient everybody-gets-the-same-hashcode method. It's legal and correct, just slooooow.

So in order for an object to be located, the search object and the object in the collection must have *both* identical hashcode values *and* return `true` for the `equals()` method. So there's just no way out of overriding both methods *to be absolutely certain that your objects can be used in Collections that use hashing.*

The hashCode() Contract

Now coming to you straight from the fabulous Java API documentation for class Object, may we present (drum roll) the `hashCode()` contract:

- Whenever it is invoked on the same object more than once during an execution of a Java application, the `hashCode()` method must consistently return the same integer, provided no information used in `equals()` comparisons on the object is modified. This integer need not remain consistent from one execution of an application to another execution of the same application.
- If two objects are equal according to the `equals(Object)` method, then calling the `hashCode()` method on each of the two objects must produce the same integer result.
- It is *not* required that if two objects are unequal according to the `equals(java.lang.Object)` method, then calling the `hashCode()` method on each of the two objects must produce distinct integer results. However, the programmer should be aware that producing distinct integer results for unequal objects may improve the performance of hashtables.

And what this means to you is…

Condition	Required	Not Required (But Allowed)
`x.equals(y) == true`	`x.hashCode() == y.hashCode()`	
`x.hashCode() == y.hashCode()`		`x.equals(y) == true`
`x.equals(y) == false`		`No hashCode() requirements`
`x.hashCode() != y.hashCode()`	`x.equals(y)== false`	

So let's look at what *else* might cause a `hashCode()` method to fail. What happens if you include a `transient` variable in your `hashCode()` method? While that's legal (compiler won't complain), under some circumstances an object you put in a collection won't be found. The exam doesn't cover object serialization, so we won't go into any details here. Just keep in mind that serialization saves an object so that it can be reanimated later by deserializing it back to full objectness.

But danger Will Robinson—remember that transient variables are not saved when an object is serialized. A bad scenario might look like this:

```
class SaveMe implements Serializable{
  transient int x;
  int y;
   SaveMe(int xVal, int yVal) {
      x = xVal;
      y = yVal;
   }
  public int hashCode() {
     return (x ^ y); //Legal, but not correct to
                     // use a transient variable
  }
  public boolean equals(Object o) {
     SaveMe test = (SaveMe)o;
     if (test.y == y && test.x == x) { // Legal, not correct
       return true;
     } else {
        return false;
     }
  }
}
```

Here's what could happen using code like the preceding example:

- Give an object some state (assign values to its instance variables).
- Put the object in a HashMap, using the object as a key.
- Save the object to a file using object serialization without altering any of its state.
- Retrieve the object from the file through deserialization.
- Use the deserialized (brought back to life on the heap) object to get the object out of the HashMap.

Oops. The object in the collection and the *supposedly* same object brought back to life are no longer identical. The object's transient variable will come back with a default value rather than the value the variable had at the time it was saved (or put into the HashMap). So using the preceding SaveMe code, if the value of *x* is 9 when the instance is put in the HashMap, then since *x* is used in the calculation of the hashcode, when the value of *x* changes the hashcode changes too. And when that same instance of SaveMe is brought back from deserialization, `x == 0`, *regardless of the value of x at the time the object was serialized.* So the new hashcode calculation will give a *different* hashcode, and the `equals()` method fails as well since *x* is used as one of the indicators of object equality.

Bottom line: transient variables can really mess with your equals and hashcode implementations. Either keep the variable nontransient or, if it *must* be marked transient, then don't use it in determining an object's hashcode or equality.

CERTIFICATION OBJECTIVE

Collections (Exam Objective 9.1)

Make appropriate selection of collection classes/interfaces to suit specific behavior requirements.

Can you imagine trying to write object-oriented applications without using data structures like hashtables or linked lists? What would you do when you needed to maintain a sorted list of, say, all the members in your *Simpsons* fan club? Obviously you can do it yourself; Amazon.com must have thousands of algorithm books you can buy. But with the kind of schedules programmers are under today ("Here's a spec. Can you have it all built by tomorrow morning?"), it's almost too painful to consider.

The Collections Framework in Java, which took shape with the release of JDk1.2 (the first *Java 2* version) and expanded in 1.4, gives you lists, sets, and maps to satisfy most of your coding needs. They've been tried, tested, and tweaked. Pick the best one for your job and you'll get—at the least—reasonably good performance. And when you need something a little more custom, the Collections Framework in the java.util package is loaded with interfaces and utilities.

So What Do You Do with a Collection?

There are a few basic operations you'll normally use with collections:

- *Add objects* to the collection.
- *Remove objects* from the collection.
- *Find out if an object (or group of objects)* is in the collection.

- *Retrieve an object* from the collection (without removing it).
- *Iterate* through the collection, looking at each element (object) one after another.

Key Interfaces and Classes of the Collections Framework

For the exam, you won't need to know much detail about the collections, but you *will* need to know the purpose of the each of the key interfaces, and you'll need to know *which* collection to choose based on a stated requirement. The collections API begins with a group of interfaces, but also gives you a truckload of concrete classes. The core interfaces you need to know for the exam (and life in general) are the following six:

Collection	Set	Sorted Set
List	Map	Sorted Map

Figure 7-2 shows the interface and class hierarchy for collections.

The core concrete implementation classes you need to know for the exam are the following ten (there are others, but the exam doesn't specifically cover them):

Map Implementations	Set Implementations	List Implementations
HashMap	HashSet	ArrayList
Hashtable	LinkedHashSet	Vector
TreeMap	TreeSet	LinkedList
LinkedHashMap		

Not all collections in the Collections Framework actually implement the Collection interface. In other words, *not all collections pass the IS-A test for Collection.* Specifically, none of the Map-related classes and interfaces extend from Collection. So while SortedMap, Hashtable, HashMap, TreeMap, and LinkedHashMap are all thought of as *collections,* none are actually extended from Collection-with-a-capital-C. To make things a little more confusing, there are really *three* overloaded uses of the word "collection":

- collection (lowercase 'c'), which represents *any* of the data structures in which objects are stored and iterated over.

FIGURE 7-2 The collections class and interface hierarchy

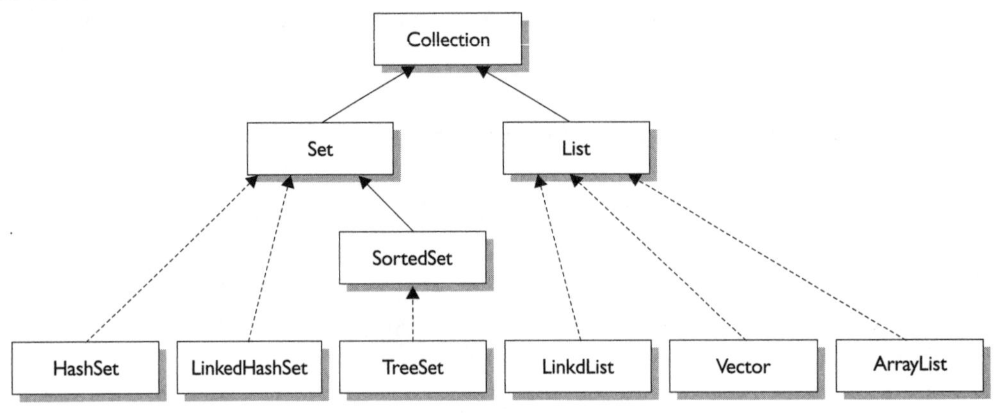

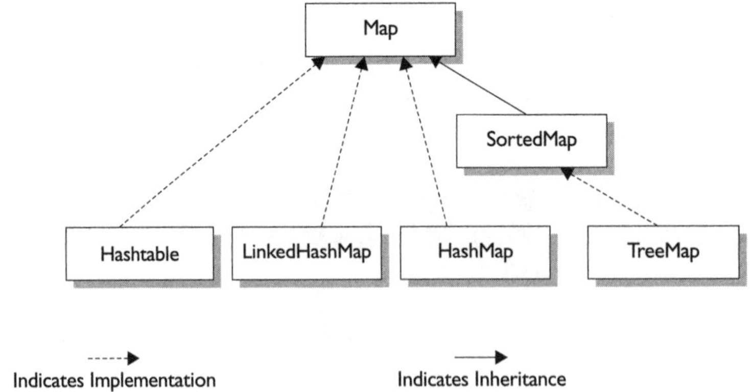

Indicates Implementation   Indicates Inheritance

- Collection (capital 'C'), which is actually the java.util.Collection interface from which Set and List extend. (That's right, *extend,* not implement. There are *no* direct implementations of Collection.)
- Collections (capital 'C' and ends with 's'), which is actually the java.util.Collections *class* that holds a pile of static utility methods for use with collections.

exam Watch

You can so easily mistake "Collections" for "Collection"—be careful. Keep in mind that Collections is a class, with static utility methods, while Collection is an interface with declarations of the methods common to most collections including `add`**,** `remove`**,** `contains`**,** `size`**, *and*** `iterator`**.**

Collections come in three basic flavors:

Lists	*Lists* of things (classes that implement List)
Sets	*Unique* things (classes that implement Set)
Maps	Things with a *unique ID* (classes that implement Map)

Figure 7-3 illustrates the structure of a List, a Set, and a Map.
But there are subflavors within those three types:

Sorted	Unsorted	Ordered	Unordered

An implementation class can be unsorted and unordered, ordered but unsorted, or both ordered *and* sorted. But an implementation can never be sorted but unordered, because sorting is a specific type of ordering, as you'll see in a moment. For example,

FIGURE 7-3

Lists, Sets, and Maps

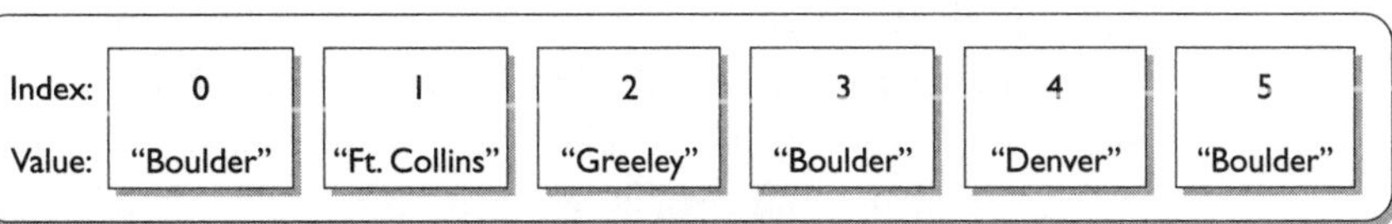

List: The salesman's itinerary (Duplicates allowed)

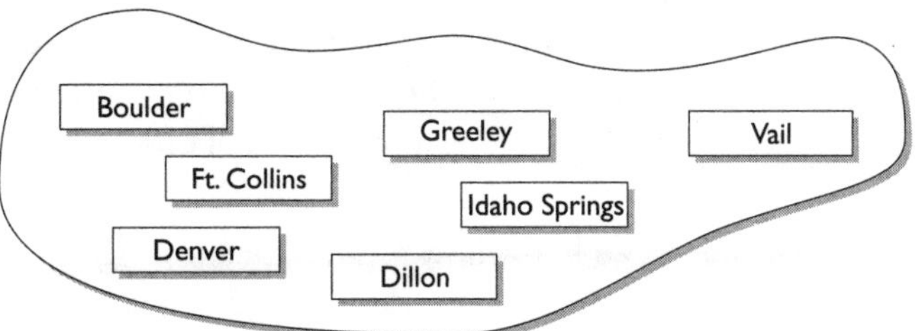

Set: The salesman's territory (No duplicates allowed)

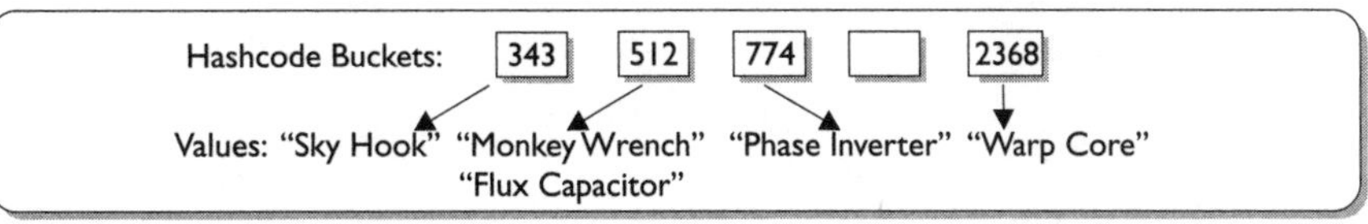

HashMap: the salesman's products (Keys generated from product IDs)

a HashSet is an unordered, unsorted set, while a LinkedHashSet is an ordered (but not sorted) set that maintains the order in which objects were inserted.

Maybe we need to be explicit about the difference between sorted and ordered, but first we have to discuss the idea of *iteration.* When you think of iteration, you may think of iterating over an array using, say, a *for* loop to access each element in the array in order ([0], [1], [2], etc.). Iterating through a collection usually means walking through the elements one after another starting from the first element. Sometimes, though, even the concept of *first* is a little strange—in a Hashtable there really *isn't* a notion of first, second, third, and so on. In a Hashtable, the elements are placed in a (as far as you're concerned) chaotic order based on the hashcode of the key. But *something* has to go first when you iterate; thus, when you iterate over a Hashtable there will indeed be an order. But as far as you can tell, it's completely arbitrary and can change in an apparently random way with further insertions into the collection.

Ordered When a collection is ordered, it means you can iterate through the collection in a specific (not-random) order. A Hashtable collection is not ordered. Although the Hashtable itself has internal logic to determine the order (based on hashcodes and the implementation of the collection itself), *you* won't find any order when you iterate through the Hashtable. An ArrayList, however, keeps the order established by the elements' index position (just like an array). LinkedHashSet keeps the order established by insertion, so the last element inserted is the last element in the LinkedHashSet (as opposed to an ArrayList where you can insert an element at a specific index position). Finally, there are some collections that keep an order referred to as the *natural order* of the elements, and those collections are then not just ordered, but also *sorted.* Let's look at how natural order works for sorted collections.

Sorted You know how to sort alphabetically—*A* comes before *B*, *F* comes before *G*, etc. For a collection of String objects, then, the *natural order* is alphabetical. For Integer objects, the natural order is by numeric value. And for Foo objects, the natural order is, um, we don't know. There *is no natural order* for Foo unless or until the Foo developer provides one, through an interface that defines how instances of a class can be compared to one another. For the exam, you don't need to know *how* to define natural order for your classes, only that you know there *is* such a thing as natural order and that it's used in sorted collections.

So, a sorted collection means *a collection sorted by natural order.* And *natural order is defined by the class of the objects being sorted* (or a supertype of that class, of course).

If you decide that Foo objects should be compared to one another (and thus sorted) using the value of their *bar* instance variables, then a sorted collection will order the Foo objects according to the rules in the Foo class for how to use the *bar* instance variable to determine the order. Again, you don't need to know *how* to define natural order, but keep in mind that *natural order* is not the same as an ordering determined by insertion, access, or index. A collection that keeps an order (such as insertion order) is not really considered sorted *unless it uses natural order* or, optionally, the ordering rules that you specify in the constructor of the sorted collection.

Figure 7-4 highlights the key distinctions between ordered and sorted collections.

FIGURE 7-4

What it means to be ordered or sorted

```
import java.util.*;
public class Ordered {
  public static void main(String [] args) {

    LinkedHashSet lhs = new LinkedHashSet();
    lhs.add ("Chicago");
    lhs.add ("Detroit");
    lhs.add ("Atlanta");
    lhs.add ("Denver");

    Iterator it = lhs.iterator();
    while (it.hasNext() ) (
      System.out.println("city " + it.next());
    }
  }
}
```

Output is

Chicago
Detroit
Atlanta
Denver

A LinkedHashSet, ***ordered*** by order of insertion

```
import java.util.*;
public class Sorted {
  public static void main(String [] args) {

    TreeSet ts = new TreeSet();
    ts.add ("Chicago");
    ts.add ("Detroit");
    ts.add ("Atlanta");
    ts.add ("Denver");

    Iterator it = ts.iterator();
    while (it.hasNext() ) (
      System.out.println("city " + it.next());
    }
  }
}
```

Output is

Atlanta
Chicago
Denver
Detroit

A TreeSet, ***sorted*** alphabetically

Now that we know about ordering and sorting, we'll look at each of the three interfaces, and then we'll dive into the concrete implementations of those interfaces.

List

A List cares about the index. The one thing that List has that nonlists don't have is a set of methods related to the index. Those key methods include things like `get(int index)`, `indexOf()`, `add(int index, Object obj)`, etc. (You don't need to memorize the method signatures.) All three List implementations are ordered by index position—a position that *you* determine either by setting an object at a specific index or by adding it *without* specifying position, in which case the object is added to the end. The three List implementations are described in the following section.

ArrayList Think of this as a growable array. It gives you *fast iteration* and *fast random access*. To state the obvious: it is an ordered collection (by index), but not sorted. You might want to know that as of version 1.4, ArrayList now implements the new RandomAccess interface—a marker interface (meaning it has no methods) that says, "this list supports fast (generally constant time) random access." Choose this over a LinkedList when you need fast iteration but aren't as likely to be doing a lot of insertion and deletion.

Vector Vector is a holdover from the earliest days of Java; Vector and Hashtable were the two original collections, the rest were added with Java 2 versions 1.2 and 1.4. A Vector is basically the same as an ArrayList, but `Vector()` methods are synchronized for thread safety. You'll normally want to use ArrayList instead of Vector because the synchronized methods add a performance hit you might not need. And if you *do* need thread safety, there are utility methods in class Collections that can help. Vector is the only class other than ArrayList to implement RandomAccess.

LinkedList A LinkedList List is ordered by index position, like ArrayList, except that the elements are doubly-linked to one another. This linkage gives you new methods (beyond what you get from the List interface) for adding and removing from the beginning or end, which makes it an easy choice for implementing a stack or queue. Keep in mind that a LinkedList may iterate more slowly than an ArrayList, but it's a good choice when you need fast insertion and deletion.

Set

A Set cares about uniqueness—it doesn't allow duplicates. Your good friend the `equals()` method determines whether two objects are identical (in which case only one can be in the set). The three Set implementations are described in the following sections.

HashSet A HashSet is an unsorted, unordered Set. It uses the hashcode of the object being inserted, so the more efficient your `hashCode()` implementation the better access performance you'll get. Use this class when you want a collection with no duplicates and you don't care about order when you iterate through it.

LinkedHashSet A LinkedHashSet is an ordered version of HashSet that maintains a doubly-linked List across all elements. Use this class instead of HashSet when you care about the iteration order; when you iterate though a HashSet the order is unpredictable, while a LinkedHashSet lets you iterate through the elements in the order in which they were inserted. Optionally, you can construct a LinkedHashSet so that it maintains the order in which elements were last *accessed*, rather than the order in which elements were inserted. That's a pretty handy feature if you want to build a least-recently-used cache that kills off objects (or flattens them) that haven't been used for awhile. (LinkedHashSet is a new collection class in version 1.4.)

TreeSet The TreeSet is one of two sorted collections (the other being TreeMap). It uses a Red-Black tree structure (but you knew that), and guarantees that the elements will be in ascending order, according to the *natural order* of the elements. Optionally, you can construct a TreeSet with a constructor that lets you give the collection your *own* rules for what the *natural order* should be (rather than relying on the ordering defined by the elements' class).

Map

A Map cares about unique identifiers. You *map* a unique *key* (the ID) to a specific *value*, where both the *key* and the *value* are of course *objects*. You're probably quite familiar with Maps since many languages support data structures that use a *key/value* or *name/value* pair. *Where* the keys land in the Map is based on the key's hashcode, so, like HashSet, the more efficient your `hashCode()` implementation, the better access performance you'll get. The Map implementations let you do things like search for a value based on the key, ask for a collection of just the values, or ask for a collection of just the keys.

HashMap The HashMap gives you an unsorted, unordered Map. When you need a Map and you don't care about the order (when you iterate through it), then HashMap is the way to go; the other maps add a little more overhead. HashMap allows one null key in a collection and multiple null values in a collection.

Hashtable Like Vector, Hashtable has been in from prehistoric Java times. For fun, don't forget to note the naming inconsistency: HashMap vs. Hashtable. Where's the capitalization of "t"? Oh well, you won't be expected to spell it. Anyway, just as Vector is a synchronized counterpart to the sleeker, more modern ArrayList, *Hashtable is the synchronized counterpart to HashMap.* Remember that you don't synchronize a *class,* so when we say that Vector and Hashtable are synchronized, we just mean that the key *methods* of the class are synchronized. Another difference, though, is that while HashMap lets you have null values as well as one null key, a *Hashtable doesn't let you have anything that's null.*

LinkedHashMap Like its Set counterpart, LinkedHashSet, the LinkedHashMap collection maintains insertion order (or, optionally, access order). Although it will be somewhat slower than HashMap for adding and removing elements, you can expect faster iteration with a LinkedHashMap. (LinkedHashMap is a new collection class as of version 1.4.)

TreeMap You can probably guess by now that a TreeMap is a *sorted* Map. And you already know that this means "sorted by the *natural order* of the elements." But like TreeSet, TreeMap lets you pass your *own* comparison rules in when you construct a TreeMap, to specify how the elements should be compared to one another when they're being ordered.

exam Watch

Look for incorrect mixtures of interfaces with classes. You can easily eliminate some answers right away if you recognize that, for example, a Map can't be the collection class you choose when you need a name/value pair collection, since Map is an interface and not a concrete implementation class. The wording on the exam is explicit when it matters, so if you're asked to choose an interface, choose an interface rather than a class that implements that interface. The reverse is also true—if you're asked to choose an implementation class, don't choose an interface type.

Whew! That's all the collection stuff you'll need for the exam, and Table 7-2 puts it in a nice little summary.

TABLE 7-2 Collection Interface Concrete Implementation Classes

Class	Map	Set	List	Ordered	Sorted
HashMap	X			No	No
Hashtable	X			No	No
TreeMap	X			Sorted	By *natural order* or custom comparison rules
LinkedHashMap	X			By insertion order or last access order	No
HashSet		X		No	No
TreeSet		X		Sorted	By *natural order* or custom comparison rules
LinkedHashSet		X		By insertion order or last access order	No
ArrayList			X	By index	No
Vector			X	By index	No
LinkedList			X	By index	No

exam watch

Be sure you know how to interpret Table 7-2 in a practical way. For the exam, you might be expected to choose a collection based on a particular requirement, where that need is expressed as a scenario. For example, which collection would you use if you needed to maintain and search on a list of parts, identified by their unique alphanumeric serial where the part would be of type Part? Would you change your answer at all if we modified the requirement such that you also need to be able to print out the parts in order, by their serial number? For the first question, you can see that since you have a Part class, but need to search for the objects based on a serial number, you need a Map. The *key* ***will be the serial number as a String, and the*** *value* ***will be the Part instance. The default choice should be HashMap, the quickest Map for access. But now when we amend the requirement to include getting the parts in order of their serial number, then we need a TreeMap–which maintains the*** *natural order* ***of the keys. Since the*** *key* ***is a String, the*** *natural order* ***for a String will be a standard alphabetical sort. If the requirement had been to keep track of which part was last accessed, then we'd probably need a LinkedHashMap.***

But since a LinkedHashMap loses the natural order (replacing it with last-accessed order), if we need to list the parts by serial number, we'll have to explicitly sort the collection, using a utility method.

Now that you know how to compare, organize, access, and sort objects, there's only one thing left to learn in this sequence: how to get *rid* of objects. The last objective in this chapter looks at the garbage collection system in Java. You simply won't believe how many garbage collection questions are likely to show up on your exam, so pay close attention to this last section. Most importantly, you'll need to know what is and is not guaranteed and what you're responsible for when it comes to memory management in Java.

CERTIFICATION OBJECTIVE

Garbage Collection (Exam Objectives 3.1, 3.2, 3.3)

State the behavior that is guaranteed by the garbage collection system.
Write code that explicitly makes objects eligible for garbage collection.
Recognize the point in a piece of source code at which an object becomes eligible for garbage collection.

Overview of Memory Management and Garbage Collection

This is the section you've been waiting for! It's finally time to dig into the wonderful world of memory management and garbage collection.

Memory management is a crucial element in many types of applications. Consider a program that reads in large amounts of data, say from somewhere else on a network, and then writes that data into a database on a hard drive. A typical design would be to read the data into some sort of collection in memory, perform some operations on the data, and then write the data into the database. After the data is written into the database, the collection that stored the data temporarily must be emptied of old data or deleted and re-created before processing the next batch. This operation might be performed thousands of times, and in languages like C or C++ that do not offer automatic garbage collection, a small flaw in the logic that manually empties or deletes the collection data structures can allow small amounts of memory to be improperly reclaimed or lost. Forever. These small losses are called *memory leaks*, and over many thousands of iterations they can make enough memory inaccessible that programs will eventually crash. Creating code that performs manual memory management cleanly and thoroughly is a nontrivial and complex task, and while estimates vary, it is arguable that manual memory management can *double* the development effort for a complex program.

Java's garbage collector provides an automatic solution to memory management. In most cases it frees you from having to add any memory management logic to your application. The downside to automatic garbage collection is that you can't completely control when it runs and when it doesn't.

Overview of Java's Garbage Collector

Let's look at what we mean when we talk about garbage collection in the land of Java. From the 30,000 ft. level, garbage collection is the phrase used to describe automatic memory management in Java. Whenever a software program executes (in Java, C, C++, Lisp, etc.), it uses memory in several different ways. We're not going to get into Computer Science 101 here, but it's typical for memory to be used to create a stack, a heap, in Java's case constant pools, and method areas. The *heap* is that part of memory where Java objects live, and it's the one and only part of memory that is in any way involved in the garbage collection process.

exam Watch

A heap is a heap is a heap. For the exam it's important to know that you can call it the heap, you can call it the garbage collectible heap, you can call it Johnson, but there is one and only one heap.

So, all of garbage collection revolves around making sure that the heap has as much free space as possible. For the purpose of the exam, what this boils down to is deleting any objects that are no longer *reachable* by the Java program running. We'll talk more about what *reachable* means, but let's drill this point in. *When the garbage collector runs, its purpose is to find and delete objects that cannot be reached.* If you think of a Java program as in a constant cycle of creating the objects it needs (which occupy space on the heap), and then discarding them when they're no longer needed, creating new objects, discarding them, and so on, the missing piece of the puzzle is the garbage collector. When it runs, it looks for those discarded objects and deletes them from memory so that the cycle of using memory and releasing it can continue. Ah, the great circle of life.

When Does the Garbage Collector Run?

The garbage collector is under the control of the JVM. The JVM decides when to run the garbage collector. From within your Java program you can ask the JVM to run the garbage collector, but there are no guarantees, under any circumstances, that the JVM will comply. Left to its own devices, the JVM will typically run the garbage collector when it senses that memory is running low. Experience indicates that when your Java program makes a request for garbage collection, the JVM will usually grant your request in short order, *but there are no guarantees.* Just when you think you can count on it, the JVM will decide to ignore your request.

How Does the Garbage Collector Work?

You just can't be sure. You might hear that the garbage collector uses a *mark and sweep* algorithm, and for any given Java implementation that *might* be true, but the Java specification doesn't guarantee any particular implementation. You might hear that the garbage collector uses *reference counting;* once again maybe yes maybe no. The important concept to understand for the exam is *when does an object become eligible for garbage collection.* To answer this question fully we have to jump ahead a little bit and talk about *threads.* (See Chapter 9 for the real scoop on threads.) In a nutshell, every Java program has from one to many threads. Each thread has its own little execution stack. Normally, you (the programmer), cause at least one thread to run in a Java program, the one with the `main()` method at the bottom of the stack. However, as you'll learn in excruciating detail in Chapter 9, there are many really cool reasons to launch additional threads from your initial thread. In addition to having its own little execution stack, each thread has its own lifecycle. For now, all we need to know is that threads can be alive or dead. With this background information we can now say with stunning clarity and resolve that, *an object is eligible for garbage collection when no live thread can access it.*

Based on that definition, the garbage collector does some magical, unknown operations, and when it discovers an object that can't be reached by any live thread it will consider that object as eligible for deletion, and it might even delete it at some point. (You guessed it, it also might *not* ever delete it.) When we talk about *reaching* an object, we're really talking about having a *reachable* reference variable that refers to the object in question. If our Java program has a reference variable that refers to an object, and that reference variable is available to a live thread, then that object is considered *reachable.* We'll talk more about how objects can become unreachable in the following section.

Can a Java application run out of memory? Yes. The garbage collection system attempts to remove objects from memory when they are not used. However, if you maintain too many live objects (objects referenced from other live objects), the system can run out of memory. Garbage collection cannot ensure that there is enough memory, only that the memory that is available will be managed as efficiently as possible.

Writing Code That Explicitly Makes Objects Eligible for Collection

In the previous section, we learned the theories behind Java garbage collection. In this section, we show how to make objects eligible for garbage collection using actual code. We also discuss how to attempt to force garbage collection if it is necessary, and how you can perform additional cleanup on objects before they are removed from memory.

Nulling a Reference

As we discussed earlier, an object becomes eligible for garbage collection when there are no more reachable references to it. Obviously, if there are no reachable references, it doesn't matter what happens to the object. For our purposes it is just floating in space, unused, inaccessible, and no longer needed.

The first way to remove a reference to an object is to set the reference variable that refers to the object to `null`. Examine the following code:

```
1. public class GarbageTruck {
2.   public static void main(String [] args) {
3.     StringBuffer sb = new StringBuffer("hello");
4.     System.out.println(sb);
5.     // The StringBuffer object is not eligible for collection
6.     sb = null;
7.     // Now the StringBuffer object is eligible for collection
8.   }
9. }
```

The StringBuffer object with the value `hello` is assigned the reference variable *sb* in the third line. To make it eligible, we set the reference variable *sb* to `null`, which removes the single reference that existed to the StringBuffer object. Once line 6 has run, our happy little `hello` StringBuffer object is doomed, eligible for garbage collection.

Reassigning a Reference Variable

We can also decouple a reference variable from an object by setting the reference variable to refer to another object. Examine the following code:

```
class GarbageTruck {
   public static void main(String [] args) {
      StringBuffer s1 = new StringBuffer("hello");
      StringBuffer s2 = new StringBuffer("goodbye");
      System.out.println(s1);
      // At this point the StringBuffer "hello" is not eligible
      s1 = s2; // Redirects s1 to refer to the "goodbye" object
      // Now the StringBuffer "hello" is eligible for collection
   }
}
```

Objects that are created in a method also need to be considered. When a method is invoked, any local variables created exist only for the duration of the method. Once the method has returned, the objects created in the method are eligible for garbage collection. There is an obvious exception, however. If an object is returned from the method, its reference might be assigned to a reference variable in the method that called it; hence, it will not be eligible for collection. Examine the following code:

```
import java.util.Date;
public class GarbageFactory {
   public static void main(String [] args) {
      Date d = getDate()
      doComplicatedStuff();
      System.out.println("d = " + d);
   }

   public static Date getDate() {
      Date d2 = new Date();
      String now = d2.toString();
      System.out.println(now);
      return d2;
   }
}
```

In the preceding example, we created a method called `getDate()` that returns a Date object. This method creates two objects: a Date and a String containing the date information. Since the method returns the Date object, it will *not* be eligible for collection even after the method has completed. The String object, though, will be eligible, even though we did not explicitly set the *now* variable to `null`.

Isolating a Reference

There is another way in which objects can become eligible for garbage collection, *even if they still have valid references!* We think of this scenario as *islands of isolation.* A simple example is a class that has an instance variable that is a reference variable to another instance of the same class. Now imagine that two such instances exist and that they refer to each other. If all other references to these two objects are removed, then even though each object still has a valid reference, there will be no way for any live thread to access either object. When the garbage collector runs, it will discover any such *islands* of objects and will remove them. As you can imagine, such islands can become quite large, theoretically containing hundreds of objects. Examine the following code:

```
public class Island {
  Island i;
  public static void main(String [] args) {

    Island i2 = new Island();
    Island i3 = new Island();
    Island i4 = new Island();

    i2.i = i3;    // i2 refers to i3
    i3.i = i4;    // i3 refers to i4
    i4.i = i2;    // i4 refers to i2

    i2 = null;
    i3 = null;
    i4 = null;

    // do complicated, memory intensive stuff
  }
}
```

When the code reaches `// do complicated,` the three Island objects (previously known as i2, i3, and i4) have instance variables so that they refer to each other, but their links to the outside world (i2, i3, and i4) have been nulled. These three objects are eligible for garbage collection.

This covers everything you will need to know about making objects eligible for garbage collection. Study Figure 7-5 to reinforce the concepts of objects without references and *islands of isolation.*

FIGURE 7-5 Objects eligible for garbage collection

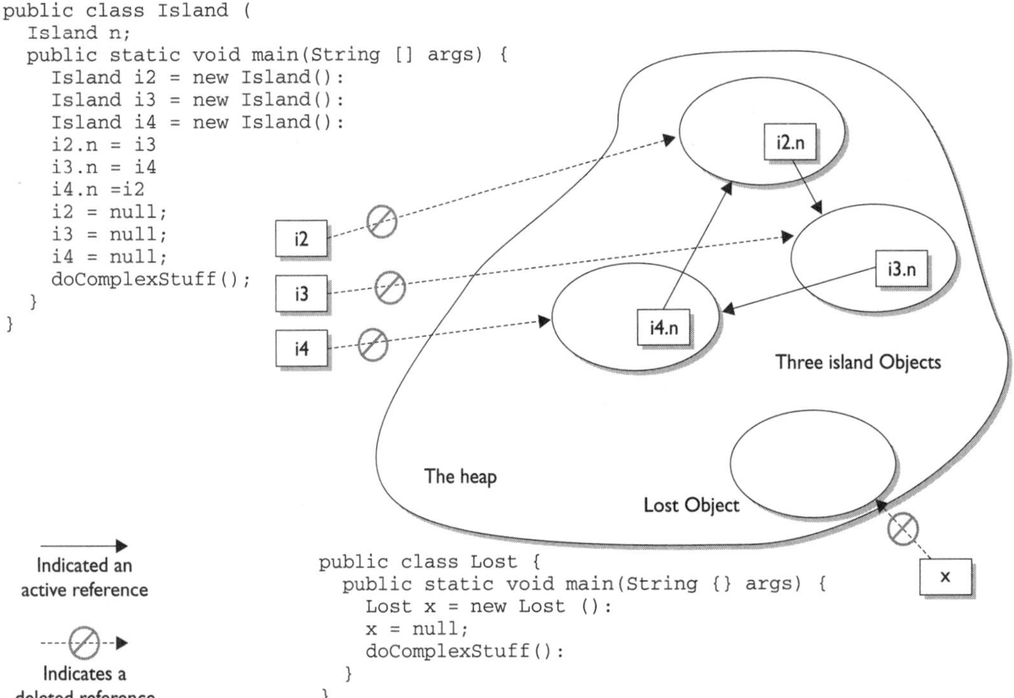

Forcing Garbage Collection

The first thing that should be mentioned here is, contrary to this section's title, *garbage collection cannot be forced.* However, Java provides some methods that allow you to request that the JVM perform garbage collection. For example, if you are about to perform some time-sensitive operations, you probably want to minimize the chances of a delay caused by garbage collection. But you must remember that the methods that Java provides are *requests*, and not demands; the virtual machine will do its best to do what you ask, but there is no guarantee that it will comply.

exam Watch

In reality, it is possible only to* suggest *to the JVM that it perform garbage collection. However, there are no guarantees the JVM will actually remove all of the unused objects from memory. It is essential that you understand this concept for the exam.

The garbage collection routines that Java provides are members of the Runtime class. The Runtime class is a special class that has a single object (a Singleton) for each main program. The Runtime object provides a mechanism for communicating directly with the virtual machine. In order to get the Runtime instance, you can use the method `Runtime.getRuntime()`, which returns the Singleton. Alternatively, for the method we are going to discuss, you can call the same method on the System class, which has static methods that can do the work of obtaining the Singleton for you. The simplest way to ask for garbage collection (remember—just a request) is

```
System.gc();
```

Theoretically, after calling `System.gc()`, you will have as much free memory as possible. We say *theoretically* because this routine does not always work that way. First, the JVM you are using may not have implemented this routine; the language specification allows this routine to do nothing at all. Second, another thread (again, see Chapter 9) may perform a substantial memory allocation right after you run the garbage collection.

This is not to say that `System.gc()` is a useless method—it's much better than nothing. You just can't rely on `System.gc()` to free up enough memory so that you don't have to worry about the garbage collector being run. The certification exam is interested in guaranteed behavior, not probable behavior.

Now that we are somewhat familiar with how this works, let's do a little experiment to see if we can see the effects of garbage collection. The following program lets us know how much total memory the JVM has available to it and how much free memory it has. It then creates 10,000 Date objects. After this, it tells us how much memory is left and then calls the garbage collector (which, if it decides to run, should halt the program until all unused objects are removed). The final free memory result should indicate whether it has run. Let's look at the program:

```
import java.util.Date;
public class CheckGC {
   public static void main(String [] args) {
      Runtime rt = Runtime.getRuntime();
      System.out.println("Total JVM memory: " + rt.totalMemory());
      System.out.println("Before Memory = " + rt.freeMemory());
      Date d = null;
      for(int i = 0;i<10000;i++) {
         d = new Date();
         d = null;
      }
      System.out.println("After Memory = " + rt.freeMemory());
      rt.gc();   // an alternate to System.gc()
      System.out.println("After GC Memory = " + rt.freeMemory());
```

```
    }
}
```

Now, let's run the program and check the results:

```
Total JVM memory: 1048568
Before Memory = 703008
After Memory = 458048
After GC Memory = 818272
```

As we can see, the VM actually did decide to garbage collect (i.e. delete) the eligible objects. In the preceding example, we suggested to the JVM to perform garbage collection with 458,048 bytes of memory remaining, and it honored our request. This program has only one user thread running, so there was nothing else going on when we called `rt.gc()`. Keep in mind that the behavior when `gc()` is called may be different for different JVMs, so there is no guarantee that the unused objects will be removed from memory. About the only thing you *can* guarantee is that if you *are* running very low on memory, the garbage collector will run before it throws an `OutOfMemoryException`.

Cleaning Up Before Garbage Collection—the Finalize() Method

Java provides you a mechanism to run some code just before your object is deleted by the garbage collector. This code is located in a method named `finalize()` that all classes inherit from class Object. On the surface this sounds like a great idea; maybe your object opened up some resources, and you'd like to close them before your object is deleted. The problem is that, as you may have gathered by now, you can't count on the garbage collector to ever delete an object. *So, any code that you put into your class's overridden `finalize()` method is **not** guaranteed to run.* The `finalize()` method for any given object might run, but you can't count on it, so don't put any essential code into your `finalize()` method. In fact, we recommend that in general you don't override `finalize()` at all.

Tricky Little Finalize() Gotcha's

There are a couple of concepts concerning `finalize()` that you need to remember.

- For any given object, `finalize()` will be called only once by the garbage collector.
- Calling `finalize()` can actually result in saving an object from deletion.

Let's look into these statements a little further. First of all, remember that `finalize()` is a method, and any code that you can put into a *normal* method you can put into `finalize()`. For example, in the `finalize()` method you could write code that passes a reference to the object in question back to another object, effectively *uneligiblizing* the object for garbage collection. If at some point later on this same object becomes eligible for garbage collection again, the garbage collector can still process this object and delete it. The garbage collector, however, will remember that, *for this object*, `finalize()` already ran, and it will not run `finalize()` again.

Now that we've gotten down and dirty with garbage collection, verify that the following scenarios and solutions make sense to you. If they don't, reread the last part of this chapter. *While awake.*

SCENARIO & SOLUTION	
I want to allocate an object and make sure that it never is deallocated. Can I tell the garbage collector to ignore an object?	No. There isn't a mechanism for marking an object as undeletable. You can instead create a static member of a class, and store a reference to the object in that. Static members are considered live objects.
My program is not performing as well as I would expect. I think the garbage collector is taking too much time. What can I do?	First, if it really is the garbage collector (and it probably isn't), then the code is creating and dropping many references to many temporary objects. Try to redesign the program to reuse objects or require fewer temporary objects.
I am creating an object in a method and passing it out as the method result. How do I make sure the object isn't deleted before the method returns?	The object won't be deleted until the last reference to the object is dropped. If you return the object as a method return value, the method that called it will contain a reference to the object.
How do I drop a reference to an object if that object is referred to in a member of my class?	Set the member to `null`. Alternatively, if you set a reference to a new object, the old object loses one reference. If that is the last reference, the object becomes eligible for deletion.
I want to keep objects around as long as they don't interfere with memory allocation. Is there any way I can ask Java to warn me if memory is getting low?	Prior to Java 1.2, you would have to check the amount of free memory yourself and guess. Java 1.2 introduced soft references for just this situation. This is not part of the Java 2 exam, however.

FROM THE CLASSROOM

Advanced Garbage Collection in Java 2

Up to this point, we have been discussing the original Java memory management model. With Java 2, the original model was augmented with *reference classes.* Reference classes, which derive from the abstract class *Reference,* are used for more sophisticated memory management. (You will not need to know the advanced management model for the exam.) The Reference class is the superclass for the *WeakReference, SoftReference,* and *PhantomReference* classes found in the java.lang.ref package.

By default, you as a programmer work with strong references. When you hear people talking about references (at parties, on the bus), they are usually talking about *strong references.* This was the classic Java way of doing things, and it is what you have unless you go out of your way to use the Reference classes. Strong references are used to prevent objects from being garbage collected; a strong reference from a reachable object is enough to keep the referred-to object in memory.

Let's look at the other three types of references:

- **Soft references** The Java language specification states that soft references can be used to create memory-sensitive caches. For example, in an image program, when you make a change to the image (say, an Image object), the old Image object can stick around in case the user wants to undo the change. This old object is an example of a *cache.*
- **Weak references** These are similar to soft references in that they allow you to refer to an object without forcing the object to remain in memory. Weak references are different from soft references, however, in that they do not request that the garbage collector attempt to keep the object in memory. Unlike soft references, which may stick around for a while even after their strong references drop, weak references go away pretty quickly.
- **Phantom references** These provide a means of delaying the reuse of memory occupied by an object, even if the object itself is finalized. A *phantom* object is one that has been finalized, but whose memory has not yet been made available for another object.

Objects are placed into one of several categories, depending on what types of references can be used to get to the object. References are ordered as follows: strong, soft, weak, and phantom. Objects are then known as *strongly reachable, softly reachable, weakly reachable, phantom reachable,* or *unreachable.*

- **Strongly reachable** If an object has a strong reference, a soft reference, a weak reference, and a phantom reference all pointing to it, then the object is considered strongly reachable and will not be collected.

- **Softly reachable** An object without a strong reference but with a soft reference, a weak reference, and a phantom reference, will be considered softly reachable and will be collected only when memory gets low.
- **Weakly reachable** An object without a strong or soft reference but with a weak or phantom reference, is considered weakly reachable and will be collected at the next garbage collection cycle.
- **Phantom reachable** An object without a strong, soft, or weak reference but with a phantom reference, is considered phantom reachable and will be finalized, but the memory for that object will not be collected.
- **Unreachable** What about an object without a strong, soft, weak, or phantom reference? Well, that object is considered unreachable and will already have been collected, or will be collected as soon as the next garbage collection cycle is run.

— Bob Hablutzel

CERTIFICATION SUMMARY

As you know by now, when we come to this point in the chapter (the end), we like to pause for a moment and review all that we've done. We began by looking at the `hashCode()` and `equals()` methods, with a quick review of another important method in class Object, `toString()`.You learned that overriding `toString()` is your opportunity to create a meaningful summary (in the form of a String) of the state of any given instance in your classes. The `toString()` method is automatically called when you ask `System.out.println()` to print an object.

Next you reviewed the purpose of == (to see if two reference variables refer to the *same object*) and the `equals()` method (to see if two objects are *meaningfully equivalent*). You learned the downside of not overriding `equals()`—you may not be able to find the object in a collection. We discussed a little bit about how to write a good `equals()` method—don't forget to use `instanceof` and refer to the object's significant attributes. We reviewed the contracts for overriding `equals()` and `hashCode()`. We learned about the theory behind hashcodes, the difference between legal, appropriate, and efficient hashcoding. We also saw that even though wildly inefficient, it's legal for a `hashCode()` method to always return the same value.

Next we turned to collections, where we learned about *Lists, Sets, and Maps,* and the difference between ordered and sorted collections. We learned the key attributes of the common collection classes, and when to use which. Finally, we dove into garbage collection, Java's automatic memory management feature. We learned that the heap is where objects live and where all the cool garbage collection activity takes place. We learned that in the end, the JVM will perform garbage collection whenever it wants to. You (the programmer) can request a garbage collection run, but you can't force it. We talked about garbage collection only applying to objects that are *eligible*, and that *eligible* means "inaccessible from any live thread." Finally, we discussed the rarely useful `finalize()` method, and what you'll have to know about it for the exam. All in all one fascinating chapter.

TWO-MINUTE DRILL

Here are some of the key points from Chapter 7.

Overriding hashCode() and equals()

- ❑ The critical methods in class Object are `equals()`, `finalize()`, `hashCode()`, and `toString()`.
- ❑ `equals()`, `hashCode()`, and `toString()` are public (`finalize()` is protected).
- ❑ Fun facts about `toString()`:
  - ❑ Override `toString()` so that `System.out.println()` or other methods can see something useful.
  - ❑ Override `toString()` to return the essence of your object's state.
- ❑ Use == to determine if two reference variables refer to the same object.
- ❑ Use `equals()` to determine if two objects are *meaningfully equivalent.*
- ❑ If you don't override `equals()`, your objects *won't* be useful hashtable/hashmap keys.
- ❑ If you don't override `equals()`, two different objects can't be considered *the same.*
- ❑ Strings and wrappers override `equals()` and make good hashtable/hashmap keys.
- ❑ When overriding `equals()`, use the `instanceof` operator to be sure you're evaluating an appropriate class.
- ❑ When overriding `equals()`, compare the objects' *significant* attributes.
- ❑ Highlights of the `equals()` contract:
  - ❑ *Reflexive:* `x.equals(x)` is `true`.
  - ❑ *Symmetric:* If `x.equals(y)` is `true`, then `y.equals(x)` must be `true`.
  - ❑ *Transitive:* If `x.equals(y)` is `true`, and `y.equals(z)` is `true`, then `z.equals(x)` is `true`.

- *Consistent:* Multiple calls to `x.equals(y)` will return the same result.
- *Null:* If `x` is not `null`, then `x.equals(null)` is `false`.

- If `x.equals(y)` is `true`, then `x.hashCode() == y.hashCode()` must be `true`.
- If you override `equals()`, override `hashCode()`.
- Classes HashMap, Hashtable, LinkedHashMap, and LinkedHashSet use hashing.
- A *legal* `hashCode()` override compiles and runs.
- An *appropriate* `hashCode()` override sticks to the contract.
- An *efficient* `hashCode()` override distributes keys randomly across a wide range of buckets.
- To reiterate: if two objects are equal, their hashcodes must be equal.
- It's *legal* for a `hashCode()` method to return the same value for all instances (although in practice it's very inefficient).
- Highlights of the `hashCode()` contract:
  - *Consistent:* Multiple calls to `x.hashCode()` return the same integer.
  - If `x.equals(y)` is `true`, then `x.hashCode() == y.hashCode()` must be `true`.
  - If `x.equals(y)` is `false`, then `x.hashCode() == y.hashCode()` can be either `true` or `false`, but `false` will tend to create better efficiency.
- Transient variables aren't appropriate for `equals()` and `hashCode()`.

Collections

- Common collection activities include adding objects, removing objects, verifying object inclusion, retrieving objects, and iterating.
- Three meanings for "collection":
  - collection—Represents the data structure in which objects are stored
  - Collection—`java.util.Collection`—Interface from which Set and List extend
  - Collections—A class that holds static collection utility methods

- Three basic *flavors* of collections include *Lists, Sets, Maps*:
  - Lists of things: Ordered, *duplicates allowed,* with an *index*
  - Sets of things: May or may not be ordered and/or sorted, *duplicates not allowed*
  - Maps of things with keys: May or may not be ordered and/or sorted, *duplicate keys not allowed*
- Four basic *subflavors* of collections include *Sorted, Unsorted, Ordered, Unordered.*
- Ordered means iterating through a collection in a specific, nonrandom order.
- Sorted means iterating through a collection in a *natural* sorted order.
- Natural means alphabetic, numeric, or programmer-defined, whichever applies.
- Key attributes of common collection classes:
  - ArrayList: Fast iteration and fast random access
  - Vector: Like a somewhat slower ArrayList, mainly due to its synchronized methods
  - LinkedList: Good for adding elements to the ends, i.e., stacks and queues
  - HashSet: Assures no duplicates, provides no ordering
  - LinkedHashSet: No duplicates; iterates by insertion order or last accessed (new with 1.4)
  - TreeSet: No duplicates; iterates in *natural* sorted order
  - HashMap: Fastest updates (key/value pairs); allows one null key, many null values
  - Hashtable: Like a slower HashMap (as with Vector, due to its synchronized methods). No null values or null keys allowed
  - LinkedHashMap: Faster iterations; iterates by insertion order or last accessed, allows one null key, many null values (new with 1.4)
  - TreeMap: A sorted map, in *natural* order

Garbage Collection

- In Java, garbage collection provides some automated memory management.
- All objects in Java live on the *heap.*

- The *heap* is also known as the *garbage collectible heap.*
- The purpose of garbage collecting is to find and delete objects that can't be reached.
- Only the *JVM* decides exactly when to run the garbage collector.
- You (the programmer) can only *recommend* when to run the garbage collector.
- You can't know the G.C. algorithm; *maybe* it uses mark and sweep, *maybe* it's generational and/or iterative.
- Objects must be considered *eligible* before they can be garbage collected.
- An object is eligible when no live thread can *reach* it.
- To reach an object, a live thread must have a live, reachable reference variable to that object.
- Java applications can run out of memory.
- Islands of objects can be garbage collected, even though they have references.
- To reiterate: garbage collection can't be forced.
- Request garbage collection with `System.gc();` (recommended).
- Class Object has a `finalize()` method.
- The `finalize()` method is guaranteed to run *once and only once* before the garbage collector deletes an object.
- Since the garbage collector makes no guarantees, *`finalize()` may never run.*
- You can uneligibilize an object from within `finalize()`.

SELF TEST

The following questions will help you measure your understanding of the material presented in this chapter. Read all of the choices carefully, as there may be more than one correct answer. Choose all correct answers for each question.

HashCode and equals() (Exam Objective 9.2)

1. Given the following,

```
x = 0;
if (x1.hashCode() != x2.hashCode() )  x = x + 1;
if (x3.equals(x4) )  x = x + 10;
if (!x5.equals(x6) ) x = x + 100;
if (x7.hashCode() == x8.hashCode() )  x = x + 1000;
System.out.println("x = " + x);
```

and assuming that the equals () and hashCode() methods are property implemented and x1 – x8 are all of the same type, if the output is "`x = 1111`", which of the following statements will always be true?

A. `x2.equals(x1)`

B. `x3.hashCode() == x4.hashCode()`

C. `x5.hashCode() != x6.hashCode()`

D. `x8.equals(x7)`

2. Given the following,

```
class Test1 {
  public int value;
  public int hashCode() { return 42; }
}
class Test2 {
  public int value;
  public int hashcode() { return (int)(value^5); }
}
```

which statement is true?

A. class Test1 will not compile.

B. The Test1 `hashCode()` method is more efficient than the Test2 `hashCode()` method.

C. The Test1 `hashCode()` method is less efficient than the Test2 `hashCode()` method.

D. class Test2 will not compile.

E. The two `hashcode()` methods will have the same efficiency.

3. Which two statements are true about comparing two instances of the same class, given that the `equals()` and `hashCode()` methods have been properly overridden? (Choose two.)

   A. If the `equals()` method returns `true`, the `hashCode()` comparison == must return `true`.

   B. If the `equals()` method returns `false`, the `hashCode()` comparison != must return `true`.

   C. If the `hashCode()` comparison == returns `true`, the `equals()` method must return `true`.

   D. If the `hashCode()` comparison == returns `true`, the `equals()` method might return `true`.

   E. If the `hashCode()` comparison != returns `true`, the `equals()` method might return `true`.

4. Which class does not override the `equals()` and `hashCode()` methods, inheriting them directly from class Object?

   A. java.lang.String

   B. java.lang.Double

   C. java.lang.StringBuffer

   D. java.lang.Character

   E. java.util.ArrayList

5. What two statements are true about properly overridden `hashCode()` and `equals()` methods?

   A. `hashCode()` doesn't have to be overridden if `equals()` is.

   B. `equals()` doesn't have to be overridden if `hashCode()` is.

   C. `hashCode()` can always return the same value, regardless of the object that invoked it.

   D. If two different objects that are not meaningfully equivalent both invoke `hashCode()`, then `hashCode()` can't return the same value for both invocations.

   E. `equals()` can be true even if it's comparing different objects.

Using Collections (Exam Objective 9.1)

6. Which collection class allows you to grow or shrink its size and provides indexed access to its elements, but whose methods are not synchronized?

A. java.util.HashSet

B. java.util.LinkedHashSet

C. java.util.List

D. java.util.ArrayList

E. java.util.Vector

7. Which collection class allows you to access its elements by associating a key with an element's value, and provides synchronization?

A. java.util.SortedMap

B. java.util.TreeMap

C. java.util.TreeSet

D. java.util.HashMap

E. java.util.Hashtable

8. Given the following,

```
TreeSet map = new TreeSet();
map.add("one");
map.add("two");
map.add("three");
map.add("four");
map.add("one");
Iterator it = map.iterator();
while (it.hasNext() ) {
    System.out.print( it.next() + " " );
 }
```

what is the result?

A. one two three four

B. four three two one

C. four one three two

D. one two three four one

E. one four three two one

F. The print order is not guaranteed.

9. Which collection class allows you to associate its elements with key values, and allows you to retrieve objects in FIFO (first-in, first-out) sequence?

A. java.util.ArrayList

B. java.util.LinkedHashMap

C. java.util.HashMap

D. java.util.TreeMap

E. java.util.LinkedHashSet

F. java.util.TreeSet

Garbage Collection (Exam Objectives 3.1, 3.2, 3.3)

10. Given the following,

```
1.  public class X {
2.    public static void main(String [] args) {
3.      X x = new X();
4.      X x2 = m1(x);
5.      X x4 = new X();
6.      x2 = x4;
7.      doComplexStuff();
8.    }
9.    static X m1(X mx) {
10.     mx = new X();
11.     return mx;
12.   }
13. }
```

After line 6 runs. how many objects are eligible for garbage collection?

A. 0

B. 1

C. 2

D. 3

E. 4

11. Which statement is true?

A. All objects that are eligible for garbage collection will be garbage collected by the garbage collector.

B. Objects with at least one reference will never be garbage collected.

C. Objects from a class with the `finalize()` method overridden will never be garbage collected.

D. Objects instantiated within anonymous inner classes are placed in the garbage collectible heap.

E. Once an overridden `finalize()` method is invoked, there is no way to make that object ineligible for garbage collection.

12. Given the following,

```
1.    class X2 {
2.      public X2 x;
3.      public static void main(String [] args) {
4.        X2 x2 = new X2();
5.        X2 x3 = new X2();
6.        x2.x = x3;
7.        x3.x = x2;
8.        x2 = new X2();
9.        x3 = x2;
10.       doComplexStuff();
11.     }
12.   }
```

after line 9 runs, how many objects are eligible for garbage collection?

A. 0

B. 1

C. 2

D. 3

E. 4

13. Which statement is true?

A. Calling `Runtime.gc()` will cause eligible objects to be garbage collected.

B. The garbage collector uses a mark and sweep algorithm.

C. If an object can be accessed from a live thread, it can't be garbage collected.

D. If object 1 refers to object 2, then object 2 can't be garbage collected.

14. Given the following,

```
X3 x2 = new X3();
X3 x3 = new X3();
X3 x5 = x3;
x3 = x2;
X3 x4 = x3;
```

```
17.  x2 = null;
18.  //  insert code
```

what two lines of code, inserted independently at line 18, will make an object eligible for garbage collection? (Choose two.)

A. `x3 = null;`

B. `x4 = null;`

C. `x5 = null;`

D. `x3 = x4;`

E. `x5 = x4;`

15. Given the following,

```
12.  void doStuff3() {
13.     X x = new X();
14.     X y = doStuff(x);
15.     y = null;
16.     x = null;
17.  }
18.  X doStuff(X mx) {
19.       return doStuff2(mx);
20.  }
```

at what point is the object created in line 13 eligible for garbage collection?

A. After line 15 runs

B. After line 16 runs

C. After line 17 runs

D. The object is not eligible.

E. It is not possible to know for sure.

SELF TEST ANSWERS

Strings (Exam Objective 9.2)

1. ☑ B. By contract, if two objects are equivalent according to the `equals()` method, then the `hashCode()` method must evaluate them to be ==.
☒ A is incorrect because if the `hashCode()` values are not equal, the two objects *must not* be equal. C is incorrect because if `equals()` is not true there is no guarantee of any result from `hashCode()`. D is incorrect because `hashCode()` will often return == even if the two objects do not evaluate to `equals()` being true.

2. ☑ C. The so-called "hashing algorithm" implemented by class Test1 will always return the same value, 42, which is legal but which will place all of the hash table entries into a single bucket, the most inefficient setup possible.
☒ A and D are incorrect because these classes are legal. B and E are incorrect based on the logic described above.

3. ☑ A and D. A is a restatement of the `equals()` and `hashCode()` contract. D is true because if the `hashCode()` comparison returns ==, the two objects might or might not be equal.
☒ B, C, and E are incorrect. B and C are incorrect because the `hashCode()` method is very flexible in its return values, and often two dissimilar objects can return the same hash code value. E is a negation of the `hashCode()` and `equals()` contract.

4. ☑ C. java.lang.StringBuffer is the only class in the list that uses the default methods provided by class Object.
☒ A, C, D, E, and F are incorrect based on the logic described above.

5. ☑ C and E are correct.
☒ A, B, and D are incorrect. A and B are incorrect because by contract `hashCode()` and `equals()` can't be overridden unless both are overridden. D is incorrect; `hashCode()` will often return the same value when hashing dissimilar objects.

Using Collections (Exam Objective 9.1)

6. ☑ D. All of the collection classes allow you to grow or shrink the size of your collection. ArrayList provides an index to its elements. The newer collection classes tend not to have synchronized methods. Vector is an older implementation of ArrayList functionality and has synchronized methods; it is slower than ArrayList.
☒ A, B, C, and E are incorrect based on the logic described above; C, *List* is an interface.

7. ☑ E. Hashtable is the only class listed that provides synchronized methods. If you need synchronization great; otherwise, use HashMap, it's faster.
☒ A, B, C, and D are incorrect based on the logic described above.

8. ☑ C. TreeSet assures no duplicate entries; also, when it is accessed it will return elements in *natural order*, which typically means alphabetical.
   ☒ A, B, D, E, and F are incorrect based on the logic described above.

9. ☑ B. LinkedHashMap is the collection class used for caching purposes. FIFO is another way to indicate caching behavior. To retrieve LinkedHashMap elements in cached order, use the `values()` method and iterate over the resultant collection.
   ☒ A, C, D, E, and E are incorrect based on the logic described above.

Garbage Collection (Exam Objectives 3.1, 3.2, 3.3)

10. ☑ B. By the time line 6 has run, the only object without a reference is the one generated as a result of line 4. Remember that "Java is pass by value," so the reference variable `x` is not affected by the `m1()` method.
    ☒ A, C, D, and E are incorrect based on the logic described above.

11. ☑ D. All objects are placed in the garbage collectible heap.
    ☒ A is incorrect because the garbage collector makes no guarantees. B is incorrect because *islands* of isolated objects can exist. C is incorrect because `finalize()` has no such mystical powers. E is incorrect because within a `finalize()` method, an object's reference can be passed back to a live thread.

12. ☑ C. This is an example of the *islands of isolated objects*. By the time line 9 has run, the objects instantiated in lines 4 and 5 are referring to each other, but no live thread can reach either of them.
    ☒ A, B, D, and E are incorrect based on the logic described above.

13. ☑ C. This is a great way to think about when objects can be garbage collected.
    ☒ A and B assume guarantees that the garbage collector never makes. D is wrong because of the now famous *islands of isolation* scenario.

14. ☑ C and E. By the time line 18 is reached, `x2` is null, `x3` and `x4` refer to the object created in line 12, and `x5` refers to the object created in line 13. Any kind of redirection of `x5` will leave the second object without a reference.
    ☒ A, B, and D are incorrect because the first object has two references; changing one of the references will not cause the first object to become unreachable.

15. ☑ E is correct. A copy of a reference to the line 13 object is passed to the `doStuff2()` method. We don't know what goes on in that method; it's possible that the reference is passed to other live objects.
    ☒ A, B, C, and D are incorrect based on the logic described above.

8

Inner Classes

CERTIFICATION OBJECTIVES

- Inner Classes
- Method-Local Inner Classes
- Anonymous Inner Classes
- Static Nested Classes
- ✓ Two-Minute Drill
- Q&A Self Test

Inner classes (including static nested classes) appear throughout the exam. Although there are no official exam objectives specifically about inner classes, the objectives related to declarations (1.2 and 4.1) and instantiation (6.3) include inner classes. More importantly, the code used to represent questions on virtually *any* topic on the exam can involve inner classes. Unless you deeply understand the rules and syntax for inner classes, you're likely to miss questions you'd otherwise be able to answer. *As if the exam weren't already tough enough.*

This chapter looks at the ins and outs (inners and outers?) of inner classes, and exposes you to the kinds of (often strange-looking) syntax examples you'll see scattered throughout the entire exam. So you've really got two goals for this chapter—to learn what you'll need to answer questions testing your inner class knowledge, and to learn how to read and understand inner class code so that you can correctly process questions testing your knowledge of *other* topics.

So what's all the hoopla about inner classes? Before we get into it, we have to warn you (if you don't already know) that inner classes have inspired passionate love 'em or hate 'em debates since first introduced in version 1.1 of the language. For once, we're going to try to keep our opinions to ourselves here and just present the facts as you'll need to know them for the exam. It's up to you to decide how—and to what extent—you should use them in your own development. We mean it. Not even our tone will betray our true feelings about them. (OK, OK, we'll tell you! We believe they have some powerful, efficient uses in very specific situations, including code that's easier to read and maintain, but they can also be abused and lead to code that's as clear as a cornfield maze, and to the syndrome known as "reuseless"...*code that's useless over and over again.*)

Inner classes let you define one class within another. They provide a type of scoping for your classes since you can make one class *a member of another class.* Just as classes have member *variables* and *methods*, a class can also have member *classes.* They come in several flavors, depending on how and where you define the inner class, including a special kind of inner class known as a "top-level nested class" (an inner class marked `static`), which technically isn't really an inner class. Because a static nested class is still a class defined within the scope of another class, we're still going to cover them in this chapter on inner classes.

Unlike the other chapters in this book, the certification objectives for inner classes don't have official exam objective numbers since they're part of other objectives covered elsewhere. So for this chapter, the Certification Objective headings represent the four inner class *topics* discussed in this chapter, rather than four official exam *objectives*:

- Inner Classes
- Method-local Inner Classes
- Anonymous Inner Classes
- Static Nested Classes

CERTIFICATION OBJECTIVE

Inner Classes

You're an OO programmer, so you know that for reuse and flexibility/extensibility you need to keep your classes specialized. In other words, a class should have code *only* for the things an object of that particular type needs to do; any *other* behavior should be part of another class better suited for *that* job. Sometimes, though, you find yourself designing a class where you discover you need behavior that belongs in a separate, specialized class, but also needs to be intimately tied to the class you're designing.

Event handlers are perhaps the best example of this (and in fact, one of the main reasons inner classes were added to the language in the first place). If you have a GUI class that performs some job like, say, a chat client, you might want the chat-client–specific methods (accept input, read new messages from server, send user input back to server, etc.) to be in the class. But how do those methods get invoked in the first place? A user clicks a button. Or types some text in the input field. Or a separate thread doing the I/O work of getting messages from the server has messages that need to be displayed in the GUI. So you have chat-client–specific methods, but you also need methods for handling the "events" (button presses, keyboard typing, I/O available, etc.) that drive the calls on those chat-client methods. The ideal scenario—from an OO perspective—is to keep the chat-client–specific methods in the ChatClient class, and put the event-handling *code* in a separate event-handling *class*.

Nothing unusual about that so far; after all, that's how you're *supposed* to design OO classes. As *specialists*. But here's the problem with the chat-client scenario: the event-handling code is intimately tied to the chat-client–specific code! Think about it: when the user presses a Send button (indicating that they want their typed-in message to be sent to the chat server), the chat-client code that sends the message needs to read from a *particular* text field. In other words, if the user clicks Button A, the program is supposed to extract the text from the TextField B, *of a particular ChatClient instance.* Not from some *other* text field from some *other* object, but specifically the text field that a specific instance of the ChatClient class has a reference to. So the event-handling code needs access to the members of the ChatClient object, in order to be useful as a "helper" to a particular ChatClient instance.

And what if the ChatClient class needs to inherit from one class, but the event-handling code is better off inheriting from some *other* class? You can't make a class extend from more than once class, so putting all the code (the chat-client–specific code and the event-handling code) in one class won't work in that case. So what you'd really like to have is the benefit of putting your event code in a separate class (better OO, encapsulation, and the ability to extend a class other than the class the ChatClient extends) but yet still allow the event-handling code to have easy access to the members of the ChatClient (so the event-handling code can, for example, update the ChatClient's private instance variables). You *could* manage it by making the members of the ChatClient accessible to the event-handling class by, for example, marking them public. But that's not a good solution either.

You already know where this is going—one of the key benefits of an inner class is the "special relationship" an *inner class instance* shares with *an instance of the outer class.* That "special relationship" gives code in the inner class access to members of the enclosing (outer) class, *as if the inner class were part of the outer class.* In fact, that's exactly what it means: the inner class *is* a part of the outer class. Not just a "part" but a full-fledged, card-carrying *member* of the outer class. Yes, an inner class instance has access to all members of the outer class, even *those marked private.* (Relax, that's the whole point, remember? We want this separate inner class instance to have an intimate relationship with the outer class instance, but we still want to keep everyone *else* out. And besides, if you wrote the outer class, then you also wrote the inner class! So you're not violating encapsulation; you *designed* it this way.)

Coding a "Regular" Inner Class

We use the term *regular* here to represent inner classes that are *not*

- static
- method-local
- anonymous

For the rest of this section, though, we'll just use the term *inner class* and drop the *regular*. (When we switch to one of the other three types in the preceding list, you'll know it.) You define an inner class within the curly braces of the outer class, as follows:

```
class MyOuter {
   class MyInner { }
}
```

Piece of cake. And if you compile it,

```
%javac MyOuter.java
```

you'll end up with *two* class files:

MyOuter.class
MyOuter$MyInner.class

The inner class is still, in the end, a separate class, so a class file is generated. But the inner class file isn't accessible to you in the usual way. You can't, for example, say

```
%java MyOuter$MyInner
```

in hopes of running the main method of the inner class, because a *regular* inner class can't have static declarations of any kind. *The only way you can access the inner class is through a live instance of the outer class!* In other words, only at runtime when there's already an instance of the outer class to tie the inner class instance to. You'll see all this in a moment. First, let's beef up the classes a little:

```
class MyOuter {
   private int x = 7;

  // inner class definition
   class MyInner {
      public void seeOuter() {
         System.out.println("Outer x is " + x);
      }
   } // close inner class definition

} // close outer class
```

The preceding code is perfectly legal. Notice that the inner class is indeed accessing a private member of the outer class. That's fine, because the inner class is also a member of the outer class. So just as any member of the outer class (say, an instance method) can access any other member of the outer class, private or not, the inner class—also a member—can do the same.

OK, so now that we know how to write the code giving an inner class access to members of the outer class, how do you actually use it?

Instantiating an Inner Class

To instantiate an instance of an inner class, *you must have an instance of the outer class* to tie to the inner class. There are no exceptions to this rule; an inner class instance can never stand alone without a direct relationship with a specific instance of the outer class.

Instantiating an Inner Class from Within Code in the Outer Class

Most often, it is the outer class that creates instances of the inner class, since it is usually the outer class wanting to use the inner instance as a helper object, for its own personal, private use. We'll modify the `MyOuter` class to instantiate an instance of `MyInner`:

```
class MyOuter {
   private int x = 7;
   public void makeInner() {
      MyInner in = new MyInner();
      in.seeOuter();
   }

   class MyInner {
      public void seeOuter() {
         System.out.println("Outer x is " + x);
      }
   }
}
```

You can see in the preceding code that the `MyOuter` code treats `MyInner` just as though `MyInner` were any other accessible class—it instantiates it using the class name (`new MyInner()`), and then invokes a method on the reference variable (`in.seeOuter()`). But the only reason this syntax works is because the outer class instance method code is doing the instantiating. In other words, *there's already an instance of the outer class—the instance running the* `makeInner()` *method.* So how do you instantiate a MyInner object from somewhere outside the `MyOuter` class? Is it even possible? (Well, since we're going to all the trouble of making a whole new subhead for it, as you'll see next, there's no big mystery here.)

Creating an Inner Class Object from Outside the Outer Class Instance Code Whew. Long subhead there, but it does explain what we're trying to do. If we want to create an instance of the inner class, we must have an instance of the outer class. You already know that, but think about the implications… it means you can't instantiate the inner class from a `static` method of the outer class (because, don't forget, in static code *there is no* `this` *reference*) or from any other code in any other class. Inner class instances are always handed an implicit reference to the outer class. The compiler takes care of it, so you'll never see anything but the end result—the ability of the inner class to access members of the outer class. The code to make an instance from anywhere outside nonstatic code of the outer class is simple, but you must memorize this for the exam!

```
public static void main (String[] args) {
     MyOuter mo = new MyOuter();
     MyOuter.MyInner inner = mo.new MyInner();
     inner.seeOuter();
}
```

The preceding code is the same regardless of whether the `main()` method is within the `MyOuter` class or some *other* class (assuming the other class has access to `MyOuter`, and since `MyOuter` has default access, that means the code must be in a class within the same package as `MyOuter`).

If you're into one-liners, you can do it like this:

```
public static void main (String[] args) {
      MyOuter.MyInner inner = new MyOuter().new MyInner();
      inner.seeOuter();
 }
```

You can think of this as though you're invoking a method on the outer instance, but the method happens to be a special inner class instantiation method, and it's invoked using the keyword `new`. Instantiating an inner class is the *only* scenario in which you'll invoke `new` *on* an instance as opposed to invoking new to *construct* an instance.

Here's a quick summary of the differences between inner class instantiation code that's *within* the outer class (but not static), and inner class instantiation code that's *outside* the outer class:

- **From inside the outer class instance code**, use the inner class name in the normal way:

  ```
  MyInner mi = new MyInner();
  ```

- **From outside the outer class instance code (including static method code within the outer class)**, the inner class name must now include the outer class name,

  ```
  MyOuter.MyInner
  ```

  and to instantiate, you must use a reference to the outer class,

  ```
  new MyOuter().new MyInner(); or outerObjRef.new MyInner();
  ```

  if you already have an instance of the outer class.

Referencing the Inner or Outer Instance from Within the Inner Class

How does an object refer to itself normally? Using the `this` reference. Quick review of `this`:

- The keyword `this` can be used only from within instance code. In other words, not within static code.
- The `this` reference is a reference to the currently-executing object. In other words, the object whose reference was used to invoke the currently-running method.
- The `this` reference is the way an object can pass a reference to itself to some other code, as a method argument:

  ```
  public void myMethod() {
     MyClass mc = new MyClass();
     mc.doStuff(this);  // pass a ref to object running myMethod
  }
  ```

Within an inner class code, the `this` reference refers to the instance of the inner class, as you'd probably expect, since `this` always refers to the currently-executing object. But what if the inner class code wants an explicit reference to the outer class instance the inner instance is tied to? In other words, *how do you reference the "outer this"?* Although normally the inner class code doesn't need a reference to the outer class, since it already has an implicit one it's using to access the members of the outer class, it would need a reference to the outer class if it needed to pass that reference to some other code as follows:

```
class MyInner {
    public void seeOuter() {
        System.out.println("Outer x is " + x);
        System.out.println("Inner class ref is " + this);
        System.out.println("Outer class ref is " + MyOuter.this);
     }
   }
```

If we run the complete code as follows:

```
class MyOuter {
   private int x = 7;
   public void makeInner() {
      MyInner in = new MyInner();
      in.seeOuter();
   }
   class MyInner {
      public void seeOuter() {
         System.out.println("Outer x is " + x);
         System.out.println("Inner class ref is " + this);
         System.out.println("Outer class ref is " + MyOuter.this);
      }
   }
  public static void main (String[] args) {
      MyOuter.MyInner inner = new MyOuter().new MyInner();
      inner.seeOuter();
   }
}
```

the output is

```
Outer x is 7
Inner class ref is MyOuter$MyInner@113708
Outer class ref is MyOuter@33f1d7
```

So the rules for an inner class referencing itself or the outer instance are as follows:

- To reference the inner class instance itself, from *within* the inner class code, use `this`.
- To reference the *"outer this"* (the outer class instance) from within the inner class code, use <NameOfOuterClass>.`this` (example, `MyOuter.this`).

Member Modifiers Applied to Inner Classes A regular inner class is a member of the outer class just as instance variables and methods are, so the following modifiers can be applied to an inner class:

- `final`
- `abstract`
- `public`
- `private`
- `protected`
- `static`—*except* `static` *turns it into a top-level nested class rather than an inner class.*
- `strictfp`

CERTIFICATION OBJECTIVE

Method-Local Inner Classes

A regular inner class is scoped inside another class' curly braces, but outside any method code (in other words, at the same level as an instance variable is declared). But you can also define an inner class within a method:

```
class MyOuter2 {
     private String x = "Outer2";

     void doStuff() {
        class MyInner {
           public void seeOuter() {
           System.out.println("Outer x is " + x);
```

```
            } // close inner class method
         } // close inner class definition
       } // close outer class method doStuff()

 } // close outer class
```

The preceding code declares a class, MyOuter2, with one method, `doStuff()`. But *inside* `dostuff()`, another class, `MyInner`, is declared, and it has a method of its own, `seeOuter()`). The code above is completely useless, however, because *it never instantiates the inner class!* Just because you *declared* the class doesn't mean you created an *instance* of it. So if you want to actually *use* the inner class (say, to invoke its methods), then you must make an instance of it somewhere *within the method but below the inner class definition.* The following legal code shows how to instantiate and use a method-local inner class:

```
class MyOuter2 {
     private String x = "Outer2";
     void doStuff() {
        class MyInner {
           public void seeOuter() {
             System.out.println("Outer x is " + x);
           } // close inner class method
        } // close inner class definition
        MyInner mi = new MyInner();   // This line must come
                                      //after the class
        mi.seeOuter();
      } // close outer class method doStuff()
} // close outer class
```

What a Method-Local Inner Object Can and Can't Do

A method-local inner class can be instantiated only within the method where the inner class is defined. In other words, no other code running in any other method—inside or outside the outer class—can ever instantiate the method-local inner class. Like regular inner class objects, the method-local inner class object shares a special relationship with the enclosing (outer) class object, and can access its private (or any other) members. However, *the inner class object cannot use the local variables of the method the inner class is in.* Why not?

Think about it. The local variables of the method live on the stack, and exist only for the lifetime of the method. You already know that the scope of a local variable is limited to the method the variable is declared in. When the method ends, the stack frame is blown away and the variable is history. But even after the method completes, the inner class object created within it might still be alive on the heap if, for example, a reference to it was passed into some other code and then stored in an instance variable. Because the local variables aren't guaranteed to be alive as long as the method-local inner class object, the inner class object can't use them. *Unless the local variables are marked final!* The following code attempts to access a local variable from within a method-local inner class:

```
class MyOuter2 {
     private String x = "Outer2";
     void doStuff() {
        String z = "local variable";
        class MyInner {
           public void seeOuter() {
           System.out.println("Outer x is " + x);
           System.out.println("Local variable z is " + z);   // Won't Compile!
           } // close inner class method
        } // close inner class definition
      } // close outer class method doStuff()
} // close outer class
```

Compiling the preceding code *really* upsets the compiler:

```
MyOuter2.java:8: local variable z is accessed from within inner class;
needs to be declared final
            System.out.println("Local variable z is " + z);
                                                        ^
```

Marking the local variable *z* as `final` fixes the problem:

```
final String z = "local variable";   // Now inner object can use it
```

And just a reminder about modifiers within a method: the same rules apply to method-local inner classes as to local variable declarations. You can't, for example, mark a method-local inner class `public`, `private`, `protected`, `static`, `transient`, and the like. The only modifiers you *can* apply to a method-local inner class are `abstract` and `final`. (But of course, never both of those at the same time as with any other class or method.)

exam Watch

Remember that a local class declared in a static method has access to only static members of the enclosing class, since there is no associated instance of the enclosing class. If you're in a static method there is no 'this', so an inner class in a static method is subject to the same restrictions as the static method. In other words, no access to 'instance variables'.

CERTIFICATION OBJECTIVE

Anonymous Inner Classes

So far we've looked at defining a class within an enclosing class (a regular inner class), and within a method (a method-local inner class). Finally, we're going to look at the most unusual syntax you might ever see in Java, inner classes declared without any class name at all (hence the word *anonymous*). And if that's not weird enough, you can even define these classes not just within a method, but within an *argument* to a method. We'll look first at the plain old (as if there is such a thing as a *plain old* anonymous inner class) version (actually, even the plain old version comes in two flavors), and then at the argument-declared anonymous inner class.

Perhaps your most important job here is to *learn to not be thrown when you see the syntax*. The exam is littered with anonymous inner class code; you might see it on questions about threads, wrappers, overriding, garbage collection, and you get the idea.

Plain Old Anonymous Inner Classes, Flavor One

Check out the following legal-but-strange-the-first-time-you-see-it code:

```
class Popcorn {
   public void pop() {
      System.out.println("popcorn");
    }
}
class Food {
   Popcorn p = new Popcorn() {
     public void pop() {
        System.out.println("anonymous popcorn");
      }
    };
}
```

Let's look at what's in the preceding code:

- We define two classes, Popcorn and Food.
- Popcorn has one method, pop().
- Food has one instance variable, declared as type Popcorn.
- That's it for Food. Food has *no* methods.

And here's the big thing to get:

- The Popcorn reference variable refers *not* to an instance of Popcorn, but to *an instance of an anonymous (unnamed)* ***subclass*** *of* Popcorn.

Let's look at just the anonymous class code:

```
2. Popcorn p = new Popcorn() {
3.     public void pop() {
4.       System.out.println("anonymous popcorn");
5.     }
6.   };
```

Line 2 Line 2 starts out as an instance variable declaration of type Popcorn. But instead of looking like this:

```
Popcorn p = new Popcorn(); // ← notice the semicolon at the end
```

there's a curly brace at the end of line 2, where a semicolon would normally be

```
Popcorn p = new Popcorn() { // ← a curly brace rather than semicolon
```

You can read line 2 as saying,

"Declare a reference variable, *p*, of type Popcorn. Then declare a new class which has no name, but which is a *subclass* of Popcorn. And here's the curly brace that opens the class definition…"

Line 3 Line 3, then, is actually the first statement within the new class definition. And what is it doing? Overriding the `pop()` method of the superclass `Popcorn`. This is the whole point of making an anonymous inner class—to *override one or more methods of the superclass!* (Or to implement methods of an interface, but we'll save that for a little later.)

Line 4 Line 4 is the first (and in this case *only*) statement within the overriding `pop()` method. Nothing special there.

Line 5 Line 5 is the closing curly brace of the `pop()` method. Again, nothing special there.

Line 6 Here's where you have to pay attention: line 6 includes a *curly brace closing off the anonymous class definition* (it's the companion brace to the one on line 2), but there's more! Line 6 also has *the semicolon that ends the statement started on line 2.* The statement where it all began. The statement declaring and initializing the `Popcorn` reference variable. And what you're left with is a `Popcorn` reference to a brand new *instance* of a brand new, just-in-time, anonymous (no name) *subclass* of `Popcorn`.

exam Watch

The closing semicolon is often hard to spot. So you might see code on the exam like this:

```
2. Popcorn p = new Popcorn() {
3.   public void pop() {
4.     System.out.println("anonymous popcorn");
5.   }
6.  } // ← Missing the semicolon needed to end statement on 2!!
7. Foo f = new Foo();
```

You'll need to be especially careful about the syntax when inner classes are involved, because the code on Line 6 looks perfectly natural. We're not used to seeing semicolons following curly braces (the only other time it happens is with shortcut array initializations).

Polymorphism is in play when anonymous inner classes are involved. Remember that, as in the preceding Popcorn example, we're using a superclass reference variable type to refer to a subclass object. What are the implications? You can only call methods on an anonymous inner class reference that are defined in the reference variable type! This is no different from any other polymorphic references, for example,

```
class Horse extends Animal{
   void buck() { }
}
class Animal {
   void eat() { }
}
class Test {
   public static void main (String[] args) {
      Animal h = new Horse();
      h.eat();  // Legal, class Animal has an eat() method
      h.buck();  // Not legal! Class Animal doesn't have buck()
   }
}
```

So on the exam, you must be able to spot an anonymous inner class that—rather than overriding a method of the superclass—defines its own new method. The method definition isn't the problem, though; the real issue is how do you invoke that new method? The reference variable type (the superclass) won't know anything about that new method (defined in the anonymous subclass), so the compiler will complain if you try to invoke any method on an anonymous inner class reference that is not in the superclass class definition.

Check out the following, illegal code:

```
class Popcorn {
   public void pop() {
      System.out.println("popcorn");
    }
}
class Food {
   Popcorn p = new Popcorn() {
      public void sizzle() {
        System.out.println("anonymous sizzling popcorn");
      }
      public void pop() {
```

```
            System.out.println("anonymous popcorn");
         }
      };
      public void popIt() {
         p.pop();  // OK, Popcorn has a pop() method
         p.sizzle();  // Not Legal! Popcorn does not have sizzle()
      }
   }
```

Compiling the preceding code gives us,

```
Anon.java:19: cannot resolve symbol
symbol  : method sizzle  ()
location: class Popcorn
      p.sizzle();
       ^
```

which is the compiler's way of saying, "I can't find method `sizzle()` in class `Popcorn`," followed by, "Get a clue."

Plain Old Anonymous Inner Classes, Flavor Two

The only difference between flavor one and flavor two is that flavor one creates an anonymous *subclass* of the specified *class* type, whereas flavor two creates an anonymous *implementer* of the specified *interface* type. In the previous examples, we defined a new anonymous subclass of type `Popcorn` as follows:

```
Popcorn p = new Popcorn() {
```

But if `Popcorn` were an *interface* type instead of a *class* type, then the new anonymous class would be an *implementer* of the *interface* rather than a *subclass* of the *class*. Look at the following example:

```
interface Cookable {
   public void cook();
}
class Food {
   Cookable c = new Cookable() {
      public void cook() {
        System.out.println("anonymous cookable implementer");
     }
   };
}
```

The preceding code, like the Popcorn example, still creates an instance of an anonymous inner class, but this time the new just-in-time class is an implementer of the `Cookable` interface. And note that this is the only time you will ever see the syntax,

```
new Cookable()
```

where `Cookable` is an *interface* rather than a non-abstract class type. Because think about it, *you can't instantiate an interface,* yet that's what the code *looks* like it's doing. But of course it's not instantiating a `Cookable` object, it's creating an instance of a new, anonymous, implementer of `Cookable`. So you can read this line,

```
Cookable c = new Cookable() {
```

as "Declare a reference variable of type `Cookable` that, obviously, will refer to an object from a class that implements the `Cookable` interface. But, oh yes, we don't yet *have* a class that implements `Cookable`, so we're going to make one right here, right now. We don't need a name for the class, but it will be a class that `implements Cookable`, and this curly brace starts the definition of the new implementing class."

One more thing to keep in mind about anonymous interface implementers—*they can implement only **one** interface.* There simply isn't any mechanism to say that your anonymous inner class is going to implement multiple interfaces. In fact, an anonymous inner class can't even extend a class and implement an interface at the same time. The inner class has to choose either to be a subclass of a named class—and not directly implement any interfaces at all—*or* to implement a single interface. By directly, we mean actually using the keyword `implements` as part of the class declaration. If the anonymous inner class is a subclass of a class type, it automatically becomes an implementer of any interfaces implemented by the superclass.

exam Watch

Don't be fooled by any attempts to instantiate an interface except in the case of an anonymous inner class. The following is not legal,

```
Runnable r = new Runnable(); // can't instantiate interface
```

whereas the following is legal, because it's instantiating an *implementer* ***of the*** `Runnable` ***interface (an anonymous implementation class):***

```
Runnable r = new Runnable() {  // curly brace instead of semicolon
   public void run() { }
};
```

Argument-Defined Anonymous Inner Class

If you understood what we've covered so far in this chapter, then this last part will be simple. If you *are* still a little fuzzy on anonymous classes, however, then you should reread the previous sections. If they're not completely clear, we'd like to take full responsibility for the confusion. But we'll be happy to share.

OK, if you've made it to this sentence then we're all going to assume you understood the previous section, and now we're just going to add one new twist. Imagine the following scenario. You're typing along, creating the Perfect Class, when you write code calling a method on a `Bar` object, and that method takes an object of type `Foo` (an interface).

```
class MyWonderfulClass {
   void go() {
      Bar b = new Bar();
      b.doStuff(AckWeDon'tHaveAFoo!); // Don't try to compile this at home
   }
}
interface Foo {
   void foof();
}
class Bar {
   void doStuff(Foo f) { }
}
```

No *problemo*, except that you don't *have* an object from a class that implements `Foo`. But you can't instantiate one, either, because *you don't even have a* ***class*** *that implements* `Foo`, let alone an instance of one. So you first need a class that implements `Foo`, and then you need an instance of that class to pass to the `Bar` class' `doStuff()` method. Savvy Java programmer that you are, you simply define an anonymous inner class, *right inside the argument.* That's right, just where you least expect to find a class. And here's what it looks like:

```
class MyWonderfulClass {
  void go() {
    Bar b = new Bar();
     b.doStuff(new Foo() {
       public void foof() {
          System.out.println("foofy");
         } // end foof method
      }); // end inner class def, arg, and end statement
   } // end go()
} // end class

interface Foo {
```

```
13.     void foof();
14. }
15. class Bar {
16.     void doStuff(Foo f) { }
17. }
```

All the action starts on line 4. We're calling `doStuff()` on a `Bar` object, but the method takes an instance that IS-A `Foo`, where `Foo` is an interface. So we must make both an *implementation* class and an *instance* of that class, all right here in the argument to `doStuff()`. So that's what we do. We write

```
new Foo() {
```

to start the new class definition for the anonymous class that implements the `Foo` interface. `Foo` has a single method to implement, `foof()`, so on lines 5, 6, and 7 we implement the `foof()` method. Then on line 8—whoa!—more strange syntax appears. The first curly brace closes off the new anonymous class definition. But don't forget that this all happened as part of a method argument, so the close parenthesis ')' finishes off the method invocation, and then we must still end the statement that began on line 4, so we end with a semicolon. Study this syntax! You *will* see anonymous inner classes on the exam, and you'll have to be very, very picky about the way they're closed. If they're argument local, they end like this,

```
});
```

but if they're just plain old anonymous classes, then they end like this:

```
};
```

Regardless, the syntax is not what you use in virtually any other part of Java, so be careful. Any question from any part of the exam might involve anonymous inner classes as part of the code.

CERTIFICATION OBJECTIVE

Static Nested Classes

We saved the easiest for last, as a kind of treat :)

You'll sometimes hear static nested classes referred to as top-level nested classes, or *static inner classes,* but they really aren't inner classes at all, by the standard definition of an inner class. While an inner class (regardless of the flavor) enjoys that *special relationship* with the outer class (or rather the *instances* of the two classes share a relationship), a static nested class does not. It is simply a non-inner (also called "top-level") class scoped within another. So with static classes it's really more about name-space resolution than about an implicit relationship between the two classes.

A static nested class is simply *a class that's a static member of the enclosing class,* as follows:

```
class BigOuter {
   static class Nested { }
}
```

The class itself isn't really "static;" there's no such thing as a static class. The `static` modifier in this case says that the nested class is *a static member of the outer class.* That means it can be accessed, as with other static members, *without having an instance of the outer class.*

exam Watch

Just as a static method does not have access to the instance variables and methods of the class, a static nested class does not have access to the instance variables and methods of the outer class. Look for static nested classes with code that behaves like a nonstatic (regular inner) class.

Instantiating a Static Nested Class

The syntax for instantiating a static nested class is a little different from a normal inner class, and looks like this:

```
class BigOuter {
   static class Nested { }
}
class Broom {
   public static void main (String [] args) {
     BigOuter.Nested n = new BigOuter.Nested(); //Use both class names
   }
}
```

CERTIFICATION SUMMARY

You're on the home stretch now; just one more chapter follows this one. You've learned all about inner classes (including static nested classes), and you're aware that they'll show up throughout the exam, regardless of the topic. You're comfortable with the sometimes bizarre syntax, and you know how to spot legal and illegal inner class definitions.

We looked first at "regular" inner classes, where one class is a member of another. You learned that coding an inner class means putting the class definition of the inner class inside the curly braces of the enclosing (outer) class, but outside of any method or other code block. We learned that an inner class *instance* shares a special relationship with a specific *instance* of the outer class, and that this special relationship lets the inner class access all members of the outer class, including those marked `private`. You learned that to instantiate an inner class, you *must* have a reference to an instance of the outer class.

Next we looked at method-local inner classes—classes defined *inside* a method. We saw that the code for a method-local inner class looks virtually the same as the code for any other class definition, except that you can't apply an access modifier the way you can to a regular inner class. You also learned why method-local inner classes cannot use nonfinal local variables declared within the same method—the inner class instance may outlive the stack frame, so the local variable might vanish while the inner class object is still alive. We showed you that to *use* the inner class you need to instantiate it, and that the instantiation must come *after* the class declaration in the method.

We also explored the strangest inner class type of all—the *anonymous* inner class. You learned that they come in two forms, normal and argument-local. Normal, ho-hum, anonymous inner classes are created as part of a variable assignment, while argument-local inner classes are actually declared, defined, and automatically instantiated *all within the argument to a method!* We covered the way anonymous inner classes can be either a *subclass* of the named class type, or an *implementer* of the named interface. Finally, we looked at how polymorphism applies to anonymous inner classes: you can invoke on the new instance only those methods defined in the named class or interface type. In other words, even if the anonymous inner class defines it's own new method, no code from anywhere outside the inner class will be able to invoke that method.

As if we weren't already having enough fun for one day, we pushed on to static inner classes, which really aren't inner classes at all. Known as static nested classes (or top-level nested classes), a nested class marked with the `static` modifier is quite similar to any other non-inner class, except that to access it, code must have access to both the nested and enclosing class. We saw that because the class is static, no instance of the enclosing class is needed, and thus the static nested class *does not share a special relationship with any instance of the enclosing class.*

We've finished the inner class tour, and now it's up to you to review the Two-Minute Drill and *take the Self Test.* We can virtually guarantee that if you can't answer these questions correctly, you probably can't pass the exam. On the bright side, though, a strong knowledge of inner class syntax and behavior should get you through some of the exam's *toughest* questions. And did you know that recent studies show that intense mental effort—like working on logic puzzles—can actually increase the synaptic connections in your brain? *This* chapter's Self-Test qualifies as "intense mental effort," and might be covered under some health insurance plans.

TWO-MINUTE DRILL

Here are some of the key points from the certification objectives (which for this chapter, means the four inner class topics).

Inner Classes

- A "regular" inner class is declared *inside* the curly braces of another class, but *outside* any method or other code block.
- An inner class is a full-fledged member of the enclosing (outer) class, so it can be marked with an access modifier as well as the `abstract` or `final` modifiers (but of course, never both `abstract` and `final` together—remember that `abstract` means it *must* be subclassed, whereas `final` means it *cannot* be subclassed).
- An inner class instance shares a special relationship with an instance of the enclosing class. This relationship gives the inner class access to *all* of the outer class' members, including those marked `private`.
- To instantiate an inner class, you must have a reference to an instance of the outer class.
- From code within the enclosing class, you can instantiate the inner class using only the name of the inner class, as follows:
  `MyInner mi = new MyInner();`
- From code outside the enclosing class' instance methods, you can instantiate the inner class only by using both the inner and outer class names, and a reference to the outer class as follows:
  `MyOuter mo = new MyOuter();`
  `MyOuter.MyInner inner = mo.new MyInner();`
- From code within the inner class, the keyword `this` holds a reference to the inner class instance. To reference the *outer this* (in other words, the instance of the outer class that this inner instance is tied to) precede the keyword `this` with the outer class name as follows:
  `MyOuter.this;`

Method-Local Inner Classes

- ❑ A method-local inner class is defined within a method of the enclosing class.
- ❑ For the inner class to be used, you must instantiate it, and that instantiation must happen within the same method, but *after* the class definition code.
- ❑ A method-local inner class cannot use variables declared within the method (including parameters) unless those variables are marked `final`.
- ❑ The only modifiers you can apply to a method-local inner class are `abstract` and `final`. (Never both at the same time, though.)

Anonymous Inner Classes

- ❑ Anonymous inner classes have no name, and their type must be either a subclass of the named type or an implementer of the named interface.
- ❑ An anonymous inner class is always created as part of a statement, so don't forget to close the statement after the class definition, with a curly brace. This is one of the rare times you'll see a curly brace followed by a semicolon in Java.
- ❑ Because of polymorphism, the only methods you can call on an anonymous inner class reference are those defined in the reference variable class (or interface), even though the anonymous class is really a subclass or implementer of the reference variable type.
- ❑ An anonymous inner class can extend one subclass, *or* implement one interface. Unlike non-anonymous classes (inner or otherwise), an anonymous inner class cannot do both. In other words, it cannot both extend a class *and* implement an interface, nor can it implement more than one interface.
- ❑ An argument-local inner class is declared, defined, and automatically instantiated as part of a method invocation. The key to remember is that the class is being defined within a method argument, so the syntax will end the class definition with a curly brace, followed by a closing parenthesis to end the method call, followed by a semicolon to end the statement:
  `});`

Static Nested Classes

- ❑ Static nested classes are inner classes marked with the `static` modifier.
- ❑ Technically, a static nested class is *not* an inner class, but instead is considered a top-level nested class.
- ❑ Because the nested class is static, it does not share any special relationship with an instance of the outer class. In fact, you don't need an instance of the outer class to instantiate a static nested class.
- ❑ Instantiating a static nested class requires using both the outer and nested class names as follows:
  `BigOuter.Nested n = new BigOuter.Nested();`
- ❑ A static nested class cannot access nonstatic members of the outer class, since it does not have an implicit reference to any outer instance (in other words, the nested class instance does not get an *outer this* reference).

SELF TEST

The following questions will help you measure your understanding of the dynamic and life-altering material presented in this chapter. Because this chapter spans so many different objectives, the questions here are not organized in specific objective categories. Read all of the choices carefully. Choose all correct answers for each question. Take your time. Breathe.

1. Given the following,

```
public class MyOuter {
   public static class MyInner {
      public static void foo() { }
   }
}
```

which statement, if placed in a class *other* than MyOuter or MyInner, instantiates an instance of the nested class?

A. `MyOuter.MyInner m = new MyOuter.MyInner();`

B. `MyOuter.MyInner mi = new MyInner();`

C. `MyOuter m = new MyOuter();`
`MyOuter.MyInner mi = m.new MyOuter.MyInner();`

D. `MyInner mi = new MyOuter.MyInner();`

2. Which two are true about a static nested class?

A. You must have a reference to an instance of the enclosing class in order to instantiate it.

B. It does not have access to nonstatic members of the enclosing class.

C. Its variables and methods must be static.

D. It can be instantiated using `new MyOuter.MyInner();`.

E. It must extend the enclosing class.

3. Which constructs an anonymous inner class instance?

A. `Runnable r = new Runnable() { };`

B. `Runnable r = new Runnable(public void run() { });`

C. `Runnable r = new Runnable { public void run(){}};`

D. `Runnable r = new Runnable() {public void run{}};`

E. `System.out.println(new Runnable() {public void run() { }});`

F. `System.out.println(new Runnable(public void run() {}));`

4. Given the following,

```
class Boo {
   Boo(String s) { }
   Boo() { }
}
class Bar extends Boo {
   Bar() { }
   Bar(String s) {super(s);}
   void zoo() {
   // insert code here
   }
}
```

which two create an anonymous inner class from within class Bar? (Choose two.)

A. `Boo f = new Boo(24) { };`

B. `Boo f = new Bar() { };`

C. `Boo f = new Boo() {String s; };`

D. `Bar f = new Boo(String s) { };`

E. `Boo f = new Boo.Bar(String s) { };`

5. Given the following,

```
1.class Foo {
2.   class Bar{ }
3.}
4.class Test {
5.    public static void main (String [] args) {
6.        Foo f = new Foo();
7.        // Insert code here
8.    }
9.}
```

which statement, inserted at line 5, creates an instance of Bar?

A. `Foo.Bar b = new Foo.Bar();`

B. `Foo.Bar b = f.new Bar();`

C. `Bar b = new f.Bar();`

D. `Bar b = f.new Bar();`

E. `Foo.Bar b = new f.Bar();`

6. Which two are true about a method-local inner class?

A. It must be marked `final`.

B. It can be marked `abstract`.

C. It can be marked `public`.

D. It can be marked `static`.

E. It can access private members of the enclosing class.

7. Which is true about an anonymous inner class?

A. It can extend exactly one class and implement exactly one interface.

B. It can extend exactly one class and can implement multiple interfaces.

C. It can extend exactly one class or implement exactly one interface.

D. It can implement multiple interfaces regardless of whether it also extends a class.

E. It can implement multiple interfaces if it does not extend a class.

8. Given the following,

```
public class Foo {
   Foo() {System.out.print("foo");}
   class Bar{
      Bar() {System.out.print("bar");}
      public void go() {System.out.print("hi");}
   }
   public static void main (String [] args) {
      Foo f = new Foo();
      f.makeBar();
   }
   void makeBar() {
     (new Bar() {}).go();
   }
}
```

what is the result?

A. Compilation fails.

B. An error occurs at runtime.

C. `foobarhi`

D. `barhi`

E. `hi`

9. Given the following,

```
1.public class TestObj {
2.  public static void main (String [] args) {
3.    Object o = new Object() {
4.       public boolean equals(Object obj) {
5.        return true;
6.       }
7.    }
8.     System.out.println(o.equals("Fred"));
9.   }
10.}
```

what is the result?

A. An exception occurs at runtime.

B. `true`

C. `fred`

D. Compilation fails because of an error on line 3.

E. Compilation fails because of an error on line 4.

F. Compilation fails because of an error on line 8.

G. Compilation fails because of an error on a line other than 3, 4, or 8.

10. Given the following,

```
1. public class HorseTest {
2.   public static void main (String [] args) {
3.    class Horse {
4.       public String name;
5.       public Horse(String s) {
6.         name = s;
7.       }
8.     }
9.   Object obj = new Horse("Zippo");
10.    Horse h = (Horse) obj;
11.    System.out.println(h.name);
12.  }
13. }
```

what is the result?

A. An exception occurs at runtime at line 10.

B. `Zippo`

C. Compilation fails because of an error on line 3.

D. Compilation fails because of an error on line 9.

E. Compilation fails because of an error on line 10.

F. Compilation fails because of an error on line 11.

11. Given the following,

```
 1. public class HorseTest {
 2.   public static void main (String [] args) {
 3.    class Horse {
 4.       public String name;
 5.       public Horse(String s) {
 6.         name = s;
 7.       }
 8.     }
 9.    Object obj = new Horse("Zippo");
10.    System.out.println(obj.name);
11.  }
12. }
```

what is the result?

A. An exception occurs at runtime at line 10.

B. `Zippo`

C. Compilation fails because of an error on line 3.

D. Compilation fails because of an error on line 9.

E. Compilation fails because of an error on line 10.

12. Given the following,

```
public abstract class AbstractTest {
   public int getNum() {
      return 45;
   }
   public abstract class Bar {
     public int getNum() {
       return 38;
     }
   }
   public static void main (String [] args) {
      AbstractTest t = new AbstractTest() {
         public int getNum() {
           return 22;
         }
       };
```

```
            AbstractTest.Bar f = t.new Bar() {
               public int getNum() {
                 return 57;
               }
             };
             System.out.println(f.getNum() + " " + t.getNum());
         }
    }
```

what is the result?

A. 57 22

B. 45 38

C. 45 57

D. An exception occurs at runtime.

E. Compilation fails.

SELF TEST ANSWERS

1. ☑ A. MyInner is a static nested class, so it must be instantiated using the fully-scoped name of MyOuter.MyInner.
   ☒ B is incorrect because it doesn't use the enclosing name in the `new`. C is incorrect because it uses incorrect syntax. When you instantiate a nested class by invoking new on an instance of the enclosing class, you do not use the enclosing name. The difference between A and C is that C is calling new on an instance of the enclosing class rather than just new by itself. D is incorrect because it doesn't use the enclosing class name in the variable declaration.

2. ☑ B and D. B is correct because a static nested class is not tied to an instance of the enclosing class, and thus can't access the nonstatic members of the class (just as a static method can't access nonstatic members of a class). D uses the correct syntax for instantiating a static nested class.
   ☒ A is incorrect because static nested classes do not need (and can't use) a reference to an instance of the enclosing class. C is incorrect because static nested classes can declare and define nonstatic members. E is wrong because…it just is. There's no rule that says an inner or nested class has to extend anything.

3. ☑ E is correct. It defines an anonymous inner class instance, which also means it creates an instance of that new anonymous class at the same time. The anonymous class is an implementer of the Runnable interface, so it must override the `run()` method of Runnable.
   ☒ A is incorrect because it doesn't override the `run()` method, so it violates the rules of interface implementation. B, C, and D use incorrect syntax.

4. ☑ B and C. B is correct because anonymous inner classes are no different from any other class when it comes to polymorphism. That means you are always allowed to declare a reference variable of the superclass type and have that reference variable refer to an instance of a subclass type, which in this case is an anonymous subclass of Bar. Since Bar is a subclass of Boo, it all works. C uses correct syntax for creating an instance of Boo.
   ☒ A is incorrect because it passes an *int* to the Boo constructor, and there is no matching constructor in the Boo class. D is incorrect because it violates the rules of polymorphism—you cannot refer to a superclass type using a reference variable declared as the subclass type. The superclass is not guaranteed to have everything the subclass has. E uses incorrect syntax.

5. ☑ B is correct because the syntax is correct—using both names (the enclosing class and the inner class) in the reference declaration, then using a reference to the enclosing class to invoke `new` on the inner class.
☒ A, C, D, and E all use incorrect syntax. A is incorrect because it doesn't use a reference to the enclosing class, and also because it includes both names in the `new`. C is incorrect because it doesn't use the enclosing class name in the reference variable declaration, and because the `new` syntax is wrong. D is incorrect because it doesn't use the enclosing class name in the reference variable declaration. E is incorrect because the `new` syntax is wrong.

6. ☑ B and E. B is correct because a method-local inner class can be abstract, although it means a subclass of the inner class must be created if the abstract class is to be used (so an abstract method-local inner class is probably not useful). E is correct because a method-local inner class works like any other inner class—it has a special relationship to an instance of the enclosing class, thus it can access all members of the enclosing class.
☒ A is incorrect because a method-local inner class does not have to be declared final (although it is legal to do so). C and D are incorrect because a method-local inner class cannot be made `public` (remember—you cannot mark any local variables as `public`), or `static`.

7. ☑ C is correct because the syntax of an anonymous inner class allows for only one named type after the `new`, and that type must be either a single interface (in which case the anonymous class implements that one interface) or a single class (in which case the anonymous class extends that one class).
☒ A, B, D, and E are all incorrect because they don't follow the syntax rules described in the response for answer C.

8. ☑ C is correct because first the Foo instance is created, which means the Foo constructor runs and prints "`foo`". Next, the `makeBar()` method is invoked which creates a `Bar`, which means the Bar constructor runs and prints "`bar`", and finally the `go()` method is invoked on the new Bar instance, which means the `go()` method prints "`hi`".
☒ A, C, D, E, and F are incorrect based on the program logic described above.

9. ☑ G. This code would be legal if line 7 ended with a semicolon. Remember that line 3 is a statement that doesn't end until line 7, and a statement needs a closing semicolon!
☒ A, B, C, D, E, and F are incorrect based on the program logic described above. If the semicolon were added at line 7, then answer B would be correct—the program would print "`true`", the return from the `equals()` method overridden by the anonymous subclass of Object.

10. ☑ **B.** The code in the HorseTest class is perfectly legal. Line 9 creates an instance of the method-local inner class Horse, using a reference variable declared as type Object. Line 10 casts the Horse object to a Horse reference variable, which allows line 11 to compile. If line 10 were removed, the HorseTest code would not compile, because class Object does not have a *name* variable.
☒ A, C, D, E, and F are incorrect based on the program logic described above.

11. ☑ E. This code is identical to the code in question 10, except the casting statement has been removed. If you use a reference variable of type Object, you can access only those members defined in class Object.
☒ A, B, C, and D are incorrect based on the program logic described above and in the previous question.

12. ☑ A. You can define an inner class as `abstract`, which means you can instantiate only concrete subclasses of the abstract inner class. The object referenced by the variable *t* is an instance of an anonymous subclass of AbstractTest, and the anonymous class overrides the `getNum()` method to return `22`. The variable referenced by *f* is an instance of an anonymous subclass of `Bar`, and the anonymous Bar subclass also overrides the `getNum()` method (to return `57`). Remember that to instantiate a `Bar` instance, we need an instance of the enclosing AbstractTest class to tie to the new `Bar` inner class instance. AbstractTest can't be instantiated because it's abstract, so we created an anonymous subclass (non-abstract) and then used the instance of that anonymous subclass to tie to the new Bar subclass instance.
☒ B, C, D, E, and F are incorrect based on the program logic described above.

9

Threads

CERTIFICATION OBJECTIVES

- Defining, Instantiating, and Starting Threads
- Preventing Thread Execution
- Synchronizing Code
- Thread Interaction
- ✓ Two-Minute Drill
- Q&A Self Test

CERTIFICATION OBJECTIVE

Defining, Instantiating, and Starting Threads (Exam Objective 7.1)

Write code to define, instantiate, and start new threads using both java.lang.Thread and java.lang.Runnable.

Imagine a stockbroker application with a lot of complex behavior that the user initiates. One of the applications is "download last stock option prices," another is "check prices for warnings," and a third time-consuming operation is, "analyze historical data for company XYZ."

In a single-threaded runtime environment, these actions execute one after another. The next action can happen *only* when the previous one is finished. If a historical analysis takes half an hour, and the user selects to perform a download and check afterward, the warning may come too late to, say, buy or sell stock as a result.

We just imagined the sort of application that cries out for multithreading. Ideally, the download should happen in the background (that is, in another thread). That way, other processes could happen at the same time so that, for example, a warning could be communicated instantly. All the while, the user is interacting with other parts of the application. The analysis, too, could happen in a separate thread, so the user can work in the rest of the application while the results are being calculated.

So what exactly *is* a thread? In Java, "thread" means two different things:

- An instance of class java.lang.Thread
- A thread of execution

An instance of Thread is just…an object. Like any other object in Java, it has variables and methods, and lives and dies on the heap. But a *thread of execution* is an individual process (a "lightweight" process) that has its own call stack. In Java, there is *one thread per call stack*—or, to think of it in reverse, *one call stack per thread.* Even if you don't create any new threads in your program, threads are back there running.

The `main()` method that starts the whole ball rolling runs in one thread, called (surprisingly) the *main* thread. If you looked at the main call stack (and you can, anytime you get a stack trace from something that happens *after* main begins, but not within another thread) you'd see that `main()` is the first method on the stack—the method at the bottom. But as soon as you create a *new* thread, a new stack materializes and methods called from *that* thread run in a call stack that's separate from the `main()` call stack. That second new call stack is said to run concurrently with the main thread, but we'll refine that notion as we go through this chapter.

You might find it confusing that we're talking about code running *concurrently*—as if in *parallel*—yet you know there's only one CPU on most of the machines running Java. What gives? The JVM, which gets its turn at the CPU by whatever scheduling mechanism the underlying OS uses, operates like a mini-OS and schedules *its* own threads regardless of the underlying operating system. In some JVMs, the java threads are actually mapped to native OS threads, but we won't discuss that here; native threads are not on the exam. Nor is an understanding of how threads behave in different JVM environments required knowledge. In fact, the most important concept to understand from this entire chapter is

When it comes to threads, very little is guaranteed.

So be very cautious about interpreting the behavior you see on *one* machine as "the way threads work." The exam expects you to know what is and is not guaranteed behavior, so that you can design your program in such a way that it will work regardless of the underlying JVM. *That's part of the whole point of Java.*

on the job

Don't make the mistake of designing your program to be dependent on a particular implementation of the JVM. As you'll learn a little later, different JVMs can run threads in profoundly different ways. For example, one JVM might be sure that all threads get their turn, with a fairly even amount of time allocated for each thread in a nice, happy, round-robin fashion. But in other JVMs, a thread might start running and then just hog the whole show, never stepping out so others can have a turn. If you test your application on the "nice turn-taking" JVM, and you don't know what is and is not guaranteed in Java, then you might be in for a big shock when you run it under a JVM with a different thread scheduling mechanism.

The thread questions on the exam are among the most difficult. In fact, for most people they *are* the toughest questions on the exam, and with four objectives for threads you'll be answering a *lot* of thread questions. If you're not already familiar with threads, you'll probably need to spend some time experimenting. Also, one final disclaimer: *This chapter makes no attempt to teach you how to design a good, safe, multithreaded application!* You're here to learn what you need to get through the thread questions on the exam. Before you can write decent multithreaded code, however, you really need to study more on the complexities and subtleties of multithreaded code.

With that out of the way, let's dive into threads. It's kind of a bad news/good news thing. The bad news is that this is probably the most difficult chapter. The good news is, *it's the last chapter* in the Programmer's Exam part of the book. So kick back and enjoy the fact that once you've finished learning what's in this chapter, and you've nailed the self-test questions, you're probably ready to take—and pass—the exam.

Making a Thread

A thread in Java begins as an instance of java.lang.Thread. You'll find methods in the Thread class for managing threads including creating, starting, and pausing them. For the exam, you'll need to know, at a minimum, the following methods:

```
start()
yield()
sleep()
run()
```

The action all starts from the `run()` method. Think of the code you want to execute in a separate thread as *"the job to do."* In other words, you have some work that needs to be done, say, downloading stock prices in the background while other things are happening in the program, so what you really want is that *job* to be executed in its own thread. So if the *work* you want done is the *job*, the one *doing* the work (actually executing the job code) is the *thread*. And the *job always starts from a* `run()` *method* as follows:

```
public void run() {
  // your job code goes here
}
```

You always write the code that needs to be run in a separate thread in a `run()` method. The `run()` method will call other methods, of course, but the thread of execution—the new call stack—always begins by invoking `run()`. So where does the `run()` method go? In one of the two classes you can use to define your thread job.

You can define and instantiate a thread in one of two ways:

- Extend the java.lang.Thread class
- Implement the Runnable interface

You need to know about both for the exam, although in the real world you're much more likely to implement Runnable than extend Thread. Extending the Thread class is the easiest, but it's usually not a good OO practice. Why? Because subclassing should be reserved for classes that extend an existing class, because they're a more specialized version of the more general superclass. So the only time it really makes sense (from an OO perspective) to extend Thread is when you have a more specialized version of a Thread class. In other words, because *you have more specialized thread-specific behavior.* Chances are, though, that the thread work you want is really just a job to be done *by* a thread. In that case, you should design a class that implements the Runnable interface, which also leaves your class free to extend from some *other* class.

Defining a Thread

To define a thread, you need a place to put your `run()` method, and as we just discussed, you can do that by extending the Thread class or by implementing the Runnable interface. We'll look at both in this section.

Extending java.lang.Thread

The simplest way to define code to run in a separate thread is to

- Extend the Thread class.
- Override the `run()` method.

It looks like this:

```
class MyThread extends Thread {
   public void run() {
     System.out.println("Important job running in MyThread");
   }
}
```

The limitation with this approach (besides being a poor design choice in most cases) is that if you extend Thread, *you can't extend anything else.* And it's not as if you really need that inherited Thread class behavior, because in order to use a thread you'll need to instantiate one anyway.

Keep in mind that you're free to overload the `run()` method in your Thread subclass:

```
class MyThread extends Thread {
   public void run() {
     System.out.println("Important job running in MyThread");
   }
   public void run(String s) {
      System.out.println("String in run is " + s);
  }
}
```

But know this: *the overloaded* `run(String s)` *method won't be called unless you call it.* It will not be used as the basis of a new call stack.

Implementing java.lang.Runnable

Implementing the Runnable interface gives you a way to extend from any class you like, but still define behavior that will be run by a separate thread. It looks like this:

```
class MyRunnable implements Runnable {
   public void run() {
     System.out.println("Important job running in MyRunnable");
   }
}
```

Regardless of which mechanism you choose, you've now got yourself some code that can be run by a thread of execution. So now let's take a look at *instantiating* your thread-capable class, and then we'll figure out how to actually get the thing *running.*

Instantiating a Thread

Remember, every thread of execution begins as an instance of class Thread. Regardless of whether your `run()` method is in a Thread subclass or a Runnable implementation class, you still need a Thread object to do the work.

If you extended the Thread class, instantiation is dead simple:

```
MyThread t = new MyThread();
```

There are some additional overloaded constructors, but we'll look at those in a moment.

If you implement Runnable, instantiation is only slightly less simple. To have code run by a separate thread, *you still need a Thread instance.* But rather than combining both the *thread* and the *job* (the code in the `run()` method) into one class, you've split it into two classes—the Thread class for the *thread-specific* code and your Runnable implementation class for your *job-that-should-be-run-by-a-thread* code.

First, you instantiate your Runnable class:

```
MyRunnable r = new MyRunnable();
```

Next, you get yourself an instance of java.lang.Thread (*somebody* has to run your job…), and you *give it your job*!

```
Thread t = new Thread(r);  // Pass your Runnable to the Thread
```

If you create a thread using the no-arg constructor, the thread will call its own `run()` method when it's time to start working. That's exactly what you want when you extend Thread, but when you use Runnable, you need to tell the new thread to use *your* `run()` method rather than its own. The Runnable you pass to the Thread constructor is called the *target* or the *target Runnable.*

You can pass a single Runnable instance to multiple Thread objects, so that the same Runnable becomes the target of multiple threads, as follows:

```
public class TestThreads {
   public static void main (String [] args) {
     MyRunnable r = new MyRunnable();
     Thread foo = new Thread(r);
     Thread bar = new Thread(r);
     Thread bat = new Thread(r);
   }
}
```

Giving the same target to multiple threads means that several threads of execution will be running the very same job.

Besides the no-arg constructor and the constructor that takes a Runnable (the target, the instance with the job to do), there are other overloaded constructors in class Thread. The constructors we care about are

- Thread()
- Thread(Runnable target)

- Thread(Runnable target, String name)
- Thread(String name)
- Thread(ThreadGroup group, Runnable target)
- Thread(ThreadGroup group, Runnable target, String name)
- Thread(ThreadGroup group, String name)

You need to recognize all of them for the exam! A little later, we'll discuss some of the other constructors in the preceding list.

So now you've made yourself a Thread instance, and it knows which `run()` method to call. *But nothing is happening yet.* At this point, all we've got is a plain old Java object of type Thread. *It is not yet a thread of execution.* To get an actual thread—a new call stack—we still have to *start* the thread.

When a thread has been instantiated but not started (in other words, the `start()` method has not been invoked on the Thread instance), the thread is said to be in the *new* state. At this stage, the thread is not yet considered to be *alive*. The "aliveness" of a thread can be tested by calling the `isAlive()` method on the Thread instance. In a nutshell, a thread is considered *alive* at some point after it has been started (you have to give the JVM a little time to get it set up as a thread once `start()` is called), and it is considered *not alive* after it becomes dead. The `isAlive()` method is the best way to determine if a thread has been started but has not yet completed its `run()` method.

Starting a Thread

You've created a Thread object and it knows its target (either the passed-in Runnable or itself if you extended class Thread). Now it's time to get the whole thread thing happening—to launch a new call stack. It's so simple it hardly deserves its own subhead:

```
t.start();
```

Prior to calling `start()` on a Thread instance, the thread (when we use lowercase *t*, we're referring to the *thread of execution* rather than the Thread class) is said to be in the *new* state as we said. The new state means you have a Thread *object* but you don't yet have a *true thread.* So what happens after you call `start()`? The good stuff:

- A new thread of execution starts (with a new call stack).

- The thread moves from the *new* state to the *runnable* state.
- When the thread gets a chance to execute, its target `run()` method will run.

Be *sure* you remember the following: You start a *Thread*, not a *Runnable*. You call `start()` on a Thread instance, not on a Runnable instance.

exam watch

There's nothing special about the `run()` method as far as Java is concerned. Like `main()`, it just happens to be the name (and signature) of the method that the new thread knows to invoke. So if you see code that calls the `run()` method on a Runnable (or even on a Thread instance), that's perfectly legal. But it doesn't mean the `run()` method will run in a separate thread! Calling a `run()` method directly just means you're invoking a method from whatever thread is currently executing, and the `run()` method goes onto the current call stack rather than at the beginning of a new call stack. The following code does not start a new thread of execution:

```
Runnable r = new Runnable();
r.run();  // Legal, but does not start a separate thread
```

The following example demonstrates what we've covered so far—defining, instantiating, and starting a thread:

```
class FooRunnable implements Runnable {
   public void run() {
      for(int x =1; x < 6; x++) {
        System.out.println("Runnable running");
      }
   }
}
public class TestThreads {
   public static void main (String [] args) {
     FooRunnable r = new FooRunnable();
     Thread t = new Thread(r);
     t.start();
   }
}
```

Running the preceding code prints out exactly what you'd expect:

```
% java TestThreads
Runnable running
Runnable running
Runnable running
```

```
Runnable running
Runnable running
```

(If this isn't what you expected, go back and reread everything in this objective.)

So what happens if we start multiple threads? We'll run a simple example in a moment, but first we need to know how to print out which thread is executing. We can use the name method of class Thread, and have each Runnable print out the name of the thread executing that Runnable object's `run()` method. The following example instantiates a thread and gives it a name, and then the name is printed out from the `run()` method:

```
class NameRunnable implements Runnable {
   public void run() {
        System.out.println("NameRunnable running");
         System.out.println("Run by "
          + Thread.currentThread().getName());
      }
   }
public class NameThread {
   public static void main (String [] args) {
     NameRunnable nr = new NameRunnable();
     Thread t = new Thread(nr);
     t.setName("Fred");
     t.start();
   }
}
```

Running this code produces the following, extra special, output:

```
% java NameThread
NameRunnable running
Run by Fred
```

To get the name of a thread you call—who would have guessed—`getName()` on the thread instance. But the target Runnable instance doesn't even *have* a reference to the Thread instance, so we first invoked the static `Thread.currentThread()` method, which returns a reference to the currently executing thread, and then we invoked `getName()` on that returned reference.

Even if you don't explicitly name a thread, it still has a name. Let's look at the previous code, commenting out the statement that sets the thread's name:

```
public class NameThread {
   public static void main (String [] args) {
```

```
        NameRunnable nr = new NameRunnable();
        Thread t = new Thread(nr);
        // t.setName("Fred");
        t.start();
    }
}
```

Running the preceding code now gives us:

```
% java NameThread
NameRunnable running
Run by Thread-0
```

And since we're getting the name of the current thread by using the static `Thread.currentThread()` method, we can even get the name of the thread running our main code,

```
public class NameThreadTwo {
    public static void main (String [] args) {
      System.out.println("thread is "
       + Thread.currentThread().getName());
    }
}
```

which prints out

```
% java NameThreadTwo
thread is main
```

That's right, the main thread already has a name—*main.* (Once again, what are the odds?) Figure 9-1 shows the process of starting a thread.

Starting and Running More Than One Thread

Enough playing around here; let's actually get *multiple* threads going. The following code creates a single Runnable instance, and three Thread instances. All three Thread instances get the same Runnable instance, and each thread is given a unique name. Finally, all three threads are started by invoking `start()` on the Thread instances.

```
class NameRunnable implements Runnable {
    public void run() {
        for (int x = 1; x < 4; x++) {
            System.out.println("Run by "
             + Thread.currentThread().getName());
        }
     }
```

```
}
public class ManyNames {
   public static void main (String [] args) {
     // Make one Runnable
     NameRunnable nr = new NameRunnable();
     Thread one = new Thread(nr);
     one.setName("Fred");
     Thread two = new Thread(nr);
     two.setName("Lucy");
     Thread three = new Thread(nr);
     three.setName("Ricky");
     one.start();
     two.start();
     three.start();
   }
}
```

FIGURE 9-1

Starting a thread

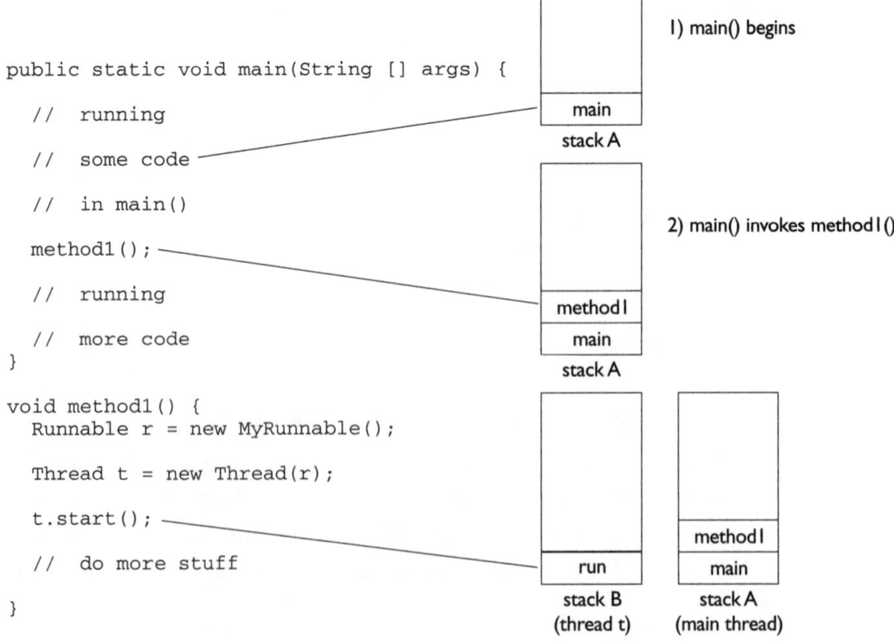

Running this code produces the following:

```
% java ManyNames
Run by Fred
Run by Fred
Run by Fred
Run by Lucy
Run by Lucy
Run by Lucy
Run by Ricky
Run by Ricky
Run by Ricky
```

Well, at least that's what it prints on *one* machine—the one we used for this particular example. (OK, if you insist we'll tell you—it's a Macintosh G4 Titanium running OSX. Yes Virginia, there *is* UNIX on the Mac.)

But the behavior you see above is not guaranteed. This is so crucial that you need to stop right now, take a deep breath, and repeat after me, "The behavior is not guaranteed." You need to know, for your future as a Java programmer as well as for the exam, that there is nothing in the Java specification that says threads will start running in the order in which they were started (in other words, the order in which `start()` was invoked on each thread). And there is no guarantee that once a thread starts executing, it will keep executing until it's done. Or that a loop will complete before another thread begins. No siree Bob. Nothing is guaranteed in the preceding code except this:

Each thread will start, and each thread will run to completion.

But how that happens is not just *JVM* dependent; it is also *runtime* dependent. In fact, just for fun we bumped up the loop code so that each `run()` method ran the loop 300 times rather than 3, and eventually we did start to see some wobbling:

```
public void run() {
      for (int x = 0; x < 300; x++) {
         System.out.println("Run by " + Thread.currentThread().getName());
      }
 }
```

Running the preceding code, with each thread executing its run loop 300 times, started out fine but then became nonlinear. Here's just a snip from the command-line output of running that code. To make it easier to distinguish each thread, I put Fred's output in italics and Lucy's in bold, and left Ricky's alone:

```
Run by Fred
Run by Fred
Run by Fred
Run by Fred
Run by Fred
Run by Fred
Run by Fred
Run by Fred
Run by Fred
Run by Fred
Run by Lucy
Run by Ricky
Run by Fred
Run by Ricky
Run by Fred
Run by Ricky
Run by Fred
Run by Ricky
Run by Fred
Run by Ricky
... it continues on ...
```

Notice that Fred (who was started first) is humming along just fine for a while and then suddenly Lucy (started second) jumps in—but only runs once! She does finish later, of course, but not until after Fred and Ricky swap in and out with no clear pattern. The rest of the output also shows Lucy and Ricky swapping for a while, and then finally Lucy finishes with a long sequence of output. So even though Ricky was started third, he actually completed second. *And if we run it again, we'll get a different result.* Why? *Because its up to the scheduler, and we don't control the scheduler!* Which brings up another key point to remember: *Just because a series of threads are started in a particular order doesn't mean they'll run in that order.* For any group of started threads, order is not guaranteed by the scheduler. And duration is not guaranteed. You don't know, for example, if one thread will run to completion before the others have a chance to get in or whether they'll all take turns nicely, or whether they'll do a combination of both. There is a way, however, to start a thread but tell it not to run until some other thread has finished. You can do this with the `join()` method, which we'll look at a little later.

A thread is done being a thread when its target `run()` *method completes.*

When a thread completes its `run()` method, the thread ceases to be a thread of execution. The stack for that thread dissolves, and the thread is considered *dead.* Not dead and *gone,* however, just *dead.* It's still a Thread *object,* just not a *thread of execution.* So if you've got a reference to a Thread instance, then even when that Thread instance is no longer a thread of execution, you can still call methods on the Thread instance, just like any other Java object. What you can't do, though, is call `start()` again.

Once a thread is dead, it can never be restarted!

If you have a reference to a Thread *t,* and its `run()` method has finished, calling `t.start()` won't restart it.

So far, we've seen three thread states: *new, runnable,* and *dead.* We'll look at more thread states before we're done with this chapter.

The Thread Scheduler

The thread scheduler is the part of the JVM (although most JVMs map Java threads directly to native threads on the underlying OS) that decides which thread should run at any given moment, and also takes threads *out* of the run state. Assuming a single processor machine, only one thread can actually *run* at a time. Only one stack can ever be executing at one time. And it's the thread scheduler that decides *which* thread—of all that are eligible—will actually *run.* When we say *eligible,* we really mean *in the runnable state.*

Any thread in the *runnable* state can be chosen by the scheduler to be the one and only *running* thread. If a thread is *not* in a runnable state, then it cannot be chosen to the *currently running* thread. And just so we're clear about how little is guaranteed here:

The order in which runnable threads are chosen to run is not guaranteed.

Although *queue* behavior is typical, it isn't guaranteed. Queue behavior means that when a thread has finished with its "turn," it moves to the end of the line of the runnable pool and waits until it eventually gets to the front of the line, where it can be chosen again. In fact, we call it a runnable *pool,* rather than a runnable *queue,* to help reinforce the fact that threads aren't all lined up in some guaranteed order.

Although we don't *control* the thread scheduler (we can't, for example, tell a specific thread to run), we can sometimes influence it. The following methods give us some tools for *influencing* the scheduler. Just don't ever mistake influence for control.

exam Watch

Expect to see exam questions that look for your understanding of what is and is not guaranteed! You must be able to look at thread code and determine whether the output is guaranteed to run in a particular way or is indeterminate.

Methods from the java.lang.Thread Class Some of the methods that can help us influence thread scheduling are as follows:

```
public static void sleep(long millis) throws InterruptedException
public static void yield()
public final void join()
public final void setPriority(int newPriority)
```

Note that both `sleep()` and `join()` have overloaded versions not shown here.

Methods from the java.lang.Object Class Every class in Java inherits the following three thread-related methods:

```
public final void wait()
public final void notify()
public final void notifyAll()
```

The `wait()` method has three overloaded versions (including the one listed here).

We'll look at the behavior of each of these methods in this chapter. First, though, we're going to look at the different states a thread can be in. We've already seen three—*new*, *runnable*, and *dead*—but wait! There's more! The thread scheduler's job is to move threads in and out of the *running* state. While the thread scheduler can move a thread from the running state back to runnable, other factors can cause a thread to move out of running, but *not* back to runnable. One of these is when the thread's `run()` method completes, in which case the thread moves from the running state directly to the dead state. Next we'll look at some of the other ways in which a thread can leave the running state, and where the thread goes.

Thread States

A thread can be only in one of five states (see Figure 9-2):

- **New** This is the state the thread is in after the Thread instance has been instantiated, but the `start()` method has not been invoked on the thread. It is a live Thread object, but not yet a thread of execution. At this point, the thread is considered *not alive.*
- **Runnable** This is the state a thread is in when it's eligible to run, but the scheduler has not selected it to be the running thread. A thread first enters the runnable state when the `start()` method is invoked, but a thread can also return to the runnable state after either running or coming back from

a blocked, waiting, or sleeping state. When the thread is in the runnable state, it is considered *alive.*

- **Running** This is it. The "big time." Where the action is. This is the state a thread is in when the thread scheduler selects it (from the runnable pool) to be the currently executing process. A thread can transition out of a running state for several reasons, including because "the thread scheduler felt like it." We'll look at those other reasons shortly. Note that in Figure 9-2, there are several ways to get to the runnable state, but only *one* way to get to the running state: the scheduler chooses a thread from the runnable pool.
- **Waiting/blocked/sleeping** OK, so this is really three states combined into one, but they all have one thing in common: the thread is still alive, but is currently not eligible to run. In other words, it is not *runnable*, but it might *return* to a runnable state later if a particular event occurs. A thread may be *blocked* waiting for a resource (like I/O or an object's lock), in which case the event that sends it back to runnable is the availability of the resource—for example, if data comes in through the input stream the thread code is reading from, or if the object's lock suddenly becomes available. A thread may be *sleeping* because the thread's run code *tells* it to sleep for some period of time, in which case the event that sends it back to runnable is that it wakes up because its sleep time has expired. Or the thread may be *waiting*, because the thread's run code *causes* it to wait, in which case the event that sends it back to runnable is that another thread sends a notification that it may no longer be necessary for the thread to wait. The important point is that one thread does not *tell* another thread to block. There *is* a method, `suspend()`, in the Thread class, that lets one thread tell another to suspend, but the `suspend()` method has been deprecated and won't be on the exam (nor will its counterpart `resume()`). There is also a `stop()` method, but it too has been deprecated and we won't even go there. Both `suspend()` and `stop()` turned out to be very dangerous, so you shouldn't use them and again, because they're deprecated, they won't appear on the exam. Don't study 'em, don't use 'em. Note also that a thread in a blocked state is still considered to be *alive.*

FIGURE 9-2

Transitioning between thread states

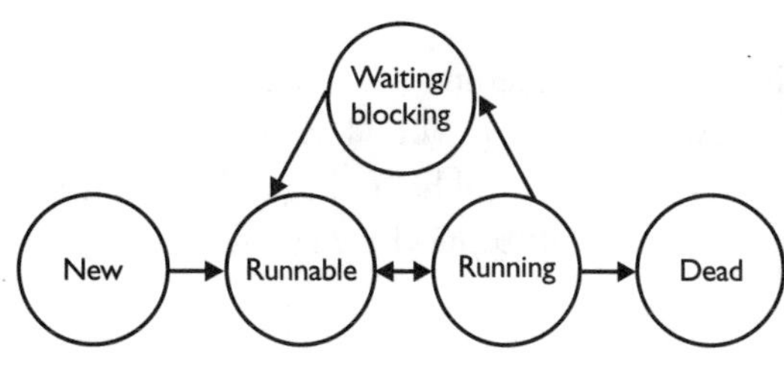

- **Dead** A thread is considered dead when its `run()` method completes. It may still be a viable Thread object, but it is no longer a separate thread of execution. Once a thread is dead, it can never be brought back to life! (The whole "I see dead threads" thing.) If you invoke `start()` on a dead Thread instance, you'll get a runtime (not compiler) exception. And it probably doesn't take a rocket scientist to tell you that if a thread is dead, it is no longer considered to be *alive*.

CERTIFICATION OBJECTIVE

Preventing Thread Execution (Exam Objective 7.2)

Recognize conditions that might prevent a thread from executing.

This objective has been the source of a lot of confusion over the last few years, because earlier versions of the objective weren't as clear about one thing: we're talking about moving a thread to a nonrunnable state (in other words, moving a thread to the blocked/sleeping/waiting state), as opposed to talking about what might *stop* a thread. A thread that's been stopped usually means a thread that's moved to the dead state. But Objective 7.2 is looking for your ability to recognize when a thread will get kicked out of running but not sent back to either runnable or dead.

For the purpose of the exam, we aren't concerned with a thread blocking on I/O (say, waiting for something to arrive from an input stream from the server). We *are* concerned with the following:

- *Sleeping*
- *Waiting*
- *Blocked because it needs an object's lock*

Sleeping

The `sleep()` method is a static method of class Thread. You use it in your code to "slow a thread down" by forcing it to go into a sleep mode before coming back to runnable (where it still has to beg to be the currently running thread). When a thread sleeps, it drifts off somewhere and doesn't return to runnable until it wakes up.

So why would you want a thread to sleep? Well, you might think the thread is moving too quickly through its code. Or you might need to force your threads to take turns, since reasonable turn-taking isn't guaranteed in the Java specifications. Or imagine a thread that runs in a loop, downloading the latest stock prices and analyzing them. Downloading prices one after another would be a waste of time, as most would be quite similar, and even more importantly—it would be an incredible waste of precious bandwidth. The simplest way to solve this is to cause a thread to pause (sleep) for five minutes after each download.

You do this by invoking the static `Thread.sleep()` method, giving it a time in milliseconds as follows:

```
try {
     Thread.sleep(5*60*1000);   // Sleep for 5 minutes
} catch (InterruptedException ex) { }
```

Notice that the `sleep()` method can throw a checked InterruptedException (which you'll usually know if that were a possibility, since another thread has to explicitly do the interrupting), so you're forced to acknowledge the exception with a handle or declare. Typically, you just wrap each call to sleep in a *try/catch*, as in the preceding code.

Let's modify our Fred, Lucy, Ricky code by using sleep to *try* to force the threads to alternate rather than letting one thread dominate for any period of time. Where do you think the `sleep()` method should go?

```
class NameRunnable implements Runnable {
   public void run() {
      for (int x = 1; x < 4; x++) {
         System.out.println("Run by "
          + Thread.currentThread().getName());
         try {
           Thread.sleep(1000);
         } catch (InterruptedException ex) { }
      }
    }
}
public class ManyNames {
   public static void main (String [] args) {
     // Make one Runnable
     NameRunnable nr = new NameRunnable();
     Thread one = new Thread(nr);
     one.setName("Fred");
     Thread two = new Thread(nr);
     two.setName("Lucy");
     Thread three = new Thread(nr);
```

```
        three.setName("Ricky");
        one.start();
        two.start();
        three.start();
    }
}
```

Running this code shows Fred, Lucy, and Ricky alternating nicely:

```
% java ManyNames
Run by Fred
Run by Lucy
Run by Ricky
Run by Fred
Run by Lucy
Run by Ricky
Run by Fred
Run by Lucy
Run by Ricky
```

Just keep in mind that the behavior in the preceding output is still not guaranteed. You can't be certain how long a thread will actually run *before* it gets put to sleep, so you can't know with certainty that only one of the three threads will be in the runnable state when the running thread goes to sleep. In other words, if there are two threads awake and in the runnable pool, you can't know with certainty that the least-recently-used thread will be the one selected to run. *Still, using* `sleep()` *is the best way to help all threads get a chance to run!* Or at least to guarantee that one thread doesn't get in and stay until it's done. When a thread encounters a sleep call, it *must* go to sleep for *at least* the specified number of milliseconds (unless it is interrupted before its wake-up time, in which case it immediately throws the InterruptedException).

Just because a thread's `sleep()` expires, and it wakes up, does* not *mean it will return to running! Remember,* when a thread wakes up it simply goes back to the runnable state. *So the time specified in `sleep()` is the* minimum *duration in which the thread won't run, but it is not the* exact *duration in which the thread won't run. So you can't, for example, rely on the `sleep()` method to give you a perfectly accurate timer. Although in many applications using `sleep()` as a timer is certainly good enough, you must know that a `sleep()` time is not a guarantee that the thread will start running again as soon as the time expires and the thread wakes.

Remember that `sleep()` is a static method, so don't be fooled into thinking that one thread can put another thread to sleep. You can put `sleep()` code anywhere, since *all* code is being run by *some* thread. When the executing code (meaning the currently running thread's code) hits a `sleep()` call, it puts the currently running thread to sleep.

EXERCISE 9-1

Creating a Thread and Putting It to Sleep

In this exercise we will create a simple counting thread. It will count to 100, pausing one second between each number. Also, in keeping with the counting theme, it will output a string every ten numbers.

1. Create a class and extend the Thread class. As an option, you can implement the Runnable interface.
2. Override the `run()` method of Thread. This is where the code will go that will output the numbers.
3. Create a *for* loop that will loop 100 times. Use the modulo operation to check whether there are any remainder numbers when divided by 10.
4. Use the static method `Thread.sleep()` to pause. The *long* number represents milliseconds.

Thread Priorities and Yield

To understand `yield()`, you must understand the concept of thread *priorities.* Threads always run with some priority, represented usually as a number between 1 and 10 (although in some cases the range is less than 10). The scheduler in most JVMs uses *preemptive, priority-based* scheduling. *This does not mean that all JVMs use time slicing.* The JVM specification does not require a VM to implement a time-slicing scheduler, where each thread is allocated a fair amount of time and then sent back to runnable to give another thread a chance. Although many JVMs do use time slicing, another may use a scheduler that lets one thread stay running until the thread completes its `run()` method.

In most JVMs, however, the scheduler does use thread priorities in one important way: If a thread enters the runnable state, and it has a higher priority than any of the threads in the pool and higher than the currently running thread, *the lower-priority running thread usually will be bumped back to runnable and the highest-priority thread will be chosen to run.* In other words, at any given time the currently running thread usually will not have a priority that is lower than any of the threads in the pool. *The running thread will be of equal or greater priority than the highest priority threads in the pool.* This is as close to a guarantee about scheduling as you'll get from the JVM specification, so you must never rely on thread priorities to guarantee correct behavior of your program.

Don't rely on thread priorities when designing your multithreaded application. Because thread-scheduling priority behavior is not guaranteed, use thread priorities as a way to improve the efficiency of your program, but just be sure your program doesn't *depend* ***on that behavior for correctness.***

What is also *not* guaranteed is the behavior when threads in the pool are of equal priority, or when the currently running thread has the same priority as threads in the pool. All priorities being equal, a JVM implementation of the scheduler is free to do just about anything it likes. That means a scheduler might do one of the following (among other things):

- Pick a thread to run, and keep it there until it blocks or completes its `run()` method.
- Time slice the threads in the pool to give everyone an equal opportunity to run.

Setting a Thread's Priority A thread gets a default priority that is *the priority of the thread of execution that creates it.* For example, in the code

```
public class TestThreads {
  public static void main (String [] args) {
   MyThread t = new MyThread();
   }
}
```

the thread referenced by *t* will have the same priority as the *main* thread, since the main thread is executing the code that creates the MyThread instance.

You can also set a thread's priority directly by calling the `setPriority()` method on a Thread instance as follows:

```
FooRunnable r = new FooRunnable();
Thread t = new Thread(r);
t.setPriority(8);
t.start();
```

Priorities are set using a positive integer, usually between 1 and 10, and the JVM will never change a thread's priority. However, the values 1 through 10 are not guaranteed, so if you have, say, ten threads each with a different priority, and the current application is running in a JVM that allocates a range of only five priorities, then two or more threads might be mapped to one priority. *The default priority is 5.*

The Thread class has three constants (static final variables) that define the range of thread priorities:

```
Thread.MIN_PRIORITY  (1)
Thread.NORM_PRIORITY  (5)
Thread.MAX_PRIORITY  (10)
```

So what does the static `Thread.yield()` have to do with all this? Not that much, in practice. What `yield()` is *supposed* to do is make the currently running thread head back to runnable to allow other threads of the *same* priority to get their turn. So the intention is to use `yield()` to promote graceful turn-taking among equal-priority threads. In reality, though, the `yield()` method isn't guaranteed to do what it claims, and even if `yield()` *does* cause a thread to step out of running and back to runnable, *there's no guarantee the yielding thread won't just be chosen again over all the others!* So while `yield()` might—and often does—make a running thread give up its slot to another runnable thread of the same priority, there's no guarantee.

The Join() Method

The nonstatic `join()` method of class Thread lets one thread "join onto the end" of another thread. If you have a thread B that can't do its work until another thread A has completed *its* work, then you want thread B to "join" thread A. This means that thread B will not become runnable until A has finished (and entered the dead state).

```
Thread t = new Thread();
t.start();
t.join();
```

The preceding code takes the currently running thread (if this were in the `main()` method, then that would be the main thread) and *joins* it to the end of the thread referenced by *t*. This blocks the current thread from becoming runnable until after the thread referenced by *t* is no longer alive. You can also call one of the overloaded versions of join that takes a timeout duration, so that you're saying, "wait until thread *t* is done, but if it takes longer than 5,000 milliseconds, then stop waiting and become runnable anyway." Figure 9-3 shows the effect of the `join()` method.

So far we've looked at three ways a running thread could leave the running state:

- A call to `sleep()` Guaranteed to cause the current thread to stop executing for at least the specified sleep duration (although it might be *interrupted* before its specified time).

FIGURE 9-3 The `join()` method

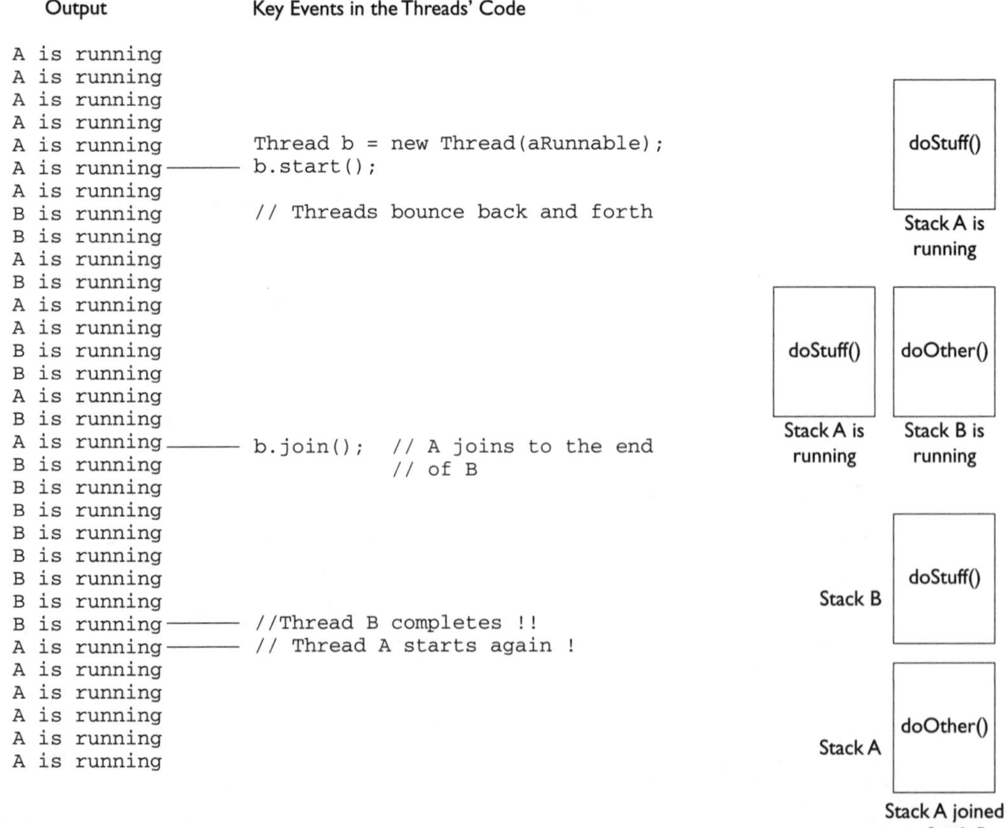

- A call to `yield()` Not guaranteed to do much of anything, although typically it will cause the currently running thread to move back to runnable so that a thread of the same priority can have a chance.
- A call to `join()` Guaranteed to cause the current thread to stop executing until the thread it joins with (in other words, the thread it calls `wait()` on) completes. If the thread it's trying to join with is not alive, however, the current thread won't need to back out.

Besides those three, we also have the following scenarios in which a thread might leave the running state:

- The thread's `run()` method completes. Duh.
- A call to `wait()` on an object (we don't call `wait()` on a *thread*, as we'll see in a moment)
- A thread can't acquire the *lock* on the object whose method code it's attempting to run.

To understand the two critical execution stoppers, you need to understand the way in which Java implements object locking to prevent multiple threads from accessing—and potentially corrupting—the same data. Since these are covered in the next two objectives (7.3 and 7.4), be sure you study these so you'll recognize when a running thread will stop (at least temporarily) running.

CERTIFICATION OBJECTIVE

Synchronizing Code (Exam Objective 7.3)

Write code using synchronized wait, notify, and notifyAll to protect against concurrent access problems and to communicate between threads.

Can you imagine the havoc that can occur when two different threads have access to a single instance of a class, and both threads invoke methods on that object…and those methods modify the state of the object? In other words, what might happen if *two* different threads call, say, a setter method on a *single* object? A scenario like that might corrupt an object's state (by changing its instance variable values in an inconsistent way), and if that object's state is data shared by other parts of the program, well, it's too scary to even visualize.

But just because we enjoy horror, let's look at an example of what might happen. The following code demonstrates what happens when two different threads are accessing the same account data. Imagine that two people each have a checkbook for a single checking account (or two people each have ATM cards, but both cards are linked to only one account).

In this example, we have a class called Account that represents a bank account. To keep the code short, this account starts with a balance of 50, and can be used only for withdrawals. The withdrawal will be accepted even if there isn't enough money in the account to cover it. The account simply reduces the balance by the amount you want to withdraw:

```
class Account {
   private int balance = 50;
   public int getBalance() {
      return balance;
   }
   public void withdraw(int amount) {
      balance = balance - amount;
   }
}
```

Now here's where it starts to get fun. Imagine a couple, Fred and Lucy, who both have access to the account and want to make withdrawals. But they don't want the account to ever be overdrawn, so just before one of them makes a withdrawal, he or she will first check the balance to be certain there's enough to cover the withdrawal. Also, withdrawals are always limited to an amount of 10, so there must be at least 10 in the account balance in order to make a withdrawal. Sounds reasonable. But that's a two-step process:

1. Check the balance.
2. If there's enough in the account (in this example, at least 10), make the withdrawal.

What happens if something separates step 1 from step 2? For example, imagine what would happen if Lucy checks the balance and sees that there's just exactly enough in the account, 10. *But before she makes the withdrawal, Fred checks the balance and also sees that there's enough for his withdrawal.* Since Lucy has verified the balance, but not yet made her withdrawal, Fred is seeing "bad data." He is seeing the account balance *before* Lucy actually debits the account, but at this point that debit is certain to occur. Now both Lucy and Fred believe there's enough to make their withdrawals. So now imagine that Lucy makes *her* withdrawal, and now there isn't enough in the account for Fred's withdrawal, but he thinks there is since when he checked, there was enough! Yikes. Here's what the actual banking code looks like, with Fred and Lucy represented by two threads, each acting on the same Runnable, and that Runnable holds a reference to the one and only account instance—so, two threads, one account.

The logic in our code example is as follows:

1. The Runnable object holds a reference to a single account.
2. Two threads are started, representing Lucy and Fred, and each thread is given a reference to the same Runnable (which holds a reference to the actual account).
3. The initial balance on the account is 50, and each withdrawal is exactly 10.
4. In the `run()` method, we loop 5 times, and in each loop we
   - Make a withdrawal (if there's enough in the account)
   - Print a statement *if the account is overdrawn* (which it should never be, since we check the balance *before* making a withdrawal)
5. The `makeWithdrawal()` method in the test class (representing the behavior of Fred or Lucy) does the following:
   - Check the balance to see if there's enough for the withdrawal.
   - If there is enough, print out the name of the one making the withdrawal.
   - Go to sleep for 500 milliseconds—just long enough to give the other partner a chance to get in before you actually *make* the withdrawal.
   - When you wake up, complete the withdrawal and print out that you've done so.
   - If there wasn't enough in the first place, print a statement showing who you are and the fact that there wasn't enough.

So what we're really trying to discover is if the following is possible: for one partner to check the account and see that there's enough, but before making the actual withdrawal, the other partner checks the account and *also* sees that there's enough. When the account balance gets to 10, if both partners check it before making the withdrawal, both will think it's OK to withdraw, and the account will overdraw by 10!

Here's the code:

```
public class AccountDanger implements Runnable {
   private Account acct = new Account();
   public static void main (String [] args) {
      AccountDanger r = new AccountDanger();
      Thread one = new Thread(r);
      Thread two = new Thread(r);
      one.setName("Fred");
      two.setName("Lucy");
      one.start();
      two.start();
    }
  public void run() {
   for (int x = 0; x < 5; x++) {
      makeWithdrawal(10);
      if (acct.getBalance() < 0) {
        System.out.println("account is overdrawn!");
      }
    }
 }
  private void makeWithdrawal(int amt) {
     if (acct.getBalance() >= amt) {
        System.out.println(Thread.currentThread().getName() +
                                   " is going
to withdraw");
        try {
            Thread.sleep(500);
        } catch(InterruptedException ex) { }
        acct.withdraw(amt);
        System.out.println(Thread.currentThread().getName() +
                                   " completes
the withdrawal");
     } else {
        System.out.println("Not enough in account for " +
Thread.currentThread().getName() + " to withdraw " +
  acct.getBalance())
     }
   }
}
```

So what happened? Is it possible that, say, Lucy checked the balance, fell asleep, Fred checked the balance, Lucy woke up and completed *her* withdrawal, then Fred completes *his* withdrawal, and in the end they overdraw the account? Look at the output:

```
% java AccountDanger
 1. Fred is going to withdraw
 2. Lucy is going to withdraw
 3. Fred completes the withdrawal
 4. Fred is going to withdraw
 5. Lucy completes the withdrawal
 6. Lucy is going to withdraw
 7. Fred completes the withdrawal
 8. Fred is going to withdraw
 9. Lucy completes the withdrawal
10. Lucy is going to withdraw
11. Fred completes the withdrawal
12. Not enough in account for Fred to withdraw 0
13. Not enough in account for Fred to withdraw 0
14. Lucy completes the withdrawal
15. account is overdrawn!
16. Not enough in account for Lucy to withdraw -10
17. account is overdrawn!
18. Not enough in account for Lucy to withdraw -10
19. account is overdrawn!
```

Although each time you run this code the output might be a little different, let's walk through this particular example using the numbered lines of output. For the first four attempts, everything is fine. Fred checks the balance on line 1, and finds it's OK. At line 2, Lucy checks the balance and finds it OK. At line 3, Fred makes his withdrawal. At this point, the balance Lucy checked for (and believes is still accurate) has actually changed since she last checked. And now Fred checks the balance *again*, before Lucy even completes her first withdrawal. By this point, even Fred is seeing a potentially inaccurate balance, because we know Lucy is going to complete her withdrawal. It is possible, of course, that Fred will complete his before Lucy does, but that's not what happens here.

On line 5, Lucy completes her withdrawal and then before Fred completes his, Lucy does another check on the account on line 6. And so it continues until we get to line 8, where Fred checks the balance and sees that it's 20. On line 9, Lucy completes a withdrawal (that she had checked for earlier), and this takes the balance to 10. On line 10, Lucy checks again, sees that the balance is 10, so she knows she can do a withdrawal. *But she didn't know that Fred, too, has already checked the balance on line 8 so he thinks its safe to do the withdrawal!* On line 11, Fred completes the withdrawal he approved on line 8. This takes the balance to zero. But Lucy still has a pending withdrawal that she got approval for on line 10! You know what's coming.

On lines 12 and 13, Fred checks the balance and finds that there's not enough in the account. But on line 14, Lucy completes her withdrawal and BOOM! The account is now overdrawn by 10—*something we thought we were preventing by doing a balance check prior to a withdrawal.*

Figure 9-4 shows the timeline of what can happen when two threads concurrently access the same object.

Preventing the Account Overdraw So what can be done? The solution is actually quite simple.

We must guarantee that the two steps of the withdrawal—*checking* the balance and *making* the withdrawal—are never split apart. We need them to always be performed as one operation, even when the thread falls asleep in between step 1 and step 2! We call this an "atomic operation" (although the physics there is a little outdated) because the operation, regardless of the number of actual statements (or underlying byte code instructions), is completed *before* any other thread code that acts on the same data.

You can't guarantee that a single thread will stay running throughout the entire atomic operation. But you *can* guarantee that even if the thread running the atomic operation moves in and out of the running state, *no other running thread will be able to act on the same data.* In other words, If Lucy falls asleep after checking the balance, we can stop Fred from checking the balance until *after* Lucy wakes up and completes her withdrawal.

FIGURE 9-4

Problems with concurrent access

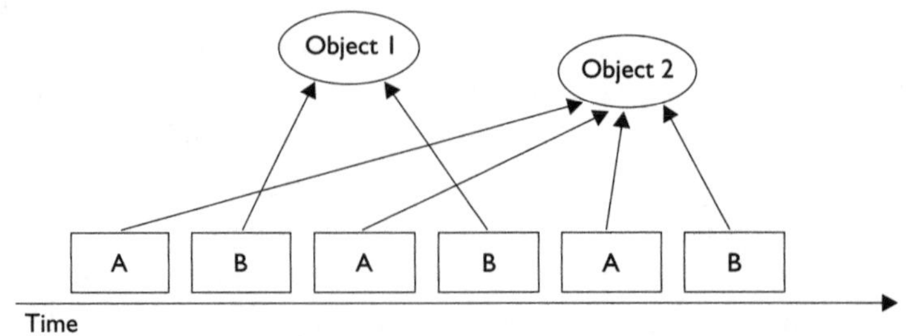

So how do you protect the data? You must do two things:

- Mark the variables `private`
- Synchronize the code that modifies the variables

Remember, you protect the variables in the normal way—using an access control modifier. It's the method code that you must protect, so that only one thread at a time can be executing that code. You do this with the `synchronized` keyword.

We can solve all of Fred and Lucy's problems by adding one word to the code. We mark the `makeWithdrawal()` method `synchronized` as follows:

```
private synchronized void makeWithdrawal(int amt) {
     if (acct.getBalance() >= amt) {
     System.out.println(Thread.currentThread().getName() +
                        " is going to withdraw");
      try {
        Thread.sleep(500);
      } catch(InterruptedException ex) { }
      acct.withdraw(amt);
      System.out.println(Thread.currentThread().getName() +
                        " completes the withdrawal");

     }
    else {
      System.out.println("Not enough in account for " +
Thread.currentThread().getName() + " to withdraw " +
acct.getBalance());
   }
}
```

Now we've guaranteed that once a thread (Lucy or Fred) starts the withdrawal process (by invoking `makeWithdrawal()`), the other thread cannot enter that method until the first one completes the process by exiting the method. The new output shows the benefit of synchronizing the `makeWithdrawal()` method:

```
% java AccountDanger
Fred is going to withdraw
Fred completes the withdrawal
Lucy is going to withdraw
Lucy completes the withdrawal
Fred is going to withdraw
Fred completes the withdrawal
```

```
Lucy is going to withdraw
Lucy completes the withdrawal
Fred is going to withdraw
Fred completes the withdrawal
Not enough in account for Lucy to withdraw 0
Not enough in account for Fred to withdraw 0
Not enough in account for Lucy to withdraw 0
Not enough in account for Fred to withdraw 0
Not enough in account for Lucy to withdraw 0
```

Notice that now the threads, Lucy and Fred, always check the account balance *and* complete the withdrawal before the other thread can check the balance.

Synchronization and Locks

How does synchronization work? With locks. Every object in Java has a built-in lock that only comes into play when the object has synchronized method code. Since there is only one lock per object, if one thread has picked up the lock, no other thread can enter the synchronized code (which means *any* synchronized method of that object) until the lock has been released. Typically, releasing a lock means the thread holding the lock (in other words, the thread currently in the synchronized method) exits the synchronized method. At that point, the lock is free until some other thread enters a synchronized method on that object.

You need to remember the following key points about locking and synchronization:

- Only *methods* can be synchronized, not variables.
- Each object has just *one* lock.
- *Not all methods in a class must be synchronized.* A class can have both synchronized and nonsynchronized methods.
- If two methods are synchronized in a class, only one thread can be accessing one of the two methods. In other words, once a thread acquires the lock on an object, no other thread can enter *any* of the synchronized methods in that class (for that object).
- If a class has both synchronized and nonsynchronized methods, *multiple threads can still access the nonsynchronized methods* of the class! If you have methods that don't access the data you're trying to protect, then you don't

need to mark them as synchronized. Synchronization is a performance hit, so you don't want to use it without a good reason.

- *If a thread goes to sleep, it takes its locks with it.*
- *A thread can acquire more than one lock.* For example, a thread can enter a synchronized method, thus acquiring a lock, and then immediately invoke a synchronized method on a different object, thus acquiring *that* lock as well. As the stack unwinds, locks are released again. Also, if a thread acquires a lock and then attempts to call a synchronized method on that same object, no problem. The JVM *knows* that this thread already has the lock for this object, so the thread is free to call other synchronized methods on the same object, using the lock the thread already has.
- *You can synchronize a block of code rather than a method.* Because synchronization does hurt concurrency, you don't want to synchronize any more code than is necessary to protect your data. So if the scope of a method is more than needed, you can reduce the scope of the synchronized part to something less than a full method—to just a block. We call this, strangely, a "synchronized block," and it looks like this:

```
class SyncTest {
public void doStuff() {
    System.out.println("not synchronized");
    synchronized(this) {
       System.out.println("synchronized");
    }
  }
}
```

When a thread is executing code from within a synchronized block, including any method code invoked from that synchronized block, the code is said to be *executing in a synchronized context.* The real question is, *synchronized on what?* Or, *synchronized on which object's lock?*

When you synchronize a method, the object used to invoke the method is the object whose lock must be acquired. But when you synchronize a block of code, you specify which object's lock you want to use as the lock, so you could, for example, use some third-party object as the lock for this piece of code. That gives you the ability to have more than one lock for code synchronization within a single object.

So What About Static Methods? Can They Be Synchronized? Static methods can be synchronized. There is only one copy of the static data you're trying to protect, so you only need one lock per class to synchronize static methods—a lock for the whole class. There is such a lock; every class loaded in Java has a corresponding instance of java.lang.Class representing that class. It's that java.lang.Class instance whose lock is used to protect the static methods of the class (if they're synchronized).

There's nothing special you have to do to synchronize a static method:

```
public static synchronized void getCount() { }
```

EXERCISE 9-2

Synchronizing a Block of Code

In this exercise we will attempt to synchronize a block of code. Within that block of code we will get the lock on an object so that other threads cannot modify it while the block of code is executing. We will be creating three threads that will all attempt to manipulate the same object. Each thread will output a single letter 100 times, and then increment that letter by one. The object we will be using is StringBuffer. We could synchronize on a String object, but strings cannot be modified once they are created so we would not be able to increment the letter without generating a new String object. The final output should have 100 As, 100 Bs, and 100 Cs all in unbroken lines.

1. Create a class and extend the Thread class.
2. Override the `run()` method of Thread. This is where the synchronized block of code will go.
3. For our three threaded objects to share the same object, we will need to create a constructor that accepts a StringBuffer object in the argument.
4. The synchronized block of code will obtain a lock on the StringBuffer object from step 3.
5. Within the block, output the StringBuffer 100 times and then increment the letter in the StringBuffer. You can check Chapter 11 for StringBuffer methods that will help with this.
6. Finally, in the `main()` method, create a single StringBuffer object using the letter *A*, then create three instances of our class and start all three of them.

What Happens if a Thread Can't Get the Lock? If a thread tries to enter a synchronized method and the lock is already taken, the thread is said to be *blocked on an object's lock*. Essentially, the thread goes into a kind of pool *for that particular object* and has to sit there until the lock is released and the thread can again become runnable/running. Just because a lock is released doesn't mean any particular thread will get it, however. There might be three threads waiting for a single lock, for example, and there's no guarantee that the thread that has waited the longest will get the lock first.

Table 9-1 lists the thread-related methods and whether the thread gives up its locks as a result of the call.

Thread Deadlock

Perhaps the scariest thing that can happen to a Java program is deadlock. Deadlock occurs when two threads are blocked, with each waiting for the other's lock. Neither can run until it gives up the lock, so they'll sit there forever and ever and ever… This can happen, for example, when thread A hits synchronized code, acquires a lock B, and then enters *another* method (still within the synchronized code it has the lock on) that's also synchronized. But thread A can't get the lock to enter this synchronized code—lock C—because another thread D has the lock already. So thread A goes off to the "waiting for the C lock" pool, hoping that thread D will hurry up and release the lock (by completing the synchronized method). But thread A will wait a very long time indeed, because while thread D picked up lock C, it then entered a method synchronized on lock B. Obviously, thread D can't get the lock B because thread A has it. And thread A won't release it until thread D releases lock C.

TABLE 9-1 Methods and Lock Status

Give Up Locks	Keep Locks	Class Defining the Method
`wait()`	`notify()` (Although the thread will probably exit the synchronized code shortly after this call, and thus give up its locks)	java.lang.Object
	`join()`	java.lang.Thread
	`sleep()`	java.lang.Thread
	`yield()`	java.lang.Thread

But thread D won't release lock C until after it can get lock B and continue. And there they sit. The following example demonstrates deadlock:

```
1.  public class DeadlockRisk {
2.     private static class Resource {
3.        public int value;
4.     }
5.     private Resource resourceA = new Resource();
6.     private Resource resourceB = new Resource();
7.     public int read() {
8.        synchronized(resourceA) { // May deadlock here
9.           synchronized(resourceB) {
10.             return resourceB.value + resourceA.value;
11.          }
12.       }
13.    }
14.
15.    public void write(int a, int b) {
16.       synchronized(resourceB) { // May deadlock here
17.          synchronized(resourceA) {
18.             resourceA.value = a;
19.             resourceB.value = b;
20.          }
21.       }
22.    }
23. }
```

Assume that `read()` is started by one thread and `write()` is started by another. If there are two different threads that may read and write independently, there is a risk of deadlock at line 8 or 16. The reader thread will have resourceA, the writer thread will have resourceB, and both will get stuck forever waiting for the other to back down.

Code like this almost never results in deadlock because the CPU has to switch from the reader thread to the writer thread at a particular point in the code, and the chances of deadlock occurring are very small. The application may work fine 99.9 percent of the time.

The preceding simple example is easy to fix; just swap the order of locking for either the reader or the writer at lines 16 and 17 (or lines 8 and 9). More complex deadlock situations can take a long time to figure out.

Regardless of how little chance there is for your code to deadlock, the bottom line is: *if you deadlock, you're dead.* There are design approaches that can help avoid deadlock, including strategies for always acquiring locks in a predetermined order. But that's for you to study and is beyond the scope of this book. We're just trying to get you through the exam. If you learn everything in this chapter, though, you'll still know more about threads then most Java programmers.

CERTIFICATION OBJECTIVE

Thread Interaction (Exam Objective 7.4)

Define the interaction among threads and object locks when executing synchronized wait, notify, and notifyAll.

The last thing we need to look at is how threads can interact with one another to communicate about—among other things—their locking status. The java.lang.Object class has three methods—`wait()`, `notify()`, and notifyAll()—that help threads communicate about the status of an event that the threads care about. For example, if one thread is a mail-delivery thread and one thread is a mail-processor thread, the mail-processor thread has to keep checking to see if there's any mail to process. Using the wait and notify mechanism, the mail-processor thread could check for mail, and if it doesn't find any it can say, "Hey, I'm not going to waste my time checking for mail every two seconds. I'm going to go hang out over here, and when the mail deliverer puts something in the mailbox, have him notify me so I can go back to runnable and do some work." In other words, wait and notify lets one thread put itself into a "waiting room" until some *other* thread notifies it that there's a reason to come back out.

One key point to remember (and keep in mind for the exam) about wait/notify is this:

> `wait()`, `notify()`, *and* `notifyAll()` *must be called from within a synchronized context! A thread can't invoke a wait or notify method on an object unless it owns that object's lock.*

Here we'll present an example of two threads that depend on each other to proceed with their execution, and we'll show how to use `wait()` and `notify()` to make them interact safely and at the proper moment.

Think of a computer-controlled machine that cuts pieces of fabric into different shapes and an application that allows users to specify the shape to cut. The current version of the application has only one thread, which first asks the user for instructions and then directs the hardware to cut that shape, repeating the cycle afterward.

```
public void run(){
   while(true){
      // Get shape from user
      // Calculate machine steps from shape
      // Send steps to hardware
   }
}
```

This design is not optimal because the user can't do anything while the machine is busy and while there are other shapes to define. We need to improve the situation.

A simple solution is to separate the processes into two different threads, one of them interacting with the user and another managing the hardware. The user thread sends the instructions to the hardware thread and then goes back to interacting with the user immediately. The hardware thread receives the instructions from the user thread and starts directing the machine immediately. Both threads use a common object to communicate, which holds the current design being processed.

The following pseudocode shows this design:

```
public void userLoop(){
   while(true){
      // Get shape from user
      // Calculate machine steps from shape
      // Modify common object with new machine steps
   }
}

public void hardwareLoop(){
   while(true){
      // Get steps from common object
      // Send steps to hardware
   }
}
```

The problem now is to get the hardware thread to process the machine steps as soon as they are available. Also, the user thread should not modify them until they have all been sent to the hardware. The solution is to use `wait()` and `notify()`, and also to synchronize some of the code.

The methods `wait()` and `notify()`, remember, are instance methods of Object. In the same way that every object has a lock, every object can have a list of threads that are waiting for a signal (a notification) from the object. A thread gets on this waiting list by executing the `wait()` method of the target object. From that moment, it doesn't execute any further instructions until the `notify()` method of the target object is called. If many threads are waiting on the same object, only one will be chosen (in no guaranteed order) to proceed with its execution. If there are no threads waiting, then no particular action is taken. Let's take a look at some real code that shows one object waiting for another object to notify it (take note, it is somewhat complex):

```
 1.  class ThreadA {
 2.     public static void main(String [] args) {
 3.        ThreadB b = new ThreadB();
 4.        b.start();
 5.
 6.        synchronized(b) {
 7.           try {
 8.              System.out.println("Waiting for b to complete...");
 9.              b.wait();
10.           } catch (InterruptedException e) {}
11.        }
12.        System.out.println("Total is: " + b.total);
13.     }
14.  }
15.
16.  class ThreadB extends Thread {
17.     int total;
18.
19.     public void run() {
20.        synchronized(this) {
21.           for(int i=0;i<100;i++) {
22.              total += i;
23.           }
24.           notify();
25.        }
26.     }
27.  }
```

This program contains two objects with threads: ThreadA contains the main thread and ThreadB has a thread that calculates the sum of all numbers from 0 through 99. As soon as line 4 calls the `start()` method, ThreadA will continue with the next line of code in its own class, which means it could get to line 12 before ThreadB has finished the calculation. To prevent this, we use the `wait()` method in line 9.

Notice in line 6 the code synchronizes itself with the object *b*—this is because in order to call `wait()` on the object, ThreadA must own a lock on *b*. For a thread to call `wait()` or `notify()`, the thread has to be the owner of the lock for that object. When the thread waits, it temporarily releases the lock for other threads to use, but it will need it again to continue execution. It is common to find code such as the following:

```
synchronized(anotherObject) { // this has the lock on anotherObject
   try {
      anotherObject.wait();
      // the thread releases the lock and waits
      // To continue, the thread needs the lock,
      // so it may be blocked until it gets it.
   } catch(InterruptedException e){}
}
```

The preceding code waits until `notify()` is called on *anotherObject.*

```
synchronized(this) {
   notify();
}
```

This code notifies any thread currently waiting on the *this* object.

The lock can be acquired much earlier in the code, such as in the calling method. Note that if the thread calling `wait()` does not own the lock, it will throw an `IllegalMonitorStateException`. This exception is not a checked exception, so you don't have to *catch* it explicitly. You should always be clear whether a thread has the lock of an object in any given block of code.

Notice in lines 7–10 there is a `try/catch` block around the `wait()` method. A waiting thread can be interrupted in the same way as a sleeping thread, so you have to take care of the exception:

```
try{
   wait();
} catch(InterruptedException e) {
   // Do something about it
}
```

In the fabric example, the way to use these methods is to have the hardware thread wait on the shape to be available and the user thread to notify after it has written the steps.

The machine steps may comprise global steps, such as moving the required fabric to the cutting area, and a number of substeps, such as the direction and length of a cut. As an example they could be

```
int fabricRoll;
int cuttingSpeed;
Point startingPoint;
float[] directions;
float[] lengths;
etc..
```

It is important that the user thread does not modify the machine steps while the hardware thread is using them, so this reading and writing should be synchronized.

The resulting code would look like this:

```
class Operator extends Thread {
   public void run(){
      while(true){
         // Get shape from user
         synchronized(this){
            // Calculate new machine steps from shape
            notify();
         }
      }
   }
}
class Machine extends Thread {
   Operator operator; // assume this gets initialized
   public void run(){
      while(true){
         synchronized(operator){
            try {
               operator.wait();
            } catch(InterruptedException ie) {}
            // Send machine steps to hardware
         }
      }
   }
}
```

The machine thread, once started, will immediately go into the waiting state and will wait patiently until the operator sends the first notification. At that point it is the operator thread that owns the lock for the object, so the hardware thread gets stuck for a while. It's only after the operator thread abandons the synchronized block that the hardware thread can really start processing the machine steps.

While one shape is being processed by the hardware, the user may interact with the system and specify another shape to be cut. When the user is finished with the shape and it is time to cut it, the operator thread attempts to enter the synchronized block, maybe blocking until the machine thread has finished with the previous machine steps. When the machine thread has finished, it repeats the loop, going again to the waiting state (and therefore releasing the lock). Only then can the operator thread enter the synchronized block and overwrite the machine steps with the new ones.

Having two threads is definitely an improvement over having one, although in this implementation there is still a possibility of making the user wait. A further improvement would be to have many shapes in a queue, thereby reducing the possibility of requiring the user to wait for the hardware.

There is also a second form of `wait()` that accepts a number of milliseconds as a maximum time to wait. If the thread is not interrupted, it will continue normally whenever it is notified or the specified timeout has elapsed. This normal continuation consists of getting out of the waiting state, but to continue execution it will have to get the lock for the object:

```
synchronized(a){ // The thread gets the lock on a
   a.wait(2000); // The thread releases the lock and waits for notify
   // But only for a maximum of two seconds, then goes back to Runnable
   // The thread reacquires the lock
   // More instructions here
}
```

When the `wait()` method is invoked on an object, the thread executing that code gives up its lock on the object immediately. However, when `notify()` is called, that doesn't mean the thread gives up its lock at that moment. If the thread is still completing synchronized code, the lock is not released until the thread moves out of synchronized code. So just because `notify()` is called doesn't mean the lock becomes available at that moment.

Using notifyAll() When Many Threads May Be Waiting

In most scenarios, it's preferable to notify *all* of the threads that are waiting on a particular object. If so, you can use `notifyAll()` on the object to let all the threads rush out of the waiting area and back to runnable. This is especially important if you have threads waiting on one object, but for different reasons, and you want to be sure that the *right* thread gets notified.

```
notifyAll(); // Will notify all waiting threads
```

All of the threads will be notified and start competing to get the lock. As the lock is used and released by each thread, all of them will get into action without a need for further notification.

As we said earlier, an object can have many threads waiting on it, and using `notify()` will affect only one of them. Which one exactly is not specified and depends on the JVM implementation, so you should never rely on a particular thread being notified in preference to another.

In cases in which there might be a lot more waiting, the best way to do this is by using `notifyAll()`. Let's take a look at this in some code. In this example, there is one class that performs a calculation and many readers that are waiting to receive the completed calculation. At any given moment many readers may be waiting.

```
class Reader extends Thread {
   Calculator c;

   public Reader(Calculator calc) {
      c = calc;
   }

   public void run() {
      synchronized(c) {
         try {
            System.out.println("Waiting for calculation...");
            c.wait();
         } catch (InterruptedException e) {}
      }
      System.out.println("Total is: " + c.total);
   }

   public static void main(String [] args) {
      Calculator calculator = new Calculator();
      new Reader(calculator).start();
      new Reader(calculator).start();
      new Reader(calculator).start();
      calculator.start();
   }
}
```

```
27. class Calculator extends Thread {
28.    int total;
29.
30.    public void run() {
31.       synchronized(this) {
32.          for(int i=0;i<100;i++) {
33.             total += i;
34.          }
35.          notifyAll();
36.       }
37.    }
38. }
```

This program starts the calculator with its calculation, and then starts three threads that are all waiting to receive the finished calculation (lines 18–24). Note that if the `run()` method at line 30 used `notify()` instead of `notifyAll()`, there would be a chance that only one reader would be notified instead of all the readers.

exam Watch

The methods `wait()`, `notify()`, and `notifyAll()` are methods of only java.lang.Object, not of java.lang.Thread or java.lang.Runnable. Be sure you know which methods are defined in Thread, which in Object, and which in Runnable (just `run()`, so that's an easy one). Of the key methods in Thread, be sure you know which are static—`sleep()` and `yield()`, and which are* not *static—`join()` and `start()`. Table 9-2 lists the key methods you'll need to know for the exam, with the static methods shown in italics.

TABLE 9-2 Key Thread Methods

Class Object	Class Thread	Interface Runnable
wait()	start()	run()
notify()	*yield()*	
notifyAll()	*sleep()*	
	join()	

CERTIFICATION SUMMARY

This chapter covered the required thread knowledge you'll need to apply on the certification exam. Threads can be created by either extending the Thread class or implementing the Runnable interface. The only method that must be overridden in the Runnable interface is the `run()` method, but the thread doesn't become a *thread of execution* until somebody calls the Thread object's `start()` method. We also looked at how the `sleep()` method can be used to pause a thread, and we saw that when an object goes to sleep, it holds onto any locks it acquired prior to sleeping.

We looked at five thread states: new, runnable, running, blocked/waiting/sleeping, and dead. You learned that when a thread is dead, it can never be restarted even if it's still a valid object on the heap. We saw that there is only one way a thread can transition to running, and that's from runnable. However, once running, a thread can become dead, go to sleep, wait for another thread to finish, block on an object's lock, wait for a notification, or return to runnable.

You saw how two threads acting on the same data can cause serious problems (remember Lucy and Fred's bank account?). We saw that to let one thread execute a method but prevent other threads from running the same object's method, we use the `synchronized` keyword. To coordinate activity between different threads, use the `wait()`, `notify()`, and `notifyAll()` methods.

TWO-MINUTE DRILL

Here are some of the key points from each certification objective in Chapter 9. Photocopy it and sleep with it under your pillow for complete absorption.

Creating, Instantiating, and Starting New Threads

- ❑ Threads can be created by extending Thread and overriding the `public void run()` method.
- ❑ Thread objects can also be created by calling the Thread constructor that takes a Runnable argument. The Runnable object is said to be the *target* of the thread.
- ❑ You can call `start()` on a Thread object only once. If `start()` is called more than once on a Thread object, it will throw a RuntimeException.
- ❑ It is legal to create many Thread objects using the same Runnable object as the target.
- ❑ When a Thread object is created, it does not become a *thread of execution* until its `start()` method is invoked. When a Thread object exists but hasn't been started, it is in the *new* state and is not considered *alive*.

Transitioning Between Thread States

- ❑ Once a new thread is started, it will always enter the runnable state.
- ❑ The thread scheduler can move a thread back and forth between the runnable state and the running state.
- ❑ Only one thread can be running at a time, although many threads may be in the runnable state.
- ❑ There is no guarantee that the order in which threads were started determines the order in which they'll run.
- ❑ There's no guarantee that threads will take turns in any fair way. It's up to the thread scheduler, as determined by the particular virtual machine implementation. If you want a guarantee that your threads will take turns regardless of the underlying JVM, you should can use the `sleep()` method. This prevents one thread from hogging the running process while another thread starves.

- ❑ A running thread may enter a blocked/waiting state by a `wait()`, `sleep()`, or `join()` call.
- ❑ A running thread may enter a blocked/waiting state because it can't acquire the lock for a synchronized block of code.
- ❑ When the sleep or wait is over, or an object's lock becomes available, the thread can only reenter the runnable state. It will *go* directly from waiting to running (well, for all practical purposes anyway).
- ❑ A dead thread cannot be started again.

Sleep, Yield, and Join

- ❑ Sleeping is used to delay execution for a period of time, and no locks are released when a thread goes to sleep.
- ❑ A sleeping thread is guaranteed to sleep for at least the time specified in the argument to the sleep method (unless it's interrupted), but there is no guarantee as to when the newly awakened thread will actually return to running.
- ❑ The `sleep()` method is a static method that sleeps the currently executing thread. One thread *cannot* tell another thread to sleep.
- ❑ The `setPriority()` method is used on Thread objects to give threads a priority of between 1 (low) and 10 (high), although priorities are not guaranteed, and not all JVMs use a priority range of 1-10.
- ❑ If not explicitly set, a thread's priority will be the same priority as the thread that created this thread (in other words, the thread executing the code that creates the new thread).
- ❑ The `yield()` method *may* cause a running thread to back out if there are runnable threads of the same priority. There is no guarantee that this will happen, and there is no guarantee that when the thread backs out it will be *different* thread selected to run. A thread might yield and then immediately reenter the running state.
- ❑ The closest thing to a guarantee is that at any given time, when a thread is running it will usually not have a lower priority than any thread in the runnable state. If a low-priority thread is running when a high-priority thread enters runnable, the JVM will preempt the running low-priority thread and put the high-priority thread in.

- When one thread calls the `join()` method of another thread, the currently running thread will wait until the thread it joins with has completed. Think of the `join()` method as saying, "Hey thread, I want to join on to the end of you. Let me know when you're done, so I can enter the runnable state."

Concurrent Access Problems and Synchronized Threads

- Synchronized methods prevent more than one thread from accessing an object's critical method code.
- You can use the `synchronized` keyword as a method modifier, or to start a synchronized block of code.
- To synchronize a block of code (in other words, a scope smaller than the whole method), you must specify an argument that is the object whose lock you want to synchronize on.
- While only one thread can be accessing synchronized code of a particular instance, multiple threads can still access the same object's *un*synchronized code.
- When an object goes to sleep, it takes its locks with it.
- Static methods can be synchronized, using the lock from the java.lang.Class instance representing that class.

Communicating with Objects by Waiting and Notifying

- The `wait()` method lets a thread say, "there's nothing for me to do here, so put me in your waiting pool and notify me when something happens that I care about." Basically, a `wait()` call means "wait me in your pool," or "add me to your waiting list."
- The `notify()` method is used to send a signal to one and only one of the threads that are waiting in that same object's waiting pool.
- The method `notifyAll()` works in the same way as `notify()`, only it sends the signal to *all* of the threads waiting on the object.
- All three methods—`wait()/notify()/notifyAll()`—must be called from within a synchronized context! A thread invokes `wait()/notify()` on a particular object, and the thread must currently hold the lock on that object.

Deadlocked Threads

- ❑ Deadlocking is when thread execution grinds to a halt because the code is waiting for locks to be removed from objects.
- ❑ Deadlocking can occur when a locked object attempts to access another locked object that is trying to access the first locked object. In other words, both threads are waiting for each other's locks to be released; therefore, the locks will *never* be released!
- ❑ Deadlocking is bad. Don't do it.

SELF TEST

The following questions will help you measure your understanding of the material presented in this chapter. Read all of the choices carefully, as there may be more than one correct answer. Choose all correct answers for each question. Stay focused.

If you have a rough time with these at first, don't beat yourself up. Be positive. Repeat nice affirmations to yourself like, "I am smart enough to understand threads." "I can do this." and "OK, so that other guy knows threads better than I do, but I bet he can't <insert something you *are* good at> like me."

1. Given the following,

```
 1.  class MyThread extends Thread {
 2.
 3.     public static void main(String [] args) {
 4.        MyThread t = new MyThread();
 5.        t.run();
 6.     }
 7.
 8.     public void run() {
 9.        for(int i=1;i<3;++i) {
10.           System.out.print(i + "..");
11.        }
12.     }
13.  }
```

what is the result?

A. This code will not compile due to line 4.

B. This code will not compile due to line 5.

C. 1..2..

D. 1..2..3..

E. An exception is thrown at runtime.

2. Which two of the following methods are defined in class Thread?

A. `start()`

B. `wait()`

C. `notify()`

D. `run()`

E. `terminate()`

3. The following block of code creates a Thread using a Runnable target:

```
Runnable target = new MyRunnable();
Thread myThread = new Thread(target);
```

Which of the following classes can be used to create the target, so that the preceding code compiles correctly?

A. `public class MyRunnable extends Runnable{public void run(){}}`

B. `public class MyRunnable extends Object{public void run(){}}`

C. `public class MyRunnable implements Runnable{public void run(){}}`

D. `public class MyRunnable implements Runnable{void run(){}}`

E. `public class MyRunnable implements Runnable{public void start(){}}`

4. Given the following,

```
class MyThread extends Thread {

   public static void main(String [] args) {
      MyThread t = new MyThread();
      t.start();
      System.out.print("one. ");
      t.start();
      System.out.print("two. ");
   }

   public void run() {
      System.out.print("Thread ");
   }
}
```

what is the result of this code?

A. Compilation fails

B. An exception occurs at runtime.

C. `Thread one. Thread two.`

D. The output cannot be determined.

5. Given the following,

```
public class MyRunnable implements Runnable {
   public void run() {
      // some code here
   }
}
```

which of these will create and start this thread?

A. `new Runnable(MyRunnable).start();`

B. `new Thread(MyRunnable).run();`

C. `new Thread(new MyRunnable()).start();`

D. `new MyRunnable().start();`

6. Given the following,

```
class MyThread extends Thread {

   public static void main(String [] args) {
      MyThread t = new MyThread();
      Thread x = new Thread(t);
      x.start();
   }

   public void run() {
      for(int i=0;i<3;++i) {
         System.out.print(i + "..");
      }
   }
}
```

what is the result of this code?

A. Compilation fails.

B. 1..2..3..

C. 0..1..2..3..

D. 0..1..2..

E. An exception occurs at runtime.

7. Given the following,

```
class Test {

   public static void main(String [] args) {
      printAll(args);
   }

   public static void printAll(String[] lines) {
      for(int i=0;i<lines.length;i++){
         System.out.println(lines[i]);
         Thread.currentThread().sleep(1000);
```

```
            }
        }
    }
```

the static method `Thread.currentThread()` returns a reference to the currently executing Thread object. What is the result of this code?

A. Each String in the array *lines* will output, with a 1-second pause.

B. Each String in the array *lines* will output, with no pause in between because this method is not executed in a Thread.

C. Each String in the array *lines* will output, and there is no guarantee there will be a pause because `currentThread()` may not retrieve this thread.

D. This code will not compile.

8. Assume you have a class that holds two `private` variables: *a* and *b*. Which of the following pairs can prevent concurrent access problems in that class? (Choose all that apply.)

A.
```
public int read(int a, int b){return a+b;}
public void set(int a, int b){this.a=a;this.b=b;}
```

B.
```
public synchronized int read(int a, int b){return a+b;}
public synchronized void set(int a, int b){this.a=a;this.b=b;}
```

C.
```
public int read(int a, int b){synchronized(a){return a+b;}}
public void set(int a, int b){synchronized(a){this.a=a;this.b=b;}}
```

D.
```
public int read(int a, int b){synchronized(a){return a+b;}}
public void set(int a, int b){synchronized(b){this.a=a;this.b=b;}}
```

E.
```
public synchronized(this) int read(int a, int b){return a+b;}
public synchronized(this) void set(int a, int b){this.a=a;this.b=b;}
```

F.
```
public int read(int a, int b){synchronized(this){return a+b;}}
public void set(int a, int b){synchronized(this){this.a=a;this.b=b;}}
```

9. Which class or interface defines the `wait()`, `notify()`, and `notifyAll()` methods?

A. Object

B. Thread

C. Runnable

D. Class

10. Which two are *true*?

A. A static method cannot be synchronized.

B. If a class has synchronized code, multiple threads can still access the nonsynchronized code.

C. Variables can be protected from concurrent access problems by marking them with the `synchronized` keyword.

D. When a thread sleeps, it releases its locks.

E. When a thread invokes `wait()`, it releases its locks.

11. Which three are methods of the Object class? (Choose three.)

A. `notify();`

B. `notifyAll();`

C. `isInterrupted();`

D. `synchronized();`

E. `interrupt();`

F. `wait(long msecs);`

G. `sleep(long msecs);`

H. `yield();`

12. Given the following,

```
 1.  public class WaitTest {
 2.     public static void main(String [] args) {
 3.        System.out.print("1 ");
 4.        synchronized(args){
 5.           System.out.print("2 ");
 6.           try {
 7.              args.wait();
 8.           }
 9.           catch(InterruptedException e){}
10.        }
11.        System.out.print("3 ");
12.     }
13.  }
```

what is the result of trying to compile and run this program?

A. It fails to compile because the IllegalMonitorStateException of `wait()` is not dealt with in line 7.

B. 1 2 3

C. 1 3

D. 1 2

E. At runtime, it throws an IllegalMonitorStateException when trying to wait.

F. It will fail to compile because it has to be synchronized on the *this* object.

13. Assume the following method is properly synchronized and called from a thread A on an object B:

```
wait(2000);
```

After calling this method, when will the thread A become a candidate to get another turn at the CPU?

A. After thread A is notified, or after two seconds.

B. After the lock on B is released, or after two seconds.

C. Two seconds after thread A is notified.

D. Two seconds after lock B is released.

14. Which two are *true*?

A. The `notifyAll()` method must be called from a synchronized context.

B. To call `wait()`, an object must own the lock on the thread.

C. The `notify()` method is defined in class java.lang.Thread.

D. When a thread is waiting as a result of `wait()`, it release its locks.

E. The `notify()` method causes a thread to immediately release its locks.

F. The difference between `notify()` and `notifyAll()` is that `notifyAll()` notifies all waiting threads, regardless of the object they're waiting on.

15. Assume you create a program and one of your threads (called backgroundThread) does some lengthy numerical processing. What would be the proper way of setting its priority to try to get the rest of the system to be very responsive while the thread is running? (Choose all that apply.)

A. `backgroundThread.setPriority(Thread.LOW_PRIORITY);`

B. `backgroundThread.setPriority(Thread.MAX_PRIORITY);`

C. `backgroundThread.setPriority(1);`

D. `backgroundThread.setPriority(Thread.NO_PRIORITY);`

E. `backgroundThread.setPriority(Thread.MIN_PRIORITY);`

F. `backgroundThread.setPriority(Thread.NORM_PRIORITY);`

G. `backgroundThread.setPriority(10);`

16. Which three guarantee that a thread will leave the running state?

A. `yield()`

B. `wait()`

C. `notify()`

D. `notifyAll()`

E. `sleep(1000)`

F. `aLiveThread.join()`

G. `Thread.killThread()`

17. Which two are true?

A. Deadlock will not occur if `wait()/notify()` is used.

B. A thread will resume execution as soon as its sleep duration expires.

C. Synchronization can prevent two objects from being accessed by the same thread.

D. The `wait()` method is overloaded to accept a duration.

E. The `notify()` method is overloaded to accept a duration.

F. Both `wait()` and `notify()` must be called from a synchronized context.

G. `wait()` doesn't throw a checked exception.

H. `sleep()` can throw a runtime exception.

18. Which two are valid constructors for Thread?

A. `Thread(Runnable r, String name)`

B. `Thread()`

C. `Thread(int priority)`

D. `Thread(Runnable r, ThreadGroup g)`

E. `Thread(Runnable r, int priority)`

19. Given the following,

```
class MyThread extends Thread {
   MyThread() {
     System.out.print(" MyThread");
   }
   public void run() {
     System.out.print(" bar");
   }
   public void run(String s) {
      System.out.println(" baz");
  }
}
public class TestThreads {
  public static void main (String [] args) {
  Thread t = new MyThread() {
    public void run() {
```

```
          System.out.println(" foo");
        }
      };
      t.start();
    }
  }
```

what is the result?

A. `foo`

B. `MyThread foo`

C. `MyThread bar`

D. `foo bar`

E. `foo bar baz`

F. `bar foo`

G. Compilation fails.

20. Given the following,

```
public class SyncTest {
   public static void main (String [] args) {
     Thread t = new Thread() {
       Foo f = new Foo();
       public void run() {
         f.increase(20);
       }
     };
     t.start();
   }
}
class Foo {
  private int data = 23;
   public void increase(int amt) {
       int x = data;
       data = x + amt;
    }
}
```

and assuming that data must be protected from corruption, what—if anything—can you *add* to the preceding code to ensure the integrity of data?

A. Synchronize the run method.

B. Wrap a synchronize(*this*) around the call to `f.increase()`.

C. The existing code will not compile.

D. The existing code will cause a runtime exception.

E. Put in a `wait()` call prior to invoking the `increase()` method.

F. Synchronize the `increase()` method

21. Given the following,

```
public class Test {
  public static void main (String [] args) {
    final Foo f = new Foo();
   Thread t = new Thread(new Runnable() {
         public void run() {
        f.doStuff();
       }
   });
   Thread g = new Thread() {
    public void run() {
         f.doStuff();
      }
     };
     t.start();
     g.start();
  }
}
class Foo {
   int x = 5;
  public void doStuff() {
     if (x < 10) {
       // nothing to do
      try {
         wait();
      } catch(InterruptedException ex) { }
     } else {
      System.out.println("x is " + x++);
      if (x >= 10) {
         notify();
       }
    }
  }
}
```

what is the result?

A. The code will not compile because of an error on line 12 of class Foo.

B. The code will not compile because of an error on line 7 of class Foo.

C. The code will not compile because of an error on line 4 of class Test.

D. The code will not compile because of some other error in class Test.

E. An exception occurs at runtime.

F. *x* is 5
x is 6

SELF TEST ANSWERS

1. ☑ C. Line 5 calls the `run()` method, so the `run()` method executes as a normal method should.
   ☒ A is incorrect because line 4 is the proper way to create an object. **B** is incorrect because it is legal to call the `run()` method, even though this will not start a true thread of execution. The code after line 5 will not execute until the `run()` method is complete. **D** is incorrect because the *for* loop only does two iterations. **E** is incorrect because the program runs without exception.

2. ☑ A and D. Only `start()` and `run()` are defined by the Thread class.
   ☒ B and **C** are incorrect because they are methods of the Object class. **E** is incorrect because there's no such method in any thread-related class.

3. ☑ C. The class correctly implements the Runnable interface with a legal `public void run()` method.
   ☒ A is incorrect because interfaces are not extended; they are implemented. **B** is incorrect because even though the class would compile and it has a valid `public void run()` method, it does not implement the Runnable interface, so the compiler would complain when creating a Thread with an instance of it. **D** is incorrect because the `run()` method must be *public*. **E** is incorrect because the method to implement is `run()`, not `start()`.

4. ☑ B. When the `start()` method is attempted a second time on a single Thread object, the method will throw an IllegalThreadStateException (you will not need to know this exception name for the exam). Even if the thread has finished running, it is still illegal to call `start()` again.
   ☒ A is incorrect because compilation will succeed. For the most part, the Java compiler only checks for illegal syntax, rather than class-specific logic. **C** and **D** are incorrect because of the logic explained above.

5. ☑ C. Because the class implements Runnable, an instance of it has to be passed to the Thread constructor, and then the instance of the Thread has to be started.
   ☒ A is incorrect. There is no constructor like this for Runnable because Runnable is an interface, and it is illegal to pass a class or interface name to any constructor. **B** is incorrect for the same reason; you can't pass a class or interface name to any constructor. **D** is incorrect because MyRunnable doesn't have a `start()` method, and the only `start()` method that can start a thread of execution is the `start()` in the Thread class.

6. ☑ **D.** The thread MyThread will start and loop three times (from 0 to 2).
☒ **A** is incorrect because the Thread class implements the Runnable interface; therefore, in line 5, Thread can take an object of type Thread as an argument in the constructor. **B** and **C** are incorrect because the variable *i* in the *for* loop starts with a value of 0 and ends with a value of 2. **E** is incorrect because of the program logic described above.

7. ☑ **D.** The `sleep()` method must be enclosed in a `try/catch` block, or the method `printAll()` must declare it `throws` the InterruptedException.
☒ **A** is incorrect, but it would be correct if the InterruptedException was dealt with. **B** is incorrect, but it would still be incorrect if the InterruptedException was dealt with because all Java code, including the `main()` method, runs in threads. **C** is incorrect. The `sleep()` method is static, so even if it is called on an instance, it still always affects the currently executing thread.

8. ☑ **B** and **F.** By marking the methods as `synchronized`, the threads will get the lock of the *this* object before proceeding. Only one thread will be either setting or reading at any given moment, thereby assuring that `read()` always returns the addition of a valid pair.
☒ **A** is incorrect because it is not synchronized; therefore, there is no guarantee that the values added by the `read()` method belong to the same pair. **C** and **D** are incorrect; only objects can be used to synchronize on. **E** is incorrect because it is not possible to select other objects to synchronize on when declaring a method as `synchronized`. Even using *this* is incorrect syntax.

9. ☑ **A.** The Object class defines these thread-specific methods.
☒ **B, C,** and **D** are incorrect because they do not define these methods. And yes, the Java API does define a class called Class, though you do not need to know it for the exam.

10. ☑ **B** and **E. B** is correct because multiple threads are allowed to enter nonsynchronized code, even within a class that has some synchronized methods. **E** is correct because a `wait()` call causes the thread to give up its locks.
☒ **A** is incorrect because static methods can be synchronized; they synchronize on the lock on the instance of class java.lang.Class that represents the class type. **C** is incorrect because only methods—not variables—can be marked `synchronized`. **D** is incorrect because a sleeping thread still maintains its locks.

11. ☑ **A, B,** and **F.** They are all related to the list of threads waiting on the specified object.
☒ **C, E, G,** and **H** are incorrect answers. The methods `isInterrupted()` and `interrupt()` are instance methods of Thread. The methods `sleep()` and `yield()` are static methods of Thread. **D** is incorrect because `synchronized` is a keyword and the `synchronized()` construct is part of the Java language.

12. ☑ D. 1 and 2 will be printed, but there will be no return from the wait call because no other thread will notify the main thread, so 3 will never be printed. The program is essentially frozen at line 7.
☒ A is incorrect; IllegalMonitorStateException is an unchecked exception so it doesn't have to be dealt with explicitly. **B** and **C** are incorrect; 3 will never be printed, since this program will never terminate because it will wait forever. **E** is incorrect because IllegalMonitorStateException will never be thrown because the `wait()` is done on *args* within a block of code synchronized on args. **F** is incorrect because any object can be used to synchronize on and, furthermore, there is no *this* when running a static method.

13. ☑ A. Either of the two events (notification or wait time expiration) will make the thread become a candidate for running again.
☒ B is incorrect because a waiting thread will not return to runnable when the lock is released, unless a notification occurs. **C** is incorrect because the thread will become a candidate immediately after notification, not two seconds afterwards. **D** is also incorrect because a thread will not come out of a waiting pool just because a lock has been released.

14. ☑ A and D. A is correct because the `notifyAll()` method (along with `wait()` and `notify()`) must always be called from within a synchronized context. **D** is correct because a thread blocked on a `wait()` call releases its locks, so another thread can get into the synchronized code and eventually call `notify()` or `notifyAll()`.
☒ B is incorrect because to call `wait()`, the thread must own the lock on the object that `wait()` is being invoked on, not the other way around. **C** is wrong because `notify()` is defined in java.lang.Object. **E** is wrong because `notify()` will not cause a thread to release its locks. The thread can only release its locks by exiting the synchronized code. **F** is wrong because `notifyAll()` notifies all the threads waiting on a particular locked object, not all threads waiting on *any* object.

15. ☑ C and E. In **E**, the constant Thread.MIN_PRIORITY is the lowest priority that a thread can have, and the background thread should have a very low priority or the lowest. Answer **C** is correct because 1 is a low (and usually the minimum) value, although for code clarity it is recommended to use the Thread.MIN_PRIORITY.
☒ A and **D** are incorrect because there are no such variables in the Thread class. **B** is incorrect; using MAX_PRIORITY would make other threads have fewer chances of getting a turn of the CPU, even to the point of freezing until the numerical processing is finished. **F** is incorrect because the thread would still compete for the CPU time and even delay other threads. **G** is incorrect because 10 is the value of MAX_PRIORITY, so *i* would be equivalent to answer **B**.

16. ☑ **B, E,** and **F. B** is correct because `wait()` always causes the current thread to go into the object's wait pool. **E** is correct because `sleep()` will always pause the currently running thread for *at least* the duration specified in the sleep argument (unless an interrupted exception is thrown). **F** is correct because, assuming that the thread you're calling `join()` on is alive, the thread calling `join()` will immediately block until the thread you're calling `join()` on is no longer alive.

☒ **A** is wrong, but tempting. The `yield()` method is not guaranteed to cause a thread to leave the running state, although if there are runnable threads of the same priority as the currently running thread, then the current thread will *probably* leave the running state. **C** and **D** are incorrect because they don't cause the thread invoking them to leave the running state. **G** is wrong because there's no such method.

17. ☑ **D** and **F. D** is correct because the `wait()` method is overloaded to accept a wait duration in milliseconds. If the thread has not been notified by the time the wait duration has elapsed, then the thread will move back to runnable even *without* having been notified. **F** is correct because `wait()/notify()/notifyAll()` must all be called from within a synchronized, context. A thread must own the lock on the object it's invoking `wait()/notify()/notifyAll()` on.

☒ **A** is incorrect because `wait()/notify()` will not prevent deadlock. **B** is incorrect because a sleeping thread will return to runnable when it wakes up, but it might not necessarily resume execution right away. To resume executing, the newly awakened thread must still be moved from runnable to running by the scheduler. **C** is incorrect because synchronization prevents two or more threads from accessing the same object. **E** is incorrect because `notify()` is not overloaded to accept a duration. **G** and **H** are incorrect because `wait()` and `sleep()` both declare a checked exception (InterruptedException).

18. ☑ **A** and **B** are both valid constructors for Thread.

☒ **C, D,** and **E** are not legal Thread constructors, although **D** is close. If you reverse the arguments in **D**, you'd have a valid constructor.

19. ☑ **B** is correct because in the first line of main we're constructing an instance of an anonymous inner class extending from MyThread. So the MyThread constructor runs and prints " MyThread". The next statement in main invokes `start()` on the new thread instance, which causes the overridden `run()` method (the `run()` method defined in the anonymous inner class) to be invoked, which prints " foo".

☒ **A, C, D, E, F,** and **G** are all incorrect because of the program logic described above.

20. ☑ F is correct because synchronizing the code that actually does the increase will protect the code from being accessed by more than one thread at a time.
☒ A is incorrect because synchronizing the `run()` method would stop other threads from running the `run()` method (a bad idea) but still would not prevent other threads with *other* runnables from accessing the `increase()` method. **B** is incorrect for virtually the same reason as A—synchronizing the code that *calls* the `increase()` method does not prevent other code from calling the `increase()` method. **C** and **D** are incorrect because the program compiles and runs fine. **E** is incorrect because it will simply prevent the call to `increase()` from ever happening from this thread.

21. ☑ E is correct because the thread does not own the lock of the object it invokes `wait()` on. If the method were synchronized, the code would run without exception.
☒ A, B, C, and D are incorrect because the code compiles without errors. **F** is incorrect because the exception is thrown before there is any output.

EXERCISE ANSWERS

Exercise 9-1: Creating a Thread and Putting It to Sleep

The final code should look something like this:

```
class TheCount extends Thread {
   public void run() {
      for(int i = 1;i<=100;++i) {
         System.out.print(i + "  ");
         if(i % 10 == 0)
            System.out.println("Hahaha");
         try {
            Thread.sleep(1000);
         } catch(InterruptedException e) {}
      }
   }

   public static void main(String [] args) {
      new TheCount().start();
   }
}
```

Exercise 9-2: Synchronizing a Block of Code

Your code might look something like this when completed:

```
1.  class InSync extends Thread {
2.     StringBuffer letter;
3.
4.     public InSync(StringBuffer letter) {
5.        this.letter = letter;
6.     }
7.
8.     public void run() {
9.        synchronized(letter) {
10.          for(int i = 1;i<=100;++i) {
11.             System.out.print(letter);
12.          }
13.          System.out.println();
14.          // Increment the letter in StringBuffer:
15.          char temp = letter.charAt(0);
16.          ++temp;
17.          letter.setCharAt(0, temp);
18.       }
19.    }
20.
21.    public static void main(String [] args) {
22.       StringBuffer sb = new StringBuffer("A");
23.       new InSync(sb).start();
24.       new InSync(sb).start();
25.       new InSync(sb).start();
26.    }
27. }
```

Just for fun, try removing lines 9 and 18 then run the program again. It will be unsynchronized, and watch what happens.

Part II

The Developer's Exam

CHAPTERS

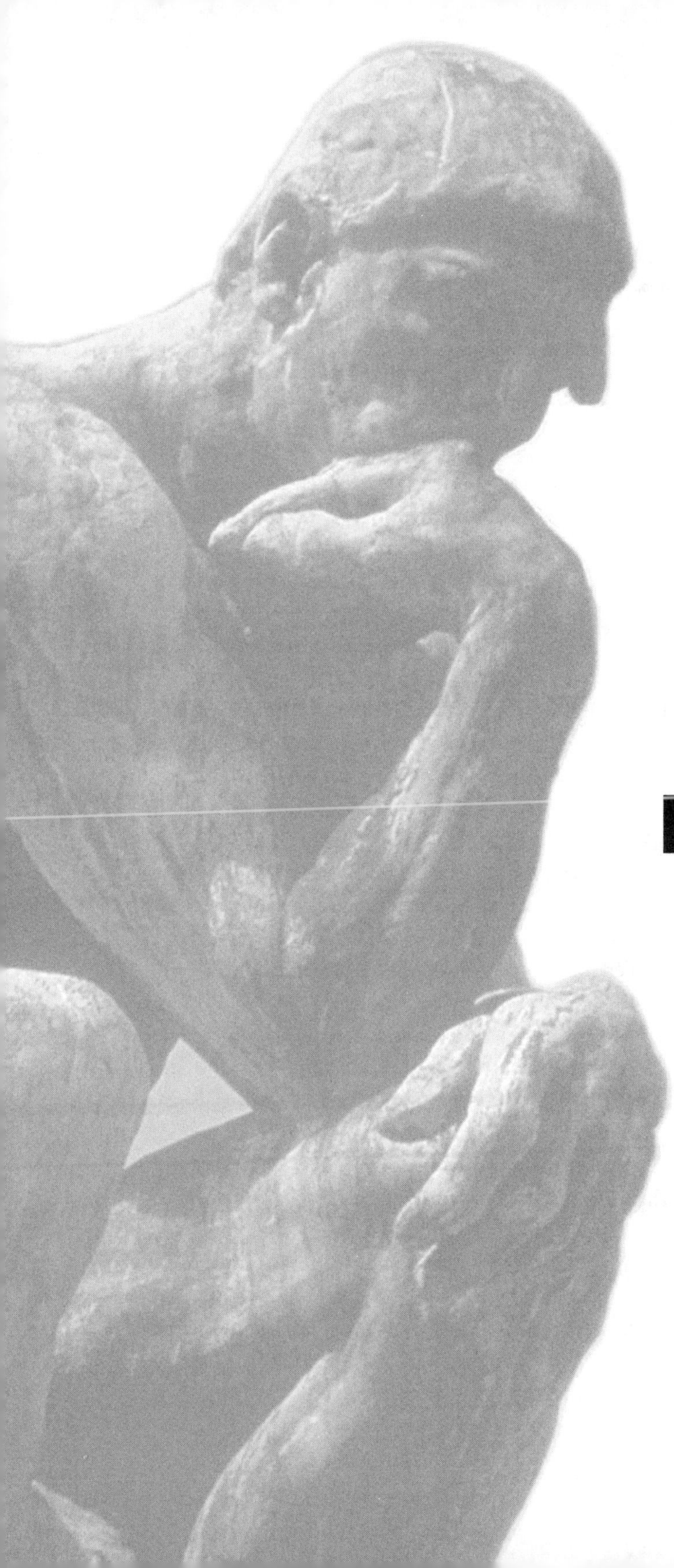

JAVA™ 2

SUN™ CERTIFIED PROGRAMMER & DEVELOPER

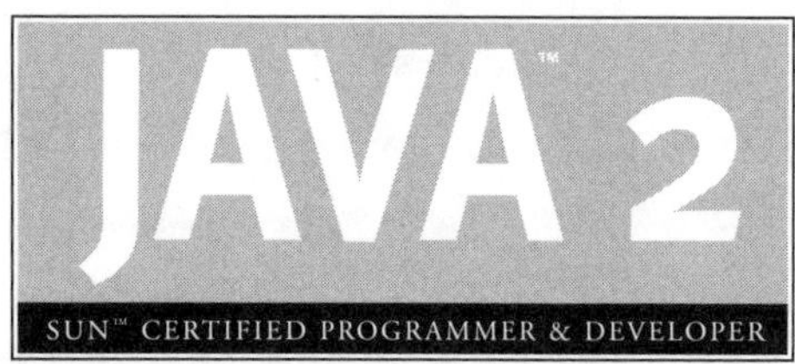

10

Introduction to the SCJD

CERTIFICATION OBJECTIVES

- Understand the Sun Certified Java Developer Exam Process

CERTIFICATION OBJECTIVE

Understand the Sun Certified Java Developer Exam Process

OK, so now you know everything about the language. But can you actually *build* something in it? You'll hear that argument from some who've never taken (or passed) the programmer's exam. Obviously, they don't understand how darn difficult the programmer's exam actually is, but nonetheless there *is* something to the claim that, "just because you know how the compiler and VM work does not mean you can develop software." The Developer exam, which is unique in the IT exam world, lets you answer that question (most often posed by a prospective employer).

In the Developer exam, you get to put your code where your mouth is by developing a software application. In fact, the Developer exam isn't even a multiple-choice test but rather a project that you build, given a (somewhat sketchy) specification. You're told what to build, with some general guidelines, and then it's up to you to implement and deliver the program. You have an unlimited amount of time in which to finish the project (as of this writing), but there *is* a short follow-up essay exam (taken at an authorized testing center, just as the Programmer exam is). The follow-up questions are largely used to verify that it was *you* (not your hotshot programmer brother-in-law who owed you big time) who did the work. In other words, the follow-up exam asks essay questions that only the project developer could answer (for example, "Justify your design choice on…").

First, we'll lay out the facts of the exam—how it works, how you do it, etc., and then we'll dive into what you need to know to pass it. Keep in mind that the actual knowledge you need to pass cannot be stuffed into a book this size, even if we made the book big enough to crush a car. Being a programmer is one thing, but being a *developer* is quite another. And you can't become a developer just by memorizing some facts. Study and memorization can work for passing the Programmer's exam—but that's OK because the programmer's exam is designed to verify that you're smart and that you really know the language. A prospective employer doesn't have to train you in Java if you've passed the programmer's exam. But if your employer wants to verify that you can follow a spec and implement a well-designed, maintainable, *correct* application, then you need either previous experience successfully building one or more Java applications or you need to pass the SCJD.

The next seven chapters (in other words, the rest of the book) show you what you'll need to know and do to pass the exam, but it's up to you to do the heavy lifting. And unless you're already well-versed in some of the topics (Swing, Threads, RMI, etc.) then you'll need to do some outside reading and practice in those technologies. We're focusing here on what the exam assessors are looking for in your finished project.

How Does It Work?

The exam has two parts, The Assignment and The Essay. You must successfully pass both parts to become certified.

The Assignment

Once you register for the Developer's exam, you're given instructions for downloading your assignment. There are many possible assignments that you might get. The assignment is a 9- or 10-page document with instructions for completing the project. Instructions include both the application specification and requirements for implementation and delivery. It also includes notes about how the application will be marked (evaluated, graded, assessed).

The Essay

Once you've submitted your assignment, you should immediately register for the essay portion of the certification. You can't register until after you've submitted your completed assignment, but the sooner the better once you have submitted it. You really want to take the essay portion while the application you just completed is still fresh in your mind. The essay portion will feel somewhat familiar to you—it takes place in an authorized Prometric testing center, just as the Programmer's exam does. You have 90 minutes to complete the essay portion, and it normally involves just a handful (about five) questions.

The Assessment

Once you've submitted both your assignment and the follow-up essay, the two pieces will be sent to the assessor for grading. It might be four weeks or so before you learn the results.

Are You a Good Candidate?

If you haven't yet passed the Programmer's (SCJP) exam, then stop right now and go get certified. You *must* pass the Programmer's exam before you're allowed to register for the Developer exam. So we figure that you'll read the first part of the book, take the Programmer's exam (passing, of course), then come back at some point and start reading this part. That means by the time you're reading this part, this book should already be dog-eared, marked-up, scratched, bent, and possibly dusty (from that dry spell between taking the Programmer's exam and going for the Developer exam).

If you got to this paragraph, then we assume you're already a Sun Certified Java Programmer. But are you ready for the Developer exam? Well, the good news is that you don't *need* to be ready when you *register* for the exam. You've got plenty of time to complete the assignment once you download it. So unlike the Programmer's exam, you don't have to wait until you're at top form for passing the exam. You can download the assignment, analyze what you'll need to learn to complete it, and then get to work. Sun (and most candidates) estimates that it takes between 90 and 120 hours of solid work to complete the exam, and that assumes you're already familiar with all the necessary technologies (networking, database, threads/locking, Swing, etc.). Some people work for three weeks straight, as if the project were their full-time job. Others work on it when they can, in their spare time, and might take several months to actually finish it. Of course, there's always the chance that you download it and discover you're way over your head and unlikely to get up-to-speed within a year. But if you've passed the Programmer's exam and you're willing to commit the time to work on it (plus whatever additional time you need to learn any required technologies you're not familiar with), then we say go for it…if you've got the money (we'll get to that in the next section).

Having said all that, we don't recommend registering until you've read the rest of this book. It'll give you a better idea of what's really involved, and you might decide to wait a while if you're still a beginner at some of these technologies. But if you're comfortable with at least three of the following, chances are you're ready to at least download the assignment:

- Swing and GUI design
- Networking issues: sockets and RMI
- Database issues: searching and record-locking
- Writing clear, maintainable code
- OO design and development

How Much Does It Cost?

All you need is $250 (US dollars) and you're in business…for the first part. The SCJD is in two parts, remember: the exam assignment (the specification that you download, implement, and submit) and the follow-up essay. The follow-up exam is an additional $150. So you're looking at $400 total to get your certification. There's no partial certification, so submitting your exam doesn't get you anywhere unless you successfully take the follow-up exam. In other words, you can't be certified without spending the $400.

How Long Does It Take?

As of this writing, there is no time limit specified for completing the assignment once you've downloaded it, but we don't advise waiting more than a year, as the requirements *could* change. Plus, there's a new requirement (although these requirements could change at any time so check the Sun website frequently at http://suned.sun.com for updates) that you must not use a version of Java that is deemed "out of date." The current definition of *out of date* is that your version must not have been superceded by a new production version for more than 18 months by the time you make your submission. What that means is that if your version has been out for less than 18 months, you're fine. If your version is older than 18 months (in other words, its official public release was more than 18 months ago), then the version released directly *after* your version must be less than 18 months old. So don't take forever is what we're saying, or you could find yourself rewriting your application. It's not good enough for your program to *run* on newer versions; you need to indicate in your exam which version you've compiled and tested on.

What's the Exam Deliverable?

Chapter 17 covers this in picky detail, but the short version is: a JAR file. As of this writing, you must submit the entire application, including compiled working classes, source code, and documentation in a single JAR file. Your assignment instructions will specify *exactly* how you must submit it and the most important rule is that *you must not deviate in any way from the submission instructions.*

Can I Develop with an IDE?

You can, but everything you submit must be *your own creation.* In other words, no auto-generated code. So use an IDE as an editor but not as a GUI-building tool or something that implements your networking. And whatever you do, be sure to test on a machine other than your development machine! When using an IDE (or not, but there's more of a danger when using an IDE) you can end up being sheltered and protected from things like classpath issues, which allow your program to run fine on your machine and then blow up (OK, just *fail* to run) at runtime on another system.

How Is It Graded?

Once you've completed both the assignment and the essay exam, an assessor takes both pieces and performs the assessment. Your project is first assumed to be correct and is given a starting point value (currently 155 points, but this could change). Then points are deducted through a variety of audits. For example, you might get 12 points deducted for issues with your coding conventions, and perhaps another 15 (out of a possible, say, 18 points) for problems with your record-locking or search algorithm. That subtracts 27 from your starting total of 155, and leaves you with 128 points. Currently, the exam requires 124 points to pass, so you'd be good with 128. Your instructions will give you an idea of the relative importance of certain evaluation (audit) criteria, but you won't know the specific values for specific violations. DISCLAIMER: the point values mentioned here are merely examples of how the exam is graded; they are *not* the actual point values used in the assessment. The only thing you will know with certainty is the relative importance of different aspects of your project. We'll give you one clue right now, though: code readability/ clarity and threading/locking will be extremely important. You'll almost certainly find these two areas carrying the most weight on your assignment instructions.

What Are the Exam Assessors Thinking?

OK, we aren't mind readers, and for all we know the assessors are thinking about last night's Bellbottom Bowling party as they mark your exam. But we *do* know one thing: *they aren't looking to see how clever an algorithm designer you are!* If anything, it's just the opposite. When you think of the Developer exam, don't think Lone Ranger. Instead, think *Team Player.* And don't even *think* about showing off your programming prowess by revising the specification to do something even better and cooler than what's asked for. There's a saying we have in the software world, and it will serve you well to remember it while building your Developer project: "Code as if the next guy to maintain it is a homicidal maniac who knows where you live."

exam Watch

The exam assessors aren't thinking like my-algorithm-is-bigger-than-yours code mavericks. They aren't looking for the next great breakthrough in record-locking. They aren't even looking for new, creative implementations. They are looking for development that says, "I'm a thoughtful programmer. I care about maintainability. Readability is very important to me. I want everyone to understand what's going on with the least amount of effort. I write careful, correct code. My code might not be the snappiest, and it might even incur an extra few bytes in order to make something less complex, but my logic is simple, my code and my design are clear and implement the specification perfectly, I didn't reinvent the wheel anywhere, and gosh—wouldn't you just love to have me on your team?" If your project submission says all that about you, you're in great shape.

The exam assessor looks at your code first from an entirely selfish perspective by asking, "Is this easy for me to evaluate?" Chapters 16 and 17 offer insight into what you need to do to make the assessor's job easier. Trust us on this one—they'd rather be at the beach (or skiing, mountain-biking, taking a Martha Stewart crafts workshop) than spending unnecessary time figuring out how to get your assignment working. Beginning with the "refreshed" exam assignments at the end of 2002, the requirements changed to make the submission rules much more strict, in order to benefit the assessor. If at any time you neglect to follow even a single submission requirement—say, the directory structure of your project puts the user documentation in a different folder—you'll be failed on the spot. The assessor won't make *any* allowances for misplaced files, even if the program still runs perfectly. Don't make them go *looking* for something.

Another aspect of making the assessor's life easier is what you'll learn in Chapters 11 and 12. *The little things really matter!* For example, while you might think—if you indent your code four spaces—that an occasional three-space indentation here and there is OK, what's the harm in that? The harm is in readability, and while a couple of inconsistencies in indentations might not be a big deal, adhering to the Java Coding Conventions is absolutely crucial for others looking at your code… *especially* the assessor.

We've seen people fail the exam because they put the curly braces on the line *below* the method declaration rather than immediately following the declaration (on the same line), violating the official Java Coding Conventions. While this infraction *alone* probably might not cause you to fail, the points deducted for code convention violations might be the ones that sink you where you otherwise might have squeaked by. You don't get to make very many mistakes in this exam. Just because *your* manager or *your* co-workers are tolerant of a little sloppiness here and there, the assessor won't be. Reread the preceding Exam Watch, copy it down on a post-it note, and stick it onto your bathroom mirror. Each morning, say it to yourself, "I'm a thoughtful programmer. I care…" (except say the whole thing).

What Are the Exam Assessors NOT Thinking?

If your solution works—according to the spec—then even if the algorithms might be tweaked just a little more for efficiency, you probably won't be marked down—especially if the code is clear, maintainable, and gets the job done correctly. They're also not looking for one particular solution. There is no one *right* way to implement your assignment. There are a gazillion *wrong* ways, however, and we'll be looking at some of those throughout the rest of the book. But here's one that's guaranteed to kill you (both on the exam and in the real world): *deadlock*. Remember, we talked about threads in Chapter 8, and you'd better take it all very seriously. If there's even a chance that your design could lead to deadlock (it doesn't have to actually *cause* deadlock right before the assessor's eyes) then you can probably kiss that $400 goodbye.

The bottom line is that they're *not* looking for The Perfect Solution. But they're also not looking for innovative new approaches, regardless of how clever, when well-known patterns or other solutions exist. They're especially not looking for you to reinvent the wheel or write your own, say, new and improved set of classes to replace the perfectly working core library packages.

What's the Assignment Like?

We can't give you a *real* assignment from the actual exam, of course, but here are a couple of examples to give you the *flavor* of what the specification might look like. And don't be thinking these are outlandish examples; wait 'til you see the *real* ones.

WindRider Horse Cruises

WindRider Horse Cruises (WHC) offers a variety of unique vacation trips, all on horseback. Copying the cruise ship model, WHC has 4-day, 7-day, and 14-day cruises that include all the food, drinks, and partying you can handle. (Which, after four straight days on a horse won't be much.) WindRider has grown steadily from a two-person outfit offering one cruise a month to a busy operation with several cruises running simultaneously in different parts of the world. But while the business has grown, their cruise booking software hasn't kept pace. The WindRider CEO is acting as the company's IT director, but he has some quirks. He insists on keeping the entire application—*including the database server*—homegrown. In other words, he doesn't want to buy or use a database server written by anyone but his trusted friend Wilbur. Sadly, Wilbur sustained an injury while fulfilling his *other* WindRider duties (training horses to tolerate the disco music) and that's where you come in. Your job is to build the new WindRider booking software. One restriction is that you *must* use the WindRider's existing data file format. All cruise records must stay in that format because the accounting part of the company still has software that requires that format, and you're only updating the *booking* software.

Customers must be able to call in to one of the four booking offices and request a cruise. A customer service representative then uses the new booking application (the one you're going to write) to search for and then book an appropriate cruise to meet that customer's needs. Although the data file lives on one machine, back at the head office, the three other booking offices (and possibly more in the future) need to be able to access it over a standard TCP/IP network. So there's a danger that two customer service agents could be trying to book the same cruise slot at the same time. (A cruise slot is like a 'cabin' on a real seafaring cruise. So any given cruise might have anywhere between 6 to 12 slots, and each slot represents a record in the data file.) You'll have to make sure that this doesn't happen! Overbooking would be a Really Bad Thing. (Especially for the horse.)

So the people who interact with the actual software are the customer service agents. But it's the actual cruise customers who are making the requests. For example, a customer might phone up and say, "I'd like a 4- or 7-day Horse Cruise sometime in August 2003, in the United States." The customer service agent must then use the system to perform a search for that customer's needs. The application needs to provide a list of all possible matching cruises and then also allow the agent to reserve (*book*) a cruise slot for that customer.

You must use a Swing GUI, and WindRider's CEO just happens to be dating a Computer-Human Interaction specialist, so you can bet she'll be looking for all the right characteristics of a usable GUI.

For networking, you have the choice between RMI and using regular old Java TCP sockets (with serialized objects). It's really up to you to make that decision, but you'd better be prepared to explain why you chose what you chose.

The data file format is a little ugly, not comma-delimited or anything, just a bunch of fixed-length fields. And you *must* stick to this data file exactly. We'll send it to you so you can see exactly how it's formatted and start working with it in your development. You can't change a thing about what goes into a record. You can't add a field, can't reformat the data…nothing. Your job is simply to build the actual database server that accesses the data file to allow for searching, booking, adding new cruises, etc. Oh, and don't forget about those concurrent user issues—you must lock these records in some way during use.

From his hospital bed, Wilbur sketched out what the database interface should be, and you need to follow this exactly (although you can add more, but you must *at least* provide these two methods in your public interface to the database server).

```
public void updateRecord(String[] recordData, int whichRecord) throws
LockedRecordException, NoSuchRecordException;

public int[] findByCustomerCriteria(Criteria criteriaObject);
```

But then you still need to add the methods for deleting, locking, etc. And you'll have to create the custom Exceptions and decide what should go in the Criteria class (the thing you're going to use to search the database).

Your job, ultimately, is to deliver the following:

- The customer service GUI application that they use to search and book records in the database.
- The actual database server application—the thing that actually gets into the data file and takes care of locking, etc. This is most likely the piece the GUI interacts with.
- Networking functionality so that multiple users can access this, remotely.

Confused?

That's part of the idea. You need to think through the problems, think about *new* problems not addressed in this spec, and figure out how to solve them, even in the face of incomplete information. The real world isn't perfect. Specs never seem to be complete. And the person you need to ask for clarification never seems to be at his desk when you call. Oh, and there's nobody—and we do mean *nobody*—who will reassure you that you're on the right track by implementing a particular solution. You're just going to have to roll your sleeves up and answer your own "what about <insert some scenario> ?" questions.

And boy oh boy are there issues. Both raised and unraised by this specification. The majority of the rest of this book raises those issues and gives you a lot to think about. We can't give you solutions—there *aren't* any right solutions, remember—and it wouldn't be ethical to work out all the issues here. That's the whole *point* of the Developer exam! The actual coding is quite straightforward and fairly simple. It's not like you're writing the world's greatest neural network or artificial life program. But thinking about the true business issues—about what the customer might need, what the customer service agents need, and what the business itself needs, and then planning and implementing a solution––are what this certification is all about. You'll thank us one day. And don't forget, if you get frustrated, just remember how much you like us for getting you through the Programmer certification. Which we did, or of course you wouldn't be reading this far into the book!

Overview of the Developer Exam Chapters

We're going to cover a lot of ground here, some at a high level and some a little lower. The high-level areas are the places where you need to design solutions and discover potential problems. Locking issues, for example, are handled at a high level. We'll raise issues to get you thinking, but you'll have to come up with your own designs—after all, we have no way of *knowing* what your exact assignment will be. The lower-level areas are reserved for things you must do throughout your entire application—such as coding standards, OO design, documentation, etc., and for tools such as *javadoc* and Jar. We also cover GUI usability in some depth, but it will be up to you to work out the implementations. The following is a chapter-by-chapter look at what we cover in the rest of the book:

Chapter 11: Coding Standards

As we mentioned earlier, even the failure to indent properly or line up your comments can mean the difference between passing and failing the exam. We'll cover the relevant parts of the Java Coding Conventions that you must be *very* meticulous about in every single line in every single class in your application.

Chapter 12: Clarity and Maintainability

This is where the whole Team Work mentality (or, if you prefer, the homicidal maniac thing) comes in. We'll look at what makes your code easy to read and maintain (and conversely, what makes it a *pain* to read and maintain), and cover things like reducing logic complexity, appropriate error-handling, and adhering to some fundamental OO principles.

Chapter 13: GUI Usability

Don't you just hate it when you're working in an application that makes you type things like "yes" or "no" rather than providing radio buttons? Or what about a nonstandard menu—you know, without a File and Help menu? Or worse, no menu bar at all. Or one that bombards you with dialog boxes for every little move you make. Or things that *should* scroll that don't. Or when you resize a window and things land anywhere other than where they were before. A well-designed GUI must be usable, useful, and *not* clumsy. Fortunately, there are established human interface guidelines to help inform our design, and that's what we'll look at in this chapter.

Chapter 14: Networking Issues

Hmm, what to choose…RMI or sockets? We'll cover the main points and then—even though there is definitely *not* a right choice for the exam—we'll spend most of the time on our personal favorite, RMI. And why laziness isn't necessarily a bad trait in a programmer.

Chapter 15: Database Issues

We know, we know…in the real world surely someone would just *buy* a database. Heck, there are *free* ones out there. But for the purposes of assessing your development skills, thinking through (and implementing) the tricky and subtle issues of concurrency will do nicely. So pretend, for the time being, that there *is* no such thing as a database. Or that you're the first person to have to build one. We'll look at some of the things you'll need to be thinking about in your design, and how crucial threads are to your design and implementation.

Chapter 16: Exam Documentation

Remember when we said your job was to make the assessor's life easier? (The assessor representing both the end-user and the client and the project manager of this application.) Now's your chance to shine. Or not. We'll look at everything from status messages to comments, but most of the focus is on *javadoc*, which you *must* provide for *all* repeat *all* classes and interfaces.

Chapter 17: Final Submission and Essay

"Real Women Ship" the saying goes (or something like that) and now it's time for you to call your application *finished* and package it up in a nice JAR and send it out. We'll emphasize the importance of getting your directory structures just right, and what you'll need to do at the command-line to run from the JAR in a particular way.

Key Points Summary

No time like the present to get started. But before we jump into code conventions, here's a quick summary of the points from this chapter:

- The Developer exam is in two parts, the Assignment and the Essay.
- You must complete (and pass) both parts to become certified.
- The Assignment is a set of instructions for building and delivering the application.
- Once you've submitted your Assignment, you can register for the Essay portion of the exam.
- You're given a minimum of one year to complete the Assignment (from the time you register and download it).
- Most candidates take between 90 and 120 hours to complete the Assignment.
- You're given 90 minutes on the Essay portion of the exam.
- You must be a Sun Certified Java Programmer (for Java 2) in order to register for the Developer exam.
- The certification costs $400 total ($250 for the Assignment portion and $150 for the Essay).
- You can develop with an IDE, but you must not include any IDE-generated code in your project. Every line must be coded by you.
- The Assignment is graded by giving your application a starting number of points and then deducting points for violations including minor things (curly braces in the wrong place) and major things (locking doesn't work in every situation).

- The Essay is designed largely to verify that *you* are the one who completed the Assignment. You need to understand the key issues of your design and be prepared to justify your decisions.
- The exam Assessors are more interested in the clarity and maintainability of your code than they are in your clever algorithms.
- Think like a Team Player rather than a lone coding maverick, even if it means your design and implementation are sometimes slightly less efficient, but more easily understood by others.

11

Coding Standards

CERTIFICATION OBJECTIVES

- Use Sun Java Coding Standards

CERTIFICATION OBJECTIVE

Use Sun Java Coding Standards

The Developer exam is challenging. There are a lot of complex design issues to consider, and a host of advanced Java technologies to understand and implement correctly. The exam assessors work under very strict guidelines. You can create the most brilliant application ever to grace a JVM, but if you don't cross your t's and dot your i's the assessors have no choice but to deduct crucial (and sometimes substantial) points from your project. This chapter will help you cross your t's and dot your i's. Following coding standards is not hard; it just requires diligence. If you are careful it's no-brainer stuff, and it would be a shame to lose points because of a curly brace in the wrong place. The Developer exam stresses things that *must* be done to avoid automatic failure. The exam uses the word *must* frequently. When we use the word *must*, we use it in the spirit of the exam, if you *must* you *must*, so just get on with it. Let's dive into the fascinating world of Java Coding Standards.

Spacing Standards

This section covers the standards for indenting, line-length limits, line breaking, and white space.

Indenting

We said this was going to be fascinating didn't we? Each level of indentation must be four spaces, exactly four spaces, always four spaces. Tabs must be set to eight spaces. If you are in several levels of indentation you can use a combination of tabs and (sets of four) spaces to accomplish the correct indentation. So if you are in a method and you need to indent 12 spaces, you can either press SPACEBAR 12 times, or press TAB once and then press SPACEBAR four times. (Slow down coach.) We recommend not using the TAB key, and sticking to the SPACEBAR—it's just a bit safer.

When to Indent If you indent like this, you'll make your assessor proud:

- Beginning comments, package declarations, import statements, interface declarations, and class declarations should not be indented.

- Static variables, instance variables, constructors, methods, and their respective comments* should be indented one level.
- Within constructors and methods, local variables, statements, and their comments* should be indented another level.
- Statements (and their comments) within block statements should be indented another level for each level of nesting involved. (Don't worry, we'll give you an example.)

The following listing shows proper indenting:

```
public class Indent {

    static int staticVar = 7;

    public Indent() { }

    public static void main(String [] args) {

        int x = 0;

        for(int z=0; z<7; z++) {
            x = x + z;
            if (x < 4) {
                x++;
            }
        }
    }
}
```

Line Lengths and Line Wrapping

The general rule is that a line shouldn't be longer than 80 characters. We recommend 65 characters just to make sure that a wide variety of editors will handle your code gracefully. When a line of code is longer than will fit on a line there are some *line wrapping* guidelines to follow. We can't say for sure that these are a must, but if you follow these guidelines you can be sure that you're on safe ground:

- Break after a comma.
- Break before an operator.

---

* Rules about comments are coming soon!

- Align the new line a tab (or eight spaces) beyond the beginning of the line being broken.
- Try not to break inside an inner parenthesized expression. (Hang on, the example is coming.)

The following snippet demonstrates acceptable line wrapping:

```
/* example of a line wrap */
System.out.println(((x * 42) + (z - 343) + (x % z ))
        + numberOfParsecs);

/* example of a line wrap for a method */
x = doStuffWithLotsOfArgs(coolStaticVar, instanceVar,
        numberOfParsecs, reallyLongShortName, x, z);
```

White Space

Can you believe we have to go to this level of detail? It turns out that if you don't parcel out your blank spaces as the standards say you should, you can lose points. With that happy thought in mind, let's discuss the proper use of blank lines and blank statements.

The Proper Use of Blank Lines Blank lines are used to help readers of your code (which might be you, months after you wrote it) to easily spot the logical blocks within your source file. If you follow these recommendations in your source files, your blank line worries will be over.

Use a blank line,

- Between methods and constructors
- After your last instance variable
- Inside a method between the local variables and the first statement
- Inside a method to separate logical segments of code
- Before single line or block comments

Use two blank lines between the major sections of the source file: the package, the import statement(s), the class, and the interface.

The Proper Use of Blank Spaces Blank spaces are used to make statements more readable, and less squished together. Use a blank space,

- Between binary operators
- After commas in an argument list
- After the expressions in a *for* statement
- Between a keyword and a parenthesis
- After casts

The following code sample demonstrates proper form to use when indenting, skipping lines, wrapping lines, and using spaces. We haven't covered all of the rules associated with the proper use of comments; therefore, this sample does *not* demonstrate standard comments:

```
/*
 * This listing demonstrates only proper spacing standards
 *
 * The Javadoc comments will be discussed in a later chapter
 */


package com.wickedlysmart.utilities;


import java.util.*;


/**
 * CoolClass description
 *
 * @version .97 10 Oct 2002
 * @author  Joe Beets
 */
public class CoolClass {

    /** Javadoc static var comment */
    public static int coolStaticVar;

    /** Javadoc public i-var comment */
```

```
        public long instanceVar;

        /* private i-var comment */
        private short reallyLongShortName;

        /** Javadoc constructor comment */
        public CoolClass() {
          // do stuff
        }

        /** Javadoc comment about method */
        void coolMethod() {
            int x = 0;
            long numberOfParsecs = 0;

            /* comment about for loop */
            for(z = 0; z < 7; z++) {
                x = x + z;

                /* comment about if test */
                if (x < 4) {
                    x++;
                }

                /* example of a line wrap */
                System.out.println(((x * 42) + (z - 343) + (x % z ))
                        + numberOfParsecs);

                /* example of a line wrap for a method */
                x = doStuffWithLotsOfArgs(coolStaticVar, instanceVar,
                        numberOfParsecs, reallyLongShortName, x, z);
            }
        }

        /** Javadoc comment about method */
        int doStuffWithLotsOfArgs(int a, long b, long c, short d, int e,
                int f) {
            return e * f;
        }
    }
```

How to Care for Your Curly Braces

If you format your curly braces correctly, you can distinguish your exam submittal from all the other Larrys and Moes out there. We know that this is a passionate topic for lots of folks; we're just letting you know what your assessor will be looking for, so please don't attempt to drag from us what our real feelings are about curly braces.

Curly Braces for Classes, Interfaces, Constructors, and Methods

OK, along with curly braces, we might talk a little about parentheses in this section. The opening brace for classes, interfaces, constructors, and methods should occur at the end of the same line as the declaration. The closing brace starts a new line by itself, and is indented to match the beginning of the corresponding declaration; for example,

```
public interface Curly {

    public int iMethod(int arg);
}


class Moe implements Curly {

    int id;

    public Moe() {
        id = 42;
    }

    public int iMethod(int argument) {
        return (argument * 2);
    }
}
```

Curly Braces for Flow Control (ifs and whiles, etc.)

Your flow control blocks should always be enclosed with curly braces. There are places where the compiler will let you get away with not using curly braces, such as *for* loops and *if* tests with only one statement in the body, but skipping the braces is considered uncivilized (and in fact often leads to bugs when code is enhanced later). For the exam, always use curly braces. Following is an example of how to structure all of the flow control code blocks in Java—pin this baby to your wall!

```
class Flow {

    static int x = 0;
```

```
static int y = 5;

public static void main(String [] args) {
    for (int z = 0; z < 7; z++) {          // for loop
        x = x + 1;
        y = y - 2;
    }

    if (x > 4) {
        System.out.println("x > 4");       // if test
        x++;
    }

    if (x > 5) {                           // if, else
        System.out.println("x > 5");
    } else {
        System.out.println("x < 6");
    }

    if (x > 30) {                          // if, else-if, else
        System.out.println("x > 30");
    } else if (x > 20) {
        System.out.println("x > 20");
    } else {
        System.out.println("x < 21");
    }

    do {                                   // do loop
        x++;
        System.out.println("in a do loop");
    } while (x < 10);

    while (x < 13) {                       // do while loop
        x++;
        System.out.println("in a do while loop");
    }

    switch (x) {                           // switch block
    case 12:
        x++;
        /* falls through */                // see comment at end
    case 13:
        x++;
        System.out.print("x was 13");
        /* falls through */
```

```
            case 14:
                System.out.print("x is 14");
                /* falls through */
            default:
                break;
            }

            try {                                   // try, catch
                doRiskyMethod();
                x++;
            } catch (Exception e) {
                System.out.println("doRisky failed");
            }

            try {                                   // try, catch, finally
                doRiskyMethod();
                x++;
            } catch (Exception e) {
                System.out.println("doRisky failed");

            } finally {
                x = 100;
            }
        }

        static void doRiskyMethod() {
            x = y;
        }
    }
```

You might want those *Exceptions* above to be *RuntimeExceptions*. *javac* does not mind, but *jikes* will give you a warning.

One interesting thing to notice about the example above is the use of the */* falls through */* comment in the *switch* statement. This comment should be used at the end of every *case* block that doesn't contain a `break` statement.

Our Comments About Comments

Earlier we talked about being a team player. The orientation of the exam is to see if you can create software that is readable, understandable, and usable by other programmers. Commenting your code correctly is one of the key ways that you can create developer-friendly software. As you might expect, the assessors will be looking to see if your code comments are appropriate, consistent, and in a standard form.

This chapter will focus on implementation comments; Chapter 16 will cover *javadoc* comments. There are several standard forms that your implementation comments can take. Based on the results of extensive research and worldwide polling we will recommend an approach, which we believe represents the most common of the standard approaches. If you choose not to use our recommendation, the most important thing that you can do is to pick a standard approach and stick with it.

There are several types of comments that commonly occur within source code listings. We will discuss each of them with our recommendations and other possible uses.

Block Comments

Use a block comment in your code when you have to describe aspects of your program that require more than a single line. They can be used most anywhere, as source file or method headers, within methods, or to describe key variables. Typically, they should be preceded by a blank line and they should take the following form:

```
/*
 *this is a block comment
 *it occupies several lines
 */
```

Single Line Comments

Use a single line comment in the same place you would block comments, but for shorter descriptions. They should also be preceded by a blank line for readability, and we recommend the following form:

```
/* this is a single line comment */
```

It is acceptable to use this alternate form:

```
// this is the alternate single line comment form
```

End of Line Comments

When you want to add a comment to the end of a line of code, use the aptly named *end of line* comment. If you have several of these comments in a row, make sure to align them vertically. We recommend the following form:

```
doRiskyStuff();         // this method might throw a FileNotFoundException

doComplexStuff();       // instantiate the rete network
```

It is acceptable to use this alternate form:

```
doRiskyStuff()         /* this method might throw a FileNotFoundException  */

doComplexStuff();      /* instantiate the rete network  */
```

Masking Comments

Often in the course of developing software, you might want to mask a code segment from the compiler without removing it from the file. This technique is useful during development, but be sure to remove any such code segments from your code before finishing your project. Masking comments should look like this:

```
//   if (moreRecs == true) {
//        ProcessRecord();
//   }
//   else {
//        doFileCleanUp();
//   }
```

General Tips About Comments

It is important to use comments where the code itself may not be clear, and it is equally important to avoid comments where the code is obvious. The following is a classic, from the Bad Comments Hall of Fame:

```
x = 5;            // set the variable x equal to 5
```

Comments should be used to provide summaries of complex code and to reveal information about the code that would otherwise be difficult to determine. Avoid comments that will fall out of date, i.e., write your comments as if they might have to last forever.

Declarations Are Fun

Declarations are a huge part of Java. They are also complex, loaded with rules, and if used sloppily can lead to bugs and poor maintainability. The following set of guidelines is intended to make your code more readable, more debuggable, and more maintainable.

Sequencing Your Declarations

The elements in your Java source files should be arranged in a standard sequence. In some cases the compiler demands it, and for the rest of the cases consistency will help you win friends and influence people. Here goes:

- class comments
- package declaration
- import statements
- class declaration
- static variables
- instance variables
- constructors
- methods

Location and Initialization

The following guidelines should be considered when making Java declarations:

- Within methods:
  - Declare and initialize local variables before other statements (whenever possible).
  - Declare and initialize block variables before other block statements (when possible).
  - Declare only one member per line.
  - Avoid *shadowing* variables. This occurs when an instance variable has the same name as a local or block variable. While the compiler will allow it, *shadowing* is considered very unfriendly towards the next co-worker (remember: potentially psychopathic) who has to maintain your code.

Capitalization

Three guesses. You better use capitalization correctly when you declare and use your package, class, interface, method, variable, and constant names. The rules are pretty simple:

- **Package names** The safest bet is to use lowercase when possible:

  `com.wickedlysmart.utilities`

- **Class and Interface names** Typically they should be nouns; capitalize the first letter and any other first letters in secondary words within the name:

  `Customer or CustomTable`

- **Method names** Typically they should be verbs; the first word should be lowercase, and if there are secondary words, the first letter of each should be capitalized:

  `initialize(); or getTelescopicOrientation();`

- **Variable names** They should follow the same capitalization rules as methods; you should start them with a letter (even though you can use _ or $, don't), and only temporary variables like looping variables should use single character names:

  `currentIndex; or name; or x;`

- **Constant names** To be labeled a constant, a variable must be declared static and final. Their names should be all uppercase and underscores must be used to separate words:

  `MAX_HEIGHT; or USED;`

Key Points Summary

- This is the easiest part of the exam, if you are careful and thorough you should be able to do very well in this area.
- Always indent four spaces from the previous level of indentation.
- Break long lines at around the 65 character mark:
  - Break after a comma
  - Break before an operator

- Try not to break inside inner parens.
- Use single blank lines between constructors, methods, logic segments, before comments, and after your last instance variable.
- Use blank spaces between binary operators, after commas in argument lists, after *for* expressions, between a keyword and a paren.
- Place opening curly brace on the same line as the declaration or statement.
- Put closing curly brace on a new line.
- Closing curly brace shares a line with *else*, *else if*, *do*, *catch*, and *finally*.
- Block comments start and end with /* and */, * in the middle.
- Single line comments use /* */
- End of line comments use //
- Masking comments use //
- File declaration sequence is this: comments, package, import, class, static, instance, constructors, methods.
- Initialize variables at the top of blocks; avoid variable name shadowing.
- Package names are lowercase: com.wickedlysmart.utilities.
- Classes and interfaces have capitalized nouns for names: Inventory.
- Methods and variables names start lowercase and capitalize secondary words, as in

  `doRiskyStuff(); or currentIndex;.`
- Constant names are all caps with underscores: MAX_HEADROOM.

12

Clarity and Maintainability

CERTIFICATION OBJECTIVE

- Writing Clear and Maintainable Code

CERTIFICATION OBJECTIVE

Write Clear and Maintainable Code

Now that you've made your code *readable*, does your easy-to-read code actually make sense? Can it be easily maintained? These are huge issues for the exam, worth a very significant chunk of your assessment score. We'll look at everything from class design to error handling. *Remember that you're a Team Player.* Some key areas of code clarity are covered in more detail in the Documentation chapter, so we won't discuss them here. Those areas include the importance of meaningful comments and self-documenting identifiers. The issues raised in *this* chapter are

- General programming style considerations
- Following OO design principles
- Reinventing the wheel
- Error-handling

General Programming Considerations

The coding conventions covered in the previous chapter are a great starting point. But the exam is also looking for consistency and appropriateness in your programming *style*. The following section lists some key points you should keep in mind when writing your perfectly-formatted code. Some of these will be explained in subsequent sections; several of these points are related to OO design, for example, and we cover them in more detail in that section. Once again, this is no time to debate the actual *merits* of these principles. Again, imagine you've come into a project team and need to prove yourself as a, what? Yes! *Team Player.* The first thing the team is looking for is whether you can follow the conventions and standards so that everyone can work together without wanting to throw one another out the seventh floor window and onto the cement fountain below. (Unless you're a dot-com company and your office now looks over an abandoned gas station.) These points are in no particular order, so don't infer that the first ones are more important than the last. You can infer, however, that your exam assessor will probably be asking if you've done these things appropriately.

Keep Variable Scope as Small as Possible

Don't use an instance variable when a local variable will work! Not only does this impact memory use, but it reduces the risk that an object "slips out" to some place it shouldn't be used, either accidentally or on purpose. Wait to declare a variable until just before it's used. And you should *always* initialize a local variable at the time it is declared (which is just before use), with the exception of *try/catch* blocks. In that case, if the variable is declared and assigned in the *try/catch* block, the compiler won't let you use it *beyond* that block, so if you need the variable after a *try* or *catch* block, then you'll have to declare it first *outside* the *try/catch*.

Another way to reduce scope is to use a *for* loop rather than *while*. Remember from the Programmer's exam chapters that when you declare a variable as part of the *for* loop declaration (as opposed to merely initializing a variable declared prior to the loop), then the variable's scope ends with the loop. So you get scope granularity that's even smaller than a method.

Avoid Designing a Class That Has No Methods

Objects are meant to have both state and behavior; they're not simply glorified structs. If you need a data structure, use a Collection. There are exceptions to this, however, that might apply to your exam assignment. Sometimes you *do* need an object whose sole purpose is to carry data from one location to another—usually as a result of a database request. A row in a table, for example, should be represented as an object in your Java program, and it might not always need methods if its sole job is to be, say, displayed in a GUI table. This is known as the *ValueObject* pattern. Which brings us to the next issue.

Use Design Patterns

When you use familiar patterns, then you've got a kind of shorthand for discussing your design with other programmers (even if that discussion is between your code/ comments and the other person. If you've done it right, *you* won't personally be there to talk about it, as is the case with the Developer exam). If you need a Singleton, make a Singleton—don't simply document that there is to be only one of these things. On the other hand, don't go forcing your design into a pattern just for the sake of using a pattern. Simplicity should be your first concern, but if it's a toss-up between your approach and an equally complex, well-known design pattern, go for the pattern.

Reduce the Visibility of Things As Much As Possible

In general, the more public stuff you expose to the world, the less free you are to make changes later without breaking someone else's code. The less you expose, the more flexibility you have for implementation changes later. And you *know* there are always changes. So, making variables, methods, and classes as restricted as you can while limiting what you expose to your "public interface," you'll be in good shape down the road. Obviously there are other subtle issues about inheritance (as in, what does a subclass get access to?), so there's more to consider here, but in general, be thinking about reducing your exposure (think of it as reducing your liability down the road). This is closely related to reducing the scope of variables.

Use Overloading Rather Than Logic

If you've got a method that needs to behave differently depending on the kind of thing it was actually handed, consider overloading it. Any time you see *if* or *switch* blocks testing the type of an argument, you should probably start thinking about overloading the method. And while you're at it…

Avoid Long Argument Lists

If you have a ton of arguments coming into a method, perhaps you need to encapsulate the stuff you need in that method into a class of its own type.

Don't Invoke Potentially Overridable Methods from a Constructor

You already know that you can't access any nonstatic things *prior* to your superconstructor running, but keep in mind that even *after* an object's superconstructor has completed, the object is still in an incomplete state until after *its* constructor has finished. Polymorphism still works in a constructor. So if B extends A, and A calls a method in its constructor that B has overridden, well, guess what happens when somebody makes an instance of B. You got it. The B constructor invokes its superconstructor (A's constructor). But inside the A constructor it invokes one of its own methods, but B has overridden that method. B's method runs! In other words, an object can have one of its methods invoked even *before* its constructor has completed! So while B isn't even a fully formed object, it can still be running code and even accessing its own instance variables. This is a problem because its instance variables have not yet been initialized to *anything* other than default values, *even if they're given explicit values when they're declared.* Yikes! So don't do it. If it's a final or private instance method, then you're safe since you know it'll never be overridden.

Code to Interfaces

Polymorphism, polymorphism, polymorphism. Use polymorphic arguments, return types, and variables whenever possible (in other words, declare a variable, return type, or argument as an interface type rather than a specific class type). Using an interface as the type lets you expose only the definition of *what* your code can do, and leaves the implementation flexible and extensible. And maintainable. And all the other good OO things-that-end-with-ble. But if you can't…

Use Abstract Classes When You Need Functionality to Be Inherited

If you really must have implementation code and/or instance variables, then use an abstract class and use that class as the declared polymorphic variable, argument, and return type.

Make Objects You're Finished with Eligible for Garbage Collection

You already know how to do this. Either explicitly set the reference variable to null when you have no more use of the object, or reassign a different object to that reference variable (thus abandoning the object originally referenced by it). At the same time…

Don't Make More Objects Than You Need To

Just because there's a garbage collector doesn't mean you won't have "memory issues." If you keep too many objects around on the heap, ineligible for garbage collection (but you won't, having read the preceding point), then you can still run out of memory. More likely, though, is just the problem that your performance might be slightly degraded by the overhead of both making all those objects and then having the garbage collector reclaim them. Don't do *anything* to alter your design just to shave a few objects, but pay attention in your implementation code. In some cases, you might be able to simply reuse an existing object by resetting its state.

Avoid Deeply Nested and Complex Logic

Less is more when it comes to branching. In fact, your assessor may be applying the Cyclomatic Complexity measure to your code, which considers code to be complex *not* based on lines of code, but rather on how many branch points there are. (It's actually much more complex than that. Ironically, the test for code complexity is itself a rather complex formula.) The bottom line is, whenever you see a nested *if* or anything other than very simple logic flow in a method, you should seriously consider redesigning that method or splitting functionality into separate methods.

Use Getters and Setters That Follow the JavaBean Naming Convention

That means you should use `set`<yourPropertyName> for methods that can modify a property (normally a property maps directly to an instance variable, but not necessarily) and `get`<yourPropertyName> for methods that can read a property. For example, a String variable *name* would have the following getter/setter methods:

```
setName(String name)
String getName()
```

If the property is a boolean, then you have a choice (yes, you actually have a choice) of whether to call the read method get<property> or is<property>. For example, a boolean instance variable *motorOn* can have the following getter/setter methods:

```
setMotorOn(boolean state)
boolean getMotorOn()
boolean isMotorOn()
```

The beauty of adhering to the JavaBeans naming convention is that, hey, you have to name it *something* and if you stick with the convention, then most Java-related tools (and some technologies) can read your code and automatically detect that you have editable properties, for example. It's cool; you should do it.

Don't Be a Procedural Programmer in an OO World

The two dead giveaways that you haven't really made the transition to a complete object "being," are when you use the following:

- **Really Big Classes** that have methods for everything.

- **Lots of static methods.** In fact, *all* methods should be nonstatic unless you have a truly good reason to make them static. This is OO. We don't have global variables and functions. There's no "start here and then keep executing linearly except when you branch, of course…". This is OO, and that means *objects all the way down.*

Make Variables and Methods As Self-Explanatory As Possible

Don't use variable names like x and y. What the heck does this mean: int x = 27; 27 *what*? Unless you really think you can lock up job security by making sure *nobody* can understand your code (and assuming the homicidal maniac who tries won't find you), then you should make your identifiers as meaningful as possible. They don't have to be *paragraphs.* In fact, if it takes a paragraph to explain what a variable represents, perhaps you need to think about your design again. Or at the least, use a comment. But don't make them terse! Take a lesson from the core APIs. They could have called `ArInBException`, but instead they called it `ArrayIndexOutOfBoundsException`. Is there *any* question about what that exception represents? Of course, the big Sun *faux pas* was the infamous `NullPointerException`. But despite the use of the forbidden word *pointer*, everybody knows what it means when they get it. But there could be some confusion if it were called `NPTException` or even `NullException`.

Use the Core APIs!

Do not reinvent the wheel, and do *not*—or you'll automatically fail for certain—use any libraries other than code *you* developed and the core Java APIs. Resist any temptation to think that you can build something faster, cleaner, more efficient, etc. Even if that's true, it isn't worth giving up the benefit of using standard classes that others are familiar with, and that have been *extremely, heavily tested in the field.*

Make Your Own Exception Classes If You Can't Find One That Suits Your Needs

If there isn't a perfect checked `Exception` class for you in java.lang, then create your own. And make it specific enough to be meaningful to the catcher. In other words, don't make a `BadThingHappenedException` and throw it for every possible business error that occurs in your program.

Do Not Return Error Codes!

This is Java. This is OO. If you really need to indicate an exceptional condition, use an Exception! If you really want to annoy an assessor, use error codes as return values from some of your methods. Even *one* method might do the trick.

Make Your Exceptions with a String Constructor Argument

Doing so gives you a chance to say more about what happened to cause the exception. When you instantiate an Exception, call the constructor that takes a String (or the one that takes another lower-level exception if you're doing exception chaining). When you create your *own* Exception class, be sure to put in a constructor that takes a String.

Follow Basic OO Design Principles

In the preceding section, some of the key points touched on areas we'll dig a bit deeper into here. You don't have to be the World's Best OO Designer, but you do need to follow the basic principles on which the benefits of OO depend. Obviously we can't make this a "How to Be a Good OO Designer in 10 Easy Pages." You need a lot more study and practice, which we assume you've already done. This should be old news by now, but you can bet that your assessor will be looking at these issues, so a refresher won't hurt. We're hitting the highlights of areas where you might get points deducted from your assignment.

Hide Implementation Details

This applies in so many places, but coding with interfaces and using encapsulation is the best way to do it. If you think of your code as little self-contained, pluggable components, then you don't want anyone who uses one of your components to have to think about *how* it does what it does. It all comes down to inputs and outputs. A public interface describes *what* a method needs from you, and *what* it will return back to you. It says nothing about *how* that's accomplished. You get to change your implementation (even the *class* doing the implementing) without affecting calling code. Implementation details can also be propagated through exceptions, so be careful that you don't use an interface but then put implementation-specific exceptions in the throws clause! If a client does a "search," they shouldn't have to catch an SQLException, for example. If your implementation code happens to be doing database work that can generate SQLExceptions (like JDBC code would), the client should not have to know that. It's your job to catch that implementation-specific exception and throw something more meaningful—a *business-specific* exception—back to client code.

Use Appropriate Class Granularity

A class should be of the right, you know, *granularity*. It shouldn't be too big or too tiny. Rarely is the problem a class that's too *small*; however, most not-quite-OO programmers make classes that are too *big*. A class is supposed to represent a *thing* that has state and behaviors. Keep asking yourself, as you write each method, if that behavior might not be better suited for some *other* thing. For example, suppose you have a Kitchen class that does all sorts of Kitchen things. Like Oven things and Refrigerator things, etc. So now you've got Kitchen things (Kitchen being a *room*) and Refrigerator things and Oven things all in the same class. That's three different things. Classes (and thus the objects instantiated from them) really should be *specialists*. They should do the kinds of behaviors that a *thing* of that type *should* do, and no more. So rather than having the Kitchen class include all the code for Refrigerator and Oven behaviors, have the Kitchen class *use* a Refrigerator and Oven in a HAS-A relationship.

This keeps all three classes simple, and reusable. And that solves your naming problem, so that you don't have to name your do-everything Kitchen class *KitchenFridgeOven*.

Another possible cause of a Big Class is that you've got too many inner classes defined. *Too many* meaning some of the inner classes should have been either top-level classes (for reuse) or simply methods of the enclosing class. Make sure your inner or nested classes really need to be included.

Limit Subclassing

If you need to make a new subclass to add important functionality, perhaps that functionality should really be in the parent class (thus eliminating the need for the subclass—you just need to *fix* the superclass). When you feel the need to extend a class, *always* look at whether the parent class should change, or whether you need *composition* (which means using HAS-A rather than IS-A relationships). Look in the core Java API for a clue about subclassing versus composition: the core API inheritance hierarchy is *really* wide but very shallow. With a few exceptions (like GUI components), most class hierarchies are no more than two to three levels deep.

Use Appropriate Method Granularity

Just as classes should be specialists, so too should methods. You'll almost certainly be docked points for your assignment if your methods are long (although in some cases, especially in your Swing GUI code, long methods aren't necessarily a reflection of bad design). In most cases, though, the longer the method the more complex, because often a long method is a reflection of a method *doing too much*. You're all programmers so we don't have to hammer the point about smaller modular functionality—*much* easier to debug, modify, reuse, etc. Always see if it makes sense to break a longer method up into smaller ones. But while in a deadline crunch you might get away with long methods in the *real* world (feeling guilty of course), it won't fly for your Developer assignment.

Use Encapsulation

Your assignment will be scrutinized for this most fundamental OO principle. Expect the assessor to look at the way in which you've controlled access to the state of your object. In other words, the way you've protected your instance variables with setters and getters. No need to discuss it here, just do it. Allow access to your data (except for constants, of course) *only* through more accessible methods. Be careful about your access modifiers. Having a nice set of accessor methods doesn't matter if you've left your variables wide-open for direct access. Again, make things as private and scope-limited as you can.

Isolate Code That Might Change from Code That Won't Have To

When you design your classes, be sure to separate out the functionality that might change into separate classes. That way, you restrict the places where you'll have to track down and make modifications as the program evolves.

Don't Reinvent the Wheel

Why would you want to? Well, most people end up doing it for one of two reasons:

- They believe they can do it *better.*
- They didn't know there already *was* a wheel.

You need to be certain that you

- Get it out of your head that you can do it better, regardless of whether you actually *can.* A better mousetrap (to completely mix metaphors here) isn't what's required. A solid, maintainable design *is.*
- Always look for an existing solution first!

Use Core APIs

Always always always check the core APIs, and know that occasionally you might find the class you're looking for in a package *other* than where you'd expect it. So be sure to really search through the APIs, even digging into packages and classes you might think are a little off the path. Sometimes a solution can be where you least expect it, so stay open to approaches that aren't necessarily the ones you would normally take. Flipping through a reference API book can help. A method might catch your eye and even if it turns out *not* to be your solution, it might spark an idea about a different solution.

In some cases, you might not find *exactly* what you're looking for, but you might find a class you can extend, thus inheriting a bunch of functionality that you now won't have to write and test (subject to the warnings about subclassing we mentioned previously).

Using core API's (besides being essential for the exam) lets you take advantage of a ton of expertise and testing, plus you're using code that hundreds of thousands of other Java developers are familiar with.

Use Standard Design Patterns

We can't tell you which ones you'll actually need for your assignment; that depends on both your assignment and your particular approach. But there are plenty of standard design patterns that let you take advantage of the collective experience of all those who've struggled with your issue before you (although usually at a fairly abstract level—that's usually where most patterns do their work). So while the core APIs let you take advantage of someone else's implementation code, design patterns let you take advantage of someone else's *approach to a problem.*

If you put a gun to our heads, though, we'd probably have to say that Singleton should be way up on your list of things to consider when developing your assignment. But you *might* also take a look at MVC (for your client GUI), Façade, Decorator, Observer, Command, Adapter, Proxy, and Callback, for starters. Pick up a book on design patterns (the classic reference is known as the "Gang of Four" (GOF) book,

Design Patterns: Elements of Reusable Object-Oriented Software, by Erich Gamma, Richard Helm, Ralph Johnson, and John Vlissides) and take time to step back and look at where your program might be trying to do something well-solved by a design pattern. The patterns don't tell you how to construct your algorithms and implement your code line by line, but they can guide you into a sound and maintainable design. Perhaps most importantly, as design patterns are becoming more and more well-known, developers have a common vocabulary to discuss design trade-offs and decisions.

We believe that the use of design patterns has recently become more important in the exam assessment than it has been in the past, due in large part to their growth in popularity.

Handle Errors Appropriately

You'll be evaluated for appropriate and clear error-handling throughout your project. You might do really well with it in your GUI and then fall down in your server, but it matters everywhere in your program.

Don't Return Error Codes

This is Java. Using error codes as return values, rather than using exceptions, is a Really Bad Idea. We're pretty sure your exam assessor knows that.

Don't Send Out Excessive Command-Line Messages

Don't be too verbose with your command-line messages, and be sure not to leave debugging messages in! Your command-line messages should include only what's necessary to verify the startup of your programs and a *very* minimal amount of status messages that might be crucial if the program fails. But in general, if something goes wrong that you *know* could go wrong, you should be handling it with exceptions.

Whatever you do, don't use command-line messages to send alert messages to the user! Use a proper dialog box if appropriate.

Use Dialog Boxes Where Appropriate

On the other hand, don't use dialog boxes for every possible message the user might need to know about. If you need to display information to the user that isn't of an urgent nature (urgent being things like a record-locking problem or if you need to offer a "Are you sure you want to Quit?" option). In many cases, a dialog box is what you'll use to alert the user when something in your program has caught an exception, and you need user input to deal with it appropriately. The use of dialog boxes from a usability perspective will be covered in more detail in Chapter 13.

Throw Checked Exceptions Appropriately

There's a correct time and place for throwing checked exceptions, and being *reluctant* to throw them can be just as bad as throwing them carelessly.

- Use runtime exceptions for programming errors.
- Use checked exceptions for things that your code might recover from (possibly with help from the user).
- Checked exceptions are *only* for truly exceptional conditions.
- Do not use exceptions for flow control! Well, not if you hope to do well both on the exam and in real life.

Remember, checked exceptions sure don't come for free at runtime; they've got overhead. Use them when, *but only when*, you need them.

Create and Throw Your Own Exceptions When Appropriate

Make use of standard exceptions when they make sense, but never hesitate to create your own if appropriate. If there's a reasonable chance that an exceptional condition can be recovered from, then use a checked exception and try to handle it. Normally, the exceptions that you create can be thought of as Business Exceptions—in other words, things like "RecordLockedException" or "InsufficientSearchCriteriaException". The more specific your exception, the more easily your code can handle it, and you get the benefit of providing specific catch blocks, thus keeping the granularity of your catch blocks useful. The opposite of that strategy would be to simply have everything in one big *try* block that catches `Exception` (or worse, `Throwable`!).

Catch Low-Level Implementation Exceptions and Throw a Higher-Level Business Exception

Say you catch an SQLException (not likely on the Developer exam). Do you throw this back to a client? Of course not. For a client, it falls into the category of "too much information." The client should not know—or care—that the database server happens to be using SQL. Instead, throw back to the client a more meaningful custom business exception that he or she can deal with. That more meaningful *business* exception is defined in your public interface, so the client is expecting it as a possibility. But simply passing a low-level exception all the way to a client reflects a poor design, since it couples the client with implementation details of the server—that's *never* a good idea in an OO design.

Make Your Exception Classes with a String Constructor (As Well As a no-arg) for Providing Additional Meaning

Every Exception class you develop should have both a no-arg constructor and a constructor that takes a String. Exception inherits a `getMessage()` method from Throwable, and it returns the String of that message, so you can pass that message back to your super constructor and then the catcher can query it for more information. The message's main use, however, is to provide more information in the stack trace. So the more detailed your message (usually about the state of key parts of the system at the time the Exception occurs), the more helpful it will be in diagnosing the problem.

Never, Ever, Ever *Eat* an Exception

By *eat* we mean the following horrible practice:

```
try {
   doRiskyThing();
} catch(Exception e) {}
```

See what's missing? By catching the exception and then not handling it in any way, it goes completely unnoticed, as if it never occurred. You should at the *least* print the stack trace. Putting something like this in your exam project might be the death blow.

Announce ALL Your Exceptions (Not Their Superclasses) in Method Declarations

Your method should declare the exact, specific Exception types that it can throw, as opposed to declaring a supertype. The following code shows an example:

```
class MyException extends Exception { }
class FooException extends MyException { }
class BooException extends MyException { }
public class TestException {
   public void go() throws MyException {  // Usually BAD to do this
     boolean x = true;
     if(x) {
      throw new FooException();
     } else {
      throw new BooException();
   }
  }
}
```

In the preceding code, class `TestException` declares a method `go()` that declares a `MyException`. But in reality, it might throw a `BooException` or it might throw a `FooException`. This is perfectly legal, of course, since both exceptions are subclasses of the declared exception. But why bother throwing two different exceptions if you don't declare it? Surely you don't want to force the catcher to insert logic to figure out *what* kind of exception they got? This doesn't mean that `catch` code won't sometimes do this, but it should be up to the catcher, not the thrower, to make that choice.

Key Points Summary

That wraps up our look at clarity and maintenance issues, and here's a list of the key points. Cut it out and tape it to your wall next to all the other incredibly valuable pages you've ripped from this book and taped to your wall. We're thinking of just offering wallpaper so you can leave your book intact.

General Programming Considerations

- Avoid designing a class that has no methods.
- Use design patterns.
- Reduce the visibility of things as much as possible.
- Use overloading rather than logic.
- Avoid long argument lists.

- Don't invoke potentially overridable methods from a constructor.
- Code to interfaces.
- Use abstract classes when you need implementation functionality.
- Make objects you're finished with eligible for garbage collection.
- Don't make more objects than you need to.
- Avoid deeply nested and complex logic.
- Use getters and setters that follow the JavaBean naming convention.
- Don't be a procedural programmer in an OO world.
- Make variable and method names as self-explanatory as possible.
- Make your own Exception classes if you can't find one in the API to suit your needs.
- Don't return error codes.
- Make your exceptions with a String message.

Follow Basic OO Design Principles

- Hide implementation details.
- Use appropriate class granularity.
- Use appropriate method granularity.
- Use encapsulation.

Don't Reinvent the Wheel

- Use core APIs.
- Use standard design patterns.

Handle Errors Appropriately

- Don't return error codes.
- Don't send out excessive command-line messages.
- Use dialogs boxes where appropriate.

- Throw checked exceptions appropriately.
- Create and throw your own exceptions when appropriate.
- Catch low-level implementation exceptions and throw a high-level business exception instead.
- Make your own custom exception classes have a String constructor (to take a detail message).
- Never, ever, eat an exception.
- Announce all your exceptions, not just their supertypes.

13

Designing the Graphical User Interface

CERTIFICATION OBJECTIVE

- Creating a Usable and Extensible GUI

CERTIFICATION OBJECTIVE

Creating a Usable and Extensible GUI

There are several key aspects of GUI design that you need to consider when designing and implementing the GUI for your project. At a high level, they can be broken down into two main areas of focus:

1. Designing the GUI to be usable and friendly from the end user's perspective.
2. Designing and implementing the GUI to be reliable, and maintainable from the programmer's perspective.

This chapter will focus almost entirely on the *first* point—ease of use for the end user. We start with a very brief overview of the technical issues you probably want to address in implementing your GUI for this project. After that brief overview, we dive into the topic of usability.

An Overview of Technical Considerations for Your GUI

Most of your GUI work on the exam assignment will be focused on usability. But for the final review, you might be asked to justify not just the user-friendliness, but also the technical considerations you took into account when designing and building your GUI. This section gives you a brief overview of some of the technical issues you need to keep in mind.

Required Technologies

Your instruction packet will probably require you to use certain technologies to implement your GUI for this project. If, for instance, your instructions indicate that you are to use Java Swing components and specifically the JTable component, not only do you have to use them, but you also need to use them appropriately. Before jumping in to implementing your GUI, you need to understand the strengths and weaknesses of the technologies you are using. In addition, each of the required technologies is meant to be used in a certain fashion—for instance, if you're going to use a JTable, you'll want to use the appropriate models and listeners. The bottom line is, don't use a widget until you really understand how Sun intended for you to use it.

Model–View–Controller

Your exam instructions will probably say that the GUI you build should be flexible and relatively easy to extend. If so, you'll probably end up considering the Model–View–Controller (MVC) design pattern. We recommend that you *do* consider the MVC approach. If you are familiar with it, so much the better. If you are not, this is a good opportunity to study it. The MVC pattern has plenty of benefits:

- It's very popular, and you're bound to run into it sooner or later.
- It anticipates that end users will ask for iteration after iteration of changes to the GUI design, and it reduces the development impact of those iterations. (You *know* how those end users are!)
- It scales well to large teams.
- It anticipates Java's "write once run anywhere" philosophy, reducing the effort required to port your GUI layer to additional environments such as browsers or mobile devices.

Event Handling, Listeners, and Inner Classes

If you're instructed to use Swing (and we can virtually guarantee you will be), you must understand the Listener paradigm. Be certain that you understand how Swing components are meant to handle events, and how components relate to their models and their listeners. In addition, you should understand how inner classes are used to help implement these capabilities.

Introduction to Usability Design

Traditionally, the assessors for the developer's exam have given a good deal of weight to the quality of the GUI. To pass the exam, your GUI should embody a host of wonderful attributes, including

- It should follow presentation standards.
- It should be easy to learn and easy to use.
- It should behave as GUIs are expected to behave.

The rest of this chapter covers key aspects of usability design and implementation for the GUI portion of your project. As an added bonus, this chapter discusses GUI design aspects that will be applicable across most of the GUI projects you encounter. Once again, we are approaching this topic with our infamous 80/20 perspective; this chapter provides the core information you need to design GUIs that are easy to learn, easy to use, and ergonomically friendly. There are eight steps to designing a great GUI:

1. Understand the business function and build use-cases.
2. Follow the general principals of good screen design.
3. Choose the appropriate widgets for your GUI.
4. Create the basic page layout(s).
5. Create appropriate menus and navigational elements.
6. Create crisp and informative GUI messages.
7. Use colors responsibly.
8. Test your GUI iteratively.

1. Use-Cases and the Business Function

The Sun developer's exam is by its nature an artificial exercise. We all understand that there are no real end users and no real business with real issues being addressed here. The rest of this section is written assuming that you're creating a solution for a real scenario. So, for the exam, you'll just have to pretend that *you* are the user, the business manager, etc. Even though you're a one-person band, you can follow this process—at least for the exam.

Interviews, Observation, and Iteration

A GUI will *always* be better if it's designed with the help of the end-user community. No matter how many businesses you've helped to automate, or how many killer GUIs you've built in the past, end-user input is essential. Although there are many ways of interacting with the end user, the three ways that offer the best return are

- Observing the end user performing *the process that you hope to automate.* From now on we'll just call it *the process.*

- Interviewing the end user about the process that he or she performs—what information is used, what decisions are made, what steps are taken, and what is created.
- Reviewing your results, and refining your implementation, with the user, over and over again at every stage of development.

Creating Use-Cases

A very effective approach to designing a GUI is to create "use-cases" with the user as you work through the observation and interview stages. Use-cases let you encapsulate the transactions that the end user performs over and over again in his or her job.

Let's say that you're creating a system to help customer service representatives (CSRs) at a company that sells PCs over the phone. After talking with the CSRs and watching them work, you might discover that they perform the following tasks over and over again in the context of working with their clients:

- Create a new customer record.
- Modify information in an existing customer record.
- Place a new order.
- Modify an existing order.
- Cancel an order.

Each of these activities can be considered a *use-case*. Once you've generated a list of use-cases for your application, the next step is to flesh them out. We like to use 4 × 6 cards for this. Each use-case is listed on its own card, and then for each card we add the following headings:

- **Find** How do you find the information you need to perform the use-case?
- **Display** What information is needed for the use-case to be completed?
- **Verification** What processes support verifying that the use-case is completed properly?
- **Finalization** What processes and information are necessary to complete the use-case?

The next step is to work with the end users to answer the four questions listed on each use-case card. When the cards have been completed and reviewed, they form the basis for designing the GUI.

Screen Mockups

The next step is to use your deck of 4 × 6 cards to generate *hand-drawn* screen mockups. Don't worry about making these mockups look good—that's handled later. Just get them down on paper quickly; they're just temporary. It's tempting to get ahead of yourself here and want to jump in and start writing code. Avoid the temptation! If done correctly, this first whack at screen design will produce screens that will absolutely *not* be what you'll want the final system to look like. In this phase, you want to quickly sketch out a rough screen for *every* heading on *every* card. If we've done the math right, that means you'll have four mock screens for every use-case; Find, Display, Verification, and Finalization.

It's hard not to get ahead of yourself here, because you'll quickly realize that a lot of these mockup screens look a whole lot like each other. That's a good thing. By reviewing these mockups with the end users, you'll discover that with just a little tweaking you can solve many different use-case steps with a single display. In our previous example, we had five use-cases, so it might seem reasonable to expect that you can represent all 20 different use-case steps with three or four displays.

2. Principles of Good Screen Design

Once we've got a rough idea what the system's individual displays ought to look like, it's time to move to the next level of design. At this stage in the design, our goal is to create mockup displays that do more than simply satisfy the requirements of the use-cases. We also want to design screens that will be easy to learn, easy to use, and will not irritate the end users over time. Here is a list of principles that will assist you in creating screens that your users (*and assessors*) will love.

Balance and Clutter

Well-designed displays tend to be balanced. By balanced, we mean that the content is approximately balanced left to right and top to bottom. Another attribute of good-looking displays is that they avoid the feeling of being cluttered. We return to the issue of clutter again later, but for now we mean that the screen elements should be neatly aligned. Figure 13-1 shows some examples of cluttered and poorly balanced displays, and then an orderly and well-balanced display.

Logical Groups and Workflow

Often a display can be thought of as many individual elements that can be placed into a few logical groups. For instance customer name, street address, city, state, and ZIP code are all individual elements, but it's natural for users to view these individual elements as a group, thought of as "customer address." Grouping elements together in a natural way is a good practice—there will be less mental strain on the user, data entry errors will be reduced if the display's tab sequence produces the shortest possible "travel" between elements, well-ordered groups tend to be more visually appealing, and, finally, natural groups are easier to learn.

FIGURE 13-1 The dos and don'ts of an orderly and balanced display

Cancel

Bad Balance

Cancel

Clutter

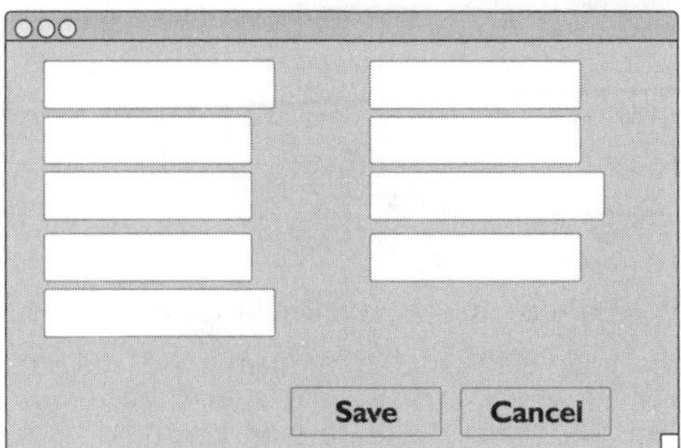

Balance and Order

You should also consider conditioned scanning patterns. In Western cultures, information is typically presented from left to right, and from the top down. These sequences are not universally recognized, however, so you should consider local cultural factors when designing a display.

Navigation and Commands

Good GUI displays typically let the user issue a variety of commands to the system. For now, we split GUI commands into two broad categories: commands that cause an action to take place within the current display (*action commands)*, and commands that make the system jump to a new display (*navigational commands*). A good rule of thumb is that action commands can occur wherever related elements are being displayed, but that navigational commands will appear only in the menu bar or toolbar, or at the bottom of the display.

When designing screen commands, simple language is the best. As a developer you know, for instance, that displaying the contents of a customer record on a display may actually require several programming steps. You don't want a button that says: "Create a search string, query the database, verify that good data was received, and, finally, display the result." Instead, you probably want something like a command button that says: "Find Customer." We'll talk more about good messages in a later section.

3. Choosing Your Widgets, JTable, and What Army?

We already mentioned that you'll probably have to use standard Swing components to implement your GUI, and that specifically you'll have to use the JTable component for a key part your main display. In addition, the second part of the exam (the follow-up essay) may ask you to describe why you made the widget (component) selections you made. Swing is a very rich GUI toolkit, and the instructions leave you with a lot of leeway in deciding which Swing components you should use for most of your application. In this section we describe many of the more common Swing components that are available, and when you should consider using them.

- **JLabel** Labels are strings of text used to identify other widgets. They are typically placed to the left or above the widget being labeled.
- **JButton** Buttons are rectangular-shaped widgets that are used to initiate actions by the system. A button can be used to initiate either an action

command or a navigational command. The nature of the command controlled by the button is typically displayed as a "label" inside the boundary of the button.

- **JTextField** and **JTextArea** Text fields and text areas are rectangular-shaped widgets that are used to either display textual data supplied by the system or as an area into which the user can type in data. Use a text field when you need no more than a single line, and a text area when the amount of data might exceed a single line. Text areas can have scroll bars (via the support widget called JScroll Pane), while text fields cannot. Text fields and text areas are typically festooned with a label placed above or to the left of the widget.
- **JRadioButton** This widget is named after the buttons found in car radios back in the good ol' days. These mechanical arrays of buttons were designed so that each one, when pressed, would tune the radio to a particular station. One of the key features of these radio buttons was that only *one* button could be depressed (in other words, *be active*) at a time. When an *inactive* button was pressed, the currently *active* button would be undepressed, and functionally move to the inactive state. The radio button widget works in much the same way; use it when you want the user to *choose one and only* one option from a list of options.
- **JCheckBox** This widget is often associated with radio buttons. It has a slightly different look and feel, and a different (albeit related) functionality. Like a radio button, the check box widget presents the user with a list of options. Unlike the radio button widget, the check box widget allows the user to select as many or as few choices as she or he wants. So, radio buttons are mutually exclusive, but check boxes are not.
- **JList** This widget presents the user with a list of entries, set inside a rectangle that can have a scroll bar. The entries are arranged in rows, one entry per row, so that the user can use a vertical scroll bar to search the list if there are more entries than can be displayed at one time. The list widget allows the user to select as few or as many entries as she or he wants.
- **JComboBox** This widget is part text field, part list (a *combo*, get it?). When not selected, the combo box resembles a text field with a down arrow button appended to its right end. The user can choose to key data into the field portion of the widget (like a text field), or choose the down arrow, which will cause a temporary list-like widget to appear. The user can select an option from this

temporary list in the same fashion that a normal list selection is made. Once the selection is chosen, it is placed into the text area of the widget and the list portion disappears.

- **JSlider** These widgets present a (typically horizontal) control that lets the user adjust the setting of any system feature whose possible values can be mapped to a range. Typical uses for sliders would be to control display brightness, or for volume (sound) control.
- **JProgressBar** These widgets present a (typically horizontal) display that allows the system to interactively indicate the progress of some system function that takes a noticeable time to complete. This widget is used to give feedback to the user so that she or he will know the system is still working, and roughly how much longer before the system will be finished with its task.
- **JTabbedPane** This widget allows the developer to pack a lot of display functionality into a small space. The analogy is that of looking at the tabs at the top of an open file drawer. When a tab is selected, an entire window of display elements associated with that tab is displayed to the user. When another tab is selected, the current tab display disappears and is replaced with a new set of elements. This widget is typically used when you need to support many infrequently used display elements. Application preferences or parameters are typically accessed via a tabbed pane widget.
- **JTree** This complex widget allows the system developer to create a traversable tree structure similar to what is presented by the Macintosh Finder or the Windows Explorer applications. This widget allows for arbitrarily large data structures to be represented and accessed. Trees are often used to represent directory structures on a hard drive or for a computer network, or any other data structure that involves nested lists of information.
- **JTable** This very complex widget is used to display and update arbitrarily large tables of information. In this usage, a table is typically a two-dimensional array of rows and columns. Generally, a table is structured so that each row of elements represents a collection of related information (often a row from a database). In this scheme, each column represents an element in the collection. You'll probably be required to use JTable in your project.
- **JMenuBar** Almost all good GUI displays include a menu bar widget. This (usually horizontal) widget is most commonly found at the top of the screen

directly under the title bar. The menu bar lets the developer arrange a wide variety of commands and system settings into logical groups. Menu bars are a part of almost every GUI display, and we look at them more closely in a few sections.

- **JToolBar** The toolbar widget is typically located directly beneath the menu bar. It displays a series of icons, each of which acts like a button, initiating an action or navigational instruction for the system.

Figure 13-2 illustrates the look and feel of this wonderful array of GUI widgets.

4. Screen Layout for Your Project

Now that we've developed our use-cases, mocked up some trial screens, equipped ourselves with an arsenal of Swing widgets (or components to be proper), and

FIGURE 13-2

Explosion at the widget factory

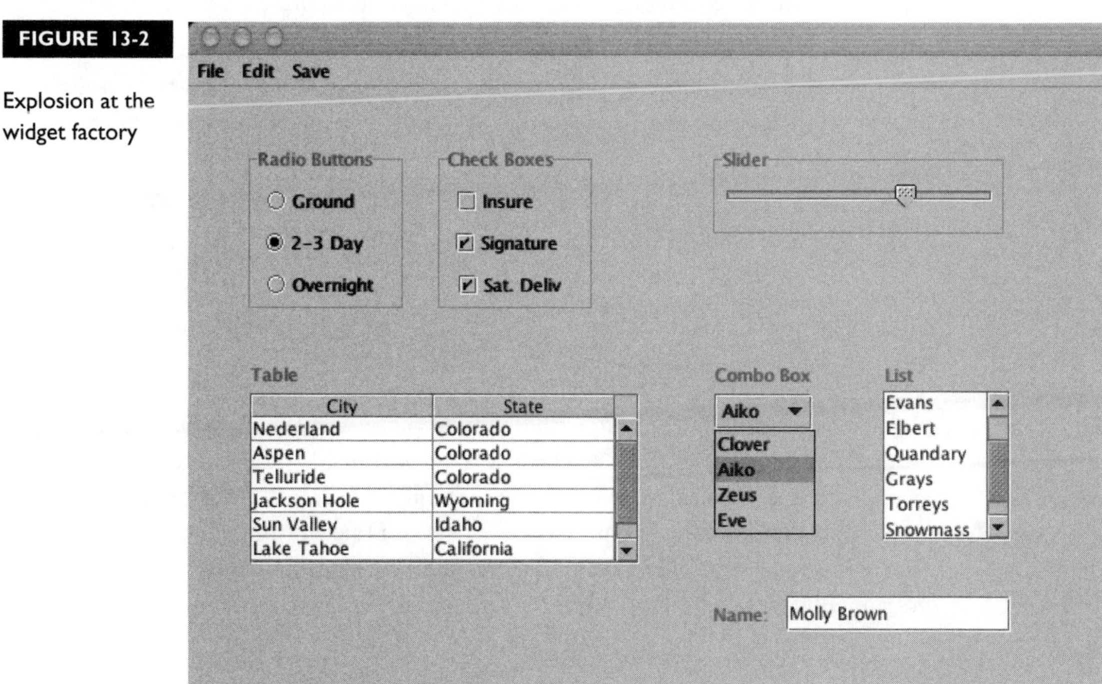

learned a little something about layout principals, it's time to put all of these pieces together! Hooray! Wait, wait, it's still not quite time to warm up your compiler—we're going to do a little more work with paper and pencil first. This phase of the design is concerned with designing the main portion of your GUI displays. The idea is to take the rough displays you designed in phase 1 and apply the rules of phase 2 and the widgets of phase 3 to these displays. When you're working on this phase, the following tips will help you create solid screen layouts:

- Remember, the user's eye will flow from left to right and from top to bottom. As much as possible, the standard path through the display should follow this natural flow.
- Try to make the display as visually pleasing as possible:
  - Don't jam too many elements into a single screen. White space and borders help keep a display looking clean, orderly, and less overwhelming.
  - Group related elements. You'll often want to place a labeled border around such a group.
  - Imagine invisible gridlines running vertically and horizontally through the display and align your groups and elements along these gridlines whenever possible.
- While other arrangements are acceptable, it's almost never wrong to right-justify text field labels and left-justify their respective text fields around the same vertical line. (See Figure 13-3.)
- Place your menu bar and toolbar (if applicable) at the top of the screen (more in the next section).

Figure 13-3 illustrates examples of many of the concepts we've been discussing. Notice that the name and address elements are grouped logically, and that they are aligned along a vertical line. The client preferences are accessible through a tabbed pane; this example shows a typical use for a set of radio buttons. On the lower left we've aligned two related combo boxes, and the navigational buttons are horizontally aligned in the bottom right of the display.

5. Menus and Navigation

Just about any standard application has menus and navigation buttons to let the user make choices and move to other windows. You'll need to pay particular attention to

FIGURE 13-3

An example of design elements

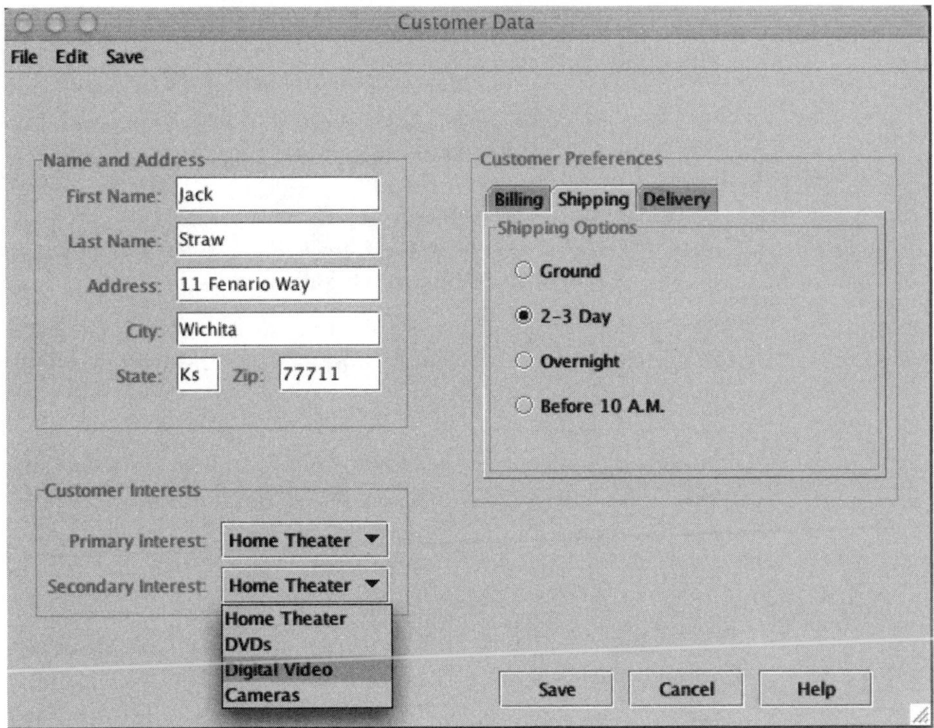

your menus and navigation features; no matter how attractive and easy-to-use you believe your GUI to be, you'll still have points deducted if you don't follow standard conventions.

Menus and Menu Bars

Menus are a powerful (and necessary) part of almost all GUIs. We focus our attention on the most common implementation of menus, the *menu bar*. An application's main menu bar is almost always located at the top of the display—sometimes directly under an application's title bar, and sometimes separate from the application's main window and docked to the top of the display.

You're familiar with the standard menu bar. Several of its more consistent entries are typically located toward the left end of the bar and include File, Edit, and View. Each entry in the menu bar represents a collection of related capabilities. Clicking on one of the entries on the menu bar will cause a specially formatted widget (a *menu*) that resembles a list widget to appear beneath the menu bar entry. The entries in these lists each represent a system capability. The most common capabilities available through menu entries are

- A navigational command such as Close (close the current document), Print (move to the Print display to initiate a print session), or Exit (end the application)
- An action command such as Spell Check (invoke the built in spell checker) or Copy (copy the currently highlighted data to the clipboard)
- Alter a system setting or parameter, such as Show Toolbar (displays the application's toolbar by default) or View Normal (display the current data in the default mode).

Within a menu, entries should be grouped in logical subsets, and each subset is typically delineated with a horizontal line or a double space. Menu commands should be left-justified, and it is common and appropriate to display keyboard shortcut commands, whenever they are available, to the right of the menu entry. Each application will have its own unique set of menus on the menu bar, but several of the menus will be very consistent from application to application. These most consistent menus are the File and the Edit. File will vary a bit from application to application, but it will almost always include commands (menu items), for New, Open, Save, Print, Close, and Exit. These commands refer to the current document or project as a whole. Edit can vary also, but will typically include commands for Undo, Redo, Cut, Copy, Paste, Clear, Select, and Find. These *editing* commands are used to modify portions of the active document or project. Not to give anything away here, but not having a standard menu bar with standard menus and menu items will cost you *big time* on your exam score.

Navigational Buttons

The second most common way to provide navigational capabilities within a GUI is through the use of navigational buttons. Navigational buttons are typically placed on the bottom (or sometimes the right side) of the active window. Navigational buttons typically act on the entire active window; examples include the Save button on a File dialog window, or the Print button on a Print dialog window. In both cases, activating the button causes a system action to take place, *followed by a navigation* to a different window in the application. Sometimes a navigational button will serve a solely navigational function such as Close, which closes the current window and returns the user back to the previous window.

6. Messages, Feedback, and Dialog Boxes

Messages and feedback are essential ways of communicating with your user, and your exam assessor will pay close attention to the way you handle keeping the user informed. The clarity, conciseness, and attitude of your messages can have a huge effect on whether users perceive your application as friendly and easy to use.

Messages and Feedback

Messages and other feedback are the primary ways that you (as the developer) have to respond to the user as she or he is using your application. Use messages to provide warnings when something has gone wrong or might be about to go wrong. Use messages to offer more information about activities that the system is performing (such as "37 occurrences found"), and use messages to display the status of an operation ("Search complete, no matches found").

Feedback tends to supply the user with information that the system has generated; for instance, if you key in a customer number and initiate a search, when the system returns with the customer's name and address that information is considered *feedback*. You also use feedback to tell the user that a lengthy operation is in progress, or that there's a problem with a current activity. Feedback can also be as subtle and useful as the blinking cursor bar that lets the user know where he or she currently is on the display.

Here are some tips for messages and feedback that will make your users smile:

- Try to use short, positive words and phrases.
- Use active voice whenever possible: "Print the file by choosing Print now", as opposed to "The file will be printed by choosing Print".
- Minimize the use of jargon or abbreviations in your messages.
- Ranges should be listed from smaller to larger and from now into the future.
- Action verbs should come first: "*Display* active customers" instead of "Active customer *display*".
- If the user selects an option that you think will require more than a few seconds to complete, give the user some sort of indication of status and progress. A system that locks up and gives the user no idea of whether progress is being made or an error has occurred is considered rude and unfriendly.

- If the user makes a mistake that can be caught immediately, it is appropriate to give them some sort of instant feedback such as warning noise or a blinking element.

Dialog Boxes

One of the nice usability features of a GUI is that the user has a great deal of flexibility in terms of sequencing tasks. For the most part, all elements on the screen are available to him or her at all times. However, when you create your *use-cases* and your mockup screens, you might run into situations that call for a strict sequence of events to take place. Counter to the normal GUI flexibility, there will be times when, for a particular action to take place, you have to follow a fixed path. An obvious case is when the user chooses to save his or her work. When the *save* request is made, no other work on the active project should take place until the save is either completed or abandoned. We use the term *nonmodal* to describe a GUI's typical openness. With a fixed-path situation like the *save* operation described above, the term is, not surprisingly, *modal*. In the GUI world, a modal sequence is one that can't be interrupted.

We know you're familiar with the typical sequence of events when you go to save some work, say a text document or perhaps a spreadsheet. When you make the *save* request, the system typically displays a small window in the center of the screen, known as a *dialog box*. Once the *save file* dialog box has been displayed, no other application actions can take place until the dialog box has been dismissed. This locking out of other actions is called *modal* behavior. When you create a dialog box, you have the choice to make it either modal or nonmodal. Always make it nonmodal as the default. However, there are times when a dialog box really should be modal—but use this only when absolutely necessary. Another good example of an appropriate use for a modal dialog box is when the user wants to open a network connection. Once the request is made, no other activity in the program can be allowed until the dialog box is answered.

Think carefully about whether each of your user dialog boxes should be modal or nonmodal. Most importantly, use dialog boxes only when you need to ask or tell the user something important. Few things annoy an end user more than a barrage of dialog boxes for every little thing when a simple display message will do. On the other hand, urgent, critical messages *should* use dialog boxes. When the user chooses to *quit*, for example, the system should give him or her a chance to cancel that request. Never take drastic action without first confirming it with the user!

7. How to Use Colors in Your GUI

The use of colors in GUIs is a controversial topic. Used correctly, colors can add aesthetic value and provide visual clues as to how to use and interpret an application. Used incorrectly, colors can be visually distracting, irritating, and confusing. In addition, poor color selections can make attractive displays ugly. In general, it is best to design your displays in monochrome and add only small color highlights. More ambitious color designs should be attempted only when you have the time to study the subject thoroughly. Here are some tips that will give your application good, conservative color usage:

- Begin by designing your displays in monochrome.
- Generally backgrounds should use lighter colors than foregrounds.
- When finding colors that work well together, start by choosing the background colors first, and then finding foreground colors to match those.
- Choose colors that are understated rather than bold. Bold colors might make striking first impressions, but they will age quickly and badly. (Remember, you don't want to irritate your end users, or the assessor!)
- Choose just a few colors to accent your application.
- Try to use color to support themes or logical connections.
- Avoid relying on cultural meanings for colors, red may mean "stop" in the Americas, but it has very different meanings in other parts of the world.
- Reds, oranges, and yellows tend to connote action.
- Greens, blues, and purples tend to connote stability.
- When users see different elements of the same color, they will associate those elements to each other, so be careful!

8. How to Test Your GUI

In this section we're going to talk about two different kinds of testing:

- Design testing, which occurs during the design phase of the project
- Code testing, which occurs once the coding phase is complete

There are other distinctions that are often drawn in the arena of testing, unit testing, system testing, regression testing, and so on. We're going to stay at a higher level and discuss design testing and code testing.

Testing Your GUI's Design

In general, the more people you show your GUI design to, the better your ultimate GUI will be. A difficulty in GUI design is that as the designer, you become too close to the application, and it becomes difficult for you to take the perspective of a new user. So, the best way to test a GUI design is to run it by users, let them ask questions, ask them questions, gauge their reactions. Do they seem to use the displays naturally, or do they stumble around looking for the correct sequences? Here are some tips to help you get the most out of your design testing:

- Test your design iteratively, in many stages:
  - Walk through the design when it's on paper.
  - Your paper designs should include use-case flows, and incorporate dialog boxes and warnings.
  - Show users your displays when all that exists are the widgets, with no real logic working.
- Prototype particularly crucial aspects of the application, and do usability testing on those key segments before the rest of the application is complete.
- Get feedback as frequently as possible—you won't be the one using this system, and the people who *will* should have a strong voice in its design.
- The corollary is don't do too much work without getting some feedback. The process should be one of constant refinement, and as such you don't want to invest too much time in a design that the users dislike.
- Make your widgets do the right thing:
  - If you are using a component that can scroll, make it scroll.
  - Avoid using *lists* or *combo boxes* for entries that have extensive ranges. For example, don't use a list for entering a user's year of birth.
  - As a corollary, if the only valid entries for a field come from a list somewhere (like a database), show the user the list if they want to see it (maybe a combo box)—don't make the user guess (for instance, a list of sales territories).

- When finding and opening a file, use a modal dialog box.
- Keep your navigation buttons in a well-aligned group.

Testing Your GUI's Code

Testing GUI code can be extremely challenging. By their very nature, GUIs are flexible in their behaviors; even simple GUIs offer billions of possible paths through their features. So how do you test all of these paths? Well, you really can't, but you can hit the high points, and there are approaches that will help you produce a solid application with a finite amount of testing. The key is to approach your testing from several radically different perspectives; the following tips will help you to create a robust and effective test plan:

- One avenue of testing *must* be use-case testing:
  - Have the users run through the system using copies of live work orders and scenarios.
  - If certain scenarios are missing from a set of live work orders, create simulated work orders to test the remaining system features/use-cases.
  - If possible, have the users test the system in parallel with their *live* activities. You will want to create duplicate databases for these parallel tests, and for sure there will be overhead, but parallel testing is a very effective way to test not only for bugs, but also to verify that the system can handle all of the scenarios that the users will run across.
- As the developer, it can be hard to really put your system through its paces, but if you pay attention to your own gut reactions, you can determine those areas where you are afraid to try to break things. Wherever you hesitate to tread, tread heavily.
- Enter invalid data everywhere.
- Test the limits of any data ranges that might exist.
- Force shutdowns of your system at critical stages to determine if transactions are properly encapsulated.

Key Points Summary

Some fun facts to remember when designing and implementing your project's GUI are shown next.

Technical GUI Considerations

- Issues with Swing and JTable
- MVC and why it helps extensibility
- The event-handling model
- Inner classes

Usability Key Points

- Use standard GUI presentation styles.
- Make it easy to learn and easy to use.
- Make it behave as standard GUIs are expected to behave.
- Develop *use-cases* to help define the scope of your GUI's capabilities.
- Document the four phases of each use-case: Find, Display, Verification, Finalization.
- The first several iterations of screen design should be with pencil and paper.

When designing screens, keep the following points in mind:

- Screens should be balanced and clutter-free.
- Elements should be grouped logically.
- Standard workflow should tend to go left to right, top to bottom.
- Action commands should be placed near their logical counterparts.
- Navigation commands should be placed in the menu or tool bars, or at the bottom of the screen (perhaps on the right side).
- Choice of widgets is important—they should match their standard use.
- Your project will probably call for you to use a JTable.
- Try to align your screen elements along invisible vertical and horizontal lines.
- When aligning labels and text fields, right-justify the labels and left-justify the fields—they will converge on a vertical line.
- When designing your menus, keep them as standard and predictable as possible; there are de facto standards that should be respected.

Feedback Principles

- Use short phrases, and positive, short words.
- Minimize the use of jargon and abbreviations.
- Ranges should be described from small to large, now to future.
- Forewarn the user when the system embarks on time-intensive functions. For really slow processes, use a status indicator.
- For the most part your GUI should be nonmodal; consider using dialog boxes when the system becomes, temporarily, modal.

Using Color

- The basic design should be monochrome.
- Backgrounds should be lighter than foregrounds.
- When matching colors, start with the background color.
- Avoid bold colors—they don't age well.
- Choose just a few colors to accent your application, then use them sparingly.
- It's OK to use colors to support themes or logical connections.
- Remember that users will make logical connections when colors match, even if there aren't any logical connections to be made.

Testing Tips

- Include users in the design process.
- Design and review incrementally.
- Consider walkthroughs with no logic behind the widgets.
- Consider walkthroughs of prototypes of key components.
- Test all the use-cases.
- Test in parallel with live systems.
- Focus on testing the areas you are most afraid to test.
- Test with invalid data, and data at the limits of ranges.
- Test by forcing shutdowns at critical stages.

Well, that wraps up our guide to user-friendly GUI design. *Now* all you need to do is learn Swing. Be prepared to spend some time—a lot of time—fiddling with layout managers and the subtleties of JTable. And although you *can* develop Swing applications without really understanding Swing's underlying MVC architecture, you *might* be asked to discuss it in your follow-up essay, so you might as well dig in and learn it all. You won't, however, need to become expert in every single component (widget) in the Swing package. As long as you're familiar enough with all the components to determine which ones best suit your desired behavior (really the *user's* desired behavior), you'll be in good shape for the exam even if you *don't* know anything else about the components you don't use in your final project.

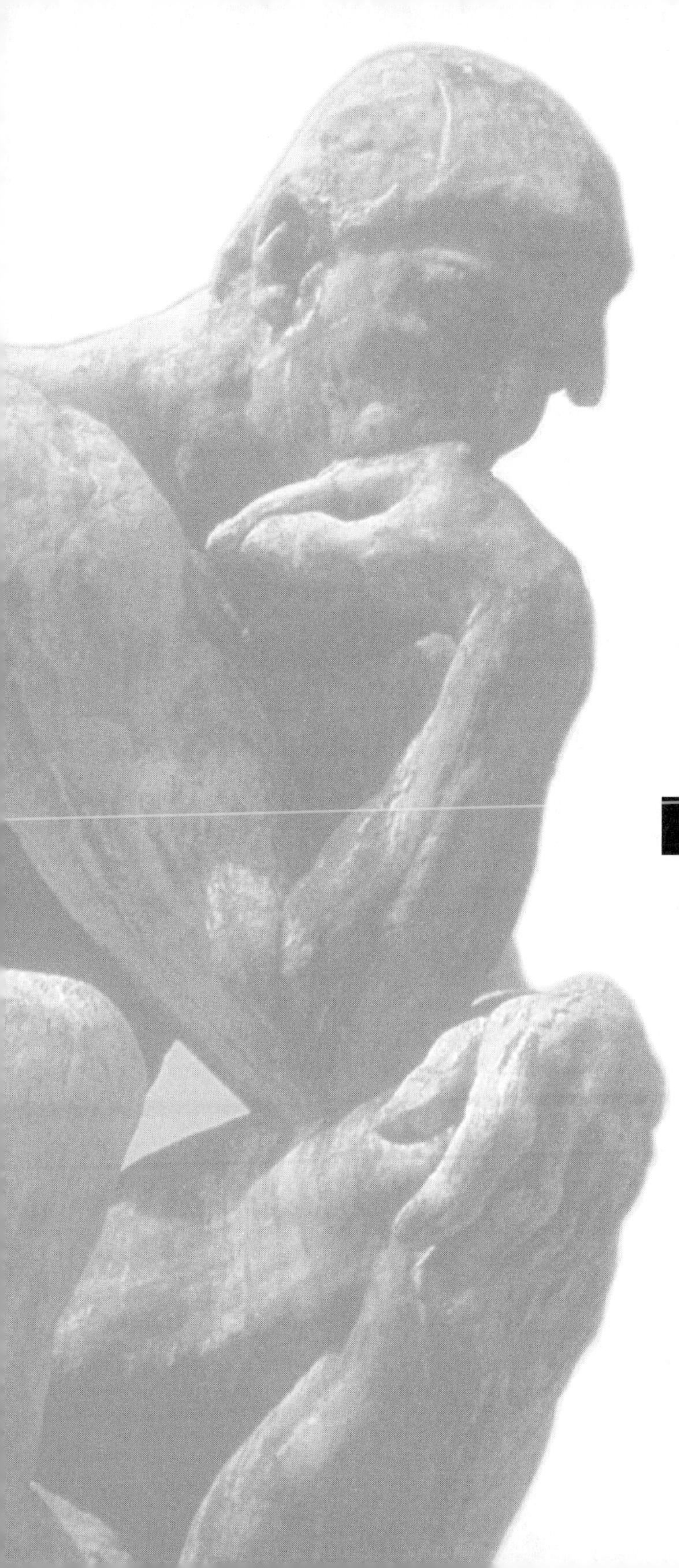

JAVA™ 2

SUN™ CERTIFIED PROGRAMMER & DEVELOPER

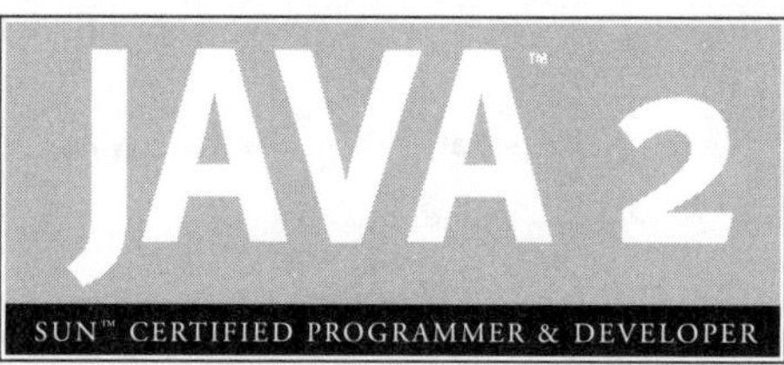

14 Networking Issues

CERTIFICATION OBJECTIVE

- Understand Networking Issues

CERTIFICATION OBJECTIVE

Understand Networking Issues

It is better to know some of the questions than all of the answers.

–James Thurber

Good questions outrank easy answers.

–Paul A Samuelson

If you don't ask the right questions, you don't get the right answers. A question asked in the right way often points to its own answer. Asking questions is the ABC of diagnosis. Only the inquiring mind solves problems.

–Edward Hodnett

Clever as you are, I bet you've figured out where this is heading…the Developer exam is about *you* figuring out solutions to the problem/specification you're given as your assignment. So, any attempt on our part to offer suggested potential solutions would, in our humble opinion, be defeating the whole point of the certification. However, given that this *is* a book about preparing for the exam, we can offer you questions. Things to think about. But we will start with a briefing on the core technologies involved: Serialization, Sockets, and RMI. There's far more to learn about these than we could possibly say here, so we're not even going to *attempt* to give you a crash-course. We're assuming that you're familiar with the technologies, and that you'll do whatever research and experimentation you need to learn to use them correctly. We will, however, do a simple review and then look at issues you'll need to consider when you build your project.

RMI and Sockets

As of this writing, the Developer exam expects you to know about networking. Well, not just *know* but actually *develop* a network server that allows remote clients to get information from a database (which you will *also* write).

Normally, building a simple network server presents you with two choices: RMI or Sockets. If your assignment asks you to make a choice, rest assured that there is *not one right answer*. You will need to think through the tradeoffs, make a choice, and document your decision.

One simple way to look at the difference is this:

Sockets are low-level, RMI is high-level.

In other words, RMI is a higher-level system that *uses* Sockets underneath. Whichever you choose, you'll need to be very comfortable with it, and you'll need to justify your choice.

Serialization

Somehow you're going to have to move a client *request*—made on one machine—across a wire to another machine. For your assignment, that "machine" might be only a virtual machine running on the same physical computer, but the Big Issues are the same whether the two machines (the client and the server) are on the same physical box or not. Two JVM's might as *well* be on two different boxes, with one key exception—the classpath. If two instances of a JVM are started on the same computer, they may well have access to the *same stuff,* and sometimes that masks a problem with your application. So, whatever you do, test test test on two different *physical* machines if you can.

What form is the client request? Well, remember from Chapter 10 when we looked at the Horse Cruise system. A client might want to request a cruise based on a certain date or horse criteria (easy horse, short horse, fast horse, etc.), or perhaps both. Ultimately, that request can take any form before you ship it from the client to the server; that's up to you, but let's say you're going to use a String. That String needs to be packaged up, shipped out, and land at the other end. When it's picked up at the other end, *the other end has to know how to use it.*

So we're really looking at *two* issues: how to pack and unpack it for shipping, and then how to make sure it makes sense to the program on the other end (the server). The packing and unpacking is easy—Serialization. Whatever object(s) you ship over the wire, they can be sent simply as *flattened* objects (*serialized*) and then they get brought back to life (*deserialized*) on the other end, and once again become real objects on the heap. So the object traveled from one heap to another. Well, it wasn't even the *object* that traveled, but a *copy* of the object.

OK, so the client makes a request for, say, a Horse Cruise on such and such a date. Now what? We put the client request into a String, serialize it, and ship it out (we haven't yet said whether this would be through RMI or straight Sockets) and the server picks it up, deserializes it, and uses it as an object. *Now* what? The client obviously needs a *result* from the request. Whatever that result actually is, you'll stuff it in an object (or group of objects) and ship it back following the same process—serialize it, ship it to the client, client deserializes it and uses it in some meaningful way (most likely, presenting the Horse Cruise search results in a GUI).

So now we know what form the request and result take (serialized objects), but we still need to know *how to ship it from point A to point B* (in other words, from client to server and from server to client). That leaves us with only one real question: do we use Sockets or RMI?

Sockets

Given that Sockets are simply the end-points of a connection between two devices, you aren't limited to shipping only serialized objects over the wire. In fact, the Socket has no idea *what's* coming—it just sees a stream of bytes. When the server gets the bytes, it's up to your server code to figure out what those bytes are supposed to mean. Are they in fact serialized objects? Then deserialize them…but in what order are they coming over? The server needs to know. And if they're *not* serialized objects, the server needs to know exactly what *is* in those bytes, in exactly which order, so it can do the appropriate *read* and get the bytes into some form a little more useful (Strings, numbers, etc.). And for that, you'll need a *protocol.* The client code developer and the server code developer will have to get together in advance and come to an agreement on what these bytes mean, in other words, how they're supposed to be interpreted. Of course, in the Developer exam, you're writing both the client and the server, so you only have to agree with *yourself.*

RMI

The beauty of RMI is that the protocol is already agreed on by both ends—it's just objects moving from one place to another (*copied* into the new location, but we're just going to say *moved* because it's easier to think about). In other words, we've already decided on the protocol for what the bytes mean, and the protocol is serialized objects. And since we've established *that,* then the client and server don't even have to do the serialization/deserialization—RMI takes care of it.

The tradeoffs, then, are already shaping up: using Sockets lets you have whatever protocol you want, but you have to do all the heavy lifting, while using RMI restricts the protocol to serialization. But with that flexibility removed, RMI can do most of the heavy lifting. By *heavy lifting,* we mean things like establishing the Socket connections, packing up the bytes, sending an output stream from one place to another, then receiving it and unpacking it and so on.

RMI is much simpler than Sockets. But simplicity never comes for free, of course, so it's also a little slower. You have to decide in all of this which is most important, but here's a hint: think Team Work. Again, there's no right answer; the assessor isn't going to prefer one over the other, because it depends on your goal and need (or in some cases, all things being equal, just which you prefer). But whichever you choose, you need to justify in your documentation (and possibly on the essay portion of the exam) why you chose one over the other.

The rest of this document looks at some of the things you'll need to think about when implementing your solution. They are in no particular order, so don't infer any relative importance from the order in which they're listed.

Questions to Ask Yourself

Ask yourself these questions as you design and implement your Exam solution.

- Serialization sends the entire object graph from point A to point B, for all instance variables that are not marked transient. Is your object large? Do you really *need* all that data to be shipped?
- Have you marked everything transient except the state you truly need on the other end?
- Have you investigated leaving most of the state transient and then reconstructing it by stepping into the deserialization process? The process of implementing your own private `readObject()` method can help. (Think of a private `readObject()` as kind of like a constructor, except instead of constructing an object for the first time, the private `readObject()` is involved in *re*constructing the object following serialization.)
- Are the superclasses of your serialized class also serializable? If not, they'll need a no-argument constructor, so be certain that this fits your design.
- Do you have any final transient variables? Be careful! If you use *blank* finals, you're in big trouble because the variable will come back to life *with a default value* since the constructor won't run when deserializing an object. And since it's final, you'll be stuck with that value.
- Have you thought about versioning issues? When an object is serialized, remember, the class needs to be present at the location where the object is being *de*serialized. What happens if the class has been modified? Will the

object still be usable if it was serialized from one version of the class and deserialized using a *different* version? Consider declaring an explicit serial version ID in all your serializable classes to reduce versioning issues.

- What happens if your database schema changes? Will your protocol have to change as well? Will your remote interface need to change?
- Have you looked for relevant design patterns? Not that we're suggesting anything, but have you looked into, oh, I don't know, say, the Command and Proxy patterns?
- Have you thought about *how* the client should get the stub class? When the client does a lookup in the RMI registry, remember, it's the stub object that gets shipped, and the client will need it. Dynamic code downloading is by far the coolest and most flexible, but unless your project specification appears to need it, it may well be more work than you need to provide.
- Have you thought about how the classes for your return types and arguments will get shipped? Are you certain that both the client and server will have all the classes they need for objects that will be shipped across from requests and results? Remember, if you've followed the rules for maintainability, you're most likely using interface types in your code, even though at runtime you'll be deserializing objects from classes that implement the interface…so the class of the implementation object needs also to be on the machine that's deserializing the object.
- How should you start the RMI registry? You can start it from the command-line, or you can start it programmatically, but you'll need to decide what's right (unless your assignment instructions/specification explicitly requires one way over the other).
- How should you shut *down* the registry?
- What happens if you need a remote object to stop being available to a client, while everything is still running? Have you looked into different options for binding and unbinding objects in the registry?
- How does the server know when a client is finished with an object? Does it even *need* to?
- What happens if a client crashes *after it locked a record.* How will you know the client is gone versus just taking a long time? Will you use a timeout

mechanism like a distributed lease that the client has to renew periodically to say, "I'm still alive!"? What about the state of the record?

- Have you looked at the `java.rmi.server.Unreferenced` interface to see if it does anything you can use?
- Have you considered bandwidth limitations if a client request turns up a lot of results?
- If you're using Sockets, do you have any potential issues with platform-specific line endings?
- How will the server know that a particular client asking to update a record is in fact the *same* client that got the lock on that record? In other words, how will you identify the client to the server in a unique way? Don't count on using the thread ID; remember that RMI makes no guarantees that it will keep the same thread for each request from a particular client.
- For that unique client ID, can you use something like web browsers use like a cookie mechanism? If so, *how* can you guarantee that one client won't have the same ID# as another client? Have you considered how you might generate your own unique identifiers? Would `random()` alone do the trick?

exam watch

There's a class you can look at in the Jini distribution, com.sun.jini.reggie.RegistrarImpl.java, that generates universally unique identifiers.

- Have you considered the possibility of distributed deadlock?
- How will you provide thread-safety in your server? Will it be at the remote object level or in your actual database? Remember, RMI doesn't guarantee that more than one thread won't be accessing your remote object.
- Have you thought about how much caffeine you'll need to complete this project?
- Have you begun to forget why you even wanted to *be* a Sun Certified Java Developer? (That's natural. We all go through that.)

For the tricky networking issues you'll encounter as you get into the specifics of your project, the best resource we can suggest is the Big Moose Saloon at javaranch.com. The saloon is a threaded discussion board with more than 16,000 posts in the Developer Certification section. Anything you might struggle with has already been struggled with by dozens of others who are willing to offer guidance.

Key Points Summary

We're not going to summarize the points we made under the Questions to Ask Yourself heading; they're *already* bullet points. But here's a quick summary of the key points around RMI and Sockets:

- Your exam assignment will require networking. Most likely you'll be asked to choose between RMI and Sockets.
- Sockets are low-level, RMI is high-level.
- RMI uses Sockets to do its work.
- To move an object from one JVM to another, you need to serialize it.
- Serialization flattens an object by packaging up the object's state.
- An object's serializable state consists of all nontransient instance variables.
- Sockets are the end-points of a connection between two networked devices.
- You can send a stream of bytes between Socket connections, but you'll need an agreed-upon protocol to know what those bytes mean.
- RMI uses serialization as the protocol, so you don't need to read and manipulate the bytes in your code.
- RMI is simpler to implement than using plain Sockets.
- Sockets offer more flexibility in protocol than does RMI.
- Ask yourself all the questions on the "Ask Yourself" list.

15

Database Issues

CERTIFICATION OBJECTIVE

- Understand Database Issues

CERTIFICATION OBJECTIVE

Understand Database Issues

Judge a man by his questions rather than his answers.

–Voltaire

A prudent question is one-half of wisdom.

–Francis Bacon

You're on your own for the other half.

–The Authors

As with the previous chapter, this chapter asks—you got it—questions. Some will seem obvious, some won't. But this is the area where your solution to the problem is going to have the greatest impact on your score. You're going to be asked to build a database. From scratch. And since there will be concurrent clients (or at least the *possibility* of concurrent clients), you'll have to be certain—dead certain—that you correctly manage record locking.

How you implement your searching, updating, and locking mechanism is entirely up to you. Again, there is definitely no One Right Answer for your solutions to these issues. But however you choose to do it, be certain that the logic is sound. For example, even if *you* never experience deadlock during testing, if there's even the slightest possibility (no matter how remote the chance) that it could happen, you could easily fail the exam even if nearly everything else in your application is perfect.

The two biggest issues are locking and searching, but locking is where the Big Money really is. We'll start with a brief overview of the key concepts, followed by yet another inspiring list of thought-provoking questions.

Building a Database

If you remember from Chapter 10, *you're* the one who has to build the database; the client's too cheap or neurotic to invest in a commercial database, even a free one. So what *is* a database? That depends on your assignment, but for the purposes of the exam, software-that-lets-you-access-a-set-of-records will do. You have some data, in some file format somewhere, with a known schema, and your job is to write an application that allows that data to be searched and modified. You might also need to add and delete records.

So the concept is simple: the client makes a request, based on some search criteria, and your database returns a result. Sometimes the client might want to, say, book a Horse Cruise, in which case one or more records will have to be updated. And you might need to insert a new cruise or delete a cancelled cruise. Regardless of the actual scenario, the Really Big Issue is

How do I protect the data from concurrent access?

In other words, *how do I lock the records?*

exam Watch

Your locking design and implementation decisions (and execution) are the most important parts of your Developer assignment. Spend the greatest percentage of your time making sure you have a sound solution. Be sure you've met any requirements in your assignment document that pertain to locking and unlocking. If part of your assignment specification is vague or ambiguous, you need to make an interpretation (your best guess about what to do) and then document your assumption and strategy.

And remember, the clients could be either local or remote (in other words, on the same machine as the database or on a machine somewhere else on the network), so you'll have to think of issues related to *both* of those scenarios. Locking is crucial, but fortunately the Developer exam isn't asking you to implement a complete distributed transaction system using the two-phase commit protocol. In fact, this is much simpler than transactions, but it will require you to understand the fundamental issues surrounding concurrent access to data. Remember the bank account example from Chapter 9? The one where the husband and wife both shared the same account? If you're not absolutely clear about how to handle synchronization, then reread that chapter. In order to correctly implement your locking strategy, you're going to need a solid grasp on synchronization, `wait()`, `notify()`, and `notifyAll()`. So, ready for some questions? Once again, these are in no particular order.

Questions to Ask Yourself

We've split these into two categories, searching and locking. But there's a lot about searching that also falls into the category of GUI issues (Chapter 13). Specifically, you'll need to be certain that your end-users *know* how to build a search query, and that's discussed in Chapter 13.

Searching

- How *easy* is it for clients to perform a search? Assuming the GUI itself is user-friendly (and we have a lot to say about that in Chapter 13), what about the criteria?
- How are the search criteria items represented? A String? A CriteriaObject?
- How does a client know exactly what they can base a search on?
- Does your search support boolean matches? Does it need to?
- The database won't necessarily be indexed, so have you thought about other ways to make the search as efficient as possible?

exam Watch

Don't sacrifice clarity and simplicity for a small performance gain. If the performance gain is big, then redesign so that you can have a reasonably efficient algorithm that is also clear and maintainable.

- Have you documented your search algorithm?

exam Watch

If you find yourself writing a* lot *of documentation to explain your search algorithm, there's probably something wrong with the design.

- Is the documentation of your search algorithm easy to read and understand?
- When the client submits a search query, is a specific piece of the search criteria explicitly matched to a particular field? Or do you search all fields for each search?
- If you're using 1.4, have you investigated whether regular expressions would help?
- What happens if nothing matches the client's search criteria?
- Will it need to be an *exact* match?
- Could there be a scenario in which too many records match the search criteria?
- Have you considered bandwidth issues when designing and implementing the format of the search criteria requests and server results? Are you shipping things over the wire that are bigger than they need to be?
- Is your search capability flexible for the end-user?

- Is your search capability flexible for future changes to the program?
- How much code, if any, would have to change if the database schema changes? Have you isolated the places where changes can occur to avoid maintenance problems?
- Are you absolutely certain that you've met the searching requirements defined in your assignment specification? Go back and reread them. Slooooooooowly.

Locking

- Are you absolutely certain that your locking scheme works in all possible scenarios?
- Does your exam assignment specify a particular kind of locking with respect to reads and writes?
- What happens when a client attempts to get a record and the record is already locked? What does the client experience?

exam watch

This is crucial. Think long and hard about what you want to happen.

- How will you keep track of which records are locked?
- How will you keep track of *who* locked each record? Do you need to know that?
- How will you uniquely identify clients in such a way that you *can* know which client locked which record? Is it the server's responsibility or the client's?
- Have you considered whether the ID of a thread is appropriate to uniquely identify a client?
- Have you considered whether a `Math.random()` number is appropriate to uniquely identify a client?
- If a client makes a request on a locked record, how will you verify that it's the same client who holds the lock?
- What happens if a client attempts to use a locked record when that client is *not* the client holding the lock?

- Is it possible to have a record locked for too long a time? How much time is *too long*?
- Is there anything you can or should do about the duration of a lock?
- What happens if a client goes down without releasing a lock?
- Does the server need a way to *know* a client went down? (As opposed to simply taking their sweet time or if they're on a painfully slow connection.)
- Is there any possibility of a deadlock? Where two or more clients are waiting for each other's locks?

exam Watch

Check for this more than you check for anything else.

- Are you correctly using `wait()`, `notify()`, and `notifyAll()`?
- Are you clear about the implications of `notify()` versus `notifyAll()`?

exam Watch

If not, go back and read Chapter 9.

- Are you relying on a nondeterministic thread mechanism such as priorities and/or yielding to guarantee your threads will behave properly?
- Are you synchronizing on the right objects?
- Are you *sure?*
- *Are you really really really sure?*
- Is everything that needs to be thread-safe, thread-safe?
- Have you made sure that things that don't need to be thread-safe, *aren't*? (You already know that synchronization carries a performance hit.)
- Have you selected appropriate data structures for implementing your lock scheme?
- Are you absolutely certain that you've met the locking requirements defined in your assignment specification?
- Would you like to revise your answers to the last two questions from Chapter 14?

16

Exam Documentation

CERTIFICATION OBJECTIVE

- Understand the Sun Certified Java Developer Exam Documentation Requirements

CERTIFICATION OBJECTIVE

Understand the Sun Certified Java Developer Exam Documentation Requirements

We know that you all know the benefits of thorough, accurate, and understandable documentation. There may be some of you out there who wish that documentation wasn't an integral part of a programmer's job. There may be others of you who are thrilled to write documentation, to exercise a different part of your brain, to help your fellow programmers, to capture (hey you, in the back, stop laughing!) your company's technical assets. Well, whatever your inclination, you're going to have to write good, solid documentation to support your project if you want to have any chance of passing this exam. It turns out that proper documentation plays as big a role in determining your exam score as many of the software aspects themselves.

The assessors will be expecting several pieces of documentation when you submit your exam. They are discussed briefly in the exam packet you receive from Sun; we will go into them more thoroughly in this chapter. The five areas of project documentation that we will cover are

- Developer's Documentation
- End User Documentation
- *javadoc*
- The Developer Choices File
- Comments and the Version File

Developer's Documentation

This area of the project's documentation is the most open ended. Your assessor is most interested in the final results of your project; these optional documents represent the design work that you did as you were working on the project. Documentation that you might consider providing in this section includes UML diagrams, schema documentation, algorithm documentation, flow diagrams, prototype plans, and test results. Given that the rest of the standalone documentation is to be submitted via ASCII text files or HTML, we recommend the same here.

End User Documentation

Your assessor is going to wear at least two hats when reviewing your project. (This makes her appear taller than she really is.) Initially, she will review your project from the standpoint of an end user. Once the end user review is complete, she will put on her 'techie' hat and dive into your code and technical documentation. But (and this is a big but), if she can't get through the end user portion easily and with no problems, she probably has no choice but to fail the project. It won't matter how unbelievably fabulous your code is, she'll never see it if the end user experience is challenging.

The actual end user documentation should be pretty easy; all it has to do is describe how to install, launch, and run your project. You will probably be told exactly how the application must be installed and launched, and from the end user's perspective, those tasks will have to be incredibly easy and relatively option free, so there won't be much to document. The key will be to document how to use the programs once they have been launched. When documenting the GUIs, the most important concepts to remember are

- Keep it simple.
- Keep it concise.

The GUIs themselves, if designed properly, should be very easy to use, so there is no need to go on and on.

The end user documentation can take several forms. The install and launch documentation must be provided in either an ASCII text file or as HTML. Make sure to follow the naming conventions described in your instructions! The GUI documentation can be added to either of these files, or it can be provided as online help.

javadoc and You

One of Java's more wonderful features is *javadoc*. While we're sure that all of you are well versed in the use of *javadoc*, and use it religiously, we are bound to review it here on the off chance that this bit of Java technology has somehow eluded you.

An Overview of *javadoc*

When you crank up your browser to look at the Java API documentation (let's say you've forgotten what arguments the `setInitialContextFactory`

`Builder()` method takes), you are really looking at the output of the *javadoc* utility. Most likely, that online documentation was created by the guy who actually wrote that method for that class (in this case the NamingManager class). *javadoc* is a utility for programmers to use to help other programmers use their programs. (We'll get off our soapbox in a minute.)

Every programmer should use *javadoc*. Even if you're a one-man shop, someday you'll want to refresh your memory on how a certain method works, and the very *javadoc* that you wrote months earlier will be right there to help you out. If you work with other programmers, then *javadoc* is truly a miracle. When you add *javadoc* comments to your code as you are creating it, you have an instant answer for anyone who wants to bug you about how your code works. (If the cute programmer in the cubicle next to you wants help, you can always provide additional assistance.) Likewise, if you're trying to update a class that was written by somebody else, you'll be grateful for their *javadoc* documentation, especially if for some reason that programmer is no longer around.

At a high level, *javadoc* comments are nothing more than specially formatted comments that you add in certain, very specific places in your code. When you run the *javadoc* utility on your Java files, it takes those comments, and the appropriate adjacent code, and creates HTML-based API documentation, just like you see on your browser.

If you've never used *javadoc* (gasp!), we recommend trying some experiments once you've read through more of this chapter. It's very useful to write a little code, produce some *javadoc*, and compare the two. With a little practice your *javadoc* comments will look just like those created by those 'think-tank' boys at Sun. Earlier, we promised to get off our soapbox; consider us officially off.

A Summary of the Project's *javadoc* Requirements

To pass the developer's exam, your code must include *javadoc* comments. Once your code is properly commented, you must then run the *javadoc* utility against it and include the resulting *javadoc* files in the *docs* directory for your project. Specifically, your *javadoc* comments might document some of the classes and interfaces you are submitting, including class, interface, constructor, method, constant, and exception comments. Your instructions will specify which elements you must document.

A Brief Tutorial on the Use of *javadoc*

It has often been said that if you know 20 percent of a certain technology you can accomplish 80 percent of everything that you ever have to do with it. That said, we're going to describe for you what is, in our humble opinion, the most crucial 20 percent of the commands provided by the *javadoc* utility. If you want to know more about *javadoc* we recommend starting with these two links:

http://java.sun.com/j2se/1.4/docs/tooldocs/solaris/javadoc.html, and
http://java.sun.com/j2se/javadoc/writingdoccomments/index.html

The Structure of a Comment As you will soon see, a single comment can grow to quite a large size. Comments can contain a wide variety of elements, but there are some restrictions to the order in which you can place these elements. To begin, the first line must start with /** (the / must be in column 1), all of the rows that contain descriptive content start with an * in column 2, and the closing delimiter is */ with the * in column 2. Finally, remember that the member declaration follows immediately after the *javadoc* comment. This format will hold true for any multiline *javadoc* comment used in documenting classes, interfaces, constructors, methods, instance variables, or exceptions; for example,

```
/**
 * the descriptive section
 * of a multiline javadoc comment
 */
public class Test {
```

A comment can contain two main sections: the description section followed by the tag section. Both sections are optional. When used, the descriptive section can contain any free form text following the column 2 *, and can span multiple lines.

The tag section of the comment begins with the first occurrence of a '@' that starts a new line of the comment (ignoring the leading *). There are two types of tags: *standalone* and *inline.* A standalone tag has the general form @tag. An inline tag has the general form { @tag }. Inline tags can be included in the descriptive section of the comment, but once a standalone tag has been encountered in a comment, no more descriptive text can be used in that comment; for example,

```
/**
 * the descriptive section
 * we're still in the descriptive section
 * {@link doStuff doStuff} and
 * after this line the tag section will begin:
 * @author  Joe Beets  (the leading @ marked the beginning
 * of the tag section
```

```
 * @version  2.1
 */
```

Launching *javadoc*, and Exciting *javadoc* Capabilities

We're not forgetting our orientation toward 80/20, and at the same time we want to let you know about some of *javadoc*'s other capabilities. Think of this as a high-level briefing.

- **Doclets** *javadoc*'s output format is determined by a 'doclet'. The default, standard doclet is built-in to *javadoc*, and produces the HTML API documentation normally associated with *javadoc*. If you want to create custom output you can subclass the standard doclet, or you can write your own doclet. For the adventurous, you can create XML or RTF; we know one guy who used *javadoc* to capture all his favorite beef jerky recipes. A good placed to start your doclet odyssey is at:

  http://java.sun.com/j2se/1.4/toolodocs/javadoc/overview.html

- **Command-line Cornucopia** Let's look at a few simple examples of calling *javadoc*:

  To run *javadoc* against all the java files in the current directory,

  ```
  % javadoc *.java (we tried to start with an easy one.)
  ```

  To run *javadoc* on a package called com.testpkg, first move to the parent directory of the fully qualified package (in other words, the directory containing the package), then

  ```
  % javadoc -d /home/html-dest com.testpkg
  ```

  In this case we used the –d flag to indicate the destination directory for the HTML output. So the command line reads, "Run *javadoc*, put the output in a directory called home/html-dest, and run the utility against all of the java files in the com.testpkg package."

- **Other Capabilities** *javadoc* has a wide range of command line options, in fact, a huge range of command-line options…so many that there is a facility that allows you to store your command-line options in a file. Let's cover some of options you might find useful for your project:

  - **`-windowtitle`** Allows you to specify the description that appears in the title bar of your browser window. See Figure 16-1.

FIGURE 16-1

Example of a custom title bar and header

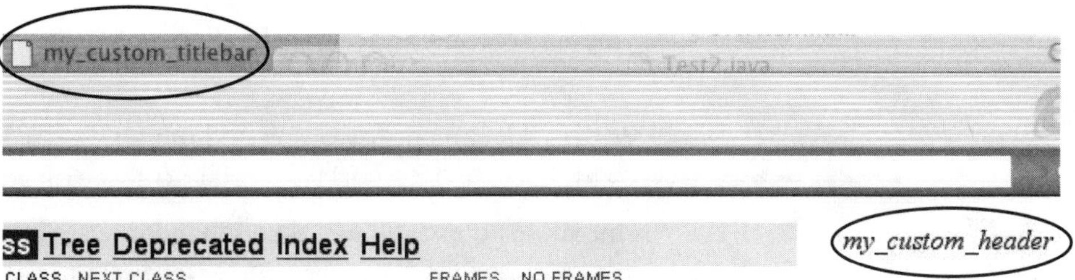

ss ClassTags

.lang.Object

- **`-header`** Allows you to specify a description that appears in the top right of your class documentation. See Figure 16-1.
- **`-footer`** Allows you to specify a description that appears in the lower right 'footer' area of your class documentation. See Figure 16-2.
- **`-bottom`** Allows you to specify a description that appears in the bottom of your class documentation. See Figure 16-2.

The following collection of command-line arguments allow you to specify which classes and members are documented, based on their access modifiers:

- **`-public`** Documents only public classes and members.
- **`-protected`** This is the option if you don't specify a command-line argument. It documents only protected and public classes and members.

FIGURE 16-2

Example of a custom footer and bottom

ClassTags

public **ClassTags**()

Class Tree Deprecated Index Help

PREV CLASS NEXT CLASS FRAMES NO FRAMES

SUMMARY: INNER | FIELD | CONSTR | METHOD DETAIL: FIELD | CONSTR | METHOD

my_custom_footer

my_custom_bottom

- **`-package`** Documents package level (default), protected, and public classes and members.
- **`-private`** Documents *all* classes and members. (`private means "everything," including things marked private.)`

Here are some more potentially useful command line arguments:

- **`-help`** Displays online help—a good way to access all of these options.
- **`-source 1.4`** Enables *javadoc* to handle assertions if you have used them in your code. Use it for documenting code that you've *compiled* using the -source 1.4 flag.

The World's Shortest Review of HTML Tags

Inside your *javadoc* comments you can format your text using standard HTML tags. The following (exhaustive) list of tags should be enough for you to properly document your project.

- `<a href=> </a>` The anchor tag will allow you to link your *javadoc* to a URL, for example, <a href="http://www.wickedlysmart.com/newindex.html">Go to Wickedly Smart</a>
- `<code> </code>` This tag will tell the *javadoc* utility to use code style font (probably courier) for the enclosed content, perfect for indicating code snippets in your comments.
- `<pre> </pre>` This tag will tell the *javadoc* utility to maintain the formatting of the enclosed content. This is very useful if you want to include a multiline code snippet in your *javadoc* and maintain the formatting (indenting, spacing, etc.).

The following code snippet was run through the *javadoc* utility, and Figure 16-3 shows a portion of the API style documentation that was generated. Notice that the *javadoc* utility ignored the formatting of the paragraph documentation, but preserved the formatting of the code snippet inside of the <pre> tag. Also notice how the <a href> tag was formatted to produce a live link to a website.

```
/**
 *  An example of HTML tags in a javadoc comment.
```

```
 *
 *   The <code>Byte</code> class wraps a primitive type
 * <code>byte</code> in an object.  An object of type
 * <code>Byte</code> contains a single field whose type
 * is <code>byte</code>.
 *
 * <pre>
 * int doStuff() {
 *     if (x < y) {
 *         x = 42;
 *     }
 * }</pre>
 *
 * @see <a href="http://wickedlysmart.com">Go to Wickedly Smart</a>
 */
public class Tags { }
```

FIGURE 16-3 Common HTML tags enhancing *javadoc* API output

Class Tags

```
java.lang.Object
  |
  +--Tags
```

---

public class **Tags**
extends java.lang.Object

An example of HTML tags in a Javadoc comment. The `Byte` class wraps a primitive type `byte` in an object. An object of type `Byte` contains a single field whose type is `byte`.

```
 int doStuff() {
     if (x < y) {
         x = 42;
     }
 }
```

See Also:
Go to Wickedly Smart

Useful *javadoc* Tags for Classes and Interfaces

Here are some useful *javadoc* tags for classes and interfaces:

- `@author` You can provide from zero to many author tags in your class comments. Although, given the nature of the exam, we'd advise zero or one. There are no formatting rules for the content after these tags. By default, author information is not included in the final API documentation; it will only be seen by people reading your source code. If you want to include the author information in your final *javadoc* output, you must run *javadoc* with the `-author flag.`
- `@version` This tag allows you to tie into Source Code Control Systems, which will automatically provide accurate versioning and date updates. Given that this is a one-person project, we recommend that if you use this tag, you insert your own manual version and date information. By default, version information is not included in the final API documentation; it will only be seen by people reading your source code. If you want to include the version information in your final *javadoc* output, you must run *javadoc* with the `-version` flag.

Useful Tags for All *javadoc* Comments

Here are some useful tags for all *javadoc* comments:

- `@see` This tag allows you to add a "See Also" entry to your *javadoc*. These entries are extremely flexible; you saw one in action in Figure 16-3, providing an intro to a URL link. `@see` can also be used to preface character strings (for instance referring to a reference book), or it can be used to preface other members in the same or other classes. Figure 16-4 shows the `@see` tag used in several different ways. There are many more wonderful possibilities that the `@see` tag offers, but we're sticking to our 80/20 guns.
- `@link` This tag is similar to `@see;` however, it creates an inline link with a label. These inline links allow online users of your API documentation to navigate quickly through your content using the hypertext links you have created with `@link.`

The following code snippet shows an example of how to use the links we just discussed. Figure 16-4 illustrates how the code sample was converted into *javadoc*.

In this case *javadoc* was run with two flags, `-version` and `-author;` without these flags the final output would not have included that information.

```
/**
 *  An example of class and interface tags
 *  link to testMethod {@link TestJD2#testMethod testMethod}
 *
 *  @author  Joe Beets
 *  @version  1.02
 *
 *  @see "The Fortran Coloring Book"
 */
public class ClassTags { }
```

Useful Tags for Constructors and Methods

Here are some useful tags for constructors and methods:

- `@param` This tag allows you to add method or constructor argument names and a description for the argument to the 'Parameters' section of the *javadoc*.

FIGURE 16-4 Class and interface tags in action

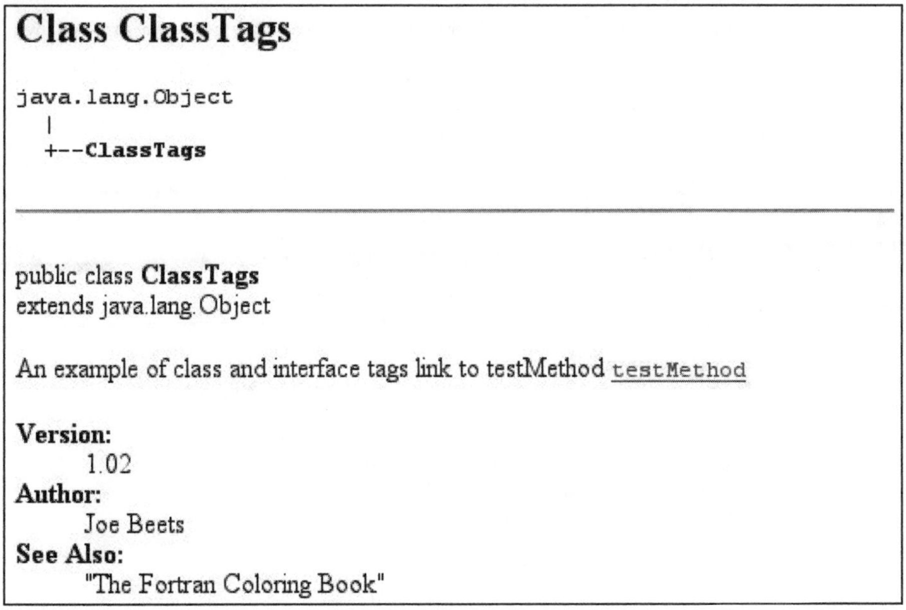

Class ClassTags

```
java.lang.Object
  |
  +--ClassTags
```

---

public class **ClassTags**
extends java.lang.Object

An example of class and interface tags link to testMethod `testMethod`

Version:
1.02
Author:
Joe Beets
See Also:
"The Fortran Coloring Book"

- `@return` This tag allows you to add a method return description to the 'Returns' section of the *javadoc*.
- `@exception` This tag has the same functionality as the `@throws` tag. They allow you to add a 'Throws' subheading to the *javadoc* for the constructor or method being documented. These tags take the exception class name and a description of the exception.

The following code example and Figure 16-5 demonstrate method and constructor tags in action:

```
/**
 * link to {@link TestJD#jdMethod jdMethod}
 * @param custId takes an int representing the customer ID
 * @return returns the answer to everything
 * @throws FooException throws a Foo exception
 */
public int method1(int z) throws FooException {
```

javadoc Comments for Classes

The *javadoc* comment for the class must directly precede the class declaration. This comment is used to describe the purpose of the class and its capabilities. It may also describe, at a high level, how the class is implemented. The Java API often includes a class comment that can run several pages long. That level of detail is probably not necessary, but it's a good idea to provide a paragraph or two of explanation. Later on in the class you will be documenting your constructors and methods, so this is

FIGURE 16-5

Method and constructor tags in action

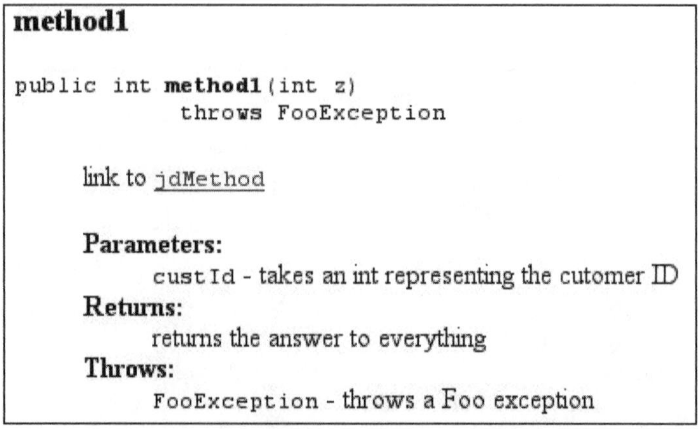

method1

```
public int method1(int z)
            throws FooException
```

link to `jdMethod`

Parameters:
`custId` - takes an int representing the cutomer ID

Returns:
returns the answer to everything

Throws:
`FooException` - throws a Foo exception

not the appropriate place for that documentation. The following is an example of a class level *javadoc* comment:

```
/**
 * The <code>Byte</code> class wraps a primitive type <code>byte</code>
 * in an object.  An object of type <code>Byte</code> contains a single
 * field whose type is <code>byte</code>.
 *
 * In addition, this class provides several methods for converting a
 * <code>byte</code> to a <code>String</code> and a <code>String</code>
 * to a <code>byte</code>, as well as other constants and methods
 * useful when dealing with a <code>byte</code>.
 *
 * @author  Joe Beets
 * @version .997
 *
 */
public class ByteSample {
```

There are several things to notice in the above example. First, notice the use of the tags `<code>` and `</code>`. These tags tell *javadoc* to use a different font (probably a courier font) for the content between the tags, to indicate a code snippet. The next things to notice are the `@author` and `@version` tags whose purposes were described in the previous "Useful Tags for Constructors and Methods" section.

javadoc Comments for Interfaces

The *javadoc* comment for an interface must directly precede the interface declaration. This comment is used to describe the purpose of the interface. The Java API often includes an interface comment that can run several pages long. That level of detail is probably not necessary, but it's a good idea to provide a paragraph or two of explanation. The following is an example of an interface level *javadoc* comment:

```
/**
 * The <code>Runnable</code> interface should be implemented by any class
 * whose instances are intended to be executed by a thread.  The class
 * must define a method of no arguments called <code>run</code>.
 *
 * This interface is designed to provide a common protocol for objects
 * that wish to execute code while they are active.  For example,
 * <code>Runnable</code> is implemented by class <code>Thread</code>.
 * Being active simply means that a thread has been started and has not
 * yet been stopped.
 *
 *
 * @author  Joe Beets
```

```
 * @version .997
 *
 */
public interface RunnableSample {
```

javadoc for Constructors

The *javadoc* comment for a constructor must directly precede the constructor declaration. This comment is used to describe the purpose of the constructor. When creating a comment for a constructor, it's a good idea to provide a paragraph or two of explanation. The following is an example of a constructor comment from the Java API:

```
/**
 * Constructs a newly allocated <code>Byte</code> object that represents
 * the <code>byte</code> value indicated by the <code>String</code>
 * parameter.  The string is converted to a <code>byte</code> value in
 * exactly the same manner used by the <code>parseByte</code> method
 * for radix 10.
 *
 * @param s the <code>String</code> to be converted to <code>Byte</code>
 * @throws NumberFormatException If the <code>String</code> does not
 * contain a parseable <code>byte</code>.
 */
 public Byte(String s) { }
```

javadoc for Methods

The *javadoc* comment for a method must directly precede the method's declaration. This comment is used to describe the purpose of the method. When creating a comment for a method it's a good idea to provide a paragraph or two of explanation. The following is an example of a method comment from the Java API:

```
/**
 * Returns a new <code>String</code> object representing the specified
 * <code>byte</code>.  The radix is assumed to be 10.
 *
 * @param b the <code>byte</code> to be converted
 * @return  the string representation of the specified <code>byte</code>
 */
public static String toString(byte b) {
```

javadoc for Exceptions

The *javadoc* comment for an exception must directly precede the declaration of the method that throws the exception. This comment is a part of the overall comment for the method in question. This comment is used to describe the class of the exception thrown along with a description of why the exception might be thrown. The Java API often includes an exception comment that can run a page long. That level of detail is probably not necessary, but it's a good idea to provide a paragraph or two of explanation. After a brief discussion of using *javadoc* for variables, we will give an example of a method that throws an exception and the *javadoc* to support that. In this case, we used `@exception` and in an earlier example we used @throws; they work the same way. Finally, see Figure 16-6 to see how this *javadoc* looks in a browser.

javadoc for Variables

The *javadoc* comment for a variable must directly precede the variable declaration. This comment is used to describe the purpose of the variable. The most common reason to use *javadoc* for a variable is for constants (`static final` variables). Constants are often used to represent minimum or maximum values. When documenting a constant it's a good idea to provide a sentence or two of explanation. The following code listing and Figure 16-6 show an exception throwing method and a related constant.

```
/** Minimum allowable Radix is 2 */
public static final int MIN_RADIX = 2;

/**
 * Parses the string argument as a signed byte in the radix specified
 * by the second argument.  The characters in the string must all be
 * digits, of the specified radix.  The resulting <code>byte</code>
 * value is returned.
 * <pre>
 * An exception of type <code>NumberFormatException</code>
 * is thrown if any of the following situations occur:
 *   - The first argument is <code>null</code> or is
 * a string of zero length.
 *     - The radix is either smaller than {@link Tags#MIN_RADIX
 *  Character.MIN_RADIX}
 *     - Any character of the string is not a digit</pre>
 * @param s the <code>String</code> containing the <code>byte</code>
 *  representation to be parsed
 * @param radix the radix to use while parsing s
 * @return the <code>byte</code> value represented by the string
 * argument in the specified radix
 * @exception NumberFormatException If the string does not contain a
 * parseable <code>byte</code>.
 *
 */
public static byte parseByte(String s, int radix) throws
      NumberFormatException
```

FIGURE 16-6 Documenting exceptions and constants

Field Detail

MIN_RADIX

```
public static final int MIN_RADIX
```

Minimum allowable Radix is 2

parseByte

```
public static byte parseByte(java.lang.String s,
                             int radix)
                      throws java.lang.NumberFormatException
```

Parses the string argument as a signed byte in the radix specified by the second argument. The characters in the string must all be digits, of the specified radix. The resulting `byte` value is returned.

```
An exception of type NumberFormatException is thrown if any of the following situations occurs:

  - The first argument is null or is a string of zero length.
  - The radix is either smaller than Character.MIN_RADIX
  - Any character of the string is not a digit
```

Parameters:
`s` - the `String` containing the `byte` representation to be parsed
`radix` - the radix to use while parsing s
Returns:
the `byte` value represented by the string argument in the specified radix
Throws:
`java.lang.NumberFormatException` - If the string does not contain a parsable `byte`.

The Developer's Choices Document

One of the key pieces of documentation you must provide when you submit your project is the document that reviews and justifies the choices you made during the design phase of your project. This document is affectionately referred to as the 'Choices' document. Your instruction packet will tell you exactly what this document must be named and where it must be located. The intention of this document is to *briefly* explain and justify the thinking you did while designing and implementing your application. In Chapters 14 and 15 we gave you lists of things to think about while designing your application. Those lists can give you good clues as to what to talk about in this document. You will have to make sure that a lot of situations are handled correctly when you design this application. In some cases, there is no perfect solution, and you will have to consider the tradeoffs and weigh the pros and cons of several possible solutions to a problem. This is the place to review those tradeoffs and pros and cons!

As is hinted at in the instruction packet, the assessors are looking for solutions that are understandable and maintainable. If you come up with a new search algorithm that is 3 percent faster than a well-known solution, you'd better be careful. Your solution had better be really clear and really easy to understand, or you might be penalized for a solution that is a bit slower, but is well known and clear. That said, you will probably have to think about database implementation issues, networking issues (RMI vs. sockets), record-locking issues, and GUI design issues in the course of this project. You may well have other design issues also. Without creating a masters thesis, describe them all in the 'Choices' document.

The Return of Comments and the Versions File

We're almost finished with *javadoc*, but there are still a couple of issues to look at. Besides correctness of your *javadoc*, your documentation should be clear and helpful. Remember, the easier it is for the assessor to figure out what your code is doing, the better your chances for a good score on the exam.

Just a Little More About Comments

We spent a lot of time in this chapter discussing the nuts and bolts of *javadoc*. Now let's spend just a little time discussing the style of the comments that you should create. There is a definite art to proper code commenting—we wish we could say it was a science, but it's not. The key points to remember for this exam are

- Make sure your code comments and clear and concise.
- Make sure the comment you are about to type is necessary.

Keep in mind that the best Java code is to a large degree self-documenting. If you find yourself documenting a lot of your code, think about these things:

- Are your variable names self-descriptive?
- Are your method names self-descriptive?
- Do you find yourself explaining why you wrote your code a certain way?

- Do you just really love to type?
- Remember some of the best Java code you've ever read, how little commenting it needed, and how clear it was.
- Is excessive commenting making up for a muddy design?

Lest We Forget, the Versions File

Not much to say here really. In the interest of being complete, we somewhat redundantly offer this advice. The instruction packet will probably ask you to provide a very small document in which you will list the version of the JDK that you used, and on which host platform(s) you developed and tested your project. Do as you're told. :)

Key Points Summary

Here, in a handy portable format, are the highlights from this chapter:

- You'll probably want to include these six forms of documentation (plus anything else the instructions ask for):
  - The Developer's Documentation—design docs.
  - End User Documentation—how to install and run the application.
  - *javadoc*—the programmer's technical inline comments.
  - The Choices Document—the architect's design choices and tradeoffs.
  - Inline code comments—in addition to the *javadoc*.
  - The Version file—SDK version used and hardware platform(s) used.
- Developer's documents are probably optional documents; include them if they briefly and clearly aid in understanding your project.
- End User documents; keep them simple and concise.

***javadoc* highlights:**

- It's how the Java API was created.
- It generates HTML.
- It's mandatory for your project.

- Comments can have a descriptive section and a tag section.
- Tags can be inline `{@tag}`, or standalone `@tag`.
- *javadoc* has a huge arguments library.
- You can store your command line arguments in a file.
- You can use HTML tags in your *javadoc*.
- Not all *javadoc* tags can be used for all class members.
- You can document the following members in *javadoc*:
  - Classes
  - Interfaces
  - Constructors
  - Variables
  - Methods
  - Exceptions
- The Choices document describes architectural decisions that you make:
  - Database design
  - Networking design
  - GUI design
  - Record-locking design
- Keep your code comments clear and concise.
- Try to make your variable and method names self-documenting.
- Are your comments propping up a muddy design?
- Don't forget your Versions file.

17

Final Submission and Essay

CERTIFICATION OBJECTIVE

- Preparing the Final Submission

CERTIFICATION OBJECTIVE

Preparing the Final Submission

You've built your project, and now the Big Day is finally here. Submission time. Your exam instructions include very specific details for submission, and you must follow them *exactly. Pay attention: any deviation from the submission instructions can mean automatic failure.* For example, if your instructions say that you must be able to run your application with a specific command,

```
java -jar runme.jar server
```

you had better have a JAR named `runme.jar`, and it better take a command-line argument "server", and it better include a manifest that specifies the class within `runme.jar` that holds the `main()` method.

In this short chapter we'll look at a typical submission requirement, and walk through how to build the final JAR along with a project checklist. Finally, we'll look at some examples of the kinds of essay questions you might see on your follow-up exam.

File Organization

Imagine the following submission instructions; yours will probably be very similar:

- All project files must be delivered in one, top-level Java Archive (JAR) file.
- The top-level, project JAR must be named **project.jar**.
- The project JAR must contain the following files and directories:
  - An *executable* JAR named **runme.jar** that contains the complete set of classes.
  - The **code** directory, which must hold the source code for your project, with all source files organized within directories reflecting the package structure of the classes.
  - A version file named **versionInfo.txt**. This must be a plain ASCII text file describing the specific version of J2SDK that you used (example: java version "1.3.1").
  - A copy of the data file, exactly as specified in the schema instructions, named **db.db**.

- The **docs** directory, which must hold all project documentation including:
  - A design decision document named **designChoices.txt**, an ASCII text file documenting design decisions.
  - End-user documentation for the server and client, unless you have used an online help system within your application. The help documents may consist of multiple HTML files but must begin with an HTML file user guide.
  - *javadoc* HTML files for all classes and interfaces. All public classes, interfaces, and members must be documented.
  - Developer documentation, optional.

Figure 17-1 illustrates the directory structure that matches the sample instructions above.

FIGURE 17-1 Sample directory structure for project submission

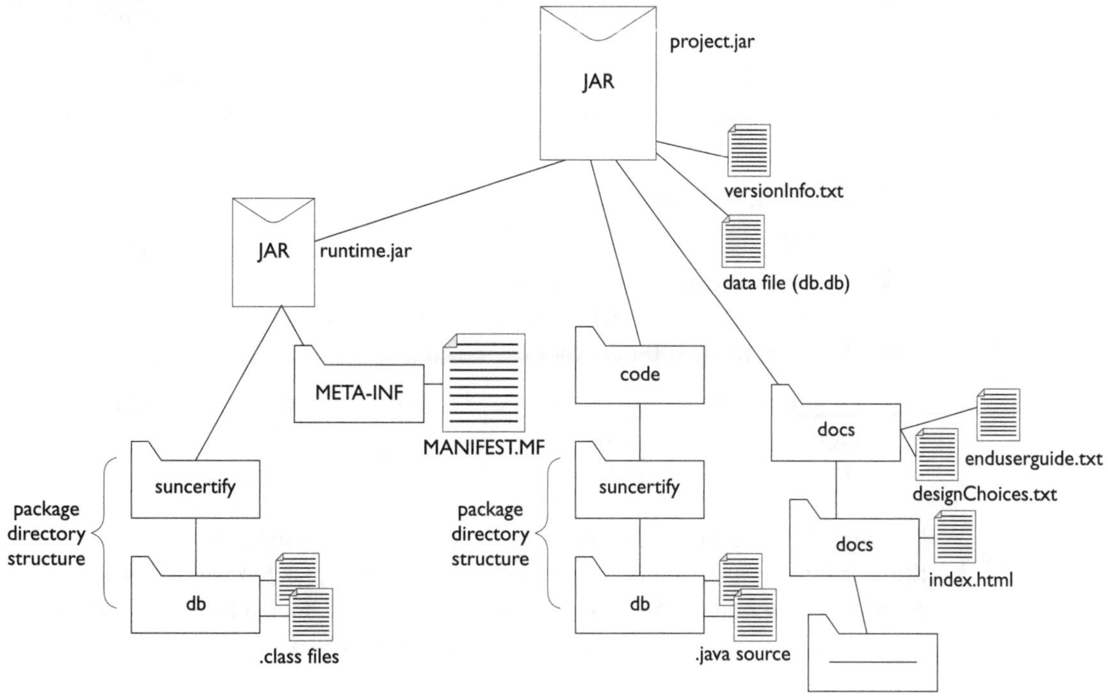

Creating the Executable JAR

An executable JAR is a JAR file that contains at least two things:

- A class file with a `main()` method.
- A manifest file that specifies *which* class in the JAR has the `main()` method. (Remember, you might have dozens of classes in your application JAR file.)

Creating the Manifest You can let the *jar* tool create both a manifest file (`MANIFEST.MF`) and the manifest directory (`META-INF`), but you'll need to put your information into the manifest file. The *jar* tool has a command that lets you specify your own text file as a place to find text that will be merged into the *real* manifest file. In other words, you won't actually *create* the manifest file yourself but you'll build a text file that has the stuff you want to *add* to the "official" manifest file the *jar* tool will create. This is not the only way to make your manifest file, but it's usually the simplest, and the end-result is the same: the `MANIFEST.MF` file will declare that you have a class with a `main()` method.

Assume the following structure for the examples we're going to walk through:

- **Main class name,** `suncertify.db.ExamProject` You have a class named ExamProject, in the `suncertify.db` package, and it holds the `main()` method for your application.
- **Working directory,** `/project` This is the directory one level *above* your package structure.
- **Manifest file name,** `Manifest.MF` This is not the *real* manifest file but rather your text file that holds the text you want to merge into the *real* manifest file that the *jar* tool will create.
- **Manifest file contents** The manifest file you'll write (as an ASCII text file) contains just a single line:
  `Main-Class: suncertify.db.ExamProject`

exam Watch

Be certain to insert a carriage return at the end of that single line! If there is not a* newline *below the main line, the manifest file will not work correctly. And be certain to include the* fully-qualified name *of the main class (*`suncertify.db.ExamProject` *as opposed to just* `ExamProject`*).

Creating the JAR We've got our application classes in their appropriate directory structure (matching the package structure). We've got our manifest file, `Manifest.MF`. We're in a working directory that is one level *above* the package, so if you listed the contents of the current directory it would include a directory named `suncertify` (the first directory in the package hierarchy).

So let's run the *jar* tool:

```
jar -cvmf Manifest.MF runme.jar suncertify/db
```

This creates a JAR file, named `runme.jar`, in your current directory. It includes all files that are in the `suncertify/db` directory (the package) and it also includes the directories themselves (`suncertify` and `db`). Plus, it takes the manifest file (`Manifest.MF`), reads its contents, and puts them into the *real* manifest file named `MANIFEST.MF,` that it puts in a directory named META-INF. At the command-line, you'll see the following when you run the `jar` command as follows:

```
jar -cvmf Manifest.MF runme.jar suncertify/db
added manifest
adding: suncertify/db/(in = 0) (out= 0)(stored 0%)
adding: suncertify/db/ExamProject.class(in = 617) (out= 379)(deflated 38%)
```

Of course in your *real* project, you'll have more than one class. Using the preceding `jar` command, you'll see the manifest being added, the directory structure being added (in this case, `suncertify/db`), and all files in the `db` directory (in this case, just the `ExamProject.class`).

More Fun with jar Tool What does that `-cvmf` mean? What else can you do with *jar* tool? The main purpose of the *jar* tool is to create archive files based on the ZIP format. It's a handy way to deliver an application, especially when it contains, for example, 4,234 classes. You *could* deliver all 4,243 to your end-users, but just *one* file is a little simpler. JAR files are also handy when you're shipping something over a network, where *one* fat file will ship faster than a ton of individual ones.

You can do all the things you'd expect to do with an archive format: make one, extract files from one, and look inside one (to display, but not extract, the contents). Table 17-1 lists examples of the basic *jar* tool commands. Assume that the JAR file name will be `MyJar.jar` and the class file we'll put in the JAR is `MyClass.class.`

TABLE 17-1 Basic *jar* Tool Commands

To create a JAR	`jar -cf  MyJar.jar MyClass.class`
To extract the contents of a JAR	`jar -xf MyJar.jar`
To view the contents of a JAR	`jar -tf MyJar.jar`
To create a JAR with your own manifest	`jar -cmf myManifest.mf MyJar.jar MyClass.class`
To create a JAR that contains all files within a directory	`jar -cf MyJar.jar suncertify/db`

The key *jar* tool switches are described here:

c	Create a new JAR file
v	Verbose—print out messages while JARring
t	List the contents of a file (in other words, display a *table*)
f	Stands for archive file name
m	Manifest—you are specifying your own text file whose contents should be put into the *real* manifest file.

Running the Executable JAR

Now that you've made your JAR file and it's got your complete package structure—with your main class in its appropriate directory (matching the package hierarchy)—and you've got a manifest inside that says *which* of your classes in the JAR has *the* `main()` method, it's a snap to run it from the command-line:

```
java -jar runme.jar
```

This works only if…

- Inside `runme.jar` there's a manifest.
- Inside the manifest, it specifies which class has a `main()` method, using the Main-Class entry:
  `Main-Class: suncertify.db.ExamProject`
- The manifest Main-Class entry specifies the fully-qualified name of the class (in other words, you must include the package structure).

- The ExamProject class is located inside the directory structure matching the package hierarchy. In other words, immediately inside the JAR there is a `suncertify` directory that contains a `db` directory, and the `db` directory contains the `ExamProject.class` file.

What About Command-Line Arguments? Your project's main application will almost certainly need command-line arguments. They might be used to pass host names and/or port numbers, or a variety of other configuration information. Most likely, though, your instructions will restrict you to a very small list of command-line arguments. For example, you might be instructed to use something like the following:

- Use `server` to have the application launch the network server.
- Use `client` to have the application launch the GUI client.
- The default—no argument—tells the application to run in *standalone* mode. (*Standalone* mode means your GUI must access the database *without* going through the network server. In other words, without RMI or sockets.)

Passing arguments to the command-line of your main class looks like this:

```
java -jar runme.jar  server
```

So anything you type *after* the JAR name is a command-line argument that gets passed straight on through to the `main()` method of your main class. In the example above, the ExamProject `main()` method would get the string server at `args[0]`.

Running javadoc on Your Package Chapter 16 describes the details of *javadoc*, but we thought a little reminder about running *javadoc* on your package might be helpful here. For this example, assume that

- Your class files are in the `suncertify/db` directory.
- Your working directory is one level *above* the start of the package (in other words, one level above the `suncertify directory)`.
- You have created a directory called `javadocs` and placed it within the docs directory.

To create javadocs for all classes in the `suncertify.db` package and have them placed in the `docs/javadocs` directory (where they'll need to be in our sample packaging instructions), run the following command from the directory one level *above* both `docs` and `suncertify`:

```
javadoc -d ./docs/javadocs suncertify.db
```

The Follow-Up Essay

Immediately after submitting your project (which means uploading it to the location you're given in your instructions), you should schedule your follow-up essay exam! We can't emphasize strongly enough that you should take your follow-up exam at the earliest possible moment. The fresher the project is in your mind, the easier it will be. You take the follow-up exam just as you did the Programmer's exam—in a Prometric Testing Center, where you answer questions in a computer application.

Rather than multiple-choice questions, however, your follow-up consists solely of essay questions. One of the main purposes of the follow-up is to see that indeed *you* are the one who wrote the application. So, you'll get questions related to the design and implementation decisions you had to make along the way. Once you've completed your essay exam, the results of the essay along with your submitted project are sent to an assessor and the fun begins. Well, for the assessor anyway. You, on the other hand, have to sit there pulling your hair out until you get your results. *Which could take as long as six weeks!* Unlike the Programmer's exam, where the results show up instantly, before you even leave the testing center, the Developer exam is marked by a real, *live* (which is a good thing, we're told...dead assessors have too many issues) human being. They'll use your essay questions to understand what's really happening.

Follow-Up Essay Questions

You never know what kind of questions you're going to get. Be prepared to describe *anything* that you might have had to consider in your design or implementation. The following questions don't necessarily reflect the actual exam questions, but they do suggest what you need to think about when preparing. We recommend that you relax about the follow-up! You've done the crucial work by designing and building your application, and assuming you—and not your cousin Chad who owes you—did the project yourself, you shouldn't have any trouble with the follow-up. Remember, there is NO ONE RIGHT ANSWER. There is, however, a *wrong* answer: the answer that contradicts the design, structure, and implementation of your application. As long as you're consistent, however, you should have nothing to fear from this part of the exam. The following questions can help you prepare for the follow-up:

- How did you decide which GUI components to use in your client application?
- Describe your design tradeoffs, and final decision, for choosing RMI or Sockets.
- Describe your event-handling mechanism and why you chose to do it that way.
- Describe your overall locking scheme and why you chose that approach.
- What design patterns did you use on this application?
- What aspects of your design allow for future modifications?
- Describe your threading and synchronization decisions.

Once you've submitted your follow-up assignment and taken your follow-up essay exam, take a deep breath, relax, and consider a refreshing alcoholic beverage. Or three. You're done! Now all that's left is the staggeringly torturous, endless, agonizingly slow, *wait* for the results. And after that, and after you've recovered from the "no more certifications for me no matter what you hear me say" phase, you can start planning your *next* certification effort.

In the meantime, don't count your chickens until you've reviewed the following key points summary. And *then* you're done. (Well, except for re-reading the threads chapter.) (Not to mention learning the exotic subtleties of the JTable.)

Key Points Summary

- Follow your project submission instructions *perfectly.*
- Your project will probably require you to package up all files in a single JAR.
- Your application should be (your instructions will confirm this) an executable JAR.
- You will need to submit both source code and class files.

- Class files will be in the executable JAR, while source code will be in a specific directory, probably named "code".
- Your instructions will give you the exact layout of the top-level project JAR including where to place the documentation, code, design choices document, and user guide.
- To create an executable JAR, you need a class with a `main()` method and a manifest with a Main-Class entry.
- The Main-Class entry indicates which class in the JAR has the `main()` method that should be executed, and it looks like the following:
  `Main-Class: suncertify.db.ExamProject`
- The *jar* tool will create a manifest; you will create a text file and specify to the *jar* tool that it should take your text file and incorporate its contents into the *real* manifest.
- The real manifest is `META-INF/MANIFEST.MF.`
- To run the *jar* tool on all the classes in a package, place them in a new JAR named `runme.jar` and include your own manifest file information, using the following command:

  ```
  jar -cvmf Manifest.MF runme.jar suncertify/db
  ```

- To run the executable JAR, use the following command-line:

  ```
  java -jar runme.jar
  ```

- You can also pass command-line arguments to the `main()` method in the main class by placing them after the JAR name as follows:

  ```
  java -jar runme.jar  standalone
  ```

- The purpose of the follow-up essay is designed to verify that *you* are the one who actually developed the assignment application.
- Schedule your follow-up essay exam *as soon as you upload/submit your assignment.*
- The fresher the project is in your mind, the better for taking the follow-up essay exam.
- For the follow-up essay, be prepared to describe and defend choices you made while designing and implementing your application.

- It's completely natural to (on many occasions) *regret* the decision to try for this certification in the first place. The feeling will pass. When it does, *get busy*, it'll be back.
- We wish you luck, success, caffeine, and plenty of sleep.
- When you've received your certification, tell us! Drop a success-story to certified@wickedlysmart.com.

A

About the CD

The CD-ROM included with this book comes complete with MasterExam and the electronic version of the book. The software is easy to install on any Windows 98/NT/2000 computer and must be installed to access the MasterExam features. You may, however, browse the electronic book directly from the CD without installation. To register for a second bonus MasterExam, simply click the Bonus Material link on the Main Page and follow the directions to the free online registration.

System Requirements

Software requires Windows 98 or higher and Internet Explorer 5.0 or above and 20 MB of hard disk space for full installation. The Electronic book requires Adobe Acrobat Reader. To access Online Training from LearnKey, you must have RealPlayer Basic 8 or Real1 Plugin, which will automatically be installed if you decide to purchase and launch additional online training.

Installing and Running MasterExam

If your computer CD-ROM drive is configured to auto run, the CD will automatically start up upon inserting the disk. From the opening screen you may install MasterExam by pressing the MasterExam buttons. This will begin the installation process and create a program group named "LearnKey." To run MasterExam use Start | Programs | LearnKey. If the auto run feature did not launch your CD, browse to the CD and Click RunInstall.

MasterExam

MasterExam provides you with a simulation of the actual exam. The number of questions, types of questions, and the time allowed are intended to be an accurate representation of the exam environment. You have the option to take an open-book exam, including hints, references, and answers; a closed-book exam; or the timed MasterExam simulation.

When you launch MasterExam, a digital clock display will appear in the upper-left corner of your screen. The clock will continue to count down to zero unless you choose to end the exam before the time expires. To register for a second bonus

MasterExam, simply click the Bonus Material link on the Main Page and follow the directions to the free online registration.

Electronic Book

The entire contents of the Study Guide are provided in PDF format. Adobe's Acrobat Reader has been included on the CD.

LearnKey Additional Training

The Additional Training link will allow you to access online training from Osborne.Onlineexpert.com. Sessions for LearnKey courses may be purchased directly from www.LearnKey.com or by calling (800) 865-0165.

The first time you run the Training, you will required to register with the online product. Follow the instructions for a first-time user. Please make sure to use a valid e-mail address.

Prior to running the Online Training you will need to add the Real Plugin and the RealCBT plugin to your system. This will automatically be facilitated to your system when you run the training the first time.

Help

A help file is provided through the Help button on the main page in the lower-left corner. Individual help features are also available through MasterExam and LearnKey's Online Training.

Removing Installation(s)

MasterExam is installed on your hard drive. For best results for removal of programs use the Start | Programs | LearnKey | Uninstall options to remove MasterExam.

If you want to remove the Real Player, use the Add/Remove Programs icon from your Control Panel. You may also remove the LearnKey training program from this location.

Technical Support

For questions regarding the technical content of the electronic book, or MasterExam, please visit www.osborne.com or e-mail customer.service@mcgraw-hill.com. For customers outside the 50 United States, e-mail international_cs@mcgraw-hill.com.

LearnKey Technical Support

For technical problems with the software (installation, operation, removing installations), and for questions regarding any LearnKey Online Training content, please visit www.learnkey.com or e-mail techsupport@learnkey.com.

Glossary

Abstract class An abstract class is a type of class that is not allowed to be instantiated. The only reason it exists is to be extended. Abstract classes contain methods and variables common to all the subclasses, but the abstract class itself is of a type that will not be used directly. Even a single abstract method requires that a class be marked `abstract`.

Abstract method An abstract method is a method declaration that contains no functional code. The reason for using an abstract method is to ensure that subclasses of this class will include an implementation of this method. Any concrete class (that is, a class that is not abstract, and therefore capable of being instantiated) must implement all abstract methods it has inherited.

Access modifier An access modifier is a modifier that changes the visibility of a class or member of a class (method, variable, or nested class).

Anonymous inner classes Anonymous inner classes are local inner classes that do not have a class name. You create an anonymous inner class by creating an instance of a new unnamed class that is either a subclass of a named class type or an implementer of a named interface type.

API Application programmers interface. This term refers to a set of related classes and methods that work together to provide a particular capability. The API represents the parts of a class that are exposed (through access controls) to code written by others.

Array Arrays are homogenous data structures implemented in Java as objects. Arrays store one or more of a specific type and provide indexed access to the store.

Automatic variables Also called method local or stack variables. Automatic variables are variables that are declared within a method and discarded when the method has completed.

Base class A base class is a class that has been extended. If class D extends class B, class B is the base class of class D.

Blocked state A thread that is waiting for a resource, such as a lock, to become available is said to be in a blocked state. Blocked threads consume no processor resources.

Boolean expression An expression that results in a value of *true* or *false.* Typically, this involves a comparison (e.g., x > 2) or a boolean condition such as (x < 5 && y > 3), but can also involve a method with a boolean return type.

boolean primitives A primitive *boolean* value can be defined only as either *true* or *false.*

Call stack A call stack is a list of methods that have been called in the order in which they were called. Typically, the most recently called method (the current method) is thought of as being at the top of the call stack.

Casting Casting is the conversion of one type to another type. Typically, casting is used to convert an object reference to either a subtype (for example, casting an Animal reference to a Horse), but casting can also be used on primitive types to convert a larger type to a smaller type, such as from a *long* to an *int.*

char A char is a 16-bit unsigned primitive data type that holds a single Unicode character.

Character literals Character literals are represented by a single character in single quotes, such as 'A'.

Child class *See* Derived class.

Class A class is the definition of a type. It is the blueprint used to construct objects of that type.

Class members Class members are things that belong to a class including methods (static and nonstatic), variables (static and nonstatic), and nested classes (static and nonstatic). Class members can have any of the four access control levels (public, protected, default (package), and private).

Class methods A class method, often referred to as a static method, may be accessed directly from a class, without instantiating the class first.

Class variable *See* static variable.

Collection A collection is an object used to store other objects. Collections are also commonly referred to as containers. Two common examples of collections are HashMap and ArrayList.

Collection interface The collection interface defines the public interface that is common to Set and List collection classes. Map classes (such as HashMap and Hashtable) do not implement Collection, but are still considered part of the collection framework.

Collection framework Three elements (interfaces, implementations, and algorithms) create what is known as the collection framework, and include Sets (which contain no duplicates), Lists (which can be accessed by an index position), and Maps (which can be accessed by a unique identifier).

Comparison operators Comparison operators perform a comparison on two parameters and return a boolean value indicating if the comparison is *true.* For example, the comparison 2<4 will result in *true* while the comparison 4==7 will result in *false.*

Constructor A method-like block of code that is called when the object is created (instantiated) Typically, constructors initialize data members and acquire whatever resources the object may require. It is the code that runs before the object can be referenced.

continue statement The *continue* statement causes the current iteration of the innermost loop to cease and the next iteration of the same loop to start if the condition of the loop is met. In the case of using a *continue* statement with a *for* loop, you need to consider the effects that the continue has on the loop iterator (the iteration expression will run immediately after the *continue* statement).

Deadlock Also called deadly embrace. Threads sometimes block while waiting to get a lock. It is easy to get into a situation where one thread has a lock and wants another lock that is currently owned by another thread that wants the first lock. Deadlock is one of those problems that are difficult to cure, especially because things just stop happening and there are no friendly exception stack traces to study. They might be difficult, or even impossible, to replicate because they always depend on what many threads may be doing at a particular moment in time.

Deadly embrace *See* Deadlock.

Decision statement The *if* and *switch* statements are commonly referred to as decision statements. When you use decision statements in your program, you are asking the program to calculate a given expression to determine which course of action is required.

Declaration A declaration is a statement that declares a class, interface, method, package, or variable in a source file. A declaration can also explicitly initialize a variable by giving it a value.

Default access A class with default access needs no modifier preceding it in the declaration. Default access allows other classes within the same package to have visibility to this class.

Derived class A derived class is a class that extends another class. If class D extends class B, then class D "derives" from class B and is a derived class.

do-while loop The *do-while* loop is slightly different from the *while* statement in that the program execution cycle will always enter the body of a *do-while* at least once. It does adhere to the rule that you do not need brackets around the body if it contains only one statement.

Encapsulation Encapsulation is the process of grouping methods and data together and hiding them behind a public interface. A class demonstrates good encapsulation by protecting variables with private or protected access, while providing more publicly accessible setter and/or getter methods.

Exception Exception has two common meanings in Java. First, an Exception is an object type. Second, an exception is shorthand for "exceptional condition," which is an occurrence that alters the normal flow of an application.

Exception handling Exception handling allows developers to easily detect errors without writing special code to test return values. Better, it lets us handle these errors in code that is nicely separated from the code that generated them and handle an entire class of errors with the same code, and it allows us to let a method defer handling its errors to a previously called method. Exception handling works by transferring execution of a program to an exception handler when an error, or exception, occurs.

Extensibility Extensibility is a term that describes a design or code that can easily be enhanced without being rewritten.

final class The `final` keyword restricts a class from being extended by another class. If you try to extend a final class, the Java compiler will give an error.

final method The `final` keyword applied to a method prevents the method from being overridden by a subclass.

final variables The `final` keyword applied to a variable makes it impossible to reinitialize a variable once it has been assigned a value. For primitives, this means the value may not be altered once it is initialized. For objects, the data within the object may be modified, but the reference variable may not be changed to reference a different object or null.

Finalizer Every class has a special method, called a finalizer, which is called before an object is reclaimed by the Java VM garbage collector. The JVM calls the finalizer for you as appropriate; you never call a finalizer directly. Think of the finalizer as a friendly warning from the virtual machine. Your finalizer should perform two tasks: performing whatever cleanup is appropriate to the object, and calling the superclass finalizer. Finalizers are not guaranteed to be called just because an object becomes eligible for garbage collection, or before a program shuts down, so you should not rely on them.

Floating-point literals Floating-point literals are defined as double by default, but if you want to specify in your code a number as float, you may attach the suffix *F* to the number.

Floating-point numbers Floating-point numbers are defined as a number, a decimal symbol, and more numbers representing the fraction. Unless a method or class is marked with the *strictfp* modifier, floating-point numbers adhere to the IEEE 754 specification.

for loop A *for* loop is used when a program needs to iterate a section of code a known number of times. There are three main parts to a *for* statement. They are the *declaration and initialization* of variables, the *boolean test expression*, and the *iteration expression*. Each of the sections are separated by a semicolon.

Garbage collection The process by which memory allocated to an object that is no longer reachable from a live thread is reclaimed by the Java VM.

Guarded region A section of code within a *try/catch* that is watched for errors to be handled by a particular group of handlers.

HashMap class The HashMap class is roughly equivalent to Hashtable, except that it is not synchronized and it permits null values (and one null key) to be stored.

Heap Java manages memory in a structure called a heap. Every object that Java creates is allocated in the heap, which is created at the beginning of the application and managed automatically by Java.

Hexadecimal literals Hexadecimal numbers are constructed using 16 distinct symbols. The symbols used are 0, 1, 2, 3, 4, 5, 6, 7, 8, 9, A, B, C, D, E, and F.

Identifiers Identifiers are names that we assign to classes, methods, and variables. Java is a case-sensitive language, which means identifiers must have consistent capitalization throughout. Identifiers can have letters and numbers, but a number may not begin the identifier name. Most symbols are not allowed, but the dollar sign ($) and underscore (_) symbols are valid. *See also* Reference variable.

if statement An *if* statement tests an expression for a boolean result. This is achieved by using one or more of Java's relational operators (>, ==, etc.) inside the parentheses of the statement to compare two or more variables.

import statement Import statements allow us to refer to classes without having to use a fully qualified name for each class. Import statements do not make classes accessible; all classes in the classpath are accessible. They simply allow you to type the class name in your code rather than the fully qualified (in other words, including the *package*) name.

Inheritance Inheritance is an object-oriented concept that provides for the reuse and modification of an existing type in such a way that many types can be manipulated as a single type. In Java, inheritance is achieved with the `extends` keyword.

Inner classes Inner classes are a type of class and follow most of the same rules as a normal class. The main difference is an inner class is declared within the curly braces of a class or even within a method. Inner classes are also classes defined at a scope smaller than a package. *See also* Anonymous inner classes; Local inner classes; Member inner classes. Static inner classes are not actually inner classes, but are considered top-level *nested* classes.

Instance Once the class is instantiated, it becomes an object. A single object is referred to as an "instance" of the class from which it was instantiated.

Instance variable An instance variable is belongs to an individual object. Instance variables may be accessed from other methods in the class, or from methods in other classes (depending on the access control). Instance variables may not be accessed from static methods, however, because a static method could be invoked when no instances of the class exist. Logically, if no instances exist, then the instance variable will also not exist, and it would be impossible to access the instance variable.

instanceof comparison operator The *instanceof* comparison operator is available for object variables. The purpose of this operator is to determine whether an object is of a given class or interface type (or any of the subtypes of that type).

This comparison may not be made on primitive types and will result in a compile-time error if it is attempted.

Interface An interface defines a group of methods, or a public interface, that must be implemented by any class that implements the interface. An interface allows an object to be treated as a type declared by the interface implemented.

Iterator An iterator provides the necessary behavior to get to each element in a collection without exposing the collection itself. In classes containing and manipulating collections, it is good practice to return an iterator instead of the collection containing the elements you want to iterate over. This shields clients from internal changes to the data structures used in your classes.

Java source file A file that contains computer instructions written in the Java programming language. A Java source file must meet strict requirements; otherwise, the Java compiler will generate errors. Source files must end with a .java extension, and there may be only one public class per source code file.

Java Virtual Machine (JVM) A program that interprets and executes Java bytecode (in most cases, the bytecode that was generated by a Java compiler). The Java VM provides a variety of resources to the applications it is executing, including memory management, network access, hardware abstraction, and so on. Because it provides a consistent environment for Java applications to run in, the Java VM is the heart of the "write once run anywhere" strategy that has made Java so popular.

javac Javac is the name of the java compiler program. This Java compiler processes the source file to produce a bytecode file.

java.lang package The java.lang package defines classes used by all Java programs. The package defines class wrappers for all primitive types such as Boolean, Byte, Character, Double, Float, Integer, Long, and Short, as well as String, Thread, and Object. Unlike classes in any *other* package, classes in the java.lang package may be referred to by just their class name, without having to use an import statement.

JVM *See* Java Virtual Machine.

Keywords Keywords are special reserved words in Java that cannot be used as identifiers for classes, methods, and variables.

Local inner classes You can define inner classes within the scope of a method, or even smaller blocks within a method. We call this a local inner class, and they are often also anonymous classes. Local inner classes cannot use local variables of the method unless those variables are marked final.

Local variable A local variable is a variable declared within a method. These are also known as automatic variables. Local variables, including primitives, must be initialized before you attempt to use them (though not necessarily on the same line of code).

Members Elements of a class, including methods, variables, and nested classes.

Method A section of source code that performs a specific function, has a name, may be passed parameters, and may return a result. Methods are found only within classes.

Method local variables *See* Automatic variables.

Modifier A modifier is a keyword in a class, method, or variable declaration that modifies the behavior of the element. *See also* Access modifier.

notify() method The methods `wait()` and `notify()` are instance methods of an object. In the same way that every object has a lock, every object has a list of threads that are waiting for a signal related to the object. A thread gets on this list by executing the `wait()` method of the object. From that moment, it does not execute any further instructions until some other thread calls the `notify()` method of the same object.

Object Once the class is instantiated it becomes an object (sometimes referred to as an instance).

Overloaded methods Methods are overloaded when there are multiple methods in the same class with the same names but with different parameter lists.

Overridden methods Methods in the parent and subclasses with the same name, parameter list, and return type are overridden.

Package A package is an entity that groups classes together. The name of the package must reflect the directory structure used to store the classes in your package. The subdirectory begins in any directory indicated by the class path environment variable.

Parent class A parent class is a class from which another class is derived. *See also* Base class.

Primitive literal A primitive literal is merely a source code representation of the primitive data types.

Primitives Primitives can be a fundamental instruction, operation, or statement. They must be initialized before you attempt to use them (though not necessarily on the same line of code).

Private members Private members are members of a class that cannot be accessed by any class other than the class in which it is declared.

public access The `public` keyword placed in front of a class allows all classes from all packages to have access to a class.

public members When a method or variable member is declared `public`, it means all other classes, regardless of the package that they belong to, can access the member (assuming the class itself is visible).

Reference The term reference is shorthand for reference variable. *See* Reference variable.

Reference variable A reference variable is an identifier that refers to a primitive type or an object (including an array). A reference variable is a name that points to a location in the computer's memory where the object is stored. A variable declaration is used to assign a variable name to an object or primitive type. A reference variable is a name that is used in Java to reference an instance of a class.

Runtime exceptions A runtime exception is an exception that does not need to be handled in your program. Usually, runtime exceptions indicate a program bug. These are referred to as unchecked exceptions, since the Java compiler does not force the program to handle them.

Shift operators Shift operators shift the bits of a number to the right or left, producing a new number. Shift operators are used on integer types only.

SortedMap interface A data structure that is similar to map except the objects are stored in ascending order according to their keys. Like map, there can be no duplicate keys and the objects themselves may be duplicated. One very important difference with SortedMap objects is that the key may not be a null value.

Source file A source file is a plaintext file containing your Java code. A source file may only have one public class or interface and an unlimited number of default classes or interfaces defined within it, and the filename must be the same as the public class name. *See also* Java source file.

Stack trace If you could print out the state of the call stack at any given time, you would produce a stack trace.

static nested classes Static nested classes are the simplest form of inner classes. They behave much like top-level classes except that they are defined within the scope of another class, namely the enclosing class. Static nested classes have no implicit references to instances of the enclosing class and can access only static members and methods of the enclosing class. Static nested classes are often used to implement small helper classes such as iterators.

static methods The `static` keyword declares a method that belongs to an entire class (as opposed to belonging to an instance). A class method may be accessed directly from a class, without instantiating the class first.

static variable Also called a class variable. A static variable, much like a static method, may be accessed from a class directly, even though the class has not been instantiated. The value of a static variable will be the same in every instance of the class.

String literal A string literal is a source code representation of a value of a string.

String objects An object that provides string manipulation capabilities. The String class is final, and thus may not be subclassed.

Superclass In object technology, a high-level class that passes attributes and methods (data and processing) down the hierarchy to subclasses. A superclass is a class from which one or more other classes are derived.

switch statement The expression in the switch statement can only evaluate to an integral primitive type that can be implicitly cast to an int. These types are byte, short, char, and int. Also, the switch can only check for an equality. This means that the other relational operators like the greater than sign are rendered unusable. *See also* Decision statement.

Synchronized methods The `synchronized` keyword indicates that a method may be accessed by only one thread at a time.

Thread An independent line of execution. The same method may be used in multiple threads. As a thread executes instructions, any variables that it declares within the method (the so-called automatic variables) are stored in a private area of memory, which other threads cannot access. This allows any other thread to execute the same method on the same object at the same time without having its automatic variables unexpectedly modified.

Time-slicing A scheme for scheduling thread execution.

transient variables The `transient` keyword indicates which variables are not to have their data written to an ObjectStream. You will not be required to know anything about *transient* for the exam other than that it is a keyword that can be applied only to variables.

Unchecked exceptions *See* Runtime exceptions.

Variable access Variable access refers to the ability of one class to read or alter (if it is not final) a variable in another class.

Visibility Visibility is the accessibility of methods and instance variables to other classes and packages. When implementing a class, you determine your methods' and instance variables' visibility keywords as `public`, `protected`, `package`, or `default`.

INDEX

Symbols

A

B

C

D

E

F

G

H

J

K

L

M

R

S

T

U

V

W

X

Y

INTERNATIONAL CONTACT INFORMATION

AUSTRALIA
McGraw-Hill Book Company Australia Pty. Ltd.
TEL +61-2-9900-1800
FAX +61-2-9878-8881
http://www.mcgraw-hill.com.au
books-it_sydney@mcgraw-hill.com

CANADA
McGraw-Hill Ryerson Ltd.
TEL +905-430-5000
FAX +905-430-5020
http://www.mcgraw-hill.ca

GREECE, MIDDLE EAST, & AFRICA (Excluding South Africa)
McGraw-Hill Hellas
TEL +30-210-6560-990
TEL +30-210-6560-993
TEL +30-210-6560-994
FAX +30-210-6545-525

MEXICO (Also serving Latin America)
McGraw-Hill Interamericana Editores S.A. de C.V.
TEL +525-117-1583
FAX +525-117-1589
http://www.mcgraw-hill.com.mx
fernando_castellanos@mcgraw-hill.com

SINGAPORE (Serving Asia)
McGraw-Hill Book Company
TEL +65-863-1580
FAX +65-862-3354
http://www.mcgraw-hill.com.sg
mghasia@mcgraw-hill.com

SOUTH AFRICA
McGraw-Hill South Africa
TEL +27-11-622-7512
FAX +27-11-622-9045
robyn_swanepoel@mcgraw-hill.com

SPAIN
McGraw-Hill/Interamericana de España, S.A.U.
TEL +34-91-180-3000
FAX +34-91-372-8513
http://www.mcgraw-hill.es
professional@mcgraw-hill.es

UNITED KINGDOM, NORTHERN, EASTERN, & CENTRAL EUROPE
McGraw-Hill Education Europe
TEL +44-1-628-502500
FAX +44-1-628-770224
http://www.mcgraw-hill.co.uk
computing_europe@mcgraw-hill.com

ALL OTHER INQUIRIES Contact:
Osborne/McGraw-Hill
TEL +1-510-549-6600
FAX +1-510-883-7600
http://www.osborne.com
omg_international@mcgraw-hill.com

LICENSE AGREEMENT

THIS PRODUCT (THE "PRODUCT") CONTAINS PROPRIETARY SOFTWARE, DATA AND INFORMATION (INCLUDING DOCUMENTATION) OWNED BY THE McGRAW-HILL COMPANIES, INC. ("McGRAW-HILL") AND ITS LICENSORS. YOUR RIGHT TO USE THE PRODUCT IS GOVERNED BY THE TERMS AND CONDITIONS OF THIS AGREEMENT.

LICENSE: Throughout this License Agreement, "you" shall mean either the individual or the entity whose agent opens this package. You are granted a non-exclusive and non-transferable license to use the Product subject to the following terms:
(i) If you have licensed a single user version of the Product, the Product may only be used on a single computer (i.e., a single CPU). If you licensed and paid the fee applicable to a local area network or wide area network version of the Product, you are subject to the terms of the following subparagraph (ii).
(ii) If you have licensed a local area network version, you may use the Product on unlimited workstations located in one single building selected by you that is served by such local area network. If you have licensed a wide area network version, you may use the Product on unlimited workstations located in multiple buildings on the same site selected by you that is served by such wide area network; provided, however, that any building will not be considered located in the same site if it is more than five (5) miles away from any building included in such site. In addition, you may only use a local area or wide area network version of the Product on one single server. If you wish to use the Product on more than one server, you must obtain written authorization from McGraw-Hill and pay additional fees.
(iii) You may make one copy of the Product for back-up purposes only and you must maintain an accurate record as to the location of the back-up at all times.

COPYRIGHT; RESTRICTIONS ON USE AND TRANSFER: All rights (including copyright) in and to the Product are owned by McGraw-Hill and its licensors. You are the owner of the enclosed disc on which the Product is recorded. You may not use, copy, decompile, disassemble, reverse engineer, modify, reproduce, create derivative works, transmit, distribute, sublicense, store in a database or retrieval system of any kind, rent or transfer the Product, or any portion thereof, in any form or by any means (including electronically or otherwise) except as expressly provided for in this License Agreement. You must reproduce the copyright notices, trademark notices, legends and logos of McGraw-Hill and its licensors that appear on the Product on the back-up copy of the Product which you are permitted to make hereunder. All rights in the Product not expressly granted herein are reserved by McGraw-Hill and its licensors.

TERM: This License Agreement is effective until terminated. It will terminate if you fail to comply with any term or condition of this License Agreement. Upon termination, you are obligated to return to McGraw-Hill the Product together with all copies thereof and to purge all copies of the Product included in any and all servers and computer facilities.

DISCLAIMER OF WARRANTY: THE PRODUCT AND THE BACK-UP COPY ARE LICENSED "AS IS." McGRAW-HILL, ITS LICENSORS AND THE AUTHORS MAKE NO WARRANTIES, EXPRESS OR IMPLIED, AS TO THE RESULTS TO BE OBTAINED BY ANY PERSON OR ENTITY FROM USE OF THE PRODUCT, ANY INFORMATION OR DATA INCLUDED THEREIN AND/OR ANY TECHNICAL SUPPORT SERVICES PROVIDED HEREUNDER, IF ANY ("TECHNICAL SUPPORT SERVICES"). McGRAW-HILL, ITS LICENSORS AND THE AUTHORS MAKE NO EXPRESS OR IMPLIED WARRANTIES OF MERCHANTABILITY OR FITNESS FOR A PARTICULAR PURPOSE OR USE WITH RESPECT TO THE PRODUCT. McGRAW-HILL, ITS LICENSORS, AND THE AUTHORS MAKE NO GUARANTEE THAT YOU WILL PASS ANY CERTIFICATION EXAM WHATSOEVER BY USING THIS PRODUCT. NEITHER McGRAW-HILL, ANY OF ITS LICENSORS NOR THE AUTHORS WARRANT THAT THE FUNCTIONS CONTAINED IN THE PRODUCT WILL MEET YOUR REQUIREMENTS OR THAT THE OPERATION OF THE PRODUCT WILL BE UNINTERRUPTED OR ERROR FREE. YOU ASSUME THE ENTIRE RISK WITH RESPECT TO THE QUALITY AND PERFORMANCE OF THE PRODUCT.

LIMITED WARRANTY FOR DISC: To the original licensee only, McGraw-Hill warrants that the enclosed disc on which the Product is recorded is free from defects in materials and workmanship under normal use and service for a period of ninety (90) days from the date of purchase. In the event of a defect in the disc covered by the foregoing warranty, McGraw-Hill will replace the disc.

LIMITATION OF LIABILITY: NEITHER McGRAW-HILL, ITS LICENSORS NOR THE AUTHORS SHALL BE LIABLE FOR ANY INDIRECT, SPECIAL OR CONSEQUENTIAL DAMAGES, SUCH AS BUT NOT LIMITED TO, LOSS OF ANTICIPATED PROFITS OR BENEFITS, RESULTING FROM THE USE OR INABILITY TO USE THE PRODUCT EVEN IF ANY OF THEM HAS BEEN ADVISED OF THE POSSIBILITY OF SUCH DAMAGES. THIS LIMITATION OF LIABILITY SHALL APPLY TO ANY CLAIM OR CAUSE WHATSOEVER WHETHER SUCH CLAIM OR CAUSE ARISES IN CONTRACT, TORT, OR OTHERWISE. Some states do not allow the exclusion or limitation of indirect, special or consequential damages, so the above limitation may not apply to you.

U.S. GOVERNMENT RESTRICTED RIGHTS: Any software included in the Product is provided with restricted rights subject to subparagraphs (c), (1) and (2) of the Commercial Computer Software-Restricted Rights clause at 48 C.F.R. 52.227-19. The terms of this Agreement applicable to the use of the data in the Product are those under which the data are generally made available to the general public by McGraw-Hill. Except as provided herein, no reproduction, use, or disclosure rights are granted with respect to the data included in the Product and no right to modify or create derivative works from any such data is hereby granted.

GENERAL: This License Agreement constitutes the entire agreement between the parties relating to the Product. The terms of any Purchase Order shall have no effect on the terms of this License Agreement. Failure of McGraw-Hill to insist at any time on strict compliance with this License Agreement shall not constitute a waiver of any rights under this License Agreement. This License Agreement shall be construed and governed in accordance with the laws of the State of New York. If any provision of this License Agreement is held to be contrary to law, that provision will be enforced to the maximum extent permissible and the remaining provisions will remain in full force and effect.